THE PAPERS OF ULYSSES S. GRANT

THE PAPERS OF

ULYSSES S. GRANT

Volume 30:

October 1, 1880–December 31, 1882

Edited by John Y. Simon

ASSOCIATE EDITOR

Aaron M. Lisec

TEXTUAL EDITOR

Cheryl R. Ragar

SOUTHERN ILLINOIS UNIVERSITY PRESS

CARBONDALE

Library of Congress Cataloging in Publication Data (Revised)

Grant, Ulysses Simpson, Pres. U.S., 1822–1885.
  The papers of Ulysses S. Grant.

  Prepared under the auspices of the Ulysses S. Grant Association.
  Bibliographical footnotes.
  CONTENTS: v. 1. 1837–1861.—v. 2. April–September 1861.—
v. 3. October 1, 1861–January 7, 1862.—v. 4. January 8–March 31,
1862.—v. 5. April 1–August 31, 1862.—v. 6. September 1–December 8,
1862.—v. 7. December 9, 1862–March 31, 1863.—v. 8. April 1–July 6,
1863.—v. 9. July 7–December 31, 1863.—v. 10. January 1–May 31,
1864.—v. 11. June 1–August 15, 1864.—v. 12. August 16–November 15,
1864.—v. 13. November 16, 1864–February 20, 1865.—v. 14. February 21–April 30, 1865.—v. 15. May 1–December 31, 1865.—
v. 16. 1866.—v. 17. January 1–September 30, 1867.—v. 18. October 1,
1867–June 30, 1868.—v. 19. July 1, 1868–October 31, 1869.—v. 20. November 1, 1869–October 31, 1870.—v. 21. November 1, 1870–May 31,
1871.—v. 22. June 1, 1871–January 31, 1872.—v. 23. February 1–
December 31, 1872.—v. 24. 1873.—v. 25. 1874.—v. 26. 1875.—v. 27.
January 1–October 31, 1876.—v. 28. November 1, 1876–September 30,
1878.—v. 29. October 1, 1878–September 30, 1880.—v. 30. October 1,
1880–December 31, 1882.

  1. Grant, Ulysses Simpson, Pres. U.S., 1822–1885. 2. United
States—History—Civil War, 1861–1865—Campaigns and battles—
Sources. 3. United States—Politics and government—1869–1877—
Sources. 4. Presidents—United States—Biography. 5. Generals—
United States—Biography. I. Simon, John Y., ed. II. Ulysses S. Grant
Association.
E660.G756   1967   973.8'2'0924   67–10725
ISBN-13: 978-0-8093-2776-8 (v. 30)
ISBN-10: 0-8093-2776-7 (v. 30)

The paper used in this publication meets the minimum requirements of
American National Standard for Information Sciences—Permanence
of Paper for Printed Library Materials, ANSI Z39.48–1992. ⊗

Published with the assistance of a grant from the National Historical
Publications and Records Commission.

Contents

═══

Introduction

———

Iɴ ᴛʜᴇ ꜰɪɴᴀʟ ᴡᴇᴇᴋꜱ of the 1880 presidential race, Ulysses S. Grant actively campaigned for the first time in his life. Stumping for James A. Garfield and the Republican ticket, Grant used New York City as his base and made forays into New Jersey, New England, and upstate New York, presiding over rallies, introducing keynote speakers such as his friend, U.S. Senator Roscoe Conkling of New York, and sometimes speaking two or three times a day to boisterous crowds. Grant found an effective strategy in defending the much-maligned carpetbagger. "All we ask is that our carpetbag fellow-citizens, and our fellow-citizens of African descent, and of every other class who may choose to be Republicans, shall have the privilege to go to the polls, even though they are in the minority, and put in their ballot without being burned out of their homes, and without being threatened or intimidated." He urged voters to "make it so that the carpet baggers can really prosper, do business and be respected and respectable in the Southern States as they are in the Western States, and help them to build up the South and make it prosperous, as the carpet-baggers of the West have done out there. We are all carpet-baggers—nothing else."

Thanks in part to Grant's efforts, Garfield won a narrow victory in New York that elected him over his Democratic opponent, Major General Winfield S. Hancock. A grateful Garfield sought

Grant's advice on policy and patronage. Grant complied on both counts, taking particular interest in cabinet appointments and relations with China and Japan. Grant also predicted to Garfield that he would experience "the least vexation any Executive has had since /60." Grant's principal advice was to reject appointing men "who were against us in the war and who have shewn no signs of change since." Grant hoped that "Garfield will give us an administration that will break up the solid south and not pander to the republican sore heads and bolters," referring to Republicans who had opposed Grant and supported Horace Greeley in 1872.

The campaign over, the Grants settled into their rooms at the Fifth Avenue Hotel, having all but decided to make New York City their new home. Grant now turned his full attention to his own affairs. He found himself at a unique disadvantage. In October, Samuel L. Clemens had welcomed him to Hartford with an astute speech about how republics treat their heroes. "You are now a private citizen, but private employments are closed against you because your name would be used for speculative purposes, and you have refused to permit that. But your country will reward you, never fear." Anxious to find his own path to prosperity, Grant sought a suitable outlet for his energies. His summer tour of western mines, made with a view toward future employment, had resulted in the "speculative" attempts Clemens mentioned. Grant turned instead to Mexico, which had been much in his thoughts since his visit the previous winter. In November, in a lengthy dinner speech, he touted prospects for Mexican railroads to a group of capitalists led by Jay Gould. This meeting, arranged by Grant's old friend Matías Romero, led to the incorporation of the Mexican Southern Railroad Co., headed by Grant, Romero, Gould, and others, and designed to open the southern state of Oaxaca to trade and development. In the early months of 1881, Grant threw himself into the new venture.

At the same time, he agreed to head a commission planning a World's Fair for 1883 in New York City. The fair foundered on issues of funding and location. Grant and others opposed a chosen site at the northern edge of Manhattan and favored Central

Park. But the public balked. "I confess that I cannot understand the universal opposition to such a use of the Park, especially as it closes the door to subscriptions which would soon place the fair on a solid financial basis." Grant soon resigned, and support for the fair evaporated.

At the end of March, Grant headed to Mexico to negotiate a charter for the Mexican Southern. Despite rumors, perhaps planted by rival promoters, that he represented annexationist forces, Grant succeeded in signing a contract that the Mexican Congress approved in late May. Wanting greater autonomy, Grant declined a Mexican subsidy for the railroad. Such scruples discouraged investors and probably delayed construction.

From Mexico City, Grant followed a political crisis developing back home. In a battle between major factions of the Republican party, Garfield sided with Secretary of State James G. Blaine over Senator Conkling in key patronage decisions. This snub of his ally angered Grant, who complained privately that "Garfield has shewn that he is not possessed of the backbone of an Angleworm." In late April, Grant openly broke with Garfield, writing that "his first act was but a deep laid scheme by somebody to punish prominent leaders for being openly friendly to me." In May, Conkling resigned from the Senate, seeking to force the issue with a fresh mandate. Grant returned from Mexico at the end of May ready to support Conkling. On arrival at New Orleans, during stops at St. Louis and Chicago, and on his way to New York City, Grant gave a series of interviews that distanced him further from the president. "Garfield is a man without backbone; a man of fine ability, but lacking stamina. He wants to please everybody and is afraid of the enmity of all the men around him." Reporters described a chilly meeting between the two men in late June at Long Branch, New Jersey. But all enmity vanished on July 2, when Garfield was shot by Charles J. Guiteau. Grant offered a frank assessment of Garfield's chances, but held out hope. He also offered a glimpse of the troubled Guiteau, who had pestered Grant during the previous winter in New York City. "Several times he waylaid me on the street or in the corridor of the hotel when I was passing through, but I would not talk to him. . . . The fellow was sharp and a ready talker, and appeared as though he had some education, but he was evidently an adventurer, a man I would not trust with anything." Garfield's decline absorbed the nation all summer, and Grant grieved with his countrymen when he died in September.

After Garfield's death, Grant again took a more active part in Republican politics under President Chester A. Arthur, a man closer to Grant's stalwart supporters. Some called for Grant's elevation to a post in the new administration. Rejecting this suggestion, Grant praised Arthur as "a man in whom I have every confidence and am satisfied the country will have also when they know him half as well as I do." For several months, Grant assisted various office seekers until the inevitable impositions associated with patronage became tiresome and he "resolved to abstain for the future from troubling the President with recommendations for appointments of any kind." Although he occasionally broke this vow, the volume of Grant's political correspondence decreased sharply. Still, he remained a significant factor in national politics and closely watched events in Washington.

In August, 1881, the Grants purchased a home on East Sixty-Sixth Street. While he continued to spend warm months along the ocean at Long Branch, and took occasional trips south and west, Grant's activities centered on the nation's financial metropolis. He was an honored guest at many dinners and gatherings, and often gave short speeches in tribute to men and ideas that he respected. Grant told members of the Lincoln Club that their organization bore "the name of one of the greatest men that our country has produced, and one who probably was better far for the time and for the occasion than perhaps any man we had in this country." "This is a country where every man has an opportunity to make a place for himself," he told the Friendly Sons of St. Patrick on another occasion. "And one reason why I am proud of my country is because there is no other nation where the poor man has such glorious opportunities as here."

Grant's own wealth appeared to grow, thanks in large part to his connection with Grant & Ward, a brokerage firm begun by his

son, Ulysses S. Grant, Jr., and Ferdinand Ward, an acquaintance
with a reputation as a financial genius. Initially brought in as a silent partner with a $50,000 investment, Grant eventually became
a full partner after committing another $50,000. While he visited
the firm's offices on Wall Street frequently and glanced over balance sheets that showed fabulous profits from apparently shrewd
contract management, Grant and his son left active operation to
Ward. Another partner, James D. Fish, president of the Marine
National Bank, also left details to Ward. In March, 1882, a false
rumor of Grant's financial failure led to a brief run on Wall Street
and may have reflected private unease about the true nature of
Ward's speculations. In November, Grant urged Arthur to increase
the money supply, a move credited with strengthening the market.

The pressures of command and of office having receded, Grant
found it easier to revisit past actions and decisions. Such reflection was evident in late 1881 when he agreed to meet Fitz John
Porter, who had long sought to overturn his dismissal from the
army for insubordination at the Second Battle of Bull Run. Grant
had blocked Porter's efforts both at army headquarters and in the
White House, and had reaffirmed his opposition as late as 1880.
Now, after hearing Porter and studying the record, Grant publicly
reversed himself. "If a solemn and sincere expression of my thorough understanding of and belief in the entire innocence of General
Porter will tend to draw the public mind to the same conviction, I
shall feel abundantly rewarded for my efforts," Grant concluded in
an article reviewing the case. Support for Porter thrust Grant into
a bitter feud with deep roots in the war and powerful antagonists
in Congress. As the controversy continued, both sides waited for
Arthur to weigh in.

With the marriage of Ulysses, Jr. (Buck), in Nov., 1880, to Fannie Chaffee, daughter of Grant's Colorado friend Jerome B. Chaffee,
all of Grant's children had found spouses. Grant described Fannie
in a letter to daughter Nellie. "Every one speaks most highly of the
young lady. She is quite pretty with all." Son Jesse had recently
married Lizzie Chapman, of San Francisco. "She is quite small with
beautiful large eyes, a very small face but prominent nose, light

auburn hair, and by some thought quite pretty. I do not think her as pretty as either Ida or Bucks wife. But she is very pleasant and not a bit spoiled. The same may be said of all your sisters-in-law." Grant's beloved circle of grandchildren soon increased. But they nearly lost their grandfather on June 29, 1882, when his commuter train from Long Branch to Manhattan plunged off a bridge into a creek, killing three. The *New York Times* reported that Grant managed to climb out of the car window. "He had lost his hat, but still had his morning's cigar between his teeth. He had received no other injury than a slight cut on the leg, and to somebody who asked him if he was hurt, he replied, 'No, I'm all right.' Then he began to direct the movements of the workmen." Grant later testified at the inquest, which found the railroad negligent.

On all accounts, Grant had reason to be pleased with his place at home and in the world. In November, the Democrats won control of the House of Representatives, a development that Grant viewed with detached apprehension. Grant now trod a wider stage. In December, he organized the city's elite to entertain a visiting Japanese prince, Emperor Meiji's uncle. In August, Arthur had appointed him commissioner to negotiate a commercial treaty with Mexico. As 1882 ended, Grant prepared to go to Washington for treaty talks, eager to further a policy close to his heart.

We are indebted to J. Dane Hartgrove and Howard H. Wehmann for assistance in searching the National Archives; to Harriet F. Simon for proofreading; and to Anastasia Saverino, Molly White, and Abigail Wheetley, graduate students at Southern Illinois University, for research assistance.

Financial support for the period during which this volume was prepared came from Southern Illinois University, the National Endowment for the Humanities, and the National Historical Publications and Records Commission.

JOHN Y. SIMON

August 16, 2006

Editorial Procedure

---

1. Editorial Insertions

A. Words or letters in roman type within brackets represent editorial reconstruction of parts of manuscripts torn, mutilated, or illegible.

B. [. . .] or [⸻ ⸻ ⸻] within brackets represent lost material which cannot be reconstructed. The number of dots represents the approximate number of lost letters; dashes represent lost words.

C. Words in *italic* type within brackets represent material such as dates which were not part of the original manuscript.

D. Other material crossed out is indicated by ~~cancelled type~~.

E. Material raised in manuscript, as "4th," has been brought in line, as "4th."

2. Symbols Used to Describe Manuscripts

AD   Autograph Document
ADS   Autograph Document Signed
ADf   Autograph Draft
ADfS   Autograph Draft Signed
AES   Autograph Endorsement Signed
AL   Autograph Letter

ALS	Autograph Letter Signed
ANS	Autograph Note Signed
D	Document
DS	Document Signed
Df	Draft
DfS	Draft Signed
ES	Endorsement Signed
LS	Letter Signed

3. *Military Terms and Abbreviations*

Act.	Acting
Adjt.	Adjutant
AG	Adjutant General
AGO	Adjutant General's Office
Art.	Artillery
Asst.	Assistant
Bvt.	Brevet
Brig.	Brigadier
Capt.	Captain
Cav.	Cavalry
Col.	Colonel
Co.	Company
C.S.A.	Confederate States of America
Dept.	Department
Div.	Division
Gen.	General
Hd. Qrs.	Headquarters
Inf.	Infantry
Lt.	Lieutenant
Maj.	Major
Q. M.	Quartermaster
Regt.	Regiment or regimental
Sgt.	Sergeant
USMA	United States Military Academy, West Point, N.Y.
Vols.	Volunteers

4. Short Titles and Abbreviations

ABPC	*American Book Prices Current* (New York, 1895–)
Badeau	Adam Badeau, *Grant in Peace. From Appomattox to Mount McGregor* (Hartford, Conn., 1887)
CG	*Congressional Globe.* Numbers following represent the Congress, session, and page.
J. G. Cramer	Jesse Grant Cramer, ed., *Letters of Ulysses S. Grant to his Father and his Youngest Sister, 1857–78* (New York and London, 1912)
DAB	*Dictionary of American Biography* (New York, 1928–36)
Foreign Relations	*Papers Relating to the Foreign Relations of the United States* (Washington, 1869–)
Garland	Hamlin Garland, *Ulysses S. Grant: His Life and Character* (New York, 1898)
Julia Grant	John Y. Simon, ed., *The Personal Memoirs of Julia Dent Grant* (New York, 1975)
HED	*House Executive Documents*
HMD	*House Miscellaneous Documents*
HRC	*House Reports of Committees.* Numbers following *HED*, *HMD*, or *HRC* represent the number of the Congress, the session, and the document.
Ill. AG Report	J. N. Reece, ed., *Report of the Adjutant General of the State of Illinois* (Springfield, 1900)
Johnson, Papers	LeRoy P. Graf and Ralph W. Haskins, eds., *The Papers of Andrew Johnson* (Knoxville, 1967–2000)
Lewis	Lloyd Lewis, *Captain Sam Grant* (Boston, 1950)
Lincoln, Works	Roy P. Basler, Marion Dolores Pratt, and Lloyd A. Dunlap, eds., *The Collected Works of Abraham Lincoln* (New Brunswick, 1953–55)
Memoirs	*Personal Memoirs of U. S. Grant* (New York, 1885–86)
Nevins, Fish	Allan Nevins, *Hamilton Fish: The Inner History of the Grant Administration* (New York, 1936)

O.R.	*The War of the Rebellion: A Compilation of the Official Records of the Union and Confederate Armies* (Washington, 1880–1901)
O.R. (Navy)	*Official Records of the Union and Confederate Navies in the War of the Rebellion* (Washington, 1894–1927). Roman numerals following *O.R.* or *O.R.* (Navy) represent the series and the volume.
PUSG	John Y. Simon, ed., *The Papers of Ulysses S. Grant* (Carbondale and Edwardsville, 1967–)
Richardson	Albert D. Richardson, *A Personal History of Ulysses S. Grant* (Hartford, Conn., 1868)
SED	*Senate Executive Documents*
SMD	*Senate Miscellaneous Documents*
SRC	*Senate Reports of Committees.* Numbers following *SED, SMD,* or *SRC* represent the number of the Congress, the session, and the document.
USGA Newsletter	*Ulysses S. Grant Association Newsletter*
Young	John Russell Young, *Around the World with General Grant* (New York, 1879)

5. *Location Symbols*

CLU	University of California at Los Angeles, Los Angeles, Calif.
CoHi	Colorado State Historical Society, Denver, Colo.
CSmH	Henry E. Huntington Library, San Marino, Calif.
CSt	Stanford University, Stanford, Calif.
CtY	Yale University, New Haven, Conn.
CU-B	Bancroft Library, University of California, Berkeley, Calif.
DLC	Library of Congress, Washington, D.C. Numbers following DLC-USG represent the series and volume of military records in the USG papers.

DNA	National Archives, Washington, D.C. Additional numbers identify record groups.
IaHA	Iowa State Department of History and Archives, Des Moines, Iowa.
I-ar	Illinois State Archives, Springfield, Ill.
IC	Chicago Public Library, Chicago, Ill.
ICarbS	Southern Illinois University, Carbondale, Ill.
ICHi	Chicago Historical Society, Chicago, Ill.
ICN	Newberry Library, Chicago, Ill.
ICU	University of Chicago, Chicago, Ill.
IHi	Illinois State Historical Library, Springfield, Ill.
In	Indiana State Library, Indianapolis, Ind.
InFtwL	Lincoln National Life Foundation, Fort Wayne, Ind.
InHi	Indiana Historical Society, Indianapolis, Ind.
InNd	University of Notre Dame, Notre Dame, Ind.
InU	Indiana University, Bloomington, Ind.
KHi	Kansas State Historical Society, Topeka, Kan.
MdAN	United States Naval Academy Museum, Annapolis, Md.
MeB	Bowdoin College, Brunswick, Me.
MH	Harvard University, Cambridge, Mass.
MHi	Massachusetts Historical Society, Boston, Mass.
MiD	Detroit Public Library, Detroit, Mich.
MiU-C	William L. Clements Library, University of Michigan, Ann Arbor, Mich.
MoSHi	Missouri Historical Society, St. Louis, Mo.
NHi	New-York Historical Society, New York, N.Y.
NIC	Cornell University, Ithaca, N.Y.
NjP	Princeton University, Princeton, N.J.
NjR	Rutgers University, New Brunswick, N.J.
NN	New York Public Library, New York, N.Y.
NNP	Pierpont Morgan Library, New York, N.Y.
NRU	University of Rochester, Rochester, N.Y.
OClWHi	Western Reserve Historical Society, Cleveland, Ohio.

OFH	Rutherford B. Hayes Library, Fremont, Ohio.
OHi	Ohio Historical Society, Columbus, Ohio.
OrHi	Oregon Historical Society, Portland, Ore.
PCarlA	U.S. Army Military History Institute, Carlisle Barracks, Pa.
PHi	Historical Society of Pennsylvania, Philadelphia, Pa.
PPRF	Rosenbach Foundation, Philadelphia, Pa.
RPB	Brown University, Providence, R.I.
TxHR	Rice University, Houston, Tex.
USG 3	Maj. Gen. Ulysses S. Grant 3rd, Clinton, N.Y.
USMA	United States Military Academy Library, West Point, N.Y.
ViHi	Virginia Historical Society, Richmond, Va.
ViU	University of Virginia, Charlottesville, Va.
WHi	State Historical Society of Wisconsin, Madison, Wis.
Wy-Ar	Wyoming State Archives and Historical Department, Cheyenne, Wyo.
WyU	University of Wyoming, Laramie, Wyo.

Chronology

October 1, 1880–December 31, 1882

━━━

1880, OCT. 6–7.   USG attended a reunion of the 21st Ill. at Decatur.

OCT. 11.   N.Y. Republicans honored USG with a torchlight parade through Manhattan.

OCT. 12.   Republicans carried elections in Ohio and Ind.

OCT. 12–15.   USG visited Providence, Boston, and Plymouth Rock.

OCT. 16.   At Hartford, Samuel L. Clemens praised USG's service to the nation.

OCT. 20.   Addressing the N.Y. Stock Exchange, USG alluded to his last visit, during the 1873 panic.

OCT. 21.   USG presided over Republican rallies at Stamford, Conn., and Jersey City.

OCT. 23.   USG testified at a court of inquiry for Lt. Col. Gouverneur K. Warren. Later, he spoke at a rally in Franklin, N.J.

OCT. 25–29.   Campaigning in upstate N.Y., USG addressed rallies at Utica, Syracuse, Auburn, Rochester, and Buffalo.

OCT. 30.   At a Staten Island rally, USG closely predicted the election's outcome.

Nov. 1.   Ulysses S. Grant, Jr., married Fannie Josephine Chaffee in New York City.

Nov. 2.   Garfield defeated Hancock. USG wrote: "The country, in my judgement has escaped a great calamity."

Nov. 11.   USG spoke at length about Mexican trade and development to leading railroad promoters assembled by Matías Romero.

Nov. 22.   USG attended the unveiling of a statue of Alexander Hamilton in Central Park.

DEC. 11.   USG toured factories at Paterson, N.J.

Dec. 14–16.   At Washington, D.C., USG addressed a Boys in Blue reception and dined at the White House.

1881, Jan. 11.   USG visited his mother and sister at Elizabeth, N.J., and addressed a parade of Zouaves.

Jan. 14.   USG accepted the presidency of the 1883 World's Fair Commission. Later, USG addressed a benefit concert for a black church.

Jan. 16.   USG attended the Saturday Club at the home of Anthony J. Drexel in Philadelphia.

Jan. 17–20.   In Albany, USG addressed the N.Y. State Assembly.

Jan. 21.   USG spoke to veterans at Troy, N.Y.

Jan. 22.   Horace Porter gave a dinner for USG at the Union League Club.

Jan. 31.   N.Y. Senator William Waldorf Astor introduced a bill to incorporate the Mexican Southern Railroad.

Feb. 1–3.   USG attended meetings of the Peabody Education Fund in Washington, D.C.

Feb. 5.   USG presided over a banquet to raise money for the 1883 World's Fair, and later subscribed $1,000 for 100 shares.

Feb. 11.   USG chaired a meeting of capitalists interested in Mexican railroad development.

Feb. 26.   USG urged that the 1883 World's Fair be located in Central Park.

Mar. 9.   Visiting Washington, D.C., USG and Julia Grant ate breakfast at the White House with President James A. Garfield.

Mar. 22.   Faced with lagging subscriptions and a dispute over the site, USG resigned from the 1883 World's Fair Commission.

Mar. 28.   USG left for Mexico to negotiate a contract for the Mexican Southern Railroad Co.

April 3.   At Galveston, the Grants and Matías Romero boarded the steamer *Whitney* for Vera Cruz.

April 22.   USG addressed a Mexico City banquet.

April 24.   In a letter from Mexico City, USG criticized Garfield over N.Y. patronage.

May 11.   USG signed a contract with Mexican officials granting concessions to the Mexican Southern Railroad Co.

June 2.   The Grants arrived at New Orleans aboard the *City of Merida*. USG praised Roscoe Conkling, who had resigned from the Senate to protest President James A. Garfield's patronage policy.

JUNE 6–11. USG extended a stop at St. Louis after Julia Grant became ill. USG attended horse races and visited his farm.

JUNE 12. Interviewed at Chicago, USG escalated his involvement in the Garfield–Conkling dispute.

JUNE 16. USG told a Pittsburgh reporter: "As a citizen I have a right to express my thoughts and will do so when it suits me."

JUNE 17. Back in New York City, USG met Conkling.

JUNE 23. USG wrote from Long Branch that Julia Grant remained ill.

JULY 2. Garfield was shot by Charles J. Guiteau.

JULY 4. Interviewed about Garfield's condition, USG recalled his own encounters with Guiteau. "He looked seedy and like a dead-beat."

JULY 4. Ulysses S. Grant 3rd was born at Chicago.

AUG. 2. USG wrote that he had purchased a home in New York City.

AUG. 4. USG's brother Orvil died at Elizabeth, N.J.

AUG. 5. Nellie Grant, daughter of Jesse Root Grant, Jr., was born at Long Branch.

AUG. 11. USG served as pallbearer at the funeral of Robert Patterson in Philadelphia.

SEPT. 6. Garfield was moved from the White House to Long Branch. At Chicago, USG told a reporter: "He should have been taken from there long ago."

SEPT. 8. USG addressed Ill. veterans at Bloomington.

SEPT. 19. Garfield died. USG was observed "weeping bitterly."

SEPT. 21. With President Chester A. Arthur, USG accompanied Garfield's body from Long Branch to Washington, D.C.

SEPT. 22. USG and Rutherford B. Hayes paid respects to Garfield in the Capitol rotunda.

SEPT. 26. Miriam Grant, daughter of Ulysses S. Grant, Jr., was born in New York City.

SEPT. 29. USG and Julia Grant moved into their new home.

OCT. 21. USG visited Washington, D.C.

Nov. 3. Fitz John Porter presented his case for reinstatement to the army to USG.

DEC. 22. Reversing his previous stance, USG wrote to Arthur favoring Fitz John Porter's cause.

1882, MAR. 8. Unfounded rumors of USG's failure sparked a run on Wall Street.

MAR. 21–28. At Washington, D.C., USG and Julia Grant attended a White House dinner and Arthur's first public reception.

APRIL 25.   USG attended the wedding of John Russell Young to Julia E. Coleman at Hartford.

MAY 4.   Arthur declined to reinstate Fitz John Porter.

JUNE 13–15.   USG attended the Army of the Potomac reunion at Detroit.

JUNE 24.   The Grants arrived at Long Branch.

JUNE 29.   USG survived a train derailment near Long Branch that left three dead.

JULY 6.   USG signed but later disavowed a letter concerning the Grant & Ward brokerage firm that authorized Ferdinand Ward to "derive what profit he can for the firm that the use of my name and influence may bring."

AUG. 7.   Arthur commissioned USG to negotiate a commercial treaty with Mexico.

AUG. 21–28.   USG and Julia Grant vacationed at Saratoga Springs, N.Y.

SEPT. 20.   The Grants left their summer home at Long Branch.

OCT. 6.   USG signed a contract to extend the Mexican Southern Railroad into Guatemala.

OCT. 10.   USG asked Edwin D. Morgan for a $30,000 loan.

OCT. 11.   USG and Julia Grant began a visit to the country home of George W. Childs, near Philadelphia.

NOV. 7.   Democrats won a majority in the House of Representatives.

NOV. 8.   USG visited a Boston industrial fair.

NOV. 22.   USG wrote to Arthur urging currency expansion.

NOV. 25.   USG attended a Saturday Club meeting at the Philadelphia home of Anthony J. Drexel.

DEC. 19.   USG hosted a dinner at the Union League Club for Prince Arisugawa Taruhito of Japan.

DEC. 22.   USG and Samuel L. Clemens addressed the New England Society dinner.

The Papers of Ulysses S. Grant
October 1, 1880–December 31, 1882

Speech

———

[*Decatur, Ill., Oct. 6, 1880*]

LADIES AND GENTLEMEN—I am not precisely aware what the order of proceedings is to be here this evening, but I know I was invited here to the reunion of the old twenty-first I[l]linois Volunteers, which was the first company I had the honor of commanding during the late rebellion. I believe the most of the survivors of that regimen[t] are here present on the platform this evening, and as the evening passes away I suppose it will be developed to my mind what is to be done here. I am very glad to meet as many of my old regiment as are here on this occasion. I suppose there are more of them, probably, still living and scattered over our distant territory, and developing the country which up to our late struggle was not occupied by the white man. I have had occasion before, in traveling all over the world, to say that war, while so much to be deplored, is not altogether an unmixed evil. There has been no where that I have been that I have not found our volunteers, no country in Europe, none in Asia or in Africa where I have been that I have not met some of our volunteers in the late war, men who, but for the change of life from their quiet homes to the field of battle, would probably have never thought of going beyond the place where they were brought up, but four years of separation from those homes has extended their ideas, enlarge[d] their views, and some of them have gone off to and introduced American commerce into distant countries, others to new territories in their restlessness of the confinement of the farms or stores and are developing now our great territories, and preparing them to become states of this Union. How much the twenty-first Illinois have contributed to this I am not aware, but I will warrant there are some of them living in every one of the new states and territories, coming all the way from there

to be present on this occasion; others so far away are so engaged
they could not be here. Gentlemen, I am very glad to see so many
of you, and I hope in the course of the evening we will be able to
hear the experience of some of you. Col. McMackin will preside
and conduct the exercises in the order in which they come.

Decatur Republican, Oct. 7, 1880. See *PUSG*, 20, 221. "The roll-call was answered to
by 125 of the 150 members of the regiment now known to be living." *Chicago Tribune*,
Oct. 7, 1880.
　　Earlier on Oct. 6, 1880, Mayor Henry W. Waggoner of Decatur, Ill., introduced
USG at the home of Richard J. Oglesby, former Ill. governor. USG replied. "Mʀ
Mᴀʏᴏʀ: It is with great pleasure I visit the city of Decatur again, after an absence of
nearly 19 years. I believe I have not been in the city not more than to pass along the
Central Railroad since 1861. It is pleasant to be here and mark the progress that has
been made in this section of the state as well as the city. I am gratified to see so many
of those who went out with me in 1861 here to-day. I thank them Mr. Mayor and you,
and the citizens for this cordial reception." *Decatur Republican*, Oct. 7, 1880.
　　On Oct. 7, after a welcoming address by Jesse H. Moore, former col., 115th Ill.,
and president, Macon County Veterans' Association, USG told an estimated 20,000
gathered at the Macon County fairgrounds ". . . that we want this whole Nation to be
a homogenious people all striving to rival each other in prosperity in developing their
relative sections, and in upholding one common flag, and one common institution—
that of freedom and of equal rights to all, without regard to race, color, section, religion or nationality, and with the speaker I believe that in some way or other that result
is to be worked out; how, I do not exactly see, but that it will be worked out in some
way I am perfectly confident, and the day will come when we will hear nothing about
the sections but will strive to rival each other as good citizens in upholding the common flag of all the states. Gentlemen, one and all, and ladies, I thank you cordially for
the reception granted me and my old regiment here to-day." *Ibid.*, Oct. 7, 1880.
　　In Oct., 1879, Decatur officials had invited USG to a reunion of the 21st Ill., to be
held the next Oct.; USG agreed, "so far as anything so far in the future could be promised." *Ibid.*, Sept. 16, 1880. In Sept., 1880, after USG wrote that the reunion would conflict with wedding plans for his son Ulysses, Waggoner and Moore visited Galena. On
Sept. 15, USG telegraphed to Moore, Decatur. "Will attend reunion in Decatur." *Ibid.*

Speech

[*Boston, Oct. 13, 1880*]

Gᴇɴᴛʟᴇᴍᴇɴ ᴏꜰ ᴛʜᴇ Mᴇʀᴄʜᴀɴᴛꜱ' Aꜱꜱᴏᴄɪᴀᴛɪᴏɴ: I do not know
precisely what the good news is I brought. That, I suppose, depends a little upon the politics of the individual. And as this is not
a party association, I should certainly say nothing on this occasion

to have a political bearing, except that I am always glad individually when the result is as it is reported this morning.[1] I do not
know that I have anything special to say this morning, except that
we know how much our success as a nation depends upon our commerce, and the commerce depends, in a large measure, upon the efforts and industry of the people engaged in trade, as all of you are.
So far as agriculture is concerned in this country, that will take
care of itself. We are getting to have intelligent farmers and culti-
vators of the soil, with their agricultural associations and county
and State fairs. The most approved agricultural machinery in the
world is found in the United States, and the most agricultural labor
is performed here with the least number of hands. It depends upon
you, gentlemen, and those in business, to find a market for those
agricultural products, and also to find occupation for the surplus
labor that is made by improved agricultural machinery. We have
got to turn our attention somewhat to the surplus labor not now
needed to cultivate the fields, and we want to find a market for our
manufactures. In my travels, it seems to me, I have seen where this
might be done with profit to those who buy of us. We do not want
them to pay us money; we want their products in exchange. I will
not say much on this occasion about how it might be accomplished
in the far East, where there is a big field; but my most recent visit
has been to our neighboring Republic, Mexico. There is a grand
field there, it seems to me, for our enterprise, and for an immense
profit to them as well as to ourselves. We are not so particularly
generous as to want to benefit our neighbors at our expense. But
when we can benefit ourselves and them, too, greatly we are the
most generous people in the world.

   I found in Mexico a country, which I had visited a good many
years ago, just on the eve of a great advance and very desirous to
extend their foreign commerce. A portion of thinking people were
alarmed a little at the approach of American population and American railroads on their borders, but they were fully alive to the
necessity and importance of railroads in their own country. They
consulted with me very freely and very confidentially, I may say,
pretty much all the time I was there, and I did and said all I could

to allay their apprehensions of danger from the approach of the universal Yankee. They have a very lively recollection of the Mexican war, which resulted in such a loss of territory. From occasional loose remarks in newspapers and by individuals, they are afraid that the approach of Yankee and American enterprise and railroads means the sloughing of this State and that. I assured them they need have no apprehension that at all events, if there is any danger at all, the best way to allay it was to cultivate the best and most intimate commercial relations between the two Republics, that if they tried to keep aloof from us, and benefit European nations by their trade to the exclusion of us, they made enemies of their neighbors. I told them that was not good policy. I told them their apprehensions were well-founded 20 years ago, because at that time we had an institution never sustained except where it existed, and that it would not exist in any country longer than it could retain political control, hence, territory where slavery could be planted was necessary to the existence of that institution, and, of course, while slavery existed they were constantly in danger of their territory being wanted to give the slaveholders political influence and supremacy in Washington. But now that institution was dead, never to be revived. We were a people of homogeneous institutions from one end of the country to the other, and there was no political advantage accruing to any political party by an accession of territory in any particular direction, and I believed it was almost the universal sentiment of our people that we wanted no territory we had to filibuster for; that if ever we acquired territory it would have to be with the consent of the people occupying that territory and our own consent. It seemed to very much satisfy those with whom I talked, and they asked me to interest myself in having American capital extended to their country to build up their roads. They would aid them with the right of way and the free admission of all the material required, and give a liberal subsidy if they could be assured of the building of the roads.

There is no secret of the capacity of Mexico for production, if you think about it. We now do an importation business of nearly $200,000,000 of tropical and semi-tropical products. Mexico could

produce the whole of them if she had railroads to give her an outlet for them, and her people have the industry to do it—a fact not
generally credited, nor did I believe it until I was there this last
time. With their climate, industry, and everything required to produce all those tropical and semi-tropical products, which, as I said,
amount to about $200,000,000 a year, and, also, increasing, as we
are increasing, in our products and wealth, we are now getting
those products from countries where they are largely produced by
slave labor. We are constantly paying into their treasuries a large
amount annually for duties, and we give them back nothing but
sterling exchange. When they want to buy anything, as they do
their manufactured articles, they go to Europe for them, and we get
comparatively nothing in return, fully 95 per cent. being paid for in
sterling exchange. Mexico is not only our neighbor, but she is a Republic. If fostered, she can produce nearly all of those articles, and
will take in exchange what our manufacturers produce. They will
take from us cotton goods, locomotives, cars, railroad iron, rolling-
stock, all the machinery necessary to the running of a railroad,
agricultural implements, wagons, carriages, musical instruments,
jewelry, clocks, watches, and a thousand and one other things too
numerous to mention. When we can pay for imports of our tropical
products with the products of our manufactories, we shall benefit
Mexico, benefit ourselves, continue to give employment to the multitude of people that we now have, and which are ever coming to
our shores, and will all be happier and better, I hope.

New York Times, Oct. 14, 1880.

On Sept. 4, 1880, Governor John D. Long of Mass. wrote to USG, Galena. "The
First Brigade of the Massachusetts Volunteer Militia is to go into camp in a few days
and it would gratify them and myself very much if you could be present. I should be
v[e]ry glad if you could come east and spend the 15th with me at my home in Hingham where an agricultural fair is to be held which would give you an opportunity to
see something of our rural life; and from there the plan is to go to camp, spend the
night and review the brigade next day. On the 17th occurs the 250th anniversary of the
settlement of Boston to which I presume you have already received an invitation from
the city authorities. In regard to the two days on which I should be glad to entertain
you I should be happy to make your coming and stay as agreeable as the courtesies of
the State will enable me to do. If you should prefer to come quietly I could arrange that
to suit your wishes. I am sure that nowhere would you be welcomed more warmly than
in Massachusetts." LS (press), Massachusetts State Library, Boston, Mass. On Sept. 10,

USG wrote to Long declining to attend the militia encampment. David Schulson, Catalogue 25 [1985], no. 37.

On Oct. 12, USG spoke at Providence, R. I., en route to Boston. "I am very glad to meet you all, and from your numbers I should suppose that the detachment of 7000 from the New York torchlight procession, which was cut off last night, had got up here and left their torches behind. I have only got one moment to stop, and it will take more time than that to make the apologies I ought to make for not saying anything." *Boston Evening Transcript*, Oct. 13, 1880. On the same evening, USG spoke after a torchlight procession in Boston. "Gentlemen—I have only just arrived. I expect to stay here to the end of the week, and if I should make you a speech I should get through with all I had to say before then; and as I expect to meet a good many people here, I should not have a word for them. And so you will all of you, therefore, have to excuse me." *Ibid.*

On Oct. 13, former Mass. governor Alexander H. Rice introduced USG at a banquet. USG replied. ". . . We are a nation that proceeds on the theory that all power is with the people. Our rulers are only servants, having only such powers as the people choose to extend to them from time to time. Other nations, I think history will bear me out in saying, have proceeded on the theory that all power is with the head of the Government, and the people have no rights, no privileges whatever, except as they are extended by the crown. It is impossible that on that theory such self-reliance, such independence as our people possess can be created except after a lapse of great time, and when the power is so far extended to the people that the crown has lost its influence. They can then begin to grow great. We started out with the experience of other nations, and commenced pretty well considering that [*apprentices*] had to boss the job. Now we have grown to manhood and have become of age, have got a history, I think with the acting President, that we, some way or other, will work through any future difficulties that may arise, and that we will go down to the end of time an example to other peoples, and furnishing a good example which many of them will feel sooner or later. . . ." *Ibid.*, Oct. 14, 1880; *New York Times*, Oct. 15, 1880.

On Oct. 14, USG spoke at Hingham, Mass. "Veterans and Ladies and Gentlemen— It affords me very great pleasure to meet you here, and I regret that we have but a few minutes to stop. I am surprised at the number of veterans I have met today in this part of Massachusetts, though I knew your State had furnished them during the war, but I supposed they had all emigrated. I have recently made a trip through some of our new Territories and States, and at least nine out of every ten men over thirty-five years of age were veterans, and I feared that the whole of them had gone from the East to develop the mines and fields of the West. But I find there are enough left here in Massachusetts to set an example to the rising generation, if need there should be for them for the purpose for which they went forth twenty years ago. But I trust there will never be an occasion of that kind again. I repeat that I am very glad to see you." *Boston Evening Transcript*, Oct. 15, 1880. On the same day, at Plymouth, USG "was escorted to Memorial Hall, where he was met by Governor and Mrs. Long and Henry B. Pierce. Judge Russell welcomed the General to the home of Miles Standish. The General replied briefly, accepting the welcome and acknowledging to courtesies extended. The sword of Miles Standish was then handed to him. From Memorial Hall the party was driven to Pilgrim Hall and thence to Plymouth Rock. From the Rock the General was taken to the national monument to the Pilgrims, whence he was driven to Davis Hall, where 800 children had gathered to greet him. . . ." *New York Herald*, Oct. 15, 1880. USG spoke. "I am very glad to see you, the school children of Plymouth. I am glad of an opportunity of visiting this historical spot. As often as I have been in Massachusetts I have never had the pleasure before, although I have been so near to it. What we see before us here in you, children, is what has made New England so famous. It is what has extended so many benefits through the new States and Territories as they have become settled. We are getting to have New England schools all through the Northwest, and I hope the day is not far distant when it will be extended to all parts of the land. When it becomes universal there will be an end to all our strife. I wish to say that I hope success may attend those schools throughout the whole country, as they have come from New England States." *Ibid.*

Also on Oct. 14, USG addressed a Republican rally at Faneuil Hall in Boston. "Gentlemen—I have no idea whatever of saying a word on political questions; in fact I do not know how I could if I should attempt it; but I came here this evening by invitation, knowing that you were to hear addresses of gentlemen who were accustomed to speech-making. But to infuse one of my speeches into this evening's proceedings would not help the matter at all, and I am here to visit you all only. I hope your meeting will meet with the greatest success." *Boston Evening Transcript*, Oct. 15, 1880. At another rally, at Tremont Temple, USG's arrival interrupted a speech by Emery A. Storrs. "Ladies and Gentlemen—The speaker who was occupying the time when I came in I have heard before. I don't know whether all of you have heard him, or whether many of you have. But I know that you will be much more pleased with what he will set before you than you would be with anything that I could say. Therefore I shall say nothing on the subject which brings you here this evening, only that I testify by my presence here my indorsement in advance of what Mr. Storrs is going to say to you." *Ibid.*

On Oct. 15, USG addressed a luncheon of the Mass. Republican Central Committee. "GENTLEMEN—I was informed when I came in here that this was rather a political body, and I understood that all the members of the committee who invited me here were members of some party, and I had an instinct that they were connected with the same party that I am. If you can tell me what good I can do in this assembly by giving my views on politics to the gentlemen present I shall be glad to do it. I heard my friend Storrs last evening describe a class of politicians with caterpillar spinal cords who need a little stiffening up or starch put into them. If any of you confess to that sort of weakness I shall be happy to speak. Well, gentlemen, you are all right then, are you? I am very much obliged to you, and I hope you will all be present on the 2d of November and of the same opinion as you are now." *New York Herald*, Oct. 16, 1880. Later on Oct. 15, USG addressed veterans. "I am very happy, gentlemen, to meet the New England Commandery of the Loyal Legion of the United States, and to be able to spend half an hour with you this evening. I think I would have done better, perhaps, in keeping the rules of this commandery than I possibly could in violating its rules by addressing you. You will have to excuse me from making any further remarks than to say how glad I am to meet you." *Boston Evening Transcript*, Oct. 16, 1880. On the same evening, USG spoke at a reception given by Dahlgren Post No. 2, Grand Army of the Republic. ". . . I have not been in a country in the four quarters of the globe, but I have met veterans. And they were not ordinary tramps, either. They knew where they were going, and what they wanted, and knew how to get home when they wanted to. I am sure while we have so much regret for the loss of so many brave men, yet by the services of those who are dead and of those living, we have accomplished a good deal that is not to be despised. We have made a country which the balance of the world did not regard as having a history. But it is now full of history, is respected abroad and honored by the common people throughout the civilized world for the example it has set of a government by the people and for the people. And if we go on for a generation or two, as we are capable of, with peace at home, there is no danger of a foreign war, because we will be so strong that nobody will want to tackle us. Ladies and gentlemen, I am very much obliged to you for listening to me for even so long as I have spoken, but I think I have kept my pledge when I said I would not detain you long." *Ibid.*

1. Republicans carried Ohio and Ind. in Oct. 12 elections.

Speech

————

[*Hartford, Oct. 16, 1880*]

MR. PRESIDENT AND GENTLEMEN OF HARTFORD—I am very proud of the welcomes that I have received at the hands of my fellow citizens from San Francisco to Boston; but this is the first occasion when I have been thrice welcomed. So much has been said in the three welcomes I have received that it leaves me little to say, except to disagree with the last speaker as to the character of the American people for generosity. I recognize their generosity, and what they have given me is more valued than gold or silver. No amount of the latter could compensate for the courtesy and kind feeling with which I have everywhere been received. I feel that you have given testimony to that to-day, and for that I thank you one and all.

New York Herald, Oct. 17, 1880. USG was welcomed to Hartford by James G. Batterson, U.S. Representative Joseph R. Hawley of Conn., and Samuel L. Clemens, who said: "I also am deputized to welcome you to the sincere and cordial hospitalities of Hartford, the city of the historic and revered Charter Oak, of which the most of this town is built. At first it was proposed to have only one speaker to welcome you, but this was changed, because it was feared that, considering the shortness of the crop of speeches this year, if anything occurred to prevent that speaker from delivering his speech you would feel disappointed. I desire at this point to refer to your past history. By years of colossal labor and colossal achievement you at last beat down a gigantic rebellion and saved your country from destruction. Then the country commanded you to take the helm of State. You preferred your great office of General of the Army and the rest and comfort which it afforded, but you loyally obeyed and relinquished permanently the ample and well earned salary of the Generalship and resigned your accumulating years to the chance mercies of a precarious existence. By this present fatiguing progress through the land you are mightily contributing toward saving your country once more, this time from dishonor and shame and from commercial disaster. You are now a private citizen, but private employments are closed against you because your name would be used for speculative purposes, and you have refused to permit that. But your country will reward you, never fear. When Wellington won Waterloo, a battle about on a level with some dozen of your victories, sordid England tried to pay him for that service with wealth and grandeur. She made him a duke and gave him $4,000,000. If you had done and suffered for any other country what you have done and suffered for your own, you would have been affronted in the same sordid way; but, thank God, this vast and rich and mighty Republic is imbued to the core with a delicacy which will forever preserve her from so degrading a deserving son. Your country loves you, your country is proud of you, your country is grateful to you. Her applauses, which have been thundering in your ears all these weeks and months, will never cease while the flag you saved continues to wave. Your country stands ready from this day forth to testify her measureless love and pride and gratitude toward you in every conceivable inexpensive way. Welcome to Hartford, great soldier, honored statesman, unselfish citizen." *Ibid.*

To Daniel Ammen

NEW YORK CITY, Oct. 17th, 1880.

MY DEAR ADMIRAL AMMEN,—

I received your letter a week ago, and have wanted to answer it ever since. But the fact is I have not been allowed a minute to myself, from the hour of rising to a late hour at night, since I arrived in this city. I am now writing with company in the room, simply to say that I received your letter, and to ask you to say to Captain Phelps that I received one from him also. Say to him that I will aid the Canal enterprise in any way that I can, and that I will at least act as a director, subscribing enough to make me eligible for the position, and that I may accept the position of president if it is tendered, and with prospects of success. But as to the latter I must leave myself free for the present, because I must either reside in a cheap place or do something to give me immediate income. While this Presidential campaign lasts, it seems as if it will be impossible for me to do more than to see people. After that I hope to have more time for the real purposes of my coming East; that is, to interest capitalists in the construction of railroads in Mexico, and the building of an inter-oceanic canal. The latter is embarrassed by Eads' ship-railroad scheme and the Parisian scheme.

I hope to see you soon. I shall probably go to Washington for a day or two before long. Please present Mrs. Grant's and my compliments to Mrs. Ammen and the children.

Yours truly,

U. S. GRANT.

Daniel Ammen, *The Old Navy and the New* (Philadelphia, 1891), p. 551. See Article, [*Feb., 1881*].

To George Nichols

———

New York City
Oct. 17th 1880.

GEO. NICHOLS, ESQ.
SEC. OF STATE, (VT.)
DEAR SIR:

I have the honor to acknowledge the receipt of the Joint Resolution of the two houses of the Legislature of Vermont, extending to me an invitation to visit the State of Vermont as a guest of the Legislature, which was handed to me in Boston. I then said to His Excellency, the Governor, that I would accept for some day during the week commencing on the 24th inst. and that I would inform the Legislature of the exact day. I now write to express my regret that I will not be able to accept the invitation so courteously extended, and to give the reason therefor. Nearly a year ago—and repeated again this fall—I received urgent invitations to visit a number of cities in the interior and Western part of this state all of which I have had to decline until this time. Now they are urgently repeated from Utica & Syracuse, and I have consented to spend several days at the two places in the course of next week. This will take as much time as I can spare from here probably during the session of the Legislature of Vermont. I thank the Legislature however for the compliment conferred by its invitation, and express the pleasure it would give me to visit Vermon[t.]

Very Respectfully &c

U. S. GRANT

ALS, Vermont Historical Society, Montpelier, Vt. On Nov. 9, 1880, the Vt. legislature passed a resolution expressing regret over USG's response. Copy, USG 3. Born in 1827, George Nichols graduated from the Vermont Medical College (1851), and served as state librarian, surgeon, 13th Vt., and Vt. secretary of state after 1865.

To Hamilton Fish

New York City
Oct. 19th /80

MY DEAR GOV.R FISH:

Will it be asking too much to request that Gen. Badeau be invited to the reception at the Union League on Saturday evening next?[1] He is stopping at Jamaica, L Island. I would be pleased to have him invited, but do not ask it if it in any way violates the rules of the club. With kind regards to Mrs. Fish and yourself,

Yours Truly
U. S. GRANT

ALS, DLC-Hamilton Fish.

On Sept. 20, 1880, Hamilton Fish wrote to George W. Childs, Philadelphia. "Private—*Confidential*—. . . It is now some months since, when I had the pleasure of a letter from you, which gave me ground to hope again soon to hear from you—I wish now to mention, in strict confidence, a matter that gives me some anxiety, & leaves me in doubt—I have written to Genl Grant letters of friendship, (one or more of which I have reason to know reached him) but have not had a line, in acknowledgment, from him since he left Europe, on his tour through Asia &c. My letters were not those of *'business,' demanding* a reply, but were letters of cordial & sincere friendship—a kind of correspondence that cannot be maintained, all on one side, & that cannot be left unnoticed, without the inevitable inference that its continuance is not desired. Self respect will not allow a sensitive person to obtrude either his presence, or his correspondence, where he may have reason to suspect that the one, or the other is unacceptable, or unwelcome—The General is soon coming East, I understand—My regard, & affection & gratitude, t[o]ward him, are the same as you have known them to be for years past. I have reason to know that I was held, by him, in regard, & am entirely unsuspicious of any word, act, or thought of mine, that should lead to any change on his part, toward me—but the fact which I have stated, remains. I fear to embarass him, by further letters. I have no right to ask if you know any cause, or can give any explanation of the withholding of acknowledgment of my letters—but I am really grieved by the suspicion that some reason must exist, & that possibly some mischief-maker may have been at work. Can you in any way, without violating any confidence under which any thing may have come to your knowledge, enlighten me as to the cause of this silence—" ALS (press), *ibid.* On Sept. 23, Childs wrote to Fish. "I have your kind note, and *know* that the General has the same affectionate regard for you that he always has expressed to me. He values your good opinion and friendship above all others, and I know how unhappy he would be if [he] realized how his wan[t] of punctuality in replying to your letters had affected you. He is but a poor correspondent at the best, and to save his credit, I had more than a hundred letters written for him when he was last in Philadel-phia Mr. Drexel was only a few days ago complaining in the same way of the Generals not answering his letters. Rest assured it is no want of affection or appreciation on his part, but a bad habit that has grown on him. . . ." ALS, *ibid.*

1. Oct. 23.

Speech

———

[*New York City, Oct. 20, 1880*]

GENTLEMEN:—This is the second time I have visited the Stock Exchange. The first time I came here I thought you were all fight-ing with one another, and if that were so it was no place for me to be, among fighting men. On this second occasion it was promised that I could sit here while you do the talking on the floor. I am pleased to see you all and wish both bulls and bears success, and that you will all come out of this without a stratch.

New York Herald, Oct. 21, 1880. On Oct. 20, 1880, USG spoke at the New York City Produce Exchange. "GENTLEMEN OF THE PRODUCE EXCHANGE:—I have no doubt you are generally in the habit of crediting what your president tells you. On this occasion, however, he is entirely mistaken in saying that I am going to make a speech. I am very much obliged to you indeed for the cordiality of your welcome, but I shall not presume to address you at length. Hereafter I advise you to believe your president in all matters except when he is talking about me." *Ibid.*

On Oct. 11, a reporter had asked USG how a Republican victory would affect the business community. "I believe that our people are prosperous now. Nothing I could say would make my opinion better known than the fact that our people are doing well. I believe that if Gen. Garfield is elected our present prosperity will continue without interruption, and that we will advance in every branch of industry. I believe that if Gen. Garfield is not elected all the good results of a long-matured and now successful business will be immediately checked. . . ." *Washington Evening Star*, Oct. 11, 1880.

Speech

———

[*Jersey City, Oct. 21, 1880*]

LADIES AND GENTLEMEN: I will do nothing more than thank you for the cordiality of your reception. I have been attending political meetings all the afternoon and evening. I presided at a Republican meeting this afternoon in Stamford, Conn., when I was called upon to make a little speech. I was at another here in Jersey City, where I astonished myself by talking at least five minutes. I had no idea of doing such a thing when I first got up. I went so far as to give some of the reasons why New-Jersey should follow Indiana and Ohio in giving Republican majorities in November next, thus securing all that has been done by the Republican Party up to this time. I went so far as to say—and I think many there believe me, too—that the Democrats, if they know their own interests, were as much interested in being defeated as we are in defeating them. One of the principles of the Republican Party, as I understand it, is that it never asks anything that it does not grant to the opposite party. We do not contend that because we are three to one in any precinct that the fourth man cannot cast his ballot as he pleases and have it honestly counted.

That is all we ask. All we ask is that our carpetbag fellow-citizens, and our fellow-citizens of African descent, and of every other class who may choose to be Republicans, shall have the privilege to go to the polls, even though they are in the minority, and put in their ballot without being burned out of their homes, and without being threatened or intimidated. All we ask is that just the same privileges shall be granted to us that we grant to the Democrats. Then, when they can beat us under those circumstances, we shall believe that they have been so purified as to be fit to govern the country—until they're turned out. The beauty of the system of free ballot is that if an Administration is not a good one the next will be of a different sort. If you are going to control elections by the use of a shot-gun and by intimidation and assassination, if you get in a bad Government it might perpetuate itself by simply being worse. That is what we want to avoid, and that is why New-Jersey is going to vote the Republican ticket on the 2d of November and follow suit with the other Northern States.

New York Times, Oct. 22, 1880. USG spoke at the Tabernacle.

On Oct. 20, 1880, USG spoke at New York City's Cooper Union. "LADIES AND GENTLEMEN: I tried my very best to slip in here quietly, without being seen in hopes of hearing something that would assure me that the right thing for me to do was to be a Republican in this canvass. I was not quite certain but what between this and the 2d of November I might have a spinal column of the sort I heard one of your speakers tell of—that is, a caterpillar column, which was a kind that he did not approve of in Republicans. I was sure, after hearing Mr. Choate and Mr. Storrs, I would require no stiffening of my spinal column, and would go away even a better Republican than when I came. If you will excuse me now, so that we may listen to them, I am sure you will all go away with the same political sentiments which they will preach and which I believe in." *New York Tribune*, Oct. 21, 1880.

On Oct. 21, USG addressed a rally at Stamford, Conn. "LADIES AND GENTLE-MEN: Under the most favorable circumstances I would be unable to make any considerable portion of this vast assemblage hear me. I am hoarse to-day. Frequent speeches make one hoarse, I believe. I made three speeches yesterday, and this one will be shorter than any one of them. I am here to preside to-day and to present some speakers who will convince you of the worth of the Republican cause. You will hear good sound arguments why you should vote the Republican ticket, and better arguments why you should not vote the other. As the first speaker I will present Mr. Torrence." *Ibid.*, Oct. 22, 1880. After remarks by Conn. Secretary of State David Torrance, USG continued. "I now introduce to you Henry C. Robinson, of Hartford, a gentleman of your State, who knows the special reasons why Connecticut should vote Republican." *Ibid.* Following former Hartford mayor Henry C. Robinson, USG spoke once more. "You have heard speakers who have pledged the Eastern States. New-York was only put down for 40,000 majority. It will go 50,000 or more. I have the pleasure of introducing a speaker from the West; we call him an orator out there. He will tell you what the great Northwest will do. He will put the majorities pretty high, and we will carry out his predictions. I introduce Mr. Storrs, of Chicago." *Ibid.*

Also on Oct. 21, USG addressed a rally at the Academy of Music in Jersey City. "LADIES AND GENTLEMEN: I believe that when I came in you were listening to a very good speech, and I suppose it was a political speech, full of good advice to people at this time. I hope so, at any rate, and that you were learning good reasons why the Republican party should be successful at the approaching election. I have been travelling around a little, not making speeches, because I cannot make one, but I have heard some in the course of my travels. I have seen the people, too, and I think that I can give to you a full assurance that the Republican ticket at the approaching election is going to have the vote of the Solid North, including New-Jersey. It used to be a common saying some years ago that New-Jersey was not in the United States; that it was a foreign land; but since that she has redeemed herself on several occasions, and she is going to again prove her allegiance to the United States on the 2nd of November. I would not say anything, if I could help it, that could be offensive to any Democrat who might be present. I like the Democrats. Some of my best friends are among the Democrats, but then I think that they ought to be satisfied with the Republicans running this Government at least until such time as they can give better assurances that they would run it in the same way—for the interest of all classes and all sections. During the Democratic war that we had—from 1861 to 1865—I always contended that the Rebels, all of whom were Democrats, were just as much interested in their defeat as we were interested in defeating them. I believe I was right then; I believe it was the interest of every foot of territory, and every person occupying every foot of territory, in this glorious Union, that the Rebellion should be put down, and that we should remain one and a united people. And I believe to-day that every Democrat that is interested in good government is as much interested in their defeat on the 2d of November as the Republicans are in defeating them. In other words, I believe in the greatest good to the greatest number, and that that good comes from our success. I hope that this audience, ladies and all, unite with me in that sentiment, and that the speaker whom I have interrupted by my entrance at this late hour will convince you of it before he gets through. I am very much obliged to you for your cordial welcome." *Ibid.* USG spoke again. "LADIES AND GENTLEMEN: I have been requested to serve as president. This is my third term. Out in Connecticut this afternoon was the second term. I was also president of a meeting held at Warren, Ohio, a short time ago. That was the first time I was ever president of a political meeting." *Ibid.*

Later, USG spoke at the Jersey City Opera House. "LADIES AND GENTLEMEN: This is the third political meeting that I have been at in Jersey City this evening, and they were all of them crowded houses. I came out of doors, and all the streets that I have been in were filled with people, from which I conclude that all of New-Jersey is in Jersey City this evening. It being a Republican occasion, an occasion of Republican rejoicing, I suppose they are all rejoicing with us in the successes we have met with in the States that have polled, and the anticipated successes in the States that are to poll; and if all the men that I have seen to-night in your streets cast their votes for the Republican candidate, I do not believe there will be any Democratic votes cast in this city at all. I know that heretofore, when you have been deficient in Jersey City and Hudson County of Democratic forces—that you were able to get in a few votes after sundown, keeping your polls open, as you do, to 6 or 7 o'clock in the evening. But I have no doubt that we will all rejoice together after the 2d of November, and that we will perpetuate this Government and Union for the benefit of all the people in the country, black and white, male and female, North and South, and make it so that the carpet baggers can really prosper, do business and be respected and respectable in the Southern States as they are in the Western States, and help them to build up the South and make it prosperous, as the carpet-baggers of the West have done out there. We are all carpet-baggers—nothing else. Why, it is only quite recently that in the State where I live—where I carpet-bagged to some years ago—had a Governor who was a native of that State. The present Governor of Illinois is a native, and is the first native of the State who has filled the office; yet I respect some of the preceding Governors, though they were carpet-baggers, for they helped to build up and make the State that baby we are so proud of. One county in Illinois—Cook County—and one in Ohio—Hamilton County—was built up entirely by the acts, the providing and the energy of these carpet-baggers, and I venture to say that these counties are so wealthy that their citizens could afford to buy them right out from the mother State, and not have to sell them again in order to pay for them. What has been the effect of the carpet-bag government in the Northwest? Let us hope that after this election carpet-baggers may go freely into the South, build up their waste places, make them happy and rich, introduce free schools—which play havoc with Democracy wherever they go; they knock Democracy higher than a kite—introduce their free schools, their energy, and their business talent, and we will have a prosperous and happy and Republican South." *Ibid.* USG was mistaken about Governor Shelby M. Cullom of Ill., who was born in Ky. in 1829 and brought to Ill. in 1830.

On Oct. 23, USG addressed a rally at Franklin, N. J. "Fellow-citizens of New-Jersey, Ladies' and Gentlemen: Even if I were in the habit of speaking I could not do so out of doors so as to make any considerable portion of the audience hear. Under no circumstances should I speak many minutes, and under the present circumstances even less. The great importance of this occasion has induced me to attend political meetings as I have never done before in my life. I have felt, as I have no doubt many of you do, that I could not see the Government in the hands of those who labored to destroy it. I believe the present occasion to be as important as any since 1865. The mission of the Republican party is not ended until a free ballot can be cast throughout this land without endangering the life, property or social position of the voter. Those who have labored to destroy this country should come to us—not we to them. As I drove up I noticed the mottoes of the two parties displayed—the Democratic, 'Tariff for Revenue only,' which means Free Trade if it means anything; and the Republican, 'Protection to Home Industries.' Now, the question of tariff is the smallest question dividing the two parties. Whatever would have pleased Northern Democrats and obtained votes would have been adopted at Cincinnati, and the 138 Southern electoral votes would have been given for it. They care nothing for tariff. You have been told it is a local question only; and here in New-Jersey they will promise to give you whatever tariff you want; but if they were in power they wouldn't consult your wishes. You will hear from the eloquent speakers to come after me many arguments for voting the Republican ticket, and on the 3d of November it will be seen that the Republican party is victorious and James A. Garfield will be President after the 4th of March next for four years." *Ibid.*, Oct. 24, 1880. In another version, USG said that Democrats "care very little about tariff; indeed, one of them has told us it is only 'a local issue' with them." *New York Times*, Oct. 24, 1880. This reference to Maj. Gen. Winfield S. Hancock, Democratic presidential candidate, drew "Cheers and laughter." *Ibid.* See David M. Jordan, *Winfield Scott Hancock: A Soldier's Life* (Bloomington, Ind., 1988), pp. 301–2. USG was followed on the platform by Edwards Pierrepont, Emery A. Storrs, and Thomas P. Ochiltree.

To Edward F. Beale

———

5th Av. Hotel, N. Y. City
Oct. 22d 1880.

MY DEAR GEN. BEALE:

Mrs. Grant received a letter from Emily asking her to accompany me when I go to Washington, and to be your guest. She will do so, but I cannot say now when we will go. If not so engaged as to detain me here, or elsewhere permanently, we we expect to spend the winter from early Jan.y in Washington. In that case we will either get a house or make some hotel arrangement. But we will pay you a visit in the mean time. It will probably be shortly

after the election. It looks to me now as if the result of the election was ~~now~~ assured. This state will certainly go republican, and
I rather think all the Northern states will go the same way. I felt
as if I could not bear the idea of the democrats getting possession
of the Gov.t, and to shew my sympathy with the cause consented to
preside at the Warren, Ohio meeting. It has caused me a world of
trouble. Letters and dispatches, and committees, are after me day
and night to go to this place and that, to some of which I have been
compelled, for my own peace of mind, to give my consent.[1] I am
glad it will all be over soon. I should not mind so much attending
these meetings only that as soon as I make my appearance there
is a universal shout for me to say something, and the people will
not be quieted without it. Speaking before the public is a terrible
trial for me, and being totally without verbal memory I cannot prepare anything in advance to say. But I cut it short and get out the
best I can, much to the disgust apparently of the democratic papers, which think that of all the country I am the least entitled to
a political opinion. If we had two National parties, neither dangerous to the prosperity and wellfare of the country, I would agree
with them in saying that it would be much more dignified for me
to keep out of the arena of politics. But our sacrifice of blood and
treasure has been too great to loose all the good results now to
save a little dignity. I sincerely believe that a democratic success
now would be almost as disastrous as a war, and that the disaster would be no less to one section, or to one party, than to the
other.

With kind regards of Mrs. Grant & myself to you and all your
family.

Very Truly yours
U. S. GRANT

ALS, DLC-Decatur House Papers.

1. On Oct. 19, 1880, N. Y. Republican leaders asked USG to address upcoming
rallies in Albany and Troy. "My impression is that it is almost a foregone conclusion that I will be sent to the northern part of the Empire State." USG then spoke
optimistically about Republican prospects elsewhere. *New York Herald*, Oct. 20,
1880.

To Marcus Petersen, Jr.

New York City
Oct. 22d 1880.

MARCUS PETERSEN, ESQ.
PRES. Y. M. R. G. [&] A. CLUB;
DEAR SIR:

Your letter of the 11th inst. probably come duly to hand, but I have been so busy, seeing people all hours of the day & night, that it did not come under my observation in time to comply with your request. I should have been very glad to have met the young republicans of Brooklyn before the election in Nov. if possible, but my time is all taken up so that it will not be possible.

Trusting, and predicting, that the result in November will be all your club can desire, I am,

Very Truly yours
U. S. GRANT

ALS, Goodspeed's Book Shop, Inc., Boston, Mass. See letter to Marcus Petersen, Jr., *et al.*, Jan. 24, 1881; *Brooklyn Eagle*, Jan. 19, 1882.

Testimony

[*New York City, Oct. 23, 1880*]

General ULYSSES S. GRANT called for the respondent, being duly sworn, testified as follows:

By Maj. ASA BIRD GARDNER, counsel for the respondent:

Question. Please state the rank and command you held in the service of the United States on the 31st of March and April 1, 1865?—Answer. I was lieutenant-general, in command of the Armies of the United States.

Q. On the 31st of March, 1865, do you recollect any circumstances, within your own knowledge, connected with the movements of General Warren's corps?—A. From actual memory I cannot fix the exact dates or hours of the day of any occurrences. That was about the time of the movement of General Warren's corps from the lines of the Army of the Potomac to re-enforce General Sheridan in the neighborhood of Dinwiddie Court-House.

Q. Do you recall the date of the battle of White Oak Ridge?— A. No; I could not fix the exact day—not from memory. Of course I know it from reading the reports.

Q. Do you recollect the circumstance of the movement by General Warren's corps upon the enemy upon the White Oak road prior to his movement to re-enforce General Sheridan?—A. I probably had better state just about what occurred. General Sheridan had been sent with the cavalry corps—his command of cavalry— to go by Dinwiddie and try to flank Five Forks; and his force not being sufficient he was obliged to fall back from his position; he reported to me the position he was in, falling back gradually and drawing the enemy out, and I thought it was a fine opportunity then, perhaps, of attacking the enemy outside of his fortifications, and so determined to re-enforce him. General Sheridan did not ask for re-enforcements. General Warren's corps was the only corps that was so situated in the line as to be drawn out conveniently and quickly, and his corps was selected for that reason. The orders which he received are all matters of record; what they are I cannot repeat from memory, but they are a matters of record and can be obtained.

Q. On the same day that General Sheridan made his movement on Five Forks from which he fell back towards Dinwiddie, do you know whether or not the Fifth Corps made any movement in the nature of a reconnaissance or assault?—A. I know they did, from reading it recently, but, answering from my personal memory, I do not recollect the exact occurrences that took place.

Q. Please look at this copy of a dispatch. Say whether you recollect sending that dispatch?—A. (Referring to dispatch.) I do not recollect it particularly, but I did send it. It is a matter of record which we have here separate from this.

Q. (By Mr. STICKNEY, counsel for the applicant.) That is not a copy of the complete file kept at your headquarters. That is Major

Gardner's copy.—A. I do not know about that. That dispatch was sent.

Maj. Asa Bird Gardner, counsel for the respondent. We will compare it with the original in the possession of the recorder.

In this connection, I will now read this dispatch to Major-General Meade from Headquarters Armies of the Unitrd State, Gravelly Run, March 31, 1865.

Mr. Stickney, counsel for the applicant. I understand the particular purpose for which this dispatch is introduced by the learned counsel. There is an expression in it which reflects severely upon General Warren. I make no objection to that dispatch going in if we can have all the dispatches of the same time relating to the same operations.

Maj. Asa Bird Gardner, counsel for the respondent. Yes; I wish to put in, though I may not be able to do so by the general this morning, but I wish to put in, from any quarter where we can find them, every dispatch that passed upon the subject of these operations, either from General Meade to General Grant, or General Grant to General Meade, or General Warren to General Meade, or General Meade to General Warren.

(Reading.)

[Telegram.]

Gravelly Run, *March* 31, 1865.

Maj. Gen. Meade:

If the enemy has been checked in Warren's front what is to prevent him from pushing in with his whole corps, attacking before giving him time to intrench or return in good order to his old line of intrenchments? I do not understand why Warren permitted his corps to be fought in detail when Ayres was pushed forward. He should have sent other troops to their support.

U. S. Grant.

A true copy from the file of copied dispatches supplied from the office for the publication of the Rebellion Records.

Loomis L. Langdon,

Brevet Lieutenant–Colonel, U. S. Army.[1]

Q. You recollect the sending of this dispatch to General Meade?—A. I do not recollect it absolutely, from my own memory, but I know it was sent from the fact that it is a matter of record, and those dispatches, I imagine, will be found, possibly, in my own handwriting.

Q. Does that recall to your recollection the movement that General Warren made which brought forth this dispatch?—A. No; not specifically. I recollect that there was disappointment with the tardiness of his moving after I had sent the orders, and dissatisfaction, but I cannot specify particularly now just what he did that was different from what I expected, except that his hour of starting was later.

Q. You refer now to the orders that you gave for him to go down and re-enforce General Sheridan?—A. Yes.

Q. I refer now to a period slightly anterior to that—his own previous movements on the day of the battle of Dinwiddie Court House, that General Sheridan fought, on the 31st of March. Do you recall any reconnaissance that was made by General Warren's corps towards the White Oak road prior to the time when he was ordered to support General Sheridan?—A. Not well enough to specify.

Q. Coming now to the morning of April 1, do you recollect the visit of Captain Warner, of the Third Artillery, to your headquarters?—A. I recollect that there were officers from Meade's headquarters over there frequently about that time.

Q. Do you recall the circumstances of sending General Babcock on any duty on that day?—A. I recollect sending a number of my staff officers, General Babcock among them, General Porter and Captain Hudson and others to General Sheridan's headquarters, so as to have information from there, as rapidly as anything might transpire, that would be important for me to know. If what you wish to get at is, to know whether I recollect about a message that I sent by one of these officers in regard to the relieving of General Warren, I recollect that specifically.

Q. Will you please state the circumstances under which that message was sent?—A. The circumstances simply are these—

Mr. Stickney, counsel for the applicant. The question itself calls for only what is proper; but I would like to call the attention of the court and the attention of General Grant to the point that it would be hardly fair, either to General Grant or to General

Warren, to go into any points which could involve any previous operations—operations in the previous history of the Army of the Potomac. Anything which General Grant has in mind now, which related directly to the situation at the time we are investigating, we shall be glad to have him state. But it would be just, neither to him nor to General Warren, to have matters brought in here which concern his opinion of General Warren, as regards former operations in the early history of the war. These, of course, should be carefully kept out here.

The WITNESS. If I should keep those out of consideration, I should have simply to say, as near as I could from memory, that I notified General Sheridan that he was authorized to relieve General Warren if, in his judgment, it was for the best interests of the service to do so; that I was afraid he would fail him at a critical moment. That was the substance of my message. I cannot recollect the words. Of course, I had to judge of that fact by my knowledge of General Warren previous to any of these movements.

Mr. ALBERT STICKNEY, counsel for the applicant. As I have argued before, the court here cannot and will not question the propriety of General Grant's act. I shall not in my argument question the propriety, in any respect, of General Grant's act in sending that message. And, as I argued before, the propriety of General Sheridan's act in relieving General Warren cannot be questioned here. The only party whose conduct is subject to investigation here is General Warren. In that point of view, it being assumed that General Grant acted upon his previous impressions, as to General Warren's character and qualifications as a commander—upon his idea of what General Warren's temperament was—and it being assumed, that he acted properly and wisely, is it fair to General Grant, or to General Warren, either, that his mere opinion of General Warren should go in here as the record, when, on the one hand, General Warren cannot go into the past history of the war to show that, as matter of fact, that opinion of General Grant was not warranted by the facts; and when, on the other hand, General Grant cannot go into past history of the war to show, upon his side, that his opinion *was* warranted by the facts? I submit now, that his mere [matter of] opinion as to General Warren's qualifications and temperament, his capacity as a soldier, everything of that sort, should not be allowed to come in here on the record, whether we look at it as a matter of justice to him, General Warren, or as a matter of justice to General Grant. It being assumed that General Grant's action was dictated by proper motives, and was wisely considered at the time.

Maj. ASA BIRD GARDNER, counsel for the respondent. The argument of my friend might have been very suitable if the applicant in the beginning of this case had restricted himself to the point that he now says he desires to restrict himself. The very first witness that was examined in this case—examined by the applicant before General Sheridan or his counsel appeared in the matter—was Captain Warner, of the Third Artillery. He was examined for the express purpose of ascertaining what were the reasons of the sending of that order by Geneal Grant through General Babcock to General Sheridan, giving him the authority to relieve General Warren, if necessary, on the day of the battle of Five Forks; and I find, in looking at the evidence of Captain Warner, this question, on page 38 of the printed record:

Q. (By the APPLICANT.) As nearly as you can judge from what took place then, was that report as to the position of General Warren's corps the occasion or cause of General Grant's sending this instruction to General Sheridan as to the relieving of General Warren?—A. That was the impression made upon me, that General Grant was disappointed to find that General Warren had not proceeded any farther, and that that led him to make these remarks. Of course I do not know, but that was the impression made upon me at the time.

Then, as shown in the record and testified to by Captain Warner, there were remarks made by General Grant, assumedly on hearing a report from Captain Warner, that General Warren had not gotten down to General Sheridan. Therefore it becomes necessary and proper, in view of the fact that the applicant has, himself, gone into this subject as to what were the reasons of General Grant's sending that order to General Sheridan, that the real reason should be stated—the court should be informed. I therefore submit that the question is proper.

Mr. STICKNEY, the counsel for the applicant. Most certainly

I cannot undertake to say no particle of irrelevant testimony has crept into this case in the several months that it has been under investigation; nor can I say with certainty, that I have not introduced, myself, testimony that is irrelevant. It is possible I may have done so. My effort has been not to do so. But we may take it for granted that I have on a number of occasions introduced testimony that will not turn out, upon critical examination, to be strictly relevant to the objects of the inquiry before this court. Now, what that particular testimony of Captain Warner was introduced for, and what it has its legitimate bearing for, was not to show what were the reasons operating in General Grant's mind at all, but what was the information then laid before him of the situation. We were not going at all into the operations of General Grant's mind, and we have to assume now, and this court will have to assume at all times, that General Grant's action was entirely appropriate. What we had a right then to show, what we attempted then to show, was the position as it was brought before him at the time he sent his message to General Sheridan as far as we could reproduce it. That testimony, then, had this legitimate bearing, and its only bearing before this court, in showing what was the position as it was then brought to General Grant's knowledge.

The WITNESS. I know it was not in consequence of any information at all brought to me or received, or opinion in regard to any of General Warren's movements at that time, that I sent this. It was simply my reflection as to General Warren in this critical position, which I then expected to make the last battle of the war, that he would probably fail him, and I wanted to warn General Sheridan of the danger he was in. The authority was not sent to General Sheridan in consequence of any report that was brought to me—it was simply that I knew General Warren's defects.

Mr. STICKNEY, counsel for the appellant. What you considered his defects.

The WITNESS (continuing). What I considered his defects. And his was the only corps I could send promptly; that corps would not have been sent if I could have gotten another one as conveniently—and I was just thinking of the consequences of a failure there, and wanted to put General Sheridan upon his guard, and I sent him that authority, so that he might feel no hesitation in removing an officer if it was necessary to his success.

Mr. STICKNEY, counsel for the applicant. Yes; that we assume— that General Grant's action was founded in a great measure upon his opinion.

The WITNESS. By my opinion entirely.

Mr. STICKNEY, counsel for the applicant. General Grant's action was dictated by his opinion of General Warren. Of course that opinion was based on his understanding of what General Warren had done in the past history of the war, upon General Warren's past acts, as they had come to General Grant's knowledge. No one would admit more readily than General Grant that he might have been misinformed upon many of those points, but whether he was or not cannot be investigated here. As far as this proposed question calls for General Grant's opinion of General Warren based upon former history, I submit that it should not be brought in before this court.

The PRESIDENT OF THE COURT. The court is of the opinion that the conduct of General Warren, or any opinion formed upon his conduct previous to the operations of the 31st, ought not to be made matter of record here. We are required simply to investigate General Warren's conduct on March 31 and April 1. Anything that may have occurred on March 31st in General Warren's conduct that influenced General Grant, might properly be made matter of record, but anything previous to that, not.

Mr. STICKNEY, counsel for the applicant. Then in view of that opinion of the court, may I ask that this expression of General Grant, as to his opinion of General Warren, which he says was based upon matters of former history, may be struck from the record?

Maj. ASA BIRD GARDNER, counsel for the respondent. I shall certainly object to anything of that kind. Here was the evidence of Captain Warner, who was brought here for the purpose of showing what were the reasons that induced General Grant to send that un-solicited authority to General Sheridan, to relieve General Warren, if he thought it was best for the interests of the service.

The PRESIDENT OF THE COURT. That occurred on the 31st, did it not?

Maj. Asa Bird Gardner, counsel for the respondent. No, sir; on the 1st of April.

The President of the Court. Anything that occurred on those two days may be taken into consideration, but previous to the 31st, not.

Maj. Asa Bird Gardner, counsel for the respondent. Captain Warner went on to say what he heard General Grant say at the time he told General Babcock to take that order to General Sheridan. Therefore as Captain Warner was brought for the express purpose of showing, and for no other purpose, what were the circumstances under which General Grant issued that order to General Sheridan, it became eminently proper that I should ask General Grant, and show to the court, whether what Captain Warner had stated was the fact or not; whether that circumstance that Captain Warner says, namely, that he brought word that part of Warren's corps had not gotten across the bridge, was the ground of General Grant's sending that unsolicited authority to General Sheridan.

The Witness. I simply say that it was not.

Major Stickney, counsel for applicant. Now recurs my application to the court to have the portions of General Grant's testimony that concern merely his opinion of General Warren—as a soldier and as a man—to have those struck from the record. And from what counsel has just said, it is very apparent that his object in asking this question is simply to weigh down General Warren with the adverse opinion of the soldier who has, certainly of American soldiers, the first reputation in the century. That opinion—it being shown here that it is an unfavorable one—that mere opinion should not appear upon the records of this court unless there is an opportunity upon the one hand for General Grant to give all the points upon which that opinion was based, and unless on the other hand an opportunity is given to General Warren to go into the history of the war and show, as matter of fact, that that opinion was not well founded. As far as the learned counsel has any purpose to ask a question which will tend to show facts and circumstances then existing, that we have no objection to; but if he goes beyond that and seeks to get upon the record an opinion of the first American soldier adversely to General Warren, for the purpose, apparently, of weighing him down with that opinion in this investigation, that should not be allowed.

Maj. ASA BIRD GARDNER, counsel for the respondent. I shall have to go still farther with my friend in this discussion. Captain Warner, as I have said before, was brought here for the express purpose of showing General Grant's mind in issuing the authority through General Babcock to General Sheridan that he could relieve Warren if he thought best. He was asked all the circumstances. He said he must have made his report in the hearing of General Grant because General Grant "immediately began to talk."

This is the language of Captain Warner:

When I returned, I made my report to General Rawlins. As near as I can recollect, the officers were around the camp-fire—the officers at headquarters of the Army of the Potomac and the officers at General Grant's headquarters all around, the same group by the fire. Whether General Grant heard my statement or whether it was immediately reported to him I don't know. At all events, he said in my presence that he wanted to relieve General Warren at _____, naming some place or time, or some battle—I do not recall it now—but that at General Meade's solicitation he did not do it, and that he was sorry now that he had not done it—had not relieved him.

Q. (By COURT.) Are you certain it was the name of a battle or the name of a town?—A. No, I cannot say. It was at some time during the campaign—had reference to some official conduct of General Warren. Either General Babcock or General Porter (who were staff officers of General Grant), I think General Porter, was getting ready to go to General Sheridan. He turned to this officer and said to him, "Tell General Sheridan if he has any occasion to relieve General Warren, not to hesitate to do so." This was given with other instructions. It was made in the presence of all the officers without any hesitation.

Q. (By APPLICANT.) As nearly as you can judge from what took place then, was that report as to the position of General Warren's corps the occasion or cause of General Grant, sending this instruction to General Sheridan as to the relieving of General Warren?—A. That was the impression made upon me, that General Grant was disappointed to find that General Warren had not proceeded any farther, and that that led him to make these remarks. Of course I do not know, but that was the impression made upon me at that time.

Q. I understand you, that the sending of the instructions to General Sheridan came immediately upon this statement's being made in General Grant's hearing?—A. It did; but I do not know that it followed from the statement. This officer was getting ready to go. The two were close together.

Q. As far as you could judge, was there any other occurrence or report which caused the Lieutenant-General to send that order at that time?—A. I don't know of any other circumstances or report. (Page 38.)

So the applicant came in here deliberately, at a special session of this court—as Captain Warner was about to sail for Europe—in order to examine Captain Warner for the express purpose of showing that General Grant sent that order to General Sheridan through General Babcock, because General Grant had heard from Captain Warner a report that Warren's forces had not gotten across Gravelly Run Creek. Now that is there as a matter of record, and carefully brought in. It is the only purpose for which Captain Warner was brought in this case—the first witness. It becomes necessary, consequently, without going into circumstances of the case at all, merely to ascertain, as we have ascertained here, through the counsel, in his queries to that witness, that that was not the reason, but that there were other reasons. General Grant has stated exactly now why. I do not choose to go into it any farther, but I have now answered Captain Warner's evidence. And if Captain Warner had not been brought here, it never probably would have occurred to me to ask General Grant anything upon the subject. But as Captain Warner was brought here especially for that purpose there is no course now but for the respondent to show that that was not the ground of the issuance of the order. And it becomes particularly material, in view of the fact that this authority came to General Sheridan unsolicited.

Mr. STICKNEY, counsel for the applicant. Taking everything that the learned counsel has said, in its fullest length and breadth, it amounts to this: that in Captain Warner's testimony there is one question and one answer which are perhaps inadmissible here, and which, if objected to at the time, would have been kept out. It may go out now. Then there is nothing on the record to be answered. The other testimony is conceded to be perfectly admissible. I cannot say that I have not introduced inadmissible testimony: let that go out, if the counsel wishes it out. My application is as to these expressions of opinion, given by General Grant upon this record— that is all I have asked to go out.

Maj. ASA BIRD GARDNER, counsel for respondent. General Grant has given the grounds upon which he sent that message; and if this had not been spread upon the record as evidence in such a form that it cannot be stricken out, as my friend now says he would like to have it out, and if it had not gone broadcast over the country through the press, then he might ask it with some propriety.

After consultation the president of the court announced the opinion of the court as follows:

The PRESIDENT OF THE COURT. The court is still of the opinion that any opinion of General Grant formed upon transactions previous to the time we are investigating should not be upon the record. General Grant has testified that he was not influenced by the facts in the verbal report as testified to by Captain Warner, and if he can give any reasons why he did send this message, based upon transactions, based upon the time within our inquiry, they can go upon the record, otherwise not.

Maj. ASA BIRD GARDNER, counsel for the respondent. Then I would like, if the court will please do so, to have indicated what there is in the evidence that has been given by the witness that is to be stricken out.

The PRESIDENT OF THE COURT. The court indicates only the general rule, that if the witness has given any testimony based upon transactions previous to the time of our inquiry, it is not to go upon record. We do not know what it is ourselves.

At the request of Major Asa Bird Gardner, the testimony of the witness was read for information.

After consultation:

The PRESIDENT OF THE COURT said: Will counsel indicate what portion of the record he thinks objectionable.

Mr. STICKNEY, counsel for the applicant. If Major Gardner is anxious to have those portions of the remarks of General Grant printed which the court say are not to be considered by them; if it will gratify him to have them printed for the purpose of getting it in the press of the country I do not object to it. I have now upon record the declaration of the court that those matters of opinion based upon previous operations are not to be regarded by the court. It will not injure me at all that those expressions of General Grant are on record if they are not to be considered. If it will please counsel to have those matters printed and go to the press and the country he can have it in that way.

Maj. ASA BIRD GARDNER, counsel for the respondent. I have not stated what the counsel says I did say. I ask the court what portion, if any, it was desirable now to strike out.

The PRESIDENT OF THE COURT. There seems to be nothing.

Mr. STICKNEY, counsel for the applicant. If that is the rule for the remaining examination of the witness—

The PRESIDENT OF THE COURT. That is the rule for the remaining examination.

The examination resumed.

By Maj. ASA BIRD GARDNER, counsel for the respondent:

Q. In consequence of the order that you sent to General Sheridan through General Babcock, do you know whether or not General Warren was relieved?

Mr. STICKNEY, counsel for the applicant. It is perfectly apparent to us that he has no personal knowledge of that. That is the fact with which the investigation starts.

Maj. ASA BIRD GARDNER, counsel for the respondent. I withdraw the question.

Q. Had you, subsequent to the sending of that order, any information as to whether General Warren was relieved or not? If so, from whom did you receive such information?

Mr. Stickney, counsel for the applicant. The fact is here conceded; we began with it; is it material to have hearsay testimony?

Maj. Asa Bird Gardner, counsel for the respondent. This is merely a preliminary question.

Mr. Stickney, counsel for the applicant. It is not material, I say.

Maj. Asa Bird Gardner, counsel for the respondent. I insist I have a right, with due respect to the court, to ask the question as preliminary.

The President of the Court. The court sees no objection to that question.

A. I could not say positively, but my recollection is that I received that information first from General Warren. I may not be right about that; I think I am.

Q. On the 1st of April what information, if any, did you receive from General Warren?—A. That he had been relieved by General Sheridan.

Q. Will you please state what he said to you at the time he made this report, and what you said to him?—A. General Warren came to my headquarters and stated that he had been relieved by General Sheridan. My answer to General Warren was substantially this: that I was not surprised, and I informed him that I had given the authority for his removal, and I also stated to General Warren that while I had a very great regard for his capacity and personal courage, yet he had certain defects which I then told him of as a subordinate commander. I believe I expressed the opinion to him that he might succeed very much better in a different sphere or command, where he would have no superior, and expressed the willingness to assign him to duty elsewhere.

Q. Is that all that you said upon the occasion?—A. I have given the synopsis. General Warren will probably recollect quite as distinctly as I do. You can take his testimony upon that.

Q. Do you recall nothing further that you at the time said to him?—A. I do not know whether I specified any particular command where he might be put. I think likely I did. General Warren probably will recollect those facts.

Q. Did you, at that time, say anything as to the reason of sending the order to General Sheridan giving him authority to relieve him?

Mr. STICKNEY, counsel for the applicant. This is going into the same point in another form.

The PRESIDENT OF THE COURT. If it occurred within the time of our investigation, very well; if it occurred previous to that, we do not want it.

Maj. ASA BIRD GARDNER, counsel for the respondent. I suppose I can get a categorical answer, and then apply the ruling of the court afterwards.

The PRESIDENT OF THE COURT. The court has decided if the witness gives a reason for anything that occurred within the time of our investigation he can answer the question; otherwise, not.

Maj. ASA BIRD GARDNER, counsel for the respondent. I will leave it for a categorical answer, and if those reasons do not come within the ruling of the court, there can be no further reply from the witness; if they do come within the ruling of the court, he can go on and say what he did say.

Mr. STICKNEY, counsel for the applicant. Then please simply say whether you stated the reason without giving us what it was. That is all that the counsel asks for.—A. I would have to say yes.

Q. Did those reasons which you then gave General Warren have reference to his conduct on the 31st of March, or on the other day, April 1st, of the battle of Five Forks; or did those reasons have reference to previous conduct of General Warren?—A. To previous conduct.

Cross examination by Mr. STICKNEY, counsel for the applicant:

Q. When you say "previous conduct," you mean, of course, your understanding of his previous conduct?—A. Certainly; of course, always my understanding.

Q. You would admit quite as readily as any other man in the world that you might have made a mistake in your judgment upon those past matters?—A. I am not ready to admit that; no, sir.

Q. What you claim is not that you cannot make a mistake, but that you did not make a mistake?—A. I have no doubt I made many mistakes, but not in that particular.

Q. In this particular you do not think you did make one?—A. No.

Q. You stated, in the beginning of your examination, that your recollection as to times and dates, and details, of course you would not go upon now.—A. No, I would not go upon them.

Q. Have you, for the purpose of giving your testimony here, examined your papers?—A. I have within two or three days. I did not have an opportunity before. General Badeau had them; but I have seen them.

Q. Has he still your original files of papers which were kept at your headquarters?—A. I think so, or he has copies of them.

Q. Do you know where the originals are?—A. I presume they are on file in the War Department.

Q. Do you mean that you turned over to the War Department your original files, or copies of them, and kept your original files—do you recollect how that was?—A. No, sir; but I presume that they are copies made by clerks in the books, and what became of the originals, that may have been written upon all sorts of bits of paper by myself, I do not know whether they are preserved or not, or whether they are on file with the General of the Army or in the War Department.

Q. Then would you be so good as to request General Badeau—he has, I believe, particularly the charge of your military papers, has he not?—A. He has copies of a large part of them.

Q. Would you do us the favor to have a search made for the original papers concerning March 31 and April 1, as far as they are in existence, and send them to the court?—A. I presume that you will find any that are in existence, of what you would call the originals, with the War Department.

Q. You think the originals themselves are there?—A. All that exist are there. I think in a very great many cases the originals were written with pencil and on any slip of paper I could get, and then copied into books; and thus the originals may not exist at all now.

Q. Can you recall at this lapse of time what the practice was—
the habit at your headquarters—as to sending dispatches to General Meade; the ones which appeared signed in your own name?—
A. They are probably nearly in every instance written by me in my
own handwriting, and telegraphed. We had a telegraph between
headquarters. They were not always sent by telegraph, but generally they would be sent by telegraph, and the original would be in
the telegraph office.

Q. Can you recall whether, as matter of custom, if General
Rawlins, for instance, would send an order or dispatch to General
Meade, would it be signed by him in his own name?—A. Yes; if
he sent it, it would be signed in his own name by him as chief of
staff.

Q. So, presumptively, the dispatches or orders that bore your
own signature?—A. (Interrupting.) Were written by myself at the
time.

Q. Can you, by referring to the copies here, refresh your recollection as to some of those events—to the copies of the dispatches?
We have not, of course, the originals.—A. In a general way—yes.

Q. Referring now to the one dispatch which the counsel has
seen fit to introduce here, and assuming, of course, as we do, that
this is a correct copy of the original, you used there the expression—(Counsel read as follows:)

I do not understand why Warren permitted his corps to be
fought in detail. When Ayres was pushed forward, he should have
sent other troops to their support.

When you wrote that dispatch, your supposition, of course, evidently was, that Warren did not push other troops to Ayres' support?—A. Of course that was the supposition.

Q. And that he did, as matter of fact, allow his corps to be
fought in detail?—A. Yes.

Q. It was upon that supposition of yours that that dispatch was
written?—A. Yes.

Q. If at the time of sending that dispatch that was not the fact,
of course you had no information of the fact being otherwise?—A.
Of course.

Q. Then the dispatch represented the situation as you were informed of it at that time?—A. As I was informed.

Q. Of course you had no personal knowledge?—A. No personal knowledge.

Q. Now come to a little later period. I will call your attention to General Meade's dispatch to General Warren, dated 4.30 p. m., March 31, which was the afternoon of the battle of Dinwiddie Court-House, when General Sheridan was engaged in front of Dinwiddie Court-House with the force of the enemy. General Meade's dispatch of that hour and date contains these words:

Word has been sent to Sheridan, and it is believed that he is pushing up. Humphreys will be ordered to push up, &c.

Do you recollect whether, at that time, 4.30 on the afternoon of the 31st of March, whether that was your information, too, of the position—that Sheridan was pushing up towards the White Oak road, instead of being driven back towards Dinwiddie. Can you recall your recollection of the position at that particular hour?—A. No; I do not think I could, at that particular hour.

Q. You notice that General Meade's dispatch speaks of Warren's trying to communicate with Sheridan. Of course, that has not reference to any movement to Sheridan's relief, but merely an effort to communicate with him while he was still advancing—is that it?—A. Yes.

Q. Will you look at this photographic map of the country around Petersburg, Dinwiddie, and Five Forks—the localities—A. I will say this, that I never was on that ground to the left, where General Sheridan was engaged. The maps were very familiar to me at the time. I knew every road and place by name, and how they were situated upon the map, but I had never been over the ground and never have been since.

Q. You went as far west as Appomattox?—A. I passed away north of that point from Petersburg, but I did not go as far west, around south, of Petersburg as Dinwiddie.

Q. You did not go down to Dinwiddie?—A. No, sir; not onto the field where these troops were engaged, at the time in controversy.

Q. Do you recall that this was one of the maps that you then had in use?—A. Yes. I recall the general features of the map. I would have to study it a little while to put my finger on places certainly.

Q. Do you recall whether you had at that time in use at your headquarters, or at General Meade's headquarters, any more detailed or accurate map of the country than that which I have shown you?—A. I think that was one of the best maps we had.

Q. That was the one in use at the headquarters of the Army, as far as your recollection is?—A. Yes.

Q. That is, at General Sheridan's, General Warren's, General Meade's, and your own?

Maj. Asa Bird Gardner, counsel for the respondent. I submit that that is hardly a proper question. The General, of course, is not called upon to answer whether General Sheridan had such a map as that unless he knew positively.

Mr. Stickney, counsel for the applicant. I ask only for the extent of his knowledge; whether he knew of any other map in use at headquarters—at Army headquarters at that time.

A. I could not state exactly, only that we had maps, and we had maps something like this.

Q. There may have been others?—A. There may have been others, and there may have been information that is not contained in the map. I may have had it myself at the time. We may have found that the maps were incorrect, in some particulars, that roads or points were not indicated upon them.

Q. Will you refer to your dispatch, March 31, dated at Dabney's Mills, to General Meade:

I send you a copy of the report just sent by Sheridan; you will see that he reports Hokes' division, which we know was in North Carolina.

If you will refer to that one [copy handed to witness], that dispatch of yours says:

Since yours was received, Colonel Porter has returned from Sheridan.[2]

Do you recollect at all the time of day that Colonel Porter got back from General Sheridan then?—A. No, sir; I could not possibly remember it.

Q. Then it also says:

He says that Devins had been driven back, in considerable confusion, south of J. Boisseau's house.

That was your information, of course, at the time?—A. That
was the information that I received and sent to General Meade.

Q. Then you also said in that dispatch:

The effort has been to get our cavalry onto the White Oak
road, west of Dabney's house.

Now, will you tell me whether the Dabney's house you there refer to was W. Dabney's, between the Claiborne road and the Crump
road?—A. No doubt it was.

Q. Then you go on:

So far this has failed, and there is no assurance that it will succeed. This will make it necessary for Warren to watch his left all
round.

That, then, was your understanding of the position at the time
you sent that dispatch?—A. This was what I thought from the information which I was receiving from that flank of the army.

Q. But that was the information that Colonel Porter had brought
you from Sheridan himself?—A. Some of the staff officers.

Q. Then, can you now recall any information of a contrary
tenor that you then had?—A. No; I cannot.

Q. Of course you have no other?—A. I do not know. If I had
any other it will be found a matter of record, I have no doubt.

Q. If you will turn also to the dispatch from General Meade to
General Grant, dated 7.40 p. m., on the same evening, March 31
[copy shown witness].

Q. Will you read over the dispatch?—A. It reads:

8.40 p. m. NORRIS,

HEADQUARTERS A. OF P., 7.40, *March 31st*, 1865.
Lieut. Gen'l GRANT:

Capt. Sheridan from Sheridan's cavalry is here, and is directed
to you by a staff officer. He reports that Gen'l Sheridan is just north
of Dinwiddie C. H., having been repulsed by the enemy's infantry on the dirt road running north, and also on the road running
northwest from north of Dinwiddie. Gen'l Sheridan states that if

he is forced to retire it will be on the Vaughn road. The staff officer leaves here to report to you.

G. G. MEADE, *Com'd'g.*

A true copy.

LOOMIS L. LANGDON,

Brevet Lieutenant-Colonel, U. S. A., Recorder.[3]

Q. Do you recollect that Captain Sheridan did come to you that evening?—A. I do not call it to mind, that especially.

Q. He states that he did?—A. I have no doubt; there is no question about the fact.

Q. Then he would have reached your headquarters shortly after 7.40 p. m.?—A. Shortly after he left General Meade's headquarters, he would have reached mine.

Q. Then, about eight o'clock that evening, according to your recollection, does that dispatch from Meade to yourself, substantially, accurately represent the position of Sheridan, as you were then informed of it?—A. I cannot answer from memory.

Q. Have you any recollection that would seem to be at variance with that?—A. I have no especial recollection on the subject; I do not recollect that dispatch. I know that General Sheridan was back, about in the position described by that.

Q. Then, taking your own dispatch to General Meade, dated at 8.40 that same evening (reads):

[Telegram.]

GRANT'S HEADQUARTERS,

March 31st, 1865—8.45 p. m.

Maj. Gen'l MEADE:

Your dispatch of 6.35 and your note of 7.30 are just received. Capt. Sheridan has reported to you the situation of affairs with Sheridan. Let Warren draw back at once to his position on Boydton road, and send a division of infantry to Sheridan's relief. The troops to Sheridan should start at once and go down Boydton road.

U. S. GRANT,

L't-Gen'l.

A true copy of the dispatch as found in the file of copied dispatches received from the office for the publication of the Rebellion Records.

LOOMIS L. LANGDON,

Brevet Lieutenant-Colonel, U. S. A.[4]

Have you any recollection now, as you reread it, of sending that dispatch?—A. No; I am about this as I am with all those dispatches. They have a familiarity, but I cannot place the minute or hour or day from recollection. But there is no question that this was mine—my own dispatch.

Q. So, evidently, your understanding of the disposition at that time was just what it states?—A. Yes.

Q. That you were sending a division of infantry to Sheridan's relief, and that Warren was to withdraw from the position that he had been previously holding?—A. Warren was to withdraw at once from his position on the Boydton road?

Q. Then at that precise point of time you had given up the idea of any offensive movement upon Warren's part, just at that moment?—A. I could not say that precisely.

Q. As nearly as you recall it?—A. There was no time after General Sheridan moved to Dinwiddie Court-House that I was not fully resolved upon making that the final blow, but I would have to change my plans according to the success attending our movements, and I have had to change perhaps here—it seems that I have had to change the position of some of General Warren's corps, in consequence of that command, being at a different position from what I hoped it would be.

Q. That, of course, we assume. But referring to [y]our purpose as to Warren's corps alone, at that precise moment, it was that it should be withdrawn?—A. Whatever this describes was my opinion upon that particular point at that moment.

Q. Then referring to General Meade's dispatch to you, dated 8.45 of the same evening:

Orders have been sent to General Warren to draw in at once to the Boydton plank road, and send, on receipt of orders, Griffin's division to report to General Sheridan, they to move down the Boydton road.[5]

You notice your own dispatch to Meade had been simply, to send a division of infantry; and he reports to you that orders have been sent, to send Griffin's division. So that was done by him on his own responsibility, as far as you recollect—that is the direction as to which division should be sent?—A. My order did not specify.

Q. Had you at that time—I suppose you had not—had you at that time, as far as you recollect, any special information as to how Griffin's division was disposed?—A. I do not recollect.

Q. Then, were you informed, at that time, that one brigade of Griffin's was away down the Crump road, by J. Boissea[u]'s, and that the rest of his division was up on the White Oak road?—A. I was fully informed, no doubt, of the position from time to time, of all the commands there, but I cannot say now as to where they were at any particular time.

Q. Did your information at that time, as you recall it, go to a detailed position of the different brigades?—A. I do not think so; hardly beyond divisions, unless there was a detachment made from a division; that might be reported.

Q. As far as you recall, had you any information at all that Griffin's was the hardest division Warren had to send on to Dinwiddie Court-House?—A. Yes.

Q. The most scattered and farthest off?—A. I do not recollect.

Q. Then you were not informed?—A. I do not remember.

Q. Will you refer to General Meade's order to Warren of 9 p. m.?

You will, by the direction of the Major General commanding, draw back at once to your position within the Boydton plank road, &c.

You will notice, I suppose, that General Meade sent you word that the order had been issued to Warren fifteen minutes before it actually had been issued, and so, of course, before Warren received it. Do you know at that time, or did you know as far as you recall, the distance between General Warren's headquarters and General Meade's, and the time it took for communication between them?—A. I do not recollect; we were changing our headquarters from time to time.

Q. Then, if you will refer to your own dispatch of ten minutes past nine to General Meade, which reads:

H'DQ'RS ARMIES OF U. S.,

Dabney's Mills, M'ch 31st, 1865—9.10 p. m.

Maj. Gen. MEADE:

I wish you would send out some cavalry to Dinwiddie to see if information can be got from Sheridan. It will only take about half the time to go from your headquarters it will take from mine and I have no one to send.

(Sgd.)   U. S. GRANT, *L't-Gen.*

A true copy from the file of of copies in possession of Major Asa Bird Gardner, U. S. A., counsel for the respondent.

LOOMIS L. LANGDON,

Brevet. Lt.-Colonel, U. S. A., Recorder.[6]

A. The probabilities are I sent that to him by telegraph, so it would go instantaneously, and because headquarters were nearer the point to be reached.

Q. That dispatch by yourself to Meade would indicate that you were just about that hour without information from General Sheridan, and wished it, and that you had no one to send for the purpose of communication?—A. Yes; and they could go from his headquarters in less time than from mine.

Q. Does your recollection agree with that?—A. If that is a part of the record no doubt it is correct.

Q. Have you any recollection what particular circumstance there was that evening which so placed you that you had no one to send to General Sheridan?—A. No, sir; I had no cavalry except a little escort at headquarters.

Q. General Meade's dispatch to Warren of 9.20 reads:

Division to be sent to Sheridan may start at once. You will be held free to act within the Boydton plank road. General Humphreys will hold to the road and the return.

I suppose you had no information at that time that Griffin's division actually had started, of course?—A. I do not recollect.

Q. Can you recall any order or direction that you had then given, at 9.20, to any other effect that General Warren at that time was to be held free to act within the Boydton plank road?—A. I cannot recollect.

Q. "Within the Boydton plank road," I suppose at that time meant to the south and east of it?—A. Yes.

Q. At 9.45 General Meade sends to you a dispatch beginning in these words: "Would it not be well for Warren to go down with his whole corps and smash up the force in front of Sheridan?"[7] and your answer to that, which is dated 10.15, reads: "Let Warren move in the way you propose, and urge him not to stop for anything."[8] As far as you recall, had there been any suggestion on either side, either from General Meade to you or from you to General Meade, before this dispatch as to Warren's moving down in the manner that is mentioned there?—A. I could not say. I can recall nothing. If there is anything it will be matter of record. It was probably in writing.

Q. At that time were you informed of General Warren's dispatch dated 8.40 p. m. to General Meade, in these words:

If we are not threatened south of Gravelly Run, east of the plank road, General Humphreys and my batteries, I think, could hold this securely and let me move down and attack the enemy at Dinwiddie on one side and Sheridan on the other.

Were you then informed that Warren had sent that dispatch to Meade?—A. I do not recollect.

Q. Were you then informed in any way that the suggestion which General Meade communicated to you as to the attack by Warren on the enemy's rear was suggested to him by Warren himself?—A. As I say, I do not recollect.

Q. Have you any information or knowledge that that movement was ever suggested by any one, either yourself or General Meade, except as the record shows, after General Warren himself suggested it to Meade?—A. I have no recollection, except as the record shows.

Q. Then, as far as your recollection goes and as the record shows, the attack by Warren in the enemy's rear was originally suggested by himself to General Meade, and then by General Meade to you?—A. I do not recollect anything about it. I say whatever the record is.

Q. Have you any recollection to the contrary?—A. No, sir; I have no recollection of the fact; I have no recollection to the contrary.

Q. You notice, too, your dispatch to General Meade of 9.45 begins in this way:

If you can get orders to Mackenzie to move his cavalry to the support of Sheridan by way of the Vaughn road, do so. I have sent the same directions to General Ord.[9]

Can you recall the reason why you requested General Meade?— A. No, sir; I cannot recollect, but I find here the letter I sent to General Ord. That very time, at 9.45, when I directed Ord to forward the cavalry of the Army of the James and send Mackenzie, at once, to Dinwiddie to support Sheridan, the cavalry and infantry were being driven into Dinwiddie. The fighting was still going on at the time I last heard from him, which was after dark. Then, at the same hour, I telegraphed Meade: (Reads.)

H'DQ'RS ARMIES OF THE U. S.,
Dabney's, March 31st, 1865—9.45 p. m.

Maj. Gen. MEADE,

    Com'd'g Army of Potomac:

If you can get orders to Mackenzie to move his cavalry to the support of Sheridan by way of the Vaughn road, do so. I have sent the same directions to General Ord. Please let me know when Griffin gets started; if he pushes promptly I think there may be a chance for cutting up the infantry the enemy have intrusted so far from home. Urge prompt movement on Griffin.

U. S. GRANT, L't-Gen.

Copy furnished Gen. Mackenzie for his guidance.

A. S. WEBB,
Bvt.-Maj. Gen., Chief of Staff.

A true copy from copy furnished Maj. Asa Bird Gardner, U. S. A., counsel for respondent.

LOOMIS L. LANGDON,
Brevet Lieutenant-Colonel, U. S. A.

Q. As far as you recollect, was the reason of your requesting General Meade to send that additional dispatch, the fact that you had alluded to before, that you had no one to send yourself?—A. It would be impossible for me to answer now from recollection just what I did. I know, through the whole of the day, from the time General Sheridan was sent off to my left flank, until Five Forks was carried, I was watching their every movement and everything that was done, doing all I could to aid. I was sending orders here and there, to one army and another, wherever I judged there was an opportunity of putting it in, and I wanted my orders promptly obeyed and generally had them. But where officers undertook to think for themselves, and considered that the officer giving them orders had not fully considered what everybody else was to do, it generally led to failure or delay.

Q. And that you did not like?—A. That I did not like.[10]

Q. Then you notice that your dispatch allowing General Meade to direct that movement of Warren (reading):

Let Warren move in the way you propose, and urge him not to stop for anything.

That is sent at 10.15.

A. That is probably correct.

Q. Then at 10.30, apparently, as our copies read, you sent this other dispatch to General Meade:

As you are sending to Sheridan, send him word of all the dispositions making to aid him, and tell him to take general direction of the forces sent to him, until the emergency for which they are sent is over.[11]

Will you examine such papers as you have and see if the date of that dispatch is correct, whether it is 10.30?

A. The dispatch is not on this memorandum. This memorandum does not appear to be a complete record.

Q. Do you recollect such a dispatch?—A. I do not.

Q. There is a dispatch dated 10.05, nearly half an hour before, and bearing your name, which would tend to show that you had already, yourself, sent a dispatch to General Sheridan direct, in writing, informing him of all the dispositions making to aid him, and telling him to take general direction of the forces sent to him, almost exactly to the same effect that you request General Meade to advise him, in this dispatch of yours to General Meade of 10.30?—A. I recollect I sent word, either written or verbal, I suppose it was in writing, to General Sheridan to take command of everything that was sent to him; take supreme command of the whole of it.

Q. Can you tell at what hour you sent that?—A. I cannot; but I presume it must have been soon after I started re-enforcements to him. [Witness here refers to memorandum.] At 10.05 I sent to Sheridan:

The Fifth Corps has been ordered to your support, &c. . . . In addition to this I have sent Mckenzie's cavalry, which will reach you by the Vaughn road. All these forces, except the cavalry, should reach you by 12 m. to-night. You will assume command, &c.[12]

Q. That dispatch purports to be dated 10.05?—A. Yes.

Q. Have you now in your mind a recollection of sending that during the evening?—A. I have recollection of sending it, but I could not fix the time or date, if I did not have something to refresh it with. I recollect the dispatch, in substance.

Q. Is that the correct hour upon it? You notice that you did not give an order to Meade, authorizing the movement, until 10.15. At 10.05 you had not ordered that or authorized it?—A. I could not say as to the date, 10.05, any further than I find it there. It is apt to be about correct.

Q. You notice that you had not then allowed a movement to be exe[c]uted, that you had not sent any dispatch allowing the movement to be executed, until fifteen minutes past ten; so the order says. You notice, too, that in that dispatch of 10.30, half an hour later, you request General Meade to send that information to General Sheridan. And will you be kind enough to have search made among the original papers to get hold of the original dispatch, if possible, and send it to the court?—A. I suppose the court could send and get them.

Q. You think they are at Washington?—A. I think they will be there. If they are in any place, they are there.

Q. Have you any recollection as to what officer took that dispatch to General Sheridan?—A. I have not. I have a very indistinct recollection about that matter. It seems to me that I sent orders to General Meade to order these troops, and immediately wrote to General Sheridan at 10.05, as it would seem from this, what was being done, and that General Meade, instead of doing promptly what he was directed to do, came over to see me. I think there was a little delay of half an hour caused in that way, before sending the orders to General Warren—I supposed sent, when this dispatch was written. I think General Meade came to see me personally. I think there was a little delay in sending General Warren his orders in consequence of that. I think that I did (as I have stated), but I will not be sure about it. I think there was a delay of that sort in sending General Warren his orders, which I did not know of at the time I wrote to General Sheridan. I think there was a delay long enough for General Meade to come to my headquarters to see me in person.

Q. If there were such a one, that would be the point to be considered?—A. Yes. I could not state it positively, but I have an indistinct recollection that there was delay in that way.

Q. Have you any recollection of a dispatch earlier than this one of your own, dated 10.15, to General Meade, or of any oral authority given earlier, authorizing and allowing General Warren's movement with his two divisions to co-operate with Sheridan?—A. I have not.

Q. Then do you remember, or can you refer us to any information that you got during the night as to Warren's actual movements?—A. I have no actual recollection, only that I have an indistinct recollection that I was very much disappointed.

Q. I am asking for information, if you please. Of course we understand that you thought that there had been great delay?—A. Yes.

Q. I want the information, if I can get it, that you had upon the point, who it came from and what it was?—A. I do not know how it came. I presume General Meade may have reported through some staff officer that Warren had not moved, or when he was moving, and the time he did move.

Q. Do you recollect that some one of Meade's staff did come to your headquarters about ten or eleven o'clock in the forenoon next day?—A. I do not recollect, because they were constantly coming.

Q. His testimony is, giving it briefly, that he brought the information at that time to your headquarters, that Warren was still delayed and hindered from crossing the stream at Gravelly Run by waiting to build a bridge.—A. I do not recollect that particular.

Q. Do you recollect getting that information at that time?— A. No.

Q. Then, as far as your recollection goes, the testimony may be entirely correct as to his report?—A. Yes. I have no doubt that it is.

Q. (By Maj. Asa Bird Gardner, counsel for the respondent). You mean on that particular point as to bringing a report there— the evidence of Captain Warner?—A. Yes.

Q. I only ask you for the information you then had as to Warren's delay?—A. I do not know from memory, but I do know from the record, which I was looking at this morning, that that information which Major Warner brought to me I had before he says that he came there.

Q. That was about what?—A. About being delayed, about building a bridge.

Q. That there had been long delay to build a bridge?—A. Yes.

Q. Then that was the information you had, that Warren had been delayed in building a bridge over Gravelly Run?—A. Yes; although I do not recollect it, I say that I had the information long before Captain Warner says that he was at my headquarters; but he was not aware probably that I did have it.

Q. Then, if the fact was that there was no delay at all for building the bridge, you were misinformed. You had no information of that, if that was the fact?—A. Of which?

Q. That there was no delay at all for the purpose of building a bridge over Gravelly Run?—A. I do not know whether there was delay or not.

Q. The fact was that there was no delay at all, but you were not informed of that?

Maj. Asa Bird Gardner, counsel for the respondent. We do not admit that.

Mr. STICKNEY, counsel for the applicant. I know you do not; I only ask what the information of the witness was.

Q. You were not informed of that; you had no information of that?—A. I do not know that I catch the question exactly.

Q. If the fact was that there was no delay at all at Gravelly Run bridge, you had no information of that?—A. Well, there was a delay.

Q. You were n[o]t there?—A. I was not there, but I think there was delay. I have no personal knowledge, except the reports that were brought to me.

Q. Those reports were that there had been a long delay?—A. Those reports were that there was delay to build a bridge.

Q. You had no information that those reports were inaccurate?—A. No, sir; not up this time, I have not.

Q. As to the operations on the morning of the 31st—I ask only as to your information of them—your understanding of it was, at the time you wrote your dispatches relating to your movements, that Warren had made an attack upon the enemy and that he had attacked only with one division instead of attacking with his whole corps?—A. Yes.

By Maj. ASA BIRD GARDNER, counsel for respondent:

Q. With relation to one of the dispatches that you have just been questioned about, namely, that dispatch from Dabney's Mills on the night of March 31st, at 10.05 p. m., to General Sheridan, that the Fifth Corps had been "ordered to your support; two divisions will go by J. Boisseau's and one down the Boydton road." A subsequent dispatch has also been shown you dated 10.15, to General Meade, to let Warren move in the way "you propose; urge him not to stop for anything, and let Griffin go in as he was first directed"; have you any recollection now whether or not you sent by a staff officer or by messenger or by telegram an order to General Meade as to the movements Warren was to make before you sent that dispatch to General Sheridan?

Mr. STICKNEY, counsel for the applicant. That is, not to Sheridan; that is, to General Meade.

Maj. ASA BIRD GARDNER, counsel for the respondent. I refer to both. Here is one to Meade at 10.15: "Let Warren move in the way you propose; urge him not to stop for anything.'" One previously

at 10.05 to General Sheridan that you had already ordered General
Warren to go down to this point?—A. I suppose there must be a
dispatch prior to that of 10.15 to Meade that I do not see here, because I had not written this one of 10.05 to Sheridan without having given the orders that it notifies him of prior.

Q. Have you any recollection now whether or not you had met
General Meade himself, or any of his staff before sending that?—
A. No; but we were constantly meeting. The possibilities were I
had given him a verbal order and he had gone back to his headquarters, and that then I have written to Sheridan that I had given
such orders. And then at 10.15 there seems to have been an order to General Meade which was anticipated by the note which he
was notified of, of 10.05. The order must have been given prior in
some way or other. But, as I say, I have an indistinct recollection
that, after Meade got the order he came over to my headquarters to
talk about it, probably, and state what he would have to leave bare
in drawing troops out, or something, I cannot tell what now; but
there has been a delay on his part in that way—a delay in communicating my orders. Probably General Webb could tell about that.
He was with me.

Q. You have also been asked as to this dispatch from General
Meade to General Warren:

[Rec'd 10.50 p. m. Nunan, 10.48.]

U. S. M. T., HD. QRS. A. OF P.,
10.15 *p. m.—M'ch* 31, 1865.

Maj. Gen. WARREN:

Send Griffin promptly, as ordered, by Boydton P. R.; but move
the balance of your command by the road Bartlett is on, and
strike the enemy in rear, who is between him and Dinwiddie. Gen.
Sheridan reported his last position as north of Dinwiddi[e] Court-
House, near Dr. Smith's, the enemy holding the cross-roads at that
point. Should the enemy turn on you, your line of retreat will be
by J. M. Brooke's & R. Boiseau's, on Boydton plank road. See one
inch maps. You must be very prompt in this movement, & get the
forks of the road at J. M. Brook's before the enemy, so as to open
to R. Boisseau's. The enemy will probably retire toward the Five
Forks, that being the direction of their main attack this day. Don't

encumber yourself with anything that will impede your progress or prevent your moving in any direction across the country. Let me know when Griffin starts & when you start.

GEORGE G. MEADE.

Maj. Gen'l.

Acknowledge receipt.

A true copy of the official copy in General Warren's file. On comparing it with the same dispatch as found in the file from the office for the publication of the Rebellion Records, it will be found that in the latter the words "south" occurs instead of "north," after the phrase "Sheridan reported his last position as," and the words "acknowledge receipt" come before the signature instead of after, as in General Warren's copy.

The dates and hours, as well as the body of General Warren's copy agree, except in the manner of spelling of proper names, with the copy of the file from the Adjutant-General's Office.

LOOMIS L. LANGDON,

Brevet Lieutenant-Colonel, U. S. Army, Recorder.

Do you know whether or not that order was obeyed?—A. I do not know; I do not remember.

Q. What information, if any, had you of that order's having been issued by General Meade to General Warren to move across the country in that way?—A. I do not remember?

By Mr. STICKNEY, counsel for the applicant:

Q. You say that, in your opinion, there must have been an earlier order to General Meade than the one that is produced here of 10.15 from you to him?—A. Yes.

Q. That is your inference?—A. That is my inference.

Q. Can you refer us now to any earlier one?—A. I cannot; only the simple fact that I wrote to Sheridan at 10.05. Certain things had been done; I infer certain orders had been given to do them. I cannot account for the 10.15 order except that General Meade was at my headquarters, and the order was given verbally and afterwards in writing.

Q. Our examination of the War Department files, General Webb's files, and General Sheridan's files do not give us any earlier order; so it is possible that that 10.05 is a mistake, that it might have been sent at a later hour. That is a possible inference?—A. That is a possible inference; instead of 10.05 it might have been 10.25.

Q. Or 10.45?—A. Yes.

Q. You have already stated you did not know of Meade's orders, and generally, cannot state whether there were any of Meade's orders to General Warren as to this movement that were brought to your notice?—A. They were all brought to my notice. There was no time during all these movements that I was not informed of everything that was done promptly.

Q. How were you informed?—A. By note, by telegraph, by messages through staff-officers, and constantly being informed every moment, almost. General Sheridan was so far separated from me that there was no telegraphic communication, but I had staff-officers. In fact my staff-officers were with General Sheridan, so that they could send notes by orderlies and then come themselves. There was a line between Sheridan and me kept up by me and by him, and orderlies from him; but between Meade and myself there was instantaneous communication.

Q. Of course you were informed with great fullness as to the movements and General Meade's instructions to subordinate commanders?—A. Yes. General Meade gave no orders that he did not have authority from me or instructions to give.

Q. Can you recall any one of those several written papers that were submitted to you, of which you had information that evening?—A. No, I cannot.

Q. As to your conversation with General Warren, when he came to your headquarters, after he had been relieved, without asking what was said; or going into details, did he ask for a court of inquiry, or to have an inquiry made?—A. I do not recollect that. My recollection is that when I said I would give him another command, his answer was, in substance, that if he was removed from the command he had he did not want any other.

Q. Can you recollect whether he asked of you to have a court of inquiry, or have an examination made of any kind?—A. I cannot recollect. That was not much of a time to be holding these courts of inquiry.

Q. Do you recollect that he did at any time?—A. I do not; it is possible he did.

The examination of this witness was here closed.

The court then, at 12.30, adjourned until Monday morning, October 25, 1880, at 11 a. m.

On the afternoon of October 24 the testimony of the last witness, General U. S. Grant, late United States Army, and Ex President of the United States, was read by him and pronounced by him to be correct as now recorded.

LOOMIS L. LANGDON,

Brevet Lieutenant-Colonel, U. S. A.

Proceedings, Findings, and Opinions of the Court of Inquiry . . . in the Case of Gouverneur K. Warren, . . . (Washington, 1883), II, 1026–46 (brackets in original). Ellipses represent legal discussions between counsel. "Among those present was General Adam Badeau, late Consul-General to London, who came with General Grant and sat at his elbow during the examination. General Grant came into the courtroom about 10 o'clock and took his seat upon the stand. He was dressed in a plain business suit. Most of his answers to the questions of the counsel were given in a quiet, unhesitating manner. Frequently in the discussions between the opposing counsel he made remarks upon the points in dispute, and once or twice in his examination by Mr. Stickney he manifested considerable feeling." *New York Tribune,* Oct. 24, 1880. See David M. Jordan, *"Happiness is Not My Companion": The Life of General G. K. Warren* (Bloomington, 2001), pp. 286–88; *Young,* II, 290; *PUSG,* 15, 21–22.

On Dec. 24, 1880, USG, New York City, wrote to Maj. Loomis L. Langdon. "I have the voucher which you sent me to be filled out for my services as witness before the court of which you are recorder. I do not return it as you request because I do not intended to present the action to receive anything." ALS (facsimile), R. M. Smythe & Co., Inc.

1. *PUSG,* 14, 274–75.
2. *Ibid.,* p. 282.
3. *Ibid.,* p. 279.
4. *Ibid.,* p. 278.
5. *Ibid.,* pp. 278–79.
6. *Ibid.,* p. 280.
7. *Ibid.,* p. 281.
8. *Ibid.*
9. *Ibid.,* p. 280.
10. USG finished this sentence: "and that kind of conduct led to the removal of one officer." *New York Tribune,* Oct. 24, 1880. Upon objection, the concluding phrase was omitted from the court record.
11. *PUSG,* 14, 280.
12. *Ibid.,* p. 289, dated 10:45.

To Elizabeth M. Borie

New York City
Oct. 24th 1880.

My Dear Mrs. Borie:

Mrs. Grant desires me to write to you to say that she will send to you by Express within a day or two some furs which she got in China as a token of her affectionate regard for an esteemed friend. I go west to-day—Sunday—so that I write in advance of the article being sent.

We will visit Phila soon where we hope to see you and to find you well. But when I visit Phila I shall miss my dear old friend. I know how you must miss him, but you have the consolation of knowing how he was esteemed by all who knew him.

With love of Mrs. Grant & myself,

yours Truly
U. S. Grant

ALS, PHi.

On Sept. 15, 1881, USG wrote to Elizabeth M. Borie. "Mrs. Grant & I were pleased to receive your letter which announces your intention of sailing for Europe on the 21st inst. I will try to do myself the pleasure of seeing you off on that occasion, and saying then how much we wish you and your party a safe trip, safe return, and benefit from the voyage and visit.—Mrs. Grant wishes to send you her love in which I join." ALS, *ibid.*

To Lt. Gen. Philip H. Sheridan

Utica, N. Y.
Oct. 25th 1880.

Dear Sheridan;

I telegraphed you yesterday for an extension of leave for Fred. to remain with me two weeks longer. A few minuets after my dispatch was sent your authority come for him to remain twelve days, the time some one els had asked for him. My reason for want-

ing him to remain with me until after the election is that I am so
pressed by committees, letters & telegrams to go to this place and
that that I would not have time to read my letters much less reply
to them if I had not some one to do this for me. I can trust Fred to
read my letters, and to answer them with no further dictation than
to say I can or I ca'nt I will or I wo'nt &c. Either one of my other
boys would answer the same purpose, but in New York City, their
home, they are busy with their own affairs, and can not escape it
except by going out of town.

When I went to Warren, Ohio, I had no idea that it was going
to entail on me so much trouble. But I feel as if it is more than this
country can or ought to bear to put in charge of it the very men
who tried to destroy it, and without repentance. If I can do any
good towards preventing this I will feel abundantly compensated
for all my trouble.—What bothers me most is that I feel like I was
only a figurehead while others are doing the work.

Since the Ia[1] & O. elections I feel that the result in Nov. is secured. There is but little doubt but that N. Y. & Conn. will go republican, and the chances are decidedly in favor of N. J. also.

I am much obliged to you for leaving Fred. with me. As soon as
the election is over my correspondence will be reduces so that I can
take care of it without assistance.

Very Truly yours
U. S. GRANT

ALS, DLC-Philip H. Sheridan.
    On Oct. [*12–16*], 1880, Chester A. Arthur telegraphed to USG, Boston. "~~There~~
Arrangements will be made for a great mass meeting at Utica the home of S. C. on
Tuesday the twenty sixth ~~of~~ instant if you can be present. ~~The Senator~~ I ~~hop~~ beg that
you will consent. I know it will be agreeable to the senator who will ~~spe~~ address the
meeting." ADf (telegram sent), DLC-Chester A. Arthur.
    On Oct. 25, USG addressed a rally. "CITIZENS OF UTICA—Under no circumstances
will I detain you long: but having a bad cold and being so hoarse that I can scarcely
speak I shall detain you even a less time. I came here to preside at a political meeting. It
is a new business for me, and if it was not for the earnestness I feel for the cause which
agitates the public mind at this time I should continue a custom which I have followed
for more than fifty years—that is, in not taking part in political meetings. But this
country has suffered so much in blood and treasure to uphold the flag of our Union
and maintain the best form of government that has ever been devised for men that it
seemed to me that I could not bear the idea of seeing the country in its legislative and

all its branches turned over to a party composed in great part of those who so recently tried to destroy it. We do not advocate the principles of the republican party because we believe they are for the good of the republican party alone and to the prejudice of the interest of the opposite party, but we proclaim them at this time because we believe they are the best for all parties. We believe that the democrats are just as much interested to-day in the success of the republican party as the republicans of the United States are. We believe further that the Southern States that were lately in rebellion are just as much interested and more interested in the success of the republican party. We all know that there is no man in the South who is not privileged to come and settle among us in the North in any section and retain his political views, and at the same time prosecute his business, whether it be professional, mercantile or what not. The Northern man has not the same privilege in the South. If he goes there to prosecute his business he must be quiet on political questions of great weight. In other words, the carpet-bagger is not a welcome citizen among them. Now, we want to see all of this changed. I, myself, am from a Northwestern State. We are all carpet-baggers in that section. The whole of it has been built up in the lifetime of many here present, and see the result of carpet-bag settlement in the Northwest. The whole of it, out of which has been grafted five or six fine States, is the gift of one of the old slave States. See the prosperity and the thrift that has been brought to these new States by these carpet baggers! They built up our Cincinnati, our Chicago, our Detroit, our Indianapolis, our Cleveland and hundreds of smaller towns of great prosperity. With the same privileges extended to carpet-baggers, the growth that has been seen in the Northwest would have been seen ere this in the Southern States. We claim that no great prosperity can overtake these until every citizen of every State is regarded as a citizen of the United States, no matter where he goes, and with the privileges of proclaiming his political principles without molestation. Now, gentlemen, I know you will hear so much more than I can say on this question and hear it so much better said that I will say no more, but will introduce as the next speaker your eminent townsman and statesman, Senator Conkling." *New York Herald,* Oct. 26, 1880.

On Oct. 26, USG addressed a rally in Syracuse. "CITIZENS OF SYRACUSE—I am here among you to-day at your request as conveyed to me through your committee, not to say much myself, but to show my interest in the cause of the republican party at the approaching election. If I did not feel a deep interest in the success of this party I would not be here. If I did not believe it was for the interest of all parties and all sections that we should succeed at this time I would not be here. Among the democrats of the North I have a great many warm personal friends, men whom I like personally as well as any friends I have under the sun. Some of them, those whom I claim as my friends, are patriotic, good men, and I believe if the democratic party was composed entirely, North and South, of such men I would still be a republican, but I would not feel so much distress if the republican party was not successful. But even admitting that all the democrats of the Northern States were of the class that I speak of (but I do not admit it), we would not be secure under a democratic administration. You all know that the bulk of the democracy is in the Southern States and that it will control if the democratic party gets in power, and it is just as impossible that the limited number of democrats of the North should control as it is that the dog's tail would wag the dog. In all instances the dog will wag the tail, and if they should get into power that tail would be so powerful that it would sweep down at one stroke all of your industries and prosperity, all of your banks and your manufactories and your industries of all sorts and descriptions. We don't want to see this. We know, with all the energy of Northern people—we all know that the North, with its great intelligence, its free schools, its energy and its industry could not be stricken not to rise again, but in rising it would suffer years of toil and disappointment. We want to avoid that, and to do that we want to elect Garfield and Arthur in November. You will probably hear, probably have heard, and probably will hear again before election day the democratic party arraigned as a party that has never advocated—certainly not in a quarter of a century—advocated or done a good act. I will not quite agree with those speakers now, but a few days ago I would; but I within a few days read an extract from a speech made by a Southern orator, whose audience happened to be composed largely of colored men, and he told them they were laboring under a great mistake in supposing that Lincoln had emancipated them. He reminded them of the fact that Lincoln's emancipation proclamation gave them—the rebels—ninety days in which to lay down their arms and to save their property, 'but they fit right straight ahead.' He says the proclamation didn't emancipate them, and hence Lincoln was not entitled to the credit of it. Now, gentlemen, I am sure I shall introduce to you a speaker—Mr. Woodford—who will give you many more reasons than I possibly can, particularly on my feet, why you should support Garfield and Arthur, on the 2d of November next." *New York Herald*, Oct. 27, 1880.

Also on Oct. 26, USG spoke at "two monster wigwams" in Auburn, N. Y. "LADIES AND GENTLEMEN—I am convinced from all I hear and see that the people—the republicans—are wide awake as to their best interests at this election. They will return the power into the hands of the people who saved the country in time of danger. We are not ready at this time to surrender the interests of this country into the hands of those who have for twenty years endeavored to destroy it. They must give up the principles for which Lee and Johnson fought before we will receive their system of doctrine. Before it will be safe to surrender our convictions they must give up the doctrine of State Rights. The democrats felt sure of 138 electoral votes at Cincinnati, no matter what nomination might be made. The democratic party does not care a cent for a platform. If a republican had been sent to the Cincinnati Convention to dictate a platform they would have accepted it. Any platform that would secure forty-seven electoral votes was what they wanted. The republican party permits a ballot to be cast by every voter. When beaten by a ballot so cast they will surrender and will submit to whatever may happen." "LADIES AND GENTLEMEN—I have just come from the wigwam across the way, where I spoke much longer than I can hope to here, and I do not know that I can say anything more than to thank you. I had one advantage at my first stopping place, as I saw no reporter present and am sure I will not get reported. But I will testify to you that I believe the best interests of the country demands, and the great uprising we have witnessed all through this country in the last two weeks and the joy we witness here to-day all indicate the people of this country are determined to maintain intact the country for which we fought and for the principles for which we sacrificed so much. I am sure I can say nothing more, and am certain not so well on the subject as the speakers you have with you to-day and who will formulate and prove this proposition. I believe that on the 2d of November this great State of New York is going to cast her vote for Garfield and Arthur and so surely as she does they will be elected. I thank you for your attention." *New York Herald*, Oct. 27, 1880. USG referred to the 138 electoral votes held by the deep South and border states, including Mo., Ky., Md., West Va., and Del. Another forty-seven was necessary to reach the 185 electoral votes required for election.

On Oct. 27, USG continued his campaign swing. "GENTLEMEN OF ROCHESTER: I esteem it a high honor to be called upon to preside here to-day. I am listening to you, gentlemen, and I cannot understand you when you are all talking at once. Neither can you hear a word of what I am saying, unless you let me do the talking for a minute or two. When the other speakers come on I hope you will keep order. I have told you that if you all talked at once I couldn't hear a word you say. Gentlemen, it is very encouraging for the cause which you and I come here to foster and advance, to see such earnestness manifested in spite of bad roads and bad weather. Since this campaign opened I have been from Illinois to Boston, passing through your own state of New York, and I find the same enthusiasm everywhere. This is convincing evidence to my notion, that the people understand the questions before us in this campaign. It seems to me an indication of determination on the part of the people of the country that the southern generals who fought so recently to destroy the Union, and who have since then experienced no change of heart, shall not administer our estates in the north, but that we are going to look after our estates ourselves. It is gratifying to me to observe that there are two topics of public importance, upon which the people have made up their minds; first, that they will have a loyal government, an honest ballot and a fair count, and secondly, that all classes are convinced of the fact that the tariff is not a local issue, but one for the benefit of agriculturists, laborers, manufacturers, and all classes alike. The farmer understands that without employment in manufactures there would not be purchasers for the products of the home markets. Now, gentlemen, not being able to hear a word of what you are saying, I will stop and introduce to you a gentleman who can give 329 reasons why the Republican party should be successful in the coming election. That gentleman is the Hon. Roscoe Conkling." *Rochester Democrat and Chronicle*, Oct. 28, 1880. Democrats had adopted the slogan "$329" to remind voters of the sum Republican presidential candidate James A. Garfield had allegedly received in the Crédit Mobilier scandal. After U.S. Senator Roscoe Conkling of N. Y. spoke for two hours, USG spoke again. "LADIES AND GENTLEMEN: You have heard as a plank of the Democratic platform, laid down here just now, that it was the work of the Democratic party to fill the gap between the aristocracy and the laboring classes in the United States of America. And you have been rightly told that we have no aristocracy. That gap was closed fifteen years ago, when slavery went out of existence in America. The only aristocracy that ever existed in this country was an aristocracy of the Democratic party, and it had its life in the ownership of human beings. I now introduce to you Colonel Pitkin, of Louisiana, who knows what that aristocracy was, and who will tell you of the disaster which it wrought in the south." *Ibid.* USG addressed the crowd once more following a speech by John R. G. Pitkin. "GENTLEMEN: The hour is late and I shall have nothing more to say to you. You will now have time to go to your suppers and prepare for the parade in the evening." *Ibid.*

On Oct. 28, USG spoke at Buffalo. "FELLOW-CITIZENS: Unless order can be restored it is not worth while for anyone to attempt to speak. I am sure that I cannot make myself heard. I am highly gratified to see the great number of people that have turned out here today. I am convinced that the people of the great State of New York are fully alive to the pending issues in this campaign. The Democratic party organized as it now is, is under the control of the Rebel Brigadiers. We want at least a National party with a policy that will prevail in all sections. We are not willing and you are not willing, and among the people of the Empire State there are men who will not submit to Southern rule. We want to be ruled by Northern people while we are alive. I predict for this State the greatest victory it has ever had and that it will be a victory from the Pacific to the Atlantic, thro[ug]hout the entire Northern States, and that we will have a different organization to contend with in the next election from what we have now. We will have an organization then to contend with which will be divided into two parties, and not by two sections of the country. We will then have a free ballot and an honest ballot, which the people of this country are determined to have, and if the South persists in a solid South they will be met by a solid North! I would make myself heard if I could and say more to you, but it is impossible, and I will now introduce to you a speaker who can make himself heard, Senator Conkling, of the State of New York." *Buffalo Commercial Advertiser,* Oct. 28, 1880. "The crowd at the great Central Wigwam this afternoon, to see Gen. Grant and hear Senator Conkling, was entirely unprecedented. The vast building, capable of holding 10,000 people, was crowded at least two hours before the time of opening the meeting. . . ." Unable to quiet the crowd, USG nearly abandoned his speech. *"Fellow Citizens:* As I cannot possibly make myself heard, I shall not say anything to you, but introduce you at once to Senator Conkling." *Ibid.* On Oct. 26, the Buffalo "Colored Citizens' Garfield and Arthur Club" and "Colored Boys in Blue" had resolved "to swell the ranks with veterans and our regular club to do honor to the greatest soldier of our nation, whose name and whose fame are the pride of any true American citizen." *Ibid.,* Oct. 27, 1880.

On Oct. 29, USG addressed a rally at Bath, N. Y. "LADIES AND GENTLEMEN—It takes more lung power than I possess to make such a large crowd of people hear me, even within four walls, but out of doors it is simply impossible. Therefore I shall leave you to those who are accustomed to speak out of doors, and who will address you upon the important issues of the day. Even if I could speak so as to be heard I take it I would be talking to an assembly who think as I do upon the issues to be settled next Tuesday. I think that Garfield and Arthur would be elected if the voting could be confined to this crowd. At least I shall hope so, and I would be willing to leave it to you, and thus save the expense of an election at least. If the ladies were allowed to vote I should be willing to abide by the result, and I hope that our opponents will be reconciled to the defeat that awaits them next Tuesday. As I have to go to the Soldiers' Home this afternoon, and attend a meeting at Elmira this evening I will therefore thank you for the cordiality of your reception to-day, hoping that I may meet you again and that we may all rejoice together next Tuesday." *New York Herald,* Oct. 30, 1880.

On Oct. 30, USG concluded his campaign tour with a speech at Staten Island, N. Y. "LADIES AND GENTLEMEN AND COMRADES: I thank you heartily for the cordiality of this greeting. It is an earnest to me that it would be a safe thing for the country to leave the election of next Tuesday entirely in the hands of this assembly. The result will be the same when the sun goes down on Tuesday next as if all parties had consented to such an arrangement, and we should save much time and expense and traveling over bad roads. It is hardly worth while for me to attempt to give you here any arguments in favor of the Republican Party. I take it that all of you know which way you are going to vote, and you will vote that way whatever I may say. I see before me a great number of the Boys in Blue, and I believe that they are going to cast their votes to bring down the solid South. Not that we bear any personal enmity toward our late foes, but we want to bring them to a just sense of the value of a good Government, of a Government where every man has the right to cast his ballot as his conscience dictates, and to have his ballot counted as it was cast. We want to show the solid South that every citizen of one of our States is a citizen of the United States, and can carry his citizenship and political sentiments with him wherever he chooses to go. I have frequently said that we are Republicans, not because success will be of any special benefit to the Republicans, but because our principles are such as to result in good to all parties in this broad land. We are all citizens of one great country, and whatever benefits the country benefits all of its citizens, Democrats and Republicans alike. Some of our views are not those of the opposite party. We believe in a tariff which protects the manufacturer, and therefore protects and pays labor. We believe that there should be no conflict between capital and labor. What benefits one also benefits the other, and anything that strikes down capital strikes down labor. We cannot all be employers. We do not believe that we can compete with foreign manufacturers unless we have a protective tariff. An opposite policy would reduce the price of labor, and we do not want to see that done. I need hardly dwell on what I believe would be the consequences of the election of Gen. Hancock. I believe that it would cause a great disturbance in the financial world. Business would be prostrated and much suffering would be caused before we could rise again. All danger of that, however, is now at an end. I have been through this State, and recently I have traveled from the Mississippi River to Boston. I never in all my life saw the same enthusiasm and determination on the part of Republicans, everywhere that I have seen this year. I shall not be surprised at any Republican majority in this State—except a small one. A small one would surprise me if under 50,000. I shall not be amazed at anything over that. My conviction is equally certain that every Northern State, with the possible exception of two—California and Nevada—will give a Republican majority. These two States are usually counted as Republican in national contests, but I don't know what local issues, like that of the tariff may be agitating them now. I want you all to remember my prediction on next Tuesday. If it appears that I am right, talk about it as much as you please. If you find that I am wrong, then treat the prediction as private and confidential." *New York Times*, Oct. 31, 1880. Democrats won Calif. and Nev.; Republicans carried all other northern states except N. J.

On Nov. 25, USG, New York City, wrote to William H. Bright, Utica lawyer and veteran, 80th N. Y. "Your letter of the 13th inst., with the names of 1,500 veterans of the late war, came duly to hand. I thank them and you for the kind expressions contained in your letter and congratulate both on the results of the late election, results largely due to the veterans of the war of the rebellion." *Ibid.*, Dec. 8, 1880.

1. Ind.

To Julia Dent Grant

Utica N. Y.
Oct. 25th 1880

DEAR JULIA:

We arrived here a little before three this morning, about an hour late as usual. I find after talking with Senator Conkling that I can not get off well without going through as far as Buffalo, and the people want me to accompany him all the week. But this I positively decline. I will leave Buffalo by the first train after the meeting there on thursday,[1] direct for New York City.

We had a good sleep here notwithstanding the late hour of arrival, not having breakfast until eleven. I slept an hour or two on the cars also. I will telegraph you two or three times between this and my return, but will not write again unless there is something special to write about. There are committees here for me from all along the line of the road to Buffalo, and letters for me from places along the line of the Erie road as I return, wanting me to go back that way.

Love to you, the boys, their wives & sweetheart.

Affectionately
U. S. G.

ALS, DLC-USG.

1. Oct. 28, 1880.

To Julia K. Fish

————

Fifth Av. Hotel,
Oct. 31st /80

My Dear Mrs. Fish:

Mrs. Grant rec'd your letter of the 23d, kindly inviting us to your house on the 4th prox. in due time, but could not answer it because of my absence, & not knowing what engagements I might have. On the 4th we have an engagement to a dinner party, and in addition I am to be at home the latter par[t] of the week to meet a gen[tleman] from Boston on a m[atter of] business. On the whole, it being now so late in the season, I think it doubtful whether we will be able to go this season We expect to remain here most of the fall & winter and hope to see much of you an[d] the Governor. I want to see the Governor very much, soon to talk to him about personal matters, and hope to have the oppertunity while he is here to cast his vote.

We would enjoy the visit to [your] country place very much [asi]d[e] from the pleasure of being with you and Govr Fish quietly, and hope yet to have that pleasure an other season, and to have a house where we can invite you.

With kindest regards of Mrs. Grant & myself to you and all your family present, I am,

Very Truly yours

U. S. GRANT

P. S. At 5 O'Clock to-morrow afternoon, U. S. Grant, Jr. will cease to be a bachilor. He is to be married to Miss Chaffee,[1] of Colorado, though a resident of this city for the past year. They—the bride & groom—leave here on the 4th for a tour.

U. S. G.

ALS, DLC-Hamilton Fish.

1. Born in 1857 in Mich., Fannie Josephine Chaffee was the daughter of former U.S. Senator Jerome B. Chaffee of Colo.

To Ellen Grant Sartoris

———

New York City
Nov. 4th 1880.

MY DEAR DAUGHTER:

The Presidential election is now over and I have time to write, and attend my own business for the first time for a month. The country, in my judgement has escaped a great calamity in the success of the republican party. A month ago the result attained was not expected.—You know Buck is married! Every one speaks most highly of the young lady. She is quite pretty with all. Fred & Ida have been with us since our arrival in New York, now nearly four weeks. They return to Chicago however this evening. It now looks as if we would make our permanent home in this city. If we do I shall be engaged in some occupation giving me a good income. I will also expect to secure a place for Fred and have him resign and come here to live. We will then be all together except you. But we will have a house and expect you and Algy to spend much of your time here. Possibly you might come here to live. Algy would not have to become a citizen if his interests were averse to it.—Buck and Jesse are both doing well in their business, and are entirely independent.—We are boarding at the Fifth Av. hotel for the present, and will continue to do so until I know I am fixed to be entirely independent. I will then purchase or lease a house. The latter is cheapest, but the former is more pleasant. I do not know whether any one has described Jesses wife? She is quite small with beautiful large eyes, a very small face but prominent nose, light auburn hair, and by some thought quite pretty. I do not think her as pretty as either Ida or Bucks wife. But she is very pleasant and not a bit spoiled. The same may be said of all your sisters-in-law.

We are all just as well as we can be and looking forward to the time when we can have you, Algy and the children with us again. With love and kisses to you all. In my next letter I want to send you a draft to get your Chrismas things with.

Yours Affectionately

U. S. GRANT

ALS, ICHi. On Nov. 3, 1880, USG complained to a reporter about time spent in interviews. "I am here on my own business, and now that the election is over I don't see why I should not be left to myself a little. As to the election, I am gratified at the result, of course; and that is all there is to say of it, it seems to me." Asked to attribute Republican victory to one cause, USG responded. "Well, in the first place, because we had the right to win. We had earned it. We had earned it by what we had done in the past for the country; and what a party has done is good earnest of what it can and will do in the future. Then, the people of the country were getting scared. They saw that a Democratic success meant domination by the South, and they did not care to be dominated and controlled by the party opposed to a free ballot and a fair count. If the South had once obtained a firm hold of the Government they would have ruined the country and nothing short of a revolution would have rescued it from their hands again." USG spoke of his role in the campaign. "I have done more talking than I ever did before in my life. . . . it is not my way to go into politics. But I felt so earnest and solicitous about the result; I saw the danger the country was drifting into; so I thought I had better take a hand in it. . . . I did or I would not have gone into the campaign. It is the first time I ever had anything to do with political campaign matters, and I never made a campaign speech before. This was my first political campaign." Asked if it would be his last, USG replied. "Very likely. But I don't pledge myself to that, mind. If anything extraordinary was to happen or any serious difficulty presented itself, the party would, of course, have my services." *New York Tribune*, Nov. 4, 1880.

To Alexander Ramsey

New York City
Nov. 10th /80

Hon. Alex. Ramsay,
Sec. of War:
Dear Sir:

I understand some changes are likely to be made in some of the heads of departments in the course of the fall and winter, by the retirement of the present heads; among them the head of the Qr. Mr. Dept. Permit me to suggest for the place Gen. Rufus Ingalls. Gen. Ingalls has unquestionably performed more service, and more valuable service, than any other officer in the Dept. I knew him well, and his services in the field. He is by far the ablest executive officer in that department, and I do not know his superior, if equal, in any other. On the ground of services rendered, and capacity for the position, I unhesitatingly recommend him to be Qr. Mr. Gen.

Very Truly yours
U. S. Grant

ALS, DNA, RG 94, ACP, 2163 1878. Brig. Gen. Montgomery C. Meigs continued as q. m. gen. See *PUSG*, 28, 194; letter to Lt. Gen. Philip H. Sheridan, Nov. 6, 1881.

On Nov. 24, 1880, USG, New York City, wrote to Secretary of War Alexander Ramsey. "If the President has not yet made a selection for the office of Chief Signal officer may I be permitted to suggest for consideration the names of Gen. Robt. Williams, of the Adj. Gen.s Dept. and Gen. C. A. Comstock of the Corps of Engineers. Either, in my judgement, would be satisfactory appointments both to the public & the department, and would prove well qualifie[d] for the position." ALS, OFH. On Dec. 15, the Senate confirmed William B. Hazen as brig. gen., chief signal officer, to succeed Albert J. Myer, who had died Aug. 24.

Speech

[*New York, Nov. 11, 1880*]

I have not arranged anything that I am going to say in order, and it may be that as I go on some questions will suggest themselves to your minds. If they do, and if you will ask me I will answer them to the best of my ability, or confess that I know nothing in the shape of an answer to the questions you may ask.

I went to Mexico last Winter for two objects. One was that I had been there a good many years ago in the war which this country unfortunately had with Mexico, and I have always felt an interest in the country from that day to this. And then I went there with the further object of seeing, if I could, how possibly we might establish relations of friendship and commerce between the two nations. I was led to that from facts which I became aware of in reference to this country. I found that we were large consumers of tropical products, and that that was increasing in a double ratio—first by an increase in our population, and then again by an increase in the wealth of our inhabitants. All those products—sugar, coffee, and tobacco being the leading articles—we derive from countries that trade but very little with us, countries that collect their revenues to a large degree by levying duties on their exports, which we have to pay, and then forcing us to ship our products to a European market to get the sterling in exchange with which to pay these bills. If I remember correctly—four years ago I could have told you accurately—but if my memory serves me right we are paying out annually $300,000,000 in current exchange, nearly all of it in sterling exchange, for such products. I believe, and was convinced after my visit to Mexico, that that country was capable of producing all that we have to import now of this character and with a large surplus to provide for our increased consumption. It is a neighboring Republic, with institutions like our own, and her wants, which must be supplied from abroad, are just such as we could furnish her. If Mexico were developed, so as to have an incentive to cultivate her soil, she would want agricultural implements and many such articles. As the people became wealthy they would want carriages and wagons, all sorts of machinery, all of the rolling stock for railroads—iron, probably, would come from England, because they would get it from there cheaper—harness, boots and shoes, clothing, and a thousand and one other articles we could furnish, so that we could pay largely for what we received in the produce of our manufactories, thereby adding to the commerce of our country and benefiting the two Republics alike. While I was there I was met with this sub-ject all the time. I found the people there very much interested in the development of their own resources. I was told that there was a good deal of hostility on the part of some people to a connection with the United States, they having in their recollection the result of the unfortunate incidents many years ago, when our Americans settled up Texas—part of Mexico at that time. That afterward led to a secession of that State from the Mexican Republic, and finally a war with the United States, which resulted in the loss of yet more territory. They felt—that is, that party felt—that they would be in danger of constantly losing territory.

To that I answered them that 20 years ago their apprehensions would have been well founded. We had existing in our country at that time an institution which was not sustained or justified by the civilized world anywhere except where the institution existed. It could not exist in a territory that was half slave and half free any longer than it could maintain political control of the country. I said, also, that they could not extend their institution North, hence their resolve and desire to acquire more territory in a southerly di-rection, where the institution of slavery could thrive, and establish new States which would give them representation in both houses. Now, our unfortunate war had extinguished that institution. We had homogeneous institutions from the North to the South, and no one section was dependent upon the acquisition of territory for the purpose of maintaining its institutions. The incentive being gone, ninety-nine out of every hundred people in the United States who think upon the subject would be indignant at the suggestion of an acquisition of territory from a friendly power by any unfair or filibustering means. I said further that if there was any danger whatever of the United States ever wanting to take territory from our neighbors, the best method in the world to secure themselves against such a result would be to cultivate friendly and commercial relations with us and not to seek to go abroad to establish rela-tions with nations beyond the seas, keeping aloof from their neigh-bors. That might lead to hostilities, and hostilities might lead to the acquisition of territory, even where people were not in favor of it at the time. The views I expressed on the subject seemed to be very favorably received, and, as I said, there was a very earnest desire on the part of the people to have railroads in their country to develop it.

There has been in this country a feeling that the Mexican people were not a class of people to develop their country, and that they have gone through a long series of years without making many advances. The assertion is made without any particular examination of the subject. From my observation, and looking at the history of the country, I think that they have done remarkably well. I think that Mexico is entitled to a great deal of credit for the position which she occupies now among the civilized nations of the earth when you consider her trials, her difficulties—trials and difficulties which it was impossible for her to avoid. Up to 1810 Mexico was a Province of old Spain. She was governed a great deal as Spain governs her Provinces now—for the purpose of getting from them all she could possibly collect, and keeping her subjects entirely ignorant of how to legislate and how to govern, simply making them producers, hewers of wood and drawers of water. Mexico, up to 1810, was governed entirely from old Spain. She was prohibited from producing anything from her soil which Spain could produce and ship to her, and all of those products had to pay a large duty when they went into Mexico. The Spaniards prevented the Mexican people from having any part in their Government, sending their own sons there to rule and to enrich themselves by large salaries and public plunder. I do not think I am overstating it, am I, Mr. Romero?

Mr. Romero—No, not at all.

It at last became so unbearable that in 1810 Mexico revolted, and the war continued until 1824 before she gained her final freedom. Then she was a people without legislative experience, without experience in governing, but free, and with a country to rule and to make laws for. The first thing she did was to adopt a Constitution something like ours, establishing a United States when there was but one State. She had to go to work and carve up the territory and make States so as to conform to the Constitution. And having no people to make laws for them, she adopted the laws which were in force—the laws of Old Spain. She prohibited the cultivation of certain articles, and so did the laws of Old Spain. She prohibited the cultivation of tobacco to one or two sections, where it was farmed out, and where the Government became the purchasers of the crop after it was raised, the manufacturers of tobacco and the salesmen of it. That perquisite was transferred to the Government of Mexico instead of to that of Old Spain. That was all the difference, or the reform, that was worked. The priests were the most educated men in the country, and had a nearer experience in governing than any other class of the people, and as any sect or any party or any kind of people would do under like circumstances, they availed themselves of the advantages which they had, and took entire control of the Government, political as well as spiritual, and so managed as to absorb all the revenues of the State and pretty much all the valuable property of the country into their own hands. And when that was becoming intolerable, so that the people were about ready to rise up in their might to overthrow the Church party—not the religion, but the claims of the clergy to the right of governing—our war with Mexico set in, which threw them back for a long period of time.

Finally, after getting over that and the effects of it, in 1855 they made war upon the Church to free themselves from their domination in civil matters. That war was going on, and had almost reached a successful close, when our rebellion set in. Then there was an intervention on the part of European powers—particularly France—which gave them another war that continued as long as ours did and a little after, so that really all the time that Mexico has had for advancement in republican institutions and republican government—to count really well—is since 1867. They have 13 years really of growth, and considering that they have been impoverished by wars, foreign and domestic, I think they have done remarkably well, and I am perfectly satisfied that with the building of railroads and of telegraphs there need be no more apprehension for the safety of capital invested in Mexico than in our own country. The building of railroads will give employment to labor and

will give rapid transit from one part of the country to another; the
telegraph will give instantaneous information of what is going on
in all parts of the country, and anything like an uprising can be
suppressed at once—suppressed in the bud. I look for a bright and
prosperous and rapid future for Mexico, and it must result in a very
large commerce with some part of the world. If we take advantage
of the time, it will accrue to the benefit of the United States more
than to that of any other country except Mexico, and Mexico will
be necessarily more than benefited any other country. At present,
owing to the lack of railroads, they have very little to export that
will bear transportation except their bullion. Their exports now, as
I learned while I was there, amount to about $25,000,000 a year.[1]
Of that sum quite or near $30,000,000 a year is in bullion, and only
about $5,000,000 of all her exports are from the product of her
soil. Even that is raised somewhere near the coast, where they can
easily get transportation. As I have said, I have no doubt that with
the building of railroads they will be able to export $200,000,000,
not a dollar of which will be bullion.

Now, as to the people, Mexico has a population of about
9,000,000, as I was informed while I was there, of which probably
7,000,000 are of the old Aztecs. They are a people who are wed-
ded to their homes. They do not like to leave, with their families,
their place of birth and the home of their ancestors. They probably occupy the same localities that their ancestors did a thousand
years ago. But they are a peaceable, quiet, innocent, inoffensive,
very religious, and virtuous people, and they are willing to work,
and are very industrious where they can see the wages coming in
Saturday night. They are a good class of labor for developing the
country around near where they live, and the men are willing to
go a distance of 20 or 30 or 40 leagues from their homes to work.
leaving their families back. With this small export, the land having no special value, the revenues of the country are very limited
indeed, about $18,000,000 being the maximum receipts of the
Government for one year—at least that was the maximum when I
was there, but Mr. Romero informs me that it has now increased to
$21,000,000.[2] At the time I looked at it, $18,000,000 was about the

extent of the revenues of the nation, with a very heavy rate of taxation, and with every effort on the part of the Government to get all
the revenue it could. With this the civil Government, including the
Army—there is no Navy to speak of—has to be maintained. Hence
it is impossible for Mexico, no matter how willing she may be, to
pay anything in her present state toward the building of railroads,[3]
and it has looked to me as though people building railroads there
with the expectation of doing any considerable portion of the work
with the subsidies they receive from Mexico will be very much
disappointed.

After the railroads are built and the country has had time to
develop as a consequence of these roads, then the country will in
all probability be rich so that she can pay. But at present it would
be impossible for her to pay any considerable amount in the shape
of subsidies to be used in the building of these roads. If there is
anything incoming from that source it is something that will have
to be waited for. The money will have to be furnished by the build-
ers of the road, and they will have to wait for the development of
the country for their subsequent returns.

Mr. Dillon[4]—Would it not be more advantageous to any set of
capitalists in the United States who set out to build a road to Mexico to build it free and independent, without loading down the Mexican people with a debt which it would be hard for them to pay?"

That is a question that railroad men can answer much better
than I could. I have had no experience in the management of railroads, except during the war. We used to build some then very suddenly, and tore them up, and we asked for no subsidies. We had no
subsidies, and we paid nobody for their work. But then, I should
think, if I were going to build a railroad myself I would rather own
the road and regulate it after it was built than to receive a subsidy
and then have the person or nation subsidizing me control me and
tell me how to run it. I think, however, that is a matter a railroad
man can tell much better than I can. Persons who expect to build
railroads in Mexico and avail themselves of the subsidies which the
Government promises them, are doomed to disappointment, or else
they have got to build the roads very slowly.

(Mr. Houston[5]—"How is it as to procuring labor?")

About that I will say that these 7,000,000 of Aztecs furnish as good labor as can be found—as industrious and willing workmen as can be found anywhere in the world—and the men will go a considerable distance from their homes and stay at work, without moving their families, however. But then, as they are scattered all over the country, as you advance you could get a new set of workmen. You could not commence at the northern border of Mexico with a set of workmen, and keep them until you got all through Mexico, but you could get new sets in the villages as you went along. Labor is now very cheap. It will, of course, enhance in value and very rapidly as the country develops. I visited, while I was there, some of the mines, and the labor is all performed there by natives.

A Mexican mining camp is a very much pleasanter sight than one of our mining camps. There is an entire absence of the drinking saloons and the gambling-houses and theatres, and the absence of bowie-knives and revolvers is very noticeable.

Mr. Houston—"What would be the cost of labor as compared with here?"

As it is now, labor would vary from 30 cents to 50 cents a day in silver. But it will enhance. Then, when you come to the labor in the terras calientas—that is, in the lowlands—where there is the yellow fever, labor would be scarce, and it would not do half the work it does on the table-lands above, and you would have to pay $1 a day. It would not average 50 cents a day—probably not as much as that.

Mr. Dillon—"It would be more desirable for capitalists here who might be interested in the construction of roads in Mexico to receive liberal charters and legislation, and build without any expectation of subsidies?"

I say that is a matter of which railroad men have to be judges. But if they wanted to build the railroad rapidly, they would have to furnish the money to build it at first, and trust to the development of the country enabling it to pay the subsidies. They cannot expect to build the road with the subsidies. In getting your Pacific road built you built 20 miles of road and turned that right in, and that could be used in the construction of another 20 miles. You had to furnish the capital only for 20 miles of road. If I were going to build a road there

I should say get a right of way without charge, exemption from taxation, and the introduction of all material used in the construction of
the road free from duty for a certain number of years, have the entire
control of fixing tariffs, &c., after it was built, and let the Government come in only when the road paid more than 10 per cent. over
cost, and say how the surplus over 10 per cent. should be divided between the Government of Mexico and the owners of the road.

New York Times, Nov. 12, 1880. USG spoke during a dinner at Delmonico's, hosted by
Matías Romero and attended by Jay Gould, Russell Sage, and other prominent railroad
financiers.

At the dinner, "Mr. Gould proposed the formation on the spot of a special committee to take into consideration the whole subject of railway communication with
Mexico. This proposition was adopted, and the followi[ng] gentlemen were informally
named as members of the committee: Chairmain, General U. S. Grant; Mr. M. Romero,
representing Mexico; Mr. C. P. Huntington, representing the Southern Pacific Railroad; General G. M. Dodge, representing the Texas Pacific Railroad; Mr. Jay Gould,
representing the Missouri, Kansas and Texas railroad; . . ." *The Two Republics*, Dec. 5,
1880. On Nov. 16, 1880, a correspondent reported from Washington, D. C., that a recent court ruling appeared to clear the way for a "grand scheme of railroad consolidation and extension" planned by Gould to "practically control the railways of the entire continent west of the Mississippi, and south to the very heart of Mexico. Another
part of the general plan is to make Gen. Grant President of the consolidated company,
first, because of his great ability to direct such a gigantic enterprise, and, secondly,
because it is believed that Gen. Grant would be able to secure from the Government of
Mexico every concession necessary to extend the road into the States of that country.
. . . Friends of Gen. Grant, cognizant of the plans above outlined, say the General has
been fully consulted in reference to the scheme, and that it is favorably regarded by
him. The present visit of Señor Romero, of Mexico, to the United States, and the recent
meeting of New-York, at which Gen. Grant made an interesting speech . . . are believed to have intimate connection with this contemplated enterprise." *New York Times*,
Nov. 17, 1880. On Dec. 23, USG chaired a meeting that presented a report "setting
forth that the members found it impossible to harmonize all the interests involved. . . .
Mr. Gould submitted a paper furnishing the basis for an agreement which he desired
to have taken as a minority report. It contained three propositions, the last of which
provided that in the event of the failure of the first and second, the respective claims
and differences of the road be submitted to Gen. Grant for decision before the 1st of
February, the decision to be accepted by both parties. . . ." *Ibid.*, Dec. 24, 1880. See letter to Matías Romero, Jan. 15, 1881.

On Jan. 28, 1881, Romero, New York City, wrote to William Henry Hurlbert,
New York World, to deny that he had represented the Mexican government at the Nov.
banquet. *New York World*, Feb. 16, 1881.

1. "$35,000,000," according to another version. *New York Tribune*, Nov. 12, 1880.
2. On Nov. 15 and 16, 1880, Edward L. Plumb, New York City, wrote to USG
transmitting reference works on Mexican commerce, laws, and geography. ADfS, CSt.
3. On Oct. 5, a committee of the Mexican Chamber of Representatives had recommended a tax on tobacco and matches to subsidize railroad construction. Printed
(in Spanish), USG 3.

4. Born in 1812 in N. Y., Sidney Dillon rose from water boy on the Mohawk & Hudson Railroad to president of the Union Pacific Railroad Co.

5. Born in 1820 in Pa., Henry H. Houston served as general freight agent for the Pennsylvania Railroad and amassed a fortune in infrastructure and real estate development.

To James A. Garfield

New York City
Nov. 11th /80

MY DEAR GEN. GARFIELD,

Now that the election is over, the result definitely known, and your election and inauguration as certain as the future is vouched safe to mortal man, I heartily congratulate you, and especially the country. I feel as shure that the nation has escaped a calamity as one can feel about untried things, by the defeat of the democratic party in the election just passed. With the unfair and unholy means resorted to by that party to carry the election it must now go into dissolution. It has been kept alive the last four years by the fact of Mr. Hayes small majority, and the necessity of having to carry three southern states to get that majority. The party knew, with the means they (it) could bring to bear, the republicans could not get another electoral vote from the south. The hope was strong of doing as well again in the north as they did the last time. They failed and must be hopelessly discouraged. I predict for you the least vexation any Executive has had since /60.

In my mind your majority was reduced in this state many thousands by the forged Chinese letter,[1] and that it lost you N. J. & Cal. A party that would resort to such means for success is not deserving, and cannot continue, to command the respect of any considerable portion of the American people. I see some of the papers, not heretofore particularly friendly to me, are mentioning my name in connection with a Cabinet position, a foreign mission, or other reward for my supposed services in the Campaign. I want to put your mind entirely at ease on this subject. As an American citizen

I felt as much interest in the result of the election as you or any one else could. I did only what I thought my duty as one who has received greater rewards from his country than any other living person. I want no reward further than the approval of the patriotic people of the land. There is no position within the gift of the President which I would accept. There is no public position which I want. If I can serve the country at any time I will do so freely and without reward. This I have great hope of being able to do by advice in relation to our affairs with Mexico and the East, especially China & Japan. There is a great future for the commerce of this country by a proper understanding with these countries.

With kind regards to Mrs. Garfield, and my congratulations to her also,

Very Truly yours
U. S. GRANT

ALS, DLC-James A. Garfield. See letter to James A. Garfield, Nov. 19, 1880.

On Nov. 15, 1880, USG attended a dinner given by William H. Beard, presidential elector for Brooklyn, and one of the "306" who had supported USG at the Republican National Convention in June. "Some one asked the General about the alleged compact which he and Senator Conkling made at Mentor with General Garfield in the dark days of the Republican canvass. General Grant smiled and remarked that if there had been anything of the kind done all the people in Mentor ought to know of it, as during the brief visit to General Garfield's house the entire population of the village seemed to be there. . . . General Grant, in response to questions asked from various parts of the table, gave interesting recitals of his impressions on the foreign lands he had visited. He was very much pleased with his travels in the East, and dwelt at considerable length on China and Japan. He spoke of the latter country in terms of great praise and of the remarkable progress the people are making. He drew a painful picture of the social and political condition of the Chinese Empire, representing the large mass of the people as virtually enslaved. When asked as to the cause of the striking difference between China and Japan, the general said that in the one the women were kept in virtual subjection and were of no account, while in the latter the women were treated with great respect and held the same place as they did in other civilized countries. An effort was made to draw the general out on the Chinese question, but he refrained from making any remarks which could be interpreted one way or the other. He believed that the Russian Empire was one of the worst governed in the world; there was no middle class and the officials were a most corrupt set. India was a most uninteresting country to visit in spite of what had been said of its attractions. In Siam, the general said he found much to interest him, and he had the pleasure of giving some advice to the young King, which relieved him from the oppression of a British Consul. The general was surprised to find that one part of Ireland was most loyal to the British Government, while the other was so disloyal, and he thought it singular that the former was the more intelligent. Summing up his impressions, General Grant said that the American people were the most ingenious in the world. The striking difference between an American and a foreigner is that the former will be able to do many things in a fairly satisfactory manner and some of them very well, while the latter can only do one thing well. The versatility of American genius was dwelt on by the General, and he instanced some exploits which were done by his volunteer soldiers during the war, which could not be accomplished by the regular standing armies of Europe. He thought that much improvement could be effected in the consular service, and he remarked that when General Garfield became President, he would take occasion to make some suggestions to him. Much could not be expected, he said, from consular servants getting $1,000 a year, but, as far as possible, they should forward the interests of American commerce. During the evening there were no set speeches, nor were any references made to local politics. The General thought that the late election would have the effect of disintegrating the Democratic party and breaking up the solid South." *Brooklyn Eagle*, Nov. 16, 1880.

On Nov. 19, John A. Bingham, U.S. minister, Tokyo, wrote to USG. "Allow me to thank you for the great service you have done by the unmatched personal influence which of merit belongs to you in securing by your efforts before the people of in Illinois, in Indiana in Ohio in New York & Massachusetts &c. the success of the Republican nominees and the great cause of the Union the Constitution & the laws against the party of disunion & treason. . . ." ADfS, Milton Ronsheim, Cadiz, Ohio. On Nov. 24, Bingham wrote to U.S. Senator John A. Logan of Ill. "Herewith I have taken the liberty to enclose in your care for transmission to our mutual friend General U. S. Grant a letter which I have written to him. . . . All honor to you & to Mr Conkling and to the other three hundred & four gallant & true men who stood immovable as a rock in the Natl. Republican Convention at Chicago for the man of the Century and the man of the people Genl Grant who, under God brought deliverance to our imperiled Country in the day of its Supreme trial. . . ." ALS, DLC-John A. Logan.

1. On Oct. 20, the *New York Truth* had published a letter, purportedly from Garfield and later proven a forgery, stating his support for Chinese immigration under the Treaty of 1868. See Allan Peskin, *Garfield* (Kent, Ohio, 1978), pp. 506–10.

To John F. Long

New York City
Nov. 12th /80

My Dear Judge Long,

I received your two letters, the one directed to Galena and the other here, the same day. In regard to the election I think the result was fortunate for the country at large, without regard to section or party. With a change, under the most favorable aspect, there would have been tinckering at the finances and tariff which would disturb business no matter whether any legislation took place or not.

In regard to negociations with Smith for a longer lease on the

farm the negociations are all on his side. I am entertaining nothing of the kind. He wrote to me a long time ago in regard to a long
lease, and I replied substantially that if I contemplated retaining
the property I would prefer a long lease, to a good tenant, to a
short one; but that I wanted to sell the property when ever there
was a market for it; that if I gave an extension I should want it arranged so as to be able to terminate it at any time by paying—or
allowing—reasonable damages for improvements made by the tenant, and which he would not get the full benefits by reason thereof.
Since that Smith has written to me—I think twice—on the subject. But I have not entertained his proposition nor do'nt intend to.
My mind is made up to sell all my Mo. property as soon as I can
get a fair offer for it. I want the money placed where it will give
me an income for my own benefit. My children are all settled and
doing well enough to be entirely independent of me. From present
indications there is no object in my saving any thing for any one
of them. Fred is in the Army and is the poorest of the lot. But he
has something outside of his pay, which I had not at his age. I will
try to go to St Louis in the spring, and if there is then a chance to
sell in a body, or by cutting up, to suit purchasers, I will sell. I care
nothing for the payments—as to when made—so that the interest
and principle are secured.

    With kindest regards to Mrs. Long and yourself

Yours Truly

U. S. GRANT

ALS, MoSHi.

To John A. J. Creswell

———

New York City

Nov. 14th /80

MY DEAR EX P. M. GEN.

    Your letter of the 12th is received. I do not expect to visit Wash-
ington now until the early days of the session of Congress. Then
only for a few days. I will be the guest of my friend Gen. Ed. F.

Beale at that time. But later in the season, probably about the middle of Feb.y,—unless so engaged as not to be able to leave here—I expect to go to Washington to remain for some time. If I can then secure good rooms at Willards I will be glad to do so. I will see Mr. Cook when I go to Washington the first time.

I hope with you that Garfield will give us an administration that will break up the solid south and not pander to the republican sore heads and bolters. He certainly will know that a thousand friends are more deserving of favors, at his hands,—I should say recognitions—than one "holyer than though art" republican who votes our ticket only when some objectionable person, hard for the party to carry, is nominated. The proportion of such is about one to a thousand.

With the love of Mrs. Grant & I to you and Mrs. Creswell,

yours Truly

U. S. GRANT

HON. JOHN ANDREW JACKSON CRESWELL

ALS, deCoppet Collection, NjP.

To Alexander Ramsey

New York City
Nov 14th 1880

HON ALEX RAMSAY
SEC OF WAR
DEAR SIR

Mrs Kennerly asks me for a letter to you to secure a place for her son in the General Service, to be employed as a Clerk. Mrs K. is the daughter of an old Army Officer, now retired, hence I give this letter, hoping that her wish in this matter may be gratified

Very Truly yours

U. S. GRANT

Copy, DLC-James A. Garfield. Florida Whiting, daughter of Daniel P. Whiting (USMA 1832), married Pierre M. Kennerly in 1860. On Nov. 16, 1880, Florida Kennerly, Washington, D. C., wrote to President-elect James A. Garfield. "General Grant an old and warm friend of my husband (now dead) has given me a letter to Gen Ramsay Sec of War a copy of which I enclose (as I am afraid the Original might get lost in the mail) Will you Dear Sir as a member of Congress extend your kindness to me a widow by giving me a letter to Sec of War in my Son's behalf (P. M. Kennerly) (a lad of 17) to enable him to get employment to assist me in supporting my three children & rest assured Dear Sir your kindness of heart will be gratefully and deeply appreciated . . ." ALS, *ibid.* Pierre M. Kennerly, Jr., was appointed laborer, War Dept.

To Ellen Grant Sartoris

New York City
Nov. 17th 1880.

DEAR NELLIE:

I enclose you herewith a draft for 100 £s to buy holiday presents for you and the children. Get Algie & the little girl something appropriate and spend the balance for yourself. I wish it was much more, and from present appearances I trust that before a year rolls by I will be in a much better condition, financially, than I ever have been heretofore. By spring we will probably be keeping house and will expect you, Algie & the children to come and spend the summer and fall with us; and the winter too if you can.

Buck and his bride have gone off for a little travel, but I do not know where they are. They will probably return next week. They have a beautiful house in this city where you with your family can always find a home when you visit the city—if we are not living here.

We are all well and send much love to all of you.

Yours Affectionately
U. S. GRANT

P. S. Your ma bought three beautiful embroidered silk dress pathes in Japan. Two of them she has had made up for herself. They are *stunners.* The third she has making up for you. When it is finished she will send it, with a few other things, to the Care of Morgan & Co. Bankers.

U. S. G.

ALS, ICHi.

To James A. Garfield

New York City
Nov. 19th 1880.

MY DEAR GENERAL:

About a week ago I wrote you a letter requiring no answer. In the evening of the same day I received yours by the hand of your former secretary.[1] Mine, although written before the receipt of yours, seemed to be about what might have been written in acknowledgement. I write now again to say that I am about as much annoyed by applications for place under your administration as if I were to be the dispenser of your patronage. Letters on this subject I tear up, and to personal appeals I make the best apologies I can. But I have had letters from persons of such standing on the subject of the Cabinet, that I must make some response to them. Now of all places within the gif[t] of the President the last one where unsolicited advice should be given is in regard to who should occupy so delicate a position as that of Constitutional adviser to the Executive. I want it understood therefore that what I say on this subject I do not want you to give weight to on my account. I have had two letters on behalf of the West, beyond the Missouri. One is in behalf of Govr Routt for the position of P. M. Gen. the other in behalf of Ex. Senator Hitchcock[2] for Sec. of the Int. They are both warm friends of mine, and could have my support for anything where I felt that it was right for me to ask. Senator H. you know as well as I do, and have known him longer. Govr Routt I probably know better. I believe him to be one of the most thoroughly honorable men in his state, and I think, from my observation out there, no one in the party exercises a greater influance. This is all I have to say in regard to this matter.

I see by the papers you are coming on to Washington? If you should come to this -city—and I hope you will—I should like to see you.

Very Truly yours
U. S. GRANT

GN. J. A. GARFIELD.

ALS, DLC-James A. Garfield. On Nov. 21, 1880, President-elect James A. Garfield, Mentor, Ohio, wrote to USG. "Your two favors of the 11th and the 19th came duly to hand—and were read with pleasure—though I confess to a feeling of disappointment, in what you say about yourself—I had hoped there might be a field in the Diplomatic Service that it would be agreeable to you to fill—But I shall certainly hope to avail myself of your Expressed willingness to aid in adjusting our relations to the two countries you name—I read, with great interest, your Speech in Boston, and later, one in New York on our relations to Mexico—which suggest new fields of Enterprise to the people of both Countries. In reference to the Choice of Heads of Departments, I am glad to receive suggestions—& will always be thankful for any you may make. But I think I can see the whole ground better in February than at an earlier day—I go to Washington soon—to look after some personal household matters. I may not be able to go to N. Y. this month; but I shall hope to visit there before the End of December— When I go I wish to see you—" ALS, Ulysses Grant Dietz, Maplewood, N. J. See Speeches, [*Oct. 13, 1880*], [*Nov. 11, 1880*].

1. In March, 1882, Thomas M. Nichol, former Garfield campaign advisor, spoke to a reporter in Chicago. "Soon after the election of 1880 General Garfield gave me a letter to deliver to General Grant. I called at Grant's room in the Fifth Avenue Hotel, in New York, to hand him the letter. We had perhaps half an hour's conversation about the campaign generally, and the Morey letter matter in particular. During the conversation Grant said there were two men that Garfield could never recognize or speak to without an entire sacrifice of his own self-respect—Hewitt and Rosecrans. He said Hewitt's conduct was outrageously indecent, but that Rosecrans' was a great deal worse, for Garfield had been the best friend he ever had. He had stood up for him, apologized for his blunders, explained and excused them, and defended him for seventeen years, when, if it hadn't been for Garfield, he would have long ago sunk out of sight into the obscurity which was all his worthlessness entitled him to. He said he hoped Garfield had found him out at last, and would let him take care of himself hereafter. He never was fit to command an army—he wouldn't, or rather *couldn't*, obey orders. He was what he (Grant) called a constitutional insubordinate, a sort of pig-headed, obstinate man, who would get a selfish prejudice into his head, and stick to it, and act on it, against the judgment and reason of everybody else, and absolutely was incapable of seeing any force in any facts or arguments in conflict with what was, for the time being, his theory. He said Rosecrans would have utterly destroyed the Army of the Cumberland, or had it destroyed, if it hadn't been for the intelligence of the army itself, and especially of such subordinate officers as Garfield and Thomas." *Chicago Evening Journal*, March 21, 1882. After USG reportedly contradicted this account, Nichols responded. ". . . I remember my call upon Gen. Grant and our conversation very clearly. . . . I handed Grant Garfield's letter, which he at once opened and read and then said, 'Well, how is Garfield?' I answered that he was quite well. He then asked me how Garfield had stood the campaign. When I answered him, he said the Democrats had directed their efforts so desperately to break down Garfield's personal character that he was afraid it might have annoyed him: that Garfield was a sensitive man, and he supposed would be easily annoyed by such a campaign. I said in answer to this that Garfield had determined early in the campaign not to allow himself to be annoyed by campaign slanders, and that the only matters that seemed to have distressed him at all was the conduct of Hewitt and Rosecrans, whom he regarded as personal friends and gentlemen of character and honor; that their conduct had been a great surprise to Garfield, and that he felt very deeply about it. To this Gen. Grant rejoined substantially in the language I gave to the

Evening Journal: . . . He then said that the Morey letter had lost the Republicans California, Nevada, and New Jersey, and had cost the party not less than 20,000 and perhaps
40,000 votes in New York. He pronounced the publication of that letter the most infamous thing that had ever been done in American politics. He said that he did not know
just what Gen. Garfield's sentiments were upon the Chinese question, but that he never
believed that he had written that letter. He understood that Garfield had voted against
the Anti-Chinese bill which passed Congress while he was out of the country; if he did
he voted right; if he (Grant) had been in Congress he would have voted against it too;
and if he had been President he would have vetoed it, just as Mr. Hayes did. To this I replied that I knew Garfield's sentiments very well on the Chinese question, and that the
Morey letter was entirely inconsistent with them; that while I assisted Gen. Garfield
with his correspondence I had occasion to answer many letters affecting the Chinese
question. I told him that I particularly remembered that of all that class of letters that
came to Gen. Garfield after his nomination making suggestions as to what subjects
ought to be treated, and how they ought to be treated in his letter of acceptance, more
of them were on the Chinese question than on any other subject. 'Do you say that people
wrote Garfield making suggestions about his letter of acceptance?' said Gen. Grant in
a surprised sort of manner. I said, 'Why, yes, dozens of them, more than a hundred, I
should think.' 'That's mighty curious,' he said: 'I was nominated for President twice,
and nobody ever made a suggestion to me about my letter of acceptance; and,' he continued, in a reflective way, 'I don't remember anything about my first letter of acceptance. I don't remember when I wrote it or what was in it. The second one I remember
by this: I was up at the Capitol when the committee handed me the formal notification
of my nomination, and I went into or was in one of the committee-rooms and got a piece
of paper and wrote my acceptance and gave it to them.'" *Chicago Tribune*, March 31,
1882. See letter to James A. Garfield, Nov. 11, 1880, note 1; *PUSG*, 23, 162.

    2. After leaving office in 1877, former U.S. Senator Phineas W. Hitchcock of Neb.
practiced law in Omaha.

Speech

————

[*New York City, Nov. 20, 1880*]

Mr. President and Gentlemen of the Lotos Club: I feel very
much embarrassed in making any response to the complimentary
remarks of your president. I do not know what in the world I have
got to say. I do not want to say that they are not deserved, and I
do not want to convince you that they are not. But if I stand here
five minutes I will prove to you that one of the remarks, at least, of
your president is untrue, without any effort on my part; and that
is when he charges me with being able to make a speech. I have no
doubt that all of you will be convinced of the fact that a misstate-
ment was then made before I sit down.

    Now in regard to the future of myself, which has been alluded to here. I am entirely satisfied as I am to-day. I am not one of those who cry out against republics, and charge them with being ungrateful. I am sure that as regards the American people as a Nation and as individuals I have every reason under the sun, if any person really has, to be satisfied with their treatment of me. I hope to have many years yet of life. I believe that I am in quite vigorous health; forty-eight years[1] of age—and have been for the last ten years. And if I can render my country any service in any way, I should certainly be very happy to do it. But as I am of the age of forty-eight years, as I say, I am beyond the period of volunteering; and if I am ever wanted in any way I shall have to be pressed into the service. But not being obstinate at all I can with confidence submit to those who have experience, for getting me anywhere that will be entirely comfortable to myself.

Now, gentlemen, I thank this club, one and all, for the courtesies of the evening. I am sorry that I am hoarse and have a bad cold and cannot talk longer and thoroughly convince you that what your president has said is not so. I wish to make one other remark. I have been sitting by the side of your president, and have heard messages coming to him from persons around the board, saying that they wanted to speak. I have about fifteen minutes of my own time left, and I will consent to give it to these volunteers.

New York Tribune, Nov. 21, 1880. USG responded to remarks by Whitelaw Reid, president, Lotos Club. ". . . Speaking rather then for his political opponents,—and for those at least of Republican faith, I am confident that I may venture so much—let me say that no wish and no act of theirs will be wanting to secure for the country the continued services of your guest. We believe the country would be most unwise—unmindful alike of her dignity and her interest,—if she failed to lay claim to this service. Let me not be misunderstood. I am speaking wholly without General Grant's knowledge, or that of any of his immediate friends, or with any reference whatever to his interests. Those will be taken care of anyway. This is no blind, broken-down Belisarius, holding out his helmet for alms[.] It is a question solely of what the Country owes to itself. Can it afford to say we have no further use for the experience gained at the head of the Army, and at the head of the Government? Why, for example, should not the Soldier of Appomattox be borne, while he lives, on the retired list of the Army? Why indeed should we not create for him the rank he has so nobly earned, and make him, while he lives, Captain-General of the Armies of the United States? Above all, why should not the Country say to him, and to every retiring President, 'Henceforth we wish your advice and your knowledge of our affairs in our highest council, the Senate of the United States. You have the wisdom that comes with experience, the moderation that comes with the exercise of power. Henceforth your future is provided for. Let all your thoughts and all your care be for your Country to the end.' To some such plan the purpose of the Country is surely turning, and neither party nor precedent should be suffered to stand in its way. Well, gentlemen, you have heard too much of my voice already, and you have lately discovered that, in spite of his life-long efforts to conceal it, your guest is an admirable speaker. . . ." *Ibid.* A collection of related newspaper clippings is in DLC-Whitelaw Reid.

On Nov. 20, 1880, Maj. Gen. John M. Schofield recorded in his diary. "Called upon General Grant at the Fifth Avenue Hotel, and had a conversation with him respecting his future. Asked him what he thought of the proposition to provide seats for life in the Senate for ex-Presidents. Genl. Grant said he did not like it at all—did not think he would take his seat in the Senate even if it was authorized. What he desires is a provision of law for his retirement on a competent salary as a *military officer*—Captain General or something of that sort (Mrs. Grant very emphatic on that point). Evidently Genl. Grant prefers that his case be considered on its own merits and not coupled with any general provision for other ex-Presidents. It was suggested that many influential democrats were desirous of joining in any proper movement to make suitable provision for Genl. Grant's future; that the only obstacle that appeared in the way of their iniating such action was his prominent candidacy (in the public mind) for the next nomination to the Presidency; that would give anything they might do the appearance of an attempt at a *bargain* with him to buy him off. Genl. Grant replied very emphatically that they need have no uneasiness on that score, or words to that effect. He was understood to mean that he had no thought of ever again becoming a candidate. But when it was suggested that some public declaration on the subject would remove all difficulty in the way of the desired action in Congress, his only reply was a more vigorous puff at his cigar. Genl. Grant understands that a measure will be introduced in Congress very soon after the session opens, to provide what he desires, and that it will receive democratic support; that the democratic party is about breaking, as the whig party did after the failure of Genl. Scott's candidacy, and that a new party will soon be organized! The action of the democratic national committee in foisting a forged letter upon the country has killed the party! The conversation was quite long, very interesting, and embraced a variety of subjects, but mostly of personal interests only. The memorandum submitted by Mr. Bigelow was not referred to in the conversation with Genl. Grant, further than above noted, for the reason that he was not prepared to entertain the proposition respecting the Senate." DLC-John M. Schofield. See letter to John A. Logan, Feb. 9, 1881.

1. USG's joke about his age (he was 58) and other remarks were greeted by laughter.

To Edward F. Beale

———

New York City
Nov. 25th /80

MY DEAR GEN. BEALE:

I find now my engagements[1] will keep me here until after the 9th of Dec. I will therefore go to Washington on Monday, the 13th.

I am busy to-day trying to get up with a correspondence which gets much behind the best I can do.

When you were here I told you that no one I talked to took any interest in the canal. The rail-road men are indifferent, but say that before the canal could be built, if commenced now, the wheat of California will be coming to the Gulf of Mexico, or New Orleans by rail cheaper than it could be transported via San Francisco to the Pacific end of the canal. Rail-roads in Mexico are receiving the enthusiastic endorsement of rail-road men with Capitol to build them, and of capitolists generally. They will be built now as fast as human labor can construct them.

With kind regards of Mrs. Grant & I to Mrs. Beale & Miss Emily,

yours Very Truly
U. S. GRANT

ALS, DLC-Decatur House Papers.

1. On Nov. 27, 1880, USG wrote to Mrs. Gray. "Mrs. Grant desires me to answer your kind note asking us to suggest a day next week or the week after when we will be disengaged and can accept an invitation to dine with you. It would be hard for me to suggest a day . . . up to that time I have a number of engagements where only gentlemen are invited; as many as it will be convenient to fill . . ." Robert F. Batchelder, Catalog 28, no. 231.

Speech

[New York City, Dec. 1, 1880]

After the very eloquent and highly-deserved eulogy of the American volunteer soldiers by Gen. Banks, I am sure you do not want any unprepared remarks of mine. This Nation, this Government—the best on the face of the earth—is indebted for its existence to the American volunteer soldiers. Too much credit cannot be given them. The very fact that the country could raise such an army as the volunteer army of the war is proof of the value of the country, and of the hold which her institutions has upon her people. This is not a Government for rulers nor for a privileged class, but it is a Government for the people and by the people, and whenever it is in danger every man springs to his feet and to arms, feeling that in fighting for his country he is fighting for himself. I believe it will never be necessary to raise such an army again, but if this country is ever threatened by any foreign foe—I cannot see how it will ever be by a domestic foe—I am sure it will at once be able to organize such an army as it found ready to save it in 1861.

New York Times, Dec. 2, 1880. USG spoke after a lecture by former Maj. Gen. Nathaniel P. Banks.

To Adam Badeau

————

New York City
~~Nov~~Dec. 4th /80

Dear Badeau:

I would advise that you drop a private note to Asst. Sec. Hay saying that you would like to have your leave extended to about the 20th, or last, of Jan.y to insure getting your book in the hands of the printer before leaving. I will be going to Washington on Monday, the 13th inst. and will speak to Hay, or Evarts, to have your leave extended if you wish. It is a pitty the book cannot be out by the holidays. Business is then suspended any many persons might read it who later will not have the time.

Sincerely yours
U. S. Grant

ALS, Munson-Williams-Proctor Institute, Utica, N. Y.
On Dec. 13, 1880, Adam Badeau, Jamaica, N. Y., wrote to John Hay, asst. secretary of state. "I have sent the Appomattox chapter to the printer, but have still the summarization and some statistics which cannot be ready under four or five weeks, I fear General Grant has told me he would see you in Washington and mention the subject to you. I do not wish, however, to apply for an extension without knowing that it will be granted. Will you let me have a line?. . ." ALS, RPB.

Speech

———

[*Paterson, N. J., Dec. 11, 1880*]

I am indeed under many obligations to you, one and all, for the
hospitalities you have extended to me this day. It has afforded me
great pleasure to visit the industries of your city which go so far to
make up the grandeur of the grandest nation which the sun shines
on, and the only one where it is comparatively easy for a man to rise
from poverty to affluence, and from any position to the highest in
society. Your industries are indeed great and I hope that they will
continue to increase. I myself come from the Northwest, from the
agricultural part of the country. We have been growing grain very
extensively and will continue to increase the volume of our production. With all this immense production, however, there are continually being ma[d]e new improvements in agricultural machinery, in
machinery which shortens the labor in the field, so that despite the
increase in production, the demand for labor has not increased in
proportion. In the future it will continue as it has been in the past,
and it is necessary that this saved and unemployed labor should find
a market somewhere. Paterson has done a great deal to supply this
market, and it deserves praise therefor. Other cities would do well to
follow in her footsteps, and the time will come when the prosperity
of a city will mainly depend upon its industries. Everything should
be done to encourage the introduction of the spindle and the trip-
hammer and the manufacture of machinery and products of every
description. It is also of great assistance to us to have an outlet for
our manufactures, to have a channel through which we can send to
the markets of others the products which we manufacture but do not
consume. I myself have been interested in this matter and have done
what I could. I have succeeded in interesting capitalists and forming
a railroad connection betwe[e]n here and Mexico, which I regard as
the great future market for our products. When I visited that country some years ago I gained an impression, which was only confirmed by a more recent visit, that that was the place to dispose of
goods which we manufactured and did not consume and from which

to receive products that were not consumed in that country. What the country wants is a healthy commerce between nations. I must in conclusion congratulate Paterson upon what she has done. I hope that her prosperity and her industries will incr[e]ase and that she will find a profitable market for all she can make.

New York Herald, Dec. 12, 1880. "Mr. Thomas Barbour, of the Barbour Flax Spinning Company, at a recent meeting of the Board of Trade of Paterson, N. J., informed that body that he had received a personal note from ex-President Grant, in which that gentleman expressed an inclination to visit the industries which have given Paterson so prominent a place in the commercial world." *Ibid.* USG spoke at a luncheon after touring textile mills, an iron works, and a locomotive works.

Endorsement

———

Major Dunn served on my Staff from 1863, while before Vicksburgh, until 1867.

He proved himself brave industrious and efficient.

He has by services in the field, richly earned the promotion for which he is here recommended,

I most cordially concur in the recommendation, and hope, when a vacancy occurs, he may be promoted

U. S. GRANT

NEW YORK CITY DEC 11 1880.

Copy, DNA, RG 94, ACP, 2187 1871. Written on a letter of Dec. 6, 1880, from Brig. Gen. John Pope, Fort Leavenworth, Kan., to President Rutherford B. Hayes recommending Capt. William M. Dunn, Jr., for asst. inspector gen. Copy, *ibid.* No promotion followed.

To Chauncey I. Filley

———

New York City
Dec. 12th 1880

MY DEAR MR. FILLEY:

As soon as I could after the receipt of your letter I visited a Photographer and had taken a profile view. I hope it is what you wanted. I send a copy with this.

Mrs. Grant joins me in kindest regards to you and Mrs. Filley.

Very Truly yours

U. S. GRANT

ALS, Frederick William Lehmann Collection, Washington University, St. Louis, Mo. Chauncey I. Filley presumably used this photograph for medals he commissioned to honor the 306 delegates who supported USG through thirty-six ballots at the June, 1880, Republican National Convention. See letter to Roscoe Conkling, June 10, 1880; Harry James Brown and Frederick D. Williams, eds., *The Diary of James A. Garfield* (East Lansing, Mich., 1967–81), IV, 488.

To *William R. Rowley*

———

New York City

Dec. 12th 1880.

MY DEAR GENERAL ROWLEY:

I was pleased to receive a letter from you and to learn that all were getting on well in Galena. Johnson wrote me in time that he could not pair with me. It was rather far to go to cast a vote in place where there was really no contest either for County, Legislative, Congressional, or State or National offices. Then too friends here—where there was debatable ground—effected to think that I might do some good for the republican ticket. Whether I did or not the ticket was sucsessful, and I think democrats as well as republicans breathed freer when the result was known.

I am kept very busy here though I have nothing in the way of my own business to do. I hope however my efforts may have something to do with the developement of rail-road, commercial & friendly relations with our sister Republic, Mexico. The subject is one of great national importance and I feel a deep interest in its success.

Remember Mrs. Grant & me kindly to Mrs Rowley, and to all our Galena friends.

Very Truly yours

U. S. GRANT

ALS (facsimile), USGA. See letter to Madison Y. Johnson, Sept. 24, 1880.

Speech

[*Washington, D. C., Dec. 14, 1880*]

LADIES AND SOLDIERS AND GENTLEMEN: It is a matter of great gratification to me to be once more here at the Capital of the Nation, where I have spent more days, more years than at any other one place since I was seventeen years of age. It is also a special pleasure to meet so many of my old comrades, who were my comrades in the dark days of the past, and who, with our absent comrades, assisted to preserve to ourselves and to our descendants our glorious country.

Since I left this city it has been my good fortune to have traveled a great deal and to meet a great many of our countrymen. I have met our comrades in every country that I have visited. In Europe, in Asia, and in Africa I have met the boys who wore the blue, and as a rule I found them maintaining the honor and dignity of our native country. I met none of them anywhere who were ashamed of their own country, or who elevated any country above their own. To my sorrow, however, I am compelled to say I did meet *some Americans* abroad who magnified the virtues of the foreign countries in which they were and belittled their own homes and institutions. I found, too, upon speaking to them, they were people who knew but very little of any country, and who, if they were compelled to earn the money they were traveling upon and spending with such free hands, would have been glad to have come back here to earn it. From my experience of them they would have found it very uphill work to have secured even a bare living in any of the countries they lauded above their own.

I come back to you, convinced that what we fought so hard for, what so many of our comrades died for, was so worthy of the sacrifice that even those who fought against us begin to appreciate that they are the gainers by their defeat, as much even as we by our success. We are glad to welcome back all these to our common country, and we are willing to accede to them all the privileges that we claim for ourselves, asking only in return that they shall regard us as their equals on their own soil, and that, too, without our being required to make an abject apology for the part we took. I expect, though, that we are so very obstinate in our views on this question that we still maintain we did right before, and if the same occasion should call us out we would do it again.

Gentlemen, when I got up before you I did not intend to say anything more than that I was very glad to see you—to see so many of you here to-night. I always rejoice and am proud of the kind receptions accorded me by our old comrades in the field.

I thank you, one and all.

Washington National Republican, Dec. 15, 1880. USG spoke at a Boys in Blue reception held at the Masonic Temple, presided over by Jacob J. Noah. After speaking, USG met many in the audience. "An interesting incident occurred during the ceremony, which only those in the immediate vicinity noticed. As a tall woman, wearing widow's weeds, approached, Judge Noah said: 'Mrs. Chisholm.' General Grant was about to salute her, as he had done others, when the Judge said: 'Mrs. Chisholm, of Mississippi.' General Grant stopped, looked in her face, which bore the marks of firm character, but upon which were traced the lines of deep and settled grief, and he took her hand in both of his, and said: 'Madam, I am glad to know you. You have my heartfelt sympathy.' Mrs Chisholm's eyes filled with tears, and, after bending low over the hands which held hers for a moment, she passed on." *Ibid.* See James M. Wells, *The Chisolm Massacre: A Picture of "Home Rule" in Mississippi* (Washington, 1878).

On Dec. 10, 1880, President Rutherford B. Hayes wrote to USG. "Mrs Hayes and I will be glad to have you and Mrs Grant ~~to~~ dine with us, with a few friends, on some evening that may be convenient to you during your coming visit to this City. ~~I go to the Brooklyn New England dinner leaving here the 20th inst. The Sunday previous, or any other day before~~ Mrs Hayes will leave Washington Friday the 17th to be absent several days. Any day prior to that time that may suit you will be agreeable to us." ADf, OFH. On Dec. 13, Monday, Hayes telegraphed to USG. "Letter received if Convenient the dinner will be given on wednesday" Telegram sent (at 10:55 A.M.), *ibid.* A reply accepting the dinner invitation for Dec. 15 is *ibid.* Jesse Root Grant, Jr., and his wife also attended.

On Dec. 16, USG visited the capitol. "Mr. Sparks, chairman of the Committee on Military Affairs, was noticed to leave the House soon after Gen. Grant entered. Mr. Sparks is a member of the sub-committee appointed to consider the bill to put Gen. Grant upon the retired list with the rank and pay of General. Gen. Bragg is also opposed to the bill, making a majority of the sub-committee against it. Mr. Myers, of Indiana, who is the father of a resolution to ascertain how much money has been paid to Gen. Grant, out of the Treasury, from his youth up, was one of the first to shake hands with him. Gen. Weaver, the Greenback candidate, was greeted with a smile and a nod by the General. Gen. Joe Johnston, of Virginia, left the chamber a few moments before Gen. Grant entered. . . . Judge Phister, of Kentucky, was observed in conversation with Gen. Grant for several minutes after the hand-shaking ceased. They were recalling boyhood days. Both attended the same school when children, enjoyed similar sports and were threshed with the same rod. . . ." *Washington Post,* Dec. 17, 1880.

To William J. Lee

WASHINGTON, D. C., *December* 16, 1880.

DEAR SIR: I would be glad to aid you in any way in my power to procure a pension for your well-deserving services during the rebellion.

I cannot specify your services so well as General Meade could, if alive, or as General George H. Sharpe, who is living, can, but I know they were hazardous and attended with much exposure to health as well as personal danger. I hope you may yet get your pension.

Very truly, yours,
U. S. GRANT.

WILLIAM J. LEE.

SRC, 48-1-821. See *HRC*, 46-2-338; *U.S. Statutes at Large*, XXIII, 589–90.
On Feb. 23, 1874, William J. Lee, Washington, D. C., wrote to USG. "I wish your attention to a very few words & I am done   1st I will Say to you that I was a Loyal Scout at your & *Genl Meads* Head Quarters army of the Potomac. 2nd I was the 1st man and the only one to mention *Mr Ruths* name to *Genl Sharpe* & the only one that *Mr Ruth* would have had any thing to do with on the Subject of information from the Enimies lines. 3 *Genl Sharpe* knows that the airaingment with *Mr Ruth* was mad through & by me. 4 Genl. George. H. Sharpe Col. Jno. McEntee & Carpt. Oliver. Jno. C. Babcock will all endorse what I say, & all I ask now is some small humble place that I can Support my family. I do not know what to ask for. But I do think I am entitled to some little consideration be it ever so small" ALS, DLC-USG, IB. See *PUSG*, 14, 87; *ibid.*, 15, 223–25.

Endorsement

Respectfully referred to the Sec. of War. I know nothing of this applicant further than what he says himself. Two of his endorsers however I know verry well, the Hon. W. H. Wadsworth,[1] & Col. Walter Evans.[2] They were both loyal Kentuckyans during the war, and republicans since. I endorse them.

U. S. GRANT

DEC. 18TH /80

AES, DNA, RG 94, ACP, 228 1881. Written on papers including a letter of Dec. 7, 1880, from James A. Cochran, Colorado Springs, to USG. "I hardly know how to approach you on this occasion being an utter stranger. I would like to be appointed a 2nd Lieutenant in the U. S. Army or Marine Corps. I was at West Point two years and would have graduated the coming June had I not resigned. I resigned in a moment of despair, because I had no capacity for mastering the French language. In mathematics I stood 27 & in French 81 at the January examination preceding my resignation. My tastes are all military, in fact I am descended from a military family, the Lewises of Western Va. I am a descendant of Gen. Andrew Lewis of revolutionary fame. Two of your best friends Hon. W. H. Wadsworth of Ky and ex-Senator Lewis of Va endorse me as worthy. It is thought a kind word from you, will secure me the place. If it was a civil office, I sought, I would not trouble you. If you speak that word, you may rest assured that I will never forget to whom I owe my success and will devote every energy of my mind and body to being worthy of the appointment." ALS, *ibid.* On Nov. 30, William H. Wadsworth, Maysville, Ky., wrote to USG. "My old Kentucky friend, John B. Cochran Esqr, now of Colorado Springs, Colo, has a fine son, James A. Cochran, who wishes to be a 2nd Lieut in our Army. The young man is worthy well reputed, & from all I can hear will do credit to the Service. His father is an old friend, always faithful to the Union, the son wishes to serve, & entitled to much consideration. He wishes me to speak this word to you, & I throw myself on yr indulgence. I wish to thank you for your great, & effectual Services in the late political campaign, Services rendered to the whole country." ALS, *ibid.* On Dec. 2, Walter Evans, Louisville, wrote to USG on the same subject. ALS, *ibid.* Related papers are *ibid.* No appointment followed.

1. See *PUSG*, 20, 4.
2. See letter to Silas F. Miller *et al.*, Nov. 9, 1879; letters to James A. Garfield, Dec. 21, 1880, Feb. 13, 1881.

To John Hay

New York City
Dec. 18 /80

DEAR SIR:

I had hoped to see you during my visit to Washington this week, but happened to be out when you called, and was so engaged while there that I did not get up to the State Dept. I left a message with Gen. Drum,—Adj. Gn of the Army—for you however, requesting an extension of Gen. Badeau's leave, to enable him to complete his book. I hope the leave may be extended for the purpose named, and that it will prove no detriment to the public service.

Very Truly yours
U. S. GRANT

Col. John Hay
Asst. Sec. of State

ALS, RPB. On Dec. 16, 1880, AG Richard C. Drum wrote to Asst. Secretary of State John Hay. "In conversation with Genl. Grant this morning, he remarked he would like to see you and especialley as he wished to speak to you of a matter in which he was interested." ALS, *ibid.* On Dec. 18, Adam Badeau, Jamaica, N. Y., wrote to Hay. "I sent my application and your note to Genl Grant, who the forwarded the despatch to the Department of state and sent me the enclosed note to you, which will explain the delay in its reception by you. I think you have about as much to do with the preparation or construction of the work as he originally or I now." ALS, *ibid.* On Dec. 31, Badeau, New York City, wrote to Hay. ". . . I heard Gen Grant talk about you yesterday, not to me, in his handsomest manner; your ability, acquiescence, character, manner all were subject of high praise . . ." AL (initialed), *ibid.*

To *William C. Roberts*

New York City
Dec. 19th /80

Wm C. Roberts, Esq.
Dear Sir:

On our return from Washington City last Friday evening[1] Mrs. Grant & I found yours and Mrs. Roberts kind invitations for us to be your guests on the occasion of the Zouaves reception, Jan. 11th /80. We are both very much obliged, and accept with pleasure if Mrs. Grant accompanies me. But at present I do not know that she will be able to do so. If she does not I will probably return by one of the late trains in the evening after the reception.

Thanking you and Mrs. Roberts for your kind invitation, I am,

Very Truly yours
U. S. Grant

ALS, NjP. On Jan. 11, 1881, USG visited Elizabeth, N. J., and dined with family and friends, including Hannah Simpson Grant and Virginia Grant Corbin, at the home of William C. Roberts. In the evening, after Zouaves led a procession to the local armory, USG thanked the crowd and briefly referred to his travels abroad. *New York Tribune,* Jan. 12, 1881. See Endorsement, June 28, 1876.

On Dec. 11, 1880, USG, New York City, had written to J. Madison Drake. "I have your letter of the 10th fixing date 10th & 11th or 12th of Jany. as the time for me to meet the Veteran Zouaves at their Armory in Elizabeth. I have an engagement for the 12th of January, but either of the two preceding days, as may suit you best I can accept for." *The Collector,* 1983, No. 892, Q-533. On Jan. 5, 1881, USG wrote to Drake regarding the arrangements for his trip. ". . . I think Mrs. Grant will not go with me. If she does she will spend the day with Mr. [O.] L. Grant." David Schulson Autographs, Catalog 80 [May 17, 1995], no. 47. On Jan. 11, William R. C. Coleman, city clerk, Elizabeth, wrote to USG. "Enclosed please find copy of resolution adopted by the City Council of the City of Elizabeth, the receipt of which please acknowledge at your own leisure, Hoping your visit to our beautiful though unfortunate City, may prove a source of unalloyed pleasure, to yourself as well as our own Citizens, . . ." ALS, Smithsonian Institution. The enclosed "Freedom of the city" is *ibid.*

Probably in 1880, USG had written to Drake. "Your note with enclosed copy of your narrative is just received, and I will take an early day to read over the thrilling account of your wanderings while escaping from a rebel prison. Please accept my thanks for the note and narrative, . . ." J. Madison Drake, *Fast and Loose in Dixie.* . . . (New York, 1880), p. 298.

1. Dec. 17.

Speech

[*Brooklyn, Dec. 21, 1880*]

MR. PRESIDENT, GENTLEMEN OF THE NEW-ENGLAND SOCIETY OF BROOKLYN: I am afraid that you are doomed to a good deal of disappointment. In one particular, however, you will not be disappointed; and that is, I shall not detain you long. We have heard from your president, also from the President of the United States, some eulogies paid to the descendants of the Pilgrims and to the people of New-England. I subscribe to all that the President has said, and would say a little more. We have heard a great deal in our country in the last fifteen years about the "carpet-baggers," and the term "carpet-bagger" has become almost a word of reproach. The New-Englander believes that when he is a citizen of one State he is a citizen of the United States, and has the right to go to any portion of the country to be a citizen there, with all the rights he had at the place of starting. In our Northern States, and particularly in the Northwestern States, we have seen the effect of carpet-baggism— the best effects of carpet-baggism—where they have been received as fully equal to a native-born citizen. We have seen growing cities that have sprung up in the lifetime of the youngest in this audience; we have seen prosperity brought from the prairie where nothing stood but what nature had planted there. It has been the work of the carpet-bagger; and the principles of the people who form this Society have done it. Without any reflection upon any section of the country, I would say that, in my judgment, there would have been very much greater prosperity in some portions of it, beside much greater contentment, if the carpet-bagger had been received in the same way he was in the Northwest. In fact, I have almost come to the conclusion that there is but very little progress or advancement in a community made up entirely of the natives of that community; that it requires a little stirring up, a little going over, a little going abroad from the place of one's nativity, to bring out the best energies.

You may take this city, you may take the suburbs across the East River or elsewhere, wherever you like, and while you may find very excellent representatives there of the sires of the men who continue their business faithfully and successfully, yet you find hardly anything that is new in the way of enterprise that is not started by some one who has come among you. So I am decidedly in favor of the principles of New-England—go where you please, obey the laws wherever you go, respect the rights of others; being free, leave others to be free to enjoy their own political and religious views, and make no distinction on account of a person's nativity.

Your president here this evening asked one conundrum which I shall not be able to answer; he said something expressive of ignorance as to where the New-Englander did not go. Well, I give it up, too. My travels have been confined to the Northern hemisphere. I have not gone to the Equator, but very close to it; and up to the 61st or 62d degree of north latitude, and I have not found the place where he did not appear. If your president wants a solution to the question he must send for Stanley; he is probably the only man who can answer it. I leave it to him. Gentlemen, I am very much obliged to you.

New York Tribune, Dec. 22, 1880. Benjamin D. Silliman presided over a dinner held at the Academy of Music.

On Nov. 24, 1880, USG, New York City, wrote to Henry Ward Beecher. "Before the receipt of your letter of the 22d inst. I had answered the invitation to meet the 'New England Society,' of Brooklyn, at their first Annual dinner, accepting so far as I could so long in advance. There is but little doubt but that I shall be in this city on the 21st of Dec. prox. and I shall make no other engagement for the evening of that day." ALS, Goodspeed's Book Shop, Inc., Boston, Mass. Beecher also spoke at the Brooklyn dinner.

On Dec. 18, USG wrote to Bartley Campbell. "Having an engagement for the evening of Dec 21st in Brooklyn, I have to decline your cauteaus invitation to witness the initial performance of your new play, 'My Geraldine' to be performed that evening." Copy, Mary Chang, Brooklyn, N. Y. See Napier Wilt, ed., *The White Slave & Other Plays by Bartley Campbell* (Princeton, 1941), pp. xlv–xlvii.

To James A. Garfield

New York City
Dec. 21st 1880.

MY DEAR GEN. GARFIELD:

I do not wish to embarrass you in the matter of appointments after your inauguration, nor now, but I take the privilege rather granted by your last letter to me to call your attention to a few persons. I do not ask their appointment to any place, but suggest some names for you to think of, and then to exercise your own judgement if wish to offer them anything. I assume you will probably want to appoint to conspicuous places a few Southern men. My own judgement is that it is a wrong to Union men, nNorth & South, to select men for such honors who were against us in the war and who have shewn no signs of change since. But if men were against us in the war and are for us now I would not make their former opposition a barrier to their recognition now. Among the southern men of ability and character, and who are with us now, I would name Gen. Wickham,[1] of Va, Judge Settle, of Fla. Col. Walter Evans, of Ky. Col. Thos Swann, of W. Va Gen. Wickham was a rebel Gen. but I believe a Union man from the start, and a republican from the close of the war. He is a man of ability and character. I do not know that he wants any position whatever. But he is a man worthy of any position. Judge Settle was also a rebel soldier, but a consistent—radical—republican ever since. He is a man of very fine ability, and I think equal to any position. He is now Judge of the U. S. Dist. Court for the Northern district of Fla. I do not know that he he wants any position, but do not doubt but he would like to be raised to the circuit Judgship if a vacancy occurred where he could be advanced to the position. ~~m~~My judgement is that if I had the power I would promote him to Judge Wood's place. Col. Evans was a Union man and Union soldier during the war, and a stalwart republican ever since, ~~h~~He is a lawyer, a man of character and ability and would make a good Solicitor Gen. Judge of a United States Dist. or Circuit Court, or Dist. Atty. I do not suppose he would want any position that would take him out of the line of his profession. Col. Thos Swann was a rebel Col. but has been a consistent republican ever since. He also is a good lawyer, a man of ability and character, and probably would not want a position unless one that kept him in the line of his profession. I mention these names simply for you to think of. It may be that no opportunity will occur to appoint either of them. I only mention them as a class from a section which you may want to recognize.

In the Army there is one man I would like you to remember. That is Gen. McKinzie, now Col. of 4th U. S. Cavalry. If you have no objection to doing so I would be glad if you would ask Mr. Hayes, in case there should be a vacancy to the rank of Brig. Gen. during his term, that he appoint McKinzie. He is a man now of forty years of age. In my judgement he would be the most capable man to command the army in case of war, now in it below the grade of Lt. Gen. He graduated head of his class in 1862 and before the close of the war, without political influence, was a Maj. Gen. Commanding a Cavalry Corps, and without a superior as such. I have nothing to say against the promotion of Miles because he has proven himself a most capable soldier and has earned all the promotion he has ever had. He ranked McKinzie as Col.

I hope you will not regard my writing this as an intrusion. I know from experience how you are embarrassed by office seekers. I have applications—made personally and by letter—sufficient to fill every place you have to give. But I shall not bother you with any of these unless I regard them as very meritorious.

With kindest regards to you and Mrs. Garfield,

Very Truly yours
U. S. GRANT

ALS, DLC-James A. Garfield. On Dec. 23 and [24], 1880, James A. Garfield wrote to USG, New York City. "Your esteemed favor of the 21st is received and read with great interest—I have been looking over the men of the South with much anxiety—There is so much division and bitterness among them, that I find it very difficult to discover a man of national reputation who will be generally acceptable to the Southern Republicans—You have not only added to my list of names, but have given me fuller knowledge of them, than I had—If I could find a man who had been with us from the beginning, I should like it best—but that I suppose is very difficult, at least, in the Cotton States— Will you please give me your opinion of Gov. Davis of Texas and Gov. Alcorn—of Mississippi?—I have quite lost track of them during the past few years—With thanks for your letter . . ." "In my letter of yesterday, I inadvertently omitted to notice what you said in reference to Gen McKinzie—Your opinion of him is so decided and favorable that I have taken the liberty to copy that portion of your letter, and Enclose it to the President, for his consideration. I knew Gen McK at Williams College, where he was a student before he went to West [Point] and have thought well of his character and abilities; but had no such means of knowing his merits as you have had—What you have said of him, may be of great service to me—" ALS (press), *ibid.*

1. See *PUSG*, 13, 395. Williams C. Wickham was active in postwar railroad development and Va. Republican politics.

Speech

[*New York City, Dec. 22, 1880*]

MR. PRESIDENT AND GENTLEMEN OF THE NEW-ENGLAND SOCIETY OF THE CITY OF NEW-YORK: I suppose on an occasion of this kind you will expect me to say something about this society, the people of New-England, and the Pilgrims who first landed at Plymouth Rock. It was my fortune last night to attend a banquet of this sort in the principal City on New-York Harbor, a city—and, gentlemen, I didn't know till I went there last night that it was the principal city,—as I said, the principal city on the Harbor of New-York—a city whose overflow has settled over all Manhattan Island, built up fine houses, business streets, and many evidences of prosperity in the suburbs, with a population thrown across the North River, perhaps, to form one-third, if not a half, of the population of the neighboring State. As I say, it was my good fortune to attend a banquet of a society of the same name—the parent society, I suppose, even including the one which is now celebrating its first anniversary in Las Vegas, New-Mexico, and I made a few remarks there, in which I tried to say what I thought of the characteristics of the people who have descended from the Pilgrims. I thought they were a people of great frugality, great personal courage, great industry, and that they possessed within themselves the qualities which built up that New-England population which has spread out over so much of this land and given so much character, prosperity, and success to us as a people and a nation. I retain yet some of the views I then expressed, and should have remained convinced that my judgment was entirely right if it was not that some speakers came after me who have a better title to speak for the people of New-England than myself, and who dispelled some of those views.

It is too many generations back[1] for me to claim to be a New-Englander. Those gentlemen who spoke are themselves New-Englanders, who have, since their manhood, emigrated to this great city that I speak of. They informed me that there was nothing at all in the Pilgrim fathers to give them the distinguishing characteristics which we attribute to them, and that it was all entirely dependent upon the poverty of the soil and the inclemency of the climate where they landed. They fell upon a sterile climate, where there were nine months of Winter and three months of cold weather, and that had called out the best energies of the men and of the women, too, to get a mere existence out of the soil in such a climate. In their efforts to do that they cultivated industry and frugality at the same time, which is the real foundation of the greatness of the Pilgrims. It was even suggested by some that if they had fallen upon a more genial climate and more fertile soil, they would have been there yet, in poverty and without industry. I shall continue to believe better of them myself. I believe the Rev. Dr. Storrs,[2] who spoke here, will agree with me that my first judgment of them was probably nearly correct. However, all jesting aside, we are proud in my section of the country of the New-Englanders and of their descendants. We hope to see them spread over all of this land and carry with them the principles inculcated in their own sterile soil from which they sprang. We want to see them take their independence of character, their self-reliance, their free schools, their learning, and their industry, and we want to see them prosper and teach others among whom they settle how to be prosperous. I am very much obliged to the gentlemen of the infant New-England Society for the reception which they have accorded to me and the other guests of this evening. I shall remember it with great pleasure, and hope that some day you will invite me again.

New York Times, Dec. 23, 1880. John C. Carter presided over a dinner at the Metropolitan Music Hall.

1. Another version has "two generations back." *New York Tribune*, Dec. 23, 1880. USG's grandfather, Noah Grant, was born in Conn.

2. Born in 1821, educated at Amherst College and Andover Theological Seminary, Richard S. Storrs was longtime pastor of Brooklyn's Church of the Pilgrims.

To Edward F. Beale

————

New York City
Dec. 23d 1880

MY DEAR GEN. BEALE:

The horses arrived on Tuesday last all right. I have no information however of the shipment of the carriages having been shipped. I spoke something to Ammen—I do not remember exactly what— about having one of them repaired in Washington, and one sold there. But this I do not want. I would like if he would ship both carriages to this city, and the best set of double harnass for the large carriage. I will have the necessary repairs done here, and sell the lighter one.

Mrs. Grant asks specially how Miss Emily is getting. We hope entirely recovered by this time. I have been kept very busy since my return from Washington, and am gratified to say now that I believe the interests of all the roads going to the Mexican border are so harmonized that there will be no conflict, and the necessary roads will be speedily built.

Very Truly Yours
U. S. GRANT

ALS, DLC-Decatur House Papers.

To William D. Cabell

———

[*New York City, Dec. 24, 1880*]

. . . The house 1116 M. St. Washington, does not belong to me, but is the property of the Rawlins children, three in number, for whom I am guardian. The youngest becomes of age in Apl. next when the estate must be divided.[1] I authorized Messrs. Fitch & Fox to sell the Washington house . . . if they can do so for a fair price before that time. I would not attempt to value the property myself, nor would I permit a portion of the lot on which the house stands, to be sold separately . . .

Charles Hamilton Auction No. 71, Sept. 20, 1973, no. 143. A Va. educator who had recently moved to Washington, D. C., William D. Cabell lived at 1114 M. St. N. W. See Cabell to Hamilton Fish, Feb. 4, 1881, DLC-Hamilton Fish.

1. See *PUSG*, 20, 97–98; *ibid.*, 23, 264–66.

To Samuel L. Clemens

———

New York City
Dec. 24th 1880.

DEAR SIR:

Since you and Dr Twichell[1] were here I have not found an hour from the hour of rising until from 12 to 2 at night when I could write a line. To-day I have staid in the whole day and devoted it to clearing off my table of the accumulated correspondence, much of which I did by casting it into the waste basket. The last letter of the day is the one enclosed. It is not all that might be said on the subject, but it opens the way for Dr. Twichell to supply the deficiency, and have it partially credited to me. Li Hung Chang is the most powerful and most influential Chinaman in his country. He professed great friendship for me when I was there, and I have had assurances of the same thing since. I hope, if he is strong enough with his govt, that the decission to withdraw the Chinese students from this country may be changed.

Very Truly yours

U. S. GRANT

SAML CLEMENT, ESQ.

ALS, CU-B. On Dec. 18, 1880, Saturday, USG, New York City, telegraphed to Samuel L. Clemens. "I will be here on Tuesday" Telegram received, *ibid*. On March 15, 1881, Clemens, Hartford, wrote to USG. "This letter is not to burden you—it requires no answer. If you respond to all letters that *do* require answers, your hands will be plenty full enough. No, this note is only to tell you (in case you do not already know it,) that your letter to Li Hung Chang has done its work, & the Chinese Educational Mission in Hartford is saved. The order to take the students home to China was revoked by the Viceroy three days ago—by cable. This cablegram mentions the receipt of your letter; & at the same time it commands the Minister Chin to take Yung Wing into his consultations.—This was not permitted before. It is an addition to the strength to the cause which cannot be overestimated. (I take these facts from a jubilant letter of Yung Wing to Mr. Twichell—a letter marked 'strictly confidential,' but Mr. T. & I considered that that prohibition could not rightfully apply to you.) So we three wish to thank you again, very sincerely, for what you have done. This achievement of yours is a most strange thing to contemplate. Without exaggeration of phrase or fact, it can be said that from No. 81 in the Fifth Avenue Hotel, you, an unofficial citizen of this republic, have changed the procedure of an empire on the other side of the globe. The Viceroy of China was in a minority in his Government, as concerns this matter; but it is plain that you & he together constitute a majority." ALS, Kent State University, Kent, Ohio. See Henry Nash Smith and William M. Gibson, eds., *Mark Twain-Howells Letters: The Correspondence of Samuel L. Clemens and William D. Howells, 1872–1910* (Cambridge, Mass., 1960), pp. 339–41; Thomas E. LaFargue, *China's First Hundred* (1942; reprinted, Pullman, Wash., 1987), pp. 43–52.

1. A graduate of Yale College (1859) and former chaplain, 71st N. Y., Joseph H. Twichell was pastor at Asylum Hill Congregational Church in Hartford, and friend of Yung Wing, diplomat and co-commissioner of the Chinese educational mission to the U.S. See Edmund H. Worthy, Jr., "Yung Wing in America," *Pacific Historical Review*, XXXIV, 3 (Aug., 1965), 265–87.

To John A. Logan

New York City

Dec. 27th /80

MY DEAR GEN. LOGAN;

I understand a bill has been introduced in Congress to retire Gen. Ord with the rank of Maj. Gen. If this be the case I hope it will pass both houses, and become a law. Gen. Ord commanded an Army during the closing months of the war, and did it gallantly and well. This should entitle him to the rank on the retired list which it was necessary to hold to exercise the command which he held in war. Ord is poor, having served all his manhood days in the Army, on small pay, with a large family to support.

Trusting that you can see your way clear to support this measure, I am

Very Truly yours

U. S. GRANT

ALS, DLC-John A. Logan. Edward O. C. Ord was retired as maj. gen. as of Jan. 28, 1881. See *HRC*, 46-3-58; *SRC*, 46-3-740.

To Edwin W. Stoughton

––––––––

[*Dec. 27, 1880*]

The horses arrived last week, but we have not had occasion yet to use a carriage and while the streets remain in this present condition we will not probably take our horses out. I am much obliged for the offer of the Landau, but I think ours will be ready by this time the streets are. I am glad to hear that you are out again, and blame myself for not calling to see you during your confinement. A Merry Christmas to you & Mrs. Stoughton

Yours very Truly

U. S. GRANT

University Archives, June 1999, No. 20529–001.

On Oct. 22, 1880, Stoughton, New York City, wrote to U.S. Representative James A. Garfield of Ohio. "Now that your Election is assured—as thank God it is—I wish to say a few words about Genl. Grant who has done so much to achieve that great national result. Some of his friends, as you may know, aware of the inadequacy of his income to enable him to live as he should, have thought of securing for him some agreeable position—such as the Presidency of a company with a handsome salary; but this upon reflection has occurred to me in view of his transcendent ability—his world wide reputation, his unprecedented service to our people and the love they bear him unworthy of him and of them. Upon consideration one great place hitherto unoccupied by any Representative of our Nation abroad has occurred to me, which he might take without abatement of his lofty position—that of Ambassador to England. . . ." ALS, DLC-James A. Garfield.

Endorsement

I most cordially endorse the advancement of those Lieutenants of the Army as have lost a limb in the service of the country, and have been retired. Shut out from promotions as they are by their retirement, and disabled for life in the service of their country, I would like to see them advanced a grade for each ten years during their lives.

U. S. GRANT

NEW YORK CITY
DEC. 29TH 1880.

AES, USG 3. Similar endorsements by Gen. William T. Sherman, Lt. Gen. Philip H. Sheridan, and four others are *ibid.* On March 30, 1880, William P. Hogarty, Washington, D. C., wrote to Sherman. "Acting upon your suggestion, I have the honor to submit for your consideration House Bill No. 4953 with accompanying Brief the full bearing of this measure will however occur to you at once. We trust you will make such alterations as will perfect the Bill and anxiously hope you may feel at liberty to approve the measure by giving it your favourable endorsement. We sincerely believe you will regard this measure as tending to the interest of the service as well as being a merited relief to those officers whose promotion in the army was stopped at the commencement of their military career by wounds which have since operated with like detriment in civil life by paralyzing their efforts to make up those reductions which follow retirement and which has left them petrified in the grade of Lieutenant without having arrested the growing wants of their families which increase with their advancing years . . ." R. M. Smythe & Co., Inc., Sale No. 186, April 22, 1999, no. 253. For Hogarty, see *SRC*, 48-1-157. In 1884, a Senate committee considering a similar bill reported that "the pay received by the class of officers referred to in the bill is now so greatly in excess of the pension which would be paid to officers similarly disabled, but who were never fortunate enough to be upon the rolls of the Regular Army, that any further increase would be unjustifiable." *Ibid.*, 48-1-315.

To James A. Garfield

New York City
Dec. 29th /80

MY DEAR GENERAL:

It will be my endeavor to give you as little annoyance (in a matter which I know from experience you will be annoyed by during your whole term of office) as possible. But I will ask one favor for an old school mate of mine of nearly fifty years ago. I ask that you consider an application from Maj. John King, of Georgetown, Brown Co. Ohio. It will be necessary for him of course to to make an application for something definite when the time comes. I will now only speak of the man and his antecedents. Maj. King, and his family, I have known as far back as my memory goes. Every member of the family, according to my memory, were anti slavery whigs until the organization of the republican party, and republicans since. John King is a lawyer, but pretty much out of practice since the war. After his discharge from the Army he held an interest with a brother-in-law in a banking business in the town where he has lived for half a century. I think I am correct in this statement. The business failed a few years since, leaving him without means, and a large family to support. To go back to his profession, at his age, handicaped in this way, is an up hill business. I do not know who the next member of Congress from his district is to be. If a republican King can get his support. If not I hope this letter will suffice without any thing from the member.

Very Truly yours
U. S. Grant

Gn. J. A. Garfield Pres. Elect

ALS, DLC–James A. Garfield. In Jan., 1881, John W. King, Georgetown, Ohio, wrote to President-elect James A. Garfield transmitting this letter and applying for a position as collector of Internal Revenue, 6th District, Ohio. ALS, *ibid.* No appointment followed. See *PUSG*, 9, 649.

To James A. Garfield

Fifth Av. Hotel,
Dec. 29th /80

My Dear Gen.

Your letter of the 24th inst. come duly to hand; but your letter of the 23d went to 58th st. and I did not receive it for several days later. You ask me about Gov. Alcorn[1] and Gen. Davis.[2] You probably are better able to judge of the ability, and the working of the mind, of the former than I am. You have seen him *in* Congress. I saw him while in Congress. I believe however that he was a Union man at heart from the beginning. But not of that offensive kind which drove him from the south into the Union Army like Davis. Davis could not have found a home in the South during the rebellion except in the ranks of either Army. He selected the Union Army, and I believe did good service. My impression is that he is a man of good ability, and entitled to the confidence and support of the republican party, and of a republican Administration.

Very Truly yours
U. S. GRANT

GN. J. A. GARFIELD.

ALS, DLC-James A. Garfield. See letter to James A. Garfield, Dec. 21, 1880.

1. Former U.S. Senator James L. Alcorn of Miss. practiced law in Friar's Point.
2. Former Governor Edmund J. Davis of Tex. chaired the state Republican committee. In Jan., 1881, Davis declined nomination as collector of customs, Galveston.

To John A. Logan

New York City
Dec. 29th 1880

DEAR GEN.

This will present to you Admiral Sands—now a retired officer of the Navy—who desires an introduction for the purpose of lauing before you the merits of a "Bill" now before Congress in which his son—also an officer of the Navy—is interested.

I speak for the Admiral a hearing, and as favorable action in the matter in which he is interested as its merits entitle it to.

Very Truly yours
U. S. GRANT

GN. J. A. LOGAN, U. S. S.

ALS, DLC-John A. Logan. In June, 1880, U.S. Senator John A. Logan of Ill. blocked action on Senate Bill No. 1210, intended to settle a dispute over relative rank among naval officers, including Commander James H. Sands, son of retired Rear Admiral Benjamin F. Sands. See *CR*, 46-2, 4587–88. On Jan. 5, 1881, Logan moved to revive the bill; despite a favorable committee report the Senate again failed to act. See *ibid.*, 46-3, 349, 1255–57; *SRC*, 47-1-671.

Testimonial

[*Galena, 1880*]

A man of great ability, pure patriotism, unselfish nature, full of forgiveness to his enemies, bearing malice toward no one he prove to be the man above all others for the great struggle through which the Nation had to pass to place itself among the greatest in the family of nations. His fame will grow brighter as time passes and his great work is better understood.

U. S. GRANT

ADS, USMA. Osborn H. Oldroyd, *The Lincoln Memorial: Album-Immortelles* (New York, 1882), p. 323. Osborn H. Oldroyd acquired such testimonials from prominent Americans between 1880 and 1882.

To Nathan Appleton

Fifth Av. Hotel N. Y
Jan.y 1st 1881

DEAR SIR:

Your letter of the 27th ult. and the relief map of the proposed Panama Canal were duly received. I note what you have to say about my taking the American Directorship The position was tendered to me, and declined on the ground that I do not believe the project feasable in the first place, and I should oppose it at any rate under any European management. My judgement is that every dollar invested in the Panama Canal, under the present scheme of a thoroughcut, or sea level, will be sunk without any return to the investors, and without a canal to promote commercial interests. If I was to advise the investment of money in the scheme I would feel that I was advocating a swindle equal to the "South Sea Bubble."

I do not accuse all the advocates—nor a very great number of them—of the de Lesseps scheme of insincerity or dishonesty, but I would be dishonest if I were to advocate it because I do not believe the proposed plan practicable with any amount of money that can be raised, nor that interest could be paid on it by all the commerce the canal could carry if built, to say nothing of the human lives that would be sacrificed in its construction.

Yours Truly
U. S. GRANT

NATHAN APPLETON, ESQR
BOSTON MASS.

ALS, The Scriptorium, Beverly Hills, Calif. On Sept. 4, 1879, a newspaper editorialized. "Mr. NATHAN APPLETON, who comes back to this country as the representative of M. DE LESSEPS in the Panama Canal project, and who, it is said, intends to stump the Atlantic States in advocacy of this great scheme, . . . is best known to the world by his connection with the banking firm of BOWLES BROTHERS & Co., into which he put several hundred thousand dollars, left to him by his father, and out of which he came a bankrupt. Since this not very hopeful business venture he has been endeavoring to regain prominence by a somewhat strained effort at personal publicity, and has written and published a number of not very interesting or instructive papers on social and economical questions. . . ." *New York Times*, Sept. 4, 1879. See *New York World*, Aug. 22–23, 1879. On Dec. 29, 1880, Nathan Appleton, Boston, wrote to USG. "I take pleasure in sending you by express one of the relief maps of the Panama Canal I have just received from Paris which I am sure will interest you, and which I ask you to accept as a New Years gift. I have hoped ever since you returned to the United States more than a year ago that I might have the pleasure of meeting you to talk about this great enterprise and the part you could take in carrying it through. It was in Paris the month of June 1879, shortly after the ~~adj~~ closing of the Canal Congress, when Mr. de Lesseps had agreed to take the lead in the new work, that I called one morning upon Admiral Baron Roncière le Noury at his apartment in the Place Vendôme to talk about it. He told me then that in his opinion an American should have the first position in the Company after Mr. de Lesseps. I told him that you were the person for the place as the most conspicuous American citizen, and I added that it gave me especial pleasure to suggest you from the great admiration I personally had for you. That same afternoon we met Mr. de Lesseps at the office of the Suez Canal Co, and he said at once, as I entered, in the presence of the Admiral, 'that is an excellent idea of yours, and I am going to offer Gen. Grant at once the first honorary presidency of the Company' This of course was all that he could properly do for an organization which was then only in embryo. I was delighted at the good news, and asked him to allow me to give it to the New York Herald, which on his permission I did, & so it went to America. You do not know, General, as I have never had the opportunity of telling you, how much I have admired you, and with what intense interest I have followed your career from the time you became prominent in the early part of the war, when I was a student at Harvard, down to the present time. I first saw you May 24. 1864 on the North Anna, the day before I was wounded, when I was on the staff of the artillery Brigade of the 5th Corps, Gen. Wainwright. My first interview with you was at the White House June or July 1870 when I had a strong letter of introduction from Minister Washburne. Our conversation was about the Canal across the American Isthmus, and I well recollect that you told me that you had studied the question with some care, and believed that the canal when built would be near and along the line of the Panama R. R. At that time I thought that a route could be found in Darien proper, as proposed by Mr Antoine de Gogorza. Subsequent explorations lead me to conclude that no canal way is feasible there, and I unhesitatingly consider Panama as the best place now known. When the Paris Congress decided in favor of the Panama route by a tremendous majority, and Ferdinand de Lesseps, the hero of Suez, agreed to undertake the work I felt that it was actually begun, and I have never changed my opinion from that time. I have always hoped that you would be the leading man in the United States in the enterprise, and that you would be his successor in the presidency of the Company. I believe by the natural laws of gravitation that sooner or later most of the stock will be owned by citizens of our country, and so, if they wish, they can transfer in the future the managing office from Paris to New York. Nor does this possibility in the least annoy Mr. de Lesseps. He wishes simply to build the canal and present it to the world, for the only ownership he recognizes is that of money as represented by the stockholders. It seems to me that it would be well worth your while to help actively this grand international work for the good of mankind. What better field is there for your talent, your activity and your influence? Now that the money has been raised of course the work will proceed at once, and indeed the scientific or technical obstacles do not appear very difficult. The contractors & engineers at Paris & on the Isthmus have been carefully making their studies for the last year & know very exactly where to commence operations & what to do, while the doctor in chief has arranged all his plans for the sanitary regulations. I trust that I shall be able to help the work in many ways, and Mr. de Lesseps has told me that I shall be commercial agent of the Company in the United States. Pray accept my apologies for the length of my letter, but it would not have been easy to make it shorter, . . ." ALS, Nellie C. Rothwell, La Jolla, Calif.

On Dec. 10, 1875, Appleton, London, had written to USG. "A few days ago in Paris I called with Mons. A. Caubert, a French gentleman who is working actively in behalf of our Centennial Exhibition, upon Mons. Ferdinand de Lesseps at the office of the Suez Canal Company. The object of my visit was to ask him informally to come to the United States next year, and when there to interest himself particularly in our proposed canal for joining the Atlantic and Pacific oceans. I was introduced to Mons. de Lesseps in Egypt at the time of the opening of the Suez Canal, having made the journey there with General N. P. Banks, and it so happened that I was the only delegate of any kind officially sent from our country, I being the representative of the Boston Board of Trade at the inauguration ceremonies. My attention was thus attracted to the canal in a way that would not otherwise have occurred, and since that time I have been watching with considerable care the progress made in the preliminary work for beginning the canal that we have to make in our own hemisphere, and you may possibly remember that I had some conversation with you on the subject in Washington early in the summer of 1870. I know very well how desirous you are that this great enterprise shall be speedily begun and carried through, and I believe we now have an exceptionally good opportunity of securing the cooperation of the one man in the world who can give it the greatest impulse—Mons. Ferdinand de Lesseps. He told me that he knew of nothing to prevent his coming to America next year and suggested that some sort of invitation would be agreeable. Now I am aware that our government cannot well undertake to make exceptional cases of individuals and give them especial invitations, but seeing in the paper that the commission appointed to decide which is the best route for the inter-oceanic canal was soon to meet, I thought that, when their decision shall have been made public, it might be possible to have an excursion party arranged, with one of our vessels put at their disposal, and Mons. de Lesseps asked as a guest, to go down to the isthmus and carefully examine the ground. I do not believe there could be any better way than this of bringing the subject of the canal to the attention of our people and of the world generally, and it might reasonably be hoped that a company for undertaking the work itself could then be formed with little difficulty. Mons. de Lesseps told me that he was to go to Egypt the latter part of this month and would not return to Paris until March, by which time I trust we shall know which route will have been concluded to be the best for our canal. I do not think we can celebrate our one hundreth anniversary of national existence in a more fitting manner than by actually beginning the work upon the canal which will open our commerce both to the East and to the West. Commending these views respectfully to your consideration . . ." ALS, DNA, RG 45, Letters Received from the President.

Speech

[*New York City, Jan. 6, 1881*]

Mr. President and Gentlemen of the New-York Press Club: I confessed to a little embarrassment this evening in being called upon, unexpectedly, to say a word before a set of such diffident men as compose, not only the Press Club, but those associated with the press of the country. I thought this was an evening that I was going to spend where all would be quiet and good order, where nobody would have anything to say. We all know the characteristic modesty of the people associated with the press. They never want to inquire into anybody's affairs—know where they are going—what they are going to do—what they are going to say when they get there—and I really thought that you would excuse me this evening; but I suppose that you will expect me to say something about the press—the press of New-York, the press of the United States, and the press of the world.

It would take a good deal to tell what it is possible for the press to do. I confess, at some period of my life, when I have read what you have had to say about me, that I have lost all faith and all hope. But since a young editor has spoken for the press, and has fixed the life-time of a generation of newspaper men at about 12 years, I have a growing hope within me that in the future the press may be able to do some of the great good, which we all admit it is possible for it to do.

I have been somewhat of a reader of newspapers for 40 years—I could read very well when I was 8 years of age—and it has given me 40 years of observation of the press and there is one peculiarity that I have observed, and that is in all of the walks of life, outside of the press, people have entirely mistaken their profession, their occupation. I never knew a Mayor of a city, or even a Councilman of any city, any public officer, any Government official; I never knew a member of Congress, a Senator, or a President of the United States who could not be enlightened in his duties by the youngest member of the press. I never knew a General to command a brigade, a division, a corps, an army, who could begin to do it as well as men far away in their sanctums, and I often wondered,—I was very glad to hear that the newspaper fraternity were ready to take with perfect confidence any office that might be tendered to them from President to Mayor, and I have often been astonished that the citizens have not tendered them, because they know all these offices would have been well and properly filled. Well, gentlemen, I am very happy to have been here with you, and I hope when a new generation, about 12 years hence, comes up, that I will again dine with the Press Club of New-York City, and that I will see that those of this generation who are so well fitted to fill all the civil offices, have all been chosen, and that there will be nothing left then to criticise. I thank you, gentlemen.

New York Times, Jan. 7, 1881.

On Jan. 10, 1881, USG spoke at the annual dinner of the Marine Society, founded in 1770 to improve maritime knowledge and to assist needy seamen and their families. "MR. PRESIDENT AND GENTLEMEN: I hardly know what to say upon an occasion of this sort. I look upon the association represented here as one representing a magnificent charity. I look upon the people before me as representatives of a trade that our Nation was once proud of, and which, unhappily, has almost disappeared from the ocean—I mean the American carrying trade. Capt. Parker has spoken of the objects of this charity. It is one which becomes the people engaged in the carrying trade. I hope the next few years will see that trade so revived as to increase the number of persons qualified to enlarge its membership, and I hope to see it so prosperous that it will not be taxed to provide for the widows and orphans of every master that may come to this port. Gentlemen, I am very glad to have met you here this evening. I will not detain you any longer, knowing that you will hear from others who are better able to entertain you." *New York Times*, Jan. 11, 1881. For James Parker, see *ibid.*, March 24, 1914.

To Horace Porter

New York City
Jan.y 8th /81

Dear Gen.

If you have not sent out your invitations for dinner next Saturday night can you not either make it for Friday evening or postpone it until after my return from Albany,[1] Saturday, the 22d? I have an invitation for Saturday evening from Phila to meet the Saturday Club.[2] I have had repeated invitations from them, and it has so happened that on all other occasions, as on this, I have had other engagements to prevent my acceptance. I will be very glad if you can postpone or advance the day for your dinner so that I may accept for Philadelphia.

Yours Truly
U. S. Grant

P. S. A verbal reply by bearer will answer every purpose.

U. S. G.

ALS, Horace Porter Mende, Zurich, Switzerland. On Jan. 22, 1881, Horace Porter hosted a dinner for USG at the Union League Club in New York City. USG, Hamilton Fish, George M. Pullman, Chester A. Arthur, and other guests signed the menu. DS, Mrs. Paul E. Ruestow, Jacksonville, Fla.

1. On Jan. 17, USG had addressed serenaders at the Executive Mansion in Albany. "Gentlemen of the Grant Club—I am glad to meet you here this evening, but I am sorry that you have been compelled to be out in the cold so much. In regard to the association of which you bear the name, individually you are members of a great political party, and no matter who heads it you have, all of you, one and all, been found in the support of the principles of that party and for the one who might be chosen to lead it. While you continue in that faith I have no doubt that the institutions of our country will be secure. At all events I am willing to leave them in your hands." *New York Herald*, Jan. 18, 1881.

On Jan. 18, USG declined an invitation for an evening engagement with an unknown correspondent. Copy, MHi.

On Jan. 19, USG addressed the N. Y. assembly. "MR. PRESIDENT AND GENTLEMEN OF THE LEGISLATURE OF THE STATE OF NEW-YORK: I feel it a great honor to be received at this Capital city and be welcomed by the Legislature of this great Empire State—a State greater in population than many of the nationalities of Europe, greater in wealth than almost any of them—than any, with probably two or three exceptions. Lest my assertion in this regard might be disputed, and the tax-lists of this State be compared with the reputed wealth of some of the nationalities of Europe, I have to state, what all of you probably know, that the taxable property of the State represents but a small percentage of its real value. Then, too, there is but very little property, either personal or real, within this State that is not the property of its citizens; but there is not a State or Territory in the Union in which there are not large amounts of taxable property, personal and real, the property of citizens of this State. It is probable that the citizens of the Empire State are possessed of more real and personal property outside the limits of the State, which is taxed elsewhere, than they own within it. Therefore, this body, representing the people of the State, represents more and greater interests than the parliaments or legislative assemblies, by whatever name they may be called, of almost any foreign country. As the guardian of so large an interest, the body assembled here before me represents the interests and legislates for the welfare of people as important in their numbers and in their wealth as meets almost any where on this globe outside of the National Capitol at Washin[g]ton and the Parliament of Great Britain. I trust and believe that the State, in submitting all her vast interests to you, gentlemen, has entrusted them to good hands, and that you, when you retire from the positions which you now hold, will do so with the respect and confidence of the constituents who sent you here. I am proud to have met you here to-day. I hope I may meet all of you on other occasions. I thank you again, gentlemen, for the cordiality of your reception." *New York Tribune*, Jan. 20, 1881.

On Jan. 20, USG addressed students at Albany High School. ". . . I hope all the children will have opportunities for education similar to those here and improve them, and I hope you will all become good and useful members of society, and return the education which you will here acquire." *New York Times*, Jan. 21, 1881.

On Jan. 21, USG addressed George L. Willard Post No. 34 in Troy, N. Y. "I am much pleased to see so many here this evening, knowing that the object for which you have met is charity to that class to which we are so much indebted, the soldiers and the families of the soldiers who fought the great struggles which we have heard of, which emancipated 4,000,000 of human beings and made a republic possible to the end of time. Your purpose is a good one, and I am delighted to see that you are so well patronized this evening. I am glad to have been able to see so many of your citizens personally. I have passed through your city frequently, but have only stopped on two previous occasions. Your city does its part in the support and aggrandizement of this great nation. In manufactures it stands as high as any other of equal population in the country. I regret that my stay is so short that I shall not be able to visit the places of industry that add so much to your credit. I hope that on some future occasion I shall be able to do so. Ladies and gentlemen, I thank you for your cordial greeting this evening." *Troy Times*, Jan. 22, 1881. See *PUSG*, 24, 178–79.

2. On Jan. 16, USG had attended the Saturday Club at the Philadelphia home of Anthony J. Drexel. "In the course of conversation allusion was made to his having been made president of the New York World's Fair and he said that he thought the project of purchasing the Main Centennial building and transporting it to New York for the

purpose of using it for the Exposition was a good idea and should be carried out if the Exhibition Company here was willing to sell it. . . . An incident of the evening at Mr. Drexel's was General Grant's immediate recognition of a veteran who had fought under him during the early part of the war. As the latter was presented and held out his left hand the General looked at him keenly for a moment and said: 'I remember, you lost your arm down in Mississippi. I am very glad to meet an old comrade.'" *Philadelphia Times*, Jan. 16, 1881.

To George W. Childs

———

NEW YORK CITY, January 10. [*1881*]

MY DEAR MR. CHILDS: I regret very much that I cannot accept your kind invitation to meet General Patterson at dinner at your house, on Wednesday, the 12th, on the occasion of his eighty-ninth birthday. I have an engagement for that day and evening in Brooklyn, which I cannot excuse myself from. Before the date was fixed I was consulted as to the time when I could attend and all the arrangements are now made, so that I must be there. I hope, however, General Patterson may have many more birthdays and that I may meet him at them and find him in full health and vigor of mind and body. I specially bespeak an invitation to his one hundredth anniversary dinner. Remember me kindly to the General and all your guests at the dinner.

Very truly yours,
U. S. GRANT.

Philadelphia Times, Jan. 13, 1881. USG served as pallbearer for Robert Patterson, who died Aug. 7, 1881. See *New York Times*, Aug. 12, 1881.

To John A. Logan

———

New York City
Jan.y 10th /81

MY DEAR GENERAL:

I have your letter of the 7th inst. There is nothing that I could consistently do for Robt. Lincoln that I would not do. I believe it would strike the public most favorably to see him in the cabinet, and no one more so than myself. But without thinking of him in that connection I have written to Storrs[1] that I would join you, and any other prominent republicans in the state, in recommending him for Atty. Gen.l. If either of these parties are settled upon I will join you in recommending them.

Very Truly yours
U. S. GRANT

GEN. J. A. LOGAN, U. S. S.

ALS, DLC-John A. Logan.
On Jan. 31, 1881, President-elect James A. Garfield wrote to U.S. Senator John A. Logan of Ill. "*Confidential* . . . your favor of the 23rd inst. came duly to hand, and your suggestions are noted. I also received the letter, Signed by yourself and the other members of the Illinois delegation.—There are several subjects connected with the organization of the new administration on which I would be glad to consult you—I cannot well visit Washington until I go to stay—and I shall be glad if you will visit me here soon—If you can do so, please advise me by letter or telegram at what time you will come—Please say nothing about you visit. Hoping to see you soon, . . ." ALS, DLC-John A. Logan.

1. Born in 1835 in N. Y., Emery A. Storrs settled in Chicago in 1859 and became a prominent lawyer, orator, and Republican official.

Speech

————

[*New York City, Jan. 14, 1881*]

I thank you and this audience for the address of welcome which has been presented to me, and I assure you I appreciate it most heartily, coming from my fellow-citizens so recently made so. I sincerely hope with you that the time is not far distant when all the privileges that citizenship carries with it will be accorded you throughout the land without any opposition, and it is a hope of mine that when they are accorded they will be exercised wisely and justly by you, and I have no fear myself but what they will be exercised as well and fully by you as by any other race enjoying the blessings and privileges of this country. Of course it is too much to expect perfection, but I have no fear that the franchise will not be exercised as carefully and judiciously by our fellow-citizens of African descent as by any others. Perhaps more care will be used because it is a boon so recently given to your race, and therefore prized more highly. I am glad to see in my travels the progress in education all over the country made by the colored people, even in the South, where the prejudice is strongest. It is rare to see a colored c[hil]d lose an opportunity to get a common school education. Education is the first great step towards the capacity to exercise the new privileges accorded to you wisely and properly. I hope the field may be open to you, regardless of any prejudice which may have hertofore existed.

New York World, Jan. 15, 1881. USG spoke during a benefit concert at Steinway Hall, after an address by John Quincy Allen "in behalf of the Colored Citizens' Association of New-York and Brooklyn." ". . . Eminently distinguishable among the events which make up the history of our struggles is the appointment of colored Americans as duly accredited representatives of the Government to Embassies and Consulates abroad. It was for you, Sir, to initiate this act of justice, and thereby to crown and complete the labors of those old anti-slavery heroes, those pioneers in the cause of human rights, that were first to break the soil and sow the seed. This act clothes you with imperishable fame, and links your name with the sainted brotherhood of Lovejoy and Lincoln, of Brown and Stevens, of Garrison and Sumner, and others of that noble band who lived and died in the cause of the down-trodden and oppressed. . . ." *New York Times*, Jan. 15, 1880. On Dec. 31, 1880, a delegation led by James M. Baxter addressed USG at the Fifth Avenue Hotel. "On the occasion of your visit to New-York last October, when a demonstration was made in your honor, in which all classes of citizens, irrespective of nationalities, vied with one another in rendering you homage, it was suggested at a meeting of colored citizens tha[t] an address be presented to you when you could conveniently receive it. We come tonight as a committee from that body of citiz[e]ns to request that you will be present on the evening of January 14 to receive the address at an entertainment for the benefit of St. Philip's Protestant Episcopal Church. The people of this country, sir, owe you a debt of gratitude, for to your sword is due the salvation of the country." *New York Tribune*, Jan. 1, 1881.

Endorsement

I have an indistinct recollection of the matters herein related, and recollect more distinctly that at the time that cattle raiders were crossing the Rio Grande I had the Sec. of State suggest to the then Mexican Minister that our troops be allowed to cross when in hot pursuit of such persons, or Indians who might come over to depridate. I think, at your suggestion, you were verbally authorized to use your discretion to cross in case of necessity, in a way not to wound the sensibility of the Mexican Government.

U. S. GRANT

JAN.Y 14TH /81

AES, DLC-USG. Written on a letter of Jan. 3, 1881, from Edward O. C. Ord, Washington, D. C., to USG, New York City. "In regard to the matter of pacification of the Mexican frontier—for which—you are somewhat responsible—It has been suggested that—as you gave me the first authority to cross my troops—in pursuit of raiders—at my request in 76—that it would be but an act of Justice to us both, to write Either Senator Maxey—who has my bill in Charge, or Senator Logan, and say so. You may not remember the conversation but it was when I asked you if you couldnt issue such an order—stating—as I did—that at that time there was a revolution in the Mexican border states, and no Mexican govt to appeal to—you replied you 'would issue the order but people would immediately accuse you of trying to get up a war with Mexico'—and then you added 'that I could go on and cross my troops—when necessary—using great care not to give just cause for war—and I promised that then should no war result from my action—Genl Should you be troubled for want of time, An endorsement of this letter and its return to me or either of the Gentlemen above named will suffice—" ALS, *ibid.* Retired in Dec., 1880, as brig. gen., Ord sought and won passage of a bill retiring him as maj. gen. on Jan. 28.

To Samuel L. Clemens

———

New York City, Jan 14, 1881

Your kind letter of the 8th inst came to hand in due time, I had delayed answering it until this time because of any doubt as to how to answer it but because of the principle reason I have for not doing what you suggest, namely, laziness. The same suggestion you make has been frequently been made to others, but never entertained for a moment. In the first place I have always distrusted my ability to write anything that would satisfy myself and the public would be much more difficult to please. In the second place I am not possessed of the kind of industry necessary to undertake such a work.

Gen. Badeau has written a history of my connection with the war, with my consent and approval, and Mr. J. R. Young has done the same of my recent travels, and it would be unfair of them for me to do any thing now that would in any way interfere with the sale of their work. Then too they have done it much better than I could if I was to try.

If I [e]ver settle down in a house of my own I may make notes which some one of my children may use after I am gone. But before I do this it will be necessary for me to be able to setle up with some one who may happen to own the premises I wish to settle down in.

I am very much obliged to you for your kind suggestions and for the friendship which inspires them and will always appreciate both. If you want to see me about this, or any other matter, at any time I beg that you will feel no hesitation in calling. I will always be glad to see you and hear you no matter whether your views and mine agree or not.

Very truly yours
U. S. GRANT

Typescript (corrected), USGA.

To Matías Romero

NEW YORK CITY, January 15, 1881.

Hon. M Romero,

DEAR SIR: On reflecting upon the best method of proceeding, and upon consultation with others, I have come to the conviction that it would be good policy for you to permit the use of your name as one of the corporators of the roads to be built in Mexico, south of the city of Mexico, and such other roads as may be connected with that system; and, also that you should suggest the names of five or six leading citizens of the state of Oaxaca, and such other states as these roads may pass through, to be associated with you. General Diaz I know personally and know him to be the most distinguished citizen of the state of Oaxaca, and deeply interested in the construction of railroads in his state and in the country at large. If his official position does not interfere with his connection with such roads, I suggest his name as one.

I am aware that there is not time now to correspond with such persons as you might suggest to get their consent to the use of their names. But as no responsibility is involved by the use of persons' names in an act of incorporation I suggest whether you cannot give such names as you think would give strength to the undertaking in your own country and inform the parties of the liberty you have taken. Should objection be raised by any whose names were so used their names could be withdrawn and others substituted. All delay in obtaining the necessary legislation in this country will be avoided by this course and time saved to get the matter before the Mexican Congress at its first meeting, if so required. Very truly yours,

U. S. GRANT.

New York World, Feb. 12, 1881. On Jan. 16, 1881, Matías Romero, New York City, wrote to USG. "I have received your letter of yesterday informing me that on reflecting upon the best method of proceeding and upon consultation with others you have come to the conviction that it would be good policy for me to permit the use of my name as one of the incorporators of the company which is to build the Oaxaca Railroad, and that I should suggest for the same purpose the names of other leading citizens of that state and of other states through which the road should pass, recommending finally that the name of General Porfirio Diaz should be used as one of such citizens. I have from the beginning, during my efforts made in this city to organize a responsible company to take hold of the Oaxaca grant, insisted that the Mexican element should be fully represented in that company and have suggested, as you are aware, some of the names which in my opinion ought to appear in the act of incorporation of said company; but I have at the same time been reluctant to allow my name to be used for that purpose, for fear that my conduct in that regard might be construed as an attempt on my par[t] to derive personal advantage from the power I hold from the state of Oaxaca to transfer the grant, and which power I intend to exercise in favor of such company as soon as it is properly organized. But as my main object is that such organization should be made with the best elements of this country, and since in your opinion, as well as that of other gentlemen who will be connected with that company, it is expedient that I should be one of the incorporators, I consent to appear as such. I have suggested from the beginning, as you are aware, the name of General Diaz, one of the most distinguished citizens of Oaxaca, as one of the incorporators from that state, but at the same time I have expressed to yourself and to other friends my fears that the use of his name might be misrepresented to him; but considering that this road has already a charter, and in taking into account the other reasons that yourself and other gentlemen have stated to me, I give his name as the first among the citizens of Oaxaca, subject to the reservations hereinafter stated. I avail myself of this opportunity to repeat here what I have before said: that I am using the names of General Diaz and of the other gentlemen whose names I suggest without consultation with them, and that it must of course be understood that they are at liberty to have their names withdrawn, if they should think proper to do so. One is Governor of the state of Oaxaca and two others are Senators from that state to the Federal Congress. The gentleman whose name I suggest in the first place as representing the state of Vera Cruz is now Secretary of the Treasury of Mexico. I will inform these gentlemen at once of what has transpired here, and under the conditions and reservations already stated I give you the following names of citizens of Oaxaca and Vera Cruz, the States within whose territory the road will pass, to be used as incorporators: General Porfirio Diaz, of Oaxaca. Francisco Mei[x]ueiro, of Oaxaca. Miguel Castro, of Oaxaca. Fidencio Hernandez, of Oaxaca. Ignacio Pombo, of Oaxaca. Ignacio Mejia, of Oaxaca. Francisco De Landero y Cos, of Vera Cruz. José Maria Mata, of Vera Cruz." *Ibid.* See Speech, [*Nov. 11, 1880*].

On Jan. 31, USG wrote to Collis P. Huntington. "You are invited to attend a meeting of the gentlemen interested in building railroads in Mexico, which will take place on Friday, the 11th of February next, at eleven oclock AM at Room 40, Fourth Floor, of No 120 Broadway, New York City." LS, Collis P. Huntington Papers, Syracuse University, Syracuse, N. Y. Also on Jan. 31, N. Y. Senator William Waldorf Astor "introduced a bill to incorporate the Mexican Southern Railroad Company. It names as the first corporators: U. S. Grant, Edwin D. Morgan, Matthias Romero, Porfirio Diaz, Miguel Castro, Edward D. Adams, Jay Gould, Thomas Nickerson, and others. The company may erect and operate railroads and telegraph lines in Mexico. The capital stock is $10,000,000." *New York Times*, Feb. 1, 1881. On Feb. 11, Romero addressed a meeting chaired by USG and attended by Jay Gould, Grenville M. Dodge, Russell Sage, and others. "Allow me to state the fact that when the railroads now in process of construction from the Rio Grande to the city of Mexico shall have been finished, the system of railways in the United States with which they are connected will not have reached one of the best and richest regions of the Mexican Republic—that which lies east and southeast of the capital. The American railroad system can be extended and I believe ought to be extended to Central and even to South America. Those who manage and direct its operations will hardly stop at the city of Mexico, but will seek for extension further south. In so doing their route will of necessity lie through the state of Oaxaca, which comprises within its territory the Isthmus of Tehuantepec, the geographical link of connection between North and Central America." Romero described the geography of Oaxaca and its principal exports, including cochineal, coffee, sugar, and tobacco. "The Oaxaca Railroad, it will be seen, would be an interoceanic line, connecting the Gulf of Mexico with the Pacific, over a distance hardly exceeding four hundred miles, though it would not be dependent upon interoceanic traffic for its profits. It would really be a first-class local road, passing through the heart of a very rich mining and agricultural country, quite thickly populated by a frugal, moral and laborious people. At the same time this road, properly called the Mexican Southern, would be a trunk line, connecting the railroad systems now in process of construction from the United States to the city of Mexico with one of the best and richest portions of the Mexican Republic and with Central America. I am myself a native of the state of Oaxaca. I know tolerably well a large portion of that state and I honestly believe that this is one of the most important and lucrative railroad lines which can be built in Mexico, although it may be a somewhat more expensive road to construct than some of the others which pass over a comparatively more level country." After detailing the likely route, Romero concluded. "The Governor of the State of Oaxaca, which commonwealth is the grantee of this line from the Federal Government, gave me, under date of September 9, 1880, a formal power of attorney, which I now hold properly authenticated, authorizing me to transfer that charter to any company which may be disposed to build the road with the privileges and under the conditions of its charter. As you, gentlemen, have shown so much interes[t] in building railroads in Mexico and many of you have already invested large amounts of money in the roads that are now being built there, and may therefore be presumed to be naturally interested in the further extension south of the Mexican system of railways, I propose to you that you should take up the Oaxaca road in connection with such other enterprises as you may engage in in that country. Should you be willing so to do, I am ready to transfer to you the charter which that state has obtained from the Federal Government and which, as I have said, I consider to offer as great inducements to investment of capital as any of the projected railroad enterprises in my country." Following Romero's address, "a resolution was adopted accepting the transfer of the charter and providing for the obtaining of such modifications in its provisions as were deemed necessary." *New York World*, Feb. 12, 1881. See letter to Jesse Root Grant, Jr., March 28, 1881.

To Rutherford B. Hayes

Albany, N. Y.
Jan.y 21st 1881

HIS EXCELLENCY, R. B. HAYES,
PRES. OF THE UNITED STATES,
DEAR SIR:

Will you permit me to say a word in behalf of Gen. C. D. MacDougall for reappointment to the office of U. S. Marshal for the Northern District of N. Y. It will not be contended that Gen. MacDougall has not filled his office with great credit to himself and to the best interests of the public service. His other services—in the field and in the state—entitle him to consideration, and I take the liberty to express a hope that he may be continued in his present office.

Very respectfully
your obt. svt.
U. S. GRANT

ALS, OFH. Born in Scotland in 1839, Clinton D. MacDougall emigrated with his parents in 1842, settled in Auburn, N. Y., served as col., 111th N. Y., and resumed a career as a banker, postmaster, and U.S. Representative (1873–77). On Feb. 13, 1877, USG nominated MacDougall as marshal, Northern District, N. Y.; on March 22, 1881, President James A. Garfield nominated MacDougall to continue as marshal.

To George C. Darling

FIFTH AVENUE HOTEL,
January 24, 1881.

Geo. C. Darling, Esq., Secretary Burns Association:

DEAR SIR—On my return from Albany I found your letter of the 17th inst. saying a carriage would be in waiting to take me to the dinner of your association. I regret to say that I will not be able to attend. My recollection is that I only accepted the invitation conditionally. My other engagements for the week are so numerous that I must be excused from this. Among the engagements made, one is for Brooklyn on Monday evening.[1] With many regrets, very truly yours,

U. S. GRANT.

Brooklyn Eagle, Jan. 26, 1881. The 1880 census lists George Darling, 28, clerk, Brooklyn, born in Scotland.

1. The Brooklyn Burns Association held their annual banquet on the anniversary of the poet's birth, Tuesday, Jan. 25, 1881.

To Rutherford B. Hayes

New York City
Jan.y 24th 1881

HIS EXCELLENCY R. B. HAYES,
PRESIDENT OF THE U. STATES:
DEAR SIR:

I take pleasure in commending to your consideration for appointment to West Point, At Large, the son of Gen. Poe, of the U. S. Army. Gen. Poe has served long and faithfully. Army officers have no Congressional districts to look to for appointments to the Military Academy, hence are entirely dependent upon the few places the President has to give for appointments for their sons.

Very respectfully
your obt. svt.
U. S. GRANT

ALS, DLC-Orlando M. Poe. Col. Orlando M. Poe (USMA 1856) served as aide to Gen. William T. Sherman. Charles C. Poe graduated from the U.S. Naval Academy in 1885.

To Marcus Petersen, Jr., et al.

———

New York City
Jan.y 24th 1881

DEAR SIRS:

By chance this moment I happened to glance at your letter of the 6th of this month, conveying to me the resolutions adopted by the "Young Mens Central Club" of Kings Co. on my acceptance of the invitation to preside at their meeting. Noticing the date— Feb.y 9th—reminded me that it would be impossible for me to attend. I have been . . . much embarrassed by accepting two or more invitations for the same evening, but none of them have I felt more than this. On the 9th Mrs. Grant and I have a special engagement which I must keep especially as heretofore her engagements have had to give way to enable me to keep mine . . . any day during the week except the 7th or 9th I would have had no other engagement to keep me away.

Hoping that the young republicans of Kings Co. may hear such words of encouragement as to strengthen their convictions that their political views are right now, and should be adhered to until in every section of our broad land their is entire freedom to think and vote as each one likes, with fear of ostricism or other harm, I am

Very Truly yours
U. S. GRANT

MARCUS PETERSEN, JR.   COM.
FRED. SCHANNING
WM C. HERBERT JR.
SAML H. ANDREWS

ALS (partial facsimile), R. M. Smythe & Co., Inc., Auction 271, May 3, 2007, no. 85. See letter to Marcus Petersen, Jr., Oct. 22, 1880; *Brooklyn Eagle*, Jan. 6, 1881. On Feb. 10, 1881, USG spoke at the Brooklyn Academy of Music. "GENTLEMEN OF THE YOUNG MEN'S CENTRAL REPUBLICAN CLUB OF BROOKLYN AND LADIES AND GENTLEMEN— I presume that I have been invited to come here this evening to present the speaker of the evening because he is a stranger to a Brooklyn audience. But I am sure there is no other city or town in the United States where his name is not familiar to a great many of our good people as a household word. After you have heard him this evening, I have no doubt but that all of you here present will remember him in the future, and it will not be necessary on other occasions to present him to you at least. Ladies and gentlemen I now have the pleasure of introducing to you the Rev. Henry Ward Beecher." *Ibid.*, Feb. 11, 1881. At a reception following his address, Henry Ward Beecher introduced USG, "saying that it had been remarked in regard to General Von Moltke, that he possessed the faculty of being silent in five languages, and the same faculty of silence had long been attributed to General Grant. But the General had lately shown himself a master of speech, . . ." USG replied "that if it should be his fortune to say anything good, it would be for the reason that he had been sitting in the neighborhood of people who had probably imbibed something stronger than Congress water or Apollonaris, and that he had been inspired by what they had drunk. As to the chaplain of the Thirteenth, the General wasn't certain whether that distinguished pillar of the church and ornament of the National Guard had or had not taken champagne under a deceptive belief that it was Apollonaris, an[d a]s a consequence had called for a speech—but, on t[he w]hole, the General was of opinion that the chaplain had been anxious to be deceived, and this accounted for the event that had occurred." *Ibid.*

On Feb. 18, USG addressed veterans of the 14th N. Y. Militia, designated the 84th N. Y. during the Civil War, at the Portland Avenue armory in Brooklyn. "VETERANS OF THE FOURTEENTH, LADIES AND GENTLEMEN:—I was not aware, until coming over from New York, that I was to say anything to-night save to formally open this fair. I am greatly pleased to be here, with my old comrades of the Fourteenth. On my arrival from the West at Culpepper Court House, in 1864, this regiment received me at the depot, and was my headquarters guard for a month or two following. I am glad to be with them to-night to testify to my appreciation of their deeds, and to say this to the citizens of Brooklyn, a part of whom they now are. Thanking you for the honor shown me, I now declare this fair formally opened." *Ibid.*, Feb. 19, 1881. Later, USG briefly addressed a Kings County Club banquet. *Ibid.*

To Frederick T. Dent

New York City
Jan.y 25th /81

DEAR FRED.

I received your letter proposing to sell your interest in the Carondelet property for $5,000 00 in due time. When I purchased that property it was not with the view of making anything for myself more than simple interest on the money invested, and what ever might be Julia's interest as one of the family. I believed from precedents in Northern Cities of rapid growth the property would be of great value in a few years. But property about St Louis has not advanced as it has about Chicago for example. There has not been a day since I made the purchase when I could have got back the money invested, with 6 pr. ct. interest. Indeed I doubt if I could get back now the money I paid without interest. For most of the property I paid in the 1st instant—all I believe except 47 Arpents got from Carlin—$200 00. After I had paid for it Burnes, Hughes son-in-law,[1] from whom I purchased, sued without giving me notice, for the widows dower, got judgement and sold the property for a song, I believe becoming the purchaser himself. When I found this out I moved to have the sale set aside, and succeeded so far as to have the property resold, when I became the purchaser, paying full price, the widow geting her dower out of the price realized. This you see has brought the property up to a price which makes it doubtful whether I will ever realize what I put into it. If a chance occurs to get my money back on that and the White Haven property I intend to avail myself of it. I want the income of it now and not for my children after I am gone.

I congratulate you on your promotion.[2] If you should desire to spend your Summers North—in case you retire—you are welcome to our house in Galena at any time we are not using it. In the summers we expect to be at Long Branch. With love of to you & Hellen from Julia & I,

Yours Truly
U. S. GRANT

ALS, ICarbS.

1. Calvin F. Burnes. See *PUSG*, 20, 145–46, 165; *ibid.*, 24, 16–20.
2. As of Jan. 2, 1881, Frederick T. Dent was made col., 1st Art.

To James A. Garfield

——

New York City
Jan.y 26th 1881

MY DEAR GENERAL:

I write to you confidentionally on a matter which I feel a deep interest in, and one in which I am sure you do. Harmony in the republican party, and at least the support of the whole party of your Administration is certainly to be desired. As you know the the papers are making and unmaking Cabinets for you. I know how impossible it is for you to prevent this. But there are some suggestions made which cause apprehension in my mind, and I know they do in the minds of others who are important factors in the party. It is generally believed that Mr Blaine has been tendered the portfolio of the State Department. I do not like the man, have no confidence in his friendship nor in his reliability. But he is—has been—a leading member of the party, and has many followers. I do not think you ought to ignore him because I do not like him. No one probably should be put in so important a place as a Cabinet position in antagonism to him. But there are others quite as important.—While it seems to be conceeded that Blaine is likely to go into the State Department it has been equally thought until quite recently that L. P. Morton, or some one from the state of New York, friendly to Senator Conkling, would take the Treasury. Now there is apprehension that the Treasure is to be given into the hands of some one from west of the Miss. This arrangement would give the state of New York a place of minor importance, or what would please some people—I know it would me—no place atall in the Cabinet. This I fear would cause a disturbance hard for the republican party to bear and bad for the country at large.

I have written thus plainly because it conveys just what I should mean if I were to use more diplomatic language. I take the liberty of writing on this subject because your letters to me invite me to do so. I hope the apprehensions which cause this letter are not well founded. There is no member of your own family more desirous of seeing your Administration a success than me. The good of the whole country requires harmonious republican government until all the results of the war are secured, and until sectional passions are allayed. We could not stand a democratic administration now, nor for many years, without a disturbance of the material interests of the Country. I do not say the appointment of Mr. Blaine would cause a disturbing influance in the party. But putting him at the head of the Cabinet, and ignoring the republican Senator from this state would.

Hoping you will receive this in the spirit in which it is sent, a spirit desiring the greatest good to the country, the party and yourself,

I am, Very Truly yours

U. S. GRANT

[G]EN. JAS. A. GARFIELD.

ALS, DLC-James A. Garfield. On Jan. 31, 1881, James A. Garfield, Mentor, Ohio, wrote to USG, New York City. "I have received your letter of Dec 29th, just forwarded to me by Maj. Geo. King of Georgetown Ohio. I will bear your suggestions in mind, and hope it will be possible for me to do something for him—I have also your letter of the 26th inst. in reference to N. Y. Affairs—I thank you for giving me the aid of your knowledge of persons whom you know better than I do—I have the strongest desire to preserve harmony in all the Elements of the Republican Party—and as far as possible, avoid antagonisms, and ill feelings—It has been my earnest wish to satisfy the views of the N. Y. Republican leaders—But the appointment of Mr. Morton, to the Treasury, encounters an express provision of the law—and even if he should go out of his banking business, it would be regarded as a violation of the Spirit of the law—I have never for a moment, thought of selecting from N. Y. for a place in the cabinet, any one who is Hostile to Senator Conkling. I have written to the Senator inviting him to visit me and confer on the subject. I hope he will do so. Of course, I must select men who will work in harmony with me, in the administration—but I shall try to avoid antagonisms, as far as I can—I had not heard, until very recently, that there were unpleasant relations between Senator Blaine and yourself—and in view of the opinion you Express of him, is is generous on your part to say that I ought not ignore him, because you do not like him. I know you will appreciate the fact that many of our leading senators are not on friendly terms, and it is quite impossible to make selections, that will please them all. I have been thinking, that in case there should be a vacancy in the Mexican or Chinese mission, you might have some person you would like to have appointed—If you have I shall be glad to have you tell me so—Thanking you for your letter, . . ." ALS, Mrs. Paul E. Ruestow, Jacksonville, Fla.

To Edward F. Beale

New York City
Jan.y 27th 1881

MY DEAR GN. BEALE;

Mrs. Grant & I received yours & Mrs Beales kind invitation to be your guest during our visit to washington next week. I go as a Trustee for the Peabody Educational Fund. The Sec. has secured rooms for all the trustees, and for their meetings, at the Rigg

House. We will only remain there to transact the business before the Board. It will be better for all of us to remain together.

Thanking you for your kind invitation, and best regards to you and all your family,

Very Truly yours

U. S. GRANT

ALS, DLC-Decatur House Papers. On Feb. 1, 1881, USG, Julia Dent Grant, Ulysses S. Grant, Jr., and Fannie C. Grant arrived in Washington, D. C. On Feb. 2 and 3, USG attended meetings of the Peabody Education Fund.

On Feb. 2, USG wrote to Julia Grant. "The Trustees, with the ladies of the party, dine here—at the Riggs House—at 7 this evening. The President & Chief Justice have other engagements and will not be at the dinner." AN (initialed, undated), DLC-USG. Written on letterhead of the Riggs House. See *Washington Post*, Feb. 3, 1881.

To Elizabeth King

———

New York City

Jan.y 27th /81

MY DEAR MRS. KING;

I received your letter proposing to sell me 160 acres of land in Mo. You are mistaken in my ability to buy for so small a sum without feeling it. While I have enough to live in Galena in a moderate way I have nothing above that without earning it. I have a gooddeal of land in Mo. about 800 acres near St. Louis. But it brings me but little above taxes. I did have also a number of other tracts through the state, but after paying taxes on them for a number of years I let them go for taxes.—Tell John that I received his letter and should have answered him. But I am my own secretary and the letters to me accumulate notwithstanding I write a great many every day. He wanted to know whether I thought he had better send my letter to Gen. Garfield[1] to him now, or whether he had better wait until he is installed in office? I think he should wait, and when he does send it it should be accompanied by his application for some definite position.

Tell Lucy's son-in-law that I do not see how I can help him. The fact is the worst thing that can be done for a young man is to get him a Government position. Such places only give a man a mere support while he holds ~~them~~ it, and unfits him for the battle of life when he is discharged. With kind regards to all my George-town friends,

Very Truly yours
U. S. GRANT

ALS, DLC-USG, IB.

1. See letter to James A. Garfield, Dec. 29, 1880.

To Lt. William W. Kimball

New York City
Jan.y 31st 1881

LT. W. W. KIMBALL, U. S. N.
DEAR SIR:

Your letter of the 23d of Jan.y was duly received. I am very busy, receive many calls and have to do all my own writing is my excuse for not answering sooner. I go to Washington to-morrow to be absent all week. Next week however I will be in town and will be pleased to see you any day you may desire to call. I am always glad to see worthy representatives of our country getting service in the Eastern countries, particularly in China & Japan, and will therefore be glad to see you and give my opinion for what it may be worth on your enterprise.

Very Truly yours
U. S. GRANT

ALS, Gilder Lehrman Collection, NHi. Born in 1848 in Maine, William W. Kimball graduated from the U.S. Naval Academy in 1869. From Dec., 1879, to Nov., 1882, Lt. Kimball was assigned to special duty, Springfield, Mass. See William B. Cogar, *Dictionary of Admirals of the U.S. Navy* (Annapolis, 1991), 2, 153–55.

To John Russell Young

————

New York City
Jan.y 31st 1881

MY DEAR COMMODORE,

Badeau sent you a letter one week ago yesterday, directed to the Herald Office, saying that he had there for you advanced sheets of his book. On Tuesday following[1] he told me that he had heard nothing from you. Thinking letters so directed might not reach you I droped you a line to the Astor House adving you of Badeau's letter. This evening he informs me that he has heard nothing from you yet.

I go to Washington in the morning to be absent until Saturday.[2] Mrs. Grant & I will spend Friday night and Saturday fore noon with Mr. Childs[3] in Phila

Yours Truly
U. S. GRANT

ALS, DLC-USG, IB.

1. Jan. 25, 1881.
2. Feb. 5.
3. On Jan. 31, USG had written to George W. Childs. "Mrs. Grant & I go to Washington tomorrow and expect to return as far as Phila. on Friday. We will stop with you or Mr. Drexel as may be most convenient for you. I take this liberty because of the kindness of you and Mr. Drexel in sending a standing invitation whenever Mrs. Grant & I visit your city. We will be obliged to return to New York on Saturday to meet the Worlds Fair Commissioners that evening. . . ." Paul C. Richards, Catalogue No. 216, Jan. 20, 1987, no. 200.

Endorsement

————

Referred to Gen. Garfield with the hope that he may be able to do some thing for Miss Van Lew after the 4th of March. She was a strong Union woman during the war, sent her slaves out of the lines—North—during the investment of Richmond to prevent their workorking in the rebel trenches, and directed two of them to get into our lines and to report to me. She also managed to send important information from time to time.

U. S. GRANT

FEB.Y 3D 1881

AES, DLC-James A. Garfield. Written on a letter of Feb. 1, 1881, from Elizabeth Van Lew, Richmond, to USG. "May I beg earnestly that you will read what I write—I am in so much trouble that I scarcely know how to make my situation known to you. The utter inability I have labored under to sell my valuable but entirely unproductive real estate has reduced me to great distress, absolute need. I tell you truly and solemnly that I have suffered for necessary food. I have not one cent in the world. I could particularize painfully to both you and myself on the straits to which I have been reduced. I believe you will have influence with Mr. Garfield—I trust Mr. Garfield remembers me himself as an earnest worker—I once ~~called~~ wrote inviting him to speak at a ratification meeting & to stay with us—~~& to stay with us~~—I have a nice letter from him in reply.—The letter I wrote and published and which you told me you kindly left on the table for Mr. Hayes,—subjected me to persecution incredible in bitterness. Some of the most uncalled for, unwarranted, cruel, malicious & bitter persecution that I endured came from my own party. As you yourself have known and suffered,—so have I. You know how some offices here have been run in the interest of certain aspirants, enemies of yours. A certain ring of this class is ruling here and strengthened lately. I do not care to write more fully. I desire a good office. I would be glad to be postmaster ~~here~~ because I understand that business. Here pardon me for saying it, but the 'Civil service' comes in as defective. I had clks—who were experts at figures—better clks than I could ever have been—Mailing clks. conversant with Mail routes,—Clks. knowing post office laws—better than I did—Letter carriers better walkers—and so of all the routine duties of the office even to the washing of spittoons,—yet as a whole there was not one single one of them who could run the office as well as I could, giving proper *care, place, & duties* to all. As regards the general supervision it seemed really to me I comprehended it better than any of them. You may call it administrative ability if you please for I suppose that was what I had & what the citizens gave & give me credit for. The present incumbent Dr. Gilmer is not yet confirmed. Dr. Gilmer is a good and honest man (owes Mr Stearns money, & Mr. Stearns interest on his money makes his earnest interest in Dr. G.) Dr. Gilmer—is a Doctor—an Editor (has been) and has a vineyard—has different ways of gaining a livelihood—and all Govt. offices are open to men.—Dr. Gilmer came from another section of the State I am a woman & what is there open for a woman to do? I was born here and have stood the brunt *alone*—of a persecution that I believe no other person in the country has endured who was not ku kluxed. ~~I h~~ I was always tolerant of difference of opinion & never discourteous, wrong only makes hate. I honestly think the Govt. should see that I was sustained if any single individual is here. The *very same social ostracism continues*—Even as regards a Mortgage on my property Mr. Grubbs—tells me that he cannot get money for me on it—as he could if owned by others—on account of political feeling—Mr. Grubbs says this is a 'fact'—I am in debt and have already been subjected to the mortification of a suit. Will you write to me—will you advise me—it will be *strictly confidential*. I trust you need no assurance from me of *our* deep interest in your welfare—" ALS, *ibid.* As of July, 1883, Van Lew clerked under the postmaster gen. in Washington, D. C. See Endorsement, Feb. 26, 1877; Elizabeth R. Varon, *Southern Lady, Yankee Spy: The True Story of Elizabeth Van Lew, A Union Agent in the Heart of the Confederacy* (Oxford, 2003), pp. 238–41.

To Chauncey I. Filley

New York City.
Feb.y 6th 1881

MY DEAR MR FILLEY:

On my return from Washington last evening I found your letter on the subject of my recommendation of Govr Routt for the position of Postmaster General. I have made no recommendations of any one for a Cabinet position, nor will I unless it should be in connection with leading representatives of the party in my own State. But what I did do—and what I would be glad to do for you— is this. I was asked to recommend the Governor for that position, and at the same time to recommend Senator Hitchcock for another Cabinet position. I wrote Genl Garfield what I had been asked to do, and said, substantially, that I knew these two gentlemen well, the former probably better than he did, the latter possibly not quite so well; if they were up for any other position than one in the cabinet I would give them a hearty endorsement. But that a Cabinet Minister occupied such a delicate position toward the Executive that I was not willing to suggest whom he should have. This may not be the exact language used by me, but it contains the idea

With kind regards of Mrs Grant and myself to you and Mrs Filley

Very Truly Yours
U. S. GRANT

Copy, DLC-James A. Garfield. In Jan., 1881, members of the Ark. legislature wrote to President-elect James A. Garfield. "The undersigned republican members of the General Assembly of Arkansas, feeling a deep interest in all measures calculated to promote the popularity and influence of successive Republican National Administrations, and through them the cultivation and dissemination of republican principles and policies among the people of our portion of the Union, in connection with citizens of other states, most respectfully ask that in selecting the distinguished Americans who are to take part in the councils of your cabinet during your administration, you will favorably consider the claims and qualifications of Hon. Chauncey I. Filley of Missouri, for the position of Post-master General. . . . If Missouri was a republican state Arkansas could not be democratic, and we feel that no one thing could contribute more to permanent republican success in Missouri, than would your action in recognizing the fitness, ability, claims, and services of Hon. Chauncey I. Filley the leading republican of Missouri, by calling him to fill the position of Post-master General during the term of your administration." DS (11 signatures), *ibid.* A related letter is *ibid.*

To James A. Garfield

New York City
Feb.y 6th 1881

MY DEAR GENERAL:

I am just in receipt of your letter. I venture to make a suggestion in regard to the position of Sec. of the Treasury. I believe the appointment of John Jacob Astor[1] would be a good one and would be well received in this state, and by the country at large.

Very Truly yours
U. S. GRANT

GN. JAS. A. GARFIELD.

ALS, DLC-James A. Garfield. On Feb. 7, 1881, USG, New York City, telegraphed to President-elect James A. Garfield, Mentor, Ohio. "Please do not consider letter of yesterday without further from me at *lest* on my account" Telegram received (at 8:10 P.M.), *ibid.*

1. Born in 1822, the third to bear his name, John Jacob Astor graduated Harvard Law School in 1842 and devoted his career to shepherding his family's large holdings and fostering the Astor Library in New York City. More active in social than political life, he joined Edwin D. Morgan, Hamilton Fish, and others in Nov., 1880, to publish "The Political Situation from a Financial Standpoint. To the People of New York," in the *North American Review*, warning that Democratic victory would undermine financial stability. On March 5, 1881, Garfield nominated William Windom as secretary of the treasury. In June, Astor reportedly declined "one of the highest and most important foreign missions." *New York Times*, June 15, 1881. See letter to Chester A. Arthur, Oct. 8, 1881.

To Thomas H. Taylor

————

New York City
Feb.y 6th 1881

Dear Sir:

I find your letter of Jan.y __ on my table, inviting me to attend the Eighth Annual Reunion of the National Association of the Veterans of the Mexican War, in Louisville, Ky. on the 22d of Feb.y inst. As this letter must have been received some time since I may have answered it, but do not remember to have done so. My engagements here however will prevent my acceptance. Thanking you for the invitation, and regreting that I cannot have the pleasure of meeting so many of my old comrades in arms, of more than a third of a century ago, I remain,

Very Truly yours
U. S. Grant

Thos H. Taylor, Esq.

ALS (facsimile), eBay, April 24, 2001. Born in 1825 in Ky., Thomas H. Taylor served in the Mexican War, as col. and act. brig. gen., C.S. Army, as deputy U.S. marshal, Ky., and as chief of police, Louisville.

To Ella Green Ward

————

Fifth Av. Hotel,
Feb.y 6th 1881

My Dear Mrs Ward;

Mrs. Grant asks me to answer your kind invitation to lunch with you on the 15th, and to say that she would be very glad to do so, and has desired very much to call on you for some time back, but that she dreads and fears getting through the streets in the lower part of the city, and across the river, in their present condition. She thinks she will have to postpone her visit to Brooklyn until the opening of Spring.

Very Truly yours
U. S. Grant

ALS, Geoffrey Ward, Boston, Mass. Ella C. Green married Ferdinand Ward in 1877. See *New York Times*, April 11, 1890. In 1880, Ward founded the Wall Street firm of Grant & Ward with partners Ulysses S. Grant, Jr., and James D. Fish. Later, USG joined the firm as a silent partner.

To John A. Logan

———

New York City
Feb.y 9th 1881

My Dear Gn. Logan:

I return you herewith Sherman's letter to you, and copy of his letter to his brother. The whole thing, in my judgement, is an afterthought. He feels ashamed of his first course and has written to his brother to hedge. He is not looking after the interests of the Army, nor do I believe he represents their feeling in regard to the bill you champion. At all events if he does, I am willing to say that under no circumstances will I accept the place if the bill passes. If it is desirable there will be no difficulty in getting the sense of the Army on it.

Very Truly yours
U. S. Grant

ALS, DLC-John A. Logan. On Jan. 10, 1881, U.S. Senator John A. Logan of Ill. introduced a bill to place USG on the army retired list, with the rank and full pay of gen., eligible for active duty during a future emergency. *CR*, 46-3, 477. On Jan. 24 and 25, the Senate debated and narrowly rejected Logan's motion to consider the bill. *Ibid.*, pp. 870–73, 901–2. A similar bill in the House of Representatives was defeated in committee. See *ibid.*, p. 38; *HRC*, 46-3-92; *SMD*, 46-3-47. On Feb. 5, Gen. William T. Sherman wrote to Logan. "I take the liberty to enclose you a copy of a letter I wrote some days ago, to my brother John Sherman which contains my deliberate opinion of the proposition you advocate with such force. I believe if you submit the Bill to retire Genl Grant with full pay, and omit for the present the clause allowing the President to put him on duty, you can succeed in passing it this session, most certainly the next. The more I think of it—the more convinced I become that to give the President the right to place General Grant on duty as a full General on our small Peace Establishment, will lead to intrigues damaging to the Army, and making the situation of both Genl Sheridan & myself most uncomfortable." ALS, DLC-John A. Logan. On Jan. 31, Sherman had written to Secretary of the Treasury John Sherman. "As my supposed action in the proposition of the President and of Senator Logan to do honor and substantial justice to General Grant has been misconstrued in high circles, I wish you at least to know the truth. I do not now, nor have I ever done a single act, or spoken a single word that can be tortured into a want of respect for General Grant, past, present, or future, but I do regard it important to the army, of which I am the General, that the Retirement of General Grant when done (as I suppose it will be in due time) may not prejudice the interests and harmony of the service. . . . The Retired List, with the substantial provision of three-fourths pay, is a noble and generous provision by the Country to old, faithful, and most worthy officers, and whatever concerns it touches the interest of every man in the Army. I will be most happy to have General Grant's name enrolled there, but my judgment is that all should be treated alike, that Congress should repeal the Law of 1870 herein quoted, thus restoring that of 1862, or that General Grant, when so retired, should await the next War, when the Government will doubtless be quick to accept his services in the eminent capacity he has demonstrated in War, as also those of many other most worthy officers whose names are on the Retired List of the Army." Copy, *ibid.* On Feb. 17, John Russell Young, New York City, wrote to Gen. Sherman. ". . . I suppose I know more than any one of General Grants real feelings about you. It was my privelege to print his opinion and I know that my publication gave him great pleasure. It would be a calamity, national, almost historical, if anything were allowed to disturb a friendship which should live as one of the most striking and beautiful in history. So when I see these mischievous paragraphs in the newspapers they give me pain.—I never heard from General Grant the expression of a desire to return to the army, and in fact, he seems whenever I see him to regard the proposed measure, whatever shape it assumes with indifference. He seems to enjoy his New York life and talks of going to Mexico next month. He is anxious to have me accompany him—but I hardly see, how after wandering so long, I can afford to wander any more. . . ." ALS, DLC-William T. Sherman. See letter to Fitz John Porter, Dec. 27, 1882; James Pickett Jones, *John A. Logan: Stalwart Republican from Illinois* (Tallahassee, 1982), pp. 142–43.

On Nov. 9, 1880, J. Pierpont Morgan, Anthony J. Drexel, George W. Childs, and one other, Philadelphia, had written to Edwards Pierrepont concerning USG. ". . . On our own knowledge we can say that his income is not sufficient to secure him in that position of comfortable independence that he should be enabled to occupy. It has occurred to us that he can be placed in this more becoming position if . . . twenty gentlemen will subscribe $5,000 each, towards a fund of one hundred thousand dollars to be invested for his benefit. In any other great nation such a fund would not be necessary as all but ours provide munificiently for their retired citizens . . . who have done the state illustrious service . . ." Charles Hamilton Auction No. 6, Jan. 14, 1965, no. 77. On Jan. 26, 1881, Childs wrote to Hamilton Fish. ". . . We have been thinking that after Congress adjourns we might make up the proposed amount and give it to the General, provided nothing is done for him by Congress. We have 18 names pledged for $5000. each and can readily obtain some more. . . ." ALS, DLC-Hamilton Fish. On Jan. 31, Edwin D. Morgan, Oliver Hoyt, and George Jones, New York City, wrote to John D. Rockefeller concerning his $1,000 subscription to the Presidential Retiring Fund. Printed circular, Rockefeller Archive Center, North Tarrytown, N. Y. On Feb. 2, Rockefeller wrote to Hoyt transmitting his contribution. ALS (press), *ibid.* On March 16, Jones, New York City, wrote to Rockefeller. "In acknowledging your prompt response to the circular with reference to your subscription to the Presidential Retiring Fund for the benefit of General Grant, I have the pleasure to announce that of the entire amount of $250,000 which has been subscribed, $216,000 has been paid in. The outstanding subscriptions are mainly those of a few subscribers for large amounts who are at present out of the country, and who have not yet had time to answer my request for payment. The amount already received has been invested by a committee of subscribers, consisting of Messrs. E. D. Morgan, Oliver Hoyt, and George Jones, and will yield an annual income of $13,160. Should the remainder be invested to equal advantage, the fund will yield over $15,000 a year. The great majority of the subscribers deem it inadvisable to make public the names of those who have contributed to the fund, and about $50,000 has been subscribed on the distinct understanding that the names of the donors shall be kept secret. . . . When it becomes necessary to provide for the ultimate destination of the fund, a meeting of the subscribers will be called." Circular, *ibid*. See *Julia Grant*, p. 323.

Speech

———

[*New York City, Feb. 11, 1881*]

GENTLEMEN: We have assembled here this evening to do honor to a gentleman who we think has contributed more than any other one man, in bringing about the result that we hoped for and all now feel so grateful for, at the last Presidential election. It is not as Republicans, but it is as patriotic citizens of this grand country, that we regard that result as so important. We feel that every man having an interest in his country, whether he be Republican or Democrat, was equally interested, although he might not have known it, with ourselves in the result which was produced. Ex-Senator Dorsey, the secretary of the Republican National Committee, led almost a forlorn hope, when he went to Indiana to conduct the campaign in the October election. To his skill and his executive ability we are largely, if not wholly indebted for the result which was attained there. For his services there, the citizens here assembled and the Republican citizens of New-York have tendered him this dinner. Now, gentlemen, I propose to you the health, long-life and prosperity of Stephen W. Dorsey.

New York Tribune, Feb. 12, 1881. As banquet chairman, USG introduced speakers including Chester A. Arthur, to whom he said "we are indebted both for the use of his name as the candidate for the second highest office in the Government, and also for his great work in the campaign in this State." *Ibid*. USG also introduced Whitelaw Reid, saying "he presumed that gentleman would want to deny that any credit was due to him in whose honor they were assembled, and would claim that the press did it all." *New York Times*, Feb. 12, 1881.

To James A. Garfield

New York City
Feb.y 13th 1881.

MY DEAR GENERAL:

Some time ago I availed myself of your kind permission to name some southern republican worthy and capable of filling, with credit, high public positions. Among others I named Col. Walter Evans, of Louisville, Ky. as a Union Soldier, and republican from the start, a capable man & lawyer, suitable by character, capacity & education for any position: but that I thought that if any position should be tendered him he would prefer it should be in the line of his profession. I do not hesitate to repeat what I then said, and to suggest his name for the position of District Attorney, for the district of Ky.

Very Truly yours
U. S. GRANT

GN. JAS. A. GARFIELD.

ALS, DLC–James A. Garfield.

To Roscoe Conkling

New York City
Feb.y 15th 1881.

MY DEAR SENATOR;

I have enquired of Capt. Miller in regard to the apt. of Wilson and removal of Buckner,[1] of Louisville. He expressed surprise that Murray[2] should approve of the confirmation of W. He says that Murray told him within the last day or two that Buckner ought not to be removed. That he was a true republican and, with his sons, worked in the same direction as the deligates sent to the convention by the state. Buckner may have democrats as guagers & storekeepers, but if he has it is because the department at Washington has been making such appointments over the head of the Collector. Miller says that Murray professed to be with the Majority in the state at the Chicago Convention, but the paper he was, and is, associated with, the Louisville Commercial, was decidedly the other way. The owners of that paper are Harlan, appointed Justice of the Supreme Court, Murray, appointed Governor of Utah, Kelley,[3] Pension Agent, the best paying office in the State, and Wilson, now nominated for Int. Rev. Collector.

Miller is a republican who has always worked for the party and contributed to it. He has never held office no+r sought office. Murray has held office nearly continuously, and may fairly be considered as favoring his business associates for office. On the whole I do not think anything would be lost by keeping Wilson out for the present.

Very Truly yours

U. S. GRANT

HON. ROSCOE CONKLING.

ALS, DLC-Roscoe Conkling.

1. On April 7, 1869, USG nominated James F. Buckner, former Ky. representative and senator, as collector of Internal Revenue, 5th District, Ky. In June, 1880, Buckner and Silas F. Miller, Louisville delegates to the Republican National Convention in Chicago, joined the 306 stalwarts who supported USG. On Jan. 22, 1881, a correspondent reported from Louisville. "The people here believe that if Buckner is removed it will be due to Secretary Sherman, as the Louisville Collector was an uncompromising Grant man, and they, therefore, will present their appeal to him as well. They cite the fact that Mr. W. S. Wilson started out a rampant Grant man, and then went over to Sherman. It is said that his position as manager of the Republican daily paper here entitles him to public pap of some sort. Col. Buckner and his sons are really the backbone and ribs of the Republican organization here, and their abandonment would be to shatter the foothold gained locally in November last, . . ." *New York Times*, Jan. 24, 1881. On Jan. 28, President Rutherford B. Hayes nominated William S. Wilson to replace Buckner. On March 27, 1882, President Chester A. Arthur nominated Lewis Buckner, son of James Buckner, to replace Wilson.

On April 18, 1883, James Buckner wrote to USG. "The bearer of this note my young friend Jno L Sehon of Louisville desires to enter the United States Army. He is a young man of fine moral character, good education, & is in every way worthy of the position he seeks. His family are my immediate neighbors in this City; I therefore speak from intimate knowledge. He believes that you could aid him, and I have cheerfully complied with his request in addressing you this note in his behalf. I have great confidence, in his integrity, courage, & patriotism. He & his friends will appreciate any courtesy extended to him." ALS, DNA, RG 94, ACP 1703 1883. On April 25, USG endorsed this letter. "I know Col. Buckner well, and esteem him highly as an original & consistent Union Man, of high personal character, and one whose recommendations would go as far with me as that of any man. ~~in~~" AES, *ibid.* John L. Sehon was appointed 2nd lt. as of Oct. 10.

2. On Jan. 15, 1880, Hayes had nominated Eli H. Murray, former col., 3rd Ky. Cav., and bvt. brig. gen., as governor, Utah Territory. Murray had served as marshal, Ky., under USG. See telegram to Alphonso Taft, Aug. 31, 1876.

3. See *PUSG*, 19, 263–64.

To John A. Logan

New York City
February 15th 1881

MY DEAR GEN.L LOGAN:

I write to you on the subject of a Cabinet position for Ill. I do not desire to give any recommendation unless it should be to join you in a recommendation. You mentioned in a letter to me the name of Rob.t Lincoln! There is nothing I could do for him, that would help him, that I would not do both for his own sake and for the profound respect and esteem in which I hold the memory of his father. But with no more means than he has it would, in my estimation, be an injury to him to give him an office that would take him from his profession.[1] To give him a position which he could not sustain himself well in might be still more injurious. Has he had the sort of practice that would enable him to prove acceptable as Atty. Gen. If so it would help him in his practice when he retired. If otherwise it would hurt him. You can judge better of his fitness than I can. If you do not want to recommend him for the Cabinet I suggest the name of Storrs to you for Atty. Gen. He is very generally recommended, I see, throughout the state, and I think from outside the state. If you wish to add your influence in his behalf I will gladly join you. If you do not I will not. General Raum's[2] name has been mentioned to me within the last day or two in connection with the Interior or Postoffice Departments. I hold him in very high esteem and if he goes into the Cabinet I will feel that both you and I have a friend *at court.*

I am constantly appealed to in regard to appointments, but will not consent to making any recommendations for important offices without consulting with,—or joining,—the representatives of the states from which the applicant comes, when these representatives are republicans. For my guidance I would be glad to get your views about Ill. representation in the Cabinet & abroad.

Very Truly yours

U. S. GRANT

ALS, DLC-John A. Logan.

    1. On Jan. 10, 1881, Robert T. Lincoln, Chicago, wrote to U.S. Senator John A. Logan of Ill., explaining his reluctance to accept a cabinet appointment. ". . . I am 37 years old, in good health and am in receipt of a professional income which not only enables me to live in comfort but added to my other small resources encourages me to think that by handling my affairs properly I may be able to make reasonable provision for my children—I like my present way of life and think I would not like a political career—If I should go into such a career—I think I would have to make up my mind to look to it for my future—In such a place as you mention my income would be considerably reduced and my expenses largely increased and the outcome of the whole matter in its relation to those dependent on me would be a constant source of anxiety—Such positions are highly honorable of course and are proper objects of ambition but they seem to me to be in the nature of luxuries which can only be properly enjoyed by men of some fortune—I am at the age in life at which I can best do the things I must do, and I am not so old but that I could ten or twelve years later enjoy an honorable political place as well as now & I think it would not be more difficult to obtain then than now if I should be in a position to take it. I think it very likely that you might be able to argue me out of my present notions by keeping my attention to the attractive side of the picture but sitting here coolly I think I am judging correctly for my own case—Feeling as I do now I should be compelled to decline any appointment and I think that inasmuch as my name has been mentioned to Gen Garfield, he ought to know my feelings. I have a letter from Mr Harlan this morning which made it necessary for me to telegraph him to see you and as he ought to know what I have written I enclose this to him asking him to give it to you. I hope that nothing that I have said will make you think that I do not feel under great obligations to you. These obligations I desire to express very warmly." ALS, *ibid.*

    2. A lawyer before the Civil War, Green B. Raum rose from maj., 56th Ill., to brig. gen., served as U.S. Representative (1867–69), and founded the Cairo and Vincennes Railroad Co. In 1876, USG appointed Raum commissioner of Internal Revenue in the wake of the Whiskey Ring scandals. See letter to John A. Logan, May 25, 1880.

Remarks

––––––

[*New York City, Feb. 16, 1881*]

    I am well aware that the sentiment of the entire country is strongly in favor of having a World's Fair held in this City in 1883.

The interest in the fair is general throughout the land, and it is felt that the Exhibition will prove of great value to the country at large. While it will prove of great value to the City of New-York, it will unquestionably advance the business interests of the entire country. The number of people who will be benefited by this Exhibition is almost incalculable. In this City every merchant will gain, while it will be of benefit to all the transportation companies—the elevated roads, the surface roads, the stages, and the hacks. And it should be remembered that the subscriptions to secure the success of this enterprise are not by any means to be regarded as in the shape of donations. My judgment is that the subscribers to the stock will receive back all their money, with a good bonus in addition. In one sense, the Fair may not be looked upon as a good investment. The investors will have to wait for some time before they will receive any returns. But the stockholders in the Centennial Exhibition had to wait four years before getting their money back, while the stockholders in the World's Fair of 1883 are only asked to wait two years and a half, when they will receive their principal back with a large interest. There is no doubt in my mind that when the Exposition is ended the subscribers will receive back, in addition to their subscriptions, a good dividend. I base this statement on the fact that if the receipts at the Centennial had been $1,500,000 more than they were, the stockholders would have recovered all that they paid out. The Fair of 1883 will be held in the midst of a population four times as large as that of Philadelphia in 1876. This population will be within easy reach of the grounds, and the price of passage to and fro will be but from 10 to 25 cents. The Centennial was held in the midst of a great financial panic, which affected not only this country but the entire world. The gate fee of 50 cents was a matter of consideration to a great many people at that time, and the traveling expenses were matters of even greater consideration in many instances. This country is now enjoying an era of unprecedented prosperity, and there is every prospect that this prosperity will continue far beyond 1883. The cost of reaching the Fair and the entrance fee will be but little to our people, compared to what it was in 1876, because now they have the money to spend, which they did not have during the Centennial. So that it looks reasonable to suppose that at least four times as many people will visit the Fair of 1883 as went to the Fair in Philadelphia. In addition to this, the good times have spread abroad, and more people living in foreign countries feel better able to travel now than there did in 1876. Our country has grown since then, and is a more desirable place to visit, and thousands will come to us from the Old World in 1883 who did not come to Philadelphia. In view of all these facts, I see no reason why the World's Fair of 1883 should not prove a grand success.

New York Times, Feb. 17, 1881. USG spoke from the chair at a meeting of the New York City World's Fair Commission. Planning for an international exhibition to commemorate the centennial of the Treaty of Paris (1783) began in 1878. In April, 1880, Congress passed a bill incorporating a commission to conduct the fair. Throughout, public opposition to a Central Park site divided organizers. See *New York Times*, May 2, 1879, Jan. 15, April 21, Nov. 19, 1880; *CR*, 46-2, 1922–24, 1955–57, 1989, 2533–37, 2545; *U.S. Statutes at Large*, XXI, 77–81.

On Jan. 13, 1881, John P. Newman, committee on organization, reported to the World's Fair Commission. "Last evening, after the adjournment of the commission, I saw General Grant and made an engagement by which he was to meet the committee at 9.30 this morning. The full committee, . . . were there, and the entire plan was unfolded to General Grant, though I confess it was a work of supererogation, for we found him very well informed. . . . Then about the site—he asked about the facilities for getting there, and for the accommodation of the people when they got there. He asked just such questions as the Executive Committee have been working at from the start, and then he said he would be happy to serve his fellow-citizens by serving as the head of the commission. He said he would be engaged for two or three months immediately to come, but after that would be at liberty to perform all the duties assigned him. . . ." *New York World*, Jan. 14, 1881. On Jan. 14, USG addressed the commissioners. "I had said to some of your members yesterday that with the understanding I had of the arrangement I would accept if I was elected, and that determination I still hold. I shall not be able to give to the duties of the position at present all of the attention I should wish, but later on will give it all possible or necessary care. I believe that you must have a certain amount of money before you can begin operations and do any corporate act. Am I right? . . . And until that is done you incur no liability and confine your work entirely to the work of securing subscriptions. I think there will be no trouble in securing the $1,000,000 necessary to begin operations and the $4,000,000 to be spent on the completion of the work of the commission. . . . I shall be in Albany next Tuesday, so I shall not be able to meet with you, but do not let my absence or my presence interfere with any work that you may have in hand. The sooner we can get to work the better." *Ibid.*, Jan. 15, 1881.

On Jan. 25, U.S. Senator Roscoe Conkling of N. Y. wrote to USG. "Mr Mullett wants and needs a position in the line of his profession. Like some of the rest of us he has been abused an belabored overmuch, and I feel very kindly toward him, & deem him a man of talent & integrity. He thinks as architect of the Worlds Fair, he could do good service, and asks me to invoke your aid and approval. I do so gladly, knowing that he has been your friend and mine. Please receive and consider his wish." ALS, USG 3.

On Feb. 5, USG presided over a banquet in his honor at Delmonico's, held to raise money for the fair. On Feb. 16, USG subscribed $1,000 for 100 shares. See *New York Times*, Feb. 6, 17, 1881.

On Feb. 23, USG presided over a meeting of the World's Fair Commission. "Before we proceed to any regular business I have a few remarks to make. When I was consulted and asked to take the presidency of this commission I made a statement that I would not be able to pay much attention to its business during the year. I intend to be absent from the city most of the time, and the probability is that I may be able to attend but one meeting more. In consultation with gentlemen outside I see great cause of apprehension as to the raising of the necessary funds. Some of the gentlemen object to the site, while some object to the manner in which the commission is conducted, and the tone is generally discouraging in the matter. There ought to be some strong movement started to bring the work of the commission before the people of the city, although at present I am not ready to make any suggestion. I think it would be well to make another effort to get the Park for the Exposition. It would be handier, and the State and city would no doubt subscribe. Philadelphia subscribed $2,500,000 for its Fair and New York City could afford to make a much larger subscription. Another objection, I find, is that the people say that when they subscribe to anything of the sort they want to know the finance committee, and they wish to elect their own committee. I believe it is a law that they have the right to do this. The question is, Would it not be better that the people of New York be informed that those who take stock can vote according to th[e] amount of that stock?" *New York World*, Feb. 24, 1881.

On Feb. 26, 1881, a reporter interviewed USG at 34 New Street. "On the second floor of that number is the office of Honoré & Grant, and there the General visits his sons several times a week while staying in New York." *New York Herald*, Feb. 27, 1881. USG predicted that the fair would fail if held at Inwood, the northernmost neighborhood on Manhattan Island. "It is as good as any other site except for the horse railways, and the connections are excellent for trains from New Haven, by way of Harlem, and for trains arriving at Jersey City and transferring their passengers to ferryboats to run to Inwood. The railways could make money by taking the whole stock of the World's Fair for the sake of the business it will create for them. They could better afford to do it than to have the Fair fail. If the Exhibition is to be held at Inwood they will need to subscribe more freely. What is needed just now is to arouse the people to enthusiasm concerning the World's Fair. . . . By locating it where it will be more easily accessible, and where it will contribute some permanent structure as an ornament for New York. . . . Our plan is to improve, not to injure, Central Park. When the people fully understand what we propose they will be enthusiastic in support of our plan. . . . It does not follow that Central Park must ever be thrown open for other exhibitions because it is used for the great World's Fair, and then chiefly for the sake of the permanent buildings to be erected. A safe exception may be made in 1883." As for permanent buildings, "there should be two, and perhaps three. . . . The Museum of Natural History building, in Ma[n]hattan square, would be completed according to the original plan of the architect, making one of the chief structures of the Fair. The Metropolitan Museum of Art building, in Central Park, would also be completed, making a structure of about equal capacity, and the promise of the completion of these two buildings would be sufficient to create much enthusiasm throughout the city in behalf of the Fair. Then if the sixty acres of the Park known as the North Meadows be taken it is possible another permanent building might be erected there. . . . Without any injury that could not be repaired by one season's growth. In fact, there is a misapprehension as to the amount of injury involved in the use of the Park we desire. When the people understand our plan they will not be prejudiced against it. The North Meadows and the Metropolitan Museum of Art grounds can be used without the least injury to the nearly eight hundred acres of the Park which remain. Even the ground we occupy will be disturbed little more than will be necessary whenever the Metropolitan Museum of Art building is completed and a large structure is erected in the North Meadows." Planners would minimize disruption "[b]y the construction of enclosures and of a temporary railway to connect them. . . . If we used the North Meadows, two in Central Park and one for Manhattan square. It would be necessary to enclose the grounds of the Metropolitan Museum of Art, and also the North Meadows. A high fence, like that enclosing the part of Fairmount Park used for the Centennial, would also surround Manhattan square." The temporary railway "would, pro[b]ably, run through the Eighty-fifth street transverse road, connecting the three enclosures and making the passage from one department of the Fair to another as convenient as it was at the Centennial. . . . The people could approach the Fair by trains on the east side as well as on the west, and after spending an hour or two in the Metropolitan Museum department could take a train across to either of the other sections without putting a foot in Central Park outside of the enclosures. . . . All that is done must be done soon. The next few weeks will determine whether an international exhibition is to be held in New York in 1883. A change in the feeling of the people must take place soon or the project must be abandoned. When I was chosen president of the commission I said that I could give little attention to its work for several months on account of my expected absence, but that next year I might be able to do more. I relied upon others to raise the funds and organize the work. If the people who wish the fair to be held at Inwood will come forward and subscribe for the stock let them do it now. If they will not, then something must be done to interest the people at large, so that they will subscribe. Whatever is done needs to be done at once. . . . I have no doubt Chicago could raise the money for this Fair within forty-eight hours. . . . They ought to have it if they wish it, provided New York is willing to give it up. But if the inhabitants of Manhattan Island can be made to interest themselves in it as they ought they will soon raise the money and go forward with the work themselves. . . . Coney Island would be accessible and healthful for visitors, but there is no prospect of establishing the Fair there. Manhattan square and Central Park contain the ground best adapted for such an exhibition. There is every prospect of a greater exhibition than the world has yet seen if New York is as enterprising as she is reputed to be. In 1876 the country was suffering from a recent panic, and there are now five who feel able to make a journey to attend an international exhibition when there was one at the time of the Centennial. The World's Fair will be at none too early a date if held in 1883, and I venture the prediction that, if as successful as it may easily be made, it will be followed by another international exhibition in some part of the world within the next six years. Had the Centennial been managed as economically as experience will enable us to manage the World's Fair of 1883 it would have paid back every dollar to its subscribers. If the people of New York will take all the stock of the World's Fair within the next month I believe the investment will prove as good as an equal sum placed at six per cent compound interest for three years. With four times as many people in its vicinity as the Centennial had, and with the advantage of a condition of prosperity in striking contrast with the distress of the country in 1876, the World's Fair of 1883, properly conducted, will undoubtedly pay a handsome profit to its stockholders. Besides, the value of such an exhibition in extending interstate and international commerce cannot be overestimated. Let the citizens of New York complete the first million dollars of subscriptions and then elect a finance committee to manage the money for them, selecting men in whom they will feel perfect confidence." *Ibid.*

On March 2, USG chaired a meeting of the executive committee. "This is probably the last meeting of the committee over which I shall be able to preside this Spring. At our last meeting a committee was appointed to ascertain if the site of the Fair could not be changed to Central Park, or, to put it more correctly, to ascertain if any portion of Central Park could be obtained, provided it was found desirable to make a change in the site. I do not know whether that committee is ready to report or not. I do not regard the location of the Fair as of so much importance as the matter of securing the subscriptions of the people. The Fair can be made a great success, in my judgment, if the money can be raised to make it so. If the money cannot be raised, the enterprise will, of necessity, be a failure. The funds necessary to enable you to organize can be secured as readily in my absence as they could be if I were here with you. I shall probably be absent for several months. I shall spend the Summer at Long Branch, where I can be called on at any time, should my presence at your meetings be necessary; but during the months of March and April, and the first half of May, I shall probably be absent from the country." *New York Times*, March 3, 1881. Following USG's remarks, Frederick L. Talcott responded that "it would be fruitless to again apply to the Commissioners for the use of the Central Park. The Park is in a Central location, it is true, but that is really the only recommendation that it has for a site. How could we transport the machinery and heavy freight to the Park, supposing we could secure the ground? We all know how long it took to move the obelisk to the ground selected for it, and that should warn us against taking the Park as a site, if it were offered to us freely. . . ." *Ibid.*

On March 12, 1881, USG spoke to a reporter. "Subscriptions have failed to come in as it was anticipated that they would, and time is getting too short to admit of further delay on uncertainties. If the fair is to be held the buildings should be ready for exhibits, especially those from distant countries, within two years. There is little time enough left for the accomplishment of the actual work now and it would be useless to attempt to go on unless we can begin very soon. I have devoted much more time to the matter than I expected or promised to when I accepted the presidency of the commission, partly because my departure from the country has been delayed a month longer than I expected and partly because I wanted to do what I could to prevent a failure of the scheme." Asked how much of the initial $1,000,000 had been subscribed, USG replied. "I do not know the exact figures, but considerably less than half that amount, and part of what has been subscribed is conditional on the holding of the fair at Inwood Park. But if another site were chosen, other subscribers, whose property would be benefited, would take the place of these. A good many prominent men will not subscribe because Inwood has been chosen, and others again will not subscribe because the value of somebody's private property will be enhanced by the fair being held near it or on it. This is one of the strongest drawbacks, and one that can be overcome only by the selection of Central Park as the site. That is public property, and the only objection to its use is the public sentiment that it should not be used for such a purpose. That, however, I think is a mistake, and a very grave mistake if it should, as appears probable, prevent the fair from being held in New York. The fair grounds could occupy the necessary space on the west side of the Park entirely fenced in from the rest of the Park without interfering with any of the walks or drives. The entrances for everything, except persons, could be on Eighth avenue, so that the Park would be in no way despoiled or turned from its usual purposes. I confess that I cannot understand the universal opposition to such a use of the Park, especially as it closes the door to subscriptions which would soon place the fair on a solid financial basis. . . . Judging from the receipts at the Centennial, I have no doubt subscribers would get their money back with a good interest. It was a period of severe depression then, so that thousands who lived within a few miles of the Centennial grounds felt hardly able to bear the loss of a day's time, or the expense of street-car fare and admission. The New York World's Fair will be held after several years of unusual prosperity, and in the centre of a population four times as great as Philadelphia's. Twice as many persons will then be able to come from a distance as in 1876, and increased business will bring proportionately as many more. I think it would be safe to say that the receipts of the fair will be four times as great as those of the Centennial. But allowing that they are only twice as great, of which there can be no doubt, subscribers would be certain of a good profit on their investment. But everybody seems [t]o hold back. The railroad, express and steamboat companies, the local transportation companies, hotels and boarding-houses—at least most of them—fail to appreciate the benefits they would receive aside from the interest on money subscribed. Several large subscriptions have been made, conditional upon a total of $4,000,000. This represents about what the necessary buildings will cost and it will be useless to begin operations with less. I presume, however, if the first $1,000,000 is not obtained by Wednesday [*March 16*] the project will be abandoned. I do not know that I can attend Wednesday's meeting, as I shall leave the city a week from next Monday and my time will be very much occupied with preparations for my journey to Mexico. I should advise a postponement until 1884. That is soon enough, anyway. But my impression is that the scheme will be given up if the Finance Committee cannot report $1,000,000 in hand by Wednesday." Asked if he would continue to lead the fair if it moved to Chicago, USG responded: "No; my interests are all here in New York or in enterprises which centre here. My two sons in civil life are here and it is convenient to be near them. Then, I am much interested in the development of the Mexican railways and in the Nicaragua canal project, although I have not a dollar at stake in any of them, nor have I any actual money interests to keep me in New York. The Mexican railways and the isthmus canal I look upon as matters of great national moment. I have been interested in their advancement and still am. After the Tehuantepec and Panama canal schemes have failed, as they surely will, the Nicaragua canal route will receive attention. The Tehuantepec route, although its situation further north than the others would greatly enhance its value, is entirely impracticable on account of the elevation that would have to be reached and the very deep cuts or ship-tunnels that would have to be constructed, which would make its expense enormous, and especially because during the dry season there would be no means of supplying the upper six or eight canal levels with water. If only one or two levels were left dry the water could be pumped up, but not for six or eight. As to M. de Lesseps's scheme, I have no doubt that every dollar invested in it will be absolutely sunk. The thing is impossible and the plan proposed simply preposterous. Sixty million dollars, I hear, have been subscribed and $12,000,000 paid in. If the canal is completed it will not cost less than $1,000,000,000. The Chagres River when in flood is as large a body of water as the Ohio at flood, and yet he proposes to stop this river by a dam 140 feet high, only letting a little water out into a ditch which is to run along by the side of the canal. The floods of the Chagres cover the whole valley from mountain to mountain to a height of twelve feet above the top of the banks of the proposed canal. The idea of stopping such a flood with a dam and backing the water up to let it evaporate is absurd. The result would be [*t*]hat half the length of the canal would be broken or washed completely away every year in the wet season and rebuilt at a cost of millions during the dry season, only to be destroyed again. The only feasible route for a canal across from the Atlantic to the Pacific is by the Nicaragua route. I have been all over the routes myself, besides having examined all the reports made regarding each of them carefully, and that is my firm conviction." *New York World*, March 13, 1881.

On March 16, amid rumors that he might resign as president, USG told a reporter. "I did not attend the meeting of the committee to-day and have not learned what took place there. I shall not decide upon any action until I am informed of to-day's proceedings. By to-morrow I shall probably have made up my mind as to the action I shall take. To have a successful fair in New York in 1883 we should have the required amount of subscription already in and let out the contracts at once. . . ." *New York Herald*, March 17, 1881.

On March 17, USG granted an interview. "I wish the Fair every success, but I find I cannot give it my personal attention, and therefore I intend making way for somebody who can give it the attention which it requires in order to make it successful. Before going away next week I will give the Commissioners an opportunity to fill my place as soon as they can find a suitable person." *New York Times*, March 18, 1881. See also *New York Herald*, March 18, 1881; letter to World's Fair Commission, March 22, 1881.

To James A. Garfield

New York City
Feb.y 18th 1881.

MY DEAR GENERAL GARFIELD:

You were kind enough in one of your letters to say that you would be glad to take advantage of my experience from travels abroad, and in another that you would be pleased to accommodate me in the matter of the appointment of a Minister to Mexico. Now I do not intend to tax your kindness by demanding, nor even by asking, anything. But I will say a few words in regard to Eastern matters, and also in regard to Mexico, for your consideration, and for such action as you may deem it advisable to take thereafter. In the first place my travels in the East convinced me that there was a large opening in that direction for an extension of our commerce; that while we purchased more of the surplus of the Eastern countries than the balance of the world probably, and more than three fourths of the exports from China & Japan, we do not sell to those countries more than two per cent of their imports. All those countries except India would prefer purchasing from us to going elswhere. This is because as a Nation, we treat these peoples, at their own homes, as if they had "rights which we were bound to respect." Other nNations, as a rule, do not treat them so, and unfortunately for us the majority of our representatives follow the example of most of the Europeans in their conduct towards the citizens of the East. The Chinese particularly,—and all other Eastern peoples to a limited extent,— are treated upon their own soil about as the Chinese are treated by the worst elements of society in our Western country. Under our extra territorial treaties, and with our Consular Courts—or rather the European Courts, and ours following their examples instead of leading—the natives find no encouragement to complain.—I would like to see this thing changed so far as we can do it. The Executive alone can not do all that is necessary to increase our trade in that direction to what it should be, but he can do much, and can, I think, cure the abuses by our citizens to a great extent. This can be effected by good appointments, with full instructions before they start out, and with instructions to our Navy in those waters to report every violation of these instructions. Now I did not see all our Consuls abroad, but I did many of them, and feel that I can answer for the whole. So far as China & Japan are concerned we have but four who ought to be allowed to remain. Gen. Stahl,[1] in Japan, is a good representative I believe. In China Mosby, O. N. Denney,[2] Consul General, Mangum[3] and Holcomb,[4] Sec. of Legation, are good representatives. Judge Bingham, in Japan, is an admirable representative so far as his physical condition will allow him to be. He is honest, patriotic, a thorough believer in his own country and fully respects the rights of the people of the country where he is. He is much respected by them, more than any any other rep Minister in Japan. But he can not make his influence effective like as he could if he was younger and could go about more. He is so infinitely more a credit to his own country than the most of the representatives there are to theirs however that he should never be removed against his consent, except to promote him. Now what I was going to suggest in this connection—and it is what I would do if I was placed where you are—is this; I would promote Judge Bingham to the Austrian

Mission, and I would appoint John Russell Young Minister to Japan. We have had no abler or more creditable Minister in Austria than Judge Bingham would make. Young would have advantages in Japan—if my notions are right—that no other man could have. He was with me in my travels, and was received by courts and the people, as a part of my suit, as no foreigners were ever received before. He knows all of my views, formed on the spot, of present abuses, and of necessary reforms. He would not only make an effective Minister so far as our relations with Japan are concerned, but his influence would be felt all over the East. The United States has a grand mission in the East and Mr. Young is the best equipped man in America to commence it. I have no interest in this matter except as a citizen feeling the greatest interest in my country. The appointment would be a pecuniary sacrifice to Mr. Young. One other change in Japan I would also suggest. It is the appointment of Edward H. House,[5] of Mass. as Consul General. Mr. House has lived for ten years in Japan. He speaks the language of the country. He is deeply interested in the welfare of those good people, and enjoys their confidence—including that of the Micado & Court—beyond any other foreigner there. He would not submit to the dictation of European representatives for a moment. He is an able man and an able writer, and would keep the Minister, and the Department at Washington, better posted in regard to all Easter matters than any other man could. His appointment would be a great stroke of policy because it would be one that would justify itself from the start. The present Consul General[6] should not be allowed to remain there a moment longer than can be helped. I will not give the reasons, but almost any American who has visited that country can. I am aware that he has an influence at home that may embarrass you in removing him. But if he must have a public position I would transfer him to Europe or Egypt.

Now in regard to the Mexican Mission. I am, as you know, deeply interested in the developement of that country, and for a twofold reason. I want to see our commerce increased in every legitimate way, and then I am deeply interested in the success of the republican form of Government. What I think of the resources of Mexico, the capacity of her people under kind treatment & judicious direction, and the advantages to us by her development it is not necessary for me to state here. I have said enough on this subject, which has gone into print, and which you have probably seen, to make it unnecessary.

The present U. S. Minister to Mexico is a very able man, one of the best lawyers in the south, and I would not ask his removal unless he should prove an obstruction to American influe[nce] in Mexico. This I do not believe possible. If however Judge Billings[7] should be rejected for the Circuit Judgeship I do not know a man in the whole south who could take his place better than Judge Morgan,[8] our Minister to Mexico. I would not suggest this however if I though[t] you had Judge Settle, of Fla. in contemplation.

Very Truly yours
U. S. GRANT

ALS, DLC-James A. Garfield. See letter to Chester A. Arthur, Dec. 5, 1881.

1. See letter to Julius Stahel, May 18, 1879.
2. See letter to Adolph E. Borie, June 6, 1879.
3. Willie P. Mangum, consul, Tientsin, died in late Feb., 1881. Mangum had been consul, Nagasaki, when USG visited Japan.
4. On Aug. 8, 1876, USG had nominated Chester Holcombe as secretary of legation and interpreter, Peking.
5. A former *New York Tribune* and *New York Herald* reporter, Edward H. House edited the *Tokio Times* at the time of USG's visit to Japan. In Sept., 1880, House and his adopted daughter, Aoki Koto, were guests of USG and Julia Dent Grant at Galena. See letter to John Russell Young, Nov. 28, 1882; *Galena Gazette*, Sept. 3, 1880; James L. Huffman, *A Yankee in Meiji Japan: The Crusading Journalist Edward H. House* (Lanham, Md., 2003), pp. 144–45, 166–71.
6. Thomas Van Buren continued as consul gen. See *PUSG*, 24, 150–57.
7. On Jan. 24, 1881, President Rutherford B. Hayes nominated Edward C. Billings as judge, 5th Circuit; the Senate took no action. See *PUSG*, 26, 58–59.
8. On Jan. 19, 1880, Hayes had nominated Philip H. Morgan as minister to Mexico. See *ibid.*, pp. 59–60.

To James A. Garfield

Dated New York Feb 19 *1881*

To GEN J A GARFIELD

The country is now in the midst of a prosperity unprecedented in all past history. It benefits labor more than capital by the new enterprises stimulated & the full employment of those already established. In my judgement the approval of the funding bill in its present shape will stop for the present all this & lead to the utter ruin of thousands of business people & enterprises I join in the belief that every effort should be made to prevent the bill becoming a law

U. S. GRANT

Telegram received, DLC–James A. Garfield. On Feb. 18, 1881, the Senate approved and sent back to the House of Representatives, with minor amendments, a bill to refund the national debt by issuing new three percent bonds in place of matured five and six percent bonds. On Feb. 19, George S. Coe, president, American Exchange Bank, New York City, wrote to [Alexander Mitchell], Milwaukee financier. "The subject of 3 pr. Ct. funding bill is stirring Wall St. to-day. With the fact staring them in the face that Banks cannot deposit lawful money & withdraw their Bonds from the department after this bill becomes law, several of our Banks have done it to-day, say 2 millions dollars. More of them will do so when they *see it*—We have telegraphed our friend T. P. Handy of Cleveland to go to Mentor and urge the 'elected,' to say to Mr Presidt Hayes that the new administration should not be embarrassed by this impracticable bill—I have got General Grant also to telegraph Garfield as follows . . . These telegrams will go to the President, without doubt. If some person could see him and show the ruinous effect of supplanting the Nat. Banking system, which will almost certainly follow the refusal of Banks to take the new bonds, it may lead to a Veto—and then an extra session of new Congress, where we are safer . . ." ALS, WHi. On Feb. 15, William G. Deshler, president, National Exchange Bank, Columbus, Ohio, had written to Mitchell. ". . . I wrote Coe, that as Genl Grant, was going into Banking in N. Y. with the Newcomb, Louisville party, that Grants, name or influence should be gotten—It could be, I am sure, if on to work at properly . . ." ALS, *ibid.* On March 3, President Rutherford B. Hayes vetoed the refunding bill. See Memorandum, [*Feb., 1881*]; *John Sherman's Recollections of Forty Years* . . . (Chicago, 1895), II, 796–801.

To Roscoe Conkling

New York City
Feb.y 20th 1881.

DEAR SENATOR:

Mr. E. F. Shepard,[1] who has been nominated for Dist. Atty. in place of Woodford asks me to write you a letter asking for his confirmation. I do not know what your notions are about the District Attyornyship, and I have none especially, except to keep out such men as Forster.[2] If Woodford is not to be retained I suppose Shepard is as good as any one els. He proposes to be,—and I think he is—a strong friend and admirer of yours, and adheres to his party even if he is disappointed. But you know much more of his fitness for the place than I do.

> Very Truly yours
> U. S. GRANT

HON. ROSCOE CONKLING U. S. SENATE

ALS, DLC-Roscoe Conkling.

1. Born in 1833 in N. Y., Elliott F. Shepard founded the state bar and was its first president. On Feb. 18, 1881, President Rutherford B. Hayes nominated Shepard as U.S. attorney, Southern District, N. Y. On Feb. 24, a correspondent reported from Washington, D. C., on efforts to collect tax from railroads owned by William H. Vanderbilt, Shepard's father-in-law. U.S. Representative James B. Belford of Colo. questioned placing "the Government's interests in this railway litigation in the hands of the relatives and friends of the defendants." *New York Times*, Feb. 25, 1881. Stewart L. Woodford remained U.S. attorney.

2. Born in 1838 in Mass., George H. Forster graduated Harvard College, moved to New York City, practiced law, and served in the state assembly. In 1880, Forster joined N. Y. Republicans who opposed USG's nomination at the Chicago convention. On Jan. 28, 1881, Hayes nominated Forster as U.S. attorney to replace Woodford. On the same day, a correspondent reported from Washington, D. C. "Mr. Conkling makes no secret of his opposition to the nomination, and will undoubtedly use every effort to defeat Mr. Forster's confirmation." *New York Times*, Jan. 29, 1881. On Feb. 17, Hayes withdrew this nomination.

To John A. J. Creswell

> New York City
> Feb.y 20th 1881

MY DEAR EX. P. M. G.

I will not be in Washington at the Inauguration, probably not again during the Winter or Spring. My expectation now is to go to Mexico in the next few weeks.

I spoke to the President of the new bank to be started here in relation to making your bank their Washington Agt. or correspondent. I will place the matter before the Cashier, and Directors, the first meeting we have. But the funding bill, if it becomes a law as it left the Senate, may stop new banks, and drive most of the old ones out of existance.

With kind regards of Mrs Grant & myself to Mrs. Creswell,

Very Truly yours

U. S. GRANT

ALS (facsimile), USGA.

On Feb. 25, 1881, USG, New York City, wrote to President Rutherford B. Hayes. "I am in receipt of your very kind note of the 23d, inviting Mrs. Grant & I to meet Gen. & Mrs. Garfield at dinner at the Executive Mansion, on the 3d of March. It would afford both of us great pleasure to be present on that occasion, and me especial pleasure to meet Gen. Garfield before he enters upon the arduous duties before him; but I have written declining all invitations to the Inauguration Ball & other ceremonies at that time." ALS, OFH.

Endorsement

——————

To GEN. J. A. LOGAN

Mr. Loraine is a man of good ability, has been in good circumstances until property ceased to have value in Galena, and would make a good territorial Governor. He has always been true to the republican party, and deserves well at its hands. If you can aid him in his aspirations in this you have my hearty support.

U. S. GRANT

FEB.Y 20TH 1881.

AES, DNA, RG 48, Appointment Papers, Wyoming Territory. Born in 1812 in Pa., John Lorrain settled in Galena in 1838, opened a wholesale grocery, and purchased the gas works in 1859. On Jan. 13, 1881, Elihu B. Washburne, Chicago, wrote to President-elect James A. Garfield recommending Lorrain for a territorial governorship. ALS, *ibid*. Related papers are *ibid*. No appointment followed.

To Dexter N. Kasson

——————

New York City

Feb.y 27th 1881.

CAPT. D. A. KASSON;

DEAR CAPT.

The day your lettre of the 19th inst. come to hand I had received one, in your behalf, from Gen. Rowley, and had endorsed it and forwarded to Senator Carpenter, hoping he might help you in your effort to obtain the Pension Agency. Poor man I had no idea he was then so near his end.[1] I had met him only a week or ten days before, and he and his family were then very confidant of his speedy recovery. I hope you may be successful in gaining the office you seek. Soldiers who lost their capacity for active work by their services in the field have a special claim upon the government the fought for, and there is a further special fitness in disabled soldiers paying out the Pensions to their disabled comrades.

You may use this lettre, or refer to me, or both, in your behalf.

Very Truly yours

U. S. GRANT

ALS, WHi. On Jan. 25, 1881, Edwin E. Bryant, Wis. AG, wrote to USG. "May I be permitted to recommend to your kind offices my friend and your friend, Capt. D. N. Kasson of Milwaukee, He desires the appointment of Pension Agent at Milwaukee for which he is every way qualified. He is a disabled Soldier with a noble record, and is one of the best known and most highly esteemed of Wisconsin's Veterans. Any good word you can speak for him will gratify a large number of Wisconsin Soldiers whose love for you increases with their years, and I am one of them." ALS, *ibid.* On Jan. 27, George E. Bryant, Madison, wrote to USG on the same subject. ALS, *ibid.* On Feb. 15, Colwort K. Pier, Fond du Lac, wrote to USG. "If any thing I can say or do will tend to secure the appointment of Capt D. N. Kasson of Milwaukee as Pension Agent, *that* is just what I want to say and do. In my opinion the reasons why he *should* be appointed are so numerous and so good, they can never *all* be told; and any (professed) reasons, why he should *not* be are either insufficient or false. If the writer knew how to make these expressions more earnest or stronger, they would be so made—in fullest faith such appointment when made secures to the government not only a most worthy and efficient officer, but as well the heartfelt approval of the ex-soldiers living, and the heirs of those not living, throughout the entire district." ALS, *ibid.* On Feb. 17, John H. Rountree, Platteville, wrote to USG. "Our mutual friend Captain D. N. Kassan, a wounded crippled Soldier, is well qualified to fill the office of Pension agent at Milwaukee and for that District, and is in Every way deserving of the office and I ask you as a special favor to recommend him to the incoming President, Genl. Garfield for appointment, and thereby confer a favor on me and very many of your friends" ALS, *ibid.* On Feb. 26, USG endorsed this letter. "I fully concur in recommending Capt. Kasson for the Pension Agency. It looks to me specially fitting that disabled soldiers should be selected to fill this office." AES, *ibid.* See letters to Dexter N. Kasson, June 21, 1880, Sept. 27, 1881.

1. U.S. Senator Matthew H. Carpenter of Wis. died on Feb. 24.

To Edward F. Beale

New York City
Feb.y 28th 1881.

My Dear General Beale:

Your letter of the 21st come duly to hand. From the last paragraph I expected you would be here before this, so did not answer. The packages left at your house I imagine are of little or no importance. If they are not in your way you may leave them there until I call for them.—Mrs. Grant has no photographs of her extant. I have some and send two as you request.

I have not met Keene[1] since you were here. The matter he spoke of has fallen through as a combined movement. I suppose there are a number of parties who are purchasing Mexican bonds with the expectation that they will become valuable.

Very Truly yours
U. S. Grant

ALS, DLC-Decatur House Papers.

1. James R. Keene had parlayed a successful prospecting stake into a career as a speculator, first in San Francisco and later on Wall Street. See *New York Times*, Dec. 30, 1883, Jan. 3, 1913.

To John A. Logan

New York City
Feb.y 28th 1881.

My Dear General:

In reply to your letter of some days since I have to repeat what I believe I have said to you before: that is that I would only be too glad to join you in any thing you would like to do for Robt. Lincoln both on account of his father and on his own. Your friends in Ill. are my friends and I will not ask any thing for any one there independent of you. I will join you in any recommendation from the state you choose to make for Cabinet or other high position if you ask it. I am just in receipt o[f] a letter from Littler.[1] He wants to be Solicitor of the Treasury. You know Littler much better than I do. I think him a first class man, far better fitted to be Sec. of the Treasury thatn the man whose name has been most associated with that office until within the last ten days.[2] He of course would be high up in standard for the place of solicitor.

I do not want to be in Washington at the time of the Inauguration atall; and then if I was there I would be obliged to dine at the White House on the 3d, to meet Garfield and all of Hayes Cabinet. I should like very much to meet Garfield & his wife, but I have no fancy for hobnobing with John Sherman or Schurts. But I respect the latter the most. I have not heard of his punishing innocent people because of their friendship for me.[3] I will come down for three or four days however about to-morrow week. Do not mention this to any one because if it is know I will be overcome by people who want me to help them with the President.

Very Truly yours
U. S. GRANT

GN. J. A. LOGAN, U. S. SENATE.

ALS, DLC-John A. Logan. See letter to John A. Logan, Feb. 15, 1881.

1. David T. Littler, Springfield lawyer and former collector of Internal Revenue, was a delegate to the 1880 Republican National Convention in Chicago and represented Ill. on the 1883 World's Fair Commission. Kenneth Rayner continued as solicitor of the treasury.

2. U.S. Senator William B. Allison of Iowa, an advocate of silver-backed currency, headed the list of rumored candidates for secretary of the treasury. When Allison ultimately declined, President James A. Garfield nominated William Windom. See Harry James Brown and Frederick D. Williams, eds., *The Diary of James A. Garfield* (East Lansing, Mich., 1967–81), IV, 515–16, 526, 550–53; *New York Times*, Jan. 27, Feb. 16, 28, 1881.

3. For Secretary of the Treasury John Sherman's alleged attempts to punish USG's supporters after the Chicago convention, see *New York Times*, June 17, July 3, 6, Dec. 10, 1880.

Memorandum

New York, [Feb.] *188*[*1*]

My objection to the present funding bills is that it is in the nature of a forced loan. It not only compells banks now existing to substitute three per cent bonds in place of those they now hold, but it practically forces them to continue business whether they can afford to or not by compelling them to return their own bills to withdraw their securities. If the law allowed a sufficient time for the banks to elect whether they would continue or not the bill would be releived of ~~much of its~~ its most objectionable feature, but even then it would be a blow at one branch of the business of the country which ~~may~~ might be attended with disastrous results to ~~the business of the country~~ all others where capitol is required.

It seems to me there is danger that the first effect of the present bill will be to cause a contraction of the currency to a dangerous extent by the effort National banks will make to withdraw their securities while they can, and an expansion afterwards by the government purchase of bonds with. the gold in the Treasury, and the issue of the authorized 300.000.000 dollars of three per ct. certificates. By the loss of gold from the Treasure the end may be to reduce the value of currency to the silver standard, enhance prices of all articles of consumption & wear by the difference between the intrinsic value of the gold & silver dollar in the markets of the world, and thus make the labor of the country the greatest sufferers. This in the end might produce labor strikes all over the country, entailing a National loss.

AD, ICarbS. Written on stationery of "Honoré & Grant." See telegram to James A. Garfield, Feb. 19, 1881.

Article

———

The Nicaragua Canal.

The construction of a ship-canal across the isthmus which connects North and South America has attracted the attention of governments, engineers, and capitalists, in this country and in Europe, for considerably more than half a century. The allusions to the possibility and importance of such a work made by travelers and scientists, almost from the time when America was discovered down to the day when practical investigations were commenced by the government of the United States, had left a deep impression on the public mind; and the rapid growth of the American Republic in population and wealth, the increasing commerce between the Atlantic and Pacific oceans, the long, tedious, and dangerous passage from shore to shore around Cape Horn, all tended to strengthen this impression, and to establish the conviction that the interest of the American people in the commerce of the world required a water communication, from sea to sea, across the Isthmus of Darien. It is now more than fifty years since this project first received serious consideration on this continent. Under the administration of Mr. Adams, in 1825, correspondence and negotiations commenced, which have continued up to the present time. Turning from one government to another for aid in carrying out the scheme, the people of Central America soon arrived at the conclusion that they must look to the United States for the completion of the work, and that to them especially, on account of location and institutions, belonged the right to unite with that state through whose territory the canal might run, in its construction and control. In 1830, in 1831, in 1835, in 1837, in 1839, in 1844, in 1846, in 1849, in 1858, plans were proposed to the governments of the United States, England, and France for the commencement of the work, until the breaking out of the civil war in this country presented a more important topic for consideration, and overshadowed all questions relating solely to industrial development and international commerce, and ended in results which have given new and vast interest and importance to every enterprise which can add power to the republic and advance the prosperity of its people. Stepping at once into the front rank among the powerful nations of the earth, the United States has entered, as it were spontaneously, upon a career of development almost unparalleled in the history of the world. By the growth of States along the Pacific coast, by the erection of trans-continental lines of railway, by the occupation of new lands, by the opening of new mines, by increasing mechanical and manufacturing enterprises, by the introduction of her products on an amazing scale into the commerce of the world, by her devotion to a system of finance which requires incessant industry among all classes of the people, and the cheapest possible means of intercourse and transportation, the United States has given new and deeper importance to every method by which industry can be advanced and commerce can be promoted. It is during this short period that the value of even the most expensive highways has been proved, that mountain ranges have been penetrated by costly tunnels, and distant seas have been connected by costly canals, and it has been demonstrated that the most extravagant investments in works of this description are remunerative under the vast commercial ebb and flow which characterizes the present age. Of the necessity for, and advantage of, intercommunication of every description, therefore, there seems to be no longer a doubt; and it is with this conviction that the United States government is called on to consider now once more the value and importance of an interoceanic canal on this continent.

Of the advantages of this canal to our industry and commerce it becomes us, therefore, first to speak. In this connection it should not be forgotten that the states of North and South America lying along the Pacific furnish in large abundance those commodities which are constantly supplied with markets in almost every country of Europe. Of guano and niter the trade is immense. From the ports of Chili nearly 400,000 tons of freight are shipped eastward annually. More than 1,000,000 tons of grain are shipped each year from the Pacific States and Territories. There is no doubt that more than 4,000,000 tons of merchandise find their way from these regions to the East, and require water communication in order that they may be shipped economically and profitably; and this is merchandise to which railway transportation across the continent is wholly inapplicable. The great wheat crops of California and Oregon, for instance, find their way to Liverpool around Cape Horn at the freight-rate of fifty cents per bushel—a rate which would not carry it by rail half-way to Boston or New York or Philadelphia, to be there shipped to its European destination. In addition to the commerce of the North and South American ports referred to, there may be estimated also the advantages which would accrue to the trade of Australia and the remote East Indies bound to Great Britain, and which would undoubtedly add 1,000,000 tons to the freight seeking a passage through the canal. When we consider the time and distance saved by the canal for this vast amount of merchandise by avoiding the passage around Cape Horn, and the importance in these days of rapid transit, and of a ready approach to a destined market, we can readily understand the value of the enterprise to producer and shipper and consumer alike. Leaving out of consideration the dangers and delays of the Cape, we should not forget that by the canal now proposed the distance from New York to Hong Kong is shortened 5,870 miles; from New York to Yokohama, 6,800 miles; from New York to San Francisco, 8,600 miles; from New York to Honolulu, 6,980 miles; from Liverpool to San Francisco, 6,065 miles; and from Liverpool to Callao, 4,374 miles; and we need no longer question the value of an interoceanic canal on the Western continent, as we have long since abandoned all doubt of the value of the Suez Canal to the commerce of the nations of the East. To Europeans the benefits and advantages of the proposed canal are great;—to the Americans they are incalculable. Forming, as a canal properly organized and constructed would, a part of the coast-line of the United States, it would increase our commercial facilities beyond calculation. Interfering in no way with the interests of those lines of railway which connect the Atlantic States with the Pacific, but tending rather to stimulate and increase the activity out of which their traffic grows, it would cheapen all staple transportation and add vastly to the ease and economy of emigration from the East to the farms and mines of the Pacific slope. That a canal will be of great benefit to the commerce of the United States, also, there can be no doubt. Meeting as we do a formidable competition in the carrying-trade to foreign ports, we find in our coastwise navigation an opportunity for a profitable use of American bottoms, protected by our own commercial laws. A continuous coast-line, including our eastern and western shores, therefore promises an increase of this navigation sufficient of itself to make a canal a matter of the utmost importance to our people.

In view of these advantages, the question naturally arises with regard to the most feasible route for the canal, both as regards economy of construction and convenience in use. On this point it would hardly seem as if there were room for controversy. The difficulties which surround the Panama scheme have been so frequently and so forcibly set forth, that they need not be elaborately repeated here. The floods of this region, caused by sudden and immense rain-fall, have attracted the attention of the most careless traveler, and have perplexed and confounded the scientific engineer in his attempts to provide some method by which to overcome the difficulties which they create. The impassable and unhealthy swamps lying along this route have always been considered unfit for a water-course, and so destructive to human life that labor and death seemed to have joined hands there. The necessity for long and expensive tunnels or open cuts, and for a safe viaduct, has added vastly to the expense of the route when estimated, and to the obstacles to be overcome by engineering. The most careful surveys have always developed a discouraging want of material for construction. The addition of five hundred miles to the distance between New York and the ports on the west coast of the United States by the Panama route over that of any other feasible route proposed, and the long and tedious calms which prevail in Panama Bay, have never failed to create opposition to this route in the mind of the navigator. The enormous cost of the Panama Canal, moreover, has never been denied. Considering the engineering difficulties attending the diversion of the Chagres River, and the necessary construction of an artificial lake to hold its floods, together with the tunneling, or open cuts, to which allusion has already been made, the cost of this canal cannot be less than $400,000,000, and would probably be much more—including the payment to the Panama Railroad for its concession. No American capitalist would be likely to look for dividends on an investment like this.

Turning from the Panama route, therefore, as one which, when practically considered, has but little to recommend it, either as a commercial convenience or a financial success, we are brought to the consideration of the Nicaragua route, as that to which the attention of the American public is most strongly drawn at this time. The advantages of this route are: the ease and economy with which the canal can be constructed; the admirable approaches to it from the sea, both east and west; the distance saved between Liverpool and the North American ports over that of the Panama route; and the distance saved, also, between New York and other Atlantic cities and the ports of the United States on the Pacific. The cost of the Nicaragua Canal has never been estimated above $100,000,000; indeed, Civil Engineer Menocal,[1] whose judgment and capacity have never been questioned, gives the following as his estimate of the entire cost of the work, after long and critical examination:

Western Division—from Port Brito to the Lake. Distance, 16.33 miles; estimated cost $21,680,777.00

Middle Division—Lake Nicaragua. Distance, 56.50 miles; estimated cost 715,658.00

Eastern Division—from Lake to Greytown. Distance, 108.43 miles; estimated cost 25,020,914.00

Construction of Greytown Harbor 2,822,630.00

Construction of Brito Harbor 2,337,739.00

Total. Distance, 181.26 miles; cost $52,577,718.00

A subsequent estimate, based on more recent surveys made by Mr. Menocal, has reduced this amount to $41,193,839—a reduction of $11,383,879; and by abandoning the valley of the San Juan River in favor of a direct route to Greytown,—ascertained to be entirely practicable,—the distance is reduced to 173.57 miles, the total canalization being but 53.17 miles.

It is well known that the Suez Canal, and, in fact, almost all great public works, cost far more than the estimates made by engineers. But applying this rule most liberally cannot bring the outlay on the Nicaragua route above $100,000,000. The surveys of this route, made subsequent to those of the other routes proposed, have developed extraordinary facilities for the work. Materials needed for construction are abundant throughout the entire line. The harbors of Brito and Greytown, at the western and eastern termini, are capable of being easily made convenient and excellent. The water supply from Lake Nicaragua is free from deposit and is abundant and easily obtained—the lake itself being the summit level of the canal. The rain-fall is not excessive. The climate during the trade winds is delightful. The country is capable of producing all the subsistence that would be required by the laborers employed in the construction of the canal. The local productions are valuable, and such as constitute many of the most important articles of commerce. In the construction, feeders, tunnels, and viaducts are not necessary. Dependent nowhere on streams which in the rainy season are irresistibly destructive, and in the dry season are reduced to mere rivulets, the canal would always be provided with a uniform and easily controlled supply of water.

A canal constructed on this route, and at the estimates before us, could not fail to be an economical highway as well as a profitable investment. Estimating the cost of the canal at $75,000,000, a charge of $2.50, for canal tolls and all other charges, would give a gross income of $10,000,000 on the 4,000,000 tons upon which former calculations have been based. Deducting from this $1,500,000 for the expenses of maintaining and operating the canal, we have $8,500,000 as the net earnings of the work. Any reasonable modification of these figures would give an encouraging exhibit. The liberal concessions made by the government of Nicaragua to the Provisional Interoceanic Canal Society indicate a determination on the part of that government to make the burthens of the enterprise as light as possible, and to leave its government entirely in the hands of the American projectors. While in the Panama concession provision is made for the entry and clearance of vessels at the terminal ports, with the delays and annoyances usually attending such requirements, the Nicaragua concession avoids all interference by custom-house officials, except so far as to prevent smuggling and violations of the customs laws. This concession provides: "There shall be a free zone upon each bank of the canal, of one hundred yards in width, measured from the water's edge, it being understood that the lake shores shall never be considered as the margin of the canal. Within this zone no illegal traffic shall be conducted, and the customs authorities will watch and prevent smuggling in accordance with the provisions of Article 32 [of the concession]. It is expressly understood that every vessel traversing the canal will, whenever the authorities desire it, receive on board a guard [customs officer] appointed by the government, who will, in case of discovering their violation, exercise his powers in accordance with the law." The articles of the concession also provide that the "two ports to be constructed and to serve for entrances to the canal on each ocean are declared to be free, and will be recognized as such from the beginning of the work to the end of this concession." While the administration and management of the Panama Canal, moreover, are placed in the hands of an independent company, deriving its powers from a foreign government, and organized on the plan adopted in the construction of the Suez Canal, the commerce availing itself of the benefits of the Nicaragua Canal is protected by the government of that country against all extortion. In Article 42, the concession provides that: "It is understood that the company, in the exercise of the powers here conferred, cannot make other regulations than such as are necessary for the administration and management of the canal, and before issuing these regulations will submit them to the government for its approval." In order to protect still further the interests of those using the canal, it is provided that all sums necessary to secure interest on the funded debts, obligations, and shares, not exceeding six per cent. for interest, and also a sinking fund, shall be reserved; and that "what remains shall form the net gains, of which at least eighty per cent. shall be divided amongst shareholders, it being understood, after ten years from the time the canal is completed, the company cannot divide amongst the shareholders, either by direct dividends, or indirectly, by issuing additional shares or otherwise, more than fifteen per cent. annually, or in this proportion, for dues collected from the canal; and when it is discovered that the charges in force produce a greater net gain, they will be reduced to the basis of fifteen per cent. per year." These provisions indicate not only the confidence of the projectors in their enterprise, but also the determination of the Nicaraguan government to guard against all possible injustice to the commerce finding a highway there.

That there are other advantages contained in the concession of the Nicaraguan government, and in the proposed administration and management of the Nicaragua Canal, there should be no doubt in the mind of every American who believes in the power and supremacy of his government on this continent. The concession is made to Americans, the society is made up of Americans, the corporators are Americans, and the act of incorporation is asked of an American Congress. Every step of this project recognizes the right of the United States to guard with jealous care the American continent against the encroachment of foreign powers. To this policy no nation and no cluster of adjacent nations, watchful of their own individual or collective interests, should take exception. It is the foundation of national existence everywhere. An American man-of-war, having on board the greatest naval commander of modern times, pauses for forty-eight hours at the mouth of the Bosphorus to recognize the right of an European power to control the waters of the Dardanelles and the Black Sea. It cannot be supposed for a moment that an American company, incorporated by the American government, organized on American soil, would have been allowed to construct the Suez Canal, even if it had established a branch of its enterprise in France and placed it under the supervision of a distinguished and representative French official. And so it is with us. The policy laid down in the early days of the Republic, and accepted from that time to this by the American mind, by which the colonization of other nationalities on these shores was protested against, should never be forgotten. The violation of this policy has always roused the American people to a firm assertion of their rights, and cost one American statesman, at least, a large share of the laurels he had won by long and honorable service.[2] The application of this principle even now secures safety and protection to a line of railway spanning the Isthmus, and connecting the eastern with the western waters. The assertion of this principle by a treaty made with Nicaragua in 1849 is accepted to-day by all Americans, people and officials, with entire satisfaction. The rejection of that treaty in order to prevent a collision between the United States and Great Britain, and to preserve unharmed the policy of an administration, is regarded as one of the most complicating and compromising acts of American diplomacy. The accepted and acceptable policy of the American government is contained in the doctrine announced more than half a century ago by President Monroe. It is to be found in the attitude assumed by our government in all the long diplomatic discussion which followed the ratification of the Clayton-Bulwer treaty;—a discussion in which General Cass, then Secretary of State, declared an analogous treaty as recognizing "principles of foreign intervention repugnant to the policy of the United States";—a discussion in which by negotiation Great Britain was compelled to recognize the "sovereignty of Honduras over the islands composing the so-called British Colony of the Bay Islands";—a discussion in which the President of the United States "denounced the Clayton-Bulwer treaty as one which had been fraught with misunderstanding and mischief from the beginning." "If the Senate," said the President to Lord Napier, "had imagined that the Clayton-Bulwer treaty could obtain the interpretation placed upon it by Great Britain, it would not have passed; and if I had been in the Senate at the time, it never would have passed."[3] It is in obedience to this policy that the United States has protested against the establishment by Great Britain of a protectorate in Central America, either on the Mosquito coast or on the Bay Islands. And it is in accordance with this policy that President Hayes, in his message of March 8th, 1880, declared that:

"The policy of this country is a canal under American control. The United States cannot consent to the surrender of this control to any European power or to any combination of European powers. . . . The capital invested by corporations or citizens of other countries in such an enterprise must in a great degree look for protection to one or more of the great powers of the world. No European power can intervene for such protection without adopting measures on this continent which the United States would deem wholly inadmissible. If the protection of the United States is relied upon, the United States must exercise such control as will enable this country to protect its national interests and maintain the rights of those whose private capital is embarked in the work.

"An interoceanic canal across the American isthmus will essentially change the geographical relations between the Atlantic and Pacific coasts of the United States, and between the United States and the rest of the world. It will be the great ocean thoroughfare between our Atlantic and our Pacific shores, and virtually a part of the coast-line of the United States. Our merely commercial interest in it is greater than that of all other countries, while its relations to our power and prosperity as a nation, to our means of defense, our unity, peace, and safety, are matters of paramount concern to the people of the United States. No other great power would, under similar circumstances, fail to assert a rightful control over a work so closely and vitally affecting its interest and welfare."

In accordance with the early and later policy of the government, in obedience to the often-expressed will of the American people, with a due regard to our national dignity and power, with a watchful care for the safety and prosperity of our interests and industries on this continent, and with a determination to guard against even the first approach of rival powers, whether friendly or hostile, on these shores, I commend an American canal, on American soil, to the American people, and congratulate myself on the fact that the most careful explorations have demonstrated that the route standing in this attitude before the world is the one which commends itself as a judicious, economical, and prosperous work.

I have formed the opinions expressed in this article, not from a hasty consideration of the subject, and not without personal observation. While commanding the army of the United States, my attention was drawn to the importance of the water communication I have here discussed. During my administration of the government, I endeavored to impress upon the country the views I then formed; and I shall feel that I have added one more act of my life to those I have already recorded, if I shall succeed in impressing upon Congress and the people the high value, as a commercial and industrial enterprise, of this great work, which, if not accomplished by Americans, will undoubtedly be accomplished by some one of our rivals in power and influence.

U. S. GRANT.

North American Review, CCXCI (Feb., 1881), 107–16. Tabular material expanded; brackets and ellipses in original.

On Dec. 14, 1880, U.S. Representative Levi P. Morton of N. Y. introduced a bill to incorporate the Maritime Canal Co. of Nicaragua, naming USG, Edwin D. Morgan, and Edward F. Beale among the backers. This co. succeeded the Provisional Interoceanic Canal Society, granted a concession by Nicaragua in May. On Dec. 16, in Washington, D. C., "The Nicaraguan minister and Admiral Ammen called on ex-Gen. Grant . . . in reference to the Inter-Oceanic canal scheme. The conference lasted some time, and was mutually agreeable. Ex-Gen. Grant expressed himself as confident of the ultimate success of the Nicaraguan scheme. . . ." *Washington Post,* Dec. 17, 1880. On the same day, USG spoke at length to a reporter. "I will make a little statement and you can take it down. As far back as 1865, directly after the close of the rebellion, I took an interest in what I thought was rapidly becoming a necessity—interoceanic communication for ships between the Atlantic and Pacific Oceans, and called upon Mr. Seward, then Secretary of State, for the purpose of interviewing him on the subject, if I could; but I failed to arouse the interest in the subject that I felt myself, and it was not a great while afterward before the administration began to pursue such a course as to repel me and prevent my having any communication with it that I could avoid, and the matter was dropped until I became President myself. . . . I have never supposed for a moment that the United States would permit any canal to connect the two oceans on this continent in which any European power had, or could have, the control to the exclusion of the United States. I did not suppose this country would allow that for a moment. It would be much as though the United States had gone and attempted to build and control a canal at Suez. Of course it would not be to our interest to throw any obstacle in the way of commerce; but we should control its course on this continent. . . . I think that if that canal was built it would be the route sailing vessels would take for certain parts of Asia, and of all steam vessels going there from Europe. I have no idea that any steam vessel running between Europe and Japan and Eastern China would go through the Suez Canal, if they had this route, unless it was certain ships that would be necessary to keep up certain lines, such as mail steamers, &c.; but mere freight steamers from all China and Japan would find the Nicaraguan Canal the most advantageous. All steamers going to the eastern coast of Africa would go through this. . . . All the concessions that are required are already secured. The thing now is to have Congress pass an act of incorporation, and then if the people choose to subscribe their money they can organize a company and go on and build the canal." *Washington National Republican,* Dec. 17, 1880. See *PUSG,* 15, 412–13; *ibid.,* 16, 237–38; *ibid.,* 23, 46–50; Daniel Ammen, *The Old Navy and The New* (Philadelphia, 1891), pp. 474–98; *HRC,* 46-3-224, 48–49; The Nicaragua Canal Construction Co., *The Inter-Oceanic Canal of Nicaragua . . .* (New York, 1891), pp. 10–11.

1. Born in Cuba and trained at Rensselaer Polytechnic Institute, Aniceto G. Menocal joined the U.S. Navy in 1872 as a civil engineer and surveyed canal routes in Panama and Nicaragua.

2. USG likely referred to former Secretary of State William H. Seward. See *PUSG,* 16, 129.

3. See John Bassett Moore, ed., *The Works of James Buchanan* (1908–11; reprinted, New York, 1960), X, 124–28, 136–39; Lindley Miller Keasbey, *The Nicaragua Canal and the Monroe Doctrine* (New York, 1896), pp. 248–63.

To Robert O. Fuller

————

New York City
March 4th 1881.

ROB.T O. FULLER, ESQ.

MY DEAR SIR:

In looking over old cloths to pack them away Mrs. Grant this morning found in the pocket of a coat your letter of the 15th of October, 1880, containing your check for $500 00 The letter had never been opened, hence the delay in acknowledging it. I presume the letter has been handed to me at a time when I could not read it and was therefore placed in my coat pocket where it has remained ever since, in the pocket of a coat probably not worn since my visit to Bos[ton] in Oct. last.

I am very much obliged to you for [t]he kind expressions contained in your letter, and fully appreciate your motive, but beg to return your check with many thanks

Very Truly yours
U. S. GRANT

ALS, Robert O. F. Bixby, Arlington, Va. Robert O. Fuller, Mass. senator (1872–73), was an iron merchant.

To Roscoe Conkling

————

March 5th 1881

MY DEAR SENATOR:

I have just learned the composition of the Cabinet. I confess to much disappointment. I shall try however to say but little about it for the present. On Monday[1] I will go to Washington and stop for a few days at Willards Hotel and would like to meet you, Logan & Cameron the first evening if you are all at leasure. Will you—if you will be at leasure that evening—speak to the other Senators named and ask them if they will meet me at about 9 pm. Monday.

Very Truly yours
U. S. GRANT

ALS, DLC-Roscoe Conkling.

1. March 7, 1881.

To Thomas L. James

————

New York City
March 5th 1881.

DEAR SIR:

I take pleasure in recommending A. N. Richard[1] for the position of Postmaster of Freeport, Stevenson Co. Ill. Mr. Richard is a staunch republican and has always been so. he is a very capable man and needs the place in connection with his paper to which he has devoted some years of time and some means beside. The present incumbent of the office has held it for years, and, as I understand, is not much credit to the office or to the party which he professes to support.

I understand the member of Congress from the district in which Freeport is—Maj. Hawk[2]—favors the appointment of Mr. Richards.

Very respectfully
U. S. GRANT

THE POSTMASTER GENERAL

ALS, WHi. On March 11, 1881, USG spoke at a banquet honoring Thomas L. James. "Gentlemen, I received an invitation to come here to a dinner yesterday in honor of our new Postmaster-General, and I prepared a speech which I have no doubt would have pleased you all very much. But it was adjusted to yesterday, and I can't possibly deliver it to-day. My memory is sometimes very short. I can say to all of us here and to the thousands who are not here that I think the President has shown marked good sense and good taste in the selection he has made for Postmaster-General. That is a man who commands more employes than the Secretary of War and the Secretary of the Navy combined. He is the chief of an army scattered over this broad land from one end to the other, extending to every inhabited township within the whole limits of our territory. It requires executive ability to fill that position, which we all believe our friend possesses in an eminent degree. All we can ask is that he will fill the important position to which he has been chosen just as well as we believe he will. One remark I should have made in reference to the large army of 60,000 employes of the Postmaster-General, was that if he finds any difficulty in getting people to serve him I can refer to him the applications I have received for positions under him, and I believe they will be sufficient." *New York Times*, March 12, 1881. See *PUSG*, 26, 245.

1. Born in 1841 in Ill., Alonzo V. Richards enlisted in the 7th Wis. and transferred to the U.S. Signal Corps. After the war he surveyed western lands and edited the *Freeport Journal.* On May 18, 1869, Orville E. Babcock wrote to Richards, Galena. "The President directs me to acknowledge the receipt of your letter of the 13th. and in reply to request you to deposit the keys and papers with Mr. L. S. Felt." Copies, DLC-USG, II, 1, 4. See *PUSG,* 19, 472; letter to Alonzo V. Richards, Oct. 10, 1881; letter to Henry Villard, April 24, 1883.

2. Robert M. A. Hawk rose to capt., 92nd Ill., lost his right leg at Raleigh in 1865, and served as Carroll County clerk until elected to Congress as a Republican in 1878.

To Edward F. Beale

———

New York City
March 6th 1881.

My Dear Gen. Beale;

Mrs. Grant & I go to Washingtn to-morrow to remain for two or three days. I go specially to see some of our friends who I have asked to meet me at Willard Hotel, where I have written for rooms. I received your kind invitation to make your house our home during our visit, but for the present occasion the hotel will be much more convenient, and will save Mrs. Beale the inconvenience of having her house as committee rooms, for strangers, during the whole time.

We thank you and Mrs. Beale for your invitation which, but for the nature of my visit, we would gladly accept.

Very Truly yours
U. S. Grant

ALS, DLC-Decatur House Papers.

To Jesse Root Grant, Jr.

———

March 6th 1881

Dear Jesse:

You have now been at sea eight days and are probably approaching land. To-morrow we will hope to hear of the Steamer at

Queenstown.[1] We are all well and nothing special has transpired here of special importance since you left except the inauguration of the new Pres. and the announcement of his Cabinet. The latter I do not like. But it is not my Cabinet. Your Ma & I go to Washington to-morrow to spend a few days. In two weeks we start to Mexico. I hope you have found Nellies little boy quite recovered. You Ma had a letter from Nellie a day or two since in which she says he is doing finely. I think likely that after we all get settled down at Long Branch we will leave Ida, Fanny & Lizzie—with their three good-for-nothing husbands—to run the house while your Ma & I run over and pay Nellie a visit of a few days and then take a months run over Switzerland.—After you left a dispatch come—a Cablegram—saying "Yes," supposed to be from Mr. Chapman.[2]

I hope you will be entirely successful in your business,[3] and that it may prove profitable to those who go in with you. Specially do I hope you may have success in arranging relations between your house here and London or Liverpool houses. You did not ask me for any letters of introduction and I do not know that I could have given you any of business value.

Your Ma & I send much love to Lizzie and you and hope you may have a pleasant visit, and return home soon. Give our best regards to Mr & Mrs. Chapman, and to Harry Honoré also.

Yours Affectionately

U. S. GRANT

ALS, Nellie C. Rothwell, La Jolla, Calif.

1. On March 8, 1881, the *City of Richmond*, carrying Jesse Root Grant, Jr., his wife Elizabeth Chapman Grant, mother-in-law Sarah A. Chapman, and brother-in-law and business partner Henry H. Honoré, Jr., arrived at Queenstown, Ireland, en route to Liverpool. *New York Times*, March 9, 1881.

2. On March 10, a correspondent reported from Boston that a Mass. charter had been granted to the Texas, Topolobampo, and Pacific Railroad and Telegraph Co. "The route is said to be substantially that surveyed by A. R. Owen, for the survey of which Congress was once asked to make an appropriation." A list of incorporators included William S. Chapman, Jesse Grant's father-in-law. *Ibid.*, March 11, 1881. See *PUSG*, 26, 496–97.

3. Honoré & Grant, general produce. See letter to Julia Dent Grant, June 15, 1880.

To William H. Hunt

March 9th *1881*

HON. WM H. HUNT,
SEC. OF THE NAVY:
DEAR SIR:

Sidney H. Dent is an applicant for appointment as Asst. Paymaser in the United States Navy. He is the son of Gen. F. T. Dent, U. S. Army, and the Nephew of Mrs. Grant. He is a young man twenty years of age, of good constitution and of excellent and exemplary habits and character. I would esteem it a favor if the appointment can be given.

Very respectfully
U. S. GRANT

ALS (written on Willard's Hotel stationery), Mrs. Gordon Singles, Arlington, Va. Born in 1823, William H. Hunt was raised in S. C. and Conn., attended Yale College, and settled in New Orleans, where he practiced law. On March 5, 1881, President James A. Garfield nominated Hunt as secretary of the navy. Sidney H. Dent, born Sidney Johnston Dent, was appointed War Dept. clerk. See *PUSG*, 2, 6.

To Adam Badeau

March 11th /81

DEAR GENERAL:

I will call over to see you a while this afternoon if I can. Young will not probably go to Mexico because there will hardly be a change there. If there should be a change in China or Japan he would have one of those places. I will tell you this evening about your chances for the Naval Office. Conkling is willing.

Yours
U. S. GRANT

ALS, Munson-Williams-Proctor Institute, Utica, N. Y. On [*March 6, 1881*], USG wrote to [Adam Badeau]. "Much obliged for your offer of services but company have been coming in all day, so that all I could do has been to answer a few letters. In the morning I go to Washington, and will take that occasion to talk to Conkling and the President about your transfer to New York." ALS (undated), *ibid.* See *Badeau*, p. 531; letter to James A. Garfield, March 16, 1881.

To Manning F. Force

NEW YORK CITY, *March 13, 1881.*

MY DEAR GENERAL:—I regret that I shall not be able to meet the Society of the Army of the Tennessee at its next reunion. It is my present expectation to sail from Galveston, Texas for Vera Cruz, on the steamer of April 1. I regret very much missing so many meetings of the society of the army composed of my first command in the great struggle for national existence. But my errand is one of business, and not of pleasure, and can not be postponed.

Very truly yours,
U. S. GRANT.

GENERAL M. F. FORCE.

Report of the Proceedings of the Society of the Army of the Tennessee at the Fourteenth Annual Meeting Held at Cincinnati, Ohio, April 6th and 7th, 1881 (Cincinnati, 1885), p. 14. On Dec. 17, 1881, USG wrote to Manning F. Force, Cincinnati. "I am sorry that I shall be obliged to disappoint you again. At the time of your reunion in Cincinnati I shall be in Washington City, by appointment and by invitation. I regret very much to miss the opportunity of meeting your Society on the approaching occasion, but such are my engagements that it will be impossible." *Cincinnati Commercial*, Jan. 13, 1882. The Cincinnati Society of Ex-Army and Navy Officers held its seventh annual banquet on Jan. 12, 1882.

Interview

[*New York City, March 13, 1881*]

It was in August, 1878, that I first visited St. Petersburg. The Czar was spending the Summer at his Summer Palace, between 30 and 40 miles by rail from the city in a south-westerly direction. I was invited to the 12 o'clock dinner with him, and during my visit we entered into a long conversation. Gortschakoff was present, and acted as interpreter whenever the Czar conversed in French, as he did during the interview. He formerly spoke English quite fluently, I am told, and while the greater part of our conversation was in English, he occasionally glided into French. Gortschakoff's English was as perfect as that of any American, and was without the slightest foreign accent. The Czar was then about 60 years old, and although he was said to be in delicate health, he did not look to be. In fact, his years had not told on him, and he presented the appearance of a very much younger man, than he really was. He was fully 6 feet in height, was perfectly erect, and in his military uniform he presented a commanding figure. He showed remarkable familiarity with the history and affairs of our own country, and much of our conversation was devoted to their discussion. No reference whatever was made to Nihilism, or to the troubles concerning which so much was being published in the European and especially in the English newspapers. I noticed no such unusual precautions for his personal protection as one might naturally expect to find, after hearing in other parts of Europe the rumors concerning the troubles in Russia. It was evident, however, that the Czar was somewhat nervous, as one would naturally be after so many attempts had been made upon his life. My visit to him was an agreeable one. It was the only time I ever saw him.

The next day I visited the Czarevitch at his Summer Palace, which was also some distance out of St. Petersburg, though in a more southerly direction. Mrs. Grant accompanied me. She was ushered into a room where she was received by the wife of the Czarevitch. I met the Czarevitch in an adjoining room. He speaks English perfectly, and we spent some time in conversation. He interrupted it with the remark that his wife was in the next room and would be pleased to see me. They entertained Mrs. Grant and myself in the most agreeable manner. It was more like meeting with Americans, and our visit was all the more enjoyable on that account. The Czarevitch is very domestic in his habits, and evidently is deeeply devoted to his family. He appeared to be about 40 years old, though he may have been considerably younger. I found that he was very much esteemed by the Russian people.

I visited Moscow and Warsaw and made many excursions into the country. I visited every corner of St. Petersburg alone and on foot, and I probably saw a great many things of which even many of the residents are perhaps ignorant, for I went about for the express purpose of observing the people and studying objects of interest.

The greater part of my visit to St. Petersburg, after the formalities of the reception were over, was spent in these trips. Not only in St. Petersburg and other Russian cities did I adopt this course of informing myself, but also in every other European and Asiatic city or town which our party visited. I could see nothing indicative of Nihilism or of popular discontent. Here, you know, if the people want anything, if the members of any particular trade are demanding something from their employers, as in a strike, we generally see some indications in the shape of a street parade or a collection of men on the corners—something pointing to the existence of disturbed feeling. I saw nothing of that sort in Russia, and could learn of nothing. I had heard and read so much of the confused condition of affairs before reaching Russian soil, that I fully expected to find considerable evidence of disturbance. If a man had been suddenly dropped into Russia who had never heard of Nihilism, he would certainly never have discovered its exist[e]nce from anything he could have seen at the time I was there.

New York Times, March 14, 1881. After several previous attempts, Nihilists assassinated Tsar Alexander II on March 13, 1881. "Gen. Grant said he could not see what the people of Russia would gain by it. Perhaps, he added, the fact that his eldest son is a more moral man may have an influence for the better upon the politics of the country. The Czar had been greatly harassed by his subjects, and had indeed led a miserable life. Yet he seemed to have an interest in his people, as was evidenced by his freeing the serfs. He had for a number of years, as the General knew, been willi[n]g to abdicate in favor of his son. 'It seems to me,' said the General, 'If I had been in his place I should have taken such a step some time ago, and retired altogether from the management of affairs.'" *Ibid.* Alexander III, aged 36, the former tsarevitch, succeeded his father. See *PUSG*, 28, 443–45, 453.

To John Walker Fearn

———

New York City
March 15th 81

MY DEAR MR FEARN

Your letter of the 22d of Feb'y was duly received. I could give no definite answer then because I did not know what I might be able to recommend for you. It was my intention to see the President soon after the inauguration, and to speak in your behalf then. I did so see him, and told him of your qualifications, your knowledge of languages, particularly of French, Spanish & Italian. I told him also that you had served in Mexico as Sec: of Legation when you were a young man—in ante belleum times—and that you knew the people well; that you were a lawyer by profession and that I understood you had a numerously signed recommendation for a Judgship. I said to the Pres. that I would be pleased to see you named as Minister to Mexico if Judge Morgan was to be transferred to another fied, but that I did not think he should be removed except to take some other position. I think you should send such endorsment as you have and make application for a foreign mission, or such place as would suit you.

I leave here next week for Mexico by way of Galveston. Will be ready to take the first steamer leaving the latter city in April. Will you be kind enough to inform Mr Whitney[1] of this. My party—proper—will consist of Mrs Grant & myself, Mr J. R. Young, and two servants. Mr Romero & his mother-in-law,[2] and possibly one or two others will probably accompany us. But they are not of the party, except as friends going over the same road at the same time.

Remember Mrs Grant & me kindly to cousin Fanny[3] and all the children.

Yours very truly
U. S. Grant.

Copy, DNA, RG 59, Applications and Recommendations, Hayes-Arthur. Related papers are *ibid.* See letter to James A. Garfield, March 19, 1881.

1. Charles A. Whitney headed Charles Morgan's Louisiana and Texas Railroad and Steamship Co. from offices in New Orleans.

2. In July, 1868, Matías Romero married Lucretia Allen of Philadelphia.

3. Born in 1849 in Ky., Frances (Fanny) Hewitt was the daughter of James Hewitt and Clarice Grant, USG's first cousin. Fanny Hewitt married John Walker Fearn in 1865. In April, 1880, USG and Julia Dent Grant were guests of the Fearns in New Orleans. See *PUSG*, 15, 220–21; *ibid.*, 25, 267; Frances Fearn, ed., *Diary of a Refugee* (New York, 1910), pp. 38–39, 108–12.

To James A. Garfield

New York City
March 16th 1881.

His Excellency: J. A. Garfield,
President of the U. States:
Dear Sir:

I take great pleasure in presenting to you Gen. A. Badeau, at present Consul General to London, and formerly a member of my staff. General Badeau goes to Washington specially to pay his respects to you, and to the head of the State Department before taking his departure for his post of duty.—You may be aware of the fact that General Badeau has been engaged for the last fifteen years in writing the history of the rebellion so far as my connection with it was concerned. That work is now completed and is in the hands of the publishers. It was my intention when in Washington to speak to you about Gen. Badeau. I do not remember whether I did so or not. But lest I did not I will mention here that it was my intention to ask his retention in his present place unless he might be appointed Naval Officer at this port. I would not ask this latter unless it meets the approval of the Senators from this state, and the republican members from this city & Brooklyn.

Very Truly yours
U. S. Grant

ALS, DLC-James A. Garfield. On March 23, 1881, President James A. Garfield nominated Adam Badeau as chargé d'affaires, Denmark, and Edwin A. Merritt as consul gen., London, in place of Badeau. On March 24 and 25, USG, New York City, telegraphed to Badeau, Washington, D. C. "See the President at once with my letter. Ask him to withdraw your nomination, and if ~~you~~ he cannot leave you in London ask him to give you either Italy or naval office in this city. Show him this despatch as my endorsement of you for either places" "I advise you to decline ~~London~~ Copenhagen and stick to London unless you can get naval office, Italy or some equally good place. Advise with Conkling and Platt. It would be better to come here without government appointment than to take Copenhagen" Copies, Munson-Williams-Proctor Institute, Utica, N. Y. On April 5, Badeau wrote to Garfield. "With reference the communications from General Grant which I have already had the honor to lay before you, I beg to say that I propose to return tomorrow to NewYork, unless you should desire a further interview, and there await your decision; at least until my leave of absence expires I forbear to press my considerations on my own account, as I know of none likely to add to the weight of

General Grants endorsement with his successor and friend. My address in New York will be communicated to the State Department and to your own private Secretary." ALS, DLC-James A. Garfield. On May 18, Garfield withdrew Badeau's nomination; on the same day, the Senate confirmed Merritt. See letter to John P. Jones, April 24, 1881; letter to Adam Badeau, July 27, 1881.

To James A. Garfield

New York City
March 19th 1881.

HIS EXCELLENCY
JAS. A. GARFIELD,
PRESIDENT OF THE U. S.
DEAR SIR:

I take great pleasure in commending J. R G. Pitkin of La. to your favorable consideration for any position he may apply for. Col. Pitkin is a native of La. He held the office of U. S. Marshal for his State under me *and gave the greatest satisfaction.* He has rendered valuable service in every campaign—political campaign—since the close of the war. I have known him personally for about twelve years as an earnest Republican worker. For Dist Att'y or Marshal of his state he has my earnest endorsement. For a foreign mission I also endorse him. [as worthy and capable. The Mexican Mission is his special desire. I have already named a person [1] as my choice for that mission, if there is to be a change . . . Now I am somewhat in doubt whether the person named by me . . . may not have opposed your election. He would not have opposed mine if I had been nominated. I hope he supported you. If he did not, I would not advise you to appoint him. In your place I would not appoint an opponent. I would not ask you to do what I would not do in your place . . .]

Very truly yours
U. S. GRANT.

Partial copy, DNA, RG 59, Applications and Recommendations, Hayes-Arthur; Charles Hamilton Auction, No. 41, April 23, 1970, no. 92; American Art Association, Dec. 3 and 4, 1923; Paul C. Richards, Catalog No. 55 [1970], no. 41; unidentified catalog, no. 401. On March 6, 1882, USG wrote to President Chester A. Arthur. "A vacancy existing in the Court of Claims bench, would not the appointment of Judge Morgan, Minister to

Mexico, be a good one? Morgan is an able lawyer, has had experience as a judge and is a thoroughly upright man. This would make a vacancy in the *Mexican Mission, for which Col. Pitkin has been so universally recommended by the people of the Mississippi Valley. I would be very glad to see Col. Pitkin fill the Mexican Mission* or any other position equally good." Copy, DNA, RG 59, Applications and Recommendations, Hayes–Arthur. On April 11, Arthur nominated John R. G. Pitkin as marshal, Eastern District, La. See *PUSG*, 21, 168–72.

    1. See letter to John Walker Fearn, March 15, 1881; letter to James A. Garfield, March 26, 1881.

To World's Fair Commission

—————

                              New York City, March 22, 1881.

    Gentlemen: I have the honor very respectfully to tender my resignation as President of the World's Fair Commission of 1883. I am satisfied that to make the enterprise a success will require the undivided time of whoever may hold the position of President. It will be impossible for me to devote any time to the duties of the office for a number of months to come, and I expect to be so engaged as to make it inconvenient to devote much time even at a later date. Hoping that your enterprise may meet with the greatest success, I am, very truly yours.

                                     U. S. Grant.

To the Commissioners of the World's Fair of 1883.

New York Times, March 24, 1881. See Remarks, [*Feb. 16, 1881*]. On March 22, 1881, a reporter interviewed USG at the Fifth Avenue Hotel. "In speaking of the World's Fair General Grant alluded in the kindest terms to his colleagues and to their energy in pushing forward the enterprise. He thought it better, however, to postpone the Fair until 1884 or 1885. He considered it a mistake to erect temporary buildings at so much expense. They should be put upon public grounds, so that at the close of the fair they could be used for art repositories, museums, menageries, aquariums, winter and summer gardens and the like. He said that out of $4,000,000 or $5,000,000 to be used in erecting these edifices, a large part could be saved for public utility, like the Trocadoro building in Paris, which after the exposition remained a permanent ornament to that great city. The condition of the iron trade was such that it would be difficult to put up suitable buildings for the New York World's Fair by 1883. General Grant said further that the exhibition wanted a man at its head who could give his whole time to its business. His engagements would take him out of the country for three months—three months vital to the success of the Fair. When he should return other engagements which could not be ignored would make it difficult for him to take active part in the Fair. For these reasons General Grant said he would resign, and while the representa-

tive of the HERALD was in the room he wrote a letter of resignation and sent it by special messenger to one of the members of the committee. It will probably be presented at
the regular meeting of the Executive Committee, to be held at half-past three o'clock
to-day. General Grant spoke of the proposed extra session of Congress. He said he
hoped that there would be no extra session. His position was that while Congress might
be considering the Funding bill, new legislation would be sure to creep in, and members would introduce special bills in which they would be personally interested, and
which would be of no importance to the country. Such legislation could be postponed
until next fall, when it would not be so certain to affect the business of the country. The
new Congress would be republican, but the opposition would be strong, especially with
political power so evenly divided, and it would exert its prerogative to criticise and oppose the administration which should have a fair trial until December, when there
would be plenty of time for legislation and discussion. When General Grant was informed that the Senate Finance Committee had expressed an opinion against the calling of an extra session he was highly gratified. The question was asked if the veto of the
Funding bill would justify an extra session. General Grant replied that it was doubtful
if the next Congress would act wisely on the bill, and the tendency to make an attack
on national banks would do more harm than would be overbalanced by any possible
good. He spoke very earnestly of the present financial situation. He thought we had the
best banking system in the world, and he believed that the financial policy of the country should look forward to a perpetuation of the currency laws for a considerable time
at least. He thought the government should issue a loan of $1,000,000,000 at three and
a half per cent for an indefinite time, which would serve as a basis for our currency and
be a safe investment for banks, trust funds, estates, &c. The time might come when the
people would wish to pay off this loan. General Grant said he was not eager to have it
paid, and he thought the country would be financially sounder if it carried for a generation at least this $1,000,000,000 debt. He said the raid upon the national banks was
only a part of that system of financial policy which had been trying ever since the beginning of the war to attain some intangible, indefinite, fantastical result at the expense of the best interests of the country. So much had been done in safeguarding the
credit of the nation that it was the highest wisdom and patriotism to resist every scheme
to affect it. He was sure the country could safely trust the administration to carry on
public affairs until the next regular meeting of Congress. General Grant also referred
to the argument in favor of a three percent loan deduced from the high rate of consols
and from the success of the French Republic in offering its recent loan of 200,000,000f.
The high rate of English consols was a temporary incident. France offered their loan at
between eighty-two and eighty-three. The American government should never sell a
bond except at par. It was too much to expect that American credit would do better
than the credit of England. In speaking of his proposed visit to Mexico the General
said he would be accompanied by his wife, his son, Ulysses S. Grant, Jr., and his wife,
Mr. Romero, the Mexican Minister, and probably one or two personal friends. He did
not expect to remain longer than three months, and on his return he would go directly
to his cottage in Long Branch. He had about made up his mind to live in New York, and
he would probably take up his residence here at the close of the summer season. Allusion was made to the New York appointments. The General expressed himself pleased
with President Garfield's nominations, especially with that of General Woodford for
the District Attorneyship. He was also glad that Mr. Jones, of Illinois, had been nominated Marshal for the Northern district of that State. This appointment would be particularly gratifying to General Logan, and he (Grant) was glad that President Garfield
had shown a disposition to recognize the republican party as a unit and to consider the

wishes of men like Logan in Illinois and Conkling in New York. During the conversation reference was made to the news from China and Japan and the perplexing complications arising out of the Loochoo question. General Grant hoped that peace would be preserved. He spoke of those countries with a great deal of interest, and he said he hoped that in two years he would be able to pay Japan another visit. He would then have an opportunity to see the country thoroughly and to visit some of his friends in both China and Japan. He would travel in a more quiet manner than when he journeyed around the world. He felt the greatest possible interest in the welfare of those countries, and he thought that there was no part of the foreign policy of the present administration where more effective and brilliant work could be done than in guarding and extending our relations with China and Japan. Allusion was made to the Chinese Treaty with the United States. The General said that he had not studied the treaty carefully, but he thought there were one or two points open to criticism. It was right to control the emigration question—a subject about which China would never embarrass us—but we ought to be careful before we limit our commercial future by placing any unnecessary restriction upon commerce." *New York Herald*, March 23, 1881. On March 28, a correspondent reported that weeks earlier USG had sought the support of New York City lawyer and former judge Henry Hilton, an early backer turned critic. "General Grant called on the Judge, to win him over, if possible. Hilton refused to be converted, and warmly attacked the charter, showing up its weak points, particularly that the management of the fair is given to an executive committee appointed by the commissioners who are not necessarily stockholders. Hilton argued that this was absurd, since the control ought to be in the representatives of stockholders. Their agent manifested considerable surprise. 'Haven't you read the charter?' asked the Judge and the President of the Commision answered no. The Judge then attacked Inwood, the site chosen, saying that it is a swamp, malarious, too far from the city, and altogether unfit for the purpose. This also surprised the General. 'Hadn't he visited Inwood?' 'He hadn't.' Whether he went out to Inwood is not stated, but he failed to enlist Judge Hilton in the enterprise, and soon bloomed out into a determined opponent of the Inwood site, which, it ought to be said, had been selected before his election to the Presidency." *Chicago Inter-Ocean*, March 29, 1881. Also on March 28, a reporter interviewed Clinton B. Fisk. "Several weeks ago Gen. Grant and I had a long talk over the matter across the way in his son's office, and we both arrived at the conclusion that the people of New-York don't want a World's Fair. . . ." *New York Times*, March 29, 1881.

To *William R. Rowley*

———

New York City
March 24th 1881

MY DEAR GEN.L ROWLEY:

On Monday[1] Mrs. Grant & I start for Mexico. On our return, about the 1st of June, we hope to take Galena in our way and to spend a few days with our friends. As I go this time entirely on business however, I may find it necessary to hasten back to this city without stoping. In this event we will hope to run out later to see you all. Tell Mr. Ryan that the weather has been so wreched that Mrs. Grant & I have not been able to get out as far as the Sacred Heart, to visit his daughters yet; but if it does not rain to-morrow afternoon we are going then.[2]—My visit to Mexico last year has resulted in the building of rail-roads in that country to an extent far beyond my most sanguine expectation at the time. The Mexicans have a country of vast resources, and these roads will develope them to the mutual benefit of both republics. We are now buying vast amounts of tropical products, sugar, coffee, tobacco, and numerous other articles, from countries that take but little from us, other than sterling exchange, all of which Mexico can furnish just as well and for which she will want the products of our manufacturies and soil. I go on business, of course, connected these enterprizes.—We go by way of St. Louis, thence by Iron Mountain R. R. to Galveston and across to Vera Cruz.—Give Mrs. Grants and my best regards to Mrs. Rowley, your daughter[3] and all our Galena friends.—If you should want to drop me a line a letter addressed to the care of Judge J. F. Long, St. Louis, Mo. or to Postmaster, Galveston, would reach me.

Very Truly yours
U. S. GRANT

ALS, ICarbS.

    1. March 28, 1881.
    2. James M. Ryan, Galena meat packer, had two daughters attending the Academy of the Sacred Heart, overlooking Manhattanville, north of New York City.
    3. Estelle Rowley, age 20 in the 1880 census.

To Ellen Grant Sartoris

New York City
March 24th 1881.

MY DEAR DAUGHTER:

I received your very nice letter a day or two ago. Almost before it left England Jesse & Lizzie must have been with you. I hope they

got to London before you left. We are glad to hear that little Algie
has recovered. I shall miss him at Long Branch during the summer.
I had counted on him and his little cousin Julia accompanying me
in my drives. But I hope yet we will have a house here in this city
by fall where you, Algie and all the children[1] can come and spend
the Winter with us. Buck & Fannie have abandoned the idea of going to Europe this spring, and have concluded to go to Mexico with
us instead. This will be very pleasant both for your ma & me.—I
hope Jesse will be successful in the business which takes him to England. But I confess that I have no clear idea of what his business is.
But he is clear headed, has very good judgement, and I know will
not misrepresent anything. How are you pleased with Lizzie? We
are delighted with her. In fact we are pleased with all our children
and children-in-law. We start to Mexico on Monday next[2] and may
be gone two months. If you write to your Ma or me soon—and
you must write—direct to the care of the U. S. Minister, Mexico.
Fred was here the past week, and only left last night. He is getting
ready to resign and go into rail-roading as President.[3] I will be
delighted when I have no near relative in government employment,
particularly if they are doing well.—You Ma joins me in love to
you, Algie & the children.

Yours Affectionately

U. S. GRANT

ALS, ICHi.

1. Algernon E. and Vivien M. Sartoris were joined by a sister, Rosemary Alice
Sartoris, born Nov. 30, 1880.
2. March 28, 1881.
3. "The sale of the Texas Western Narrow Gauge Railroad was confirmed in the
United States Circuit Court to-day, . . . It is in contemplation to transfer the road to a
new company. Gen. U. S. Grant, H. Victor Newcomb, of Louisville; John B. Alley, of
Boston, and Fred D. Grant are believed to be named in connection with the directory
to be formed, . . ." "A dispatch from Houston, Texas, gives further details of the sale
of the Texas Western Narrow-gauge Railroad, under foreclosure of mortgage. Col.
W. B. B[o]tts was the purchaser at $100,000. A new company will be formed with H.
H. Honore, of Chicago, as President. It is said that Col. Fred D. Grant will probably
resign from the Army to take charge of the road as Chief Engineer, . . ." "Col. Fred
Grant will leave here to-day with his family for New-York, where he goes to assume
the Presidency of the Texas Western Narrow Gauge Railroad Company. . . . Col. Grant
will make his head-quarters in New-York, but much of his time will be spent in Texas."

New York Times, April 7, 8, 29, 1881. On leave since April 1, Frederick Dent Grant resigned his army commission as of Oct. 1.

To James A. Garfield

New York City
March 26th 1881

HIS EXCELLENCY:
JAS. A. GARFIELD:
PRESIDENT OF THE UNITED STATES
DEAR SIR:

This will present Mr. Walter Fearn, of New Orleans, whos name I gave for the Mexican Mission in case there should be a vacancy there. I infer now that there is not likely to be a vacancy in that Mission [Mr. Fearn is an accomplished gentleman, speaks the French, Spanish & Italian languages about as fluently as his own, had experience years ago as Secretary of Legation, has traveled much in Europe, and in every way is appropriate for a foreign appointment. In a letter to Mr. Pitkin I stated that since my recommendation of a gentleman for the Mexican Commission it had occurred to me that the person named may have opposed your election.[1] I hoped he had not. Mr. Fearn informs me that he did nothing to oppose you. He was very much] disappointed at the result of the Convention which made the nomination. If under these circumstances you can appoint Mr. Fearn to a suitable Mission I will feel under obligation. I do not know whether the Belgian Mission is to be vacant or not. If so Mr. Fearn would be an ornament to that Mission as he would be to Italy. I would not name the latter place in opposition to Gen. Badeau.

Judge Hunt, of your Cabinet, is well acquainted with Mr Fearn.

Very Truly
U. S. GRANT

ALS (partial facsimile), Christie's Sale No. 1139, Oct. 9, 2002, no. 135; Sotheby Parke Bernet, Sale No. 4748E, Part Five, Dec. 4, 1981, no. 1141.

1. See letter to James A. Garfield, March 19, 1881.

To Robert T. Lincoln

———

New York City
March 26th 1881

HON. ROBT LINCOLN:
SEC. OF WAR:
DEAR SIR:

A classmate of mine, and a General in the rebellion, Gen. I. F. Quinby, has a son, Arnot Quinby, who he is very anxious should have an appointment to the Military Academy. I take pleasure in commending him to the President for an appointment, At Large, if there are vacancies to fill for the coming June, or for June 1882. Young Quinby will be seventeen years of age in June, just bearly eligible for for the present year, and quite young enough for 1882.

Very Truly yours
U. S. GRANT

ALS, DNA, RG 94, Correspondence, USMA. Related papers are *ibid.* Arnot Quinby did not attend USMA.

To Jesse Root Grant, Jr.

———

New York City
March 28th /81

DEAR JESSE:

We leave this am. at Eight O'Clock for Mexico, Via St. Louis & Galveston.

Everything now seems to be in good shape for our rail-road enterprize. I have accepted the Presidency of the company, and now nothing is wanting except some changes to the consession. Freds road too seems to be fairly under way.[1] He will probably accompany me as far as Houston, Texas, so as to be present at the sale of the finished part of his road, on the 5th prox.—I hope you are having success in your business enterprize. I cannot say however that I know what your business is.—I hope you see a good deal of

Nellie. We have not had a letter from her written since your arrival
in England, though we got one written about that time in which she
expressed great anxiety about seeing you and Lizzie.—Your Ma & I
send much love to both you and Lizzie, and Nellie and her children.

Affectionately Yours

U. S. GRANT

ALS, ICHi.

On March 18, 1881, USG wrote to Collis P. Huntington *et al.* "The meeting of the
Incorporators of the Mexican Southern Railroad Company called for March 19th 1881,
at 3. P. M., is postponed until such time and place as may be fixed by further notice
from the Chairman." LS, Collis P. Huntington Papers, Syracuse University, Syracuse,
N. Y.; Goodspeed's Book Shop, Inc., Boston, Mass.; Mrs. Walter Love, Flint, Mich.;
Gallery of History, Las Vegas, Nev.; Edwin D. Morgan Papers, New York State Library, Albany, N. Y. On March 23, USG wrote to Huntington *et al.* "A meeting of the
incorporators of the Mexican Southern Railroad Company, for the purpose of organization, will be held on Thursday, the the 24th day of March (inst.) at 7.30 O'Clock P. M.
of that day, at No. 77, Clinton Place, New York City. You are respectfully invited to attend." LS, Collis P. Huntington Papers, Syracuse University, Syracuse, N. Y.; Edwin D.
Morgan Papers, New York State Library, Albany, N. Y.; DLC-USG, IB. See letter to
Matías Romero, Jan. 15, 1881.

On March 14, Thomas P. Ochiltree had written to Ulysses S. Grant, Jr. "I deem
it my duty to give you some information, (for your guidance,) in regard to a new relation I see you have gone into with certain parties in a Rail Road enterprise. 1st Genl (!)
Barnes of Texas—This man is unscrupulous, visionary, and hypocritical, *pretending*
to be the supporter of Genl Grant, (during the late exciting contest at Chicago,) he
sent repeated urgent & importunate appeals to Governor Davis (by telegraph from
Washington,) 'for Gods sake dont nominate Grant—it will ruin the country &c &c'—
'support Blaine with the whole Texas delegation' &c' &c.' *Now,* finding out that Genl
Grant has influence in Mexico, this cunning old Fox has worked his way into a connection with you so as to use your influence with your father and to trade on your
name—' 2d The man J. B. Price has been connected with the late 'Star route scandal'
at Washington, and in every other robbery in the Post Office Department for the past
fifteen years; He bears a most unenviable reputation amongst his brother contractors
for gross unreliability and general dishonesty of character; In a word he is one of the
most disreputable of men, &, outside of his 'shyster mining associates', great wonder
has been expressed at his being associated with such respectable names as those of Col
Buck and yourself in this Railway enterprise: I am perfectly willing that this communication should be shown to either of the foregoing individuals, for I can substantiate
all I have said regarding both." ALS, USG 3.

On March 23, J. & W. Seligman & Co., New York City, wrote to USG. "Learning
that you propose leaving shortly for Mexico, we take the opportunity, with your kind
permission, of presenting certain facts to the Mexican Government, which are not only
of interest, but, if carried out, will unquestionably exert a very beneficial effect upon
Mexico and its industries. We believe that Mexico has now arrived at that stage when
serious consideration should be given toward making some legitimate and reasonable
provision for regulating and meeting its recognized debt. The growing interchange of

commodities with the United States, the rapid and unprecedented construction of railroads into Mexico by United States capital, the increase in the revenues of Mexico itself: all point to a gradual era of prosperity such as Mexico has as yet never attained. In order to place her credit on a stable basis, thereby giving proof to the civilized world of her intention and ability to meet her interest payments, it will be necessary, at once, to make some provision toward effecting this object, and which, if wisely administered, will, without difficulty, place her national credit on a safe basis. In thus referring to this matter, we beg to state that we have the co-operation of the Messrs. Rothschilds and their associates in Europe, and the principal holders of the Mexican Bonds in the United States, thus representing probably a majority of Bondholders, who are all willing to enter into any honest plan for funding the present debt, provided they receive assurance in shape of special liens, that the same will be carried out; and authorize you, dear sir, to make such advances as will lead to an attainment of their wishes. . . . Another plan which we would suggest, would be the exchanging of these Bonds against good lands in Mexico, on such basis and conditions as will be mutually satisfactory. In such an exchange, it will, of course, be necessary for the Mexican Government to give clean and valid titles to such lands, with exemption from any State burdens, thus giving the Bondholders in exchange a perfectly and perpetually secure investment. We have already shown the importance of the State of Mexico taking some immediate action in this matter, as this feeling of security is only wanting to justify large immigration into Mexico, and at the same time, a safe home investment for Mexican capitalists themselves. We feel confident, dear sir, that this mission could not be entrusted to more able and influential hands; and we feel assured that you, who always have been such a friend of Mexico and have taken such an interest in its domestic affairs, will give this matter your earnest attention. . . . P. S. We have just received a cable from our London house, in which the Messrs. Rothschilds suggest that it might be advisable for the Mexican Government to pay 1½ per cent. yearly for three years, 2 per cent. for 5 years and 3 per cent. thereafter. Also, that the United States and the French Consuls should act as Trustees for the Bondholders." TLS, *ibid.*

1. See letter to Ellen Grant Sartoris, March 24, 1881, note 3.

To John Russell Young

[*March, 1881*]

Dear Com.

I telegraphed you to-day asking you to dine with me at six this evening. Not hearing from you I fear you were out. If you can not come will you read the enclosed papers and return them to me. You can see what I would like. I would like to see in the Heral in the morning a short editorial calling for justice to Japan—by the speedy restoration of her own funds, wrongly taken from her.

Yours &c.

U. S. Grant

ALS, DLC-John Russell Young. In an editorial, "Japan and the Indemnity," the *New York Herald* supported a bill to return the U.S. share of the Shimonoseki indemnity fund, paid by Japan to foreign powers after an 1863 naval skirmish. ". . . Ex-President Grant, having been in Japan when he studied the question, knows it minutely, and makes an appeal for its passage as due to the honor of America, not to speak of justice to Japan. . . ." *New York Herald*, March 4, 1881. On March 3, 1881, the final day of the Congressional session, the Senate passed the bill; the House failed to act. See *CR*, 46-3, 2399–2402; "Justice to Japan," *New York Times*, March 2, 1881; *PUSG*, 25, 290; letter to Charles G. Williams, July 24, 1882.

To Samuel L. Clemens

Galveston, Texas,
April 1st 1881.

My Dear Mr. Clemens;

Myself and party arrived here this noon. After getting the dust washed off and a bite to eat, I wrote the enclosed note under many difficulties. I have had no minuet of time without callers, and among them the inevitable reporter. If you will shew this letter to Young Wing, and he approves of it, and then forward it to Li Hung Chang, I will be much obliged to you.

I regret much not reading your letter when it was received. Had I done so I would have arranged for a meeting with you and friends no matter what I had to do. But the fact is, when your letter come I was much behind in my correspondence, and as soon as I looked at the address I put it in my pocket, with a number of others, to be attended to as soon as I got time. This is not a very good excuse for such treatment, but it has the merit of being the exact fact.

Please let me hear from you at your pleasure. My address will be Care U. S. Minister, City of Mexico.

Very Truly yours
U. S. Grant

ALS, CU-B. On April 22, 1881, Samuel L. Clemens, Hartford, wrote to USG. "I was sorry you had to write your letter on the wing, when you might have been resting in Galveston instead of working, if I had only had wit enough to so mark the back of my letter to you as to call your immediate attention to it. Your letter to the viceroy has gone at a fortunate time, for it will strengthen his hands at a needed season. I make the following extract from a letter just received by Rev. Mr. Twitchell, from Yung Wing: . . .

This is all the news I have, General. It is not official, still I suppose it is trustworthy. I thought I would send it to you, because you may not get our journals in Mexico, or at least may be too busy to examine them closely." Ellipsis in original, *Washington Post*, April 28, 1902. Supplied by Noble E. Dawson in a letter to the editor. See letter to Samuel L. Clemens, Dec. 24, 1880; letter to Li Hung-chang, April 1, 1881.

On April 1, USG had arrived at Galveston by train, en route to Vera Cruz via the steamer *Whitney*, departing on April 3. A reporter asked USG whether the Mexican Southern Railroad would "be a part of what is known as the Gould system?" USG answered. "Yes; Mr. Gould is one of the stockholders and a director in the line." USG explained that the termini would be "[t]he City of Mexico and Tehuantepec, the line passing through Oajaca. At the City of Mexico, connection will be made with all the roads centering there and diverging toward the north. Upon these construction is being pushed as rapidly as possible, 10,000 men being now employed on the line of the Mexican Central. Before the end of the year there will be 50,000 laborers at work on railroads throughout the Republic. . . . There are sufficient brains, energy and money at hand to accomplish the results that are sought." As for completion, "Circumstances will largely control that; of course no time will be lost, and delays will be avoided as much as possible." USG then characterized Mexican reaction to "the inroad of American capital." "Favorable. The great body of the people—the intelligent masses, who govern and control everywhere—have come to see that their interests lie in this direction. They have not the requisite means for this development, and, therefore, are glad to see the presence of American capital." USG addressed Mexican concern about annexation. "I do not fear anything on that score. When I visited Mexico I found something of this feeling, but I proved conclusively, I think, to their minds the folly of such a fear. I told them of the change which had taken place in our institutions. Twenty years ago, when slavery was in existence, there might have been a feeling favorable to the acquisition of this territory, for the reason [th]at, with any growth slavery might at[t]ai[n,] it would have required additional room in th[is] direction, as its spread in others had been ch[ec]ked. But the abolition of that institution had e[ffect]ually destroyed this argument for acquisition, and at this time I was satisfied that the American people would oppose the acquirement of further possessions except upon terms honorable and satisfactory to all. Again, as another argument, I showed that we consume $200,000,000 worth of tropical and semi-tropical fruits, which we now obtain from countries that, in the first place, employ slave labor, which is distasteful to us; then they impose heavy duties, which we have to pay, and, in the end, they deal in return with us only to the extent of receiving our sterling exchange. This trade, I argued, they could control and command, and by an interchange of products and trade relations could be established equally and mutually profitable and satisfactory." Asked if hostile press reports reflected strong opposition, USG replied. "No—not to a serious extent. The Mexicans understand their own press, and know how to gauge it. It is our own press which can do us harm. The New York Sun has been opposing this enterprise, but that means me. It is not so much opposition to the railroad as it is to me personally. The World and other leading journals have treated the enterprise fairly. . . . Of course, some of the foreigners will oppose it, but their numbers or influence are not dangerous. . . . The Government has made greater concessions than should have been made; greater than she will be able to pay. . . . Already attention has been directed to the increase of the agricultural features. Large sugar, coffee and wheat plantations are now being opened, and these will be opened and widened upon an extended scale. Land and labor are cheap, and the native population, finding a means of transportation for their products, will all the more readily engage in these pursuits. The traffic between the two countries will develop immensely with the progress of carrying facilities. . . . The whole country will experience it. Texas first and more immediately, but the influence will be general." Asked where the projected system of railroads connecting the U.S. and Mexico would find an ocean outlet, USG responded. "Galveston, of course, if you can get deep water. You have a city here already and have all the advantages of geographical location. If your efforts to deepen your harbor are successful, the railroads will naturally point to this place. [I]f not, they will have to seek some other port. However, I learn that the engineer in charge of the works is confident of success." *Galveston News*, April 2, 1881. "Here the conversation drifted into a discussion of the narrow-gauge system, which Gen. Grant pronounced to be the most valuable as pioneer roads, on account of their cheapness of construction and the fact that from their own earnings they could be changed to the standard gauge. From his remarks further in this strain the impression was not made that he considered it extremely probable there would soon be a national or international network of this system. At present the charter of the Mexican Southern calls for a narrow-gauge line." *Ibid.* See *ibid.*, April 3, 1881; Lynn M. Alperin, *Custodians of the Coast: History of the United States Army Engineers at Galveston* (Washington, 1977), pp. 37–51.

To Samuel L. Clemens

Galveston, Texas
April 1st 1881.

My Dear Mr. Clemens;

In my letter to-day to Viceroy Li Hung Chang I did not make use of an argument in favor of the Chinese looking to the United States both for men & money to carry out internal improvements rather than to the English, or any other European power, which I would have used in conversation. It is this. They have nothing to fear from the United States in the way of interference in their home affairs. The Viceroy understands very well that with Europeans if given an "Inch they will take an Ell;" they are domineering in their intercourse with the Eastern powers. Too many of our representatives in that ~~country~~ section follow the example of the English in their treatment and manner towards natives of the East; but in this they are not sustained by their Government. In fact until my trip to the East the Government has never been informed of the indignities the people there are subjected to by foreigners. I informed the State Department on my return of it, and wrote to Gen. Garfield, before his inauguration, on the same subject. Since that I have also conversed with him, and advised him of orders that should be issued through the Navy Department, ~~to Ministers & Consu~~ to officers stationed in the Chinese & Japanese waters, and through the State Department to Ministers and Consuls, to put a stop to it so far as our countrymen are concerned. If you choose you might "talk" this to Young Wing in your own way. It is an argument that he could well use if he favors American influence rather than European.

On my return to New York I will be very glad to meet you with Young Wing, and any others you, or he, choose to bring, to talk on this subject.

Very Truly yours
U. S. GRANT

ALS, CU-B.

To Li Hung-chang

———

Galveston Texas, April 1st., 1881.

My dear Friend: I am now at this place—Galveston—ready to debark for Mexico, our neighboring Republic. Mexico, like the Eastern countries, has been without railroads to this time but now has commenced a complete system, under American auspices, and with American capital. I am on my way there in the interest of these American roads.

At present but two steamers monthly pass between this city and Mexico. Just the day beofore I was obliged to leave New York City in order to connect with the steamer now about to depart, I learned for the first time that your great country was contemplating the building of four great trunk lines of rail roads. I was delighted to hear this, and if I had not been obliged to hurry off would have made it my duty and pleasure to have seen the Chinese representatives to our country, to offer my assistance in any way that might be useful.

You no doubt remember the conversations we had on the importance of railroads to develop the resources of a country; to give employment to the millions, and to give strength to a country against an outside enemy, as well as to suppress internal insurrections. At your request I repeated what I had said to Prince Kung. I little then dreamed then that China was likely so soon to contemplate what I then suggested. If what I now learn is true, it will afford me pleasure if I can be of service to you in this enterprise. I will be back in New York City before this letter can reach you. I will be very glad to hear from you then.

If China contemplates what I hope she does—the building of railroads—I would advise an examination of our system before adopting any other. I think we build railroads faster than any other country; build them quite as well, and build better locomotives and other rolling stock.

England can furnish the rails cheaper. For civil engineers, especially those engaged in the construction of railroads and all connected with them, the American engineer is unsurpassed. Should a foreign loan be required it can be effected in the United States, through an American Syndicate as well as elsewhere.

I repeat: if I can help China in matters of internal improvement, either in suggesting persons for employment in laying out roads; building them, or running them after being built; to construct and superintend the necessary workshops for repairs; or in suggesting parties here to negotiate any loan that may be wanted, I will be glad to render such service.

With renewed assurances of my high regard, and best wishes for you and your country I am,

Faithfully yours

U. S. GRANT.

Typescript, DLC-John Russell Young.

On May 26, 1881, Li Hung-chang, Tientsin, China, wrote to USG. "I beg to thank you for your letter of Feb. 3rd, enclosing the reply of the Winchester Arms Company and some of their pamphlets. I am having the latter translated and believe they will give me all needful information regarding the Winchester and the Hotchkiss arms. This information will be of value to me when I next require to purchase arms and I thank you for your kindness in furnishing it. It is very gratifying to read what you say of the present prosperity of your country, and it is my earnest wish that it may be permanent. Your industries and manufactures develop with surprising rapidity into vast proportions, and this must make your people peaceful and happy. China is also, I am happy to say, enjoying peace and prosperity. The danger of a war with Russia has passed away, and the country has been free from the calamities of famines and floods. The Treaties lately made with the United States have given great satisfaction, especially the one which forbids dealing in Opium. Whenever you have opportunity I beg that you will express to your countrymen how gratified my government is at this blow against Opium, which has always been a great curse to my Country & which has been spreading its evil influence with alarming rapidity. With such moral support as this Treaty gives, China may now make a successful stand against her enemy—opium—, and may hope ere long to banish it from her borders. I trust, also, that you will find occasion to recommend to your Government that Mr. Denny be appointed to succeed Minister Angell at Peking when the latter retires in the autumn. Mr. Denny's appointment would be very acceptable to my Government and would also give me great pleasure because of the regard I have for him. I feel sure that he would fill the office with peculiar ability. Hoping that you may long enjoy health and happiness and that I may yet have the pleasure of meeting you and again enjoying the privilege of your Counsel . . ." LS, USG 3. See Robert R. Swartout, Jr., *Mandarins, Gunboats, and Power Politics: Owen Nickerson Denny and the International Rivalries in Korea* (Honolulu, 1980), p. 8.

To John Russell Young

——————

Galveston, Texas
April 2d 1881.

MY DEAR COMMODORE:

We arrived here yesterday, after passing through one of the severest snow storms of the year in Ohio & Indiana, to find pleasant but cool weather. We will get of from here about noon to-day with a smooth sea which I hope will continue to Vera Cruz. I wish you were along to make up the Boston party. We found Mr. Chaffee here awaiting us to accompany us to Mexico. You would just make the four. We may undertake to teach Romero.

Will you be kind enough to see that Mr Murphy received the enclosed letter. I do not mail it to him because I believe there is another Hon. Thom Murphy[1] in the city with whom I do not correspond.—I hope Badeaus case will come out right, and that the whole political situation in Washington will take such shape as to

give Garfield peace of mind and the country quiet. If he did take
the benefits of treason he should not reward it.

Very Truly yours
U. S. GRANT

ALS, DLC-John Russell Young.

    1. Possibly Thomas Murphy, Democratic leader in the 20th Assembly District,
New York City. See *New York Times,* May 21, 1906.

To Edward F. Noyes, Adam Badeau, et al.

————

City of Mexico,
Apl. 10th 1881

    I take pleasure in presenting General Cyrus Bussey, of New
Orleans, La. to General Noyes, U. S. Minister to France, Gen.
Badeau, Consul General, London and to my personal acquaintances in United States Service in Europe, as a gentleman and representative American who they will be pleased to meet. Gen Busey
served in the war of the rebellion—Union Army—with credit and
has been a successful business man in the south ever since He will
appreciate any attention he may receive as I will also.

Very Truly
U. S. GRANT

ALS, IaHA.

Speech

————

[*Mexico City, April 22, 1881*]

    Gentlemen: Having always felt a great interest in Mexico, and
having a very vivid recollection of my visit here many years ago,
I felt a great anxiety to return to the country to see it again. In
gratification of that feeling I returned here about one year ago. I

then had no object in view further than to visit the country and to
see what changes had taken place since I had visited it before. On
my arrival here, however, I found many of the citizens, and particularly the President, interested very much in the matter of railroads
as a means of developing the resources of the country. This was a
feeling that I heartily entertained myself, and what was intended in
the first instance as a visit of pleasure became one of duty in trying
to establish sentiments of confidence and good feeling between the
citizens of the two neighboring republics. We having railroads under construction at that time which were rapidly approaching the
frontiers of this country, I said what I could in favor of a system of
railroads which should connect the two republics. I had in view the
establishing of close commercial relations which I was then satisfied, and am now satisfied, will produce also friendly personal relations. The then President entertained sentiments similar to my
own and I promised him that on my return to the United States I
would try to interest American capitalists, and particularly those
engaged in developing the railroad system of the United States,
in Mexican affairs. On my return in frequent conversations, interviews with newspaper men and, in remarks made at receptions, I
alluded to, and found it a very easy matter to awaken a deep interest in, the subject. Already the result is seen in a system of railroads
which will form principal trunk lines for the country north of the
city of Mexico. In the course of time, judging from the experience
we have had in the United States, many other lines will be found
equally, important in the development of the country and in developing the business of these main trunk lines. Indiana, the smallest
one of our states west of the Alleghany mountains and containing
a population of only about one-fourth of that of Mexico has already
in successful operation more than [*the*] number of miles of railroad
tha[*t are*] now in contemplation in this Republic, including all those
now seeking grants, so far as I am informed. Yet they find it necessary to build more roads every year to keep up with the growing
demands of her business and I have no doubt that such will be also
the experience of Mexico when all the roads now in contemplation
are built. You will find that they have created a necessity for oth-

ers, and that they are only the commencement of a grand system of roads yet to be constructed.

I also conceived the idea that for the full development of this country, lines south of the city of Mexico as well as those north, were highly important.

I have interested the same class of capitalists on this subject also and they have chosen me as the President of what is know as the Mexican Southern road. I hope that it will meet with as much favor with the citizens of this country as it has with the capitalists of ours, and that the road will speedily be built, and the development of that rich section of this country will immediately commence.

I have no interest there personal to myself, but am very desirous of rendering my own country, this country and the republican form of Government a service whenever it is in my power to do so.

I have long been of the opinion that the United States and Mexico should be the warmest of friends, and enjoy the closest commercial relations. This country is a complement of our own; we produce all of the northern cereals, and fruits of the temperate zone. Mexico, in addition to furnishing the same commodities, can furnish all those of a tropical nature; we are naturally large consumers of the articles which Mexico is capable of producing, and which we can not ourselves produce. Our importations of these articles—sugar, coffee and tobacco being the leading ones, but embracing many others, such as dye-woods, tropical fruits mahogany and other valuable woods,—amounts now to over $200.000,000 a year. We get but very few of these articles from Mexico but we would like to get more, or all of them if possible, because it would not only benefit a neighboring republic, but it would be a very great advantage to ourselves, in as much as we could pay for them, partly or in whole, in articles which we can produce to better advantage than can Mexico. At all events so large a balance would not be left to be paid in coin. Then too, as I have said on frequent occasions, in the United States we now get these articles from countries which collected revenue by levying duties upon exports. Mexico, like the United States, encourages the exportation of her products, and puts no tax upon their going out of the country. We would save this amount in making our purchases here instead of making them where we do now. That alone would be of very great advantage to us as a nation,—but no more desirable than seeing the progress of institutions which we pride ourselves upon and which we are glad to see encouraged wherever they exist.

I look upon the railroads which are now being built as vastly important to Mexico, and I wish to see them prosper, and realize to the capitalists who build them a good return for the money invested and result in the development of the resources of Mexico. Those which I represent on this occasion, lying south of the city of Mexico, will be, in my judgment, of very great aid to the roads which are now being built. Instead of being in competition with them, they will be feeders to them. In fact, whatever goes to the development and growth of a country, goes to increase the business of the railroads of that cou[n]try. Progress in Mexico throughout all its ports, means business for the railroads.

There is no railroad enterprise now in operation and none spoken of, that I feel the one I have in contemplation will conflict with, and none to which I would not lend my aid to their success in any way in my power, and I hope this kindly feeling is reciprocated by those interested in the railroads now building towards the roads in contemplation of which I have the honor of being President. I predict, with the building of these roads, a development of the country will take place such as has never been witnessed in any country before. Mexico commences her internal improvements where it has taken Europe and the United States fifty years of toil, expenditure and invention to reach. With her great natural resources, and the open market of the world for her comodities, her development must be what I have just predicted.

While these railroads will furnish transportation through the interior and, for many, articles, from one republic to the other, yet the great line of commerce will necessarily be from the different searports, particulary those upon the Gulf of Mexico. At the present time there is but one harbor upon the Gulf within Mexican territory where vessels of any considerable draft can come in close proximity to the shore, namely Vera Cruz. It will be found that, to keep up with the march of progress, you will have to look for more ports, and that the demands for them will probably grow more rapidly than the country will find means to provide for. The road which I represent looks to the opening of a new port, Anton Lizardo, which I do not look upon as conflicting at all with the interest of the main port of the republic, Vera Cruz. On the contrary that port now, even in the anticipation of what is to take place in the near future, is hardly capable, of transacting the business that it is called upon to transact, and I hope an enterprise which I have just heard of, that of enlarging the capacity of Vera Cruz, may be commenced and carried forward as rapidly as men and money can carry it on. With the contemplated improvements, I predict its capacity will be wholly inadequate to the demands made upon it. It is my desire to get the present grant executed so as to start from Vera Cruz, running by, or near Anton Lizardo so that the advantages of two ports may be had when they become necessary. A railroad between the two ports would always be highly desirable. Our experience in the United States has been that wherever we can find an inlet that can, by the expenditure of money, be made to admit large vessels, it is to our advantage, and to the advantage of the whole country to enlarge their capacity so as to admit vessels, and instedd of being rivals, and in competition with well established and old ports, it only seems to increase the business of the old ones. The United States now expends millions of dollars annually in improvements of harbors, and in making additional harbors.

She is at this time expending large sums in the creation of four new harbors in the state of Texas, in addition to the expenditures for the improvement in progress at Galveston, the only harbor in the state now admitting vessels of considerable draft.

With the developments which are now in contemplation and which I hope to see speedily realized, the revenues of Mexico will increase from eighteen to twenty millions, as they now are, to fifty millions, and upon a very greatly diminished rate of taxation.

There is nothing, in my opinion, to stand in the way of Mexican progress and grandeur, and wealth, but the people themselves. I do not anticipate their opposition, but fully expect their active support. I think that I answer for nine-tenths of the people of my own country when I say that we have no sinister motives whatever, we have no designs nor desires that are inimical to the honor and credit of this great republic.

I am aware that some of the papers of Mexico, as well as, possibly, some in the United States, have made allusion to the possibility of the annexation of Mexican territory to the United States. On that subject I know that there are no grounds whatever for apprehension. While I was President of the United States representatives of the republic of Santo Domingo applied to me for annexation, declaring that such was the desire of the government and the wish of all the people of the island. This proposition came to me several times before I considered it at all. At length fearing what had been said to me might be merely the statements of designing men willing to sell their, country for private gain, I determined, quietly and without the k[n]owledge of the agents of Santo Domingo, to send thither agents of my own to discover the real feeling of her people. By this means I verified the statements that ninety nine hundredths of her citizens were anxious for the proposed annexation. They were fully alive to the subject, had thought over it, and such a consummation was the brightest of their dreams. They desired, as they expressed it, to become a part of the great republic. I then entered into a teatry with that country (which has all the capacities of the best part of Mexico,) and submitted it to the Senate of the United States for ratification. It was with great difficultty notwithstanding my position as head of the government, that I could get the question considered at all by the Senate, and when I did, it was defeated by an overwhelming majority.

I am sure that even if it could be shown that all the people of Mexico were in favor of the annexation of a portion of their territory to the United States, it would still be rejected. We want no more land. We do want to improve what we have, and we want to see our neighbors improve, and grow so strong that the designs of any other country could not endanger them.

Mexico has the elements of development and wealth such as no other country possesses, at all events to so high a degree. Her proximity to the equator, with her elevated plains enables her to produce the fruits of all latitudes. Her mines are the richest in the world and she possesses every climate from the tropical to the frigid in near proximity to each other. With the contemplated improvements in internal communication she must advance beyond the dream of her most patriotic citizens. So far as I am concerned I will be very glad if I can contribute to this result.

I hope that we may be the warmest of friends, and that the two republics may exist always.

The Two Republics, April 24, 1881. USG spoke at a banquet held in his honor at the Tivoli del Eliseo by Mexican senators and representatives from Oaxaca. "Upon being called, General Grant rose and said that he had prepared a speech for the occasion, that it had been translated into Spanish and that Mr. Romero would read it. This being done, Mr. Juan Fenochio, Member of Congress from Oaxaca, replied in English." *Ibid.* See *New York World*, April 26, May 12, 1881; David M. Pletcher, *Rails, Mines, and Progress: Seven American Promoters in Mexico, 1867–1911* (Ithaca, N. Y., 1958), p. 163.

To James A. Garfield

City of Mexico
Apl. 24th 1881.

The President:
Dear Sir:

The privilege which you gave me of writing to you, before and after your inauguration, and the deep interest I feel in the success of the republican party,—believing that it should controll the country until all the results of our costly war were fully admitted by all political parties—induces me to write you this letter. I write it as an earnest well wisher of my country, and of you individually. I believe sincerely that with such an administration as you can give, and have the opportunity of giving, you will have no competitor for the nomination in /84, and that your re-election will be much easyier than your election. But this cannot be by giving the administration over to the settlement of *other peoples* private grievances, nor by recognizing factions as the party. When I saw the batch of

appointments made correcting what I believed a grievous mistake
of your immediate predecessor, I felt that you had struck the key
note of success. When the appointments of the next day went in
I was saddened and thought it would have been much better, or
rather not half so bad, if you had continued the policy of Mr. Hayes
in recognizing disgruntled factions, who support the party only
when they are made the leaders of it, as the party. It is always the
fair thing to recognize the representatives chosen by the people.
The Senators from New York were chosen against all the power
an administration of their own party could bring to bear. It is fair
to suppose that their Senators represent at least their party within
the state. To nominate a man to the most influential position within
the gift of the President, ~~without consu~~ in their state, without consulting them, would be an undeserved slight. To select the most
obnoxious man, to them, in the state is more than a slight. Mr.
Robertson[1] did not support the nominee of the republican party in
1872—I think he did not—when that nominee received the unanimous vote of his party. He gave indications at the convention which
nominated you, that if the nominee of 1872 were nominated in /80
he would not support the ticket, although he went as a deligate to
that convention pledged to support that candidate. I am disposed,
so far as I am concerned, to ignore, if I cannot forget, all wrongs
perpitrated against me personally, for the general good. But insults
and wrongs against others for the crime of having supported me I
do feel and will resent all that it is in my power to resent. I gave
you a hearty and strong support, in the presence of an assembled
croud, the moment your nomination was sent over the wires. I continued that support up to the night preceding the election. I claim
no credit for this for it was my duty. I had been honored as no other
man had by the republican party and by the nation. It was my duty
to serve both. But I do claim that I ought not to be humiliated by
seeing my personal friends punished for no other offence than their
friendship and support. I do hope and trust you may see this matter
in the same light I do, and if you do not, believe at least that I have
no other object in writing to you at this time than to serve you, the

party and the nation you represent. The republican paty has gone through four years of trials hard to bear, and it may not be able to withstand four years more. I sincerely trust it may not be put to the test.

I shall send this letter through my friend Senator Jones, of Nevada, to insure it reaching your hands without going through the hands of a Secretary, to be read perhaps before it reaches you.

With sincere regard, and my best wishes for you and your administration, I am

Very Truly yours

U. S. Grant

Gen. J. A. Garfield President of the U. States.

ALS, DLC-James A. Garfield. On May 15, 1881, President James A. Garfield wrote to USG. "Yours of the 24th April was handed to me by Senator Jones the night before last. I was, and always will be, glad to hear your suggestions on an subject connected with the public welfare—I am in hearty accord with every expression in your letter touching the welfare of the country, and the success of the Republican party—You are, however, under serious misapprehension in reference to my motives and purposes concerning the NewYork appointments, and I beg to refer, in detail to the points in your letter, omitting, for the present, that which is personal to me—You say that success cannot be achieved by 'giving the administration over to the settlement of other people's private greivances'—You do me great injustice to suppose that I am capable of permitting such use of the power entrusted to me. It has not been done nor will it be—I have no thought of making any appointment to injure you—While I heartily agree with you when you say that you 'ought not to be humiliated by seeing my [your] personal friends punished for no other offence than their friendship and support', I am sure you will agree with me that able worthy and competent men should not be excluded from recognition because they opposed your nomination at Chicago. That I had no purpose to proscribe your friends in N. Y, but every disposition to deal justly and at the same time cultivate their friendly feelings towards my administration, appears from the fact that I selected for a very important cabinet position one of your warm supporters, and gave ten other important position to your friends in N. Y. most of whom had been strongly recommended by one or both of the Senators & by other friends of yours—In making a selection of a Collector of the Port of N. Y. an office more national than local, I sought to secure the services of a gentleman of eminent ability, and at the same time to give just recognition to that large and intelligent element of N. Y. Republicans who were in in accord with the majority of the Chicago Convention. For this, I am assailed by some of your indiscreet friends. As I said in the Chicago Convention, it needed all grades and shades of Republicans to carry the Election—So it needs the support of all good republicans to make the administration successful—In this connection, let me correct two errors of fact into which you have inadvertently fallen—Judge Robertson did not, as you suppose, oppose your Election in 1872, nor did he declare, in the Chicago Convention that he would not support you if nominated—He was elected State Senator in 1872, running on the same ticket with you—At Chicago, on the roll-call, before any nominations had been made, he voted to support the nominee of the Convention whoever he might be—Now, while I agree substantially with you, that 'it is always the fair thing to recognize the representatives chosen by the people', I am not willing to allow the power of the Executive, in selecting persons for nomination to be restricted to the consideration of those only who may be suggested by the Senators from the state from which the selection is to be made—I feel bound, as you did, when President, to see to it that local quarrels for leadership shall not exclude from recognition men who represent any valuable element in the Republican party. It is my purpose to be just to all; and while I am incapable of discriminating against any Republican because he supported you, I am sure you will agree with me that I ough[t] not to permit any one to be proscribed because he did not support you— Before Judge Robertson's nomination I had reason to know that it was the wish of both the N. Y. Senators that the Collector should be changed—I knew that in Senator Platts recent election, he had received the support of Judge Robertson both in the caucus and in the Senate, & I had reason to believe, and did believe that the nomination would be satisfactory to him, and to the Governor of the State, (both of whom, were your warm Supporters,) and that that it would be eminently satisfactory to a ~~majority~~ large body of N. Y. Republicans—I had no reason to suppose that Mr. Robertson was regarded as a personal enemy by Senator Conkling—Judge Robertson had twice ~~supported~~ voted for Mr Conkling for U. S. Senator, and had supported him for the Presidency at Cincinnati, so long as the N. Y. delegation presented his name. He occupied a leading and distinguished position in his state and party—His fitness for the Collectorship had not been, and is not, questioned. Notwithstanding all this when, on the day after the nomination I heard that it was objected to by Senator Conkling, I made an appointment for a conference with him, Senator Platt and the Vice President, on the subject, and waited an hour and a half beyond the time they had fixed. They did not call—nor has Senator Conkling called to see me since—The course of subsequent events has placed the question far beyond the personal fate of Judge Robertson as a nominee—The issue now is, whether the President, in making nominations to office shall act in obedience to the dictation of the Senators from the state where the office is to be exercised. I regard this assumption as at war with the Constitution, and destructive of the true principles of administration—To submit to this view, would be to renounce the trust I have undertaken—My dear General, I can never forget your great services during the late campaign. They were given ungrudgingly asnd as whole-heartedly as I always gave you mine, when our positions were reversed before the people—You supported me without condition or attempted stipulation; and my heart warms generously in response to any request or desire of yours—In this connection, I may say that I shall be glad if I find myself able to carry out your wish in reference to Gen. Badeau—Be assured that whatever concerns your happiness and prosperity, will always be a matter of sincere interest to me—" ALS (brackets in original), Mrs. Paul E. Ruestow, Jacksonville, Fla. Roscoe Conkling prepared a memorandum rebutting this letter. "I. *James*. Whitelaw Read & Blaine put him into the Cabinet. No N. Y. Senator or friend of Genl Grant had any knowledge of it till it was arranged. II 'Ten other important positions given to your friends in N. Y. &c.' This paragraph is false. 1. L. P. Morton was appointed on a bargain made in August '80 to induce him to raise & pay money. No senator consulted, no one asked the appointmnt. 2. Pearson P. M. at N. Y. an utter surprise. No senator or other friend of Genl G. asked or wanted it, or even knew of it. Pearson had no political position—Jame's son in law. 3. Woodford, Tenney & McDougall re-appointments—

wholly aside from any request of senators—and except McD holding slight relation to Stallwart Republicans—Payn a stalwart was withdrawn as marshall of Southen Dist., & Knox a Tilden Democrat put in his place. These are all the general appointments—The rest of the list must be made up of local officers recommended from the localities and by Members of the House. III Garfield sought 'a gentleman of eminent ability &c. for Collector. 1. Merritt in midst of his term. Hayes & Sherman had certified just before going out that he was a model collector. It is utterly false that either Senator ever asked his removal. The avowed purpose was to snatch the office, in violation of oftrepeated pledges and give it to Robertson as a reward for betraying a trust & inciting other men to do so too. 2. Robertson, aside from other objections never had an hours experience fitting him for the *official* duties of the place. His sole industry for 20 years has been manipulating politics, hunting patronage, & representing certain RailRoads who have bought his elections to the legislature No one pretends his fitness, & 7000 firms remonstated against the change. Robertson & his intimates never in 72 supported Genl Grant until after the North Carolina election. Depew ran on the Democratic ticket for Lt Govenor, & Robertson was at heart for him—3. Garfield had over & over again stated that the collector if new appointmnt should be mad should be satisfactory to Senators & the porganization they represented. Sunday before the Tuesday when the nomination was made, he said to one of the senators, & by him sent word to the other & to the Vice President, that before any action was taken he would send for them for consultation, & wished them to then be prepared withholding all papers & suggestions meanwhile—The act not only sudden but secreted from all including Cabinet officer from the state. 4 Garfield denied to R. C. that he ever heard or thought that Platt would be for any of the Robertson bolters at Chicago. IV The statement about an appointment is false. McVaigh & James proposed a talk to hear Garfield repeat what he told them. No invitation from G. & when James messenger went to say that they would not call that evening, Garfield evinced surprise & said there was no appointmn & he should be out." AD, USG 3. On June 20, in New York City, USG recalled receiving Garfield's letter. ". . . He was on the steamer and about to leave the harbor of Vera Cruz when the Postmaster of that city boarded the vessel and handed him the President's letter. This letter, he said, was in a desk in his office down town. His time had been so much occupied since his arrival in this City that he had not had an opportunity to write a reply to it, as it certainly required an acknowledgment. It was certainly a most polite and friendly letter, he said, and he intended to reply to it at length, as it deserved to be treated. The General pointed to pen, ink, and paper on the round table in the centre of the room, and said that he had already begun his answer to the President. When asked whether he was willing to give the President's letter for publication, he said that he did not feel that it would be the proper thing for him to do. His attention was called to that part of the Washington dispatch which read that the President would decline to give the two letters for publication unless the consent of Gen. Grant was obtained. 'The President has my free and full permission to publish the letters,' said the General, adding, 'My letter to him was not marked confidential, and he is at perfect liberty to give it to the newspapers.' The General said that the letters would explain themselves, and that nothing further was necessary to be said upon that point. He thought that when the charge was publicly made that he was inconsistent in the matter of what is now called 'Senatorial courtesy,' it was time for him to say something upon that subject. The statement had been paraded in some of the newspapers that he did not recognize such a thing as Senatorial courtesy at the time the appointment of Mr. William E. Simmons as Collector of the Port of Boston was agitated. That statement, said the

General, was unsupported by the facts. Charles Sumner and George S. Boutwell were the Senators from Massachusetts at that time. During his first term as President Mr. Boutwell was Secretary of the Treasury. He had long known and admired Mr. Boutwell, and when that gentleman became one of his Cabinet officers the strong friendship which had existed was more closely cemented and a positive affection for each other was engendered. He had the greatest respect for Mr. Boutwell's opinions. He knew him to be a man of marked ability and one upon whom calumny could not rest. Mr. Sumner had from the first, continued the General, seen fit not only to harshly criticise the conduct of the Administration, but at times acted as though he wished to ignore the President altogether. At no time did Mr. Sumner consult him upon any subject, make a suggestion to him, or enter a protest about anything. The Senator from Massachusetts put himself outside the pale of respect from the Administration by his treatment of it. He never personally urged the appointment or rejection of any man, but contented himself with wholesale abuse of the President. During the General's second term as President Mr. Boutwell was a Senator from Massachusetts. Mr. Simmons was urged for the Collectorship of the port of Boston, and Senator Sumner at once opened his batteries upon him. A powerful influence was brought to bear to bring about the appointment and confirmation of Mr. Simmons. Unnumbered petitions in his favor were sent to the President from some of the best business men and others of Massachusetts, but there was an element at work that sought the overthrow of Mr. Simmons because he, a mere plebeian, as it were, was a candidate for an office that had been held by such a man as Gov. Lincoln and other men of proud ancestry. Gen. Butler, who was at that time, said the General, a true and tried Republican, strongly urged the appointment of Mr. Simmons. Some of Senator Boutwell's constituents were emphatic in their disapproval of the appointment of Mr. Simmons, and two of the members of the House of Representatives opposed it. Senator Boutwell was urged by these gentlemen and others to refuse to give his sanction to the selection of Mr. Simmons, but all the petitions for and against Mr. Simmons received by the Senator were laid before the Senate by him, and he said that he merely wished the Senators to decide upon the facts; as far as he (Mr. Boutwell) was concerned, he should neither urge nor oppose the appointment of Mr. Simmons. 'If Senator Boutwell had at any time asked me,' added the General, 'to withdraw the nomination of Mr. Simmons, I should have promptly acceded to his request. I believed in Senatorial courtesy then just as I believe in it now.' Mr. Simmons was, said the General, a man who believed that the office of Collector of the Port of Boston elevated him, and was not one of those who thought he added honor and dignity to the office by accepting it. He was not a figure-head such as is found in the daily walks of men, one who is merely at the head and who allows others to do the work. He began to study the Custom-house in all its branches, and made himself proficient in all of them. He was one of the most active men who ever held the position. The General believed that the record would bear him out when he said that nine-tenths of the petitions and communications received by the President, the Senate, and Mr. Boutwell favored most earnestly the selection of Mr. Simmons for the position which he so ably filled. . . ." *New York Times*, June 21, 1881. See following letter; *PUSG*, 25, 46–50; Harry James Brown and Frederick D. Williams, eds., *The Diary of James A. Garfield* (East Lansing, Mich., 1967–81), IV, 561–70, 583–87, 590–97, 613–16; Allan Peskin, *Garfield* (Kent, Ohio, 1978), pp. 557–72.

1. On March 23, Garfield had nominated William H. Robertson, N. Y. senate president *pro tem*, as collector of customs, New York City.

To John P. Jones

————

CITY OF MEXICO, April 24.—Dear Senator.—I see by the latest dispatches received here from the capital that the dead lock in organizing the senate has not yet been broken, and that nothing has been done by the president to allay the bitterness which must be engendered by his most recent appointments.

When the first batch of nominations for New York was sent in, I was delighted. I believed the president had determined to recognize the republican party and not a faction, but his nominations of the next day convinced me that his first act was but a deep laid scheme by somebody to punish prominent leaders for being openly friendly to me. I can not believe that Garfield is the author of this policy. I give him credit for being too big a man to descend to such means for the punishment of men who gave him a hearty support in his election and who are disposed to give him the same now, for the offense of having had former preferences for some one else for the office which he now holds. But Garfield is president and is responsible for all the acts of his administration.

Conkling and Platt are the chosen senators from the great state of New York, and that, too, against all opposition of an administration created by the same party that elected them. This should give them all the stronger claim to be consulted in the matter of appointments in their state. When it comes to filling the most influential office in their state without consulting these senators it is a great slight. When he selects the most offensive man to be found, it becomes an insult and ought to be resented to the bitter end. I sincerely hope the president will see this and correct his mistake himself and restore harmony to the party. He owes this to himself and to those without whom he could not have been elected. Nobody believes he could have carried the state of New York without the active support of the present senators. Their passive support would not have answered. Without the state of New York Garfield would not now be president. This rewarding Robertson is not only offensive to the New York senators, but it is offensive to the New York republicans.

The change of Badeau and Cramer, the two appointments in which I felt a strong personal interest was very distasteful to me. The first because of our personal relations and my wish that he should be kept where his office would support him until he finishes some work he is engaged upon and which he could do without interfering with his public duties. The second because it was at the expense of removing the son of my old secretary of state who never had his superior—certainly never for moral worth—in the department. It is true that Fish resigned, but he did this from a sense of honor supposing it to be the duty of representatives abroad to give the new administration the opportunity of saying whether they were wanted or not. Very truly yours,

U. S. GRANT.

New York Herald, May 19, 1881. On May 31, 1881, President James A. Garfield wrote to USG. "I have just heard from Senator Chaffee that he is likely to see you immediately on your return from Mexico. I avail myself of his kindness to send by him a copy of a letter which I addressed to you in reply to yours of April 24th, and which I fear did not reach you before you left Mexico. I send this because I am desirous that you should not misunderstand the facts and the motives upon which I have acted in relation to recent events here Soon after I had written you, I saw from your letter to Senator Jones which appeared in the newspapers, that you supposed that Mr Fish was removed from his position at Switzerland. You will probably have seen before this the correspondence between Mr. Fish and the State Department He had sent in his resignation to Mr. Evarts before the close of the last Administration, and renewed it soon after I came in. He had stated so to me that his resignation was not forced. When I became satisfied that he actually wished to quit the office (but not until then) I nominated Mr. Cramer, wholly because I desired to carry out your wish by giving him a more [—] climate I shall be glad to see you at any time and confer with you freely concerning the general situation." ALS (press), DLC-James A. Garfield. This letter was endorsed: "Not sent Withheld upon reflection" E, *ibid.* See previous letter; telegram to James H. Work, [*May 16–17, 1881*].

On March 23, Garfield had nominated Michael John Cramer as chargé d'affaires, Switzerland, in place of Nicholas Fish, resigned. On March 25, Hamilton Fish, New York City, wrote to Nicholas Fish, Berne. "Yesterday I received your telegram requesting to ask for Berlin, London &c—on the day before Cramer had been nominated as Chargé at Berne—Badeau transferred from London Consulate to Copenhagen Chargé-ship, &c &c—on the Evening of the Announcement of these nominations Genl Grant came to see me, & asked whether I had been advised of what was about to be done, & if you had asked to be relieved, or any other provision made for you—He was very much annoyed that his Brother in Law should displace you, unless you were promoted, or otherwise provided for—I told him that I was not advised whether you had or had not actually resigned—that I had understood from a letter received some time since that you purposed tendering a resignation, & that you had written to John Hay to that effect, that I thought you would not object to *exchanging* your present position, &

would not be unwilling to take an Assist Secretaryship in the Department—Hearing that I was not sure that you had tendered a resignation he proposed telegraphing to Garfield to withdraw Cramer's nomination—to this I could not consent, especially in the absence of any definite knowledge as to what you had done in the matter, & in fact, as to what you *really wished*—you had alluded to a *temporary* appointment to Vienna—such appointment was, of course, an impossibility to ask—. . ." ALS (press), DLC-Hamilton Fish.

To Ellen Grant Sartoris

City of Mexico
Apl. 26th 1881.

DEAR DAUGHTER:

We are still here, and expect to remain for a month yet. The business which brought me seems to be progressing favorably enough, but there are always delays in transactions with Governments. Buck and his wife are with us, but will return home by the Steamer of the 8th of May. Bessie Sharp is also with us and will remain until we return. Going back we will probably stop for a few days at St. Louis and again in Galena. I am very much interested in the work I am now engaged, and feel that it will result in developing the resources of this great country, and in increasing the commerce of our own vastly, as well as benefiting all commercial nations. Fred. is engaged on a road running through Texas and Mexico, to the Gulf of California, and the papers announced, has resigned from the Army. Buck is also interested in his road and the one with which I am connected.

We have not heard from Jesse since a short time after his arrival in England. I would write to him, but I expect he will be away from there before a letter could reach him.[1] If he is still there give him & Lizzie our love. I hope he has been successful in the business which took him to England. Jesse has ability and I think he will develope business capacity.

We hope to be in a good house—of our own—at the close of the season at Long Branch, and will expect you, Algie and the children to come over and spend the Winter with us. I am disappointed

that little Algie is not to be at Long Branch the coming Summer
to take me out riding. I thoug[ht] he would drive for me when I
got tired. Tell him his little cousin Julia will be there and will be
much disappointed not to see him and his little sisters, and Aunt
Mahitable Ann.[2]

    With love and kisses to you all from your Ma & I

Yours Affectionately

U. S. GRANT

ALS, NN.

    1. Jesse Root Grant, Jr., and his wife Elizabeth returned from Europe on May 26,
1881. *New York Times*, May 27, 1881.
    2. Lottie Hough played Mehitable Ann in "The Yankee Legacy" at the Olym-
pic Theatre on Broadway, Nov.-Dec., 1863. See *Calendar*, Feb. 18, 1864 (*PUSG*
Supplement).

Speech

———

[*Mexico City, April, 1881*]

    My own experience in civil office after the great rebellion in
our country has convinced me that there may be periods when it is
impossible, for a time at least, to carry out all the laws, no matter
how good they may be, and no matter how well calculated for the
good of the people. We have found that the case where society has
been well organized for a great many years, and I can very well appreciate how the government may pass the very best of laws for the
protection and toleration of opinions—religious and secular—and
yet that it may take some little time before it is able to execute
those laws to the fullest extent in the presence of a prejudice of cen-
turies' standing. I believe the work which Mexico is now engaged
in, and which, by the aid of American capital and enterprise, goes
on so rapidly, will soon render this government able to execute all
its laws and give all the protection that its laws promise. But at this
time, as heretofore, the means of communication are so limited,
and the method of transmitting information so slow, that violence
may be done almost in the immediate neighborhood and the guilty

parties escape before news of it can reach the central government. All this we hope will rapidly be corrected.

I recognize in the labors of the missionaries here in Mexico a service that is of immense value in the development of the country at large, and in preparing the minds of the people of Mexico for the changes that are taking place and that will, in my judgment, go on so rapidly. I hope you will continue in your good work and meet with great success—especially in the matter of education. Of course, I do not confine my wish for your success to the matter of education alone, but I think that covers the broadest field. It prepares the mind of the people to judge for themselves, and to exercise a judgment of their own in regard to religious as well as to civil matters. The conversion of a people in entire ignorance to a new religion does not amount to nearly as much as to educate and then convert them, because that will be something real, as it would be to so great an extent if the result of mere excitement or emotion. I regard education as the great beginning to religious enlightenment.

I thank you, gentlemen, for what you have said, and for what you have done.

Chicago Inter-Ocean, May 2, 1881 (datelined April 19). Charles W. Drees, superintendent of Methodist missions in Mexico, headed a delegation of Protestant ministers welcoming USG. "... As you are doubtless fully aware, the laws of Mexico with reference to liberty of conscience and religious worship, as contained in the constitution of 1857 and the laws of reform of later date, are very complete and satisfactory, in their form and in the right impartially secured to all. You are also no doubt aware that these laws extend to the Federal Government the prerogative and impose upon that government the obligation to secure their faithful observance. We are glad to recognize in the government in general a disposition to secure to us our rights; still it not unfrequently happens that the local authorities are un[favor]ably disposed, and fail to discharge toward us their duty. We have very recently in the city of Queretaro suffered from the lack of suitable protection on the part of the local authorities. In Apizaco, wi[t]hin a few days past, one of our ministers, a Mexican, was cruelly assassinated. We mention these facts to you fully understanding that your presence in Mexico is simply in the capacity of a private citizen; and it is not in our thought to ask on your part any interference on our behalf. We only desire to mention these circumstances to you as we would wish that our position, together with the character and importance of our work, should be understood and appreciated by all our fellow countrymen, and especially by the official representatives of our government in Mexico...." *Ibid.*

On June 3, 1876, U.S. Representative William A. Phillips of Kan. had written to USG. "I enclose a letter from my brother, who is a Missionary under the American

Board in Mexico. I believe he has the entire confidence of the Board, and would refer you to Drs Dixon and Kendall of New York. I learned, that at the instigation of some Catholic priests he was mobbed, and nearly killed a few weeks ago. I communicated with the Secretary of State, at the time, and had an acknowledgment of the receipt of my letter, and the information that Foster had been communicated with. It will be seen by the enclosed letter that Minister Foster has taken a rather singular view of the case Nearly two years ago a Missionary under the American Board, a companion of my brother, was killed, in a similar war. My brother, has I learn, organised a large number of Protestant churches. This is the real secret, of the matter. He is neither turbulent nor indiscreet. Maxwell Phillips was a theological student in 1862. In the spring of that year he left college.—entered the Union Army, Organised a company, was mustered as Lt. and rose to be eCapt. was a good officer, has three severe wounds on his person, but has never claimed any privilege for them. Within a week of his muster out he entered College, and is now a missionary. I cannot sympathise with Mr Foster's decision. Neither can I with the idea that the higher phase of American civilization shall be arrested by a few bigoted priests Neither can I with the idea that an American citizen shall not be, or *can not be* protected in what is legitimate and just Pardon me for this long note. It is not, merely a personal matter. It involves far more than the missionary in question. It involves what is of the utmost moment to every American Citizen" ALS, DNA, RG 59, Miscellaneous Letters. On May 10, Maxwell Phillips, San Luis Potosi, Mexico, had written to William Phillips. ". . . Minister Foster makes another statement, which I desire to refer thro[ugh] you to the Secretary of State, namely as missionaries we are not entitled to the same proteccion as other citizens of the [U. S.] because our position is an exceptiona[l] one, because our work involves in suc[h] especial dangers that the U. S. Governme[nt] cannot concede to us as its citizens any more protection than simply to reque[st] the Mexican Governmt to protect us if it can. . . ." ALS, *ibid.*

To H. Victor Newcomb

City of Mexico
May 3d 1881.

VICTOR NEWCOMB, ESQ.
PRES. U. S. NATIONAL BANK,
NEW YORK CITY:

DEAR SIR:

I take pleasure in presenting to your acquaintance Mr Robt. Geddes, of the London Bank of Mexico and South America, who passes through New York City on his way to England. The bank Mr. Geddes has been in charge of in this city is one of high standing, and must grow in importance now with the introduction of foreign capital. As the United States, or her citizens, are now the most numerously represented in the enterprises going on in this country of any ~~other~~ foreigners, it has occurred to me that the exchange between this country and ours must grow to great importance. I have suggested to Mr. Geddes the idea of presenting this introduction to you with the ~~idea~~ view of seeing if a correspondence could not be effected between the U. S. National Bank, of New York, and the bank here for the purpose of conducting the matter of exchange between the two countries.

Very Truly yours

U. S. GRANT

ALS, Gilder Lehrman Collection, NHi. Born in 1844 in Louisville, H. Victor Newcomb succeeded his father as president, Louisville and Nashville Railroad, then moved to New York City and established the United States National Bank of New York, with USG as a director. See *New York Times*, Aug. 31, 1901, Nov. 4, 1911.

To Adam Badeau

City of Mexico
May 7th 1881.

DEAR GENERAL:

I received your several letters written since my departure from New York, and your telegram. The latter I answered at once saying stick to London or its equivalent. The opperator refused to send the despatch on the prepayment. I then sent my pass—which I have over the Mexican Cable & Western Union—when they received it. I supposed of course you would get the reply. I am completely disgusted with Garfield[s] course. It is to late now for him to do anything to restore him to my confidance. I will never again lend my active aid to the support of a Presidential candidate who has not strength enough to appear before a convention as a candidate, but gets in simply by the adherence of prominent candidates preferring any outsider to either of the candidates before the convention save their own. Garfield has shewn that he is not possessed of the backbone of an Angleworm. I hope his nominations may be defeat[ed] and you left where you are until you are ready to withdraw voluntarily.

I see no note of your book coming out yet. It looks as if the Appletons were in no hurry.[1]

My business here progresses favorably so far as the President
and the departments are concerned. I have hear[d] nothing yet of
any opposition in Congress. Before this reaches you I will be on my
way home.

I never would have undertaken the work I am now engaged
in for any possible gain that can accrue to myself. But I have been
much impressed with the resources of this country, and have entertained a much higher opinion of these people than the world
at large generall[y] does, and of their capacity to develope their
resources, with aid and encouragement from outside. I felt that
this developement must come soon and the country furnishing the
means would receive the greatest benefit from the increased commerce. I wanted it to be ours. Besides we want to encourage republican government, and particularly on this continent. Then too
it is an advantage for us to pay for our imports with the products
of our soil & manufactures as far as possi[b]le. This we do not do
now with countries from which we receive tropical & semi-tropical
products. Mexico can furnish all the comodities and will want in
return what we have to sell.

I will always be glad to hear from you, and will write in return
occasionally. You know I have a good many letters to write, and
probably will have to write more in the future. Bu[t] I have learned
one thing on this trip that I wish I had learned twenty years ago.
I brought along a stenographer[2] who I find no trouble whatever in dictating lette[rs,] speeches & reports. It saves a world of
trou[ble.]

With best regards of Mrs. Grant & myself

Yours Truly

U. S. Grant

ALS, Munson-Williams-Proctor Institute, Utica, N. Y.

1. Volumes 2 and 3 of Adam Badeau's *Military History of Ulysses S. Grant, From
April, 1861, to April, 1865,* published by D. Appleton & Co., went on sale by subscription
in the second week of June, 1881. At the same time, the firm reissued volume 1, first
published in 1868. See *New York Times,* June 10, 12, 1881.

2. On March 25, 1881, Friday, USG, New York City, wrote to Secretary of War Robert T. Lincoln. "May I ask the great favor of you for a sixty days absence for Mr. N. E. Dawson, of your Department, to accompany me to Mexico, as Secretary and Stenographer. His knowledge of Spanish will make him especially useful. I ask this favor with more confidence, because I believe my business to Mexico is of greater importance to the nation at large than to me or any other person individually. If Mr. Dawson comes he should meet me in St. Louis in time to take the morning train, Iron Mountain Road, for Galveston; or else come on here in time to leave with me on Monday morning. Would like very much to see him in NEW YORK before we start." Printed copy, DNA, RG 59, Applications and Recommendations, Hayes-Arthur. On the same day, Lincoln telegraphed to USG. "It will give me pleasure to give Mr. Dawson leave until June 1st to accompany you to Mexico. He will report to you Sunday Morning in New York." LS (telegram sent), *ibid.*, RG 107, Telegrams Collected (Bound); telegram received, USG 3. On March 26, Lincoln wrote to USG. "You will have already learned by my telegram of yesterday that it has given me pleasure to comply with your request respecting Mr. Dawson. I trust that you will have a very pleasant and successful journey in Mexico. I write this especially to say that my class-mate and very intimate friend, Mr. John A. Dillon of St. Louis, who has been for many years one of the editors of the *Globe-Democrat*, writes me that he has just started for Mexico, partly in the interest of the newspaper, and somewhat in the interest of Capt. Eads, who was formerly his guardian. I should be very glad to have him make your personal acquaintance while you are in Mexico, and I assure you that you will find him one of the most agreeable cultivated and intelligent men you could meet, and it may be possible that he might be of service to you, in some manner of which I, myself, have no idea" LS, *ibid.*

To John Russell Young

City of Mexico, May 12th., 1881.

MY DEAR MR. YOUNG:—The mail is just in and brings your very welcome letter. My speech, at the banquet given me here, was sent to Mr. Worke, the Secretary of our company and I suggested in my letter of transmittal that it should be given to the Associated Press.

I have seen no notice of it in home papers and do not know how it was received further than what you state and what Mr. Worke said in a dispatch.

My work here is completed very satisfactorily so far as the Government is concerned. The President and such Members of Congress as I have talked to, express no doubt about the action of Congress. I think I will be able to leave for home by the steamer of the 23rd inst.

There has been a very unscrupulous opposition here, to my getting what I asked, by agents or friends, of roads now being built by American capital; but I believe they have been defeated. They could not possibly object to the roads I represent, except on the ground that they oppose all roads they are not employed as agents of.

My interest in this Country is precisely the same I felt in the East, particularly in China and Japan. I know Mexico must develop into a powerful commercial nation, and I want our country to be the agent to bring this result about rapidly, and to build up a friendship between the two, honorable to both, and profitable at the same time. I believe sincerely that a market will spring up here for our products that will postpone the next panic for years.

I am sorry to hear that the recommendation of Badeau for a Foreign Mission is treated with levity. He is certainly as well qualified, in every way, for a Mission as Lowell, and I do not find fault with his holding the highest Mission in the gift of the President.

Badeau is a gentleman, a scholar and a man of ability and culture. He would know nothing about manipulating a convention to defeat the will of the people however nor would I.

I am sorry I did not receive Mackay's letters. I would have answered him promptly had I received them. I have no idea of what could have been their contents. Tell him if he will drop me a line to 34 New Street, I will be there before a letter from him can reach me, and I will answer him promptly.

We are all well and send our regards.

I do not wonder that Garfield dislikes the course of the Herald towards him. Facts—when they are against one—are harder to hear than falsehood and slander. It will be hard for Garfield to convince anyone that Blaine is not running his Administration, and running it to destruction fast.

Very truly yours
U. S. GRANT.

Copy (typescript), DLC-John Russell Young.

On May 11, 1881, USG signed a contract with Mexican officials setting terms and granting concessions to the Mexican Southern Railroad Co. A printed copy (in Spanish), published May 26, is in DLC-USG. See Interview, [*June 2, 1881*], note 4.

To Ellen Grant Sartoris

City of Mexico
May 16th 1881

MY DEAR DAUGHTER;

I have received your nice letter written from Paris where you had gone with Jesse & Lizzie. I am glad you like Lizzie. The business which brought me to Mexico seems to be progressing favorably and I now hope that the Congress will confirm this week what the President has approved, and let us off for home by the Steamer of the 23d inst. We are very anxious to get back because we will have to refurnish our Long Branch house before moving into it. We also expect to own a house in New York City which will have to be furnished also. I expect to make New York my home and to be a citizen of that state hereafter. Fred & Ida will live with us, for the present at least. Jesse & Buck will live with us at Long Branch. I have been contemplating an addition to my house at the Branch so as to always have room for all our children and grandchildren during the summer. We will always have room for you and the children in our city house, and hope to have you all with us next winter.—Your ma has not been well the last few days though I think nothing serious is the matter. Bessie Sharp is with us and has been great company to your Ma.[1] She likes Bessie very much. She is a very fine girl. Buck and Fannie, you knew, came with us. But they returned to the states about two weeks ago. We have not heard from them since they left Vera Cruz: but no doubt they are safely at home. I presume we will find Jesse & Lizzie in New York on our return. If they have not left when you get this give them our love, and tell them to take little Algie along to stay with us until you come over in the fall. I think we could have

him sufficiently spoiled by that time to deny his his allegiance to
England, and to make the United States his permanent home. The
latter is a much better country for a young man to make his way in.

With love and kisses from your Ma & I to you and all the
children,

yours Affectionately

U. S. GRANT

ALS, ICHi.

1. Elizabeth B. Sharp, daughter of Alexander and Ellen Dent Sharp, was born in
1861 in Mo. See *PUSG*, 2, 26. On June 15, 1876, USG attended her graduation from
the College of Notre Dame, Baltimore.

To James H. Work

———

[*Mexico City, May 16–17, 1881*]

I hope the legislature will sustain its Senators. The treatment
they have received is scandalous and ought to be ~~reproved by the
New York republicans~~ rebuked. Without New York the present
Administration could not have come into power. Without the active
support of the present Senators New York could not have been carried republican.

ADf (telegram sent, facsimile), *St. Louis Post-Dispatch*, April 27, 1890. On May 16, 1881,
U.S. Senators Roscoe Conkling and Thomas C. Platt of N. Y. resigned their seats to
protest President James A. Garfield's disregard for the tradition of senatorial courtesy.
USG's stenographer, Noble E. Dawson, later recalled. "We were sitting at a table in his
room when the news came and Gen. Grant picked up the back of a letter and wrote a telegram upon it to J. H. Work of New York, the Secretary of the syndicate of which he was
the nominal President. He addressed Work because we had a cipher telegraphic code in
common . . . It did not get through, however, and it lodged at Vera Cruz. It would have
gone through had it not been sent in cypher, but Gen. Grant was supposed by the leading financier of the United States and the leading financier of Mexico to be interested in
Mexican investments. These two great capitalists controlled the telegraph wires of both
countries and they thought the cipher dispatch was a business one and stopped it." *Ibid.*

On May 22 and June 8, Garfield wrote to Rutherford B. Hayes. ". . . The Conkling
war seems not unlikely to End in Suicide Even though reinforced by Gen Grant—Of
course, I was sorry to have a row; but it was probably inevitable—and better come now
than later . . ." "Thanks for your Kind letter—It is not pleasant to begin with a storm;
but there was no honorable way to avoid it—and I shall hope to see clearing weather
by-and-by—The attitude of Gen. Grant is most surprising—If he follows up the spirit

of his letter to Jones, he will aggravate the quarrel and perhaps injure the party; but he will very seriously injure himself—Indeed he has done so already. It is a pity that our friends in Albany do not unite on candidates—They could soon settle the N. Y. problem in that way. . . ." ALS, InHi. See letter to John P. Jones, April 24, 1881; Interview, [*June 2, 1881*]; David M. Jordan, *Roscoe Conkling of New York: Voice in the Senate* (Ithaca, 1971), pp. 379–404.

Interview

———

[*New Orleans, June 2, 1881*]

The press, and some people—Gov. Young,[1] of Ohio, for instance, seemed to think that I should abandon the right which every American citizen may exercise, to speak his mind on public concerns, and the political affairs of the country. The papers abuse me whenever I give vent to my views on public matters, which, however, I shall continue to express whenever I think proper, just like any other private citizen.

My opinion about this Conkling affair is fully given in the letter I wrote Jones (Senator Jones, of Nevada) as soon as I heard o[*f*] the way Conkling was being dealt with.[2] He has been shamefully treated, sir, and for no cause whatsoever that I can discover. What has he done or said to call forth this personal abuse?

Did Conkling make a mistake in resigning?

Certainly not, sir. It was the proper thing for him to do after such treatment[.] I am inclined to think most of these uncalled for attacks on Mr. Conkling, this general abuse, have been instigated by White House influence, but I can't say that Mr. Garfield himself urged on the attack.

He certainly should be re-elected as a vindication of his course, and would be if I had anything to do with it.

I have already expressed my opinion publicly in regard to the President's course towards Mr. Conkling, as I certainly thought I had a right to do. This is all I intended to do about it. I am not even going to New York direct, but take a trip first to St. Louis, then to Galena and Chicago, remaining a day or so at each place[.] Afterwards I shall go to New York. I see from the papers that I am expected at West Point on June 10th, but it is scarcely possible I shall get there.

Since I left the United States the press has teemed with false statements about me. I can't keep the run of all of them, and am getting used to newspaper lying, but there's that alleged statement of Gov. Young, which I just saw.[3]

Oh, it is incorrect from beginning to end, and without any basis except as to my being a director in the national banks mentioned. Then there is the statement published extensively throughout the United States that my reception in Mexico was very cold, and that my mission was likely to prove a failure.

Yes, how about that? The impression was created that you had gone to Mexico to organize a regular old fashioned revolution, which was to terminate with the annexation of that country to the United States. What gave rise to such a rumor?

I have no idea. Of course, it was all false. The welcome accorded me was cordial, and my relations with the President, his Cabinet and the most eminent men in the Republic, were very pleasant. I imagine that the reports about me were circulated in the United States by parties interested in the subsidized Mexican railroads, as my bill did not call for a subsidy. It was thought the articles would be copied by Mexican papers and prejudice Congress against my proposition. But I went everywhere, to banquets, to the houses of prominent men, and saw no signs of hostility towards me. Congress made very little objection to my bill, adopted the desired amendments, and granted me all the concessions that were asked.[4]

Such liberal minded and practical men as Romero,[5] Riva Palacio, Porfirio Diaz, President Gonzales,[6] are doing what they think best for the country and the development of its resources[.] But there are others, of course, who are more intent on bettering their own private interests than doing anything for the benefit of the Republic. However, that is not peculiar to Mexico. We have plenty of such people in the United States.

New Orleans Picayune, June 4, 1881. USG spoke aboard the *City of Merida*, quarantined below New Orleans upon arrival from Vera Cruz.

On June 5, 1881, aboard a train from New Orleans to St. Louis, USG granted another interview. "Gen. Grant affects no concealment of his annoyance at the treatment accorded Conkling; says that Conkling saved New York to Garfield, and thus saved him the presidency; that Garfield started out with the good wishes of everybody for a successful administration, and could undoubtedly have been his own successor. The country was prosperous and the people were engaged in their material affairs, but the det[er]mination of the friends of the administration, instigated by Blaine, to break down Conkling and his friends through falsehood and slander would make serious trouble. Garfield had voluntarily asked him to make recommendations as to some of his friends, assuring Grant of his desire to serve him, and of his grateful appreciation of services rendered the party. When he made the recommendations he not only found them ignored, but a systematic attempt was made to place him before the country in the attitude of having supported Garfield in the pitiful expectation of patronage. He was frank to say that he should never again support a 'dark horse.' It was generally found that they have too many mortgages on them. Although he might not oppose the candidate of his party, he would not again support any man who could not let his name and record go before the people. He had not thought that Conkling would run for re-election now, but apprehended that he had been forced into that position by the avowed determination of the administration to humiliate him by the election of its own friends. The general apprehended that the course being pursued would result in a break up of parties and in new alignments. A party long in power naturally draws to it a large class who sustain it merely for what they can make out of it; many of whom have no real devotion to principle, but would be Democrats to-morrow and declare that their sympathies were always that way if that party should come into power. The Democratic party were not united by great principles; on the contrary, were divided upon almost every issue of importance, and only act together as outs. Hayes, he observed, had volunteered the information that Conkling's downfall commenced in 1877. He apparently connected Hayes's opinion of Conkling with the fact that Conkling was not an enthusiastic believer in Mr. Hayes's election, and acquiesced in the observation that Mr. Conkling would not have been averse to a new election in 1877. He thought Mr. Hayes's declaration somewhat surprising in view of the fact that Mr. Hayes had used the power of his civil service reform administration to break Conkling down in New York, and in spite of this Conkling had been elected by a unanimous vote of the New York Legislature. Later, the power of the administration was used to oppose the election of Conkling's friend Platt without avail. Mr. Conkling paid no attention to Hayes or his opposition, treated it with contempt and succeeded in spite of it." USG discussed his recent trip to Mexico. "The reports put in circulation concerning his designs in Mexico emanated from hostile railroad interests or persons who opposed his company because they could not control it, or have its business pass through their hands. President Gonzales was very indignant when he discovered the animus of the reports, as the general took early opportunity to disabuse his mind. He had been treated with every consideration and found the most liberal disposition on the part of the Mexican authorities to encourage the development of the country. . . . It was remarked when Gen. Grant passed through New Orleans last year that he was not favorably prepossessed with Mr. Eads's ship railway plans. These objections existed in his mind until a full discussion of the subject with Mr. Eads, when he found that all of them had been fully comprehended by the great engineer, who has clearly demonstrated that they may be overcome. He had not opposed Mr. Eads's plan even before being convinced of its feasibility, and when consulted by a committee of the Mexican Congress, quickly pointed out to them the immense advantage to accrue to Mexico by the expenditure of such large sums amongst her people, and the fact, if it should be a success, that Mexico would supply the shipping of the world with her products. Gen. Grant is now evidently a strong convert to the Eads railway instead of a lukewarm observer of its construction. It was quite apparent that the ex-President had no faith in the construction of the Panama canal, and he evidently believed that Mr. Lesseps has undertaken a hopeless task. He said that for a great many years he had taken a lively interest in the question of an inter oceanic water way; he had endeavored to interest Mr. Seward and to have surveys made, but did not succeed in having a proper investigation of the subject until he became President, when he had caused a number of surveys to be made. One of the principal difficulties found at Panama was the Chagres river, which, at certain seasons, afforded a meagre supply of water, but became at other times a roaring torrent, which would pour into the canal with terrific force, carrying large trees and immense boulders, which would injure the canal and endanger the shipping." The Tehuantepec route, USG continued, "presented many attractions to Americans and would have become a popular one, owing to its proximity to the United States and the manifest advantages to this country. A great difficulty was experienced, however, with respect to the supply of water at certain seasons of the year, and by reason that vessels would have had to be 'locked up' fully 700 feet. Gen. Grant had favored the Nicaragua route for a canal, and had caused elaborate surveys to be made. It presented fewer engineering difficulties, and could be constructed at less cost than either of the other projected routes. It is quite evident, however, that the Eads ship railway has the call, and has in a great measure changed the opinions of the ex-President, which were formed before Eads's plans were known. In respect to the Crescent City the most enthusiastic believers in our future would have been satisfied with the general's estimate of the future of New Orleans. He anticipated that we would receive a large share of the commerce of Mexico, South and Central America, but thought that we should not confine ourselves to building up a commercial city, but convert New Orleans into a manufacturing city making hundreds of articles of every day use, manufacturing our own cotton, furniture, etc., and thus fo[s]tering industries which would employ our population all the year round. He was especially earnest in the opinion that our planters should spin their cotton into yarn on the plantations by improved machinery and ship the manufactured article instead of the lint. Gen. Grant referred to the Red river country and its great future. He had been stationed there in 1847, and knew many of the people along the river. His recollections of the country were of the most pleasant character, and when he came here again it would give him pleasure to revisit the scenes of his early manhood." *New Orleans Democrat*, June 7, 1881. See letter to James B. Eads, Jan. 13, 1882.

1. Born in 1832 in Ireland, Thomas L. Young settled in Cincinnati, won promotion to bvt. brig. gen. after the battle of Resaca, and entered politics, assuming the Ohio governorship after Rutherford B. Hayes became president. In 1878, Young was elected to Congress.

2. See letter to John P. Jones, April 24, 1881.

3. USG objected to a report from New York City. "Something was said by a gentleman present on Grant having accepted a large money present to keep him out of undignified political interference, and that he had rushed into print after taking some of the money, with commentaries on Garfield. 'That was a mistake,' said Gov. Young. 'As one of Grant's soldiers I admire many things about him; but he has not many followers

in his later political writings. That letter he wrote to Jones was to all intents a public letter, and it therefore looks like an attempt on Grant's part to keep communicating with the public on the direct concerns o[f] the Government. Now,' said Col Young, 'I have just discovered that Grant is receiving $10,000 a year salary as the President of the United States National Bank. I desired to have the Citizens' Bank of Cincinnati—which is the largest bank in [t]he West, with a capital of $2,000,000—made a national depository, and to that effect I made an argument before Secretary Sherman. He heard the argument and rejected the plea. When Windom came in I renewed it, and was sent to the Assistant Secretary for that purpose. The answer made to me was substantially the same under both administrations—that Gen. Grant had come to Washington in person on behalf of the United States National Bank, recently organized in New York by Newcomb and others, from which he was and is receiving ten thousand dollars a year as president, and had asked that it be made a national depository. The Government's reply was that the Government already had a sub-treasury in New York, besides two national banks—the First and the Fourth—appointed depositories, and the same condition of things existed in Cincinnati, where there were two national banks depositories and the sub-treasury also existed. The reply to me was that they had already refused an ex-President of the United States, and that they had no appropriation for the additional expense involved in another depository.' A business man standing by said: 'Grant has previously been a director in the Marine National Bank of New York, and when he was elected President of this new bank, some months ago, he retired as director from the Marine Bank, and his son Ulysses succeeded him. He is also a partner in his son's business house of Grant & Ward, and has an interest there of $50,000.'" *New Orleans Picayune*, June 4, 1881. See Interview, [*June 16, 1881*], note 3.

4. "The reporter asked Gen. Grant for a copy of his concessions, but the bill was in one of the trunks on the vessel, and was not procurable immediately. However, the following synopsis, revised by the General's secretary, Mr. Dawson, will give a fair idea of the concession to Gen. Grant: 1. The line is to start from the city of Mexico, passing by the cities of Puebla and Oaxaca, and by Tehuantepec, and to take there the best route for the frontier of Mexico with Guatemala, one branch to come from Vera Cruz and Anton Lizardo, and another to run to Huatalco. The company has a right to build a line to Tuxlta, Chiapas, San Cristobal and Comtan, in the State of Chiapas. 2. The surveys of the line are to begin within six months from the publication of the contract, and the work is to commence within six months from date. During the second year the company is to build at least fifty k[i]lometres of the road; one hundred kilometres during the third year, and one hundred and sixty kilometres during each of the seven succeeding years. The entire road is to be finished in ten years from the date of contract. 3. The road is to be built without subsidy, but the company will have the right of way and free importation of all articles needed for building during construction of the road, and for fifteen years afterward, the road and its capital and accessories to be free from all classes of duties for twenty-five years after completion. . . . 6. The tariffs can be raised to the point at which they will yield 10 per cent. of the capital represented by the road, after deducting all expenses. 7. The company has full right to mortgage the road and issue stocks and bonds, but after the lapse of ninety years from the date of contract the Mexican Government will have the right to purchase the road, paying in cash its actual value. . . . The third and sixth clauses are considered particularly favorable. Gen. Grant describes the country through which the line will run as very productive[,] rich in mines, and yielding a large variety of productions. The company is backed by tremendous capital, such men as Gould, Russell Sage, E. D. Morgan, Nickerson and

other well known capitalists being interested in the enterprise. It is estimated they can control fully $250,000,000. Surveys are now being made of the proposed route, but work will not be commenced until after the rainy season. Gen. Grant thinks that the outlook for Mexico is very favorable. He observed that much progress had been made since his last visit. . . . While in Mexico Gen. Grant obtained the right for a company, the Western Union, to lay a telegraph cable from Yucatan to Cuba. He has no personal interest in this enterprise." *New Orleans Picayune*, June 4, 1881.

5. On May 31, Matías Romero, Mexico City, had written to USG. "The house of representatives approved to day unanimously and without discusion your contract for the cable, but the Senate had no time to take it up. It will be approved by the Senate very early next session. I hope you will arrive safely home. The parties saling the Anton Lizardo and Bamba and Garrapatero property are ready to signe the deed. Mr. Payno told me to-day that to-morrow would be perfected the sale of Mrs. Smith's property. The owner of the property by Guadalupe road says that Guzman wants to buy it from him. I think he will wait for us for 15 or 20 days. In my letter of this date to Mr. Work I informe him of all which has transpired here since you left" LS, Nellie C. Rothwell, La Jolla, Calif.

6. On June 2, President Manuel González of Mexico wrote to USG thanking him for his visit. LS (in Spanish), *ibid.*

Interview

[*St. Louis, June 7, 1881*]

This Japanese boy of mine cuts a figure in the case.[1] It is not my habit to carry these medals and decorations with me. I prize them too highly to subject them to the risk of travel. On one occasion I was called upon to participate in a celebration given by the members of the Grand Army of the Republic in an Eastern city. I did not have the badge that they presented me with, and I expressed my regret. My Japanese boy heard me, but did not of course take the matter fully in. He only knew that I regretted the absence of a medal. When we were packing up at Chicago for the Mexican trip he recalled the circumstance, and about said to himself, "The General will have a medal the next time he wants one." So he put in seven which attracted his eye. The remainder were deposited in bank. I knew nothing of this, because I trust the boy implicitly in the matter of handling my baggage. This morning we opened the trunk in which he had placed them. The cases were found all right, but the contents had been removed. The burglary of the trunk had been done very neatly.

Will you remain to prosecute the cases against the two men, King and Fitzpatrick?

I don't think it will be necessary. The railroad company has undertaken the prosecution as common carriers. I will probably make a deposition establishing my ownership to the property, and that will be all that will be required of me.

Senator Conkling, whom I consider one of the ablest men in American life, was controlled by that dignity which makes him honored when he tendered his resignation. His act was not charac-terized by pettishness, as his enemies chose to say, but was that of dignity and manliness. This crusade upon Senator Conkling was commenced under the administration of the late President Hayes, when Merritt was forced into the position of Collector of New York, vice Arthur, removed by Sherman and Hayes.² Mr. Hayes' Secretary of State forced this fight, and that was in 1877. Merritt was confirmed, and the country said it was a Conkling defeat, yet the Legislature elected that fall sent him back to the seat he had honored by a unanimous vote on the first ballot. Again, Senator Kernan's term expired last year. He was a Democrat.³ Senator Con-kling went into the field; again made a personal issue, and elected a Legislature which this spring sent his man into the United States Senate. I see that Mr. Hayes in a published interview says that the decline of Senator Conkling has been steady and rapid. Two such victories as he has achieved against the Administration influence, would seem to indicate that his fall had not been very rapid.

What do you think of the present situation at Albany, and how do you reconcile the deadlock with Conkling's power in the State?

I would say that it is Administration influence, and the action of that part of the press hostile to Senator Conkling, notably the two *Tribunes*—I mean the New York and Chicago. The administra-tion may not directly do the work, but it is responsible for the spe-cious arguments, statements ingeniously calculated to mislead and false issues that are sent out from Washington.

What do you anticipate will be the result?

I can not say, as my information is gleaned entirely from such newspapers as I have received. I hope that there will be no election, that the matter of Conkling's vindication will be thrown before the people of New York, this fall.

There can, then, be only one result, the triumph of Senators Conkling and Platt?

Senator Conkling's success will mean that of his friends.

What do you think of Garfield's attitude in this matter?[4]

I think that the President has been influenced by his Secretary of State to disregard a voluntary promise and offer to consult in the matter of New York, appointments, the man who contributed to his election. He made the promise, I think, in good faith, and in the flush of gratitude, and it should have been kept or never made. The animosity of Blaine to Conkling is so well understood that it is feeble to deny that it has manifested itself in this case.

What do you think of Carl Schurz?

Well, Carl Schurz will draw an official salary without earning it with more zeal and efficiency than any man I know of. I see that he has taken charge of the New York *Evening Post,* but he will hardly succeed there. He broke down one *Post* in Detroit, and I don't know what he will do with the *Post* in New York. He is a failure anywhere you put him. He might make a success as a professional carpet-bagger moving about from one State to another, and running for Senator. He will never stay in one place any longer than it takes for the people to find him out. Then he'll have to move.[5]

St. Louis Globe-Democrat, June 8, 1881. At the close of the interview, the reporter "introduced the subject of Boss Shepherd by a reference to the condition of the streets of St. Louis, and a wish that some man like him were here to improve them. Gen. Grant said that the people who abused Boss Shepherd knew nothing of the man, and did not comprehend the nature and extent of the work he had done. He spoke of the condition of the streets and public works of Washington before Shepherd's regime, as contrasted with their present condition. It was true, he said, that there was a great deal of money expended, but the improvements were there to show for it. Boss Shepherd left Washington a very poor man, and now he (Grant) was glad to know he was doing well in mining property, and he hoped he would return to Washington a very rich man to spite the Bourbons who had opposed his every effort to make the Capital a city worthy of the nation." *Ibid.*

A planned short visit to St. Louis was extended by the illness of Julia Dent Grant. During his stay, USG attended several horse races. On June 9, 1881, USG "arrived at the track in time to witness the second race—two and a quarter miles. He proposed to Col. Hunt to bet $5—he never bet a larger sum, he said—that he could name a horse that would beat his (Hunt's) 'John Davis.' The proposition was accepted, the money was put up, Gen. Grant named 'Bancroft' and pocketed $10 at the close of the race. The General declined to stay for the hurdle race. He said he did not like hurdle races, because they were dangerous. He had seen men terribly bruised at them, and it always made him nervous to look at one. A gentleman who was present and heard this remarked that during his Mexican trip the General would not allow any of his party to witness a bull fight." *Ibid.*, June 10, 1881.

1. On March 30, USG had passed through St. Louis on his way to Mexico. "His valuable baggage was plundered between St. Louis and Texarkana . . . by John F. Fitzpatrick and E. T. King. The first named was a messenger of the Iron Mountain Express; the other was a brakeman on the road. . . . They continued to work regularly, and attended to their business as usual until about three weeks ago, when, at Texarkana, they got on a big spree, and were discharged from the employ of the company by the local Superintendent. They continued their debauch for several days, and one day they appeared reeling through the principal streets of the town, gorgeous in glittering medals and badges pinned upon the outside of their coats. . . ." *Ibid.*, June 1, 1881. "In a general conversation about this matter which followed, the General laughed heartily at the picture of the two drunken men parading the streets of Texarkana, glittering with these precious honors." *Ibid.*, June 8, 1881. The 1880 census for USG's household listed Yanada, age 21, body servant. See Speech, [*April 9, 1880*].

2. See *PUSG*, 18, 420–21; Thomas C. Reeves, *Gentleman Boss: The Life of Chester Alan Arthur* (New York, 1975), pp. 125–26, 136–41, 146–47.

3. Born in 1816 in N. Y., a Utica lawyer, Francis Kernan served one term as U.S. Representative (1863–65) and as U.S. Senator (1875–81).

4. While in St. Louis, USG was reportedly asked "why Mr. Garfield began his Administration by fighting Conkling. 'Well,' said he, 'I suppose he thought he had to fight somebody, and I have noticed that weak men always fight friends, while strong men always fight enemies.'" *St. Louis Globe-Democrat*, June 12, 1881.

5. ". . . The General evidently considers himself ill-used personally. Some time ago he was in an unenviable manner exhibited by his friends as a man without means of support and for whom something should be done. And now he is in danger of exhibiting himself as 'a man with a grievance.' The rôle of the 'silent man' became him much better." *New York Evening Post*, June 13, 1881.

To William R. Rowley

———

Palmer House, Chicago, June 12th *1881.*

MY DEAR GEN. ROWLEY:

I regret very much not being able to get to Galena this trip. I expected to have been there about last Thursday.[1] But Mrs Grant was taken sick in St Louis and was only able to move last evening; and then only in a special car where she could have her bed. We had arranged to have our car switched off on the central road for

Galena and only learned an hour or two before leaving St Louis that there would be no train along until Monday morning early, or after midnight to-night. We had therefore to come on here, and expected to go over to Galena to-night. But Mrs. Grant is not well enough to go so we will stop here for a few days and then go on to New York where business really calls me. I am very sorry not to get to Galena at this time, but it seems impossib[le.] Give my best regards to all my friends there in which request Mrs. Grant joins me.—Mrs Grant sends Eliza—her maid—o[ver] to visit her friends and to bri[ng] some things from the house. [If] you will be kind enough t[o] aid her in getting the things I will be ever so much obliged. While speaking of the house let m[e] say that we object to Mr. Ma[. . . .] taking boarders in the house. No rent is charged and therefore we can make this stipulation. We want them to enjoy the house for themselves and to keep ~~the house~~ it with the funature and grou[nds] in good condition for our use when[ever] we want it.—Instead of Eliza [*taking*] things from the house they had better [be] packed and shipped to us—by Ad[ams] Ex—to New York City. The foll[owing] are the articles: three trunks—fa[stened] securely—they in the dessing room adja[cent to] Mrs. Grants room, all the pickles, preserves jellies & wine in the pantry between the kitchen and new addition we had built last summer. Amber tinted glass bolls & saucers and silver spoons, forks with the knives. The glass is in the pantry and the silver—Mrs Grant thinks—is in the cupboard drawer in her dressing room, all the shells, and all the linnen on the enclosed list. In the library there is a paperweight, of green stone, representing an apple which might be sent. ~~Either~~ Miss Felt I think has the keys. In the beaureau drawer, in dressing room up stairs, are some fine books which might be packed up ~~and sent~~ ready to ship when we send for them. These articles can be sent to us ~~in New York~~ at Long Branch N. J by Adams Ex. the trunks to New York. You might get these things ready for shipment and I will telegraph you when to ship them.

The Ale Mrs. Grant wants you & Mrs. Rowley to keep to drink h[er] health in.

With kindest regards to you, [Mrs.] Rowley, Miss Minnie and
our fri[ends] generally

Yours very Truly

U. S. GRANT

ALS (frayed), IHi. On June 16, 1881, a correspondent reported from Galena. "Judge W.
H. Rowley, who went to Chicago to see Gen. Grant in response to a telegram from the
latter, arrived home this morning, . . ." *Chicago Tribune*, June 17, 1881.

On June 12, a reporter had interviewed USG at the Palmer House. "I accomplished my purpose, having obtained all that I went for without any great difficulty,
despite the attempts of certain newspapers and persons here to create an opposition
through talk of annexation, etc., etc. That was caused, I think, by people interested
in other roads who didn't want to see a company operating in Mexico that they didn't
control or have an interest in. The articles that were published by papers here were
copied into those of Mexico, and at first aroused a little opposition, but I went before Congress and in a short speech I told them what I wanted, and they gave me my
charter at once. One was never issued before in so short a time. The road will be in all
about 700 miles long, running from the City of Mexico through Pueblo to the Pacific
Coast, while another branch runs down to the gulf. It will be a great benefit to Mexico
in developing the resources of that country, and to the United States, because in exchange for her commodities Mexico will take such productions as we can best spare,
without draining us of our precious metals. The charter provides for the completion
of the road in ten years, but in all probability the bulk of it will be finished inside of
three. Four surveying parties are already at work. I shall very likely return there next
winter. . . . If you want to know what I think of the manner in which Mr. Conkling has
been treated by the President and his colleagues in the Senate, I will tell you without
any hesitation. I think it is most outrageous, and if you want to know where I stand in
the present contest, I will tell you that I am with Conkling and Platt. Mr. Conkling
is my friend. He has been a warm supporter of mine, but for all that I do not owe him
near so much to-day as does Garfield. It is true, Mr. Conkling did not support Garfield
in the Chicago Convention, but he saved him in November. Without New York State
Mr. Garfield could not have been elected, and without Mr. Conkling New York State
would not have gone Republican. Whenever the State has gone Republican in past
years the cause could be traced directly to Conkling and his personal efforts. When
I say that Garfield owes more to Senator Conkling than I do, I do not mean to under-
estimate the obligations I am under to him, but I was elected once without the State
of New York, and when it did go for me I would have been elected without it. When
Mr. Conkling went to Warren and commenced his vigorous campaign for the Republican party and Garfield, matters looked very serious. Defeat was almost certain. It
was then, and then only, that Republicans took heart, and from that time on the tide
of battle turned. Mr. Conkling went into the campaign because he was a Republican
and because he desired the success of his party—not because of any trade he had made
with Garfield. It was in accord with the resolutions which he offered in the National
Convention, pledging the support of every delegate to the candidates nominated, whoever they might be. This was done because several had declared that if I was nominated
they would bolt." The reporter asked about the rumored "Treaty of Mentor," referring
to USG's visit on Sept. 28, 1880, to James A. Garfield's Ohio home. "There wasn't a

word of truth in the sensational reports that were published concerning what occurred during our visit. We were in the State speaking, and in compliance with Garfield's oft-repeated request, I determined to call at Mentor, as it could be done without putting us much out of our way. Conkling said he would go with me. Arrived at Garfield's house, we found a crowd of people there—probably 150 in all. We went into the house and sat down, talked with Garfield and others present, but not a word was said by either Conkling or myself to Garfield in the way of a trade or bargain. Nor was any understanding of any kind whatever arrived at. All that we said while with Garfield was in a general way, and could be heard by those around us. In fact, it would have been impossible for us to say anything that those around us could not hear. So all this talk about the Mentor treaty was nonsense. I have no doubt but that when Mr. Conkling resigned he did so with the intention of keeping out of politics, and out of the Senate. . . . He was sick and disgusted with the condition of affairs. He had been insulted by the President and slighted by the Senate. There is, or should be, a great deal in 'Senatorial courtesy,' which means simply this, that when the President makes an appointment in any state and it fails to elicit the approval of the two Senators from that state, the matter ends there, and the nomination is rejected. If the Republican Senators from any state object to any nomination, the rest of their party is expected to support them in the matter without exception. The same is, of course, true of the Democrats. But in this case, it was a coalition against Conkling. He accepted it as such. In the first place it was an insult, and, doubtless, intended as such on the part of Garfield, to ever select for the New York Collectorship this man Robertson. He was a personal and political enemy of Conkling's, and was probably chosen for that reason." Concerning Secretary of State James G. Blaine's role in the Conkling dispute, USG said. "Well, of course I can't say about that, but I don't believe it ever would have happened if he hadn't been in the Cabinet. I know nothing personally of Conkling's purposes or intentions, having neither seen nor heard from him since this affair happened, but from my knowledge of him, and from what I have learned from those who have talked with him, I am of the opinion that he went home to stay. But, as you know, no sooner had he got out than a series of attacks were made upon him through the press and from all quarters. It was said that Conkling acted petulantly, and was inclined to sulk and play the child, because he could not have things to suit him. All these stories seemed to emanate from the White House and that locality. Even after he was out they could not let him rest in peace. Conkling is a proud man, and I presume he said, when all these contemptible stories came to his ears, 'I will show them what I can do; I will go back again; I will fight them,' and he will do it, too. They may beat him through the means last resorted to, but they can never carry New York State without him. The contest will, in all probability, be carried over to another session. . . . After Garfield was elected, he wrote me several letters filled with protestations of gratitude at what he chose to call my valuable services during the campaign, and asked me to give him a chance to repay in part the great debt he thought he owed. He said he wanted my assistance, and the benefit of my travels and experience in making his selections for foreign appointments. I finally wrote him that my brother-in-law, Cramer, was sick and wanted to get out of Denmark, and asked for his transfer to some place south of there, naming Spain, Belgium, and Portugal. He was sent to Switzerland. But you see it was all part of a plan. Gen. Badeau was known to be a friend of mine. He was sent to Denmark in order to make place for Merritt. Merritt was appointed to the New York Custom House because he was known to be an enemy of Conkling's, and for the purpose of breaking the latter up. Failing in this, Robertson, a still greater enemy, was selected to complete the work, and it was of course necessary to provide for Merritt. Hence these changes. But it is not likely that I would ask for any transfer that would endanger the son of my old Secretary of State. Fish resigned, it is true, but it was because he wanted to be promoted." *Chicago Morning News*, June 13, 1881. See *ibid.*, June 15, 1881.

In a second interview on June 12, USG again expressed optimism for rapid growth in Mexico and in Mexican-U.S. trade. "I consider good transportation the basis of the most valuable commercial relations between the two countries." Concerning Mexican annexation, USG said. "That will never be; the country is now more settled and quiet than before in years; it is well governed, and the people see the benefits of peace, one of which is the investment of foreign capital. It is entirely safe now to invest capital in any business or industry that would thrive in Mexico. Eventually the country will be a new and strong Latin republic, combining the better Spanish elements of Central America. Anything the United States can do to help this growing republic on our southwestern border will redound to our benefit." USG spoke again about Blaine and Conkling. "There can be but little question that the Secretary of State is responsible in a great degree for the difficulty. Even if he favored the appointment of Robertson it should not have been made, for in objecting Conkling had the right of precedent and Republican usage. When I was acting as President if a single Senator from any State objected to an appointment, it was not made, although some Cabinet officer might have favored it. . . . Since my return every Republican I have met, with one exception, has held that the Senators should be sustained, and that the fight against them is unjust and hurtful to the best interests of the party. Even the Democrats acknowledge Conkling to be in the right; yet they hate him bitterly, and would like to see him beaten, for they know he is the strongest man in the Republican party, and they rightly give him the credit of being the main agent of their defeat last fall." Asked whether dissenting Republicans might form a new party, USG replied. "Well, yes, there are very apparent indications of a break-up of the old parties. The feeling is quite pronounced in the South, where the business element and the better class of people in general are desirous of seeing the solidity of that section destroyed. A new party with good leaders, sound principles, and a platform to suit the times would be popular and receive a heavy following, not only in the South but in the North as well, where there is a great deal of dissatisfaction in the ranks of both parties. The Democrats see hopeful signs in the growing division in the Republican party, and will undoubtedly try to keep up their organization in order to be prepared to take advantage of a break in the Republican ranks, and get into power through the split, like the Republicans did after Scott's defeat in 1850 [*1852*]." *Chicago Inter-Ocean*, June 13, 1881.

In a third interview on the same day, USG told a reporter that he had asked the Mexican government "for the right-of-way, [f]or protection, and to be relieved for a period of twenty-five years from paying duty on material, stock, etc., to be used in the construction and maintainance of the road. . . . The Senate granted what we asked of them by a unanimous vote, and in the House there were only two or three votes against us." An amendment provided "that the special police for the road shall be native Mexicans,—and that is as it should be, because the Mexicans know the country better, and they will also cost less." USG explained the benefits of the proposed railroad. "Well, you see, the road comes into the City of Mexico from two sides, connecting the city with the Pacific coast and the Gulf coast, and there is already a northern connection. At present there is no way of transporting the products of the country from the coast districts except on the backs of bronchos and Mexican products are not such as can bear that mode of transportation. And it would cost almost as much to build wagon-roads, such are the natural features of the country as to construct a railroad. In some regions of Mexico sugar is so plentiful that families exist on it almost wholly, and in cotton regions, not 150 miles distant, sugar is a luxury enjoyed only by the rich—there is no way of transporting it except by means of bronchos and rugged paths. With a railroad the people can derive a great profit from their surplus products and can get products not natural in their own country at a moderate cost. So the Mexican Southern will open up a big trade for this country and Mexico. . . . If the poorer classes of this country were not paid any better than is Mexican labor there would be greater danger of a revolution here than there is now in Mexico." USG again discussed Roscoe Conkling's resignation. "He has sought a reëlection because he desires to show the public that the slurs and insults thrown at him since his resignation are not indorsed by the people of New York. And I will say right here that these slurs seem in a great measure to have emanated from the White House. . . ." *Chicago Tribune*, June 13, 1881. A rival paper reported that the *Tribune* interview was gained under false pretenses. ". . . When the General saw the trick which had been played he was much displeased, and spoke of it as most dishonorable and contemptible: but, while it was a low trick, it was only in keeping with the character and practices of the man at the head of the paper, and was in perfect accord with the treatment he (General Grant) had ever received at Medill's hands. He was indignant at the treatment received at the hands of the editor of the *Tribune*, and to a reporter of THE INTER OCEAN expressed himself very freely on the subject." *Chicago Inter-Ocean*, June 14, 1881. "A REPRESENTATIVE of THE INTER OCEAN met General Grant at General Sheridan's headquarters yesterday, and the conversation turned upon the conduct of the Chicago *Tribune* toward him, so vigorously denounced by the General in his interview Monday. 'What I complain of,' said General Grant, 'is the attack by innuendo which it is customary for the *Tribune* to make upon me. It had a paragraph, for illustration, referring to the case of Hallett Kilbourne in Washington, saying that he was imprisoned for refusing to reveal the secrets of the real estate ring in that city, and that if he had done so many prominent persons would have been found connected with the fraud. Then it rings my name in, without any seeming connection, but giving the impression, or trying to without saying so, that I am in some way mixed up with those accused of dishonesty. That is contemptible, but it is after the style of the *Tribune's* attacks upon me for years. If it believes I am connected with rings, why don't it have the manliness to say so instead of suggesting such charges, and sending them out nameless and irresponsible? A newspaper that attempts to undermine reputation in this way is unworthy of the support of honorable men.' The conversation turned upon the trouble at Albany, and General Grant expressed the same opinion published heretofore. The General thinks Blaine has had a pretty large hand in the difficulty, whatever may be said to the contrary. 'Blaine,' said he, 'is a very smart man, and when I say that I do not mean talented, but smart. I haven't a doubt that the appointment of Robertson is largely owing to his efforts, though he may not have spoken to Garfield about it since the election, as some of them say.'" *Ibid.*, June 15, 1881.

On June 19, in New York City, USG repeated much of what he had said earlier about Mexico. ". . . I was exceedingly pleased with President Gonzales. All I saw of him impressed me with the fact that he was a man of great firmness, and he unquestionably did resist persons who had been regarded as all-powerful in Mexico and Mexican affairs, and what he did was exactly in the line of opposition to their remonstrances. Everything that I saw there shows that great progress is making and has been made in all directions, and I could see this change for the year that I was absent from the country. . . . I think [*the Mexican telegraph system*] would be good if it were under Government control, for it seems to be in private hands at present and they can examine any despatches they please: but I have no doubt but what the Congress will regulate that matter in time. . . . I judge that Americans are entering many lines of business there. I could see a great advance since my visit of a year ago. There are large shipments of machinery for performing the operations on the plantations, and of other agricultural implements there have been liberal shipments from this country. . . ." *New York World*, June 20, 1881.

On June 30, Matías Romero telegraphed to USG, New York City. "Number five your five received. I drew on the twenty eighth on you for twenty thousand dollars for the present enough. full answer by mail" Telegram received, USG 3. On July 1, James H. Work, secretary, Mexican Southern Railroad Co., New York City, wrote to USG, Long Branch. "I have this morning a telegram from Mr Romero of which I enclose a copy and which I understand as disposing satisfactorily of the money question in connection with the land purchases for some little time. I have also your telegram saying that you will not be in town until tomorrow, and will try and arrange a meeting of the Finance Committee for tomorrow but am a little afraid that we cannot well have a meeting of any formal character as Mr Gould is they tell me, rarely if ever in town on Saturday. I think perhaps I may be able to make about as much progress without the meeting as with it and have matters in shape for a meeting of the whole board of direction immediately after the 4th of July. I write this note to you on my first arrival at the office with the intention of adding to it if anything occurs during the day which is worth noticing." ALS, *ibid.*

On July 13 and 26, Romero wrote to USG. "I received by the New Orleans steamer your esteemed letter dated at New York on the 20th of June last, in which you ask me to see the President and Secretary of State about the unfair course that Mr. Zamacona, our Minister to Washington is following towards you. I saw at once Mr. Mariscal and he said that he would see the President about it. After having seen the President, Mr Mariscal wrote me a letter dated on the 9th instant in which he says as follows: 'The President desires me to tell you, that you say to Gen. Grant that we should be very sorry if what he says of Mr. Zamacona should be confirmed. In justice to the truth I must say that Mr. Zamacona's official letters to the State Department, do not show any hostile spirit against Gen. Grant. Should he show such hostile spirit in his private correspondence, we will try to ascertain it although it will be somewhat difficult to succeed.' I asked Mr. Mariscal whether Mr. Zamacona had sent to the State Department your interview with the *World* reporter published in the weekly *World* of the 22d instant, and he said not; and this does not show much impartiality. Your are probably aware that Mr Zamacona is an intimate friend of D. Ramon Guzman and this fact will explain his attitude towards you. As soon as I received the Weekly World I applied for an interview with the President to read it to him, and I tried to have it published in Spanish in our papers. I saw this morning the President and read to him such portion of your interview as relates to him. He was very much pleased to see what you said of him, and inquired about you and your road with great deal of interest. I ofered him a translation of the interview for its publication in the Official paper. The *Nacional* has published already portions of it, but not in full. I did not receive by yesterdays mail any private or official letter from you or from Mr. Work, and only received a telegram. I send you by this mail a complete account of all which has taken place here during last week. We have received very satisfactory news about the health of President Garfield. Payno and Amat relied upon you for the building of their roads which they have just contracted with the Mexican Goverment. Hoping that Mrs Grant is entirely recovered and my best wishes for your health and hapiness and kindest regards of Mrs. Romero and Mrs. Allen . . ." "I send you a full mail by this steamer which will inform you of all that has taken place here. Sr. Payno and Gen. Lalanne are very anxious to obtain from you a loan of $10.000 to make a deposit to garantee the organization of their Co, not the building of their road. I believe there is no danger of loosing that money in any case. If the Mexican Southern would not take that road Jesse might take it. I have telegraphed to him on the subject to day. After consultation with Chief Justice Vallarta I decided to draw the deed for Anton Lizardo in the name of the Company directly to obviate difficulties. You may consider this affair as entirely finished The work of our engineers progress satisfactorily, and they have found less difficulties than I anticipated. Your interview with the *World's* reporter has been printed in full, not only by the Official paper, but by the Monitor and other papers with wide circulation. Every body (except Guzman and clique) seem very much pleased with it. Gen. Mejia Gen. Cañedo, Father Gillow and several others have asked me to congratulate you for that ~~let~~ interview. I have drawn to day for $100.000 on Mr. Russell Sage to pay for Anton Lizardo and Bamba and Garrapatero properties. With the exchange of that amount I will have enogh to pay the engineers for some time. In great haste, . . ." ALS, Nellie C. Rothwell, La Jolla, Calif. On Aug. 6, Romero telegraphed to USG. "Twelve—Your thirteen received—Decute for A. finally signed" Telegram received, USG 3.

In July, officers of the Mexican Southern had stated their position. "The Mexican charters of the company, allowing right of way, importation of building materials free of charge, &c., do not grant any subsidy in aid of the undertaking. The managers of the company preferred not to have a subsidy, as under the present agreement they are left substantial control of their freight and passenger rates, together with exclusive posses-sion of the railroad property, which will not lapse into the hands of the government, like the subsidized roads, at the end of ninety nine years." *New York Evening Post*, July 19, 1881. See telegram to Matías Romero, [*Nov.*] 19, 1881.

1. June 9.

Interview

————

[*Pittsburgh, June 16, 1881*]

I think the treatment of the New York Senators shameful. Not only they were not given a voice in the appointments, but they were unable to retain a man in position until his term ran out. The Collector of New York was a man objectionable to the New York Senators, but they would have been satisfied if he had remained until his time expired in two years. This was denied them. I believe that the whole thing was fixed long ago. When Mr. Hayes, just before his time expired, made a long list of appointments, one or two of which were not vacant until after he went out of office, he did it to hurt Mr. Conkling's friend. Mr. Hayes knew that these appointments were obnoxious to the Legislature of New York, and he knew that, if confirmed, they would injure Conkling's friend in his canvass. Mr. Conkling succeeded in preventing their confirmation, and so it stood when Mr. Garfield came into office. Then he sent for the New York Senators and the Vice President to consult with them about the offices to be filled. He knew well, before he said a word to them, whom they would want and after talking about a desire for harmony and all that, he produced a list of names which he said he intended to send to the Senate. They were all men whom the Senators could support and Mr. Garfield knew it, and for that reason had determined to appoint them. Not a word was said about the Collectorship, and when the conference broke up there was not a shadow of trouble. Then without warning, Mr. Garfield nominates Robertson for Collector. He knew that he could not name a man in the United States more objectionable to the New York Senators, but he sent it into the Senate.

Garfield is a man without backbone; a man of fine ability, but lacking stamina. He wants to please everybody and is afraid of the enmity of all the men around him. This was why he threw a sop to Conkling and Platt. Robertson's appointment, I am sure was settled before March 4. Yes before the Chicago Convention, Robertson knew that if my nomination could be prevented he would be Collector of New York. I do not suppose that he had any direct pledge. The contract was with Blaine, and Blaine is keen and wary. Robertson, however, knew that he was to get the appointment. Blain failed, and Garfield was nominated, and the pledge to Robertson stood good. Mr. Garfield knew he had to appoint him, yet was afraid to say so. Why didn't he come out and say openly, "I am going to appoint Robertson." I do not think Blaine has personally said anything to Garfield in this matter. He wants to be in a position to say that since he has been Secretary of State he has never interfered with the appointments, and I think he can say this. He had not said anything, but through him the Robertson nomination was dictated, and through him it was insisted upon.

I have been away so much and have only the press to rely upon for information, but I do not think that the Legislature can elect [*Conkling*]. When Conkling resigned, I think it was without intention of running again. He was disgusted and wanted to get away from it.

Are you going to New York to take pa[*rt*] in the fight?

Oh, no. I have business there and am going to attend to it. I am out of politics except as a citizen who exercises his right to vote and think as he pleases.

To change the subject rather suddenly, what do you think of Jeff Davis' book?

I have only seen extracts of it in the papers, and am not conversant with all its contents. I was highly amused by his description of how he was going to escape; throw the man off the horse and the rest of it. The idea of Jeff. Davis doing a thing of that kind is absurd. A man seventy years of age, for years an invalid, a coward, for Jeff. Davis was always a mortal coward, although he had great moral courage; it was amusing.

What do you think of the attack he made on you?

I did not see that. I read his attack on Sherman[1] and Sherman's reply about the burning of Columbia, when Sherman said that if he had burned it, the world would have known it at once, as he would have told that he did, and never attempted a denial. I endorse all that Sherman said, and I think he might have gone further. I would have said, that while the Union forces did not burn Columbia, they had a perfect right to do so. That a precedent had been established by the rebels. Columbia was the capital of a rebel State, and a State which had led in the rebellion. It was fortified and could only be taken by assault. On the other hand, as soon as the rebels got above Mason and Dixie's line, they started to burn. When they got North for a few days, just across the border to Chambersburg, a town without defences, that was never garrisoned during the war and had no one in it but women, children and non-combatants, they sacked and burned the town. Then they pushed on to York, Pa., another town without troops or defen[*c*]es and with only women, children and non combatants in it. They demanded a sum of money, several hun-

dred thousands—I don't know the exact sum—or the town must
be sacked and burned. The money was scraped together and the
town saved, and the people are paying interest on the bonds to-
day. They never repudiated and are still carrying that debt made
by the rebels. What other precedent was necessary for burning a
[r]ebel town? But Sherman did not [b]urn Columbia. The rebels
fired it before he got there, and it was the Union forces who saved
the place from total destruction. This I would have said if I been
Sherman, but of course no two men think of the same points in
making an answer, unless they consult about it. What attack does
make on me?

In one place he refers to the difference in the loss, both of men
and money in your advance, and that of McClelland, on Richmond,
and makes a comparison in the l[a]tters favor.[2]

I captured Lee's army: McClelland didn't. I think the book will
do good. It will not affect any Union men, and may have the effect
of driving some of Davis' old associates to the right side. Davis
might have pitched into me about the burning of Jackson, Miss.
The depot and hotel were burned by my men, but not with my consent, and I stopped it at once. I did not punish anyone, for I knew
the class of men who did it. They were men captured at Shiloh and
were taken through Jackson in cattle cars, packed like matches in
a box. They stopped in front of that hotel, not to be fed, but to let
others get their food. They begged for water, but could get nothing but curses, and the crowd gathered around like Northern boys
would around a menagerie. Their treatment was such that they
swore to be revenged, if they ever had an opportunity, and when
they got back they started the fire, but the troops stopped it. Joe
Johnston set fire to every store house in Jackson before I reached
it. That was perfectly justifiable, as he could not take his provisions
and did not want them to fall into my hands, but I had to issue two
hundred thousand rations to prevent the people from starving.

While I was in quarantine, I read an interview with Tom
Young, Governor, I think he is. I suppose it was authentic, but i[t]
was a tissue of lies.[3] The thing was gotten up to treat slurringly
of me. In the first place it said that I was a director of the Marine

Bank of New York and had resigned to make room for my son, who was elected in may place. That is false. I have a son in New York, a man of some means, gathered by his own exertions. He had relations with the Marine Bank, but as a depositor and then as a stockholder, and in his business has been a borrower from the bank. He was elected, and is now a director in the bank, but until last fall I did not know that there was such an institution; I was never a director of the bank and never resigned to make way for my son. So much for that. Then Mr. Young went on to say that I was the President of the United States Bank at a salary of $10,000 a year. This is another lie. There could be nothing wrong in my taking the presidency of a bank at $10,000 or any other salary; but the fact is I am not the President of the bank. The United States Bank was started recently by a few gentlemen. Almost every one holding stock is a director, it is in fact a sort of close corporation, and only one or two stockholders are not directors, one of them being connected with another large banking establishment in a way which prevents him being a director in the United States Bank. I am a director, but I do not get a cent of salary; neither is the President salaried. That is the truth about the matter. These statements were made by Mr. Young to belittle me. Why he should do so, I can not imagine. For the last twenty years Tom Young and I have held similar views on all questions both as regards Ohio and the Nation. I cannot account for such deliberate falsehoods.

The half-breed press seem to think that I have no right to either hold or express an opinion and malign me constantly. So long as I have anything to say, o[r] do anything, I will, like Sherman speaking of the burning of Columbia, let the world know of it. As a citizen I have a right to express my thoughts and will do so when it suits me.

Pittsburg Times, June 17, 1881. USG spoke en route from Chicago to New York City.

On June 17, 1881, USG arrived in New York City, where a newspaper reported the next day. "General Grant and ex-Senator Conkling held a long consultation last night, presumably on the question of the Senatorship. The General was very out-spoken to his friends on this subject, saying that this State would be disgraced if ex-Senators Conkling and Platt are not sent back to Washington. He talked very bitterly of the

treatment he and his friends had been subjected to by the Administration. Of the offices filled in this State by President Garfield, only about four-fifths of them have gone
to the Grant men, and the General thought that not even the other fifth should have
been filled in opposition to the wishes of the two Senators from the State. He said he
did not expect to go to Albany, and did not think his presence there would hasten the
election of Messrs. Conkling and Platt. He was here on private business, he said, and
not for political considerations. The $250,000 raised for him by his friends, with the
accumulated interest, is to be presented by the committee in a few days. Mr. Childs, of
Philadelphia, will come to New-York to assist in the presentation." *New York Tribune*,
June 18, 1881.

1. See Jefferson Davis, *The Rise and Fall of the Confederate Government* (New York,
1881), II, 627–29.
2. *Ibid.*, p. 526.
3. See Interview, [*June 2, 1881*], notes 1 and 3. On June 18, U.S. Representative
Thomas L. Young of Ohio wrote to USG. "I was pained to read in the National Associated Press dispatches of this morning what purports to be an interview with you,
published in THE PITTSBURG TIMES, wherein you take occasion to allude to me as a
'liar,' because you read what purported to be an 'interview' of mine in some newspaper
at New Orleans, wherein I was quoted as saying that you were connected with certain
banks, and that you were the President of one of them. In your interview, as published,
you admit all, and exactly what I did say—that you are a Director in the United States
National Bank of New York City. This I know from official sources. I never said you
were the salaried President of the bank, or that you were connected with any other
bank, because I did not know it. The conversation occurred among a party of gentlemen, all of whom, so far as I know, are your admirers. It turned on your Mexican
railroad enterprise, and the part relating to the banking business was only an incident
of it. There was in the company a prominent newspaper correspondent, and he made
the conversation the basis of the *interview* you take exceptions to. In your interview
you are made to say that I intended to 'speak slurringly of you,' and to 'belittle' you.
Now, sir, you know that when you speak to a journalist, and give him what you intend
for the public, that it is printed all over the country: and this fact must be my excuse
for printing this letter, to do myself the justice to say that from the commencement of
your brilliant career as a soldier until the close of your public life as President of the
United States, I was an humble admirer and friend. In 1868 I went as a delegate from
this district to Chicago to help make you the nominee for President. In 1872 I went to
Philadelphia to assist in the same grand purpose. In these political campaigns I spent
my time, money and best effort for your success. During the eight years of your Presidency I never asked you for an official favor for myself or any of my relations or friends.
I loved you as a soldier, and still admire you as a man, and your assumption now that
I have lied about you, or that I want to 'belittle' you, is both unkind and unjust to me.
There is but one man in this great nation could ever succeed in 'belittling' the great
soldier and statesman of whom our nation is justly proud, and that man is—*not* your
humble friend." *Pittsburg Times*, June 20, 1881. "Gen. Grant has replied to the recent
letter of Representative Young, of Ohio, and informed him that the newspaper statements of his language in speaking of him were greatly exaggerated. The letter was
addressed to Gen. Young, in Washington, and has been forwarded to him in Mexico,
where he now is." *New York Times*, July 4, 1881.

To Ellen Grant Sartoris

———

New York City
June 23d 1881

MY DEAR DAUGHTER:

Your Ma and I got back to the city a week ago. Our trip to Mexico was a very pleasant one; the climate there is always delightful and very healthy. But returning, the weather was very warm after we left Vera Cruz, and became warmer all the way to St Louis. At St Louis your Ma was taken sick—or rather seemed to break down—and has not been able to set up much since.[1] I think there is nothing serious the matter, but she will require rest. We are now at Long Branch, staying with Jesse—until our house is ready to go into. That will be about a week from now. We expected to have Fred & wife, Buck & wife and Jesse & wife with us this summer. But Jesse has taken a cottage, expecting Mr & Mrs. Chapman to stay with him. But they are still in England and may not be back until the summer is pretty well passed. While Fred. was in Texas Ida got frightened and went to her sisters in Chicago. She will not be able to come on before the 1st of August. Buck, I understand, bought a farm in Westchester Co. about one & a half hours from the city, and may go there for the summer.[2] So after all we may be entirely alone this Summer, or the most of it. In Chicago, on our way here we received four letters from you. Since our return we have had another, and several from Badeau in which you are mentioned. One from you to Buck is now before me. We expect to buy a house in the City during the Summer, and to have it ready to move into by the end of the season at Long Branch. Of course we will expect to see you all then. I expect little Algie will be so pleased with his native land, and the nice horses I expect him to drive me out with, that he will want to remain. If he does we will keep him.—Give our love to Algie & the children from us all.

yours Affectionately
U. S. GRANT

ALS, Catherine Barnes, Philadelphia, Pa.

1. On May 2, Eliphalet N. Potter, president, Union College, Schenectady, N. Y., had written to USG inviting him to attend commencement and participate in "the laying of the corner-stone of the new building for recitation rooms, library, &c." *New York Times*, May 4, 1881. A correspondent later reported that USG "has telegraphed to President Potter that he will not be able to attend, on account of Mrs. Grant's illness." *Ibid.*, June 21, 1881.

2. Ulysses S. Grant, Jr., completed this purchase in Aug., 1881. See letter to Daniel Ammen, Oct. 11, 1881; *New York Times*, Sept. 14, 1881; J. Thomas Scharf, *History of Westchester County, New York*, . . . (Philadelphia, 1886), II, 513.

To Julia K. Fish

New York City
June 24th 1881.

DEAR MRS. FISH;

Your letter of the 17th inst. to Mrs. Grant; kindly inviting us to your house, was rec'd only last night, at Long Branch. It had been to Washington, the direction being Fifth Ave. Hotel, Washington, by mistake. Mrs. Grant got back here quite sick though I think nothing serious. She seems very much broken down without anything in particular being the matter. Probably rest is what she wants more than any thing els. This she will have a good opportunity of getting at Long Branch. She would not have been able to accept your kind invitation if she had received it because she was—and is—confined to her bed most of the time. My last visit to Mexico was one of business, and having just returned, I was busy here so I could not have accompanied her. I will however try to run up for a day, some time soon, myself just to see how the Governor is improving in farming. When he has leisure I hope he will give the world the benefit of "What he knows about farming," in one volume. It will be worth as much as Greeleys book [1] and I promise it shall have a prominent place in my library. We will hope to see you and the Governor at our little place at Long Branch during the summer.

With kindest regards of Mrs. Grant & myself,

Very Truly yours
U. S. GRANT

ALS, ICarbS. On June 27, 1881, Hamilton Fish wrote to USG. "Mrs Fish's mistake in the address of her letter, was not wholly unnatural. Like ~~the rest of us~~ so very many others she wanted you to have been in Washington, &, woman-like, what she wanted, was in her mind, & she confounded a White House on the Fifth Avenue, with one further South. She shewed me your letter, you are quite right about the farming. My book is not yet ready, but when you see it, you will learn many things, about farming, you never before knew. I think of adding for the benefit of the Settlers on your Rail-Road a chapter on 'Mexican farming' & the various uses to which the 'maguey' (in particular) & other products of the region may be profitably applied—We are pained to hear of Mrs Grant's illness—but hope that rest will soon entirely restore her health & strength. You are very good to promise us a visit—we shall be delighted to have you. I have to be in NewYork on Thursday, & again on the 4th July—on or about the 7th Mrs Fish goes to Newport to pass two or three weeks with Mrs Webster—If you come before she goes, let me know when to meet you at the Station—if you cannot, we shall hope to see you later With regard to 'Politics,' the less said the better. I do not feel like voting for another Ohio man for the Presidency, unless h[e] has removed out of the State, & learned something elsewhere. We have elected three Presidents from Ohio—one did not live—the second might as well not have lived, & the third—well 'enough said'—With kindest regards from my wife & me to Mrs Grant . . . I am reading Badeaus last volumes—They are very interesting, & the style is admirable. In a merely literary view, they are superior to the first—" ALS (press), DLC-Hamilton Fish.

1. Horace Greeley published *What I know of Farming* in 1871.

To Robert T. Lincoln

New York City
June 24th 1881.

HON. ROBT LINCOLN, SEC. OF WAR:
MY DEAR MR. SEC.

I take pleasure in presenting to your acquaintance Gn. J. M. Withers, of Ala. The General has been an acquaintance of mine for a number of years, is a graduate of West. Point, and a gentleman I highly respect. If you can facilitate attention to the business he may have it will be appreciated as a favor.

Very Truly yours
U. S. GRANT

ALS, Goodspeed's Book Shop, Inc., Boston, Mass. Active after the Civil War in Mobile politics, Jones M. Withers moved to Washington, D. C., to work as a claims agent. See *PUSG*, 5, 251; Speech, [*April 9, 1880*], note 1.

To Edward F. Beale

New York City
June 25th 1881.

My Dear General Beale:

Your kind letter of the 22nd inst. and Emily's to Mrs. Grant, of about the same date, come duly to hand. Mrs. Grant is much better than when we arrived here, but is by no means well. She seems to be more broken down than having any thing specific the matter. She will hadve a good chance to rest at Long Branch this Summer which is probably what she needs more than anything els.—I hope we will meet you and Mrs Beale at Long Branch during the Summer.—I am as yet without anything to drive, but I expect to have something by the last of next week. Buck & I living together we will have carriage teams enough, but I want something for my own driving.

Please present Mrs. Grant's and my kindest regards to Mrs Beale & Miss Emma.

Very Truly yours
U. S. Grant

ALS, DLC-Decatur House Papers.

To George S. Canfield

New-York, June 30, 1881.
Col. George S. Canfield, Adjutant-General, Toledo, Ohio:

Dear Sir: I have your letter of the 28th of June. I have answered the invitation to be at Clyde on the 22d of July, at the unveiling of the McPherson statue, that I am not able to say positively that I will be able to be present on that occasion, but if I can leave New-York at that time I shall certainly be there. My respect for Gen. McPherson was so great that I want to do everything I can to express my appreciation of the man and of his services while living. I hope the Ohio soldiers who served under him will turn out on that occasion in great number.

> With great respect, &c.
> U. S. Grant.

New York Times, July 12, 1881. Former drummer boy, 21st Ohio, George S. Canfield was a Toledo journalist. See following letter.

To Rutherford B. Hayes

———

> New York City
> July 19th 1881,

My Dear Gen. Hayes:

I have your letter of the 16th of July conveying the kind invitation of Capt. Temmon [1] for me to be his guest during the ceremonies of the unveiling of the McPherson statue, and of Mrs Hayes & yourself for me to return by the way of Fremont and be your guests for as long a time as I can stop. I regret very much that I cannot be at Clyde on the 22d but it is impossible. I have guests staying with me for the week, and besides business connected with my recent trip to Mexico are about culminating so that, for the present, I cannot well be out of reach of this city for a single day. I regret not being able to meet the Ohio Veterans on the coming occasion, and still more my inability to testify to the high regard I feel for the memory of McPherson who was for so long a time a member of my household.

Thanking Capt. Temmon Mrs. Hayes & yourself for your kind invitation, I am

> Very Truly yours
> U. S. Grant

ALS, OFH. On June 25, 1881, USG, New York City, wrote to Rutherford B. Hayes. "Your letter of the 17th inst. come duly to hand, but I have only just this moment seen it. I answered General Buckland, of the committee in charge of the ceremonies at the unveiling of the McPherson Statue, a few days since to the effect that it was not probable that I would be able to go to Clyde on the 22nd of July, but that if I could go any place at that time I would go there." ALS, *ibid.*

1. John M. Lemmon, former capt., 72nd Ohio, practiced law in Clyde, Ohio. See Charles Richard Williams, ed., *Diary and Letters of Rutherford Birchard Hayes* (Columbus, 1922–26), IV, 11–12.

To John M. Hamilton

NEW YORK CITY, July 22, 1881.

My dear Governor:

Your letter of the 19th inst., conveying an invitation from the Soldiers' Reunion Association of Illinois to attend a reunion to be held in Bloomington from the 7th to 9th of September, is received. I would gladly accept if I could. I have received several other invitations to attend reunion and fairs in the State during the coming fall, and have had to partially decline them all or to accept on condition I can be in the State at the dates named. I hope to get to Illinois for a visit of a week or ten days in the fall, but feel certain I will not be able to go as early as September. I regret very much not being able to meet the veterans of Illinois on the occasion of their reunion, and will not now wholly decline because, if so situated as to be able to go on the 7th or 8th, I will do so, even if it should make a second trip necessary. Very truly yours,

U. S. GRANT.

Gov. J. M. Hamilton, Chairman Com, &c.

Bloomington Pantagraph, Aug. 2, 1881. A Bloomington, Ill., lawyer and veteran of the 141st Ill., John M. Hamilton was elected Ill. senator in 1876 and lt. governor in 1880. On July 29, 1881, USG wrote to Hamilton. "I have your second letter of July 26th, urging your invitation for me to be present at the soldiers' reunion in the fall. I have a very great desire to be there on that occasion, and shall make an effort to gratify that desire. The day fixed for the reunion is earlier than I had expected to go West, but I shall endeavor to arrange it so as to be there at the time specified, viz.: from the 7th to 9th of September." *Ibid.*

On Sept. 8, USG spoke at Bloomington. "It can be said of the veteran that he would not ask anything of his government that he would deny to any citizen except his pension, and he expects that it be given to Union soldiers only." *Ibid.*, Sept. 9, 1881.

To Adam Badeau

———

New York City
July 27th 1881

MY DEAR GN. BADEAU:

I am just this day in receipt of two letters from you of the latter part of June. Why they have been so long coming I cannot conceive.—A few days after your letters were written, as you know— the dastardly attempt was made upon the Presidents life. This of course has put a stop to all communication on the subject of foreign appointments—in fact all Presidential appointments. I had told Porter before this terrible crime that I though probably you had better after all accept the Copenhag[en] appointment for the ~~Presiden~~[t] present. Whether Porter had an opportunity to mention the subject before the wounding of the President or not I do not know.—This attempt upon the life of Gn. Garfield produced a shock upon the public mind but little less than that produced by the Assasination of Mr Lincoln. The intensity of feeling has somewhat died out in consequence of the favorable reports of the patients condition from day to day; but now more alarm is being felt for his safety. I my self have felt until within the last three or four days that there was scarsely a doubt about his recovery. Now however I fear the chances are largely against it. But by the time this reaches you more certainty will be felt one way or the other. The crime is a disgrace to our country, and yet cannot be punished as it deserves.

I have been very busy though not accomplishing much, which must be my excuse for not writing sooner.

Very Truly yours
U. S. GRANT

ALS, Munson-Williams-Proctor Institute, Utica, N. Y. See letter to James A. Garfield, March 16, 1881.

On June 15, 1881, Adam Badeau, London, wrote to President James A. Garfield transmitting a set of his recently published *Military History of Ulysses S. Grant*. ". . . I trust it may not be inappropriate for me to add how much I regret that the moment of the appearance of a work, which from its subject and authority I have hoped might be accepted as national, should also have been the moment when I seem to be in disfavor with my government. I have however had opportunities of observing closely the difficulties and embarassments that beset a Chief Executive, . . ." ALS, DLC–James A. Garfield.

On June 3, Badeau had written to Gen. William T. Sherman. ". . . I suppose I shall be in America before a great while, as the President has selected the time of the appearance of what I hope will be accepted as a national work, to relieve me from civil office, against the protest of General Grant, and indicating by his offer of another but ~~useless~~ desirable place, that no dissatisfaction exists in regard to the discharge of my functions in that post which I leave. I cannot say that I have not hitherto received my deserts, but I could have wished that I should not seem rebuked or ignored by my government at the very moment of the completion of the task which is the result of twenty years of my life. . . ." ALS, DLC–William T. Sherman. On June 21, Sherman wrote to Badeau. ". . . I understand that you have declined the mission to Denmark. You know that I am frank and honest, and you will not mistake my meaning when I say, unless you are sure of an income from your books or pen, you ought to have accepted that mission. It may be a sinecure. It was what General Hugh Ewing had, when President Grant turned him out to make room for Cramer. It brought down on me the power of the Ewing family, because it was naturally supposed that I had or ought to have had enough personal influence with General Grant to have spared General Hugh Ewing, who was one of my Division Commanders at Vicksburg, and who was displaced to make room for General Grant's brother-in-law. But of course General Grant did not think of me or any body in that connection. Somebody had to provide for Cramer: and now again trouble arises to provide him a place at the expense of Mr. Fish's son and of yourself. . . ." Copy, *ibid.* On July 13, Badeau wrote to Sherman. ". . . As to Copenhagen, I put myself in that matter entirely in Gen Grants hands, and followed his advice implicitly. I hear however that the President was still not averse to doing something to please me, when he was attacked by Guiteau. . . ." ALS, *ibid.* See *PUSG*, 19, 363–64; letter to Adam Badeau, March 7, 1882.

1. On July 2, Charles J. Guiteau shot Garfield at the Baltimore & Potomac Railroad station in Washington, D. C. On the same day, USG, Long Branch, telegraphed to Secretary of War Robert T. Lincoln. "Please despatch me the condition of the President. News received conflicts. I hope the most favorable may be confirmed. Express to the President My deep Sympathy & hope that he may speedily recover." Telegram received, DLC–James A. Garfield. On July 2 (twice) and 3, Lincoln telegraphed to USG. "The President's condition is very serious and excites our gravest apprehensions. There is internal hemorrhage The Surgeon's are evidently very anxious and guarded in their expressions. He is perfectly clear in mind and desires me to thank you for your telegram which I gave to him in substance." "At this hour, ten fifteen, the President's condition is improved. In the judgment of all the attending physicians the change is marked and hopeful" "Eleven thirty: The President's condition is greatly improved. He secures sufficient refreshing sleep, and during his waking hours is cheerful and inclined to discuss pleasant topics. Pulse 106, ~~Tem~~ with more full and soft expression. Temperature and respiration normal." Copies, DNA, RG 107, Telegrams Collected (Bound).

On July 4, USG spoke to a reporter. "It is hard to express an opinion. Of course my hopes are all for a favorable result. After the President rallied from the shock I really believed he might recover. But later news yesterday gave me great anxiety. I have known a great many cases of men shot very much in the same way where the ball was lodged where it could not be found. The men would rally after the shock and then suddenly change for the worse, contrary to the expectations of the patient and physicians and then die in a few hours. I remember the case of General Walker, who was down in the Mexican War. He received an internal wound not unlike that of the President.

Every one thought the would die, but he rallied and lingered along two or three months. Like the President, he could not turn over in bed, but he determined to live, and finally insisted on being taken home. He was carried from the City of Mexico 250 miles on a stretcher to Vera Cruz, and from there by water to New York, then up the Hudson River to his home in Troy. He remained in the same condition several months, then finally got well, fought in the war of the Rebellion and was ki[l]led. Why, I got my promotion to First Lieutenant through the death of a man who was wounded in the same way. As I remember it, the wound was almost precisely the same as that of General Garfield. The Lieutenant was shot from a horse after we had got into the City of Mexico. He retained his natural color, his respiration, pulse and temperature were almost normal, he was cheerful and he had no idea of dying. He even laughed and joked about it and said that after he got well he should never be careless again. Suddenly his complexion changed to that of a corpse and in a few hours he was dead. So, you see, you cannot really tell anything about what result may follow such a shot. If the President should live two or three days longer with his strong constitution and absolutely correct habits, I should expect he would eventually recover. . . . I did intend to go [*to Washington, D. C.*] this morning and Mrs. Child was going with me. It was an impulse when I firs[t] got up to run down on the next train and see the President, and I had my bag packed for the trip[.] Then I learned that no one was allowed to see him except his physicians, nurses and Mrs. Garfield, so that my going would not do him any good, while I get as trustworthy news of his condition here as I could there. . . . I communicated with him through Mr. Lincoln and received his reply. If he had expressed a wish to see me I would leave on the next train. . . . It was simply the act of a lunatic who was disappointed because he couldn't get what he wanted. I have seen this fellow Guiteau several times. When I was at the Fifth Avenue Hotel last winter he sent his card up to my room one day as coming from Chicago. My son, who was then on General Sheridan's staff, happened to be in my room, and I asked him if he knew this Guiteau. 'Yes,' he said, 'he is a sort of a lawyer and dead-beat in Chicago. Don't let him come up. If you do he will bore you to death.['] I sent word down I would not see him. After that he sent his card up frequently, sometimes every day for several days in succession. I always returned the same reply, that I would not see him. Several times he waylaid me on the street or in the corridor of the hotel when I was passing through, but I would not talk to him. Finally he wrote me a letter saying that he wanted me to help him obtain the appointment as Minister to Austria; that he was about to marry a woman in New York worth a million dollars, and that if he was appointed Minister he could support the position with proper dignity. He further said he had the support of Henry Ward Beecher, General Sherman and others whom I have forgotten. I paid no attention to the letter; soon after he sent his card up again. I sent back the same answer as always before—that I would not see him. He followed the waiter up when he took t[h]e card, however, saw where my room was, and when he got my answer came to the door and knocked. Supposing it to be a servant I said, 'Come in.' When he entered I knew him at once, and said to him, 'I said I would not see you.' 'All I want,' said he, 'is your name. I don't want you to trouble to write anything at all.' 'But I don't know you,' I said, 'and I wont give you my name for any purpose whatever. That is sufficient.' He still remained and repeated about the same words he had said to me in his letter concerning the Austrian Mission, and the support of Mr. Beecher, General Sherman and others. 'I was in the campaign,' he said. 'Didn't you get a copy of the speech I sent you?' 'There were a good many people in the campaign,' I said. He finally went away greatly disappointed and after he had gone my son told me that the fellow was already married and tha[t] there was no truth in his story of marrying a New York woman worth a million. I never saw him afterwards. He looked seedy and like a dead-beat. Possibly I was influenced in my opinion by my son. The fellow was sharp and a ready talker, and appeared as though he had some education, but he was evidently an adventurer, a man I would not trust with anything." About the political impact of Garfield's possible death, USG said. "Nothing tha[t] I [c]an se[e] except to disappoint— seriously disappoint—some men who want office. The places they want will be filled by men equally as competent. As to General Arthur, the shameful and villainous manner in wh[i]ch he has been slandered by the bitter newspapers known as the 'half-breed' press has given many of the people the idea that he is a monster. The trouble is that he is but little known to the people generally. I know him to be a man of common sense and clear-headed, with good associates—a man of integrity." *New York World*, July 5, 1881. Shot in the back at Molino del Rey, Capt. William H. T. Walker, USMA 1837, was transported to Albany, N. Y., by way of Vera Cruz and New Orleans. On July 22, 1864, Walker, C.S.A. maj. gen., was killed near Atlanta. See Russell K. Brown, *To the Manner Born: The Life of General William H. T. Walker* (Macon, Ga., 2005). For 1st Lt. Sidney Smith, see *Memoirs*, I, 162; *PUSG*, 1, 147.

To Philo Parsons

NEW-YORK, 1881, July 29.
Philo Parsons, Esq., Chairman of the Reception Committee, &c., Detroit:
DEAR SIR: I have your kind letter of July 18, only just received, inviting me to attend the State Agricultural Fair in September coming. I have a very great desire to visit the State of Michigan and the city of Detroit, a place where I spent a few very pleasant years, and it so happened that I have scarcely had an opportunity since leaving there in 1851 to revisit it. I will be present on the occasion of your annual fair if possible, but from the fact that I partially promised to be present at a soldiers' reunion in Illinois from the 7th to the 9th of September it may be doubtful whether I can stay long enough in the West to be in Michigan from the 19th to the 23d, or if I should return immediately to New-York from the soldiers' reunion whether I will be able to leave my business so soon after to go to Detroit; but if it is possible for me to be there I shall, and will regret very much my inability to go if it should turn out that I am unable to do so.

Truly yours,
U. S. GRANT.

New York Times, Aug. 4, 1881. Philo Parsons was a banker and former president, Detroit Board of Trade.

To Philip Lee et al.

———

NEW YORK Aug. 1, 1881

Messrs. P. Lee, J. G. Morrison, J. W. Melton, Committee, Jacksonville, Ill.:

GENTLEMEN—Yours of the 26[t]h ult. invi[t]ing me to attend the annual reunion of the "Central Illinois S[o]ldiers' and Sailors' Union" on the 10[t]h ins[t]. was duly received, and in reply I desire to say that I shall probably attend a reunion at Bloomington, Ill. If I do it will be the only occasion on which I will be able to attend a soldiers' meeting during the coming fall in the northwest. That is to be a grand reunion, I understand, of all the veterans of the state, and I shall expect to meet those of Jacksonville at Bloomington on that occasion.

Truly Yours,
U. S. GRANT.

Jacksonville Journal, Aug. 1, 1885. See letter to John M. Hamilton, July 22, 1881. Philip Lee, former capt., 101st Ill., was a wagon maker, John G. Morrison, former sgt., 101st Ill., a lawyer, and John W. Melton, 5th Ill. Cav., city clerk of Jacksonville, Ill.

On Aug. 1, 1881, USG wrote to Joshua L. Chamberlain, Brunswick, Maine. "Yours of the 29th ult, enclosing invitation to a reunion of the Maine Soldiers on Aug. 23–25 was duly received, and in reply I desire to express my regrets that my engagements are such that I shall not be able to attend—" LS, DLC-USG, VIII.

To Maj. Gen. John M. Schofield

———

New York, Aug 1 *1881*

GEN. J. M. SCHOFIELD.
DEAR GENERAL:—

Your letter of the 12th of July has just been handed me by Col. Wherry of your staff. I have read it carefully, together with the article from the "Toledo Democrat." The lapse of time since the event spoken of in that article is so great that I feel some hesitation in answering your letter, and the article from the Democrat, as I might do if I had access to the archives at Washington; but writing from memory I think I can say with great positiveness there was never any despatch from you to me, or from you to anyone in Washington, disparaging Gen Thomas' movements at Nashville. On the contrary my recollection is that when I met you on your way to Wilmington, North Carolina, subsequent to the battle of Nashville, you explained the situation at Nashville prior to Gen Thomas' movement against Hood, with a view of removing the feeling that I had that Thomas had been slow. I was very impatient at that time with what I thought was tardiness on the part of Gen Thomas, and was very much afraid that while he was lying there at Nashville and not moving his army, that Hood might cross the Tennessee River either above or below the City of Nashville, and get between him and the Ohio River, and make a retrograde movement of our army at Nashville a necessity, and very much embarrass and delay future operations of the armies. Laboring under this feeling and impression I was telegraphing Gen Thomas daily, and almost hourly, urging him to move out and attack Hood, and finally became so impatient that I contemplated his removal and the substitution of another officer in his place; but this feeling on my part was not added to by any despatches from any person from the scene of action except those from Gen Thomas himself. I have certainly no recollection of receiving any despatches from Nashville during the time spoken of in the Article in the Democrat from any person but Gen Thomas himself. I feel very sure that if any despatches had been received from you, I should now recollect it, and I am free to say that it would have created a prejudice to your disadvantage if I had received such despatches

This much you are at liberty to use in any way you may deem proper.

The other reflections which the author of the article here alluded to against you I of course am not called upon to say anything in regard to. The fact is your subsequent promotions are proof positive that I entertained none of the views set forth to your disadvantage in this article.

Very Truly Yours,
U. S. GRANT

LS, CSmH. This is the first of many subsequent letters written on stationery of the Mexican Southern Railroad Co. On July 12, 1881, Maj. Gen. John M. Schofield, London, wrote to USG, New York City. "For a long time I have been made aware of the fact that a base falsehood was secretly circulated through out the country, to the effect that, while General Thomas' army was at Nashville in Dec 1864 I endeavored in some way to influence you or somebody in Washington to remove him from the command and to place me in his stead. I have not heretofore been able to defend myself against this slander because of its secrecy. But now, for the first time within my Knowledge, this falsehood has made its appearance in public print, in the form of an article in the Toledo Northern Ohio Democrat,' copied into the New York Times of June 22d, of which I send you a slip. You, my dear General, are probably the only man now living who is able to make an authoritative statement of the facts in respect to this matter, such as must be accepted without question. I hope, therefore, it is not asking too much to request you to give me in a form which I may use publicly, a full and explicit statement of the facts in respect to this accusation. Perhaps you may also be able to recall the substance of a conversation of between you & me, on the subject of the delay of Thomas to attack Hood at Nashville, which occurred on the Naval steamer on our way from Hampton Roads to Cape Fear River when we went down to see Admiral Porter and General Terry while my troops were delayed by the ice in the Potomac. In that conversation I tried to justify Thomas' delay during the storm at Nashville, and I thought perhaps succeeded in modifying to some extent your opinion on the subject. If you are able to recollect the substance of that conversation, a statement of it would be an effective answer to the malicious charge that I was not faithful to Thomas as my Commanding officer. Not Knowing where you may be when this letter reaches the United States I send it to Col Wherry, to be sent you by mail or handed you by one of my aids as may be most convenient. Please do me the great favor to send to Wherry, or the other officer who may call upon you, an answer which he may use in public refutation of the malicious charge which has been made against me. He can then send it to me. The vipers are taking advantage of my absence to publish falsehoods and give them a ~~good~~ long start of the truth which must be sent in pursuit." Copy, DLC-John M. Schofield. On Aug. 3, 1881, Capt. William M. Wherry, New York City, wrote to the editor. "THE TIMES having given prominence to certain adverse criticisms upon Major-Gen. Schofield, now absent in Europe, and especially to a statement by Gen. Steedman, copied from the Toledo *Northern Ohio Democrat*, will you in justice to Gen. Schofield publish the accompanying letter from Gen. Grant to Gen. Schofield, in response to a request from the latter that Gen. Grant would give his recollection in refutation of the statement that Gen. Schofield had attempted at Nashville to influence Gen. Grant against Gen. George H. Thomas?" *New York Times*, Aug. 4, 1881. Born in 1836 in Mo., Wherry won distinction at Wilson's Creek in 1861, and served as Schofield's longtime aide-de-camp.

On Sept. 15, 1880, in advance of the Society of the Army of the Cumberland reunion at Toledo, Schofield had written at length to Henry M. Cist, society secretary, offering "a few brief historical reminiscences . . . to correct the misapprehensions of those who have tried to write history respecting my relations to Gen. Thomas and the Army of the Cumberland. . . . It is due to the memory of Gen. Thomas, no less than to Gen. Schofield, to put on record the fact that in all those operations from Pulaski to Nashville, including the battle of Franklin, the commanding General in the field was left that freedom of action which properly belonged to his rank and command. While all his intended movements were promptly reported to his superior at Nashville by telegraph, and all received full and unqualified approval, in no case were those movements made at the instance of Gen. Thomas, and in very few cases could his approval be received in time to influence action. Every movement was made by Gen. Schofield in the exercise of his proper discretion, or at his instance with Gen. Thomas's approval. Especially was this true of the battle of Franklin, with which Gen. Thomas had absolutely no more to do than had Gen. Sherman or Gen. Grant. Those who, through a mistaken zeal for the reputation of a beloved commander, have during all these years represented Gen. Thomas as commanding at the battle of Franklin and during the previous operations have done him even more than any other a great injustice by attempting to give him a credit which his noble nature would have scorned to claim for himself, and by thus placing him in the unsoldierly position of trying to command an army in the field while sitting in his office at Nashville, from 20 to 50 miles away. . . . It has been quite generally, but very erroneously, represented that Gen. Logan was ordered to supersede Gen. Thomas in the chief command at Nashville. On the contrary, the dispatch from Gen. Grant at City Point to Gen. Halleck in Washington was that Gen. Thomas should turn over his command to Gen. Schofield. . . . A correct understanding of this true state of the case is necessary to a due appreciation of what transpired at Nashville at that time, where it was perfectly understood both by Gen. Thomas and Gen. Schofield. It was known that Gen. Schofield enjoyed the confidence of Gen. Grant more fully than Gen. Thomas did at that time. Gen. Schofield had just won an important victory over superior numbers at Franklin, for which Gen. Grant gave him full credit, while censuring Gen. Thomas for supposed unnecessary delay in not immediately taking full advantage of that victory by reinforcing Schofield and assuming aggressive action. . . ." *Ibid.*, June 6, 1881. Schofield claimed that at a Dec. 9, 1864, meeting of senior commanders in Nashville, he had led others in supporting Maj. Gen. George H. Thomas's decision to delay action, even though by opposing Thomas he might have succeeded him in command. Schofield's letter to Cist was "accidentally mislaid" and not presented to the society. "Gen. Schofield thereupon caused it to be printed privately, and sent it to a number of Army officers." *Ibid.* Interviewed on June 12 and 13, 1881, Marcus P. Bestow, former maj. and asst. AG under Brig. Gen. Thomas J. Wood, criticized Schofield's letter and his conduct at the battles of Franklin, Tenn., and Nashville. *Ibid.*, June 13, 14, 1881. Also in [*June*], James B. Steedman wrote to the *Toledo Democrat*. ". . . There are four living witnesses—Gens. Wood, Smith, Wilson, and Steedman—who were in the council of war held in the St. Cloud Hotel, in Nashville, presided over by Gen. Thomas, all of whom can testify that Gen. Schofield states a deliberate falsehood when he says that, as the ranking officer next to the commanding General, he waived his right to speak last and promptly sustained Gen. Thomas. The truth is Gen. Schofield did not speak at all until all the other Generals had given their opinions, and then only said he would obey orders. Gen. Thomas knew three days before the battle of Nashville that Schofield was playing the part of Judas, by telegraphing to Gen. Grant at Washington disparaging suggestions about the action of Thomas, saying in one dispatch: 'It is the opinion of all our officers with whom I have conversed that Gen. Thomas is too tardy in moving against the enemy.' It was known to a number of our officers that, pending the battle, . . . Schofield was intriguing with Grant to get Thomas relieved in order that he might succeed to the command of our army as the General next in rank to Thomas. . . . In the name of the grand hero who sleeps in his honored grave, we protest against the recognition of the false, infamous claim of Schofield, whom we brand as the slanderer of both the living and dead soldiers of the Army of the Cumberland. We do not say that Schofield is a rank coward, but we can, from personal knowledge, safely state that he possesses the 'rascally virtue called caution' in an eminent degree. . . ." Reprinted, *ibid.*, June 22, 1881.

On Aug. 19, Schofield, Rigi-Kulm, Switzerland, wrote to Gen. William T. Sherman. ". . . General Grant has given me the desired letter about that slander. Assuming that he would do so I some time ago authorized Wherry to place the whole matter in the hands of Cox and ask him to do what he might think best about it at the Chattanooga meeting, and telling him I would not say any thing further on the subject at present. My object was to give the Cumberland Society an opportunity to do what is right if they want to do it. . . ." ALS, DLC-William T. Sherman. See letters to John A. Logan, Jan. 25, Feb. 14, 1884; John M. Schofield, *Forty-Six Years in the Army* (New York, 1897), pp. 236–39, 293–98.

To Ellen Grant Sartoris

New York City
Aug. 2d 1881.

MY DEAR DAUGHTER:

I did not see your Ma's letter to you which you do not quite understand. But what she ment to say is about this. When she wrote we had no house, and if we did not succeed in making a purchase we would be boarding at a hotel. In that case she wanted a visit. But now we have bought a beautiful house up by the Park. We will commence furnishing it about the middle of September, and will no doubt have every thing comfortable by the 10th of Oct. We will want you, Algy and all the children to come so as to be here at that time or as soon after as possible. Fred & Ida and you and your children will have all of the 3d floor. In that there are four large bed rooms.—The picture of your little girl is beautiful. I have no doubt but she & little Algie will be so much spoiled that they will not want to go back to England. They will be much pleased too with their little cousin Julia. The park is so handy that the children will be able to walk out there with their nurses to play when ever the weather is good.

All are very well and send much love to you, Algie and all the children.

Affectionately yours
U. S. GRANT

ALS, ICHi. USG's new home at 3 East 66th Street was located near Fifth Avenue and Central Park. See letter to John A. Logan, Feb. 9, 1881; letter to Ellen Grant Sartoris, Sept. 29, 1881.

On Aug. 12, 1881, C. Seton Lindsay, New-York Life Insurance Co., wrote to USG. "Regarding the house you have bought (subject to a Mtge. to this Company) I have just heard by accident—and of course do not know how true it may be—that you desire to pay of the loan, but the Company are unwilling to accept it—If you would permit me to call—I could make a proposal which perhaps might be acceptable to you—if you really desire to have your house free and clear at once—At any rate there would be no harm done—nor much time lost—if nothing came of it—" ALS, ICarbS.

To Benjamin F. Felt

————

90 Broadway
New York City
Aug. 9th 1881

MY DEAR MR. FELT.

Will you be kind enough to ship as freight to the address D. S. Hess & Co.[1] Nos 35 & 37 West 23d Street, New York City, the articles I have stored, by your kindness, with you. If it is not too much trouble I will feel obliged if you will send me to this office the number of packages and the date when shipped.

I have purchased a house here and hope, by the end of the season at Long Branch, to have it furnished and ready to receive any of my Galena friends who may chance to visit this City. We shall hope to see you or any members of your family who may be coming eEast.

Very Truly yours
U. S. GRANT

ALS, Mrs. Walter J. Ehrler, Galena, Ill. Born in 1821 in N. Y., Benjamin F. Felt, a Galena grocer, was the younger brother of Lucius S. Felt, who had helped to manage USG's Galena affairs until his death in 1876.

1. Interior decorators and furniture makers.

To Mary S. Logan

————

New York City
Aug. 12th 1881

MY DEAR MRS. LOGAN;

Mrs. Grant told me last evening that she had a letter from you which she wished me to read and answer saying for you to come directly to our house the moment you arrived. I forgot to read the letter hence can only say that we will be delighted to see you. If you come by Phila and arrive in time to take the 3 35 train for Long Branch you will avoid coming by this city. There are also other trains—a number every day—any of which if you will take, and telegraph us the hour of leaving Phila some one will meet you at the station. The station for you to get out at will be "West End Station."

Fred leaves here to-morrow night for Chicago and will be returning with his small but important family—now that there is a boy in it [1]—about Wednesday next. [2] With kind regards to the General & all your family,

Very Truly yours
U. S. GRANT

ALS, DLC-Logan Family Papers.

    1. Ulysses S. Grant 3rd was born July 4, 1881.
    2. Aug. 17.

To Lucy M. Porter

New York City
Aug. 15th 1881

MY DEAR MRS. PORTER:

I have your letter from Hopkinsville. I received your previous letters but did not see what I could do I felt that I could not ask anything of this Administration, in fact that my asking anything would not help the party interceded for. Having gone out of long public life and now just settling down again I have every thing about a home to purchase anew and am therefore involved in debt for the time being, as so far as I can see, for a good while to come. I have also others more or less dependent upon me beside my own immediate family. None of them fortunately are dependent upon me at present, and it looks now as if they never will be. But we cannot tell what the future may bring forth. I would be glad to help you if in my power, and to this end I have written to-day, in your behalf to the Sec. of the Treasury, who I believe is friendly to me. I would advise you to write to him also, marking your letter personal as I have done mine. In my case doing this and writing my own name on the envelope, under the word "personal" I feel sure the Sec. himself will open and read it. I wrote on the back of your letter.

If you write to me direct your letter to No 90 Broadway, New York City

Very Truly yours
U. S. Grant

ALS, DNA, RG 56, Applications. See following Endorsement.

Endorsement

———

[Aug. 15, 1881]

Hon. Wm Windom,
Sec. of the Treas.

This letter is from the daughter of Ex Governor and Ex Senator Morehead of Ky.[1] She is also the Widow of an Officer of my old regiment, the 4th U. S. Infantry. She is a woman of rare talent and of the most outspoken loyalty during the War. For the eight years while I was President she was Post-Master of Louisville, Ky. In that position she saved enough to purchase a place a little out of the City, but she was obliged to sacrifice it to save an unworthy son.[2] She is now, as you will see from this letter, in deep distress. If you can give her a position you will bring joy to a very worthy and capable woman.

Very Truly yours
U. S. Grant

AES, DNA, RG 56, Applications. Written on a letter of Aug. 9, 1881, from Lucy M. Porter, Hopkinsville, Ky., to USG. "I have no right I know to trouble you so much with my affairs. But please have patience with me and pardon my many importunities for help. I am appalled at the prospect which is before me. I don't know what is to become of me. I have no one to help me and am at a loss to know how to make a start to help myself. General, is there nothing you can do for me? I think I could do copying as well as any one and if there is no other way of aiding me, I would be so thankful if you could get me a place as copyist. Any thing that would afford the bread would be acceptable. Since my return to Kentucky I have been visiting my tried and true friends, Col. Sam. Starling's family. You must have heard of Col. Starling during the war as one of the most influential of Ky. loyalists. His widowed daughter residing with him, (Mrs. Payne) is my particular friend and has made me so comfortable at this, her delightful country home for five weeks past, that I have some what recovered from the effects of my sufferings on account of James. Mrs. Payne is an oracle of goodness, and has the reputation of being the most intellectual woman in Ky, and the whole family are and have ever been your most ardent admirers. Unless you can again extend a helping hand to me I dare not contemplate what my lot may be. My son and his wife have voluntarily cut themselves off from me, *entirely*; and of course, should I ever have any means again, I would be the only one to enjoy the benefits and would be enabled to provide for the future by careful savings. I am passionately fond of Gardening and delight in horticulture, and at my little country place was making much more than a support. If my son had only left me my home, or if I had only a rented place, and a little start in the world I could live well and make a little fortune. And if you could only procure me General (or some trusted friend) for me) a place that would enable me to settle myself in a little country home near a city I would soon be perfectly independent. I earnestly beg General that you will let me hear from you and oh! if possible let me hear some thing that will give hope and encouragement. I was in St Louis a few days after you and Mrs. Grant were there. I am glad to learn that Mrs. Grant ihas quite recovered from the illness she suffered from in St Louis Please present my affectionate and respectful regards to her. And for your self General please accept my most respectful regards." ALS, *ibid.*

On Aug. 17, Secretary of the Treasury William Windom wrote to USG, Long Branch. "I have the honor to acknowledge the receipt of the letter of Mrs. G. M. Porter, of the 9th instant, applying for appointment to a position in this Department, with your favorable recommendation thereon. And in reply to inform you that her name has been placed on the special list, with a view to her appointment when it shall be practicable." LS, *ibid.* On Aug. 20, Windom wrote to USG that he had appointed Porter "temporarily to a clerkship at with compensation at the rate of $900 per annum." DfS, *ibid.*

In [*Dec., 1867*], Jesse Root Grant had written to Secretary of the Treasury Hugh McCulloch. "The Lady I spoke to you about and for whom I asked a Clerkship, is the widow of the late Judge Bruce Porter of Covington Ky—The only Daughter of the late Ex-Governor, & U. S. Senator—Mrs Lucy Porter has lost her Father, Mother, six brothers two Husbands & two children—And has now no relation to care for her but a son about 18 a Midship man now at Anapolis She is highly educated & accomplished, very beutiful, about 40 years of age. And unfortunately reduced in circumstances—If you can give her a situation, that will support her untill her son graduates, you will confer a favor on a worthy Lady"—ALS (undated, stamped Dec. 16), *ibid.* Related papers are *ibid.* See letter to Charles J. Folger, Dec. 28, 1881.

1. Born in 1797, James T. Morehead rose in Ky. politics as a protegé of John J. Crittenden.

2. 1st Lt. James M. Gore resigned as of June 30, 1881. See *PUSG,* 19, 249.

To Robert T. Lincoln

———

New York City
Aug. 28th 1881

My Dear Mr. Secretary:

I am just in receipt of your letter of yesterday stating the grounds on which Lt. Blair's application for leave of absence has been, thus far, dectined. When I made my endorsement I knew of-course none of the facts stated in your letter. It places the matter in a new light, and I do not feel that I could urge his claims any further. In your place I do not know exactly how I would act; but it is probably that I should say to him that in its present form his applications for a years leave of absence is declined. If however he chose to tender his resignation to take effect at the end of a year, requesting a leave of absence up to that time, it would be considered. I do not ask you however to change your decision on my account.

Very Truly yours

Hon. Rob.t Lincoln Sec. of War.

AL, DNA, RG 94, ACP, 2959 1877. On Aug. 23, 1881, 2nd Lt. Frank P. Blair, St. Louis, wrote to USG, New York City. "*Personal* . . . The extremity of my need is my only excuse for troubling you. I am a graduate of West Point & a (1877) & a 2nd Lt. of Arty. I am ambitious to become a lawyer & have studied law for four years. To tide me over the first dull period of practice, I have applied for a year's leave of absence, intending to resign at its expiration. As my father at his death left nothing, & as I have been unable to save anything (having turned over all surplus to the family) this leave would materially advance my prospects. Genl. Sherman interposes, however, saying that to give me such a leave would 'Establish a bad precedent.' I need not tell you that Genl. Sherman in his press of business, must have misapprehended the facts in my case, for it is certainly not an uncommon thing to grant officers such leaves. Besides my graduating leave, I have had only about a month's leave in more than four year's time. A word from you to Mr. Secy. Lincoln would end my anxiety. I need not say that I shall ever be ready to answer my country's call in time of need. No one of my blood was ever ungrateful for a kindness. I shall prove no exception." ALS, *ibid.* On Aug. 26, USG endorsed this letter. "Referred to General Sherman. If I had it in my power to grant this leave I should unhesitatingly do it. It is a favor I would grant any graduate of West Point asking it, knowing that there is no trouble in getting all the 2d Lts. the Army wants, in time of peace, and believing graduates render their country better service, at such time, in Civil life than they can in the Army, and that in case of war they are all the better for their Civil pursuits. I would be still further induced to grant this him on account of the father's Civil service at the breaking out of the war, and his military service after." AES, *ibid.* On Aug. 27, Secretary of War Robert T. Lincoln wrote to USG. "I have this morning the letter of Lieut. F. P. Blair to yourself, bearing your endorsement and recommendation of his request that he should be granted a year's leave of absence. It is needless to say that I attach very great importance to a recommendation from yourself, especially in a matter of this character, but I judge that you are not entirely familiar with the facts in the case, and therefore write this note to know whether you adhere to the recommendation after what I shall tell you in this case. Lieut. Blair was appointed a cadet at West Point as the son of his father, and in recognition of his father's services I suppose, to a great extent. He graduated in 1877, took his graduating leave until December of that year, then served with his Artillery regiment in New York Harbor for about a year and a half, that is, until August 1879, was then as a special favor, and again as a recognition of his claim to kindness as the son of Gen. Blair, designated as the Professor of Military tactics at the University of Missouri, his own state, at Columbia; the tour of duty being three years, which will expire a year from now. He presented a short time ago, an application for leave of absence for one year, accompanied by his resignation, worded to take effect at the expiration of that leave, if granted. Before his application was received by me, he withdrew the resignation, but renewed the application for a year's leave, stating in that application no reason therefore, and giving no expression of his intended course thereafter. It became then a simple question whether it was proper, in view of possible applications from other officers of similar Military history, to grant Lieut Blair, having served only a year and a half with his regiment, and having had for two years what is considered a 'soft' place, a year's leave of absence, and this too, when his services are needed at the University, because it is, under the law, entitled to an officer, and if he goes away, another officer will have to be selected and taken from his company and assigned there—not an easy thing to do at this time, as our troops are nearly all actively engaged in service against the Indians. It seemed to me that it was improper to grant his application, and thereby make a precedent for future action. Judge Blair was in to see me yesterday on the subject. I told him that of course I had nothing but the warmest feelings towards himself and towards all members of his family, for obvious reasons, but that it seemed that young Mr. Blair was pressing too much and too often the considerations which lead everybody to feel kindly towards him, and to an extent which might cause him to be considered an object of special favoritism, and which might be embarrassing hereafter to myself and my successors in passing upon similar applications from other officers. In his present application he does not present his resignation, nor has he intimated to me the slightest intention of doing so. On the contrary, he has withdrawn his expressed intention to do so. I do not mean to say that he does not, in good faith, intend to resign at the end of the year. As to that I know nothing except what he says in his letter to you, but in his official papers he expresses no such intention, and if the leave was granted, he would be at perfect liberty, so far as the records of this Dep't are concerned, to again at the end of the leave, make an application for a leave of absence of such length, as should be satisfactory to him, accompanied ~~in this case~~ then by his resignation, and based on it and if made, it would undoubtedly be pressed by Judge Blair upon the same considerations which he used with me yesterday. I confess that I feel embarrassed in this matter, and I would be glad if you would drop me a word as to your views upon the considerations which I have stated." LS (press), Robert T. Lincoln Letterbooks, IHi. Granted leave from Sept. 1, Blair resigned as of Sept. 1, 1882.

To Joachim H. Siddons

New York, Aug 29 1881

J. H. SIDDONS
LE DROIT PARK WASHINGTON D. C.
DEAR SIR:

I have your letter of the 25th of August requesting from me data and information to enable you to write up the even[ts] of my two terms in the Executive office of t[he] Nation. I kept no journal, retained no archives, and have nothing in my possession whic[h] would give you any of the information desire[d.] I was entirely satisfied to perform my duties to the best of my ability, and leave the archive[s] of the various departments and bureaus under me to furnish all the history that I deem necessary.

Truly Yours.—

U. S. GRANT

LS, General Grant National Memorial, New York, N. Y. Joachim H. Siddons (also J. H. Stocqueler), British-born author, clerked in the P. O. Dept. See *New York Tribune*, Oct. 8, 1881.

To Clara D. McClellan

[Chicago, Sept. 6, 1881

MY DEAR MRS. MCCLELLAN: Your letter to Mrs. Grant & myself kindly extending to us an invitation to be your guest at the time of the marriage[1] . . . reached me here. Mrs. Grant is not with me, and we will not be able to attend . . . Mrs. Grant will be very busy furnishing our new house to get it ready to go into at the end of the season at Long Branch; and I will not be able to remain absent from New York long enough to attend. . . . Mrs. Grant was much disappointed that she did not get to Galena on our return from Mexico. We had fully expected to make a visit there . . . but Mrs. Grant was taken sick in St. Louis. . . .] I expected to have got to Galena this trip. But in this I am now disappointed. I left Long

Branch last Saturday morning expecting to get the evening train from New York for Chicago, intending to go directly on to Galena, and from there to Bloomington on Wednesday—to-morrow. But when I got to the cars in Jersey City there was not a single berth to be obtained in the sleeping car, and two nights was too much to set up. I returned therefore to the city and started West the next day.—Please present my kindest regards to Mr. McClellan.

Very Truly yours

U. S. GRANT

ALS (partial facsimile), Christie's Sale No. 7086, June, 1990, no. 69.

On Feb. 22, 1885, Clara D. McClellan, Galena, wrote to Julia Dent Grant. "Mr. McClellan and I have felt very much distressed at the reports current in the Western papers, in regard to the General's health. We comfort ourselves by thinking that it is the nature of the Chicago press to exaggerate and hope that references to the General's ill health are exaggerated too. I hope you will not mind my letting you how much I have admired the courage with which you have borne everything. I have felt that you were both *heroic*. I suppose you do not contemplate ever coming back to Galena to live. The place is rough, but I have found the people most cordial and hearty. Your home on the hill still waits for you. Mr. Smith writes his sermons in the library, but I must confess tobacco is more truly king in these clerical days, than during the military régime, nor is the tobacco as good, if I am any judge. Mrs Felt's house is closed for the winter. She has gone to Denver to see Kitty & her baby. Think of Kitty with a baby! Isn't it incomprehensible? I do not see much of Mrs. Rowley. She is very domestic, and now that the Soldier's Monument is paid for, and there are no more *festibles*—as she called them—to organize, she rests on her laurels. I wish I might hope for a line from you, telling us how the General is, and a word or two about yourself Mr. McClellan & I both enjoyed the Century article so much. The General's style seems to me perfection. Will you both accept Mr. McClellan's expression of esteem and regard, as well as those of Your sincere friend" ALS, USG 3. In Feb., 1882, Katherine L. (Kitty) Felt had married Moses Hallett, U.S. District Judge, Colo. See letter to Horace Porter, Nov. 26, 1879; Speech, [*April 27, 1880*], note 1.

1. On Sept. 15, 1881, Susan M. Felt married Master Joel A. Barber, U.S. Navy, in Galena. USG and Julia Grant telegraphed their congratulations. See *Galena Gazette*, Sept. 16, 1881; *PUSG*, 21, 73.

To Wayne MacVeagh

———

DATED, NEWYORK 20 REC'D AT LONG BRANCH, N. J.
To WAYNE MACVEAGH SEP 20 *188[1]*

Please Convey to the bereaved family of the Prest my heartfelt sympathy & sorrow for them in their deep affliction a Nation will mourn with them for the loss of a chief magistrate so recently

called to preside over its destiny I will return to L B in the morning to tender my services if they can be made useful

U S GRANT

Telegram received, DLC-James A. Garfield. On Sept. 19, 1881, 10:35 P.M., President
James A. Garfield died at Long Branch. An hour later, at the Fifth Avenue Hotel, USG
told a reporter. "You will please excuse me from a consideration of this sad news at this
time. It comes with terrible force, and is unexpected. What can I say? There is nothing—absolutely nothing—to be said under circumstances such as these." *New York
Times*, Sept. 20, 1881. USG later retired to a private office, "weeping bitterly. . . . Col.
Fred Grant said to THE TIMES's reporter that though he had seen his father under many
trying circumstances he had never before known him to be so terribly affected." *Ibid.*

On Sept. 6, doctors had moved Garfield by train from the White House to Long
Branch. On the same day, USG, Chicago, spoke to a reporter about progress on the
Mexican Southern Railroad, then commented on Garfield's condition. "I think such
a removal was absolutely necessary, not only because the President desired it, but because such a course was the only one to be taken under the circumstances. During the
months of August and September the White House is one of the most unhealthy places
in the world. He should have been taken from there long ago. Scarcely any of the people who stay there during these months but suffer from chills and fever. An unhealthy
breeze continually blows from the flats to the south of the White House. I remember
that during my administration several of the attaches of the White House died during
the summer from the effects of this disease ladened wind. . . . I think this removal will
do him great good, and if he eventually recovers, it will be due to his removal from the
White House." Asked about "the inability clause in the Constitution," USG replied. "I
have no doubt that that condition of affairs exists to-day requiring the Vice President
to act, but then there is no provision in the Constitution, nor has any effort been made
by Congress to make one, showing how the disability shall be declared. While such a
state of affairs existed, it would be wholly inappropriate for the Vice President unasked
to make a move toward assuming the duties of the Presidential chair. I suppose really
what should be done in a case of this kind—if anything were done at all, and I don't
think it is necessary—would be for the attending physicians to certify to the Cabi[n]et
that in their opinion the President is unable to perform the duties required of him.
Then the Cabinet, as a whole, might consider the certificate of the physicians, and forward it to the Vice President, with a request that he come forwar[d] to act as President
during the disability of the President. There is nothing legal about it, but I don't see
that there could be any other way in which it could be done. I don't think there is any
necessity, however, of now calling upon the Vice President. The government can get
along well enough until the meeting of Congress, as there is no necessity that the Vice
President should act until just about that time. It is very evident now that the President
can hardly be in a condition by the convening of Congress to make it safe for him to
have the trouble and responsibilities of the office on his hands." USG discussed press
hostility toward Vice President Chester A. Arthur. "They are but a few of your excellent people who attacked him at the time he was nominated—such men, for instance, as
Medill, editor of a sheet called the *Tribune*, and his faithful follower, a man by the name
of Shuman. These men have attacked Mr. Arthur until some people who do not know
him have really been convinced that he is what they have represented him to be. I think
it is a misfortune that you have got such men as those attached to daily newspapers in
a world made up of such people as this is. Still, we will survive this misfortune, as we

have survived other misfortunes." *Chicago Inter-Ocean*, Sept. 7, 1881. For Andrew Shuman, Chicago editor and Ill. lt. governor (1877–81), see *Chicago Tribune*, May 6, 1890. Probably on the same day, USG said of Garfield: "I have not been very sanguine about him any of the time since he was shot. His wound is a terrible one, and many a man would have died from the first shock. If they can prolong his life and he gains strength, he may yet recover." USG repeated his suggestion for an eventual informal transfer of power to the vice president. "The Government is doing very well under the heads of the different departments, and doubtless will continue to do so until the convening of Congress. When Congress meets in December something may have to be done. . . . I think the plan I have mentioned would be acceptable to the American people, and that is all that is required in the premises." *New York Times*, Sept. 9, 1881.

To John F. Long

———

New York City
Sept. 24th 1881

MY DEAR JUDGE LONG:

Your letter of the 15th of ~~s~~Sept. come duly to hand as did the one previously written by you. As I have been away from my office nearly continuously for three weeks,—and at the odd times when I did get there finding a mass of letters to answer which could not well be overlooked—I have had no fair chance to write to you before. I am very much obliged for your interest in my affairs. I shall not push the sale of my St. Louis property this year. But as soon as I can dispose of it I will do so. I would like the income the money would give me. As I have said before present indications are that it is not necessary for me to look out for accumulating to give to my children. At present they are all more than self supporting. I will authorize—do authorize—Gn. ~~Colender~~ Cavender [1] to dispose of the White Haven farm—all of mine & Mrs. Grants property there—for the sum of $100.000.00; $20,000.00 in Cash, the ballance on any time the purchasers may want, with 6 pr ct. interest and security upon the land. The Carondelet property I might keep a little longer.

If I can help you with the new ~~a~~Administration I will be glad to do so. Your having favored the Hancock ticket will no doubt raise an opposition. But I think I can say that your opposition was not to Arthur, and that probably the greatest opposition [*to*] you will come from persons who would ha[ve] opposed the ticket if [—] had

have had with [—] at the head of the ti[cket] his own first choi[ce.]
With kind regards to [—] the members of your f[ami]ly.

Very Truly yours

U. S. GRANT

ALS (facsimile), CSmH. While in St. Louis in June, 1881, USG planned to visit his
farm. "The continued illness of Judge Long, who has the farm in charge, has caused
this visit to be postponed from day to day until the General had given up visiting the
old homestead, but yesterday Judge Long notified the General that he desired to withdraw from the management of the farm, as he was growing old and unable to shoulder
so much responsibility. Thereupon the General appointed Gen. John S. Cavender to
take charge of the place, and this necessitated a trip to the country in order to post the
new agent on the condition and demands of the farm." "The trip was made rapidly, a
very short time being occupied in inspecting the farm, which was found in good condition. It is no longer exclusively a stock-farm. Some of its acreage is devoted to pas-
ture, the remainder is planted in corn and wheat. It yields its owner a revenue of about
$2,000 a year." *St. Louis Globe-Democrat*, June 11, 12, 1881.

1. N. H. native and former col., 29th Mo., John S. Cavender sold real estate with
partner Edward S. Rowse. See *PUSG*, 7, 522–23; letter to Cavender & Rowse, April 27,
1883; *St. Louis Post-Dispatch*, Feb. 23, 1886.

To Dexter N. Kasson

New York, Sept 27 *1881*

CAPT D. N. KASSON
MILWAUKEE, WIS.
DEAR SIR:

Your letter of the 15th of Sept, was no doubt duly received (the
previous letter I have no recollection of having received), but as I
have been out of my office most of the time since your letter came
to hand, and the few times I have been in it having large mails to
attend to and people to see, I have overlooked your letter until the
present. When you come to New York City as you say you expect
to do early in October, I should be very glad to meet you. My residence is No 3 East 66th. St where generally I will be found in the
Evening. During the day I am generally at my office, which is at
No 90 Broadway. I will be glad to meet you at either place.

Apologizing for not answering your letter sooner, I am,

Very Truly Yours

U. S. GRANT

LS, WHi.

On Nov. 19 and Dec. 17, 1881, USG wrote to Dexter N. Kasson, Milwaukee. "Your letter of the 12th of Nov. was duly received. I will take pleasure in suggesting to Senator Howe your endorsement for the position of Pension Agent. There will be no appointments made, I am sure, until sometime after the meeting of Congress and I advise you to write to Senator Howe and inform him of the contents of this letter." "I expect to go to Washington between the 5th and 10th of January to remain there from a week to ten days. I should be very happy to meet you and Gen. Bryant if you should be there at that time, and to render you all the assistance I can then in person. That I shall do, whether you are present or not." LS, *ibid.* See letter to Dexter N. Kasson, Feb. 27, 1881; letter to Timothy O. Howe, Jan. 13, 1882.

To Fitz John Porter

New York, September 27, '81.

Gen. F. J. Porter, 119 *Liberty street, N. Y.*

Dear General—Your letter of the 17th of September was handed to me at Long Branch the day after the death of the President.[1] Since that time I have had no opportunity of seeing you, and hence have deferred writing until this time. For a few days I will be so busily employed that I am not able now to appoint a time for the conference which you desire to have with me, but as soon as I can fix a day I will take great pleasure in doing so, and will hear what you have to say in regard to the matter alluded to in your letter, and will endeavor to listen without prejudice, and if convinced that I was wrong in former opinions entertained, and possibly expressed,[2] I would be willing to correct them.

Very truly yours,

U. S. Grant.

General Grant's Unpublished Correspondence in the Case of Gen. Fitz-John Porter (n. p., n. d.), p. 7. On Sept. 17, 1881, Fitz John Porter wrote to USG, Long Branch. "I have been told that you have entertained and sometimes expressed opinions reflecting upon the integrity of my military acts while in the Army. While I have always been unwilling to believe these reports, I cannot help taking them to heart, as I am willing to acknowledge that it would be a matter of wonder if you did not entertain opinions adverse to me, considering the light under which you may have, if you did, express them. Desirous always of having the good opinion of an eminent soldier, but only through his honest convictions of my worthiness of it, I would be very glad and highly gratified, if at a time and place convenient to you, you would favor me with an interview and an opportunity of presenting facts to me[e]t any objection you may have to my acts—hoping as I do to remove all such unfavorable impressions, and believing that if I can do so, it would be none the less gratifying to you." ALS (press), DLC-Fitz John Porter.

On Oct. 31, USG, New York City, wrote to Porter. "Since my letter to you I have been so busy with correspondence and callers each day, that I have not been able to designate a particular time to see you. If you will call any day, however, at my office 90 Broadway abou[t] eleven oclock I will give you the interview desired, and will keep persons from coming in my office during the time you are with me." LS, *ibid.* Porter drafted a reply to USG on this letter, dated Nov. 2 from internal evidence. "I thank you for your kind letter of the 31st which, in consequence of absence, till this morning, I have just read. I shall avail myself of your offer to-morrow (Thursday) at 11. O'Clock—" ADfS (undated), *ibid.* Porter described his interview with USG in "Memorandum of efforts to obtain favorable action in my case from Gen. U. S. Grant." ". . . I was present at Genl Grant's room. 90. Broadway at the hour fixed—and in few minutes entered upon our conversation. I said. the press had published at various times professed interviews with him giving—He then interupted me and said that many interviews had been reported of him in which he was said to have depracating remarks of me—He asserted that he had in some cases he never had the interviews and for all of them he denied having made the remarks reported—I said—Your denial is sufficient—I am perfectly satisfied—Now, it has been reported to me that he had said, on one occasion when Senator Randolph presented my appeal to him, that he had thoroughly examined my case and was satisfied I deserved to be shot. I had asked Randolph if such an interview had taken place—and he had said no—and had never heard of it, till he saw it in the papers—that I put no faith in the report—but even if not true, it was very annoying, & very unjust and if he had ever thought such should have been my fate, I wanted to know on what ground he drew his conclusion, as I was sure I could convince him of his error. He promptly said—he had 'never used such an expression & never thought it. I did conclude on one occasion, in reading your appeal and receiving a letter from Gen Pope at the same, that you had failed to make an attack because of the superior enemy in your front, and that I should do nothing to re open the case.' I said 'I was not surprised at his conclusion with Gen Pope's letter before him, but I would satisfy now of the error of his opinion then formed—I was glad to receive his denial of his having said I should have been shot. His denial was sufficient.' I then gave him the facts in the case, and after some conversation on several pointts, I asked him if he had the report of the Board and looked into the case. He said that he had not—that Board's report came out as he was preparing to go abroad or after he left—at all events he recollected but little of it & knew or heard but little prior to his arrival at San Francisco—when he heard much through Mrs McDowell & a few others—He promised to read the Report & any other papers I should send him & would, when read, give me his candid opinion on his idea of the merits of the case. In speaking of the receipt of the 4.30 order—I explained the discovery of the dispatches brought forward by McDowell, as according to him, having been found by one of his Military family—Col Shriver—He interrupted—did he say Col Shriver found them—I replied—yes—He so said before the Board—but I know or have been that—He broke in—Why Mrs McDowell told me she found them & gave them to Genl McD— who, at once, said that they were important & he would produce them—I said—I was aware that Mrs McD found them—but for three days nothing was known of them, when Mrs McD— suddenly let the fact out to one the aides—and in that way the dispatches became known. . . ." D, *ibid.* See *PUSG,* 25, 91–93; *SED,* 46-1-37.

On Nov. 4, Porter wrote to USG. "If, after you have read the Report of the Board and my letter to Gen Cox, you should need any further light or information or proof to sustain anything put forth, by the Board or by me, I shall be very glad to give it. Yesterday I saw plainly that your impressions of the facts in the case were incorrect—and I am anxious that you should see the facts in their true light—and the more so, as this matter was once in your hands to act upon but you did not act upon, I presume, because of such impressions as you expressed yesterday. I will try to present my case and proofs to you clearly & dispassionately believing you will receive them as dispassionately—and free from prejudice and with as great a desire to undo any wrong unintentionally done, as you would have done right in the first case. My statement sent to you yesterday was mainly written in 1863—added to, as time sustained my views, by proofs—and but slightly altered by my counsel for presentation to the Schofield Board—The foot notes were added after the adjournment of the Board, and when the Senate was printing the Proceedings. My case will come before Congress at the opening of the session—It will, so long as I live, and till adjusted, be before the Government. I have always believed & felt it was the duty of the Administration to adjust it, under present laws, by one simple administrative act, and a nomination to the Senate, and to satisfy the administration of the justice of its act in so doing, I have always sought as you know the decision of a Board of Army Officers, skilled in war & of undoubted integrity,—and, if you will recollect, that when Acting Sec of War, I offered then to submit the whole matter to you and to abide your decision after consideration of the evidence. I did hope that the last administration, after giving me the Board and receiving the result of their deliberations, would have given to me, as they did to Dr Hammond, their favorable action. The Boards deliberately expressed convictions that the court martial had been led by misinformation into errors, and that I was free from all blame and more than that—and also that it laid no blame upon any one for the wrong under which I—as well as all I hold dear—had suffered many years—I had hoped would have caused the powers that then were to have done what was just—to have at once carried out the recommendation of the Board by one simple act of authority and of law, and a nomination to the Senate—& have thus saved the country the spectacle of a partisan discussion & support of injustice now m[ade] manife[st]. Pardon these lines, if I have gone too far—and consider them the excess of zeal of one whose aim of life is to vindicate his name from reproach—for his own sake—the sake of wife & children—the sake of the Army, the country & the government which he offered his life on many fields to sustain, . . ." ADfS and ADfS (press), DLC-Fitz John Porter. Probably on the same day, Porter wrote to USG. "I enclose a copy of my defence before the Court Martial, written by Mr Eames—& prepared from the imperfect evidence of fact on the record—but at that time, with the obstacles thrown in the way of getting evidence—all the evidence I could bring forward—It is substantially the same argument as now made." ADfS (undated), *ibid.* See *O.R.*, I, xii, part 2 (Supplement), 1075–1112. On Nov. 9, Porter wrote to USG. "I intended but accidentally omitted sending you the other day, the map referred to in my letter to Genl Cox. Genl Cox's letter to me Genl Garfield, and all our corresponce though in some degree private, are at your service to read if you desire them. I have nothing to conceal and am ready to prove my unwavering loyalty & integrity wherever properly called into question" ADfS, DLC-Fitz John Porter.

1. Sept. 20.
2. On Dec. 16, 1880, a correspondent had reported USG's remarks concerning Porter made while visiting New Orleans the previous spring. "Soon after my inauguration the first time, one of Porter's intimate friends came to me and urged me to take steps for a reopening of his case. He brought with him a mass of documents which, it

was claimed, would show Porter's action in a better light. I took the papers and went through them. When he called again for an answer, I told him that when I urged a reopening of that case I would also urge the hanging of Porter. That's the last I heard of the case. They waited until Hayes got in before they brought up their new evidence again. I had another case of the same kind. An officer of the Twenty-first Illinois, the regiment I first took command of, was dismissed the service, and as soon as I was elected President he came to me to have his case retried. He didn't get it, but I see he has been successful since then. I haven't much sympathy with a man who staid at home after being dismissed as an officer, and then, after the war is over, comes in with a claim for pay. If he should enlist after being dismissed I might think he was a patriot." Concerning the military commission that tried Porter, USG said that it "was composed of conservative men. I doubt if an equal number of prominent officers less likely to be unjustly severe could be found in the Army. They were men more disposed to be merciful than severe. After going into all the details and sifting all the evidence, they concluded Gen. Porter should be shot. There was no difference of opinion among them—the conclusion was unanimous. President Lincoln was responsible for the modification of sentence. He interceded in behalf of Porter, not for Porter's sake, but as a matter of public policy. He wrote to the commission urging them to spare Porter's life. The feeling in the Army of the Potomac at that time was such that Mr. Lincoln was afraid of the effect of the execution of an officer of Porter's rank. So the commission dismissed him from the service with loss of pay, although they believed the evidence warranted a more severe punishment." Questioned on new evidence from C.S.A. sources, USG replied. "This is the evidence of the enemy, and amounts to this, that if Porter had gone into the fight he would have been whipped. That sort of evidence is not worth a great deal. You can always prove by a General that he would have won in a fight that never took place. Many a General who was sure of success has been whipped. An enemy may be able to see flaws in a General's plans that he does not see. The confidence of the enemy that they could have whipped Porter is no excuse for Porter's failure to fight." Unwilling to call Porter a traitor, USG continued. "It did not look well for Porter to stay out of the war after his dismissal. As his loyalty was in question, he would have done well to vindicate it by going into the Army as a private, if he could go in no other way. The country needed the services of every able-bodied man. Porter staid at home, and now comes forward, years after, and asks for pay. If a man loves his country, he will serve it when in danger; and if he can't be a General he will be a private soldier." *New York Times*, Dec. 17, 1880.

To Ellen Grant Sartoris

New York City
Sept. 29th 1881

My Dear Daughter:

Your nice long letter of Sept. 14th is received. Your Ma & I will be glad to see you as soon as you can come. We go into our house to-day, but with but little furniture. It will be two or three weeks before the furniture is all in. With all the pretty things we picked up on our trip around the world I think it will look very pretty.— Your Ma said something about what I was to say in refferrence to your proposition to bring over certain bed linnen and your silver ware. I am sure if I attempt to tell you what I will make a mistake. However we have much to purchase in the way of both articles. If you bring over what you do not want in the way of linnen on hand we can use it to advantage, and will pay you for it what we would have to pay elsewhere. If you will bring over a Silver Waiter, Ice pitcher slop bowl, in fact pretty comple set for 24 people, including knives & forks, we will take them.—I will tell your ma as near as I can what I have written here and if it is not correct she must write.—One thing I am sure I am right in saying. Your Ma says to bring over but one girl with you. Our difficulty is more for servants room than anything else. Ida has but one girl who nurses the babe and does all she has to do. You will find your Mas Maid always ready, and then little Algee & I will take care of ourselves and help greatly in looking after the balance of the family.

With kind regards to Mr Sartoris, Sr. and love to all the balance of you,

Affectionately

AL (signature clipped), ICHi.

To William Windom

———

New York City,
Sept. 30th. 1881.

Hon W. Windom:
Sec. of the Treas.
Dear Sir:

I understand that the Collector of Int. Rev. for the 6th. district of Ohio has tendered his resignation.

The Member of Congress from the district in which the office is located is a democrat. It is the district in which I was born, and the office should be located in the town where I lived until my entrance into the Military Academy. For this reason, I venture to suggest the name of Chas. D. Thompson[1] for the position. I have known the family of Mr. Thompson—the father, grand-father, uncles and aunts—ever since I have known anyone. All have been trusty and trusted citizens. And although the present applicant was born since I left Ohio, my visits to my old home have made me sufficiently acquainted with him to warrant me in endorsing him as in every way worthy and fit for the place.

Very Truly Yours,
U. S. GRANT.

Copy, George T. Campbell, Georgetown, Ohio. George P. Dunham replaced James Pursell as collector of Internal Revenue, Sixth District, Ohio.

1. The 1880 census for Brown County, Ohio, lists Charles D. Thompson, age 38, livery business.

To Chester A. Arthur

———

New York City
Oct. 4th 188[1]

GEN. C. A. ARTHUR, PRESIDENT OF THE U. STATES;
DEAR GEN.

An introduction from me to you of Paul Strobach,[1] of Ala. is not necessary. But I write a line to ask if you will not see and converse with him on Alabama affairs. I know Ala. republicanism is badly represented in Washington by Governor Reynolds,[2] of *Ala. from from Iowa*, and Ex. Senator Warner[3] of *Ala*. from *Ohio*. As you are no doubt aware Mr Strobach is a contestant for a seat in Congress, and is a member of the Nat. Committee. He, with Geo. Turner,[4] Chairman Rep. State Comm. are the most competant and reliable men in the state to obtain information from, of a a political nature.

Very Truly yours
U. S. GRANT

ALS, DLC-Chester A. Arthur.

1. Born in Austria about 1831, Paul Strobach emigrated to the U.S. after 1860, settled in Montgomery, and served in the Ala. House of Representatives (1868–72). In 1880, Strobach represented Ala. on the Republican National Committee and ran for Congress, later unsuccessfully contesting his defeat. See *HMD*, 47-1-17; *HRC*, 47-1-1521; Sarah Woolfolk Wiggins, *The Scalawag in Alabama Politics, 1865–1881* (University, Ala., 1977), pp. 124–25.

2. Born in 1826 in Ohio, Robert M. Reynolds taught in Ill. and Iowa, served in the 1st Iowa Cav., and settled in Ala., where he entered politics. Reynolds held several posts under USG and was appointed 1st auditor by President Rutherford B. Hayes. See *PUSG*, 24, 43–45.

3. On Nov. 6, 1880, Willard Warner wrote to USG. "I write to express my sincere acknowledgements for the great service you have done the country and the Party in the canvas just closed, and for the brave word you said for the Carpet-Baggers—so called of the South, whose all was bound up in this contest. Myself and associates have a quarter of a million of dollars invested here, which would have been greatly reduced in value in the Event of Democratic success. Now all looks bright and Encouraging. The Tariff question will yet divide and break the solid south. General, you sorely wounded and humiliated me in the matter of the Mobile collectorship, though I believe with great reluctance and without unkind feeling, and I long ago ceased to think of the matter. The *real* Carpet-Baggers who fought me then, have mostly left the state & the remainder will soon follow. I am out of politics so far as office is concerned. With kind regards to Mrs. Grant, . . ." ALS (press), Tennessee State Library and Archives, Nashville, Tenn. Warner, who managed an iron works in Tecumseh, Ala., had opposed USG's nomination in June. See *PUSG*, 21, 21; *ibid.*, 22, 350–51; *New York Times*, May 22, 1880, May 31, 1884.

4. Born in 1850 in Mo., George Turner, a wartime telegrapher, studied law and settled in Mobile, where he served as marshal under USG and Hayes. With Strobach, he led Ala.'s pro-USG delegates at the 1880 convention. See *ibid.*, Jan. 27, 1932.

To James D. Brady

NEW YORK, Oct. 4, 1881,

JAMES D. BRADY, esq., Chairman Republican State Executive Committee, Petersburg, Va.;

DEAR SIR: Your letter of the 10th of September was duly received, but not answered at the time because of my absence from the city. I was busy on my return, and have only just come across your letter again. A a rule I am averse to taking any part in political matters outside of the State in which I reside, except where they become national in their character. I do regard the present contest in Virginia as being national, and therefore justifying me and all other lovers of their country, without regard to section, in expressing an opinion. In conversations on the subject I have openly and frequently expressed my sympathy with General Mahone and the Readjusters, so called, in their present contest. I have never been a sympathizer with repudiation in any form, but in the present instance the virtue claimed by the Democracy of the State of Virginia I regard as all assumed. They have had control of the State for quite a number of years, and, as I understand the politics of the State, they not only have made no effort to pay the interest upon their State debt, but they have prohibited taxation beyond a certain percentage, which looks to a determination to pay no part, principal or interest. In other words, while they are in favor of acknowledging the whole debt, principal and interest, they are opposed to paying any part of either. Hence, on this point between the two, I much prefer those who are willing to acknowledge as much of the debt as they think they can pay, and who want to bind themselves to provide for the interest and the acknowledged principal when it becomes due. But in this contest there is a much more important issue at stake. I regard the success of what is called the Readjusters as working the emancipation of all the voters of the State, and when that is secured it is a matter of much less difference which party succeeds. It is patent to my mind that at present and for some years back, while there is an acknowledgment of the right of the colored citizen to vote, there is a determination that his vote shall not decide the success of a political party. When this freedom of the ballot is given to all legal voters Virginia will be in a condition to invite immigration of people who will add greatly to the resources as well as to the population of the State. The interests of all citizens will then become so great that no fear need be entertained of bad government, no matter which political party may have the ascendancy.

Truly yours,

U. S. GRANT.

Washington National Republican, Oct. 17, 1881. In [*Feb., 1881*], USG discussed the Va. Readjuster party with George C. Gorham, editor, *Washington National Republican*. "As I understand it, the debt payers have a great deal to say about paying everything, but never paying, while the readjusters say they will pay all that can be paid." Quoted in a letter from Gorham to William Mahone, Feb. 8, 1881, in Nelson Morehouse Blake, *William Mahone of Virginia: Soldier and Political Insurgent* (Richmond, 1935), p. 194. See *ibid.*, p. 205; *PUSG*, 11, 236; *ibid.*, 27, 91–92; Jane Dailey, *Before Jim Crow: The Politics of Race in Postemancipation Virginia* (Chapel Hill, 2000), pp. 81–84.

To Chester C. Cole

———

New York, Oct 4 *1881*

JUDGE C. C. COLE
DES MOINES IA
DEAR SIR:

Your letter of the 28th of September was duly received. I am very much obliged to you and other friends for the sentiments expressed in your letter, but I assure you that I would not accept the position of which you speak, nor any other which could be tendered by the Executive. Of course if I supposed that I could render any marked service to my country, I would accept any position where that service could be rendered; but we are now in a prosperous condition; we will have at the helm of state a man in whom I have every confidence and am satisfied the country will have also when they know him half as well as I do, and therefore it is not necessary that I should occupy any official position Please present Mrs Grants and my kindest regards to Mrs Cole and the other members of your family.

Very Truly Yours.
U. S. GRANT

LS, IaHA.

To Chester A. Arthur

———

New York City,
Oct. 8th 1881

MY DEAR MR. PRESIDENT:

I have just heard—there is a rumor to this effect—that the Secretaryship of the Treasure has been tendered to Gov. Boutwell and that he has declined. I hope the rumor of the declination is unfounded. But I drop you a line to ask, if the rumor is true, and he will not reconsider, whether you have thought of John Jacob Astor for the place.

I hope you will excuse the suggestion.

Very Truly yours

U. S. GRANT

GN. C. A. ARTHUR PRESIDENT OF THE U. S.

ALS, DLC-Chester A. Arthur. On Oct. 24, 1881, President Chester A. Arthur nominated Edwin D. Morgan as secretary of the treasury. When Morgan declined, Arthur nominated Charles J. Folger. On Dec. 18, a correspondent reported from Washington, D. C. "Ex-Senator Boutwell, it is reported, has been tendered the Navy portfolio, but is not inclined to accept it. Mr. Boutwell is believed to desire an appointment as United States Circuit Judge, . . ." *New York Times*, Dec. 19, 1881. See *ibid.*, Jan. 4, 1882. George S. Boutwell continued as agent and counsel before the French and American Claims Commission. For John Jacob Astor, see letter to James A. Garfield, Feb. 6, 1881.

To Alonzo V. Richards

———

New York, Oct 10 *1881*

ALONZO V. RICHARDS ESQ

FREEPORT ILL.

DEAR SIR:

Your letter of Oct. 1st was duly received. If you will get the endorsement of the Member of Congress from your district Maj. Hawk I will take great pleasure in doing what I can to secure for you the Post office in Freeport Ill., and that without waiting for the expiration of the term of the present incumbent. My own impression is that the present Postmaster has been too long in his present place and ought to be removed without any hesitation, and if I could have my way I know he would be.

Very Truly Yours,

U. S. GRANT

LS, WHi. On Jan. 3, 1882, USG wrote to Alonzo V. Richards, Freeport, Ill. "Since the receipt of your letter of the 20th of December I have had an opportunity of talking with the Asst. Postmaster General in regard to your case, and have fully posted him, and believe that he fully sympathises with you. Although I cannot promise I hope that you will not be disappointed." LS, *ibid.* On Jan. 12, USG telegraphed to Richards. "Advise short petition signed by best & most prominent citizens" Telegram received

(at 1:30 P.M.), *ibid.* On April 12, President Chester A. Arthur nominated Smith D. At-
kins, former col., 92nd Ill., and Freeport lawyer and editor, to continue as postmaster.
See letter to Thomas L. James, March 5, 1881.

To Daniel Ammen

———

NEW YORK CITY, Oct. 11th, 1881.

MY DEAR ADMIRAL AMMEN,—

We have now been in our new house nearly three weeks, and
are beginning to get things in shape to receive all our worldly
goods. Fred and his family will constitute a part of our family, and
for the winter we expect Nellie and family. The other two boys are
keeping house, Buck in his own house, and Jesse in a rented one.
Buck has taken the "farming fever," and has purchased about two
hundred acres on the Harlem Railroad, in Westchester County,
about an hour from the city. He was fortunate enough to purchase
from a city merchant who has recovered from the fever, and was
able to purchase cheap. The farm is improved with fine stone fences
around nearly all the fields, with barns for fifty to one hundred head
of horses and cattle, a fine stone house with twenty-one rooms, all
furnished, and large and small fruit already bearing. The house was
rented out for the summer for one thousand dollars, and the land to
a farmer on halves. Buck got one-half the rent for the house, and all
the rent for the land, and got the whole for twenty-seven thousand
five hundred dollars, less than the house and furniture would cost
to replace. He is already beginning to stock up, and will no doubt
be much pleased for a few years at least.

We are now ready to receive our goods from the navy-yard,
Washington. May I ask if you will be kind enough to have them
shipped to me at No. 3, E. 66th Street, by express? I enclose you
the receipts for the goods, with the numbers on the boxes. In addition to the goods receipted for, there was a large family portrait
sent some time after the other goods, and for which we have no receipt. Will you be kind enough to have all the pictures sent to care
of Goupil, corner 22d Street and Fifth Avenue?

I wrote to you some days ago, saying that the buggies and harness at your farm might be sent to McDermot for sale, but asking you to accept the light buggy with harness, for your use about the farm.

With kind regards to all your family, very truly yours,

U. S. GRANT.

Daniel Ammen, *The Old Navy and the New* (Philadelphia, 1891), p. 552. On Oct. 17, 1881, Monday, USG wrote to Daniel Ammen. "The articles you were kind enough to have shipped for me all came to hand, in good order, on Saturday last. If you will be kind enough to have the balance of my goods at the navy-yard shipped as freight, I will be very much obliged. With kind regards to all your family," *Ibid.*

To Robert T. Lincoln

New York City,
Oct. 18th 1881.

To THE SEC. OF WAR:
DEAR SIR:

I have the honor to make application through you to The President for an appointment to West Point for Ulysses Grant Sharp, of the Army, for 1882. Young Sharp cannot make application through any member of Congress because his father is an officer of the Army, and cannot claim any special Congressional district as his residence.

Very respectfully
U. S. GRANT

ALS, DNA, RG 94, Correspondence, USMA. On Oct. 24 and 26, 1881, Secretary of War Robert T. Lincoln wrote to USG. "I have your letter of October 18th instant, making application for the appointment to the Military Academy of Ulysses Grant Sharp for 1882. It will give me pleasure to bring the matter personally to the attention of the President, although the chance for an appointment at large for the next examination in June, 1882, is small, as there will be regularly only four vacancies, and President Garfield nominated the four regular candidates to fill them, and also three alternates." "Since writing you my note of the 24th instant, respecting the appointment of a cadet at-large at West Point, I am informed by the Adjutant General that there are no cadets at-large in the class which will graduate in 1883 and 1884, so that, except for casualties occurring by the death, resignation or discharges of cadets at-large already appointed, and excepting one alternate for next year, the President will have no appointment at-large to make for any class prior to that entering in 1885, for which year there will be six appointments to be made." LS (press), Robert T. Lincoln Letterbooks, IHi. Ulysses Grant Sharp did not attend USMA. See Margaret Sharp Angus, *A Biography of Dr. Alexander Sharp, Major and Paymaster; His Antecedents and Descendents* (Kingston, Ontario, 1988), pp. 241–42.

To Edward F. Beale

————

New York City,
Oct. 26th 1881

MY DEAR GEN. BEALE;

Instead of writing the letter for Hutchison you ask I endorse your letter and send it directly to the President. I have no doubt but it will produce the desired effect.

I have become so accustomed to travel with my little Jap, who looks after every thing, that being without him on my last visit I come off leaving my baggage at the station without think to get it checked. It was telegraphed for however, and is now here.

With kindest regards to Mrs. Beale & Miss Emily,

Very Truly yours
U. S. GRANT

ALS, DLC-Decatur House Papers.

On Nov. 30, 1881, USG telegraphed to Edward F. Beale. "Cant you, Mrs Beale and family come this week and make us a visit as long as you can stay" Telegram received, *ibid.*

To William S. Harney

————

New York, Oct 28 *1881*

GEN. W. S. HARNEY
3518 WASHINGTON AVE
ST LOUIS MO.
DEAR SIR:

Your letter of the 24th of October is at hand. I had already written and put in a word in behalf of your friend Mr Sturgeon for retention in the place he now holds. I have little doubt but what he will be retained. I am sorry to hear that your sight is growing weak and hope you may have many years yet of good health and that I may have the good fortune to meet you again. If you should visit this City I hope you will come directly to our house.

Very truly Yours,

U. S. GRANT

LS, MoSHi. On Oct. 24, 1881, William S. Harney, St. Louis, wrote to USG. "You were kind enough to appoint my esteemed friend Isaac H. Sturgeon of this city Collector of Internal Revenue, upon my earnest recommendation to succeed a man who had abused your confidence by proving false to the trust you reposed in him. I have known Mr. Sturgeon, (as I think you have) for over thirty years, as one of the best citizens of St. Louis, and to day feel the same zealous interest in the welfare and hapiness of himself and his family that I did when I so urgently urged upon you his appointment as a great personal favor to me—He has acquitted himself well in his position as I ~~new~~ knew he would, and is unversally esteemed, No one can justly ask his removal to make place for some one else—if any one should, it must be simply to get him out of the way, to make place for some unscrupulous person that could perhaps repeat the scandals perpetrated on your administration by his predecessor who violated your confidence. Mr. Sturgeon is politically, (as I suppose you know) a stalwart in his Republican sentiments, but always a gentleman in his deportment towards those differing with him. All concur that he has made the best Collector the government has had since the office was created, and I am sure you will agree with me, that it is desirable to retain such an officer—As a friend I urgently beg of you to Commend Mr. Sturgeon to President Arthur for retention in office—I assure you that any kindness shown to Mr. Sturgeon I appreciate as done to me personally—In his welfare and hapiness I feel the deepest interest, and you will do me great personal kindness to interest yourself for me in his behalf—. . . P. S. I am obliged as you will see to employ an amanuensis, my sight is very bad, my warmest love to Mrs. Grant and yourself, with sincere wishes for your continued prosperity—I see you are expecting your children to spend Thanksgiving day with you—remember me to each one and say to my little friend Mrs Sartoris, she still holds a warm place in the heart of her old friend Gen'l Harney—" Copy, *ibid.* Isaac H. Sturgeon continued as collector of Internal Revenue, 1st District, Mo. See *PUSG,* 26, 239.

To William R. Rowley

New York City,
October 30, 1881.

MY DEAR GENERAL:

We are now pretty well settled in our new house. Everything is very comfortable, and with the different articles picked up in the trip around the world, we think very pretty.

If you come east at any time come and see us and judge for yourself.

But with all we have in the house Mrs. Grant wants sent from Galena—by express—the handsome parlor books, an old brass bell, wooden sword rack, large black lacquer box, two [c]loisonne blue plaques—if you know what that means, I do not—two flower vases of silver bronze and cut glass, and any other handsome ornaments you may see.

Please have the heavy things packed separately from the glass. Probably it will be well to get someone who understands the business to pack all these articles so that they will come safely.

Tell Mr. Ryan to keep the buggy and harness for his use and when I go to Galena, I will take him out in it and show him more of his own country. The fact is I fear my assessment for losses in this year's farming will amount to more than the buggy is worth and I want to get on the right side of him so he will not come back on me for any more.

With kind regards to Mrs. and Miss Rowley, and all our Galena friends,

Very truly yours,
U. S. GRANT.

P. S. Mrs. Grant says it is not an old bell, but a beautifully carved bell from India. The Lacquer box is in the parlor.

U. S. G.

La Crosse Tribune, April 28, 1918.

To Lt. Gen. Philip H. Sheridan

New York City;
Oct. 30th 1881.

MY DEAR GENERAL SHERIDAN:

We are now nearly settled in our new house. Fred & family are with us. By the end of this week Nellie & family will be here, barring accidents at sea.[1] To make the family complete Mrs. Grant and I want you and Mrs. Sheridan to make us a visit. Come at any time that suits you best. Later in the season there will be more balls and parties, but now, or early, driving and going out to see during the day is better. We will be equally glad to see you at any time you may elect. But Mrs. Grant wants you to bring Mrs. Sheridan with you.

Very Truly yours

U. S. GRANT

ALS, DLC–Philip H. Sheridan.

1. The Sartoris family arrived on the *Elbe* on Nov. 5, 1881.

To Fitch, Fox, & Brown

New York, Oct 31 *1881*

MESS FITCH FOX & BROWN
1437 PENNA. AVE. WASHINGTON D. C.
GENTLEMEN:

I have your letter of the 29th inst, and in answer thereto will say that the terms proposed will be acceptable to me—that is to say: I relinquish my lien on the property, Mrs Coleman to borrow $12500. on it paying me out of the same the sum of $12000 and giving me a second mortgage of $3500. due in 2 or 3 years, the last mentioned sum of $3500. being secured by collateral of $50.000, stock in the Oil Co referred to.

In accepting these terms however, it is on condition that the $12,000 is sent to me ~~that is referred to~~.

Truly Yours,

U. S. GRANT

LS (facsimile), Historical Documents International, Inc. [n. d.], no. 18. On Nov. 29, 1881, USG wrote to Fitch, Fox, & Brown. "I am just in receipt of your letter of the 26th inst, inclosing cheque for $310 00, interest on the house purchased by Mrs. Coleman. Mrs. Coleman may make a loan of $10,500,—sending me $10,000 of the money—on giving such collateral security for the balance due me as you would approve of, without however making you responsible in case of failure to realize." ALS, Rochester Public Library, Rochester, N. Y.

On Feb. 7, 1884, Anna M. Colman, Washington, D. C., wrote to Fitch, Fox, & Brown. "You will remember that General Grant in May last, consented to accept four thousand dollars for his mortgage on No 2. Iowa Circle. I was disappointed in getting the money at that time which I expected, and have never since been able to command it until now. The necessity of my having control of the collateral left with you forces me to ask for the release of my note for four thousand cash. I was unable to pay the small semiannual interest due Dec. last. The judgment which forms a part of the collateral is still under appeal, and the property of the stock Company is advertised for sale on the first day of March next, in favor of the Bondholders. Both my notes are due Dec. 15— 1884 and the prospects of my being able to meet them are next to nothing but I must make one more effort to save the house. I regret exceedingly that I have been unable to meet my obligations fully and promptly, and I appreciate General Grants uniform kindness. I hereby tender you the sum of $4000. It is the utmost that I can do" ALS, IHi. On Feb. 8, Fitch, Fox, & Brown endorsed this letter. "Respectfully referred to General US. Grant who will be good enough to endorse the note enclosed without recourse. Genl Grant will please, also, inform us whether—if he accepts the $4.000—we are to require the arrears of interest of Mrs Colman" E, *ibid.* On Feb. 10, USG wrote to Fitch, Fox, & Brown. "In relation to letter from Mrs Coleman to you, referred to me, I have to say that you can accept the $4000. if it is paid promptly, in full, and without Mrs C. paying up the arrears of interest. She seems to be hard pressed and I am sure I do not desire to press her any. . . . I herewith return note endorsed without recourse as requested—" Copy (dictated to Frank F. Wood), *ibid.*

To Thomas Boles

New York, Nov 2 1881

Thomas Bowles Esq.
Dardanelle Ark.
Dear Sir:

Your letter of the 26th of October was duly received. You have been a little misinformed as to my urgency for the appointment of Dr W. W. Bailey.[1] I have known the Doctor from his infancy, as well as his father in the old Army, and if I could serve either without injustice to other parties I should always be glad to do so. But in regard to the application of Dr Bailey for the Marshalship I simply gave his father a letter of introduction to Ex Senator Clayton. Previous to that I had said to the President in writing and verbally that Senator Clayton was the most proper person I knew of to represent the Republican[s] of Arkansas, and that I should make no recommendations for that state myself unless it should be in cooperation with Gen Clayton

Truly Yours—
U. S. Grant

LS, William B. Morris, Spring Branch, Tex. Born in 1837, Thomas Boles was capt., 3rd Ark. (U.S.), joined the Republican party, and served as circuit judge (1865–68),

U.S. Representative (1868–71, 1872–73), and land receiver (1878–82). On Jan. 26, 1882, President Chester A. Arthur nominated Boles as marshal, Western District, Ark.

1. Born in 1839 at Fort Gibson, Indian Territory, William Worth Bailey served as surgeon, 1st Mo. Cav. On Nov. 19, 1875, Bailey, Fort Smith, Ark., wrote to USG. "I am an applicant for the position of one of the board of visitors at West Point in June 1876. I wrote to the Hon W. W. Belknap Secretary of War some time since asking his valuable assistance in securing my appointment; he very kindly replied to my communication and stated that he had placed my name upon file with other applicants to be presented to you for selection; at the same time adding that this action on his part did not necessarily imply that I would be successful, but he stated in addition that it would afford him great pleasure in mentioning my name favorably to you. My great desire to be present as a member of the board at the anual examination next June arrises from the fact that I have a Nephew in the Corps of Cadets, John R Williams son of the late Genl Thomas Williams; who will if nothing happens to prevent graduate at that time. He has for several years as you are doutless aware stood at the head of his Class, and so far has given you no cause to regret that through your kindness he was secured the appontmt I can only urge my claims upon the score of old acquaintance and admiration for you personally as well as being a warm supporter of your administration and will take it as a great privilege and honor if you can confer this favor upon me—" ALS, DNA, RG 94, Correspondence, USMA. On Nov. 20, Judge Isaac C. Parker, Western District, Ark., Fort Smith, wrote to USG. "Dr W Worth Baily of this place desires the appointment of examiner at the Military Academy at West Point for the next annual examination I take pleasure in saying that I believe you could appoint no one who would reflect more credit upon the position than Dr Baily He is a gentleman of fine attainments of good character and takes a lively interest in every thing pertaining to the Army. You will no ~~dout~~ doubt remember him as he was a Surgeon in our army during the war. He is the Son of Dr Baily who is an old army Surgeon I hope you will appoint Dr Baily as one of the examiners" ALS, *ibid.* No appointment followed. See *ibid.*, ACP, 4354 1875; *PUSG*, 21, 374; *ibid.*, 25, 267–68; James Bailey Parker, "The Bailey Family," *The Journal* [Fort Smith Historical Society], 17, 2 (Sept. 1993), 37–42.

To Lt. Gen. Philip H. Sheridan

New York City
Nov. 6th 1881.

MY DEAR GENERAL SHERIDAN;

I am just in receipt of your letter of the 2d of this month, and enclosure,—copy of a letter from Gen. Rucker. The matter about which you write I understood to be pretty well fixed while I was in Washington. Gen. Arthur does not seem to be a man who makes promises to be broken, and is therefore cautious not to say that he will do a thing unless he knows he can keep his word. But I think his mind was made up to retire Meigs, appoint Rucker, have the latter confirmed by the Senate, then retire him and appoint Ingalls.

Did you get a letter from me asking you and Mrs. Sheridan to come on and make us a visit? We will be glad to see you at any time. If you come on this month however I would like to know as early as possible because I want to ask Don Cameron & his wife and would like to time his invitation.[1] It might be that Mrs. Grant would like to have both at once and then I could have Cameron come while you were here. If she wants to avoid sending any one to the 4th floor then the invitation to Cameron could be given for a different time.—Mrs Sartoris is now with us as well as Fred & family. It makes it very pleasant to have all our children about us, and particularly so as they seem all to be doing so well.

With kind regards to Mrs. Sheridan and the children,

Very Truly yours
U. S. GRANT

ALS, DLC-Philip H. Sheridan. On Feb. 6, 1882, President Chester A. Arthur nominated Col. Daniel H. Rucker, father-in-law of Lt. Gen. Philip H. Sheridan, as brig. gen., q. m. gen., replacing Montgomery C. Meigs, retired. The Senate confirmed Rucker on Feb. 13. On Feb. 23, Arthur nominated Col. Rufus Ingalls to replace Rucker, also retired.

1. U.S. Senator James D. Cameron of Pa. had married Elizabeth Sherman, niece of Gen. William T. Sherman, in 1878. On Dec. 12, 1881, the Camerons joined USG and Julia Dent Grant as guests at a Patriarchs' ball held at Delmonico's. See *New York Times*, Dec. 13, 1881; Arline Boucher Tehan, *Henry Adams in Love: The Pursuit of Elizabeth Sherman Cameron* (New York, 1983).

To Simeon K. Miner

————

New York, Nov. 11 1881

S. K. MINER ESQ.
WARREN ILL.
DEAR SIR:

Your letter of the 9th inst. is received. In regard to Mr. Richards appointment to the Post-office at Freeport I think with the endorsement of the Member of Congress from that district, and what I have said on the subject, and what I intend still to say, there can be but very little doubt about his receiving that office. Whether

the present incumbent will be turned out in December or whether
he will be permitted to hold his office until the end of his term, I do
not know, but I am strongly in favor of having the change made at
once, but I cannot say positively that it will be done.

Truly Yours—

U. S. Grant

LS, WHi. Born in N. Y., Simeon K. Miner moved to Ill. in 1839 and settled in Jo Da-
viess County, where he served two terms as sheriff. In 1867, his daughter, Flora L.,
married Alonzo V. Richards. See letter to Alonzo V. Richards, Oct. 10, 1881.

To Alphonso Taft

New York City
Nov. 14th 1881.

My Dear Judge Taft:

Your letter of the 9th inst. is just opened though likely it was
delivered several days ago. My mails are so large that I do not get
through my letters often more than once a week.—There is nothing
in your desire that ought not to be gratified unless the President
has selected already some one for the vacant mission you speak of.
I shall send your letter to him at once, with a favorable endorsement, or rather letter.

With kind regards to all your family,

Very Truly yours

U. S. Grant

LS, DLC-William H. Taft. Rumored to be a candidate for the Berlin mission vacated
by Andrew D. White, Alphonso Taft was nominated as minister to Austria on April
20, 1882. See *New York Times*, Jan. 30, 1882.

To J. Federico Elmore

New York City, *November* 17, 1881.

[Private.]

My Dear Mr. Elmore: I am sorry I was not in when you
called on the 13th. As soon as I returned to the house I received

your letter and accompanying papers and expected to see you at five o'clock.

My not being in, a verbal message was sent to you to call at that hour. You may not have received it. Since you were here I hear that President Calderon has been carried off to Chili as a prisoner of war. I hope this is not true. What can I say or do beyond expressing my sympathy for Peru in her present troubles, and expressing the hope that she may yet come out of them with honor?

It seems to me, however, proper and important that the United States should step in now and say to Chili that she cannot oppress or despoil Peru of territory. She may demand indemnity and security.

With great respect, your obedient servant,

U. S. GRANT.

P. S. I return the paper you sent to my house.

U. S. G.

HRC, 47-1-1790, 182. Brackets in original. The War of the Pacific, begun in 1879 over rights to lucrative guano deposits, pitted Chile against Peru and Bolivia. By late 1880, Chile had defeated both opposing armies and occupied Lima. Negotiations for territorial and financial concessions faltered, and in Nov., 1881, President Francisco García Calderón of Peru was arrested and imprisoned at Santiago. On Nov. 18, J. Federico Elmore, Peruvian minister, wrote to Secretary of State James G. Blaine concerning García Calderón's arrest, "... a situation, which has probably no other solution than the resolute intervention of Your Excellency's Government ..." LS, DNA, RG 59, Notes from Foreign Legations, Peru. *SED,* 47-1-79, 563; *Foreign Relations, 1881,* pp. 975–76. On April 20, 1882, U.S. Representative Perry Belmont of N. Y., Committee on Foreign Affairs, questioned William Henry Hurlbert, editor, *New York World,* concerning Crédit Industriel, which Hurlbert termed "a very powerful French organization representing the French and continental bondholders of Peru, interested in extensive business with Peru, and which was disposed to enable Peru to pay any financial indemnity which might be fixed upon in negotiations for peace, in order to save Peru from the necessity of ceding her territory." "Do you remember any particular instance going to show that Mr. Blaine approved of this part of the programme of the Crédit Industriel?. . . A. I recollect an incident which made considerable impression on my mind, in consequence of the person whose name was used in connection with it as having expressed a very strong opinion against the cession of territory by Peru, being made a precedent condition of negotiations. . . . It was General Grant. . . . I have always understood from the Peruvian minister that he had an old acquaintance with General Grant; that he was Peruvian minister in China, I think, when General Grant visited that country, and was able and very glad to show him civilities at Peking at that time. . . ." *HRC,* 47-1-1790, 181–82, 186. Hurlbert was the brother of Stephen A. Hurlbut, U.S. minister to Peru, having changed the spelling of his name. On April 27, Belmont questioned

Blaine. "Will you state if any one showed you that letter of General Grant's, in which he said it was about time for the United States to step in?—A. . . . I should think it was very nearly the 1st December, Mr. Robert Randall showed me a letter from General Grant. Q. He was the counsel of the Crédit Industriel?—A. Yes, sir. . . . I was very much surprised to see that letter come out in testimony. I do not think General Grant ever thought it was to be made public, or that he was intermeddling in the matter in any way; I never so understood it." *Ibid.,* p. 232. On May 11, Robert E. Randall testified that ". . . on or about the 25th or 26th of November, Mr. Elmore communicated to me the fact that he had received such a letter. I asked him to send it to me, which he did, and on visiting Washington about the 1st of December, I read that letter to Mr. Blaine on my own personal responsibility without consulting anybody. I had no idea then that it would ever be made public, or I should not have taken that liberty. My relations with Mr. Elmore are of the closest character. They might almost be considered as those between counsel and client; I therefore took that liberty. . . . My object in showing the letter to Mr. Blaine was that he should know the opinion of an ex-President, standing in the position in which General Grant does before the world, and to show to Mr Blaine further that General Grant—who certainly must have a very positive and accurate knowledge of political affairs in South America, and consequently his opinion was worth having—entertained a very decided opinion as to the government's course; and further, to show Mr. Blaine that if there were any factions in the Republican party, so far as any faction was represented by General Grant, it was in accord with the policy which I understood Mr. Blaine to be carrying out. . . ." *Ibid.,* p. 332. See *ibid.,* pp. IV-VI; *New York Times,* Feb. 25, 1882; Herbert Millington, *American Diplomacy and the War of the Pacific* (New York, 1948).

On May 20, 1881, Jacob R. Shipherd had written to President James A. Garfield on behalf of the Peruvian Co., organized in New York City to promote the claims of Americans against Peru. *HRC,* 47-1-1790, 49–51. On May 21, Shipherd wrote to Garfield. "Since my letter of yesterday was closed, the remarkable letter of General Grant to Senator Jones has appeared in print here, and has already determined my clients to reconsider their intention to offer General Grant the presidency of this company, and I am instructed to reopen this parcel and add this intimation. Of course, my clients read General Grant's letter through business eyes only—but none the less it disturbs them. . . ." *Ibid.,* p. 52. See letter to John P. Jones, April 24, 1881. On Oct. 27, Shipherd wrote to Stephen Hurlbut urging him to press American claims. ". . . For your own satisfaction, I may say that our staff of counsel, including such representative and various men as Governor Boutwell, Senator Eaton, Senator Conkling, Collector Robertson, ex-Congressman Lord, and Senator Blair, are absolutely agreed upon this as upon every other point material to the pending issues; and the most radical suggestions of policy as yet suggested have the hearty autograph approval of General Grant, who is now one of us. . . ." *HRC,* 47-1-1790, 102; *SED,* 47-1-79, 570. The latter source omits the names. On April 10, 1882, U.S. Representative James H. Blount of Ga. questioned Shipherd about this letter during testimony before the Committee on Foreign Affairs. "You spoke of General Grant 'as one of us.' What did you mean by that—as stockholder, or what? The WITNESS. . . . I first sent the papers in this case to General Grant, I think, in June or July, while he was at Long Branch for the summer; I sent them with a note simply asking him to give them such attention as he might think proper, and that I wished at some future day to discuss the matter with him; I intended merely to bring the matter to his attention. Some time later (I should say in the latter part of September, perhaps, or in the first part of October) I had a conversation with General Grant on the subject, and I then suggested to him definitely that our people would be glad to have him become associated with us more or less prominently in the direction of the company; he replied at some length; our conversation lasted, I think, at least an hour, and in that instance, at least, I was not the chief talker. General Grant talked most of the hour. He discussed at very considerable length the general principles which he thought applicable to this case. The gist of his statement was this: 'I shall not at present consider any proposition to become pecuniarily interested with you; the disposition of the public to comment upon every business enterprise with which I become connected is such that I am increasingly indisposed to connect myself with any public corporation; but I have no hesitation whatever in expressing to you my views as to what your general rights are in the premises and what the government ought to do for you.' He then recapitulated at considerable length similar cases—cases that had occurred which had called for the interference of the Executive in behalf of the rights of American citizens in foreign countries during his own administration; he went into considerable details and said expressly, after mentioning several of the cases: 'These were much harder cases than yours. The right of the citizen to have the government interfere in his behalf in such cases was not so clear as your right is, as I understand the case.' He summed the matter up by saying: 'Mr. Shipherd, it will make no difference whether I am a stockholder with you or not, so far as my co-operation is concerned. I should do nothing for you if I were a stockholder except to aid you in securing from the government such help as in my judgment you are entitled to absolutely any way. I shall help you as a matter of fact in any and every way that I can, but solely as a citizen with reference to your rights as an American corporation. On that you may rely, and for the present please to understand distinctly that I do not wish to consider the question of becoming pecuniarily interested with you.' That conversation, I should say, was in the last of September or the first of October; I had a second and I think a third conversation with General Grant (along during October, I should say); the substance of his declarations in each instance was identical with the substance of his first declaration . . . Mr. Blount. When did General Grant become a stockholder in the Peruvian Company? The Witness. He never did. . . . Mr. Blount. You drew up a certain cable dispatch which you wanted sent to Minister Hurlbut from the State Department?. . . The Witness. . . . I sent the draft to General Grant by a messenger with a note indicating (and I will submit that note also) that I would be glad to have his judgment on this draft. His indorsement was, I suppose, simply a reply to me. It was all the reply that was sent. . . ." *HRC*, 47-1-1790, 102–3. On April 11, Blount again questioned Shipherd. "I find in a letter from you to Mr. Hurlbut, dated November 15, 1881, the following: 'Sɪʀ: Senator Blair writes me, "Hurlbut telegraphs that the Chilians have captured Calderon and carried him to Chili." The Senator adds, "There must be trouble now. Have General Grant do his duty. American influence in America is at an end if Chili can slap our face as flatly as this."' And you also say in the same letter, 'I shall consult General Grant to-day, and he and I may go to Washington on Thursday.' Did you seek to get General Grant to co-operate with you in the way indicated in that letter? The Witness. I did consult with General Grant pursuant to the purpose which I had, . . . He replied that he thought it was not necessary for him to go personally; and I think he added that it would be difficult for him to leave at the time. . . ." *Ibid.*, p. 113. See *SED*, 47-1-79, 585–86. On April 13 and 14, Belmont questioned Shipherd. ". . . you have stated in your letter of November 26, to General Hurlbut, 'I was in Washington again last week, and had a full talk with the President, at General Grant's suggestion and upon his introduction.' Was that a letter of introduction?—A. Yes, sir. Q. Will you produce that letter or a copy of it?—A. . . . I will cheerfully produce it upon the consent or approval of either General Grant, who wrote it, or the President, who received it. . . . Q. What was the date of the interview?—A. It was approximately the 18th November. . . ." *HRC*, 47-1-1790, 128, 138. See *SED*, 47-1-79, 594–95.

On May 1, U.S. Senator Henry W. Blair of N. H. testified concerning his involvement with the Peruvian Co. ". . . As late as the middle of November the State Department supposed the Peruvian Company to be composed 'of reputable gentlemen,' and General Grant introduced its president to the American Executive, as I had four months earlier to the Secretary of State. Mr. Shipherd's matters were lying around pretty loosely; but there were the elements of success in the situation, and in time his, or some American, association would have achieved it, . . ." *HRC*, 47-1-1790, 250. On May 4, Blount questioned Blair. ". . . Mr. Shipherd and the Peruvian Company have been endeavoring to use the power of this government to collect from Peru $1,200,000,000. They have, amongst other things, sought to bring to bear, and it appears in this correspondence, the name of General Grant to influence this administration to a given policy in South America for the purpose of benefiting that claim. Now, I want to know who those gentlemen are; I think it is pertinent; I do not know what may come of it. . . . The WITNESS. . . . my knowledge of General Grant's relations to, and opinions of, and inclinations in reference to these claims are derived through statements made by Mr. Shipherd to myself and from no other source, except the formal indorsement of General Grant's approval upon, as I recollect it, the demands upon Chili and Peru setting forth these very claims. . . . I saw the approval and autographic indorsement of General Grant upon a dispatch or draft of a form of dispatch which he thought was a proper one to send to our ministers in those countries, asking the good offices of our legations in favor of the claims; . . ." *Ibid.*, pp. 266–67. See *ibid.*, pp. 268–69; *SED*, 47-1-79, 683–84; "A Man of Many Schemes: Jacob R. Shipherd's Singular Career," *New York Times*, Feb. 16, 1882.

On Dec. 7, 1875, USG had written. "Will the Sec. of State please see Mr. Geo. W. Dent, of San Francisco, & oblig[?]" ANS, Hamilton Fish diary, DLC-Hamilton Fish. On the same day, Secretary of State Hamilton Fish recorded in his diary. "Mr G. W. Dent of Chicago called and brought me the annexed card—He wished to speak of the Landeau claim against Peru He states that he, Mr Hodgkins and some other parties are interested in the Claim. Tell him we have but little faith in it; . . ." *Ibid.* On April 28, John C. Landreau, Washington, D. C., had written to USG. "I have the honor to informe your Excellency of the magnitude and nature of my owne and brother's Claim against the government of Peru, whiche judging frome the evasive and dilatory action of its officials, I am persuaded will never be paid without you cause an imperative demand to be made upon that government for a prompt and full Satisfaction of the Same J T Landreau, my brother a scientist residing in Peru, proposed to me in 1858 that if I would furnish him with funds to defray his expences in prosicuting explorations in that country, I should share equally the benefit of all his discoveries, I a citizen of the United Satetes residing in the State of Louisiana accepted his proposition, and remitted to hime from time to time, no less, than eleven (11) thousands dollars for that object; In the cause of my brothers exploration on a Small,—Small uninhabited island in the Pacific ocean claimed to be within the territory of Peru he discovered a deposit of verry superior guan[o] whiche he has every reason to beleive will exceed twenty million of ton, and computing it at (30) thirty dollar per ton, less than one hal[f] the price it is selling for in the markets of th[e] world and its value beased upon these figur[es] is Six hundred million of dollars. . . ." ALS, DNA, RG 59, Miscellaneous Letters. On July

12, 1871, J. Théophile Landreau, Lima, had written on the same subject. LS, *ibid.* See
Foreign Relations, 1874, p. 800; *HRC*, 45-3-114; *New York Times*, Oct. 27, 1922.

On Aug. 2, 1876, John Landreau wrote to USG. "I have the honor respectfully
to solicit an appointment as a Consul of the United States: and refer you to the accompanying endorsements of gentlemen from my State (Louisiana) as to my ability
to discharge the duties of such office." ALS, DNA, RG 59, Letters of Application and
Recommendation. On Aug. 5, USG endorsed this letter. "Refered to the Sec. of State.
If there is a vacancy to which Mr. Landreau can be appointed I have no objection to his
receiving it." AES, *ibid.* Related papers are *ibid.*; DLC-Hamilton Fish. On Dec. 7, USG
nominated Landreau as consul, Santiago de Cuba.

On April 20, 1882, Blount questioned William Hurlbert. "Have you any knowledge or information about the ownership of the Landreau claim?—A. . . . It turned up
first, according to my information, in the second administration of President Grant, in
the year 1874. . . . I have been informed that the persons chiefly active at that time in
pressing that claim were a man named Peter Hevner, a resident, I think, of Philadelphia; Ex-Governor (I think they called him) Henry D. Cooke, of the District of Columbia; Mr. Jay Cooke, and a Mr. Joseph Carter, I think, of Philadelphia. . . . Q. Did you
ever hear that Mr. Corbin at one time owned half of the Landreau claim? I mean the
brother-in-law of General Grant.—A. Yes, sir; I have heard that. . . ." *HRC*, 47-1-1790,
185. For Shipherd's purported interest in the Landreau claim, see *ibid.*, p. 200.

To Sarah B. Leet

———

New York, Nov. 19 *1881*

Mrs. S. B. Leet
932 New York Ave. Washington D. C.
Dear Madam:

Yours of the 15th inst was duly received. I am so overrun with
applications for such recommendations that it seems impossible for
me to give them; and at the same time your husband having served
on my staff I should be very glad to do anything for you, if I could.
I know the departments are so overrun with applications that it is
almost impossible for them to make a vacancy for anybody. After
the Cabinet is in, when I am in Washington next, I will try and
think of it, to speak to one of the heads of departments.

Truly Yours—

U. S. Grant

LS, DNA, RG 56, Applications. George K. Leet died on March 26, 1881. On Nov. 16,
Sarah B. Leet, Washington, D. C., wrote to Secretary of the Treasury Charles J. Folger. "I have the honor to apply for a position in your Department. Am the widow of Col

George K. Leet. formerly of General Grants staff. I have five children, and have been left without any means of support. . . . My residence is Allegheny City Pa." ALS, *ibid.* Related papers include letters to Folger from U.S. Senator James D. Cameron of Pa. and Samuel F. Miller, U.S. Supreme Court. *Ibid.* Leet was appointed copyist, Treasury Dept., as of Dec. 20.

On Sept. 21, 1875, Orville E. Babcock, Long Branch, had written to Secretary of the Treasury Benjamin H. Bristow. "The President directs me to write this note to you and to say that he will be pleased to have Geo K Leet appointed a deputy Collector of Customs at Jersey City vice the late asst Collector (deceased)." ALS, *ibid.*, Collector of Customs Applications. On Sept. 23, Bristow wrote to USG. "I have the honor to transmit herewith for your signature, the appointment of Mr. Geo. K. Leet, as Assistant Collector of Customs at Jersey City, in the collection district of New York, vice Phineas Dummer, deceased." Copy, *ibid.*, Letters Sent. See *PUSG*, 21, 403; *ibid.*, 23, 54.

To Fitz John Porter

——————

Nov. 19th 1881.

Dear Gen.

I am in receipt of yours of this date, with copy of Gen Terry's letter. I have read the latter. It is many[1] to say the least, and exhonerates you so far as the judgement of one—and a very intelligent— member of the court goes.—I will destroy the copy of Gn. Terry's letter which you send me.

Very Truly yours
U. S. Grant

Gen. F. J. Porter

ALS, DLC-Fitz John Porter. On Nov. 19, [*1881*], Fitz John Porter, New York City, wrote to USG. "The enclosed, of course, carries no conviction, but does show that a man's convictions can be changed by the presentation of facts from bitter hostility to honest regard. No one could have been more bitterly prejudiced against me, as I knew, when he went on the board—So hostile was he, that, he told me, it was impossible for him to do me justice under any evidence, and he asked me to have him relieved by my objections—I replied that all that I desired was that he should hear my side—that I would accept his judgements—During the sessions of the board our intercourse was nothing more than the ordinary salutation when we met—I send the letter that, knowing the man, you may judge somewhat of the influences of a thorough investigation upon one mind—About a year ago I asked permission to show his letter & to use it, in case my friends or I deemed it advisable. Though intended as personal & held as such, I have shown it, under his consent given in reply, to very few—Without that consent I would not now send it to you—but I hope it will be pleasant for you to read." ALS (press), *ibid.* On Aug. 26, 1879, Brig. Gen. Alfred H. Terry, St. Paul, had written to

Porter. "Soon after the publication of the report of the Schofield board, you wrote to me thanking me as one of the Board for our action in your case. I intended to reply to your letter at once; but just then, General Sheridan desired me to accompany him on a visit to some of the posts in my department & I delayed my reply till my return to St Paul. Then, in the multitude of things to which I had to attend, I forgot to make it. I write now to say that it is not thanks, but pardon which I should ask from you. For years I did you wrong in thought and sometimes wrong in speech. It is true that this was through ignorance; but I had not the right to be so ignorant. I might have learned something, at least, of the truth had I diligently sought it. If you find anything in my action as a member of the board which you can accept as an attonement for the wrong which I did you, I shall be more than gratified" Copy, *ibid.*

1. Rendered as "manly" in a copy of USG's letter, *ibid.*

To Matías Romero

New York, [*Nov.*] 19th, 1881.

M. Romero,
Mexico.

You may formally announce in the name of the Company that according to the reports of our engineers, we find the line between the city of Oaxaca and the Gulf of Mexico practicable and acceptable.

We will commence the construction of this part of the line and that of the line to Puebla and the city of Mexico as soon as possible after having received in New York the reports of the preliminary surveys of our engineers and the definite location of the route.

There may be delay in commencing the construction, but there will be none in carrying it out when once commenced.

There is no doubt as to the complete construction of our line in a short time, if we can count on the cooperation of the Mexican people.

U. S. GRANT.

The Two Republics, Nov. 27, 1881. "Rumors unfavorable to the Mexican Southern Railway Company and its ability to construct the railway for which it holds a concession having circulated in Mexico and been transmitted to New York, General Grant has sent to Mr. Romero the following telegram." *Ibid.*

On Dec. 28, 1881, a reporter asked USG to comment on the announcement "that President Gonzalez had invited Señor Matias Romero, formerly Mexican Minister at Washington, to accept an appointment as special envoy to negotiate a reciprocity treaty of commerce with the United States." USG replied. "I know that Señor Romero, from his long and intimate acquaintance with American affairs, is just the right man in the right place. . . . [A]t present we have no commercial treaty with Mexico and there exists a great necessity for one. It will be for the interest of both countries, but I think that this country has more to gain from such a treaty than Mexico has. While our exports to Mexico have increased enormously, say several hundred per cent. in the past ten years, the increase has not by any means kept pace with our purchases of Mexican products, the increase in which has been simply marvellous, and so far as present indications go, will be still larger in the future. While this is the case, and while this Government is admitting Mexican products at [a] fair rate of duty, very many of the American articles of manufacture, notably machinery used in mining and other industries, are entirely shut out of Mexico by the duty which is so high as to be prohibitory. For this reason the mission of Señor Romero is timely and very important, as if these duties can be reduced so that our manufacturers can dispose of their products in Mexico, I am certain that the export trade to that country can be largely increased, and the people of Mexico will be supplied with articles which are much needed to develop its wonderful resources. But it is not alone to negotiate a commercial treaty that Señor Romero came here. President Gonzalez for some reason is extremely desirous that I should return to Mexico. I said, when the desire was conveyed to me, that neither for business nor for pleasure would I go again to Mexico until I could go all the way by rail. Finding that I would not go to him, President Gonzalez has sent Señor Romero to see me." Asked if Romero's mission had "any political significance," USG answered, "No, not as regards the politics of this country. It has to do principally with the affairs of this road and with regard to internal improvements generally in Mexico. I thought it probable that some Mexican public man might be sent to confer with me, but until I saw it in THE WORLD this morning I was not advised as to who the envoy would be." *New York World*, Dec. 30, 1881. For a statement questioning the accuracy of USG's comment on mining machinery, see *ibid.*, Jan. 6, 1882.

In Feb., 1882, a reporter summarized the findings of "four commissions appointed by the Mexican Southern Railway Company to make preliminary surveys, to discover the most feasible routes for the Mexican Southern on its different extensions, . . . As soon as the four divisions of engineers have finished their work the plans and profiles will be sent to the office of the company in New York to be definitely passed upon." *The Two Republics*, Feb. 5, 1882. Subsequently, the Mexican government "allowed certain modifications to the Romero-Grant railroad concession. . . ." *Ibid.*, Feb. 12, 1882. In April, an editorial noted the general belief in Mexico City "that General Grant has not succeeded in raising the necessary capital for commencing the construction of the Mexican Southern Railway. . . ." *Ibid.*, April 27, 1882. In May, a newspaper reprinted from the "official organ of the Mexican Government" an extract of a dispatch from Matías Romero, minister to the U.S. "The second point to which Gen. Grant alluded with considerable interest in a long intervi[e]w which I had with him this morning in New York, refers to the rumors set afloat regarding his supposed bankruptcy. In fact, the said rumors were published here about a month since; but no importance whatever was attributed to them, and even then he told me that they were absolutely groundless. . . . [F]or a long time past he had made up his mind not to contradict any rumors published about him, and that for this reason he had not contradicted in a formal manner those which referred to his supposed financial ruin; but that privately he had to tell his friends that it was entirely false and that he had not lost a single cent in the operations attributed to him. As in Mexico some sensation has been created with Gen.

Grant's supposed bankruptcy, and I deem it convenient for the Government to be well informed as to the real truth, I have resolved to forward to you the statements made to me this morning by the said General." *Ibid.*, May 14, 1882.

On May 14, 1883, President Manuel González of Mexico approved a new contract consolidating the Mexican Southern Railroad Co. and the Mexican Oriental, Interoceanic and International Railroad Co., headed by Jay Gould. The combination extended the Mexican Southern north from Mexico City to Laredo, and more than doubled the total length to 1,205 miles. See *HED*, 48-1-86, 39–40, 54–59. An editorial noted a new concession. "As it was found impracticable to raise money for the Mexican Southern, without a subsidy, the Government has accorded it $7,000 per mile in the new grant. This confirms the expediency of subsidies, inasmuch as General Grant was at the outset opposed to them, and would not have sought one for this line if he had not, after two years, experience, found it needful in order to enlist the aid of American and European capitalists for the speedy completion of the road." *The Two Republics*, May 31, 1883. See letter to William R. Rowley, June 12, 1881; letter to Edward F. Beale, Dec. 28, 1882.

To Lewis Wolfley

New York, Nov 19 *1881*

Louis Wolfley Esq
1309 14th St. Washington D. C.
Dear Sir:

Your letter of Nov. 2, was duly received but on account of the great number of letters I receive I was unable to answer it at the time, and have just come across it again. I remember now more of your case than I did when I wrote you before, and will be very glad to help you if it is in my power. I return you the letters from Senator Kellogg and Ex Senator West so that in case they should be of any use to you, you may use them. You are at liberty to say that it would be very gratifying to me to see you occupy such public position in your state or Elsewhere as you may ask for.

Truly Yours—
U. S. Grant

LS, DNA, RG 59, Applications and Recommendations, Hayes-Arthur. On Nov. 2, 1881, J. Rodman West, Washington, D. C., wrote to USG. "At the request of Major Lewis Wolfley I beg leave to recall to your recollection the circumstances of his being removed from the position of Assessor of Internal Revenue in Louisiana. I think you discovered subsequently that an injustice had been inadvertently done Maj. Wolfley and as he is now an applicant for an appointment by President Arthur I think you would be glad to assist in relieving him from the disadvantage of having been once removed

from office by your administration. Permit me to remind you of Major Wolfley's services in the Army—also of his efforts in behalf of the Republican cause in 1868 by a
large contribution of money to defray the expenses of the election of that year. In giving preference or rather being committed to another party, when in 1875 you offered
Maj. Wolfley the position of Collector Int. Revenue for north Louisiana I feel that I
have stood somewhat in his way, and hope that you will find it agreeable to join me
in an effort towards his reinstatement by saying a few words in his behalf." ALS, *ibid.*
On Nov. 1, U.S. Senator William P. Kellogg of La. had written to USG recommending
Lewis Wolfley, former maj., 3rd Ky. Cav., for marshal, New Mexico Territory. ALS,
ibid. No appointment followed. See Scot Wrighton and Earl Zarbin, "Lewis Wolfley,
Territorial Politics, and the Founding of *The Arizona Republican*," *Journal of Arizona
History*, 31, 3 (Autumn, 1990), 307–28.

To John P. Jones

New York City,
Nov. 25th 1881.

My Dear Senator Jones:

I give this introduction to Governor Flanders,[1] of La. at my
own suggestion and without his asking it. Governor Flanders was
a Union man in La. at the breaking out of the rebellion, and got
through the lines—without his family—the very *last chance*, in /61 &
reported to me at Cairo. He was appointed Governor of the state by
Sheridan at the time he made changes during reconstruction times.
The Governor is a man of high character, and understands Louisiana politics as well as any other man. I believe from my late visits
to the state that La. can be made a republican state—at least Anti
Bourbon state—if the Governor, Col. Pitkin & Judge Beattie,[2] and
a few such gentlemen can be understood to be having a fair hearing
in the management of affairs there, Col. Pitkin wants to be minister to Mexico. He would be unobjectionable there if there was to be
a change. I do not think there ought to be a change unless Morgan
should be put on the Bench. Even then I think Pitkin—looking to
his own interest—should stay in La. But I do not dictate to him
what is for his interest.—I hope you will present Governor Flanders to the President.

Very Truly yours
U. S. Grant

ALS, Louisiana State University, Baton Rouge, La.

1. Appointed in 1873, Benjamin F. Flanders served as asst. treasurer, New Orleans. See *PUSG*, 22, 343.

2. Judge, sugar planter, and former C.S.A. col., Taylor Beattie lost his bid for La. governor as a Republican in 1879. See William Ivy Hair, *Bourbonism and Agrarian Protest: Louisiana Politics, 1877–1900* (Baton Rouge, 1969), pp. 105, 182–83.

To Thomas B. Swann

New York City
Nov. 28th 1881.

MY DEAR COL. SWANN:

I received your ~~official~~ business letter in due time, and while I have no means to invest in real estate, and with my experience would not invest in country property, I made enquiries to ascertain whether the Ohio, Kanawha & Elk Valley rail-road was in contemplation. Mr Gould told me that the rumor that he was to build such a road was without any foundation. He said however—and seemed to speak as if his attention had been called to the matter before— that he thought very well of the prospect of such a road. If such a road was likely to be built it is possible that all three of my sons might take a limited interest in such a company as you speak of. They are of an age that they could afford to wait some years for their returns. I want all the income I can get to use along from month to month, and returns are not quick from real estate. I have a farm near St. Louis that I would sell for thirty pr. ct. less than I would have take twelve years ago, and will sell soon whether I have to make a further concession in price or not.

With kind regards to Aunt Rachel, your wife and all my Kanawha friends.

Very Truly yours
U. S. GRANT

ALS, West Virginia Archives, Charleston, West Va. Thomas B. Swann had married USG's cousin Mary W. Tompkins. On June 27, 1874, USG and Julia Dent Grant visited Swann at Charleston, West Va. *Washington Chronicle*, June 28, 1874. See *PUSG*, 24, 318–19. For railroad expansion in West Va., see Ronald L. Lewis, *Transforming the Appalachian Countryside: Railroads, Deforestation, and Social Change in West Virginia, 1880–1920* (Chapel Hill, 1998), pp. 45–80.

On April 15, 1873, Swann, Charleston, had written to USG forwarding papers from Alfred Beckley, USMA 1823, concerning the application of his son Daniel W. Beckley to USMA. ALS, DNA, RG 94, Correspondence, USMA. Daniel Beckley did not attend USMA.

In Sept., 1875, Swann wrote to USG. "Lieut. Earnest Ruffner of this County is the son of General Lewis Ruffner, an old Citizen of high Standing & great personal worth. Lieut. Ruffner is esteemed & beloved by his Friends, & as a gentleman is in every way unexceptionable. Your Excellency will remember that some eight years ago he graduated no. 1. at WestPoint. His Friends will ask for him the appointment of Professor of Mathematics at WestPoint." ALS, *ibid.* Related papers are *ibid.* No appointment followed.

On Feb. 21, 1876, Swann wrote to USG. "This will reach you by the hands of The Rev. Mr. R. T. Brown of Rockville Md Mr Brown many years ago was Rector of St John's Church at this Place. Mrs Brown is a grand-daughter of Major Cone of the Revolution & an estimable Lady. Mr Brown has a favor to ask of your Excellency, which I hope your Excellency will be disposed to Grant." ALS, *ibid.*, RG 45, Letters Received from the President. Richard Templeton Brown had served as rector, St. John's Church, Charleston, West Va. (1850–54). Geo. W. Peterkin, *A History and Record of the Protestant Episcopal Church in the Diocese of West Virginia, . . .* (Charleston, West Va., 1902), pp. 636–37.

On July 8, 1876, Swann wrote to USG. "I have a nephew, Mr. F. R. Swann, to whom I have given a thorough Collegiate education. He is moral & amiable. I would be gratified to see him in the Army. Cant you give him a Lieutenancy in the Army?" ALS, DNA, RG 94, Applications for Positions in the War Dept. On Feb. 13, 1877, Ferdinand R. Swann, Charleston, wrote to USG. "I make application for any consulship that may be vacant in Mexico—or Chili—My preference in *Mexico* is either the city of Mexico or Minatitillan, and in Chili, Talcahuano. Hoping you will consider this, . . ." ALS, *ibid.*, RG 59, Applications and Recommendations, Hayes-Arthur. In a letter stamped Feb. 15, Thomas Swann and three others wrote to USG supporting Ferdinand Swann. LS, *ibid.* No appointment followed.

On March 2, Thomas Swann, Washington, D. C., wrote to USG. "With assured confidence of your personal regards; it is with reluctance I have concluded to ask of you a personal favor. If I ask too much you have generosity to overlook it. If *entirely* pleasant to you, I would be glad, if you ask Gov. Hayes to give me a place upon The Supreme Bench. If there is any other gentleman in the South more deserving I yield to him." ALS, OFH. USG endorsed this letter. "For incoming President." AE (undated), *ibid.*

To John Russell Young

New York City
Nov. 28th 1881

MY DEAR COMMODORE

Three gentlemen are to visit my house this evening, at half past seven, who, while not altogether hostile to you yet like to antagonize you with the view of making all they can out of you. Wo'nt you come at the same hour and meet them *face to face?*

Very Truly yours

U. S. GRANT

P. S. Please say yes or no to bearer.

ALS (facsimile), USG 3.

Endorsement

I take pleasure in joining in the recommendation of Wm F Raynolds, Jr. for the appointment of Supervising Inspector of Steam vessls because I believe him well qualified for the place, and because I have a faint recollection of an injustice having been done him while I was in office. He is the nephew of a class mate and friend of mine, Gen. W. F. Raynolds,[1] now of the Corps of Engrs U. S. Army. I believe Mr. Raynolds is better qualified for the office than most of the men who can be got to accept it.

U. S. GRANT

NOV. 29TH 1881.

AES, DNA, RG 56, Applications. Written on a letter of Nov. 28, 1881, from William F. Raynolds, Jr., Canton, Ohio, to President Chester A. Arthur seeking appointment as "Supervising Inspector of Steam Vessels in the 3d district at Baltimore Md. or in the 9th district at Buffalo and Cleveland or to any other of the remaining districts of the United States preferring the 3d district." ALS, *ibid.* On Nov. 28 or 29, Raynolds, Jr., wrote to USG. "I have the pleasure of handing you herewith some of the papers I spoke of in a former communication, and which I now forward you at your suggestion and request that you may give them your consideration & endorsement and forward them to the President . . . In *1856* I went to sea on a whaling voyage was gone *four years,* visiting during that time *China Japan Australia New Zealand* The islands of the *Pacific* the *Arctic Ocean* and Coast of *Africa,* Returning in 1860. Entered the army as a *Private* in the 4th O Vols Served through West Virginia with *Gen McClellan* untill after the *Romney* Engagement when I was promoted to be *adjutant* of the *6th O V Cavalry* where I remained for near a year When by reason of sickness contracted at *'Rich mountain'* I left the regiment and came home remaining *two weeks* then Entered the *Navy* as *masters* mate participating in all the James River engagements also on the Coast of *Florida* and *Fort Morgan Mobile Bay* &c Entered the *Revenue Cutter* Service as 3d *Lieutenant* . . . Resigned in 1871, and entered the *Steamboat Inspection* Service as U S Inspector of *Hulls* at Louisville Ky remaining untill 1875, when I made room for the Father in Law of Bluford Wilson Esq (at that time Solicitor of Treasurey) who now occupies my place at

Louisville and who during the war was an UNCOMPROMISING REBEL. Entered the employ of B F Avery & Sons of Louisville in Charge of the Ill & Indiana Business of that firm. While at the Centenial at Phila in 1876, became sick by reason of chronic dyptheria contracted during the war and untill within a few months have been unfit for work. But my health being restored I desire to again be employed . . ." ALS, *ibid.* On Jan. 19, 1882, Raynolds, Jr., wrote to USG on the same subject. ALS, *ibid.* USG endorsed this letter. "Respectfully referred to the Sec. of the Treas. Mr. Raynolds would make a most excellent Inspector of Steam boats. He has filled the office before and is acquainted with its duties. May I ask the Sec. to examine his papers now on file in the Department." AES (undated), *ibid.* Related papers are *ibid.* Appointed in March as clerk, steamboat inspection service, Raynolds, Jr., was removed in Aug. because of illness.

    1. Born in 1820 in Ohio, USMA 1843, William F. Raynolds led early explorations of the Black Hills and the Yellowstone River, won bvt. brig. gen. for wartime service, and resumed surveying and engineering duties. On March 18, 1869, Lt. Col. Raynolds, Detroit, wrote to USG concerning a Mich. appointment. ALS, *ibid.*, RG 60, Records Relating to Appointments. See *PUSG*, 25, 143.

To Charles J. Folger

NEW YORK CITY,
November 30, 1881.

Hon. C. J. Folger, Secretary of the Treasury:

    The enclosed recommendation for Judge John F. Long to the President for the office of Surveyor of the Port of St. Louis has been sent to me for indorsement. Judge Long held the office for four years under me and probably made the most efficient Collector St. Louis ever had. He was the Collector himself and did not leave the office to be run by deputies. He was one of the few collectors or surveyors St. Louis has had who was able to settle up his accounts without the aid of Congress or his sureties. I have known the Judge for thirty-eight years and can indorse him strongly for the office. I know that he can have the support of the business community and can fill his bond without placing himself under obligations that would hamper him in the administration of his office. I feel sure the appointment, if made, will commend itself to the people of St. Louis, and will be in the interest of good government. Very truly, yours,

U. S. GRANT.

St. Louis Post-Dispatch, Jan. 16, 1888. See following letter.

To John F. Long

―――――

No 90 Broadway
N. Y. City
Nov. 30th 1881

MY DEAR JUDGE LONG:

I received your letter—without date—enclosing power of atty. for you to vote my stock in the Agricultural and Mechanical Association.[1] I herewith return it duly signed & witnessed.

Your endorsements for the Surveyorship have come to me. I sent them to the Sec. of the Treas. instead of to the President to whom they were directed. I send you a copy of my letter to the Sec. of the Treasury for your information.—It is not now probable that I will see the President until after the 1st of Jan.y. When I do I will talk to him about this matter, as I have done before, and urge it if necessary. With kind regards to all your family,

Very Truly yours
U. S. GRANT

ALS, MoSHi. See previous letter; letter to John F. Long, Dec. 16, 1881; letter to James Campbell, June 26, 1884.

1. Incorporated in 1855, the St. Louis Agricultural and Mechanical Association operated a zoo and museum and held indoor and outdoor fairs and horse races on its grounds.

To Fitz John Porter

―――――

[*Dec. 1, 1881*]

I will be glad to see you at any time you may call, but your papers I carried to my house to go over carefully, but as to yet I have had company every evening at the house—the only time I am there—so I have not yet examined them sufficiently to say anything. I think I can safely say however that you will not meet with opposition from me in ~~relief~~ obtaining relief from the odium of your sentence. After examining the papers before me—which I will do within a few days if I have to shut myself up for the purpose—if my judgement convinces me that you have been wronged I will say so.

U. S. GRANT

ANS, DLC-Fitz John Porter. Written on a note of Dec. 1, 1881, from Fitz John Porter, New York City, to USG. "I would be glad of an interview with you to day if agreeable—or to morrow if more convenient to you." ANS, *ibid.* On the same day, Porter again wrote to USG. "I will bide your examinations of the papers I sent you and a notice, if you will be so kindly as to send it, when you will be ready to see me. I prefer the opportunity of explaining & proving, if necessary, any doubtful points and of freely & frankly and dispassionately talking with you. I thank you for your kind assurance of to day. I am sure you will pardon my anxiety in view of my earnest desire on account of all concerned to avoid discussion personal and partizan in Congress" ADfS, *ibid.* Porter described subsequent developments in "Memorandum of efforts to obtain favorable action in my case from Gen. U. S. Grant." "Again—I wrote to Gen Horace Porter, that I would be glad if he would see the Genl & try to hasten his action—The next day Porter asked me to come to his office to get the result of the interview Porter then told me that Grant had read nearly all the papers, and was convinced of the wrongs he had done me by prolonging my vindication to the present time—& that he felt it was due to me that he should take strong action in the case & if still of the same opinion when he read all the papers—he certainly would do all his power to right me—Adding 'you know, Porter, when I am convinced of my duty, I never fail to do it'—Porter said 'I know that but I did not know what effect those Illinois people would have on you.' The Genl then indicated pointedly that no one would turn him from his duty—Porter said Grant would see him me in a few days—" D, *ibid.* On Dec. 9, Horace Porter, New York City, wrote to Fitz John Porter. "I have seen the General and if you can drop in at my office I will tell you what he says." LS, *ibid.* See letter to Fitz John Porter, Dec. 9, 1881.

To Chester A. Arthur

———

NewYork Dec 5 /81.

THE PRESIDENT:

My late travels through the East gave me an opportunity of observing, such as probably but few persons have had in this generation. It impressed me very strongly with the necessity for some action on the part of our Government which would give us an influence and an interest there commensurate with our present and prospective greatness. We labor under many disadvantages from our system of representation, which does not, in the first place give compensation sufficient to command the services of proper representatives while the European governments, and notably England,

Germany and France, are represented by men whose career is in
the diplomatic or consular service and who give the whole of their
time and their energies to the cultivation of trade between their respective countries and the East, while with us our representatives
are absolutely debarred not only from taking part in the trade of
the Eastern countries but it would be regarded as sufficient ground
for the removal of a consular officer or a minister who seemed to
take an active part in establishing trade relations between prominent houses in our country and ~~prominent houses in any of~~ the
Eastern countries, particularly if he seemed to be interested in
the welfare of any single firm. This is all wrong, but the wrong is
in the legislation and can not be ~~helped~~ wholly cured by the Executive; but it occurred to me while traveling in those countries
that much could be done in the way of establishing trade relations
between the United States and those countries by suitable instructions to ministers and consular officers. The first thing to be done
would be to secure in some of the principal places proper representatives. In view of the conversation which I had with you on this
subject, I take the liberty now of suggesting some appointments
which I think would aid us, especially in China and Japan.

Mr John Russell Young was with me in all my travels in those
countries, and, by his being with me, had access to all the places
that I had, and had the advantage of observation that he could not
have had if he had been traveling alone. My views were expressed
to him constantly upon the situation in those countries while we
were upon the spot and while the defects in our system were viv-
idly brought before me. He also had the same opportunity of observing the unfitness of many of our representatives that I had.
For this reason I would strongly urge him for the appointment of
United States Minister to Japan. I know that Mr Young in accepting this position will be making a pecuniary sacrafice, but I believe
the benefits to the country from his appointment will be a compensation to him greater than a pecuniary reward could be. I know his
appointment would be well received by the highest officials in Japan, and I know he understands the situation there well, and would
be of great assistance to whoever might be his colleague in China

The United States purchases more than 90 percent of the exports of Japan, and as near as I could learn while I was there, our sales to them are about two percent of what they import, while there is scarcely an article not produced by themselves and required for their consumption which we cannot supply as well as any European nation, and as cheaply, taking into consideration quality with the price. It was also plain to me that the Japanese would much prefer trading largely with the United States, to any of the European powers for the reason not only that we buy the most that they have to sell, but that we treat them with more respect upon their own soil than do the representatives of any of the European powers and particularly those whom most of their trade is with.

I would also recommend the appointment of Consul General O. N. Denny,[1] now at Shanghai, for Minister Resident. I saw a great deal of him while there. He is a man of intelligence, understands the Chinese people and their institutions well. From my own intercourse and observations while in China, and letters received from Viceroy Li Hung Chang, the ablest and most influential Viceroy in the entire empire, he would have more the confidence of the Chinese people and government than any person who could be appointed. I believe it is a matter of national importance that he should receive that appointment. I know Gen. Swift[2] has been urged for the position, and in many respects he may be an eminently fit man to represent his country abroad, but from letters which I have received, his course while in China was such as to very much disgust—to use the mildest term—the leading Chinese people, and his appointment th[er]e would be regarded by them as offensive.

For some of the minor places—but of importance in what ought to be a new departure in our dealings with these nations, I would suggest the appointment of Col. John S. Mosby now Consul to HongKong for Consul General.[3] Col. Mosby is a man of fine intelligence, I believe of the strictest integrity, is brave to fight the opposition which any officer in the place will meet from the representatives of European nations, and can serve us there better than any one I can think of now, taking into consideration his presen[t] information with his other qualifications. Col Mosby is from the

State of Virginia. If he should be appointed, Mr Henry McGilsey [4] would be a good substitute for him at HongKong.

For Consul at Teint-sin I would recommend William N. Peth-ick, [5] who hailed I believe formerly from the State of NewYork. He has been for many years in China, and no doubt proposes to remain there always, whether holding an official position under his government or not. He is a scholar, and only the most highly educated of the Chinese gentlemen are equally learned in their own language with Mr Pethick. He is the warm and intimate friend of Viceroy Li Hung Chang, and has for many years made the translations of information from all parts of the world into the Chinese for this cultivated Viceroy. His appointment will be taken as a special favor by the Chinese Government, while it would serve our own country most admirably.

In the matter of Consul General to Japan, in my judgment it is highly important that there should be a change in that office. The present Consul General, Gen. Van Buren I have no desire to say anything against and if he was promoted to a better position elsewhere out of Japan I would be very glad to see it. About this, however, I ask nothing special, only that I am clearly of the conviction that his place there should be filled by somebody else. For that place I would strongly urge Mr Edward H. House. Mr House I believe is a native of Massachusetts, but resided and was probably a citizen of NewYork when he first went to Japan some eleven or twelve years ago, where he has resided with the exception of two or three visits home for a year or eighteen months. He is very much interested in the Japanese people, has their confidence in a very high degree, and is better able to combat undue and improper foreign influences than any man I know in all my acquaintance. It would be a labor of love with him to serve his country there, and I believe would be productive of very great good.

In making these recommendations I am not actuated by any personal motives whatever. Mr Young is the only one who, in the proper sense of th[e] word, could be said to be a particular personal friend whom I might wish to favor. With him it has been long under consideration whether he would accept the position or not, if tendered. In the last few days, however, he has come to the conclusion that if the place is offered to him he will accept it and endeavor to serve his country faithfully. In conversations I have said to you that the present representative to Japan represents his country so well, so ably, that I would never desire his removal except to see him promoted I understand now he has tendered to him, and will probably accept, a position of Judge of a court which is to be established by the Japanese government in that Empire. In that way he will become an employé of that government, and inasmuch as they have determined to organize a mixed court, (that is a court composed of, as I understand, two foreigners and three natives) I congratulate Japan on their selection of Judge Bingham for one of these places.

There are quite a number of the smaller consulates in Japan and China that ought to be changed as rapidl[y] as good men can be found who will take their places. For my part I think it would be good policy on the part of Congress to abolish the present regulations for the consular service in all countries outside of Europe. The regulations are perhaps proper and wise so far as the European countries are concerned, but in all the other countries with which we have commercial relations I think it would be a much wiser policy if the fees of the different ports were given to the consuls, and instead of appointing them on the present plan say to the different chambers of commerce throughout the country that all these consular positions are now open to be filled by these chambers. A list of all of the ports in foreign Countries other than Europe should be published, together with the fees received at each, according to the last reports at the State department, and the Chambers of Commerce should be informed that any persons whom they were willing to constitute agents for the sale of such American goods as might be consigned to them would receive the Consular appointment from the President and would have all the fees. Holding an official position of that sort under the Government of the United States would benefit them in their trade with the peoples among whom they would be located; it would be an advertisement for them. While the fees might be very small, it would be the means of introducing American Goods and the commissions which they would receive from persons consigning goods to them, or for whom they would make purchases of the commodities of the countries to which they were accredited, might in some instances give very great compensation. This plan would serve to put us, in some degree, on a footing with representatives of the European nations in those countries. I only throw this out, however, as a suggestion and as a matter that when I meet you I should be very glad to talk much more at length upon.

Hoping that I have not fatiged you by the length of this communication, I am

Very Truly Yours.—

U. S. GRANT

P. S. As I dictated this letter to a stenographer it has been spun out much longer than I dreamed of until it was written out, and fear too long to expect you to read it while you have so much to do as at the begining of a session of Congress. I hope however, when you get a new Sec. of State you will please have him consider it.

U. S. G.

LS (postscript in USG's hand), DNA, RG 59, Applications and Recommendations, Hayes-Arthur. See letter to James A. Garfield, Feb. 18, 1881; letter to George F. Edmunds, March 14, 1882.

1. On Oct. 8, 1881, USG twice wrote to President Chester A. Arthur concerning Owen N. Denny. "To the President. Judge Denny, now Consul General of the U. States in China is the person who I spoke to you about personally as being the fittest person I know of for the Chinese Mission. His influence with the leading Chinese officials, from my own observation and from letters recently received from Viceroy Li Hung Chang, probably the leading Chinaman in the Empire, attests this." "I wish the President would see Mr. C. E. Hill personally. Mr. H. has been more than twenty years in China and can attest personally to what I have said about Judge Denny." AES and ANS, DNA, RG 59, Applications and Recommendations, Hayes-Arthur. Papers supporting and opposing Denny are *ibid.*

2. On March 24, 1880, President Rutherford B. Hayes had nominated John F. Swift, San Francisco lawyer and former Cal. assemblyman, as commissioner to negotiate a treaty with China. See Jack L. Hammersmith, *Spoilsmen in a 'Flowery Fairyland': The Development of the U. S. Legation in Japan, 1859–1906* (Kent, Ohio, 1998), pp. 158–60; Andrew Gyory, *Closing the Gate: Race, Politics, and the Chinese Exclusion Act* (Chapel Hill, 1998), pp. 213–16.

3. See letter to Charles W. Russell, Jan. 12, 1882.

4. On April 19, 1869, Israel Washburn, Jr., collector of customs, Portland, Maine, had written to Secretary of State Hamilton Fish recommending Henry McGilvery,

Belfast, Maine, as consul, Shanghai. ". . . He is an old shipmaster & well acquainted with trade at the Chinese ports. . . ." ALS, DNA, RG 59, Letters of Application and Recommendation. No appointment followed. See *HMD*, 45-2-31, 5.

5. On Feb. 2, 1880, Charles E. Hill, New York City, wrote to Secretary of State William M. Evarts recommending William N. Pethick for promotion from vice consul and interpreter to consul, Tientsin. *"Personal* . . . No foreigner any where has a tithe of the influence with Li Hung Chung that he has, this he has gained by strict integrity square manly advice and counsel, given only when asked for and then for right and justice whether pleasing to the Chinese or otherwise—They have never disregard his advice without comitting mistakes . . ." ALS, DNA, RG 59, Applications and Recommendations, Hayes-Arthur. On June 3, Hayes nominated Pethick as secretary, Chinese treaty commission. See *New York Times*, Dec. 21, 1901.

To Chester A. Arthur

New York City,
Dec. 7th 1881.

THE PRESIDENT:

Some time since I gave a letter of recommendation for a Paymastership, in the Army, to Major Amos Webster. He is both qualified and deserving. At that time I did not know W. F. Tucker, Jr. of Ill. would be, or was, an applicant for the place. I know Mr. Tucker but slightly personally but I know him well through members of my family. He is a young man of the best moral character, and in every way worthy of trust. He is the son-in-law of General Logan whos services to the country, in the field and in the two houses of Congress, richly entitle him to this favor especially as he presents a worthy man. I join therefore in the request that Mr. Tucker may receive the Apt. of Paymaster when a vacancy occurs.

Very Truly yours
U. S. GRANT

ALS, DNA, RG 94, ACP, 2669 1882. On Dec. 9, 1881, Mary S. Logan, Washington, D. C., wrote to President Chester A. Arthur. "I enclose you a letter I recieved from Gen Grant. I heard he had asked you to appoint Col Webster to the Pay Mastership soon to become vacant. And desiring to relieve you from any embarrassment in the premises, I wrote to the Gen & asked him to withdraw his friend and give our son-in-law Mr Tucker his endorsement, which he has done in a very graceful manner & for which I feel grateful to him. Mr Lincoln has also promised me to give Mr Tucker his earnest support. Mr Baker having been provided for in another direction. Now my Dear Mr President I leave the whole thing with you, and I pray you make me happy by giving the appointment to Wm F Tucker Jr and I promise you most positively to ask nothing at your hands in the future. My whole soul is enlisted in this thing. I think of little else, and it would be a sad blow to me to be disappointed. If you desire to see Mr Tucker that you may judge of his capability etc. please let me know and I will have him come on at once, as we are very proud of him, and would be pleased to have you see him. But do not wish to annoy you by personal importunities, as you must be weary of seeing people. Wishing you pre-eminent success in your administration & hoping that my loved ones may in some way be able to contribute to the same . . ." ALS, *ibid.* On Dec. 12, Arthur wrote to Mary Logan acknowledging the receipt of USG's and her letter. LS, DLC-John A. Logan. On Feb. 20, 1882, Arthur nominated William F. Tucker, Jr., as maj., paymaster. Tucker, Jr., had married Mary E. Logan in 1877.

On Nov. 5, 1881, USG endorsed Amos Webster's application for paymaster. "Major Webster was a most efficient quartermaster on my staff during the last year of the war and after to the time of my leaving the Army. Since that he has filled the office of register of wills most acceptably to the supreme court of the District. He is most admirably fitted for the office he now seeks, and I do not hesitate to indorse him for it." *SRC*, 55-2-791, 5. Similar endorsements from Col. Rufus Ingalls, Gen. William T. Sherman, Horace Porter, and Governor John D. Long of Mass. are *ibid.*, pp. 5–6. On April 15, 1882, USG wrote to Arthur recommending Webster "in case of the compulsary retirement bill becoming a law." Robert K. Black List No. 29, Sept. 1952, no. 72; ABPC, 1948, p. 546. As of July 1, 1883, Webster was chief clerk to the secretary of the treasury. See *PUSG*, 21, 468–69.

To Fitz John Porter

————

Dec. 9th 1881

GEN. F. J. PORDER;
DEAR GEN.

I have been able to give one day to the reading of the papers which you submitted to me, but have not finished them. If you will call, say next Monday, about Eleven O'Clock, I will be pleased to see you. I can say now however, from what I have read, I believe I have heretofore done you an injustice, both in thought & speach, and if of the same opinion when through the examination of your case I will regard it a most solemn obligation on my part to correct the wrong so far as I have any responsibility for it.

Very Truly yours
U. S. GRANT

ALS, DLC-Fitz John Porter. Fitz John Porter drafted a reply on this letter. "God bless you for your kind words. I will call on Monday about 11. am" ADf (undated), *ibid.* Porter described this interview on Dec. 12, 1881, in "Memorandum of efforts to obtain favorable action in my case from Gen. U. S. Grant." "I was promptly at the General's office—Almost immediately the General opened on the subject and did almost all the talking for an hour & a quarter—He repeated substantially but more strongly the points in his last letter—That he had done me great injustice by his former non investigation & causing delay in justice—& that he felt it very much—He had thought much of it & was grieved—& had considered how he could best remedy the wrong—He would write the President—but any one could do that—He would write & also see the Presd & urge him to examine the case & if convinced as he was of the wrong, to do full justice—He went over the points of the case & showed a good study of them—& familiarity with the pros & cons, & said that I did all that I should have done—and if I had done differently—or what Gen Pope—wanted, but of which I did not know, I should have done wrong. He approved of all I did—and as for despatches, he did not object to them as the Board—& thought, if I had resented some of Pope's despatches to me, I would have been justified 'especially as some of them were probably designed to trap me.' Gen Grant was fair, most manly and dispassionate throughout—and we parted with the assurance from him I should soon hear from him I left a copy of my appeal with him—he promising to confer with me as to his future action, 'if he continued of his present convictions He asked me if Genl Cox had replied to my letter—I told him he had & what the reply was. He said Cox was very narrow minded & mean,—as were all such men whose eyes were very close together. On returning to my office, I sent him a complete copy of my correspondence with Cox, with the request that he would return it when done with—Also sent him a copy of Mr Rope's book—" D, *ibid.* See John Codman Ropes, *The Army Under Pope* (New York, 1881).

On Dec. 19, USG wrote to Fitz John Porter. "I am through reading the papers you submitted to me and will be ready to meet you any morning at about 11 a. m. after to-morrow. I have seen nothing to change the views I expressed to you atin our last conversation" Copy, DLC-Fitz John Porter. On Dec. 20, Porter, New York City, wrote to USG. "Again I say, with all my heart, God bless you, for your good words just received. When your kind acts are completed, intentions or even publicly known, I know you will give your friends and mine a joy only equal[ed] by that you now give to me & those most dear to me. . . . P. S. I will call to-morrow morning shortly after 11. O'Clock" ALS (press), *ibid.* Porter described this interview in a memorandum. "He at once opened on the subject and spoke almost uninterruptedly by me—occasionally referring to some of his own matters as illustration—He said his mind was not changed but more fixedly confirmed in the opinions he had expressed—He then went over the case—minutely—& said he should write the President and urge him to examine the case carefully or get the Attorney General Mr Brewster to do so—Brewster was an old friend—and he had that morning recd a letter of thanks from him for his aid in getting the Attorney Generalship but had written him, he had not done it—He said the Judge Advocate Genl was not the proper person to consult—as he was of the Garfield ring—& would only aid to perpetuate the wrong—He said he had spoken to Mr Pierpont—at his (G's) house & told him of his convictions and intentions. He said—'there was but one objection which could be offered to your despatches. Up to the time you joined Pope all was certainly right—After that you were in Pope's presence or near him—& it might be claimed you should have sent your despatches through him—or that he should have known of them—but you were not with Pope—and the President was asking information through Burnside from you. Your misfortune was that with Pope's orders sent by you, you gave a correct condition of affairs—and it proved true, & that y̶ From all the evidence it is manifest that you were only one who knew the real state of affairs—a̶The telegrams show you did—There may have been others who did know—but they were not your superiors. I̶ I believe if you had had command the result of that campaign would have been different & that you would have won. Of course I can't say this in a letter to the Presdt but I can personally—& will.' The same kind, frank, manly manner was shown as on former occasions He said he felt that his confession of being in the wrong so long would put him an embarrasing light before the country—I said—but general what you have said, in regard to the new Evidence coming up now—No—he broke in—not so, you told me you had it—& I see that you had it—& I should have listened to you and examined it—But it matters not I shall do my duty in full. The Presd will be here this week and Logan soon—& I shall speak to both—I asked as I left—General when shall I have your letter (the one I was to send to the Presdt) 'Within an hour—he replied—if I am not too much occupied by my visitors—It will take only a half hour—but anyhow to morrow—I am now writing at 2. Pm Dec 22d—It has not yet come—but I am sure it will—For I believe in his sincerity, & manliness & I believe the act will do him g̶ as great good before the public as his course towards Lee at Appomatox—& he must see it—" D, *ibid.* See *PUSG*, 26, 71–74; letter to Chester A. Arthur, Dec. 22, 1881; letter to Fitz John Porter, Dec. 23, 1881; letter to Benjamin H. Brewster, Dec. 24, 1881.

Endorsement

If the Pension Agency is to go to Mo, I heartily join in the recommendation of A. R. Easton, Jr. for appointment to fill the office. A. R. Easton, Sr. filled the office under my Administration, and the records in Washington will shew the office in as fine condition while he filled it as any office in the country. A. R. Easton, Jr was chief clerk during that time and must therefore be thoroughly acquainted with the duties of the office.

U. S. GRANT

DEC. 12TH 1881.

AES, DNA, RG 48, Appointment Div., Letters Received. Written on a letter of Dec. 2, 1881, from John F. Long, St. Louis, to USG. "There is a movement on foot to a *division* of the 'St Louis Pension Agency,' in which event, I would be pleased to fully endorse, for the position, *Alton R. Easton, Jr.* who has had experience, as a Clerk in that office for Several years. Should the Agency be divided, & a Branch left in St. Louis, Mr. Easton will be better adapted to the position than any one now suggested. I fully endorse his application because of his Capacity, his integrity, Sobriety & honesty." ALS, *ibid.* Related papers are *ibid.* No appointment followed.

To Grenville M. Dodge

New York City.
Dec. 13th 1881

MY DEAR GENERAL DODGE:

This will present Gen. Williams, formerly a high official in the U. S. Treasury, a gentleman who was selected by the Japanese Government to organize their Treasury & Mint system of accountability when they adopted Western Civilization. He wishes to ask a favor which I hope can be granted without embarassment.

Very Truly yours
U. S. GRANT

ALS, Sheldon S. Cohen, Chevy Chase, Md. On Dec. 13, 1881, David H. Strother, consul gen., Mexico City, wrote in his journal after visiting USG at his office on Broadway. "Several persons called, one Williams just from Japan and some others seeking influence for offices." Quoted in Cecil D. Eby, Jr., " 'Porte Crayon' Meets General Grant," *Journal of the Illinois State Historical Society*, LII, 2 (Spring, 1959), 245–46. See letter to Ellen Grant Sartoris, Aug. 10, 1879, note 1.

Endorsement

~~I can not ask about this petition per Major Renos request.~~[1] But I would suggest that the President examine for himself, or through his Sec. of War or Atty. Gen. the proceeding in the case of Major Reno and then take such action as, in his judgement, is due to the Major. It seems to me, in view of the recommendation of the Court which tried Maj. Reno; of the fact that he was found "~~n~~Not Guilty" of the most serious parts of the Specifications; and that the reviewing officers—the Dept. Commander, the Judge Advocate & the General of the Army,—concur in the opinion that the court should have found the accused "Not Guilty" of the charge under which alone he could have been dismissed from the Army, is a full justification for reviewing his case at this late date.

U. S. GRANT

NEW YORK CITY,
DEC. 15TH 1881.

AES, DNA, RG 94, ACP, R314 CB 1865. See John Upton Terrell and George Walton, *Faint the Trumpet Sounds: The Life and Trial of Major Reno* (New York, 1966), pp. 294–307.

1. This line bears the notation "Erased by me. U. S. GRANT." ANS, DNA, RG 94, ACP, R314 CB 1865.

To John F. Long

———

New York City
Dec. 16th 1881.

MY DEAR JUDGE LONG;

Your letter of the 13th is received. I do not think a trip to Washington would be of an special benefit towards securing the apt. you seek. But if you would like to go it would do no harm. You would find the President affable & agreeable. The only question I take it in regard to your appointment is as to whether the President wishes to make any removals. I do not think he would re-appoint St Gem. when his times expires. [I] understand the President intends [to] come on here next week to spend [a] portion of the vacation. I shall then talk to him in regard to your interests. I shall also spend [a] week or two in Washington in January, probably going there before the 10th. If you visit there it would probably be better to do so during my visit. I could telegraph you if I thought your visit necessary. I am much obliged to you for the trouble you have taken in looking after my Mo. property. I have some hope of selling the White Haven farm between this and Spring. Would be very glad to sell the whole.

With kind regards to all your family,

Very Truly yours
U. S. GRANT

ALS, MoSHi. See letter to John F. Long, April 15, 1882.

To Charles H. Tompkins

—————

New York, Dec 17 *1881*

COL. CHAS. H. TOMPKINS—
ASST. Q. M. GENERAL
CHICAGO ILL.
DEAR COLONEL:

Your letter of the 12th of December was duly received—The letter which you request a copy of is not in my possession, but if files are kept at the Executive Mansion, as there were while I was president, it probably will be found on file there. I will send to the President a request asking him to furnish you with a copy of it.

Truly Yours—
U. S. GRANT

LS, Randy Weinstein, Great Barrington, Mass. Born in 1830, the son of Daniel D. Tompkins (USMA 1820) and great-nephew of N. Y. governor and Vice President Daniel D. Tompkins, Charles H. Tompkins entered USMA in 1847, resigned in 1849, enlisted as private in 1856, and was appointed 2nd lt. in 1861. On Jan. 24, 1881, President Rutherford B. Hayes nominated Tompkins as col., asst. q. m. gen.

To Chester A. Arthur

—————

NewYork Dec. 22. 1881.

THE PRESIDENT. WASHINGTON D. C.
DEAR SIR:

At the request of Gen Fitz John Porter, I have recently reviewed his trial and the testimony furnished before the Schofield Court of Inquiry held in 1879, giving to the subject three full days of careful reading and consideration, and much thought in the intervening time. The reading of the whole of this record has thoroughly convinced me that for these nineteen years I have been doing a gallant and efficient soldier, a very great injustice in thought, and sometimes in speech. I feel it incumbent upon me now to do whatever lies in my power to remove from him and from his family the stain upon his good name. I feel this the more incumbent upon me than I should if I had been a corps commander only, or occupying any other command in the Army than the one which I did; but as General I had it possibly in my power to have obtained for him the hearing which he only got at a later day, and as President I certainly had the power to have ordered that hearing. In justification for my injustice to Genl. Porter I can only state that shortly after the war closed his defence was brought to my attention, but I read it in connection with a sketch of the field where his offences were said to have been committed, which I now see, since perfect maps have been made by the Engineers Department, of the whole field, were totally incorrect as showing the position of the two Armies. I also read it in connection with statements made on the other Side, against GenPorter, and I am afraid possibly with some little prejudice in the case—although GenPorter was a man whom I personally knew and liked, before; but I got the impression, with many others, that there was a half hearted support of Gen Pope in his campaigns, and that GenPorter, while possibly not more guilty than others, happened to be placed in a position where he could be made responsible for his indifference, and that the punishment was not a severe one for such an offence.[1] I am now convinced that he rendered faithful, efficient and intelligent service, and the fact that he was retained in command of a corps for months after his offences were said to have been committed, is in his favor.

What I would ask in GenPorter's behalf from you, is that if you can possibly give the time, that you give the subject the same study and thought that I have given it, and act then as your judgment may dictate. But, feeling that you will not have the time for such an investigation (for it would take Several days time) I would ask that the whole matter be laid before the Attorney General for his examination and opinion.[2]

Hoping that you will be able to do this much for an officer who has suffered, for nineteen years, a punishment that never should be inflicted upon any but the most guilty, I am,

Very Truly Yours,
U. S. GRANT

LS, DNA, RG 94, ACP P228 CB 1869. On Dec. 28, 188[1], Fitz John Porter, New York City, wrote to U.S. Senator John A. Logan of Ill. "On a suggestion from General Grant and a hope on my part that you will be gratified, I send you a copy of his letter to the President in my behalf. When in September I asked Gen. Grant to study my case, I asked an interview with you, with the hope that with explanations, I could satisfy you of the misunderstandings still existing in your mind from insufficient information of the facts—and I still hope I may be given the opportunity to attempt to convince you. I also send you a copy of a private letter to me from Gen'l Terry, who was at one time so prejudiced against me as to ask me on that ground to be relieved from the Schofield, Terry, Getty Advisory Board." Typescript (misdated), DLC-Fitz John Porter. Porter endorsed this letter. "Grant should not have asked me to do this—but I did" AE (undated), *ibid.* On Jan. 4, 1882, Porter wrote to USG. "Thinking you might like to see my letter to General Logan, I send you a copy herewith. . . ." ALS (press), *ibid.* See letters to Fitz John Porter, Dec. 23, 30, 1881.

On Jan. 2, 1882, a reporter questioned USG concerning his rumored support for Porter. "Yes, Sir, those statements are correct, with the exception that I have not said anything about Gen. Porter's restoration to the Army. I am anxious to see justice done to Gen. Porter's reputation as a soldier, but the question of his being restored to the Army is something that I have nothing to do with. . . . I had fully made up my mind that the judgment of the court-martial was a just one. Recently, however, at the request of Gen. Porter, I have read over all of the testimony in the case, and also the orders and reports of the Confederate officers who were at the second battle of Bull Run. As I progressed in my reading I became very much interested in the case and found that the facts were very different from what I have hitherto believed. I am of the opinion that had all of the testimony and documents now available been brought before the court-martial there would have been no verdict against Gen. Porter. The orders of the Confederate Generals show that the Confederate army was just where Porter said it was and not where the court-martial was led to believe it was. For 19 years I have believed that the finding of the court was a just one and warranted by the facts. But now I see that I am in error, and the fact that for 12 years, when I was General of the Army and President of the United States, I had it in my power to do Gen. Porter justice and did not, makes me feel under obligations to do all that I possibly can to remove the odium and disgrace from him now. . . . I finished reading the testimony about three weeks ago, and since then I have expressed my convictions unreservedly to some of my friends. I did not expect, however, that anything would be printed in the newspapers about the matter. I communicated my conclusions, after investigating the matter, to Gen. Logan, who, as a warm personal friend of mine, I desired to understand clearly my position. I think that Gen. Porter is entirely innocent of the charges made against him, and am thoroughly satisfied that in Gen. Pope's campaign he did his duty to the very best of his ability." Asked whether he had written to President Chester A. Arthur, USG replied. "I must decline to say anything on that subject. What I do or say will all be made public in due time and through the proper channels. I shall write out my views and append my signature to them, and it is quite likely that my statement will in the course of time find its way into print. I cannot tell you when that statement will be prepared." As to Porter's reinstatement to the army, USG said. "I think justice should be done him on the facts as they exist. He has been greatly wronged, and there is scarcely any reparation that can entirely compensate him for the many years of misrepresentation and humiliation. Of course, the first step to be taken, providing the Government can be brought to see the matter in the same light that I do, is to restore to Gen. Porter his good name and give him back his reputation as a soldier, so that neither himself nor his family need longer suffer humiliation and dishonor. Ultimately he may be restored to the Army, but that is a point that I do not care to talk about. . . . Sometimes it may become the duty of a soldier to disobey orders. For instance, a commanding General may send an order to a subordinate who is a long distance off. He may not be fully acquainted with the condition of affairs at the place where his subordinate is, or during the transmission of the order circumstances may have taken on an entirely different phase. Such things have been known to happen, and very often, therefore, it becomes the bounden duty of the subordinate to disobey orders. Being in possession of knowledge of which his superior is not, and, perhaps, cannot be, he should exercise his own judgment and do what may seem to him to be right." Asked whether Porter had disobeyed orders, USG said. "I did so understand for 19 years, but now I understand that he did not disobey orders. However, I am not desirous of saying anything about the merits of the case in detail until I do so over my own signature." *New York Times*, Jan. 3, 1882.

On Jan. 6, Henry M. Rawson, New York City, wrote to USG. "your generous letter in behalf of Genl Porter, will cause warm pulsations to beat in many a soldiers heart, that had grown cold towards you. It is an honor to you, even now, to own up and repair the wrong. Had you in the court of Inquiry in regard to the Battle of Five Forks, uttered such sentiments, in regard to another of your Corps Commanders [*Gouverneur K. Warren*], it woul have done you no harm I am satisfied, that a careful study on your part, of all the evidence taken by that court, with what you know of the circumstances on April first 1865 would lead you to say, yes: it was unjust. Sherridan, Brave Impulsive Sherridan, made a mistake. As the Old Commander of the Army, I thank you for daring to be yourself, and ask for justice for Fitz John Porter. yours in Fraternity, Charrity, and Loyalty," ALS, DLC-Fitz John Porter. See Testimony, [*Oct. 23, 1880*].

On Feb. 11, Col. Henry J. Hunt, Washington, D. C., wrote to USG. "I received yours of 23d Jany: as I was leaving Washington and could not then acknowledge its receipt. Indeed it hardly required an answer, as no exception could be taken to your views on 'retirement with higher rank' I write now however for another purpose. I want to tell you how much I was gratified by your letter in regard to Gen Fitz John Porter—It had always been a puzzle and regret to me that you took an adverse view of his case. I could hardly understand it. Still there were so many other fair-minded men who condemned him, that I supposed my *knowledge* of the case, outside of its presentation to the court made that presentation clearer to me than to those who had not that knowledge For I knew, of my own knowledge, that from the moment that Porter with whom I was then serving, ascertained at Williamsburg, that Lee had left Richmond, down to the moment that he left Fredericksburg and Burnside to join Pope, that he had strained every nerve—worked day and night, to get troops to Popes support.—We worked together in embarking troops at Old Point, Hampton and Newports News: then I went to Acquia, to receive, and Porter to Fredericksburg to organise and forward them; he having promised to let me know in time to take part in the active operations His very sudden departure from Fredericksburg without forewarning me prevented me, much to my regret from taking part in the campaign that followed: But I was with Burnside when these telegrams were received, discussed them with him, and thoroughly understood the circumstances. I have never had a doubt as to Porters perfect integrity in this, or I may add, in any other matter. Under these circumstances your letter greatly pleased me, and as one of your oldest friends I wish to tell you so.—However clear your duty when you found that you had been misled, and therefore although unwitting had omitted to do justice when in your power. Still it requires a great deal of magnanimity to publicly acknowledge it That you have done this so frankly will be regarded in the future as more creditable to you than would be another great victory in the field." ALS, Porter Collection, USMA.

On March 13, William H. Moore, who served under Porter in the 126th Pa., Firth, Neb., wrote to Jacob D. Cox castigating Porter. ". . . What Gen. Grants motives are in changing his mind can only be conjectured, whether it was from his defeat at 'Chicago' and trying to gain future strength from the democratic party—or from a sense of duty to his brother officer, . . ." ALS, Oberlin College, Oberlin, Ohio.

1. See *PUSG*, 16, 550–51; *ibid.*, 17, 327–40.

2. On March 15, Attorney Gen. Benjamin H. Brewster delivered an opinion to Arthur that in Porter's case "the President has no power to review the proceedings of the court-martial and annul its sentence. It follows from this view that the President can afford the applicant no relief through a revision of the sentence in his case. That sentence involved immediate dismissal from the Army and disability to hold office thereafter. . . . The latter may be remitted by the exercise of the pardoning power, but the former cannot in any way be affected thereby. . . . Upon the general question considered the conclusion arrived at is that it is not within the competency of the President to afford the applicant the relief he has asked for—that is to say, that it is not competent for the President to annul and set aside the finding and sentence of the court-martial and to nominate to the Senate for restoration to his former rank in the Army." *SMD*, 47-1-91, 23–25. On May 4, Arthur commuted the part of Porter's sentence that prohibited him from holding public office. See *New York Times*, April 16, May 7, 1882.

To James H. Work

———

New York City,
Dec. 22 1881.

J. H. WORK, ESQ.

This book was reviewed by me, chapter by chapter, as it was being prepared for the publishers. I was submitted for a similar review also to Generals Porter and Babcock, two of the Staff Collegues of the Author. In addition to this all those chapters treating of events in which Generals Sherman and Sheridan held detached commands were submitted to these officers.[1] The Author had access to the Government, and captured and purchased archives. He also read and consulted all that was published, on both sides, before and during the time he was writing this book with the view of getting the truth. So far as I am capable of judging this is a true history of the events of which it treats. The opinions expressed of men are the Author's own, and for which no one else is responsible.

Very Truly
U. S. GRANT

P. S. General Geo. H. Thomas was dead before the events in which he held detached command took place. Otherwise those chapters relating to events after March 1864 in which he took a leading part would have been submitted to him.

U. S. G.

ALS, InU. "Mr. Work had a copy of my Military History of Grant especially bound for his library, and asked General Grant to write something in it to attest his opinion of its merits; and this letter is the inscription it contains." *Badeau*, p. 588.

    1. On Jan. 4 and Feb. 21, 1881, Lt. Col. Michael V. Sheridan wrote to Adam Badeau, New York City. "I return today the proofs. The General has read them, and while he is not perhaps satisfied as to the fullness of detail which he conceives the campaign demands, he recognizes that it is a difficult matter in a general history to enter into particulars with regard to every movement, or battle. This has struck him as to Sailor's Creek, possibly from the strong effort that was made to deprive him of the credit of that victory and to be-little its character by connecting it with the general operations of the Army of the Potomac. The bearing of that victory upon the general result of the campaign was very great for it destroyed one fourth of Lee's army, and as it was quickly conceived and happily executed, he feels it would be well if it could be done, to establish from an authoritative source, what that battle was, and who won it. If this could be shown clearly it would be satisfactory to the General, and a valuable contribution to the truth of history." "Colonel Grant returned yesterday from Newyork, and informs me that you have felt some little hurt relative to the letter I wrote you by direction of General Sheridan on January 4th., transmitting to you the proof-sheets of the last chapter of your history of General Grant. The General desires me to say that he regrets very much you should feel so, for that letter was in no way intended to reflect on your work. In directing it to be written, he only wished to bring to your notice the fact that efforts had been made (by Gen. Meade and others) to deprive him of the credit of the battle of Sailor's Creek, . . . He feels that you have rendered him full credit where ever he is deserving of it, and he desires me to assure you that the letter referred to was written in the best spirit towards yourself and as before stated with no design to cast any reflection whatever on the manner in which you have recorded these events. . . ." LS (press) and L (press), DLC-Philip H. Sheridan. See *PUSG*, 14, 440.

To Fitz John Porter

———

New York, Dec. 23 *1881*

GEN F. J. PORTER—
NEWYORK
DEAR SIR:

    I send you by the bearer the letter to the President which I hope is satisfactory, and which I expect to follow up by such course as circumstances hereafter may dictate as necessary and proper. I sincerely hope that the day is not distant when you will receive the justice which I feel sure is due to you.

I will be pleased if you will send me a copy of the Proceedings of the Board, as published by the Senate.

Truly Yours

U. S. GRANT

LS, DLC-Fitz John Porter. On Dec. 23, 1881, Fitz John Porter, New York City, wrote to USG. "Not hearing from you I fear your letter may have miscarried or I misunderstood you—you expecting me to call again—and hence I send this inquiry—though I know your thoughts and time are engrossed with other important matters. In case you should, at any time, wish information or to see me, I shall be glad to meet any call sent to me here or at 44 W. 25th St.—my winter lodgings. Please tell me if you have a copy of the Proceedings of the Board as published by the Senate in four volumes—as, if not, I will take pleasure in getting a set for you." ALS (press), *ibid.* See letter to Chester A. Arthur, Dec. 22, 1881; *SED*, 46-1-37.

To Benjamin H. Brewster

HON. BENJAMIN H. BREWSTER, Atty.-Gen.:

MY DEAR SIR,—I received your very kind letter of a few days since, in which you attribute more to me than I deserve in the matter of the President's selection of his Attorney-General, but I sincerely congratulate the President on his selection, and I was delighted when I saw the nomination sent in. Senator Cameron spoke to me on the subject of your appointment to the place when he was last in the city, now two or three weeks since, and expressed his anxiety in the matter, and I agreed with him in the propriety of the appointment. This much the Senator may have stated to the President. But I am inclined to think the appointment is the President's own, only wanting to feel assured that it would not be disagreeable to his friends. With sincere congratulations and best wishes,

U. S. GRANT.

DECEMBER 24, 1881.

Eugene Coleman Savidge, *Life of Benjamin Harris Brewster, with Discourses and Addresses* (Philadelphia, 1891), p. 179. See *PUSG*, 19, 223–25.

To Fitz John Porter

———

DECEMBER 27, 1881.

Gen. F. J. PORTER:

DEAR GENERAL—I hardly know how to advise in regard to the best time to present your petition to the President. I presume the Senator (Sewell) could see the President at the hour named, one o'clock. But the chances are he would have no opportunity to converse with him privately. I am very desirous of talking to him myself about your matter, and my conclusions regarding the wrong you have been suffering, and called yesterday on him; but others were in the room all the time I was there.[1] I shall endeavor to get an opportunity to tell him about my letter to him on your matter before he returns.

You can judge as well as I can whether it is better to have Senator Sewell call here or not.

Very truly yours,
U. S. GRANT.

General Grant's Unpublished Correspondence in the Case of Gen. Fitz-John Porter (n. p., n. d.), pp. 10–11. Born in 1835 in Ireland, William J. Sewell served as an officer of N. J. vols. during the Civil War and gained prominence as a railroad executive. After entering the U.S. Senate as a Republican (1881), he pushed legislation to restore his constituent Fitz John Porter to the army. See *CR*, 47-1, 3689, 6184–85, 47-2, 173–74, 752–55, 774–79; *New York Times*, Dec. 8, 1882.

1. President Chester A. Arthur was then visiting his home in New York City. See *New York Tribune*, Dec. 27, 1881.

To Frederick T. Frelinghuysen

———

New York City
Dec. 28. 1881

HON. F. T. FRELINGHUYSEN
SEC. OF STATE
MY DEAR MR. SEC:

I desire to call your attention to a matter that you may know all about, and I hope you do. I am interested in it for the honor of our country and as an act of justice towards a neighboring and weaker republic.

You know a joint commission was agreed upon between the United States & Mexico to adjust claims of each against unlawful seizure and depredation by the other. It is known now that two of the claims—and large ones—against Mexico were supported wholly and entirely by falsehood and perjury. I believe you will find the proofs of this in your own department. Mexico is paying up the balance against her in annual installments. Up to this time these fraudulent claimants have received their quota from the installments notwithstanding the last administration reported to Congress the injustice of allowing these claims. In January an other installment will be paid by Mexico. What I would ask is, that before paying out the money so received you examine this case and take such action as your judgment may then dictate.

I regret that my engagements have been such during the holidays that I could not accept either of the two invitations to go to NewArk to meet you. But I congratulate the President all the same upon his selection of a sec. of state.

Very truly yours

U. S. Grant

Copy, Pennsylvania History and Museum Commission, Harrisburg, Pa. On Jan. 6, 1882, Secretary of State Frederick T. Frelinghuysen wrote to USG. "I have your letter relating to the claims against Mexico, established by the Commission between the United States & Mexico It seems hard that they should be paid when established by perjury, yet the State Dept: cannot review & must obey the decision Those claims may have been sold to innocent parties & may be considered as vested—The only relief I see is by a treaty between the U. S & Mexico to have the claims reconsidered and decided anew—It will give me great pleasure to aid in this remedy, as I am sorry to see Mexico defrauded and have successful fraud. I think the mode of relief I suggest would be effective & would be happy to aid any one who will attend to the matter & æffect the result suggested." LS, *ibid.* USG endorsed this letter. "Referred to Hon. J. A. J. Creswell, 1st Nat. Bank Building Washington D. C." AE (undated), *ibid.* Allegations of perjury in the claims of Benjamin Weil, for cotton seized near Nuevo Laredo in 1864, and the La Abra Silver Mining Co., for operations suspended in Durango, led to more than two decades of dispute in Congress and in the U.S. Supreme Court. See Stephen R. Niblo, "The United States-Mexican Claims Commission of 1868," *New Mexico Historical Review,* L, 2 (April, 1975), 101–21; George E. Paulsen, "Fraud, Honor, and Trade: The United States-Mexico Dispute over the Claim of La Abra Company, 1875–1902," *Pacific Historical Review,* LII, 2 (May, 1983), 175–90.

To Charles J. Folger

———

New York City,
Dec. 28th 1881.

Hon. C. J. Folger;
Sec. of the Treas.
Dear Sir:

On the "lapse roll" in the Treasury Dept is the name of Mrs.
L. M. Porter. She has not been long in the Dept. She is a most
accomplished lady, the daughter of Ex-Governor & Ex-Senator
Morehead, of Ky. and the widow of an officer of my old regiment,
the 4th U. S. Infantry, and a special friend and companion during,
before and after, the Mexican War, and up to his death. Mrs. Porter
was conspicuous for her loyalty during the war as she is now for
her ability. I hope you may be able to retain her for it is her only
support.

Very Truly yours
U. S. Grant

ALS, DNA, RG 56, Applications. See Endorsement, [*Aug. 15, 1881*]; letter to Charles J.
Folger, June 2, 1882.

To John A. Logan

———

New York City, December 30, 1881.

My Dear General—I have your letter of yesterday. It is true
that I have re-examined the proceedings of the court marshal and
court of inquiry of Fitz-John Porter's case, and believe sincerely
that I have done him an injustice, and have so written to the President. When I gave General Porter the letter I requested him to
send you a copy. If he has not done so he will, or I will. That letter will explain all that I would otherwise write you on this subject. I reluctantly came to the conclusions I did, but was convinced

beyond all preconceived notions, and felt it due to an accused man to say so.

Very truly yours,

U. S. GRANT.

Gen. J. A. LOGAN, U. S. Senate.

General Grant's Unpublished Correspondence in the Case of Gen. Fitz-John Porter (n. p., n. d.), p. 11. USG endorsed this letter to Fitz John Porter. "Please read enclosed letter and then have it dropped in the mail." *Ibid.* U. S. Senator John A. Logan of Ill. opposed restoring Porter to the army. See *CR*, 46-2, 536–37, 1377–79, 1429–31; *ibid.*, Appendix, 47–92; James Pickett Jones, *John A. Logan: Stalwart Republican from Illinois* (Tallahassee, 1982), pp. 122–26, 141–42; letter to Chester A. Arthur, Dec. 22, 1881.

To Frederick W. Swift

———

90 BROADWAY, NEW YORK CITY.

[Dec., 1881]

My Dear Gen. Swift:

Your letter of the 28th ultimo, kindly inviting me to attend the next meeting of the Society of the Army of the Potomac, to be held in Detroit on the 7th and 8th of June next, came duly to hand. It has been my desire for a long time to revisit where I resided for two years so pleasantly and renew partially an acquaintance which was extensive there thirty years ago. I accept the invitation with pleasure, and, if in the country at the time, and so situated as to be able to get away, will spend at least the two days of the reunion with my comrades of the Army of the Potomac.

Very truly yours,

U. S. GRANT.

Detroit Free Press, Feb. 7, 1882. USG later wrote: "I accept with great pleasure; probably will reach the city on the 13th and remain until the last of the week, and Mrs. Grant with me. I retain very pleasant recollections of my two years' residence in Detroit, and of the many pleasant acquaintances I had formed at the time, and look forward with agreeable anticipations to my third visit (only the third) since 1851." *New York Times*, May 13, 1882. See Speech, [*June 15, 1882*]. Born in Conn., Frederick W. Swift moved to Detroit in 1847, entered business, and enlisted as capt., 17th Mich., rising to col. On Sept. 18, 1867, Richard A. Watts, former capt., 17th Mich., Adrian, wrote to USG, secretary of war, *ad interim.* "Enclosed please find recommendations of General's Hartranft and Burnside,—late Maj. Genl's United States Volunteers, for the promotion of Col. Swift, to the rank of Brevet. Brig. Genl. . . ." ALS, DNA, RG 94, ACP, B1359 CB 1867. On Dec. 10, Swift, postmaster, Detroit, wrote to USG accepting the bvt. promotion. ALS, *ibid.*, S1575 CB 1867. On April 13, 1871, USG nominated Swift to continue as postmaster.

To Horace Porter

[*1881–1882*]

GEN.

Can you, without inconvenience, obtain for me a pass for my nephew, Harry Grant, from here to Kansas City. I am sending him to New Mexico where I have obtained a position for him. I ask it because the two boys have to support their mother and three others—beside themselves—except what Buck & I help them, and ~~their~~ the passage is quite an item to them. I will get a ticket from Kansas City to where he is going over the Atchison & Topeka.

yours
U. S. G.

AL, Horace Porter Mende, Zurich, Switzerland. USG's brother Orvil L. Grant died Aug. 4, 1881, at Elizabeth, N. J., leaving his wife, Mary M., and four children, Harry L., Ulysses S. (known as Simpson), Jesse R., and Virginia E. Grant. Harry died Nov. 14, 1882, at Elizabeth. Simpson clerked at the U.S. Subtreasury in New York City as of July 1, 1881.

Endorsement

Does Governor Fish remember any thing of this case. I remember something of a Mr. Jacobs wanting a Consulat, or some apt. but do not call to mind the Circumstances he relates.

U. S. GRANT

JAN. 3D 1882.

AES, Nellie C. Rothwell, La Jolla, Calif. Written on a letter of Dec. 17, 1881, from Enoch Jacobs, Mount Airy, Ohio, to USG. "Excuse me for calling your attention to an old business matter. You will recollct, that in 1872, at your instance, and by the Special

request of Secretary Fish, I furnished a large amount of material from manuscript prepared for the press, for the use of the State Department—in the case of 'Senor Angulo
Guridi' an American Citizen restrained of his liberty in Santo Domingo. It was understood when I laid the case of Sen Guridi before you (Senator Wade being present) that
the manuscript thus used should be withheld from the press—and you promised that
it should be paid for. At a subsequent call you gave me an order on on Mr Secretary
Fish for $550.00—if I mistake not—which was presented, *but never paid*, because the
Secretary said there was 'no monies in his hands applicable for such purpose'. I could
have disposed of this manuscript long since, at full rates, and can do so now: But having
disposed of it, as I supposed, I felt under obligations to make no allusion to the matter
publicly. I can not now get pay for it from the Department, without your help. It should
be paid with interest—or the manuscript returned to me—thus relieving me from the
implied obligation of State secrecy. Believe that I have written this with the kindest
feelings. In all I have written of your public life or private acts, no reflection has been
made upon your integrity. Poor Guridi! I fear he was murdered by our neglect: But I
suppose you know the result of the effort made to save him." ALS, *ibid.* On Jan. 4, 1882,
Hamilton Fish, New York City, wrote to USG. "I have a very distinct recollection of
Mr Enoch Jacobs, as an applicant for a Consulate—he was appointed in January 1873
to Montevideo. But I have not the faintest recollection of any thing of the nature stated
in his note. I do not think it possible that so unusual, a thing as an order from the
President ~~for~~ on the Secretary of State, for the payment of money could have occurred
without leaving a permanent recollection—and I have no recollection of any papers
(other than his application for an appointment) or of any important information communicated to the State Department by Mr Jacobs. I have an indistinct impression that
after his arrival at Montevideo he complained of the inadequacy of the salary, and a like
indistinct impression that complaints were made of him, the precise nature of which I
do not recall—I might possibly find some memoranda in relation to this latter point, if
you think the investigation important—He ceased to be Consul at Montevideo, during
your Presidency.... P S I return Jacobs letter herewith" ALS, *ibid.* Born in 1809 in Vt.,
Jacobs settled in Ohio, edited an early Adventist newspaper, became partner in an iron
works, founded a school, and served as a recruiter and correspondent with the 12th Ky.
See Ronald L. Numbers and Jonathan M. Butler, eds., *The Disappointed: Millerism and
Millenarianism in the Nineteenth Century* (Bloomington, Ind., 1987), pp. 173–74, 181–83.

On June 27, 1871, U.S. Senator Oliver P. Morton of Ind., Indianapolis, had written
to USG. "I take great pleasure in reccommending to you E. Jacobs, Esq, who accompanied the Commissioners to San Domingo as a correspondent for the Cin *Coml* and whose
letters were characterized by unusual fairness and ability—He has lectured upon Domi-
nica since his return and is a staunch friend of annexation—He desires the appointment
of U. S. Minister at Port au Prince, and I earnestly recommend him for the position and
am confidant were he there he could be of great advantage to the country in its future
negotiations etc I trust you will find it consistent to give him the appointment—" ALS,
DNA, RG 59, Letters of Application and Recommendation. On July 5, Benjamin F.
Wade, Jefferson, Ohio, wrote to USG on the same subject. LS, *ibid.* Related papers are
ibid. On April 29, 1872, Jacobs, Waynesville, Ohio, wrote to USG. "I went to Santo Domingo in company with Dr Ames in Dec. last, and was a close observer of his public
acts, and private life. It has been an unpleasant duty for me to say, that he is notoriously
unfit for the position he occupies. His bad habits—opium eating & rum drinking—keeps
him so stupefied that he seems to me incapable of the exercise of sound judgement—and
is only moved by passion and prejudice. He has no influence with the Government—in

fact deserves none,—calls President Baez 'a damn'd nigger' behing his back, and plays the hypocrite to his face. Baez knows him thoroughly, and suffers insults to be put upon him which would not be borne by any other foreign representative. I regret not having seen you on my way home, as I wished to say many things that I can not put in writing. As you were so kind as to offer me the position of Commercial Agent at Santo Domingo, in case Ames should resign, I ~~could~~ can not allow my name to be used in such connection, after stating what I have as a matter of duty: though I hope to be remembered for some more lucrative position in the near-future of Santo Domingo. The instruments loaned me by Mr Sec'y Robeson, I left with my son at Samana, with suggestions that he keep a daily record of the Barometrical & Thermometrical changes, on land, during the Summer. My son is anxious to have charge of the American flag the next time it is raised on coal island—in connection with the position of Naval Storekeeper, in case Mr Price leaves. *Guridi.* The case of Alejandro Angulo Guridi, claiming to be a citizen of the United States, and now under the protection of Cambiazo, the Italian Consul in Santo Domingo,—I have carefully considered as to the law of the case, and am thoroughly satisfied that he is entitled to protection by the United States. The evidence, as it developed, was incorporated in my correspondence, and runs through some ten or twelve very lengthy letters, which have been withheld from the public by the 'N. Y. Tribune' and 'Cincinnati Commercial,' for the reason, let us charitably suppose, that truth would not suit their purpose just at this time. Now if I copy all this evidence in Guridi's case, and send it to the Secretary of State, while we have a commercial agent at Santo Domingo I can not hope that my judgement will triumph over constituted authority When Dr Ames asked for Guridi's pasports, a year and a half ago, Baez told him that Guridi had forfeited his American Nationality, by holding office under Santana. Guridi was given no oportunity to make a defence, and has been left in prison ever since. At this point I commenced the investigation, without fee or reward, or prospect of any, for Guridi, though a shrewd and very able lawyer, is poor. . . . He first came to the States in 1850, and rec'd his final papers from the Supreme Court in New York in 1855. He was then engaged in the practice of Law—afterwards removed to Charleston S. C where he married an American lady. He then went to Venzuela under an engagement to write for *La Republica* a weekly paper—also subsequently filled a similar engagement at Curacoa—made several visits to the island of S. D. but studiously and carefully avoided any step calculated to compromise his American Nationality. Baez and his ministers admit that Guridi is the smartest and best educated man on the Island, and that 'should he get away he might do a great deal of harm.' . . . It seems to me a matter of the utmost importance, that naturalized citizens, which comprise so large an element in our population, should have their rights clearly defined. The only case of American protection I can find in Santo Domingo, is that of Hatch who probably deserved to be shot. He owes his life to the humane offices of Gen'l Babcock." ALS, *ibid.*, Miscellaneous Letters. On Dec. 17, USG nominated Jacobs as consul, Montevideo. See *PUSG*, 21, 370.

On Feb. 14, 1877, Jacobs, Mount Airy, wrote to USG. "The Hon. William Hunter, Second Assistant Secretary of State, in his despatch No. 77, of Jan. 10th 1876, said to me—'The President is of the opinion that the public service would be promoted by a change in the Consulate at Montevideo'. This inteligence surprised me, and I soon after resigned. I had faithfully performed the duties of my office, to the satisfaction of nine out of ten, of all the parties with whom I had official dealings: But I had gained the ill will of corrupt parties among the ~~other ten~~ ballance, to whose schemes of fraud, I refused official sanction. . . . You will recollect the note you gave me in 1873, requesting Mr Fish to pay me for about $600. worth of correspondence from San Domingo, for the N. Y. Tribune, which he had solicited of me by letter, and made use of in the case of Alexander Guridi, an American citizen, deprived of his liberty by President Baez for nearly two years; and how Mr Fish turned me away with the reply—'no funds for such purposes,' thus depriving me of the large share of my winters work in 1872, & 3. You will also recollect my reporting to you direct, the delivery of your Autograph letter to President Ellauri, of Uruguay, with attendant ceremonies and a copy of my speech on the occasion,—and the indignation of the Secretary for such 'irregularity':—He had denied my right to perform any duty pertaining to the Legation, in the absence of the Minister, and had no funds to pay for such service:—Yet those services were forced upon me by the Uruguay authorities for nearly a year. When a bill had passed the House of Representatives, allowing the compensation in part for such service, it failed to pass the Senate. Pecuniarily, I have not profited by my connection with the consulate at Montevideo; but I have gained experience which I think valuable in the interests of American Commerce. Justice to myself, and the great respect I have ever cherished for our worthy President, has induced these brief hints, before the expiration of your official term." ALS, DNA, RG 59, Miscellaneous Letters.

To J. Russell Jones

New York City,
Jan.y 11th 1882

Dear Jones:

I have answered your letter of the 11th inst. accepting the conditions named therein: that is I will sell at $1200 00 pr acre, this offer holding good until Feb.y 1st, receiving one third cash, balance one & two years, with six pr. ct. in deferred payments.

Tell Doan[1] & Corwith to let me know when they come to the City and I will try to have them come to my house. There is a little balance due me which I would like to collect.

yours
U. S. Grant

ALS, Edward W. Stack, Sea Cliff, N. J. See *PUSG*, 23, 244–45; *ibid.*, 25, 265.
On Dec. 13, 1882, USG wrote to J. Russell Jones. "I hear there is a 'boom' now in Chicago property. Do you think you could get a friend of yours to take mine of my hands? and at what price? I would be glad to sell." ALS, ICU.

1. Born in 1833 in Conn., John W. Doane settled in Chicago and prospered as a coffee and tea importer, bank president, and Pullman Palace Car Co. director. On visits to New York City he lived at the Windsor Hotel, part of a colony of Chicago businessmen that included Nathan and Henry Corwith. See *New York Times*, Jan. 7, 1884, March 24, 1901.

To Charles W. Russell

————

New York, Jany 12 *1882*

Mr C. W. Russell
311 Indiana Ave Washington D. C.
Dear Sir,

I have anticipated your request con[*cerning — —*] letter without date, just received. [I have recommended Col.] Mosby, in a letter to [the President for the position] of ConsulGeneral in [China, but at the same ti]me stated to the Presi[dent verbally that I thou]ght Col Mosby would [be much better pleased] with a position at home, [and suggested two posit]ions—one of them Asst [Attorney General, and the] other District Attorney of [Virginia. I have no p]romise from the President as to [what he will] do, but presume that he will at least [be] advanced from his present position

Truly Yours.

U. S. Grant

LS (partial facsimile), Superior Auction Galleries, May 21, 1994, no. 154. Born in 1856 in Va., Charles W. Russell was an asst. to the Librarian of Congress and brother-in-law of John S. Mosby. On May 23, 1882, Russell wrote to President Chester A. Arthur. ". . . Some months ago, General Grant wrote me that he had recommended Consul Mosby for one of several positions, including that of the Shanghai consulate and that of Assistant Attorney General. I so informed Colonel Mosby, & he now writes that I must call on you & say that he doesn't want Shanghai, since the slight increase of salary would be more than off-set by the increase of expenses. If he is to stay in the East he prefers to stay in Hong-Kong, but he is anxious to return to this country, unless he could be assigned to some first-class post in Europe. I shall not be so bold as to suggest any thing as proper to be done, but, merely reminding you of the suggestions of General Grant, . . ." ALS, DNA, RG 59, Applications and Recommendations, Hayes-Arthur. Mosby continued as consul, Hong Kong. See letter to Chester A. Arthur, Dec. 5, 1881.

To James B. Eads

————

New York, Jan. 13, 1882.

Captain J. B. Eads, Washington, D. C.:—

Dear Captain—Until I met you in the city of Mexico and had conversations with you there, and subsequently, on the subject of your interoceanic ship railroad and read some of your pamphlets upon the subject, I had thought that I saw insurmountable obstacles in the way of the success of your enterprise. You so far removed my doubts about the practicability of carrying ships with cargoes securely by rail, that, while I was not sanguine that it would prove a success, I yet was not prepared to say that it might not be.

I am of that opinion still, but at the same time you gave me to understand that no guarantee was to be asked from the government until a section of ten miles of the railroad was built, and had carried a vessel of the capacity of 2,000 tons burden to the terminus at the rate of ten miles an hour and returned at the same rate of speed, and had landed the vessel safely in water, when the government was to guarantee three per cent interest upon $5,000,000. Upon the completion of a second ten miles of the railroad a vessel of 2,500 tons burden, with her cargo, was to be transported to the terminus at the rate of ten miles an hour, and again returned to the water at like speed, without injury, when a second instalment of $5,000,000 of bonds were to be guaranteed for a like interest and on the same conditions. At the completion of each section for ten miles the like test was to be applied with vessels, increasing 500 tons with each section, until one with her cargo of 4,000 tons should be transported to the terminus of the road and into the water; and on completion and the success of each section of ten miles the like interest on $5,000,000 of bonds were to be guaranteed by the government until the whole amount should reach $50,000,000.

I have felt a very great interest in the matter of communication between the Atlantic and Pacific oceans somewhere in North America, and which should be mainly under the control of the United States government and United States capital. To that end, with the valuable aid of Admiral Ammen, I had succeeded in having all of the well known lines of low level between the United States of Colombia in South America and Tehuantepec surveyed, and had submitted the result of the surveys to a board of engineers, which I convened. That board, on an examination of these various reports, reported that no other route was practicable for a ship canal as compared with the Nicaragua route. From that time on I became interested in seeing that work undertaken by an American company, not caring who it was done by so that it was done, but willing to lend my name to the enterprise because there is no problem whatever as to the practicability of the route and no difficulty in doing the work if the capital can be secured for it.

But your proposed work accomplishing the object which I had in view, and seeming to have followers who might be willing to furnish the necessary capital, I was induced on your statements to say to Admiral Ammen and to Captain Phelps that with money appropriated for the De Lesseps canal, by the way of Panama, and the following you had for your road, it was idle for us to try to enlist capital in a third enterprise of this kind, and as you asked nothing from the government more than a guarantee that your road earned three per cent upon fifty millions of capitol, if it could carry vessels of 4,000 tons burden successfully from ocean to ocean and without injury to the ships, I thought the government was running no risk whatever, and advised that we should let the matter drop until either the two enterprises under construction and in contemplation were exploded or proved a success. If yours should prove a success the Nicaragua Canal would not be wanted at all, at least not in the near future.

But I now have your bill—No. 430—before me, and see that its provisions are so entirely at variance from what I had been led to suppose you intended to ask that I feel it my duty to notify you that I shall oppose it in its present form with all my ability. I do this because I feel that I have been deceived as to what you intended to ask, and also believe that if your present bill passes the government will be made responsible for six per cent interest upon a large bonded indebtedness even if your enterprise should prove a total failure.

In the first instance the speed with which vessels were to be safely transported is changed by this bill from ten miles to six miles an hour; the rate of interest upon the bonds guaranteed is changed from three per cent per annum to three per cent semi-annually; the vessels transported of the named tonnage are to be vessels with their cargoes weighing the amount of what I supposed was to be the tonnage of the vessels. I do not think the change of ten miles to six per hour, or even to four, a serious objection; but the change in the class of vessels transported and in the rate of interest asked are very serious changes.

Then, also, in your bill you provide what I would approve of for using rivers and canals as far as it was practicable to do so, and to shorten the line of railroad simply to what would be necessary to get over the elevation dividing the two oceans. An examination of the map shows that by deepening the mouth of the Coatzacoalcos River six feet you have a navigable river for all the vessels you propose to carry for thirty miles. From thence to the foothills, through a flat and marshy country where the amount of excavation will be a minimum, you will have a still greater distance where a canal can be cheaply constructed. In like manner on the Pacific side, with a little deepening at the mouth of a slough or small lagoon, connecting with the Pacific, and by deepening between that and another lagoon inland, and a canal through a flat and low country to the foothills, in all a distance of twenty to thirty miles or more, ships of the classes you propose to carry can easily be transported. All this leaves the extent of ship rai[l]road to be built probably less than one-fourth of the entire distance across from the Gulf of Mexico to the Pacific Ocean.

Your bill provides that the same subsidy shall be guaranteed for water communication that is allowed to the railroads, and the same rate of speed—viz., six miles an hour—is not mandatory in the canal.

This would give you, by the terms of this bill, a guarantee of $5,000,000 for the first ten miles, which would be river navigation from the Gulf of Mexico, and a like sum for the first ten miles from the Pacific coast, likewise of water navigation, nearly completed by nature.

The balance of the route is to be divided up into twenty sections of equal length. Whenever any one of them is completed on either side bonds to the extent of $2,000,000 are to be guaranteed for each section so completed.

All this would insure to you or to the company that you represent a guarantee of from thirty to forty millions before it would be necessary to enter upon that portion of the work which is in any degree problematical—viz., the ship railroad. The government is bound to provide for this six per cent interest, whether the railway and canal earn it or not, for fifteen years after the completion of the road.

Now it looks to me very much as if that portion of the work about which there can be no difficulty might be completed, these thirty to forty millions of guaranteed bonds secured and the work stop entirely, and as it never would be completed, there would be a six per cent irredeemable bond for which the government would be responsible for the interest fastened upon it.

Now, I know, captain, that you are enthusiastic and have full faith in the feasibility of the work you propose. I am satisfied, further, that if the matter was left entirely to you you not only would spend every dollar that you could realize out of the bonds in proving the feasibility of your plans of transporting ships, but you would spend all the private means that you could in anyway raise, by hypothecating the second mortgage bond, or even your private estate.

But you must recollect that this is a company, will have directors, will be controlled by the capital that is put in it, and even if there was a possibility of the success of your enterprise by the expenditure of a large sum of money, the stock of this company might be held by men who would be satisfied with the thirty to forty millions they had already received and would oppose any further progress of the work or expenditure of the means, because, at the expiration of fifteen years after the completion of the work the government would cease to be responsible for either the principal or interest of these bonds.

I have felt it my duty to state these objections to you, because you had reason to understand that, while I might do nothing to favor your project (because I was not entirely satisfied with its feasibility), I would not antagonize or oppose it. Now that I have concluded that I must oppose it, you should know it first.

I was somewhat surprised when I saw Senate bill No. 550, to incorporate the Maritime Canal Company of Nicaragua, was introduced. I supposed what I had said to Admiral Ammen and Captain Phelps would probably prevent anything being done in the way of inaugurating that company until, as I suggested before in this letter, the other enterprises for interoceanic ship communication had proved a failure, and my first impulse was to write to Senator Miller, stating frankly what I had said to these gentlemen, and what my ideas were on the subject; but fortunately I was so pressed for time for a few days after the bill was introduced that I could not take the matter up, and afterward forgot it, until I saw your bill, of which I am now speaking, and I confess to you I was very glad that I had not written the letter which I had contemplated writing, and I shall take the liberty of furnishing Senator Miller a copy of this letter.

Assuring you that I have no pride in the establishing of any particular line or route for the transportation of vessels between the two oceans, but only to see the work done, and do not care by whom it is done provided it is under American auspices, and that I should wish your enterprise the same success that I would if my own name was connected with it if inaugurated on terms that were not going to make the government responsible for any failure, I am very truly, yours,

U. S. GRANT.

New York Herald, March 5, 1886. On Jan. 21, 1882, James B. Eads, Washington, D. C., wrote to USG. "I have the honor to acknowledge receipt of your letter of January 13th, in which you inform me that you feel it your duty to oppose the Ship Railway Bill. . . . Appreciating the deep interest which you had always taken in the advance of American Commerce, and remembering your great anxiety, both in public and private life, to bring about a solution of the Isthmian problem, I felt very desirous that you should fully understand my project, what I proposed to do, and what aid from the Government I regarded as necessary. Hence it was that when I met you in Mexico, and afterwards on our journey home, I discussed the whole matter freely with you. I need hardly say that when I succeeded in removing your doubts as to the practicability of the work I was greatly gratified. You point out in your letter certain objections to the bill recently introduced before Congress which, you say, have decided you to oppose its passage. You will no doubt remember that when returning home on the steamer, I handed you a copy of the bill reported by the Interoceanic Committee to the last Congress. You read the bill and I had no reason to suppose that you failed to fully understand it. The Government guarantee therein provided for, was a three per centum semi-annual guarantee, not of interest upon bonds, but of stock dividends. There were also provisions as to a canal, and payments for the same as in the case of the Railway. You remarked at the time that you did not think I would have much difficulty in passing the bill as it left no risk on the part of the Government in relation to the practicability of the railway. I now enclose you a copy of the bill I then showed you, and am satisfied that when you compare it with the bill more recently introduced, you will find that they substantially agree. If there be any difference I think that the latter bill is, in some respects, even more favorable to the Government. As I understand it you have two serious objections to the bill, and they are as follows, viz: 1st, That the Company might never complete the work, and in this case, under its guarantee, the Government would be required to pay for an indefinite period. 2d, The liability of the Government might be made to attach to a large amount, for the construction of a canal merely, and without the practicability of a Ship Railway ever having been demonstrated. I am unwilling to admit that the bill can be fairly made to bear this construction, but will not stop to argue the point, because I freely concede that the existence of the *slightest* doubt upon the subject renders a proper amendment imperative. I certainly never intended that any such construction should be placed upon the bill and shall see that the language is so changed as to make this construction impossible. I am willing that positive provisions shall be put into the bill to the effect that under no circumstances shall the Government pay upon its guarantee for a longer period than twenty years from and after the date of the testing of the first ten miles of railway and that no portion of the guarantee shall apply to any canal until the practicability of the project shall have been demonstrated by the successful transportation of a loaded vessel over ten miles of the railway. I never contemplated the construction of a canal over any considerable distance of the route, and am very sure that under no circumstances will all portions of the canal, taken together, (if indeed any canal at all be constructed,) equal a distance of ten miles. The bill certainly does not provide that the improvement of the river shall entitle the Company to the benefit of any part of the guarantee. I am satisfied that no such construction could be sustained for a moment, and yet I am entirely willing that a provision shall be incorporated into the bill concerning the matter in express language. There are other minor matters mentioned in your letter, but as you have informed me verbally that you do not regard them as important, I will not weary you by referring to them. Will you kindly advise me, by early mail, whether, if the bill be amended in accordance with the suggestions herein contained, you will not be willing to withdraw all opposition to it? I feel satisfied that I shall build the Ship Railway, and I know that I can, and will, make it a complete success. Believe me, I would be unwilling to stake my reputation upon a doubtful experiment, or identify the closing years of my life with a failure. I am deeply anxious that when the Railway is in successful operation you shall be classed among its earliest and strongest friends. Soliciting an early reply, . . ." E. L. Corthell, *An Exposition of the Errors and Fallacies in Rear-Admiral Ammen's Pamphlet Entitled "The Certainty of the Nicaragua Canal Contrasted with the Uncertainties of the Eads Ship Railway"* (Washington, D. C., 1886), pp. 47–49. Ellipsis in original. See following letter.

To Jesse Root Grant, Jr.

New York City
Jan.y 13th 1882

DEAR JESSE;

I have seen Capt. Eads Bill for his Ship railway. It is not atall what he told me, and I shall feel compelled to oppose it, in its

prsent form, with all my might. You should withdraw from all connection with it. It can not pass Congress, and if it should I would
much prefer seeing you lose all you have to making a profit out of
such a swindle as I regard this. He has changed nearly all he professed to me to ask for. He said he asked only a guarantee of 3 pr.
ct. upon $50.000.000. of bonds, for twenty (may have said longer)
years, and none of it until ten miles of road was completed, and a
ship of certain tonage, with cargo carried at a ten mile speed over
it, and returned to the water safe and sound. Then $5.000.000. was
to be guaranteed. When ten additional miles should be completed
and a vessel of larger tonnage, with her cargo, carried over at the
same rate of speed, then another $5.000.000 of bonds should be
guaranteed. In like manner, with the completion of every section of
ten miles of road, carrying at like speed, safely, vessels and cargoes
of constantly increasing tonage an additional $5.000.000 was to be
given, until the whole amount should reach $50.000.000. His bill
now provides for a river, canal & rail-road transportation of ship,
at six miles an hour, vessels and cargoes to ~~whigh~~ weigh what was
given as tonage before, and the guarantee to be three pr. ct. Semi
annually The guarantee is to be from ocean to ocean, $5.000.000
for the first ten miles from either side the balance of the distance to
be divided into twenty equal divisions and $2,000.000 bonds guar-
anteed for the completion of each of these sections. Now there is
thirty miles of river, navigable for all the classes of vessels he proposes to transport, at the Easter end. There is a long distance of
low marshy lands, easily canaled, before he comes to the foot hills.
At the Western end there are Lagoons and low lands, easily canaled for say twenty or more miles. By this bill, if it becomes a law,
he will secure $30.000.000 of bonds before he enters atall upon
the only problem there is in his enterprize. The work will not cost
$10.000.000 to this point.

Give it up by all means.

Yours Affectionat[ely]
U. S. GRANT

ALS, Chapman Grant, Escondido, Calif. See previous letter; John Y. Simon, "Ulysses
S. Grant and the Ship Railway," *ICarbS*, IV, 1 (Spring-Summer, 1978), 3–9.

On Jan. 23, 1882, Jesse Root Grant, Jr., New York City, telegraphed and wrote to James B. Eads. "Letter received. Satisfactory. Sent copy to Miller." "I showed your letter to father, and he expresses himself as satisfied with the letter, and I have just wired you to that effect. He has written to Miller explaining the error he made." E. L. Corthell, *An Exposition of the Errors and Fallacies in Rear-Admiral Ammen's Pamphlet Entitled "The Certainty of the Nicaragua Canal Contrasted with the Uncertainties of the Eads Ship Railway"* (Washington, D. C., 1886), p. 49. "Two or three weeks after this correspondence," Eads wrote to Jesse Grant. "The sub-committee (five members of the committee of commerce of the Senate) have agreed to report unanimously in favor of the Ship Railway bill, and the full committee have authorized the printing of their report before final action is taken on it. . . . In the meantime, Ammen is doing all he can to defeat us. You will see by the enclosed slip, cut from the latest New Orleans newspaper, that U. S. Grant, Sr., and U. S. Grant, Jr., still constitute the Alpha and Omega of his forces, and are to share the honor of opposing the Ship Railway bill so long as he can keep them thus prominently before Congress and the country. Of course, I regret this for several reasons: 1st. Because I do not like to see the honored name of General Grant so prominently identified with a project which will inevitably prove a failure, even should Congress fail to pass my bill. 2d. Instead of occupying the impregnable position of a patriotic promoter of an isthmian highway for ships, whose great influence, official power, and high position were directed to the solution of the question, it places him in the attitude of a partisan, opposing a project for solving the problem which is supported by an overwhelming mass of expert testimony, and which avails of a location not only admitted by every one to be much superior to Nicaragua, but in a territory in which he has already important individual interests, whose inhabitants are his friends, and who are earnestly desiring to see the consummation of the enterprise which he seems to be opposing. 3d. I regret it because it gives color to the numberless misstatements that have been published throughout the country, to the effect that I had received a letter from General Grant upbraiding me with having deceived him as to the terms of my proposition, in consequence of which he had withdrawn from the directory of my company [in which he was never interested.] No less than three different articles to this effect were shown me yesterday, cut from recent newspapers. 4th. I regret it, because having assured me in his last letter that he would throw no obstacle in the way of my measure, this use of his name by Admiral Ammen keeps in its way the most serious obstacle which it has to encounter, and furnishes to Ammen the only possible means with which he can hope to defeat my bill. He totally disregards the advice of your father and is determined to use his name as long as he will permit it. As the Ship Railway becomes more and more popular, some of the blackmailers become more and more desperate and vicious. I send you a slip referring to the republication of a scandalous letter published two or three years ago; to-day the same paper republishes the libellous statement published by a New York paper against me about three years ago, and which it afterwards retracted." *Ibid.* (ellipsis, brackets in original), p. 50. See letter to John F. Miller, Feb. 8, 1882; *New York Herald*, Jan. 18, 26, Feb. 2, 6, 1882.

On [*March*] 13, [Elizabeth Chapman Grant] wrote to [Nellie Chapman Mason], Alameda, Calif. "Dined at Mrs G's last night & General was perfectly lovely—I told him of a dream I had where I told him I was so delighted that we were in the Eads scheme & he was in the Nicaraguan—It was so nice to be in both & he scolded me & made me cry & said he would see to it that our bill didn't pass Well he laughed & said 'You know I havn't much faith in your bill' & I told him the general opinion was that it would pass & he said he believed it would pass but didn't believe it—the road—would be built for Capt Eads was always very extravagant—all of his schemes had *been very expensive*—One of the slips enclosed in Capt Eads letter which I forwarded to you explained that all fully & I will show it to Gen. G. when you return it—. . . There was no truth in the report—which probably has gone the rounds of the world—about Gen. G's note being protested nor of his failure—he is as well off as ever—so is Mrs G—J. R. Young is soon to be married to Miss Coleman of Washtn cousin to the Jewell's" AL (date supplied from envelope), USGA.

To Timothy O. Howe

New York City,
Jan.y 13th 1882,

HON. T. O. HOWE;
POSTMASTER GENERAL:
DEAR JUDGE:

I received your letter stating your judgement as to the proprity—impropriety—of appointing Capt. Kasson Pension Agt. in the Northwest. Now I have no special interest in the matter further than that I have known the Capt. for some time, specially through Gen. Rowley, of Galena, the only survivor of my original staff. General Rowley has never been tinctured with democracy even before the War. I do not think it possible that he can be deceived in regard to Capt. Kasson's political faith, past or present. I have a letter from Gen. C. S. Hamilton making the same statements in regard to the Capts political status that you do. But the weight of evidence that comes to me is the other way. I believe from all I hear that he is the choice of the soldiers who receive pensions through the agency he applies for. The present incumbent, though a wounded soldier, does not deserve it by reason of his factional disposition. Then too he has had the office a long time and, I understand, does not need it.

My judgement is that the only ground for charging democracy upon Kasson is that after the result of the Chicago Convention was announced he expressed his dissent from the action of the convention in very vigorous terms, and announced his intention of supporting the nominee of the Cincinnati convention. But this feeling wore away in a very short time and he gave all the support he could to the republican ticket.—I hope in this instance I am not mistaken & that you are, and will confess it.

Very Truly yours

U. S. GRANT

ALS, WHi. On Feb. 13, 1882, President Chester A. Arthur nominated Edward Ferguson to continue as pension agent, Milwaukee. See letter to Dexter N. Kasson, Sept. 27, 1881; letter to William F. Vilas, Feb. 25, 1882.

To Robert C. Napier

New York City

Jan.y 16th 1882

MY DEAR LORD NAPIER;

As a slight return for the honor you did me, at the close of the Abyssinian War, in sending me the bible captured in the quarters of King Theodore[1] please accept the accompanying volumes; Badeaus History of the Rebellion. The book I regard as very accurate so far as it treats of events. The author alone is responsible for what he says of individuals.

Remembering with great pleasure our meeting at Gibralter, and hoping that I may yet have the honor of returning your hospitality in my own country, I am

Very Truly yours

U. S. GRANT

TO LORD NAPIER OF MAGDALA

ALS, Ralph G. Newman, Chicago, Ill. On May 9, 1882, Robert C. Napier, Gibraltar, wrote to USG. "I have had the pleasure of receiving your kind letter of the 11 January together with the three volumes containing your History in connection with the gigantic Campaigns which you brought to so successful a conclusion. I shall read the work with the greatest interest and am truly obliged to you for the honor you have done me in presenting it to me. I most earnestly desire and hope that the wounds and sorrows, which such a conflict could not fail to entail, may be healed and that the union between the North and the South may year by year become cemented by forgiveness and kind feelings on both sides; and promote the happiness and prosperity of your great Country. Your visit to Gibraltar is remembered with great pleasure by Lady Napier and myself. With our kind regards to Mrs Grant and yourself . . ." ALS, USG 3. See letter to Frederick Dent Grant, Nov. 14, 1878, note 1.

On Nov. 26, [*1881*], Adam Badeau, New York City, had written to John Russell Young. "The General has told ~~you~~me that I might ask you to set afloat in the press—the statement that he is having bound—copies of my work to be sent to each of the potentates who entertained him during his tour round the world. He is also entirely willing that a copy of the list which he furnished you should be given to the press. I think this would be answer enough to the assaults the book has received. I trust all looks well for Japan. The country would benefit, if not you . . ." AL (initialed), DLC-John Russell Young. On Jan. 20, 1882, Young wrote to John A. Bingham, U.S. minister, Tokyo. "I am directed by our illustrious and dear friend Gen. U. S. Grant to send to your care a letter addressed to Prince Iwakura, and a package containing a copy of Badeau's History of the Rebellion. Gen. Grant further requests me to say that if you will present this letter to Prince Iwakura, and give him the books accompanying it, he will take it as a very great favor. He is anxious to show to His Highness his appreciation of the kindness extended to him while in Japan. Gen. Grant requests me to send you his warmest remembrances, and the same to the members of your family—in all of which I cordially join . . ." LS, Milton Ronsheim, Cadiz, Ohio. On May 12, Bingham wrote to USG concerning a shipment of Japanese silks, jewelry, and plates ordered by Julia Dent Grant. ". . . I beg here to add that on the 12th of March last I recd through the State Department a letter addressed to me by Mr John Russell Young dated Jany 20th 1882 covering an open note from you to His Excellency Mr Iwakura. . . . By the outgoing mail on the 20th March last I replied to Mr Young by letter addressed to him at New York & ~~told~~ informed him that the books had not reached me . . . I hope they may soon reach me as it will be a pleasure to deliver them in your name together with your note to Mr Iwakura. . . ." ADfS, *ibid.* On May 20, Bingham again wrote to USG. ". . . On Saturday the 13th inst. and after the departure of the mail on that morng for America I recd my official mail from the U. S. & found in the Pouch in good order the History of the Rebellion by Genl Badeau which on Monday morng the 15th inst I sent to Mr Iwakura together with your open note to him & a letter from myself explaining the delay in the delivery of your note & the Books. His Excellency conveyed to me through my messenger (Mr Frazier) his Sincere thanks and the assurance that he would write me—on the Subject. . . ." ADfS, *ibid.* On May 24, Iwakura Tomomi, Tokyo, wrote to USG. "I have to acknowledge the receipt of your letter dated 14th January of this year together with a copy of Badeau History of the great rebellion of 1861 to 1865 in the United States through the hands of Mr Bingham, the United States Minister residing in our city. In reply thereto permit me to tender you my most hearty thanks for your valuable present, and of which the most important portion had been readily translated into the Japanese and was presented to His Imperial Majesty the Emperor. This present I shall keep carefully forever and transmit to my posterity, more so, for it describes the detailed account of the great military career of your own." In Japanese and translation, USG 3.

On Jan. 16, USG had written to Albert, Prince of Wales, conveying a copy of Badeau's *Military History of Ulysses S. Grant* and recalling "our pleasant relations in England." Typescript, Windsor Castle. Also on Jan. 16, USG wrote a similar letter to Ashley Eden, lt. governor of Bengal, Calcutta. Gary Combs Autographs, Inc., Jan., 2007. On the same day, USG wrote to Edward Robert Bulwer-Lytton. "Recalling our very pleasant relations, when I was your guest in India—I take pleasure in sending you a copy of Badeau's History of the Rebellion,—which I trust you will accept with the assurances of my esteem" LS, Ralph G. Newman, Chicago, Ill. On April 30, Bulwer-Lytton, Stevenage, England, wrote to USG. "Your letter of the 16th of January last, and the volumes accompanying it have safely reached me through Mr Lowell. Pray accept my sincere thanks for your most obliging gift of Badeau's History of the Rebellion of the Southern states, and for the valued autograph attached to the work by the Eminent man, of whose great achievement it is so interesting a record." ALS, USG 3. See letter to Anthony J. Drexel, Feb. 16, 1879; letter to Adam Badeau, March 15, 1879.

On Dec. 12, USG wrote to James Falshaw. "Please accept the accompanying volumes as a token of remembrance of my very pleasant visit to Edinborough, in the year 1877, and of your kind hospitality to my party and myself. Hoping that we may meet at some future day, in this country, and that I may be able to return your hospitality in kind, . . ." ALS, The Scriptorium, Beverly Hills, Calif. On Jan. 11, 1883, Falshaw, Edinburgh, wrote to USG. "I thank you very much for your note of the 12th December and for the three Volumes of your distinguished 'Military history' which I shall read with much pleasure. These three volumes you are good enough to say are in token of remembrance of your visit to Edinburgh in the year 1877 I shall ever bear in mind the pleasure afforded to Lady Falshaw and myself during the time you, Mrs Grant and party were at my house. I can hardly anticipate the hope of our meeting in your Country at my time of life, 73, however gratifying such a visit would be to me.—" ALS, USG 3. See *PUSG*, 28, 260–61. For similar responses from recipients abroad, see letter to Adam Badeau, June 26, 1882.

On Feb. 23, 1882, Michael John Cramer, New York City, had written to Badeau, Washington, D. C. ". . . You have certainly succeeded in presentin[g] to the world, in a very abl[e] form, the military achievements of the greatest General of modern times; The American people may be as proud of your work as they are of Gen. Grant himself. Sincerely thanking you for your valuable present, . . ." ALS, CSmH.

1. Born in 1818, Theodore II became emperor of Abyssinia (Ethiopia) in 1855. In April, 1868, he committed suicide after British forces under Napier defeated his army at Magdala. On Sept. 14, Secretary of State William H. Seward wrote to USG. "I have the pleasure to transmit to you a letter which has been received at this Department through the United States Legation in London, together with its accompaniment which is an Abyssinian book sent to your address by General Lord Napier of Magdala." LS, DLC-USG, IB.

To Chester A. Arthur

New York City,
Jan.y 23d 1882,

THE PRESIDENT:

I take pleasure in presenting Governor Randolph, of N. J. who visits Washington no doubt principally in reference to rendering a service to Gen. F. J. Porter. He desires to meet you personally and I give him this letter cheerfully requesting that he may have that pleasure.

Of course I know a letter from me is not necessary to secure this favor because as Governor of a neighboring state, and as representative of his state in the United States Senate, you know him ~~personally~~ in a public capacity. But as I feel myself somewhat responsible for Gen. Porter's long suffering I ask an interview with one of his personal friends to the end that you may consult as to the best method of reaching a just and practical solution of the Porter case, if you should look upon the matter as I do.

Very Truly yours

U. S. GRANT

ALS, DLC-Chester A. Arthur. On Feb. 1, 1882, Secretary of State Frederick T. Frelinghuysen wrote to Theodore F. Randolph, Washington, D. C. "The President has appointed the hour of one p. m. tomorrow, Thursday, for your reception. He has read and has now in his possession Genl. Grant's letter introducing you." Typescript, *ibid.* Randolph served as Democratic governor of N. J. (1869–72) and U.S. Senator (1875–81). While in the Senate, he advocated legislation to restore his constituent Fitz John Porter to the army. See *CR*, 46-2, 1222–28.

On Feb. 13, 1882, Frelinghuysen wrote to USG. "Referring to yours of the 9th inst let me say that Mr. John Wilson has by Executive order been remanded to his position of Consul-~~General~~ at Brussels—In reply to yours of 11th inst I take pleasure in saying that I think the President will execute an instrument which after reciting the finding of the Board, will remit all pains & penalties—" Typescript, DLC-Chester A. Arthur. For John Wilson, see *PUSG*, 22, 217–19. On Feb. 22, a correspondent in Washington, D. C., reprinted a story from that day's *Washington Evening Star*. "... The decision of the Advisory Board that Gen. Porter was not only unjustly dealt with, but that if it had not been for him there would have been a great disaster to the Union Army, has had great weight with the President and his Cabinet...." *New York Times*, Feb. 23, 1882.

To J. Henry Rives

New York, Jany 23 *1882*

CAPT J. H. REEVES

LYNCHBURG VA.

DEAR SIR:

Your letter of the 19th inst is just received. In suggesting something for Mr Mosby of course I had no idea of displacing any worthy person from a position whether he was my friend or not.

I should be very glad to see Mr. Mosby, on account of the great friendship I feel for his brother, have some position that would suit him, but not at the expense of other deserving Republicans of the State.

Truly Yours

U. S. Grant

LS, PHi. On Feb. 14, 1871, USG nominated J. Henry Rives, former capt., C.S. Army, as collector of Internal Revenue, 5th District, Va., a position he still held in 1882. On Feb. 27, 1883, President Chester A. Arthur nominated William H. Mosby, brother of John S. Mosby, as postmaster, Liberty, Va. See *PUSG*, 15, 578–80.

To Andrew S. Draper

New York City

Jan.y 30th 1882.

A. S. Draper, Esq.
Chairman Com. of Arangements
Albany Grant Club;
Dear Sir:

I regret very much that I can not be with your club at its annual supper to-morrow evening. But, as stated in my former letter—dictated—I have company visiting me that I can not induce to accompany me nor am I willing to leave. The company is a gentleman and soldier who I know you would like to honor—Gen. Sheridan [1]—and who would like to partake with me your hospitalities, but who can not on this occasion as he must leave the city on Thursday morning,[2] and has other engagements for the intervening time.

Wishing you all a good time at your annual meeting, and that you may all live to enjoy many more of them, I am,

Very Truly yours

U. S. Grant

ALS (facsimile), Early American History Auctions, Inc., April 23, 2005, no. 80. Born in 1848 in N. Y., Andrew S. Draper graduated Albany Law School (1871) and served one term in the N. Y. assembly (1881–82). See letter to Horace Porter, Jan. 8, 1881; Harlan Hoyt Horner, *The Life and Work of Andrew Sloan Draper* (Urbana, Ill., 1934).

1. On Jan. 11, 1882, USG telegraphed to Lt. Gen. Philip H. Sheridan, Chicago. "When may we expect you & Mrs. Sheridan?" ALS (facsimile, telegram sent), Heritage Auction Galleries, Dec. 1, 2006, no. 25234.

2. Feb. 2.

To Adam Badeau

[*Jan., 1882*]

Dear Badeau:

I think it would be well if the Appletons would send one of their canvassers for this city to me.[1]

I hardly know how to advise you to proceed in your personal matter. But I think I would see the President and if he is not inclined to remove Marsh I would suggest the Consul Generalship of Paris or London. There may be some hesitation about the removal of the latter, but I am told there ~~sh~~would not be in regard to the former.

Very Truly yours
U. S. Grant

ALS, Munson-Williams-Proctor Institute, Utica, N. Y. See following letter.

1. "The first sentence refers to my 'Military History,' which was sold by subscription, and Grant wanted to make out a list of his personal friends to whom the canvassers might offer the book." *Badeau*, p. 537.

To Adam Badeau

New York City
Feb.y 3d 1882

Dear Badeau;

I have your letter of the 1st. It is possible the Presidents Sec.— knowing how the President is oppressed by calls—never laid your letter before him. At all events I would assume that he had not, and would lay my business before him. The President has spoken in the kindest terms of you, and suggested himself, before I mentioned it, the Italian Mission. I would suggest that you go in to see him in his office hours and say that you would not take up his time now, but if he would name a time you would like to call when he could give you a few minuets. Of course you are at liberty to use any letter or saying of mine.

Old Mr. Hamilton was in to see me a few days ago. He had just finished reading your book and was in extacies over it. He had not one word of unfavorable comment.[1]

The Appletons have not yet sent an Agent to me.—I hope you may be speedily relieved from your suspense by Presidential action.

Very Truly yours

U. S. GRANT

ALS, Munson-Williams-Proctor Institute, Utica, N. Y. See previous letter.

1. "The Mr. Hamilton spoken of was the late John C. Hamilton of New York, father-in-law of General Halleck. It was this relationship which made his commendation notable; for I had been obliged to say many things in my history, which were unfavorable to Halleck." *Badeau*, p. 537. See *New York Times*, July 26, 1882.

To Elizabeth S. Ewell

———

New York, Feby 3 *1882*

MISS ELIZABETH S. EWELL,
GEORGETOWN D. C.

DEAR MISS:

Your letter of the 1st inst together with a memorial to Congress enclosed with it, are received. I return you the latter without any comments. I am asked almost daily to make endorsements to secure compensation to the descendants or nearest of Kin of ex soldiers, for bounties pensions &c, and the number being so great I am obliged to decline. If it was not for this determination I might be inclined to give an endorsement to this memorial. I have known two of your brothers, and all that I have known of them has been highly to their credit. I should be very glad to see you get what you ask for in the memorial to Congress.

Truly Yours

U. S. GRANT

LS, Ewell Papers, College of William and Mary, Williamsburg, Va. Born in 1813 in Georgetown, D. C., Elizabeth S. Ewell was the sister of Benjamin S. (USMA 1832), Richard S. (USMA 1840), and Thomas, killed at Cerro Gordo in 1847. In July, 1882, the House of Representatives tabled a petition to pay a bounty to Thomas's survivors. See *PUSG*, 15, 154–56; *ibid.*, 17, 135–37; *Memoirs*, I, 49.

To James D. Cameron

NEW-YORK, Feb. 4, 1882.

The Hon. J. D. Cameron, United States Senate, Washington, D. C.:

DEAR SIR: It has been my intention until within the last few days to visit Washington this Winter to spend some time, and there to have a conversation with you and with Gen. Logan on the subject of the Fitz John Porter case; but having now pretty nearly decided not to go to Washington, I have determined to write, and write to you so that you may state my position to your friends and particularly to Gen. Logan, and, if you choose, show this letter to any such people.

When I commenced the examination of the Fitz John Porter case, as it now stands, it was with the conviction that his sentence was a just one, and that his punishment had been light for so hideous an offense; but I tried to throw off all prejudice in the case and to examine it on its merits. I came out of that examination with the firm conviction that an entirely innocent man had been most unjustly punished.[1] I cast no censure upon the court which tried him, because the evidence which now proves his entire innocence of disobedience of orders it was impossible to have before that court. When I completed the investigation and came to the conclusion that I did—of his innocence—my first thought was to write to Gen. Logan, because I regard him as my friend, and I am sure I am his, and he had made probably the ablest speech of his life in opposition to the bill for Gen. Porter's restoration to the Army.[2] I thought, therefore, it was due to him that I should inform him of the conclusion that I had come to after the investigation. But as the President was just about visiting this city when my letter to him was written, and it was desired to present it to him here, I requested, in lieu of a letter to Gen. Logan, to have a copy of my letter to the President sent to him. This was done.[3]

You are aware that when Gen. Logan made his speech against Gen. Porter it was in opposition to a bill pending in Congress. He, like myself, was thoroughly convinced of the guilt of Gen. Porter, and was, therefore, opposed to the bill. His investigations, therefore, were necessarily to find arguments to sustain his side of a pending question. I, of course, have no knowledge of the papers he would refer to, or would examine to find such arguments; but I know that he could have the testimony which was taken before the court-martial which convicted; probably, also, the arguments of the officer who acted as prosecutor[4] when the case was before the Schofield court,[5] and arguments that have been made by lawyers— J. D. Cox and others possibly—all of which were in opposition to Gen. Porter, as much as that of paid attorneys in cases before civil courts. But my investigation of all the facts that I could bring before me of the occurrence from the 27th of August, 1862, and for some little time prior, to the 1st of September, the same year, show conclusively that the court and some of the witnesses entirely misapprehended the position of the enemy on that day.

Gen. Porter was convicted of disobedience of an order of Gen. Pope's, dated at 4:30 P. M., on the 29th of August, to attack the enemy on his right flank, and in his rear, if possible. Dispatches of Gen. Pope of that day show that he knew Gen. Lee was coming to the support of Jackson, whom he thought commanded the only force in his front at that time, but that he could not arrive until the evening of the following day, or the morning of the day after. It was sworn to before the court that this order of 4:30 P. M. reached Gen. Porter at about 5 or 5:30 o'clock in the afternoon, but it must be recollected that this testimony was given from memory and unquestionably without any idea at the time of the occurrence that they were ever to be called upon to give any testimony in the case. Investigation shows a dispatch from Gen. Porter, dated 6 P. M. of that afternoon, which makes no mention of having received the order to attack, and it is such a dispatch as could not be written without mentioning the receipt of that order, if it had been received. There is other testimony that makes it entirely satisfactory to my mind that the order was not received until about sundown, or between sundown and dark. It was given, as stated before, to attack the enemy's right, and, if possible, to get into his rear. This was on the supposition that Jackson was there alone, as Gen. Pope had stated he would be until the evening of the next day or the morning of the day following. I believe the court was convinced that on the evening of the 29th of August Jackson with his force was there alone; but now it is proved by testimony better than sworn evidence of any persons on the Union side that by 11 o'clock A. M. of the 29th Longstreet was up and to the right of Jackson, with a force much greater than Gen. Porter's entire force. The attack upon Jackson's right and rear was, therefore, impossible without first wiping out the force of Longstreet. The order did not contemplate, either, a night attack, and to have obeyed it, even if Longstreet had not been there, Gen. Porter would have been obliged to make a night attack. But even as it was, I find that Gen. Porter, notwithstanding the late hour, did all he could to obey that order. He had previously given a command to Gen. Morell,[6] who commanded his most advanced division, or one most fronting the enemy, to throw out a skirmish line to engage the enemy or to keep him occupied, and on the receipt of this order, although at this late hour, he immediately sent orders to Gen. Morell to increase it from a skirmish line to a large force, and that he would be with him as soon as he could get there. He did actually go to the front, although it was dark, to superintend this movement, and as far as possible to prevent the enemy detaching anything from his front, thus showing a desire to obey the order strictly and to the best of his ability.[7]

I find the Schofield board acquit him entirely, but throw some censure upon him for having expressed a lack of confidence in his commanding officer. Such conduct might be censured, although if every man in the Army had been punished who had expressed lack of confidence in his superior officer many of our best soldiers would have been punished. But, in fact, if this was not stated in the summing up of the case by the board, I should not have found that he had expressed any such lack of confidence. On the contrary, to my mind now, he was zealous in giving a support to Gen. Pope, and more so, possibly, for the reason that he knew among his former Army associates there was a good deal of apprehension, to say the least, of his fitness for his new place. It must be recollected that Gen. Pope was selected from a Western army and brought East to command an army where there were a great many Generals who had had experience in a previous war, and who had, like himself, a military education, and there may (improperly) have been a feeling that it was a reflection upon them to go out of their own command to find a suitable commander; and it is also very probable that expression was freely given to that feeling. But it would be well to reflect what would have been the sentiments in the West if an officer from the Eastern army had been sent out to supersede all of them and to command them, and whether or not there might not have been some harsh criticisms, even by men who proved to be among our most gallant and devoted commanders.

Then, too, in re-examining the case, my attention was called again to Gen. Pope's early order in taking command of the Army of Virginia. I send you a copy of this order.[8] You will see that it was calculated to make the army to whom it was addressed feel that it was a reflection upon their former services and former commanders, from that of a company to the commander of the whole, and that even as amiable people as Gen. Logan and myself are would have been very apt to have made some very uncomplimentary remarks if they had been addressed by an Eastern officer sent West to command over us in our field of duty.

I commenced reading up this case with the conviction that Gen. Porter had been guilty, as found by the court, but came out of the investigation with a thorough conviction that I and the public generally had done him a fearful injustice, and entirely satisfied that any intelligent man or lawyer who will throw aside prejudice and examine the case as I have done will come to the same conclusion.

As stated in my letter to the President, I feel it incumbent upon me, in view of the positions that I have held heretofore, and my failure then to do what I now wish I had done, to do all in my power to place Gen. Porter right before the public and in future history, and to repair my own unintentional injustice.

I addressed this letter to you, knowing that you will have a desire to do just what your judgment dictates as being right in the matter, and that you will state to whomsoever it may seem to you proper and necessary my present convictions upon this case. Very truly yours,

U. S. GRANT.

New York Times, Dec. 4, 1882. On Feb. 4, 1882, USG, New York City, wrote to Fitz John Porter. "I send you my letter to Senator Cameron. Please read it and mail unless you have suggestions to make of alterations or additions. My whole object now is to benefit you, and to this end I am willing to do anything that is truthful." *The Collector*, Volume LV-A (n. d.), p. 4 (copy in DLC-Fitz John Porter). On Jan. 11, 1883, U.S. Senator James D. Cameron of Pa. spoke in favor of a bill to restore Porter to the army. *CR*, 47-2, 1091. See letter to James D. Cameron, May 29, 1882; letter to Fitz John Porter, Dec. 27, 1882; *New York Times*, Jan. 12, 1883.

1. See letter to Fitz John Porter, Sept. 27, 1881.
2. See *CR*, 46-2, Appendix, 47–92.
3. See letter to Chester A. Arthur, Dec. 22, 1881; letter to John A. Logan, Dec. 30, 1881.
4. Maj. Asa B. Gardiner.
5. See *SED*, 46-1-37.
6. George W. Morell, USMA 1835, resigned his commission (1837) and rejoined the army during the Civil War, serving as brig. gen. vols. and maj. gen. vols.
7. For USG's expanded analysis, see Article, [*Oct. 24, 1882*].
8. See *O.R.*, I, xii, part 3, 473–74.

To John F. Miller

———

NEW YORK, Feb. 8, 1882.

Hon. J. T. MILLER, United States Senate:——

DEAR SIR—I learn by the papers that it is proposed to have the Nicaragua route resurveyed before any further action is taken in the matter of an interoceanic canal by that route. This seems to me to be entirely unnecessary and intended to delay action in the interest of other enterprises. It will be remembered that I had all the known lines of low level between the two oceans surveyed and the reports of the different surveying parties submitted to a board of engineers. Before the Board reported parties were sent over the Nicaragua and Panama routes again, and after their reports were received reported in favor of the Nicaragua route. As I stated in a previous letter my great desire is to see a successful ship communication between the two oceans established under American auspices, and I did not care who received the honor or benefit of it, but I do not wish to see a plan for accomplishing this result (about the success of which there can be no doubt, except that of raising the necessary funds) defeated in the interest of schemes which are problematical to say the least.

Very truly yours,

U. S. GRANT.

New York Herald, March 11, 1882. "It has been given out here that the principal incorporators in the Nicaragua Ship Canal enterprise had abandoned it, and particularly General Grant. The following letter sufficiently indicates the General's position in that respect:—" *Ibid.* Born in 1831, John F. Miller was Ind. senator, col., 29th Ind., and brig. gen. Settling in Calif., Miller served as collector, San Francisco, and was elected U.S. Senator in 1880. See letter to Jesse Root Grant, Jr., Jan. 13, 1882.

To Chester A. Arthur

FEBRUARY 9, 1882.

Hon. CHESTER A. ARTHUR,
President of the United States.

MY DEAR SIR: Chief Engineer George Sewell, United States Navy, second in rank of chief engineers, entered the United States service during the war with Mexico, some months after Chief Engineer W. H. Shock, the present Chief of Bureau of Steam Engineering.

At present B. F. Isherwood is first, George Sewell is second, and W. H. Shock third in rank. Mr. Isherwood has held the position as Chief of Bureau of Steam Engineering during two terms, and Mr. Shock, who underranks Mr. Sewell, has held the position from before the Hayes Administration to the present time. Mr. Sewell's ability was recognized during the Mexican war in his skill in saving and curing several gunboats that had been nearly abandoned (the *Vixen*, *Spitfire*, and others) on account of there being no dry docks in that country. He was steadily promoted over all his brother engineers for his ability. During the Perry Expedition to China and Japan, Mr. Sewell was the chief engineer, and during that cruise his ability was again shown by his rapid remedies to injured vessels, no dry dock being available, a special case being the flagship *Powhatan,* which called forth letters of thanks from the Department and special praise from Chief Bonny, of Her Majesty's fleet in those waters.

During the late war Mr. Sewell's suggestions to Secretary Welles in regard to torpedoes, etc., in Charleston Harbor were adopted, for which Mr. Sewell also received a letter of thanks from the Department.

Mr. Sewell's ability is well known by all engineers out of the service as well as in the service, and his record is A 1.

Mr. Sewell's friends feel that his ability and service to his Government should be recognized now, as his age will retire him should he have to wait until the next Administration. Also, that he should be placed in his proper position (Chief of Bureau of Steam Engineering), now held by his junior in rank and ability. Mr. Sewell is a native of New York and a lifelong Republican.

I take pleasure in commending Engineer George Sewell, of the United States Navy, for the chief of his corps on the retirement, resignation, or removal of the present chief. In view of the probable appropriations for an increase in the naval armament of the Navy, it is highly important to have at the head of the Bureau of Construction an able and experienced engineer. Mr. Sewell, I believe, has demonstrated himself to be all this.

U. S. GRANT.

FEBRUARY 9, 1882.

SRC, 54-1-502, 2–3, 55-1-272, 2–3. Charles H. Loring replaced William H. Shock as engineer-in-chief, Bureau of Steam Engineering.

To Chester A. Arthur

NEW YORK CITY, *February* 10, 1882.

The PRESIDENT:

The case of Commander J. N. Quackenbush, United States Navy, sentenced to be dismissed in 1874, has just been called to my attention with the hardship attending his case by reason of inadvertency in the nomination of his successor after his sentence had been commuted.

The matter of nomination or promotion in the Army and Navy is regulated by law so that the Executive scarcely thinks to look at the nominations when they are put before him, supposing, of course, they are to fill vacancies. In this way it seems Commander Quackenbush was superseded and now finds himself in danger of being out of the Navy, by a recent decision in another case.

I remember of Commander Quackenbush but not the details of my action. I have no doubt, however, but that the Hon. George M. Robeson, then Secretary of the Navy, knows and remembers all about it.

I do know, however, the intention was not to put him out of the service, and I now recommend his nomination to the vacancy, which was kept open for him from the time of the first vacancy after the promotion of Schley.

The fact that executive action was delayed so long in the case of Commander Quackenbush, at the request of Mr. Samuel Howe,[1] shows quite conclusively that the approval of the sentence and commutation were done at one and the same time. My decision was probably given verbally to the Secretary, and the mistake in the record has been made by a clerk.

Very truly, yours,

U. S. GRANT.

HRC, 47-1-1195, 2. On June 4, 1874, Secretary of the Navy George M. Robeson wrote to USG. "I have the honor to submit herewith the record of the proceedings of a Naval General Court Martial in the case of Commander John N. Quackenbush, of the Navy, who has been found guilty of the charges of 'Drunkenness' and 'Scandalous conduct tending to the destruction of good morals' and sentenced to 'be dismissed from the Naval Service of the United States'" Copies (2), DNA, RG 45, Letters Sent to the President. On June 5, USG approved the dismissal of John N. Quackenbush. Copy, *ibid.* On June 10, USG nominated Lt. Commander Winfield S. Schley as commander to replace Quackenbush. See *New York Times*, June 8, 1895, Jan. 11, 1901; *Quackenbush v. United States*, 177 U.S. 20 (1900).

1. On Feb. 16, 1882, Robeson wrote to President Chester A. Arthur that in 1874, ". . . Mrs. Julia Ward Howe, with her niece, the wife of Commander Quackenbush,

called upon me in regard to this case, and I told them that they needed the direct action of the President, and they must go at once to him, which they did. . . ." *HRC*, 47-1-1195, 2.

Speech

[*New York City, Feb. 13, 1882*]

GENTLEMEN OF THE LINCOLN CLUB: I am very sorry you did not listen to the very sensible suggestion of Senator McDonald [1] and let Mr. Storrs, of Chicago, speak. I am sure, if you had, you would have heard something worthy of the occasion, and worthy of this club and worthy of the name the club bears. He is a citizen much longer than I have been, of the State from which Mr. Lincoln hailed. He knew Mr. Lincoln long before I did, for I never met Mr. Lincoln until I met him in March, 1864. He could tell you much better than I could all his good qualities. I will say, however, now that I am on my feet, that I like the name of your club. I like the principles upon which it is based. I like the name because it bears the name of one of the greatest men that our country has produced, and one who probably was better far for the time and for the occasion than perhaps any man we had in this country. Although when the war broke out in 1861 I was a citizen of the same State that the President belonged to, I had never met him until I came East in 1864 to take command of all the armies. I had heard very much of him. I had heard very much of his fund of anecdote. I was led to suppose that he was a man who passed away his time in telling little stories, and sometimes stories that it would hardly do to repeat except in society entirely composed of gentlemen.

I can say this: that I met him a great deal after I came here. He spent a good deal of time with me at City Point, and I saw him on intimate terms. I never heard a word from Mr. Lincoln himself that could not be said in the society of a lady. He had a fund of anecdote, but it was always to illustrate a point. I scarcely ever heard him talk in my life but that after stating the case very clearly he did not add some little anecdote to illustrate exactly what he meant, and to give point to it. I will give you one of the stories that I heard him tell, as an indication, after the surrender of Appomattox. I gave necessary orders for the parolling and releasing of prisoners and ordered General Meade to march the army to take the Brookville junction of the Richmond and Danville with the Western Road. I started back to Washington to stop the enlistments and purchasings of supplies and general expenses of the Army. The Confederate Government and the State Government of Virginia left Richmond about the same time Lee did. When they left Danville, and finding they were not pursued, they stopped for a time. I was supposed to be with the Army; but, as I say, I had gone on to Washington. After I left there I received a telegram from General Meade, which had been written by Governor Smith, of Virginia, in which he said he was the Governor of the Commonwealth of the State of Virginia, and as such he had temporarily taken the State Government to Danville. He wished to know whether he would be permitted to carry on the functions of his office unmolested. If he was not permitted to do so he wished to know whether he and his friends would be permitted to leave the country without molestation. I referred the matter to Mr. Lincoln a few moments afterward, and he said: "Well, now, I am just like my friend McGroiarty, of Springfield. He was very fond of drinking. He would drink a good deal. But his friends persuaded him to join the temperance society. But he was so much in the habit of drinking that he had to go through the motions by taking soda-water. For two or three days he held to soda-water, but he held the glass behind his back and said: 'Doctor, could you not put in a drop unbeknownt to meself?' And I knew then as well what I was to do and what I was to reply to Governor Smith's letters as well as if Mr. Lincoln had made a speech as long as the speech of Senator McDonald.[2]

New York Tribune, Feb. 14, 1882. USG spoke at the eleventh annual banquet of the Lincoln Club. See Speech, [*Oct. 31, 1879*]; *PUSG*, 14, 389; *Memoirs*, II, 532–33.

1. Born in 1832 in Pa., Alexander McDonald moved to Kan. in 1857, raised troops in the Civil War, settled in Ark. as a merchant and banker, and served as U.S. Senator (1868–71). By 1880, McDonald was in the mining business in New York City.
2. McDonald had declined to speak.

To Col. Frederick T. Dent

———

New York City
Feb.y 13d 1882.

Dear Dent;

I received last week your letter making a proposition to sell your St Louis land. I have not the money at this time to accept your proposition even if I was disposed to. But it came just at a time when I had just received the first proposition I have ever had for the purchase of the "Old Farm." The proposition comes to purchase, or lease for fifteen years. I have written Judge Long authorizing the sale of mine for $100.000 00, one fifth cash, the balance on indefinite payments secured by bond & mortgage, with 6 pr. cts payable semi annually. I have written the Judge to put your 80 acres in pro rata, and to sell if possible. If not, to see what rent the man will give. In either event to put your land in. In case of sale I will pay you all cash at just what your share amounts to. In case of lease I will buy yours and pay you the $10.000. I have also written to the Judge that I am anxious to sell all my Carondelet property even if I can only get what I paid, without interest. Property in and about St. Louis does not bring as much, and is not as ready sale as it was fifteen years ago. The city grows and seems to be prosperous. But Chicago has so far outstripped it that every thing in the West like enterprize seems to be going there and St Louis becomes more & more villege like. I have all my children here now, and six of my Grand children.[1] The boys all live here and are more than self supporting. Nellie and her husband, and two children,[2] are on a visit for the winter. I will write to you if I get anything in regard to sale or lease of land.

With love to you and family from us all,

Very Truly yours
U. S. Grant

ALS (facsimile), USGA.

1. Algernon E. and Vivien M. Sartoris; Julia and Ulysses S. Grant 3rd; Nellie Grant, daughter of Jesse Root Grant, Jr., born Aug., 1881; Miriam Grant, daughter of Ulysses S. Grant, Jr., born Sept., 1881.

2. The third Sartoris child, Rosemary Alice, born Nov., 1880, apparently remained in England. See letter to Ellen Grant Sartoris, Nov. 28, 1882.

To Adam Badeau

———

New York City
Feb.y 16th 1882.

DEAR BADEAU;

I have your letter of yesterday, and received in time yours of a few days ago. I think there is no doubt but the President is disposed to do something for you. But, to this time, he has seemed averse to making any removals, no matter how offensive the parties in place have been to him and his friends. I hope this will not continue. Exactly what to suggest I am at a loss to think of, something in Washington would suit your purpose of writing the volume[1] you speak of better than elswhere. But what is there then of sufficient dignity & compensation that would give you the time. I have no doubt but they would be glad to give you the place vacated—or to be vacated—by young Blaine.[2] If that would do suggest it to the Sec. or Asst. Sec. and no doubt it could be brought about. Refer to me in this or any other matter for your benefit.

Geo. Jones & his wife dine with me on Saturday next.[3] I will see what he might be willing to do in the direction you suggest. With a fair compensation from that quarter, your retired pay and what you might pick up in other ways might be better, pecuniarily, than an official position in Washington.

Very Truly yours
U. S. GRANT

ALS, Munson-Williams-Proctor Institute, Utica, N. Y.

1. "The volume General Grant here refers to is his political history, which, as the military work was complete, I was now about to begin." *Badeau*, p. 538. On Feb. 12, 1882, Gen. William T. Sherman wrote to Adam Badeau. ". . . I rather like the idea of your preparing a History of Reconstruction; only it seems to me that it will be a tight squeeze to get all the essential facts into a small volume of the size of Scribner. It will be better to collect the materials and allow the size to result from them. Reconstruction was a Corolary of the War—and forms a continuation of the very subject matter of your past work—and it so happens that your Hero in War was Leader in the Recon-

struction—So I see no reason why it should not form a fourth volume. In whatever you may undertake you have my best wishes." ALS (partial facsimile), *ibid.*, pp. 63, 589.

2. Born in 1855, Walker Blaine graduated from Yale College and Columbia Law School. On July 2, 1881, President James A. Garfield appointed Blaine as 3rd asst. secretary of state, "with many warm expressions of friendly regard, telling him not to consider it as done on his father's account, but on his own. The President has known him since his early childhood." *New York Times*, July 3, 1881. On July 11, 1882, President Chester A. Arthur nominated Alvey A. Adee to replace Blaine, who became asst. counsel, Court of Commissioners of *Alabama* Claims. See *ibid.*, Jan. 16, 1890.

3. "There were some conversations between Mr. George Jones and several of my friends, at this time, in regard to my joining the staff of the *New York Times*, which will explain the concluding sentences of this letter." *Badeau*, p. 538.

To Adam Badeau

————

New York City,
Feb:y 19th 1882.

DEAR BADEAU:

Yours of yesterday received. I wrote the President this morning suggesting Austria and said that your qualifications for the office were equal to those of any representative we have had at that Court in twenty years. I also said that you spoke the German, French & Spanish languages, and that I believed you did the Italian also. Am I right? I marked the letter "Personal" on the envelope, and signed my name, so that it might go direct to the President. I think I would call upon him again if I were in your place even if I did not mention the Austrian Mission. He would be apt to speak of my letter. You might speak of the rail road inspectorship.

Very Truly yours
U. S. GRANT

ALS, Munson-Williams-Proctor Institute, Utica, N. Y.

To Leonidas C. Houk

————

NEW YORK, *February* 20, 1882.

DEAR SIR: I have your letter of February 18 making inquiry in regard to money collected from disloyal citizens in the vicinity of Henderson, Tenn., in the year 1862. I have no papers whatever relating to the matter; in fact, have none relative to the war. All my official dispatches and letters will probably be found on file in the War Department. If not, General Sherman will probably have those dated during the time that I commanded in the west. My recollection in regard to the Henderson matter is that some guerrillas or rebels away from their main command set fire to a bridge near the little town of Henderson, Tenn., and, as soon as they had left, some women living in the neighborhood, who were Union in sentiment, took buckets and carried water, and put out the fire before much damage had been done.

Hearing of this I directed the commanding officer of that district to collect from disloyal persons in the neighborhood a sum of money to compensate these women for their conspicuous act of loyalty, and one which possibly may have exposed them or the male members of their families to danger at any time when Union troops might be withdrawn. I have no recollection of loyal citizens having been molested at that time, or of having ordered collections in their behalf, *but whatever the record may be made at the time it may be taken as the exact fact.* What I have stated is simply from memory. I do recollect, however, of General Sullivan saying to me some years after the war that he had still in his possession some thousands of dollars collected at that time, and wanted to know what should be done with it.

I think my recommendation to him was that he should turn it over to the War Department and get a receipt for it, and from there to be covered into the Treasuy, or be *held subject to any orders that Congress might make;* but I am under the impression he never did turn over the fund.

U. S. GRANT.

Hon. L. C. HOUK,
Chairman of the Committee on Claims, Washington, D. C.

SRC, 48-1-466, 25–26. U.S. Representative Leonidas C. Houk of Tenn., chairman, Committee on War Claims, had served with the Tenn. vols. (1861–63) and entered Congress in 1879. On July 15, 1870, William S. Hillyer, New York City, had written to Maj. Thomas M. Vincent, asst. AG. "I have the honor to acknowledge the receipt of your communication of the 12th inst., asking information as to the disposition of certain moneys turned over to me while acting provost-marshal-general of the Department of the Tennessee, by Maj. M. Smith, district of Jackson. A similar inquiry was made some two or three years ago through General Rawlins, then chief of staff, to the General of the Army. . . . In November or December, 1862, or January, 1863, General Sullivan was commanding at Jackson, Tenn. At that time a bridge was fired and some damage done to Government property by guerrillas. A Union woman extinguished the fire and saved the bridge. It was represented also that about the same time a large amount of private cotton was destroyed by these guerrillas. General Grant directed General Sullivan to make assessments and collect the same from rebel sympathizers in the neighborhood sufficient to make good the Government losses and pay a reward of (I think) $500 to the woman who extinguished the fire. General Sullivan collected a much larger sum than was required for these purposes, and reported the excess to General Grant, with a statement that parties who had had cotton destroyed by guerrillas claimed that he, General Grant, intended their losses should be made good to them out of this fund. General Grant, in reply, stated that it was not true he so intended; that the Army was not an insurance company to indemnify cotton speculators for losses in their operations, and that no part of this money rightfully belonged to them nor should be paid to them. That he did not intend that any assessment should be made in excess of an amount sufficient to indemnify the Government and reward the woman, and that his orders had been misunderstood, or exceeded. He further directed General Sullivan that Colonel Smith, in whose custody the funds were, should report and pay the same over to me with other funds belonging to his department, which was done. This is the whole case. It was thoroughly investigated by General Rawlins, under the direction of General Grant, and, as I am informed, distinctly adjudged that these parties have no claim, either legal or equitable, against the Government. . . ." *Ibid.*, pp. 24–25. On Feb. 25, 1882, USG endorsed this letter. "General Hillyer's letter, as printed above, is no doubt entirely correct. I certainly never intended any collection for the benefit of cotton purchasers." *Ibid.*, p. 25; *SRC*, 47-1-237, 3; *HRC*, 54-1-416, 3, 56-1-16, 3. On March 3, 1884, Jeremiah C. Sullivan, San Francisco, swore a deposition. "I am the General J. C. Sullivan who was in command of the Department of West Tennessee when Special Order No. 15, December 12, 1862, was issued. . . . Order No. 15 was not directed against parties who had been tried and convicted of complicity in the raid, but as against those whom I believed could control and discourage future raids; such parties as I believed to be influential and were interested in keeping the department quiet were selected and made to put up a money security, the amount based upon their ability in proportion to the loss sustained. It was not intended that such money so collected should be used in any way to reimburse any person or individual who claimed a loss by such raid. . . . In my opinion, the relief asked for should be granted, as this money was simply a bond for good behavior and compulsory assistance in helping me maintain order and quiet. Cotton purchasers were not looked upon with favor in General Grant's command, and no officer would have dared make innocent parties pay their claims. I most positively state that it was in no manner intended by me to pay or adjust any such claims." *SRC*, 48-1-466, 26–27. Claimants eventually received compensation. See *PUSG*, 6, 347–49; *HRC*, 51-1-14; *U.S. Statutes at Large*, XXXI, 1507–9.

On Dec. 5, 1875, Mrs. H. C. Walsh, Henderson Station, Tenn., had written to USG. "no doubt you will be surprised at the reception of this letter when you read I hope you will pardon me I live near Henderson Sta on the Mobile an Ohio R R lived here during the War the Federal Troops here company *B* of the *28* 49 Illinois Reg

Capt Wm P Moore Company was stationed here from July till *Oct 7th* Nov. 25 /62
when at day break 500 Rebel suprised them killed one picket an Captured all the Company a except two pickets that was sttioned near my house they was ~~fired~~ shot at they
ran to my house an I concealed them an saved their lives they set fire the R R bridge
across Sugar Creek a long bridge that c[os]t a large sum when built had it burned woul
have cut off transportation north an South they then went up to the Depot burned it
an one 100 bales of cotton I ran to the bridge an put it out a circumstanc[e] I hope
you remember my husband hid under the bridge an aided me by handing water. *Col
Stephens* was sent up an took charge of the fort he called on me an I give all the particulars of the fight . . . *Col Stephens* an Capt Moore requisition they presented me for
three thousand Dollars on the goverment Col S said he spoke had to you said I Should
be rewaded . . . last year the drouth was here an nothing raised I was compell to Mortgage my home to live hopeing to raise cotton this year an redeem my home but alas
it was ruined by the frost an we are with out money or mean an need help I am no
imposture . . . my faith is Strong that you will help me no one knows theat I appeal to
you this was Strong cession place during the war if they know they would call it van-
ity an laugh me to scorn some of them wants my land was a Col in the rebellin pleas
help me . . ." ALS (with clerical notations), DNA, RG 94, Letters Received, 2316 1876.
On May 16, 1876, Maj. Henry Goodfellow, judge advocate, wrote to Walsh "that while
the records show a raid on Henderson Station November 25, 1862, substantially as
you describe, no evidence has been found of your services in saving the bridge, but
two other persons, Miss Sarah Rankin and Miss Elizabeth Gentry, are mentioned in
orders, as having turned out with buckets and extinguished the fire. I am also directed
to inform you; that if your statement were fully substantiated, Congress alone could reward you, neither the ~~President~~ Secretary of War nor the Presidents having authority
to use the public money for that purpose" Df, *ibid.* Related papers are *ibid.*

To Adam Badeau

New York City
Feb.y 21st 1882.

My Dear General:

The boxes you refer to are at my house. They were pried open
and discovering that they contained only papers were put in the
store room where they now are.—I shall take no notice of Shipherd
for the present. He stated, truthfully, in a published interview that
I had no interest in the Peruvian Co. and never had. I do not recognize the right of reporters & sensational writers to call upon me
for an explanation whenever my name is mentioned. If I should say
anything to a reportedr it would be that the greatest ~~of~~ objection
I had to the statements of Mr Shipherd was that he associated my

name with those of Reid, Hay Shurts & Medill.[1] But this was partially relieved by the many good names on his list.

Very Truly yours

U. S. GRANT

ALS, Munson-Williams-Proctor Institute, Utica, N. Y. On June 2, 1881, Jacob R. Shipherd, New York City, wrote to Stephen A. Hurlbut, U.S. minister, Lima, listing USG among some fifty individuals and firms, including Edwin D. Morgan, William H. Vanderbilt, John Sherman, and others, "with whom I have already, or shall soon be in confidential negotiations" concerning Shipherd's Peruvian Co., organized to promote American claims against Peru. *New York Times*, Feb. 18, 1882. On Feb. 18, 1882, a reporter called on USG to ask about this letter, published as part of a Congressional inquiry. "General Grant refused to be seen, but sent word that he had nothing whatever to say upon the subject. A number of reporters had called upon him, but he had refused to say anything to any of them." *New York World*, Feb. 19, 1882. See letter to J. Federico Elmore, Nov. 17, 1881.

1. USG's antipathy toward journalists Whitelaw Reid and Joseph Medill dated back to the early days of the Civil War. John Hay had worked under Reid at the *New York Tribune*, where both had supported Carl Schurz and the Liberal Republican party.

To Edward F. Beale

New York City

Feb.y 23d 1882.

MY DEAR GN. BEALE;

Although the papers announce that I am going to Washington it is without any authority whatever. Mrs. Grant & I think a little of going to Florida for a few weeks: but if we do we will not make any stop in Washington until our return. I may, in case of our going, try to arrange to have an hour or two then to see the President. But beyond that I do not want to go there now, and it is not by any means certain that we will go to Florida, or away from here, for the present. Thank for your kind invitation and best regards to your family.

Very Truly yours

U. S. GRANT

ALS, DLC-Decatur House Papers.

To Robert T. Lincoln

———

New York City,
Feb.y 25th 1882.

HON. ROBT LINCOLN:
SEC. OF WAR;
DEAR SIR:

I write to say that I have known Surgeon John Campbell, of the army, since during the Mexican War. I regard him as a capable and deserving man in his profession, and worthy and capable for any position in his corp. I do not want to recommend specifically for promotion to the Surgeon Generalcy. But I do not think that Baxter [1] should be advanced to that place, and I think of Surgeon Campbell—as I probably said in a letter regarding Surgeon Summers [2]—that he should not be overlooked by the appointment of a junior to the position.

Very Truly yours
U. S. GRANT

ALS, DNA, RG 94, ACP, 55 1884. Surgeon Gen. Joseph K. Barnes retired as of June 30, 1882; Charles H. Crane served as surgeon gen. with the rank of brig. gen. as of July 3, 1882.

On Oct. 10, 1883, Lt. Col. John Campbell, Newport Barracks, Ky., wrote to USG. "When the office of Surgeon General of the Army was about to become vacant by the retirement of Gnl. Barnes, though you had already exerted your influence in favor of another aspirant, you were good enough to give me a letter to the President expressive of your opinion as to my fitness for the position. By telegram today I learn with great regret of the death of Genl. Crane—a friend of many years standing—You will regret it for I know you appreciated his worth. The office of Surg. General having thus again become vacant I think it no presumption for me to again aspire to the place—If there were a reasonable chance that Dr. Murray the Senior Surgeon in the Army by length of service would be appointed to the vacancy I wd. not offer myself as a candidate—But as I feel sure that the most prominent candidate will be Dr. Baxter whom neither you nor I consider the proper man for the place I have no hesitation in offering my claim for it—If you have not advocated the claim of any one else then, General—& if you consider me a suitable candidate for the place, will you not say a word to the president—by letter or otherwise in support of my candidateship?—I ask your support in opposition to every one else in the corps except Dr. Murray To his better claim on the ground of seniority I cheerfully defer" ALS, Maryland Historical Society, Baltimore, Md. On Oct. 12, USG endorsed this letter. "On reaching my office after our interview I found this letter on my desk. It is so manly I thought I would send it to you. If you choose to see the letter I wrote the Sec. of War this am you can read the retained copy any time you choose to call at my office." AES, *ibid.* On Dec. 13, President Chester A. Arthur nominated Col. Robert Murray as brig. gen., surgeon gen., to date from Nov. 23.

    1. Jedediah H. Baxter, appointed col. and chief medical purveyor as of June 23, 1874. On March 12, 1872, USG had written to the Senate. "In accordance with an Act of Congress, approved to-day, entitled 'An Act to provide for the designation of a Chief Medical Purveyor I hereby nominate Lieutenant Colonel and Assistant Medical Purveyor Jedediah H. Baxter, to be such Chief Medical Purveyor." DS, DNA, RG 46, Nominations. See *ibid.*, RG 94, ACP, 4433 1875. On Aug. 16, 1890, President Benjamin Harrison nominated Baxter as surgeon gen. ". . . It is an interesting fact that Col. Baxter was selected for the Surgeon General's office nine years ago and lost it through the assassination of President Garfield. . . ." *New York Times*, Aug. 17, 1890.

    2. John E. Summers, appointed surgeon, lt. col., as of March 17, 1880. On Dec. 10, 1874, Summers, Omaha, had written to USG. "When I was in Washington last spring and asked the kindness of you to appoint my son to West Point, I confidently expected to have the pleasure of seeing you again before I should come west, and when I was relieved from duty at Fort Monroe to come here as Medical Director, you were absent, and I tried to reach Chicago while you were there attending the marriage of your son but I failed in that, arriving in the p. m after you left: Doomed to these disappointments, and not having received any positive assurance that you would make the appointment, (but instructed on how and to make the application at once, which was done) and as the period is approaching when those appointments are usually made, I dare venture this letter as a reminder of our conversation on this subject with the hope that you will do me the kindness when the time comes as I have not been the recipient of any favor or reward for the long service rendered, some of which, and by no means the least arduous was with you at Vicksburg" ALS, DNA, RG 94, Correspondence, USMA. On Nov. 23, 1875, Summers wrote to Orville E. Babcock. ". . . When the appointments were made, you may imagine the disappointment to my son, as well as to my self . . . You recollect that while en route from Des Moines to this place I had a conversation with you on this subject, and for the reason that the President had been so completely surrounded and occupied, I had not approached him on the subject, and requested that you would learn from him what hopes I might indulge in for the appointment, which you assured me you would do. . . ." ALS, *ibid.* On Nov. 30, Babcock endorsed the docket. "The President directs that special attention be called to this case when appts are next made, as he intended to have appointed young Summers when app'ts were last made." ES, *ibid.* On Jan. 20, 1876, USG ordered John E. Summers, Jr., appointed to USMA. D, *ibid.* Summers, Jr., who did not graduate, later achieved prominence as a surgeon.

To William F. Vilas

New York City
Feb.y 25th 1882.

MY DEAR GEN. VILAS;

    Seeing a letter from you before me reminds me that I never acknowledged the receipt of yours in behalf of Kasson for the Pension Agency. I did and said all I could for Kasson and regret that he was not successful in his application. The disappointment is partially made up however in the appointment of Gen. Bryant to the Madison Postoffice. That is a double victory, a victory in getting a good man in the place and a victory in getting a "machine reformer" out.

Please express my congratulations to Gen. Bryant, and my kindest regards to Mrs Vilas and your children.

Very Truly yours
U. S. GRANT

ALS, WHi. On Feb. 2, 1882, President Chester A. Arthur nominated George E. Bryant as postmaster, Madison, Wis., to replace Elisha W. Keyes, whose commission had expired. In 1869 and 1873, USG had nominated Keyes, former Republican mayor of Madison, to continue as postmaster. In 1879 and 1881, Keyes ran unsuccessfully for U.S. Senator. For Dexter N. Kasson, see letter to Timothy O. Howe, Jan. 13, 1882.

To Adam Badeau

———

New York City,
Feb.y 27th 1882.

DEAR BADEAU:

The only objection I would have to the use of my name in connection with the Roman Fair[1] is that it would entail on me such an amount of correspondence. Thousand of unknown—to me—people in the United States would write making all sorts of enquiries about the fair; many of them having no other object than to get a letter from me.—I do not know that I shall go south. If I do it will not be this week, and I shall stop in Washington just as short a time as possible. Would see the President however.

Very Truly yours
U. S. GRANT

ALS (facsimile), R & R Enterprises, Catalog 252 (Aug., 2000), no. 41.

1. Rome did not hold a world's fair until 1887–88.

To Chester A. Arthur

————

New York City
March 4th 1882.

THE PRESIDENT:

Soon after your accession to the Presidency I suggested that Gen McKenzie ought to be made Brigadier General as soon as a vacancy occurred, and probably that a vacancy ought to be made by the retirement of Gn. McDowell. I am still of this opinion. But Gen. G. W. Getty, 3d U. S. Artillery, is an officer who has rendered conspicuous service in two wars—the Mexican war and the war of the rebellion,—and is now ellagable for retirement. I would earnestly recommend his promotion and retirement in a short time to make the vacancy for Gen. McKenzie.

Very Truly yours
U. S. GRANT

ALS, DLC-Chester A. Arthur. Maj. Gen. Irvin McDowell retired as of Oct. 15, 1882. Col. Ranald S. Mackenzie was promoted to brig. gen. as of Oct. 26. Col. George W. Getty retired as of Oct. 2, 1883. See letter to Edward F. Beale, [*March 8–10, 1884*].

To Adam Badeau

————

March 7th 1882.

DEAR BADEAU:

Your proposed letter to the President is in good enough tone; but I think I would not send it, but instead would call and say in substance the same thing. If I did send the letter I would omit what is here marked out.

AL (signature clipped), Munson-Williams-Proctor Institute, Utica, N. Y.

On April 5, 1882, USG telegraphed to Adam Badeau, Washington, D. C. "I would accept with conditions named." *Badeau*, p. 542. On April 20, President Chester A. Arthur nominated Badeau as consul gen., Havana. On Aug. 3, Thursday, Arthur wrote to USG, New York City. "I would have been glad to be able to gratify you by the appointment of General Badeau to the Italian Mission, but there were so many embarrassments in the way, (of which I will tell you when I have an opportunity) that I could not well do so. I had thought that the General was satisfied with his present place the emoluments of which certainly amount to much more than the salary of the minister to Italy I suppose however that he would rather be in Europe. It looks now like adjournment on Saturday night, which I earnestly hope for. With sincere regard for Mrs. Grant & yourself, . . ." ALS, Dartmouth College, Hanover, N. H. On the same day, Arthur nominated William Waldorf Astor as minister to Italy.

To Samuel L. Clemens

————

No 2 Wall st.
New York City
March 7th 1882

My Dear Mr. Clemens:

I have an office, not fortified though in a building known as "Fort Sherman". I will be glad to see you in my office, on either of the days named in your letter, between the hours of 11 am & 2 pm. I will also be glad to meet you in my own house any evening when not engaged. On Friday[1] I will have a little party dining with me, but have no engagement for Saturday evening.

Very Truly yours
U. S. Grant

ALS, CU-B.
    On March 11, 1882, Secretary of State Frederick T. Frelinghuysen wrote to USG. "You may inform Mr Clemens that it is not our purpose to make a change in the consulate at Toronto." ALS, *ibid.* USG forwarded this note to Samuel L. Clemens, Hartford. *Ibid.* William C. Howells continued as consul, Toronto. See Henry Nash Smith and William M. Gibson, eds., *Mark Twain-Howells Letters: The Correspondence of Samuel L. Clemens and William D. Howells, 1872–1910* (Cambridge, Mass., 1960), pp. 371, 393–95, 536.

    1. March 10.

To George W. Childs

————

[*March 14, 1882*]

On Tuesday next Mrs. Grant & I go to Washington to be the guests of the President. . . . But we may find it convenient and

agreeable—on account of the number of people who may be pressing me for my influence with the President—to leave earlyer . . .

American Art Association, Nov. 30, 1927. On March 17, 1882, Friday, President Chester A. Arthur wrote to USG. "I have your note of the 15th instant, and will look for
your coming on Tuesday next with great pleasure." LS, Ulysses Grant Dietz, Maplewood, N. J. On March 19, USG telegraphed to Edward F. Beale, Washington, D. C.
"Any day not taken by president up to friday can dine with you probably leave Washn
on Saturday" Telegram received (at 1:48 P.M.), DLC-Decatur House Papers. On March
21, George Bancroft, Washington, D. C., wrote to USG. "We have just heard of your
expected arrival in Washington today. Mrs Bancroft joins me in the request that you &
Mrs Grant will do us the honor to dine with us on Thursday next the 23d at Seven
o'clock. The President has promised us his company on that day; and your presence
with that of Mrs Grant would make the occasion all that could be desired." ALS, DLC-
Chester A. Arthur. On March 22, Arthur held a White House dinner for the Grants.
On March 27, Arthur wrote to Elizabeth Cameron. "Pardon my delay in answering
your note & thank the Senator for his kind invitation. I read your note to Gen. Grant &
he said he would be glad to go between 2 & 3 oclock this afternoon. General Beale, who
was here, said he could drive the whole party to the farm with his 'four-in-hand' team,
in what he calls his 'Omnibus',—and I presume you have heard from him in regard to
it. I could not decide until noon today whether I could go or not,—but have assumed
that we would not go today, on account of the rain & the muddy roads—It may be that
we can all go tomorrow I am glad to know that the Senator is better, . . ." ALS, J. L. M.
Curry Papers, Alabama Department of Archives and History, Montgomery, Ala. On
March 28, the Grants attended Arthur's first public reception.

To George F. Edmunds

———

New York City,
March 14th 1882.

HON. GEO. F. EDMUNDS:
U. S. SENATE:
DEAR SIR:

Mr. J. R. Young having been nominated for the Chinese Mission, and his name being before the Committee of which you are a
member, I take pleasure in giving him this letter of introduction.
As you are aware Mr Young accompanied me in my trip around
the world, and my being to a great extent the guest of the different
Eastern Nations visited, had an opportunity of seeing and studying
those peoples and their institutions as but few travelers ever have.
I believe there is a fine opportunity of extending our influence, and

our commerce, in the East, and that for this purpose Mr. Youngs appointment is the very best that could be made. I supposed that you were personally acquainted with Mr. Young, but he tells me not and therefore this letter believing that on an acquaintance you would believe as I do: that the appointment could not be bettered.

Very Truly yours

U. S. GRANT

ALS, DLC-USG. John Russell Young was nominated as minister to China on March 13, 1882, and confirmed two days later. See letter to James A. Garfield, Feb. 18, 1881; letter to Chester A. Arthur, Dec. 5, 1881. See also Young to Adam Badeau, Feb. 13, 1882, MH.

Speech

[*March 17, 1882*]

MR. PRESIDENT AND GENTLEMEN OF THE FRIENDLY SONS OF ST. PATRICK:—It is true I was made an Irish citizen, having become one in January, 1879, during a short sojourn in the city of Dublin. It is a curious fact that I was immediately affected with that modesty which is so natural to Irishmen. I therefore feel embarrassed this evening. I have not been back in America long enough to overcome it—and unless I should happen to return to the soil of my new citizenship a residence here may relieve me of this embarrassment in time; so that on some future occasion I may be able to say what I would wish. I saw a gentleman come in a few moments ago—Mr. Depew—who is able to say just what I would like to say, and I think you had better ask Mr. Depew to make a speech.[1]

This is a country where every man has an opportunity to make a place for himself. It is never inquired here what was the country of his birth, what was the country of his ancestry. That is one of the beauties of our institutions. In all my travels I came back to my own country a better American than when I went away. And one reason why I am proud of my country is because there is no other nation where the poor man has such glorious opportunities as here. Gentlemen, I am very glad I am here this evening and I leave Mr. Depew to say what I would like to say.

New York Herald, March 18, 1882. USG spoke after U.S. Senator Charles W. Jones of Fla., a native of Ireland. "General Grant alluded in a few complimentary words to the speech of Senator Jones and hoped, as he did, that Irishmen in this country would take advantage of the opportunities that are given to them here." *Ibid.*

On March 10, 1882, USG wrote. "General Grant accepts with pleasure the invitation of the Society of the Friendly Sons of St Patrick to dine with them on the occasion of their 98th Anniversary, at Delmonico, March 17th at 6 30 O'Clock." AN (facsimile), Profiles in History, Catalog 40, [Winter, 2005], no. 122b.

On April 3, at a Cooper Union rally to protest British detention of American citizens suspected as Fenians, John P. Brophy read extracts of letters from supporters. "Mr. Brophy said there was no letter from Gen. Grant, but he was authorized to present this as Gen. Grant's sentiment: 'If I were President I would protect the rights of all American citizens in foreign lands, whether native or naturalized, and when arrested charged with violating the law of any land, I would certainly demand for them an immediate trial.'" *New York Times*, April 4, 1882.

1. Born in 1834 in N. Y., a graduate of Yale College, Chauncey M. Depew was a prominent railroad lawyer and renowned dinner speaker. See Depew, *My Memories of Eighty Years* (New York, 1922), pp. 70–71.

To John A. Logan

WASHINGTON, *March* 24, 1882.

DEAR GENERAL: I understand the case of Lieutenant Campbell, late of the Army, is before the committee of which you are chairman for consideration as to the propriety of his restoration. I do not know the circumstances connected with his leaving the Army, but I want to say a word for the family, and, if possible, for the sake of the family, that he be restored. Colonel and Mrs. Campbell, the father and mother, have for many years been associated with the best families, resident and official, in this city.[1] They have but two children, a son and daughter, the latter married and living abroad.[2] They are getting old and are possessed of but small means. Colonel Campbell is a hopeless invalid, who will never again be able to do anything to aid his family. For these reasons I ask that you take as favorable a view of the case of the son as you can, consistently.

Very truly, yours,

U. S. GRANT.

General J. A. LOGAN, *U. S. S.*

SRC, 47-1-660, 25; *HRC*, 56-2-2987, 26. Charles H. Campbell attended USMA (1863–64), served in the 1st N. Y. Art., was appointed 2nd lt. in 1866, and resigned as capt. on

Feb. 15, 1881, after violating a temperance pledge. As of July, Campbell clerked in the Engineer Dept.

    1. Archibald Campbell married Mary W. Harrod in 1843. In 1872, USG nominated Campbell to the U.S.-Canadian boundary commission. See *PUSG*, 17, 306–7.

    2. Mary G. Campbell married William O. Charlton, a British diplomat, in 1873.

Endorsement

———

I concur in recommending the passage of the above bill. No pension can compensate the men who have lost one or more limbs and I should have been glad to see that class of pensioners well provided for instead of the indiscriminate pensioner,[1] many of whom are physically as good as they would have been if the war had never been fought.

U. S. GRANT

WASHINGTON D. C.
MARCH 27TH 1882.

AES, InU. Printed in *New York Times*, Dec. 22, 1882. Beginning in Dec., 1881, Congress considered legislation to increase pensions for veterans who had lost an arm or a leg. On March 2, 1883, President Chester A. Arthur signed the resulting bill. See *CR*, 47-1, 6656–58, 47-2, 3284–87, 3376–3408; *New York Times*, March 1, 1883; *U.S. Statutes at Large*, XXII, 453; *PUSG*, 28, 513; John William Oliver, *History of the Civil War Military Pensions, 1861–1885* (Madison, Wis., 1917), pp. 90–92.

    1. "As for Grant, ye gods how have the mighty fallen. As President he vetoed the equalization of bounties bill, and then approved the back-pay steal because he was benefited by it. He is perfectly willing that the Government should vote him a pension, but he accuses the poor, helpless soldier of being a fraud. If the veteran who receives a paltry pension of a few dollars a month is a thief and a fraud what is the proper name for a man who accepts a pension of $1,250 per month? Let General Grant figure this up." John M. Bannon, Chetopa, Kan., in *National Tribune*, Jan. 25, 1883. See *ibid.*, March 1, 1883; *PUSG*, 24, 12; *ibid.*, 26, 74–76.

Endorsement

———

The writer of this I have known all his life. His mother is a cousin of mine who I have known also all her life. The young man, from

failure of his eyes, desires the indulgens asked with the view of setting up in the west where he may be employed in other than clerical duties, and asks time to enable him to establish himself. If the
indulgence is one that can be granted with propriety, and without
detriment to the service, I respectfully endorse his application.

U. S. GRANT

MARCH 28TH 1882.

AES, DNA, RG 56, Applications. Charles S. Burke was born in 1856 in Galena to Helen
M. Ross and Melancthon T. Burke. See *PUSG*, 2, 8, 53. On March 28, 1882, Charles
Burke, Washington, D. C., wrote to Secretary of the Treasury Charles J. Folger. "I
have the honor to make application for six months leave of absence, with permission of
placing a substitute in my position on a portion of my salary. My reason for asking the
leave of absence is the failure of my eye sight. I have been employed in the Sixth Auditor's office, as an Examiner of Money-order accounts for seven years. When I entered
the office my sight was perfect; at the present time I am almost unable to use my eyes,
and they are in the condition set forth by the enclosed Surgeons Certificate. In support
of my request I respectfully refer you to the inclosed indorsements." ALS, *ibid.*

On Nov. 2, 1874, and June 2, 1876, USG had endorsed letters from Burke to Secretary of the Treasury Benjamin H. Bristow. "Refered to the Sec. of the Treas. This
applicant is the son of a [cous]in of mine who has been reduced from moderate affluence
to bankruptcy by fires and other losses growing out of the panic of /73." "Refered to
the Sec. of the Treas. Asks promotion. If deemed worthy, and can be promoted without
detriment to the public service would be pleased." AES, *ibid.* Related papers are *ibid.*

To Chester A. Arthur

New York City
March 31st 1882.

THE PRESIDENT:

I take pleasure in presenting to you Judge—General—M. F.
Force, of Cincinnati, Ohio, who visits Washington on business entirely non political. The General was one of Shermans most esteemed Division Commanders, and since the War has several times
been elected to a Judicial office. I am sure you will be pleased to
meet him.

Very Truly yours
U. S. GRANT

ALS, DLC-Chester A. Arthur.

To Michael A. Doyle

———

NEW YORK CITY, *March 31, 1882.*

M. A. DOYLE,
Chairman, etc.:

DEAR SIR:—In response to the invitation of the Committee on Invitations to attend the meeting of the Society of the Army of the Tennessee, to be held in St. Louis, Missouri, on the 10th and 11th of May next, I answer that it will afford me much pleasure to be there in attendance if I can so arrange. I shall try. But I have accepted an invitation to be in Detroit, where I was stationed and well acquainted when a Lieutenant in the army, at a date at this moment forgotten,[1] and if the two do not conflict, I think I will have no trouble about being in St. Louis at the time designated.

Very truly yours,
U. S. GRANT.

Report of the Proceedings of the Society of the Army of the Tennessee at the Fifteenth Annual Meeting Held at St. Louis, Missouri, May 10th and 11th, 1882 (Cincinnati, 1885), p. 222. USG did not attend this reunion. Retired St. Louis merchant Michael A. Doyle had served as 1st lt., 7th Mo.

1. See Speech, [*June 15, 1882*].

To Charles Gayarré

———

New York City
Apl. 4th 1882.

HON. CHAS GAYARRÉ:
DEAR SIR:

Your very interesting letter of the 20th of March reached here, no doubt, by due course of Mail. But my absence from this city at the time, and the large accumulation of mail matter during my absence, has kept it from view until to-day. I will send your letter to the President with a copy of this. I think you will find that President Arthur understands the situation in Louisiana, and the whole south, very well, and is fully disposed to redeem it as far as lays in his power. But you must recollect that he is much embarrassed by circumstances beyond his controll and for which he is in no way responsible. The two political parties are exactly equally balanced in the Senate—which has to confirm all his appointments—and with the Liberals, Independents & Greenbackers neither party has a working majority in the House. In Congress party fealty, I fear, ranks higher than public good. But you have been in politics yourself and know about this better than I do. Each party is trying to gain an advantage over the other to tell in future election. This constrains the President—with the small or no majority of his party in power—to satisfy the republican representatives, at least so far as appointments in their respective states are concerned. He may not do just what they want him in respect to appointments; but he cannot go diammetrically against their will. Hence the cure is with the states. If they will send representatives who truly represent the best interests, the intelligence and virtue, in the state then the National government will also be so represented. I know very well that leaders become tyranical by long success, and it becomes hard to break their power. But if the situation is as bad as you describe it in La. the time cannot be far distant when the people of substance and intelligence will raise up in their power and put none but good men on duty. When they do they will cease to look to the mere utterances of a President for relief.

Hoping that Louisiana may find the desired relief sought, and with assurances that Gen. Arthur is ready and more than willing to give his aid to bring it about, I am

Very Truly &c

U. S. GRANT

ALS, deCoppet Collection, NjP. Born in 1805, Charles Gayarré was a lawyer, politician, novelist, and leading La. historian. On Dec. 18, 1872, Gayarré, New Orleans, wrote to Evert A. Duyckinck. ". . . By the Gods, could you not get somebody to recommend me to Fish or Grant for a mission to Spain or Italy, or something else? Have you any direct or indirect influence at Court? President Pierce was very near sending me to Madrid instead of Soulé, and if he had I cannot but think that I should have cut another figure than Soulé did. If such a diplomatic mission is too high for me, I would accept a consulate to Barcelona, Havana—or anything that might take me out of this African hell. Let Grant try if I cannot do better than Sickles, . . ." Printed in "Some Letters of Charles Etienne Gayarré on Literature and Politic, 1854–1885,"

Louisiana Historical Quarterly, 33, 2 (April, 1950), 249. See "Biographical Sketch of Hon. Charles Gayarre," *ibid.*, 12, 1 (Jan., 1929), 9–27.

To John Cullen Bryant

New York City
Apl. 5th 1882

JOHN CULLEN BRYANT:
DEAR SIR:

I have the pleasure to acknowledge the receipt of yours of the 3d inst. conveying to me an invitation from the G. A. R. of Wilmington to participate with it at an open "Camp Fire" on the 8th of ~~this month~~. May. It would afford me pleasure to accept this invitation but I fear it will not be possible. I have accepted—conditionally—an invitation to be in St. Louis, Mo, on the 11th of May, the occasion being the Annual reunion of the Society of the Army of the Tennessee, and I can hardly attend both.

I thank your Post for the cordiality of the invitation.

Very Truly yours
U. S. GRANT

ALS, deCoppet Collection, NjP. See *National Tribune*, May 20, 1882. John Cullen Bryant, former private, 46th Mass., was a bookseller in Haverhill, Mass.

To Timothy O. Howe

New York City
Apl. 5th 1882.

HON. T. O. HOWE:
POSTMASTER GENERAL:
DEAR SIR:

There has been employed in your office for a number of years a lady of refinement, education and family—Mrs. Mary E. Wilcox—who I understand there is now an effort being made to have removed, and partly on the ground of being charged to Tenn. while she was not born there and has not lived there for a number of years. Mrs. Wilcox was born in the Executive Mansion because that event took place while her Uncle, or her fathers Uncle, was President of the United States, and her father & mother were a part of the Executive household. Her father, Andrew J Donalson, was always a citizen of Tenn. and I believe his daughter has always been also. But being left a widow, without means, she has been obliged to live where she can get such employment as will give her and her children a support. I hope you will give Mrs. Wilcox an opportunity of speaking for herself if her removal is in contemplation.

Very Truly yours
U. S. GRANT

ALS, DNA, RG 59, Applications and Recommendations, Hayes-Arthur. Born in 1829, Mary E. Donelson married then U.S. Representative John A. Wilcox of Miss. in 1852. Wilcox died in 1864 while serving as C.S.A. Representative from Tex. See letter to Mary E. Wilcox, April 12, 1882; *HRC*, 56-1-1880; Pauline Wilcox Burke, *Emily Donelson of Tennessee* (Richmond, 1941); Harriet Chappell Owsley, "Andrew Jackson and His Ward, Andrew Jackson Donelson," *Tennessee Historical Quarterly*, XLI, 2 (Summer, 1982), 124–39.

To Chester A. Arthur

New York City
Apl. 10th 1882

THE PRESIDENT;

To-morrow being "Cabinet day," and assuming that in all probability whatever action you propose to take in the F. J. Porter case will then be closed, I venture to address you once more upon the subject. As I have before said verbally, and in writing,[1] I take a very deep interest in this matter because I deem myself somewhat responsible for the continuous punishment of an officer of high rank in the Army, whos innocence I am now as sure of as it is possible for one to be on human evidence. I do not ask you to change any views you may entertain about the case, but I would ask that if you cannot conscientiously recommend his case favorably to congress that you can refer to the report of the Advisory Board,[2] its conclusions, and, if you choose, to what I have said and written since my recent review of the case, and leave Congress to act without the weight of Executive recommendation against it.

Very Truly yours

U. S. GRANT

ALS, DNA, RG 94, ACP, P228 CB 1869. See letter to Fitz John Porter, Dec. 27, 1882.

1. See letters to Chester A. Arthur, Dec. 22, 1881, Jan. 23, 1882.
2. See *SED*, 46-1-37.

To Jesse Root Grant, Jr.

———

Apl. 11th /82

DEAR JESSE;

Your Ma has just received your dispatch saying that you would be up on Thursday, and that you would come to us if we had room. There is one room above the library and one in the 4th floor where the nurse and babe could sleep, but there is not an other room—nor separate bed on 4th floor—for the maid. We would be delighted to to have you stay with us but you see that with Fred & Nellies families we are pretty well filled up.

Yours Affectionately

U. S. GRANT

ALS, Chapman Grant, Escondido, Calif.

To Mary E. Wilcox

———

New York City

Apl. 12th 1882.

MY DEAR MRS. WILCOX:

Your letter of the 8th inst. only reached me yesterday. While I can deeply sympatize with you I do not know how to advise or to help you. I am disappointed with the effect—lack of effect—of my letter to the Postmaster General. You might ask some of your friends to speak to the Sec. of State in your behalf. I know he has but few female clerks in his office; but you could be very serviceable there on account of your education, particularly in foreign languages.

Very Truly yours

U. S. GRANT

ALS, DNA, RG 59, Applications and Recommendations, Hayes–Arthur. On July 3, 1882, U.S. Representative William R. Moore of Tenn. wrote to Secretary of State Frederick T. Frelinghuysen. "*Private* . . . I learn, I dont know how truly, that that *Mrs Wilcox*, whose *democratic* son is already in your Dept, is seeking a position there also. As she has always been hostile to our *party* and our *cause*, I hope she may not be put in over the *Union* Soldier's widows. Will give you written proofs if desired. . . . P. S. she was formerly in P. O. D." ALS, *ibid.* As of July 1, 1883, Mary E. Wilcox clerked in the Treasury Dept. See letter to Timothy O. Howe, April 5, 1882.

On March 11, 1872, Cadmus M. Wilcox, USMA 1846, New Orleans, had written to USG. "I write to you at the request of my sister in-law Mrs Mary E Wilcox of Nashville Tennessee, to ask the appointment of Cadet at the military academy for her Son Andrew Donelson Wilcox. My Sister in law—is the daughter of Majr Donelson of Tennessee, (lately deceased) and though you may never have known him personally, yet you know of him. He was a graduate of West Point and his daughter is anxious to have her Son graduate there also. This Sister of mine was born in the White House and lived her first four or five years there, her father being the private Secretary of Genl Jackson when he was President It has been a long time General, since I have had the pleasure of meeting Mrs Grant, yet I feel quite certain that I am not forgotten by her or by yourself either, and must beg therefore to be kindly remembered to her." ALS, DNA, RG 94, Unsuccessful Cadet Applications. On Nov. 9, 1874, USG wrote. "Understanding that a vacant clerkship exists in the Court of Claims I venture to suggest to the Court the name of And. D. Wilcox—grand son of And. Jackson Donaldson—as a suitable person for the position." ANS, CSmH.

To John F. Long

———

New York City,
Apl. 15th 1882.

MY DEAR JUDGE LONG:

While in Washington I had a full conversation with the Sec. of the Treasury in regard to your appointment; the animus that seemed to move the last Administration in regard to Mo. appointments &c. and said all I could for your restoration. The Sec. seemed to pay special attention to what I said, and I observed that he took notes while I was talking. This gave me hopes that either soon, or the time of the present incumbent expires we might expect favorable action. But I received no further assurances than was given by appearances. I am much obliged to you for your interest as continuously manifested. I wish I could get rid of my St. Louis property all together or in pieces. I would sell it cheap either way, and give purchasers as much time as they wanted by paying part cash and the interest on the balance semi annually.

Please say to your daughter, Mrs. Hawkins,[1] that this answers her letter of the 7th of this month. With kind regards to all your family.

Very Truly yours
U. S. GRANT

ALS, MoSHi. See letter to Charles J. Folger, June 26, 1882.

    1. Lily Boggs Long had married Otis R. Hawken in 1857.

To Edward S. Tobey

New York City
Apl. 18th 1882.

MY DEAR MR. TOBEY:

I am in receipt of your letter of yesterday. I think there can be no possible danger of your removal from office during your term, and not then if you are endorsed by the Boston delegation. But I do not think it proper to intercede in matters of local appointments in states having republican representatives, and in fact have resolved to abstain for the future from troubling the President with recommendations for appointments of any kind.

Very Truly yours
U. S. GRANT

ALS, DLC-George H. Stuart. On March 24, 1881, Edward S. Tobey, postmaster, Boston, wrote to USG, New York City. "As you are aware I am indebted to your confidence & kindness for the commission *first* as one of the Board of Indian Commissioners, and second for my commission as Postmaster, & third you kindly invited me to accept an appointment as 'Commissioner of Indian Affairs' which circumstances compelled me to decline When I accepted my present ~~commission~~ office from you it was in a *pecuniary* sense quite unimportant, but I regarded it as in the highest degree complimentary on yr part, as also as that of Govr Jewell—The loss of a quarter of a million of dollars by the war has made this position now *very important to me* & to my family—My renomination by Presdt Hayes was advocated by *all the Bank* & Insurance Co officers in this city, & also by our leading merchants, & *no opposition* appeared from any quarter The nomination & re-nomination were *unanimously* confirmed by the Senate. I have administered the duties of the office and business as Civil Service rules prescribed in form & in detail by the Post Office Dept, & by Presdt Hayes in an *autograph* letter I have good reason to believe that the public generally are satisfied with the efficiency of the service, but I am desirous of being fortified in the favorable opinion of Presdt Garfield in order to provide against the contingency of any efforts of managing politicians & subordinate mal contents to displace me—As I have not the honor of the acquaintance of the President will it be too presuming for me to ask of you the favor of your friendly influence on my behalf either by a brief letter or in personal interviews? If you do not find it entirely consonant with your own views to comply with this suggestion, I shall of course beleive that your reasons are sufficent & still remain, as ever, with the highest esteem and friendly consideration . . . P. S. My best wishes will accompany you on your proposed visit to Mexico—I am gratified to notice that you have withdrawn from official connection with the 'World's Fair of 1883." ALS, USG 3. Tobey retained his post. See *PUSG*, 26, 361–62, 365, 374; letter to World's Fair Commission, March 22, 1881.

On April 28, 1882, Ulysses S. Grant, Jr., New York City, wrote to S. Prentiss Nutt. "The General says that he would be most happy to be of service to Mr Merril whom he appreciates highly, but in this case in addition to his unwillingness to burden the authorities with his recommendations for office, he believes that Mr Merril is bodily incapacitated from performing the duties of any office, and he is unwilling to become sponsor for Dunbar." ALS, OHi. S. Prentiss Nutt was the son of Haller and Julia A. Nutt of Natchez. Ayres P. Merrill, Jr., also of Natchez, had served as minister to Belgium under USG. See *PUSG*, 9, 215–17; *ibid.*, 16, 197–99; *ibid.*, 24, 387–88; *ibid.*, 26, 185–86.

To Maj. Gen. Irvin McDowell

New York City
May 2d /82

DEAR GENERAL:

I send you the letters requested in your letter which I found at my house this am. I will try to think of it to bring the papers which you furnished me—except the pamphlet, your defence, which I want to keep. I do not know that I care for the return of any the letters sent with this unless it may be the one from Gen. McClellan.

Very Truly yours
U. S. GRANT

ALS, MHi. On March 24, 1882, a correspondent reported from Washington, D. C. "Considerable excitement prevails in Army circles here to-night over a report, said to emanate from trustworthy sources, that the President has practically determined to place Major-Gen. McDowell on the retired list and to promote Gens. Pope and McKenzie. These changes are said to constitute one of the objects of Gen. Grant's present visit to Washington." *New York Times*, March 25, 1882. See letter to Chester A. Arthur, March 4, 1882.

To Roland Worthington

———

[New York City, May 20, 1882]

After my congratulations upon your appointment and confirmation as Collector, matters in which I felt a great interest, allow me to ask of you if consistent with your views and the public good. I have living with me a Butler a colored man by the name of Terrell. He has a son now working his way through Harvard. I believe he is now about entering the junior class. While pursuing his course of studies he has to earn his own living. This he does by work during vacation and earning what he can in the interval. he will present this letter—his name is Robert Terrell—and ask employment in the Custom House such as he can do without interrupting his course. Terrells letters show him to be a young man of good ability and of the right kind of aspirations. If you can give him a position to help him he will appreciate the kindness and I will also.

Very Truly yours
U. S. GRANT

Robert A. Siegel Auction Galleries, Inc., Sale 760A, May 28, 1994, no. 3077 (last 11 words and closing in facsimile). Roland Worthington took over the *Boston Traveler* in 1845 and eventually affiliated with the Republicans. His nomination as collector of customs, Boston, provoked Civil Service reformers. See *New York Times*, April 9, May 10, 16, 1882, March 21, 1898. Robert H. Terrell graduated from Harvard University in 1884; he later married Mary Eliza Church, who became a Civil Rights leader. See letter to Roland Worthington, July 3, 1883; letter to Harrison Terrell, June 2, 1885; Louis R. Harlan, ed., *Booker T. Washington Papers* (Urbana, Ill., 1972–89), IV, 447; Beverly Washington Jones, *Quest for Equality: The Life and Writings of Mary Eliza Church Terrell, 1863–1954* (Brooklyn, 1990).

To George W. Childs

———

N. Y. May 23d /82

MY DEAR MR. CHILDS:

There is a box—possibly two boxes—containing swords and canes which we can not find and thought possibly they had been left with you when we went abroad. May I enquire if this is the case, and if you have them will you be kind enough to express them

to us. In June Mrs. Grant and I expect to take a trip West to be gone about two weeks. Immediately on our return we will go to Long Branch for the Summer where we expect to see much of you. Our house has been so crouded this Winter that we did not have the expected visit from you & Mrs. Childs and Drexel and wife.

Very Truly yours

U. S. GRANT

P. S. During my little summer excursions you may have my fast horse exclusively for your own driving.

ALS, Georgetown University, Washington, D. C.

To James D. Cameron

NEW YORK CITY, May 29, 1882.

Hon. J. D. CAMERON, *U. S. S.:*

DEAR SENATOR—I understand the bill for the relief of Gen. F. J. Porter will be called up to-morrow, if there is a session, if not, on the first meeting thereafter. I hope you will do all that is proper to expedite a hearing and vote in his case. My feeling in this matter is intensified by my thorough conviction of Porter's innocence of the charges upon which he was convicted and the fact that I am more or less responsible for the long delay in having justice—partial justice—done him. Logan made an able speech against Porter, believing him guilty, as I did at the time, but I do not believe he will benefit himself by renewing the attack, now that an investigation, not only by an able and impartial board, acting as judges and not as defenders, unqualifiedly pronounce him innocent, but writers of history, free from prejudice or prejudiced against him, also so find.

If you can urge a vote this week, I will regard it as a special favor. The bill is a very mild one in comparison to what I think is due Porter; but perhaps it is better that it should be so.

Very truly yours,

U. S. GRANT.

General Grant's Unpublished Correspondence in the Case of Gen. Fitz-John Porter (n. p., n. d.), pp. 15–16. On May 8, 1882, U.S. Senator William J. Sewell of N. J. introduced a bill to restore Fitz John Porter to the army. On May 31, the Senate received majority and minority reports from the Committee on Military Affairs, but debate on the measure did not begin until Dec. 28. See *CR*, 47-1, 3689, 4358; *SRC*, 47-1-662; letter to James D. Cameron, Feb. 4, 1882; letter to Fitz John Porter, Dec. 27, 1882.

To Hamilton G. Howard

———

NEW YORK CITY, *June I.* [*1882*]

DEAR SIR: I have your letter of the 29th ult. Perhaps I should have written to you on the receipt of your former letter to tell you what I had done in the matter of your request. My excuse for not doing so is that I receive more letters in regard to appointments than I can possibly answer.

But as soon as your letter was received I made as favorable endorsement as I could on it, and forwarded it to the President. If I had retained a copy of my endorsement I would enclose it to you. But I did not. I remember, however, that I called the attention of the President to the services and standing of your father; to the fact also that you resided in Utah, and could, therefore, afford to accept the position, although the compensation would not justify a person from outside, competent for the place, in accepting it except as a sort of missionary work.

Very truly yours,

U. S. GRANT.

Hamilton Gay Howard, *Civil-War Echoes: Character Sketches and State Secrets* (Washington, 1907), p. 267. A lawyer and former secretary to his father, U.S. Senator Jacob M. Howard of Mich., Hamilton G. Howard was active in Detroit politics. "The first time I met General Grant after the receipt of the foregoing letter was after the lapse of several months. He was in my home city and holding a quasi-public reception. As I approached to shake his hand he was standing at rest, with his eyes looking down upon the floor, there being a cessation of callers. On my name being announced to him by the chairman of the reception committee, he quickly looked up, smiled, cordially grasped my hand, and remarked as if the subject was fresh in his mind: 'I suppose you have not heard from Washington yet. I wrote as strongly as I could to the President, but I am afraid we made a mistake in asking your appointment to be credited to Utah.' He was right. I did not get the appointment." *Ibid.*, pp. 267–68. USG visited Detroit June 13–15, 1882, for an army reunion. In Utah Territory to pursue a mining venture with his brother Charles, Howard sought appointment to the Utah Commission, established by Congress in March to prevent polygamists from voting or holding office. See *ibid.*, pp. 264–65, 298; *PUSG*, 27, 378; Howard to James A. Garfield, Jan. 17, 1881, DLC-James A. Garfield.

To Charles J. Folger

New York City
June 2d 1882.

Hon. Chas J. Folger;
Sec. of the Treas.
Dear Sir:

Mrs. Lucy M. Porter has been for some months—on my recommendation—a temporary clerk in the Navigation Div. of the Treas. She is now, I believe, discharged or about to be, while but few as worthy and none more competant will necessarily be retained. Mrs. Porter is a lady of accomplishment and talent. She is the daughter of Ex Governor and Senator Morehead of Ky.—a collegue of Clay & Crittenden in the Senate, and the widow of an officer of my old regiment. She lived in Ky. during the war and notwithstanding her surroundings she was an open and able advocate of the Union Cause. She is now somewhat advanced in life and is without a relative or friend to look to for help. As a Clerk she is abundantly able and willing to earn her support. I think there is not a more deserving case in your department than hers.

Very Truly yours
U. S. Grant

ALS, DNA, RG 56, Applications. Lucy M. Porter continued as clerk, Internal Revenue and Navigation. See letter to Charles J. Folger, Dec. 28, 1881.

To William A. Phillips

New York, June 7 *1882*

Hon Wm A. Phillips
Washington D. C.
Dear Sir,

I owe you an apology for not answering your letter of May 25th earlier but I was not able to do so at the time and with the accumulation of letters it has been misplaced until now. I would be very glad indeed to accommodate you in the matter about which you write me, but the number of applications which come to me for endorsement for public positions became so great that some two months ago, or more, I had to resolve to take no further part in matters of appointment,[1] and have so written to many persons who have asked me for my endorsement. Had I thought of it on the occasion of the President's visit to this city I would have taken pleasure in mentioning your son's application to him in person, but would prefer not to have further letters on file from me on the subject of appointments.

Very truly Yours
U. S. GRANT

ALS (facsimile), Signature House, Catalog XXX, no. 541. Journalist and lawyer William A. Phillips founded Salina, Kan., and served as territorial judge, col., Indian Home Guards, U.S. Representative (1873–79), and Cherokee lobbyist.

1. See letter to Edward S. Tobey, April 18, 1882.

To Robert E. Peterson

New York, June 8 *1882*

R. EVANS PETERSON ESQ.
ROOM 5—330—WALNUT ST.
PHILADELPHIA PA.
DEAR SIR:

Having received your letter of May 18th at the house, it was put in my pocket to respond to at my office, and it has laid there ever since, forgotten, until now. My office is No. 2. Wall St where I can usually be found between the hours of eleven and one and any time that you may be inclined to call I will be very glad to see you. On Monday Evening[1] I leave for Detroit and will be absent from the city for the balance of the week. Before and after that time I will be at the office as indicated above.

Please accept my apologies for not attending to your letter sooner.

Truly Yours
U. S. GRANT

LS, Ralph G. Newman, Chicago, Ill. Born in 1812 in Philadelphia, Robert E. Peterson was by turns a hardware merchant, lawyer, bookseller, publisher (with George W. Childs), and physician. His daughter Emma married Childs. A son, Robert E., is listed as R. Evans Peterson, engraver, in the 1880 census.

1. June 12, 1882.

To Otto von Bismarck

N. Y. City,
June 9th 1882.

HIS EXCELLENCY, PRINCE BISMARK
DEAR PRINCE

I take pleasure in presenting to you Mr. Emery A Storrs, a distinguished lawyer of Chicago Illinois, who visits Europe this Summer on a tour of pleasure and recuperation. I am sure you will be pleased with Mr. Storrs, and find him a good representative of a villege that has grown from a fronteer Indian trading post fifty years ago, to a city of 600.000 inhabitans now, with a suburb of probably 100.000 more—and fully one third as many Germans as Berlin has. Mr. Storrs is specially anxious to make your acquaintance being familiar as he is with your great and distinguished public career. He will appreciate any attention he may receive as I will to have him received as my personal friend.

Very Truly yours
U. S. GRANT

ALS, ICHi. On June 9, 1882, USG wrote to Premier Léon Gambetta of France, introducing Emery A. Storrs. ". . . Mr. Storrs will esteem it a great favor to make the acquaintance of one who has done so much for free government, and whos public acts he has watched with so much interest. . . . you will find him an able and agreeable advocate of the same principles in his own country that you advocate in yours . . ." Hudson Rogue, May, 1992, no. 34. Storrs arrived in New York City from Liverpool in Oct. See letter to John A. Logan, Jan. 10, 1881.

To Arthur MacArthur

New York City
June, 10th 1882.

Dear Judge

I have a letter from your son, Capt. McArthur,[1] requesting my interest in his behalf to get him attached to the Chinese Legation.

Since my conversation with the Captain a few weeks since, seeing the interest he has taken in Eastern affairs, and the study he has given the subject, I am not only satisfied that his selection would be the wisest that could be made, but that the appointment of such an Attache to our Chinese Legation might be attended with good results in establishing better relations with those people. I know there is a sort of morbid sensitiveness on the part of Congress and the press generally against trusting soldiers anywhere except in front of the cannon or musket. But if this matter is laid before the President I will willingly give my vews in favor of such an Appointment, and of the selection of Capt. McArthur for the place.

Very Truly yours
U. S. Grant.

Copy, DNA, RG 59, Applications and Recommendations, Hayes-Arthur. A Scottish immigrant, Arthur MacArthur served as Wis. lt. governor (1856–57) and judge before USG appointed him to the D. C. supreme court in 1870. MacArthur wrote to President Chester A. Arthur enclosing a copy of USG's letter. ". . . The occasion of the General's letter can be briefly stated. Capt Arthur MacArthur of the 13th Infantry U. S. A. has made a special study of China for several years, and has learned all that can be acquired from books concerning its history, institutions and characteristicts, and he entertains, notwithstanding recent legislation very favorable views of our relations with that great Empire. He desires to suggest to the President the expediency of a military Attachee to our Embassy in China as a step which would be attended with highly desirable results. Capt MacArthur would deem it a great privilege to be selected for this position. In that event he would make China his place of residence for years perhaps for life, in order to learn its language its military peculiarities, and all matters relating to its commercial intercourse with the United States, and generally to serve American interests in every way which a perfect knowledge and study of the Country would enable him to do. I beg to add that General Grant is quite willing to furnish his views in favor of the measure, and I have reason to believe that our minister the Hon John Russell Young will address a communication upon the subject to the Department of State. All of which is Respectfully submitted" LS (docketed June 23, 1882), *ibid.* On April 9, 1883, Secretary of War Robert T. Lincoln wrote to Secretary of State Frederick T. Frelinghuysen. "*Unofficial.* . . . I have read Mr. Young's despatch with care. I do not perceive that the War Department has any interest in sending a military attaché to our Legation to China; . . . In case it should be thought desirable that an officer should be attached to our Legation to China, I would feel bound to recommend that some officer not a captain should be selected, for the reason that Captains of Companies are especially needed with their companies, . . ." LS, *ibid.* Typed copies of USG's letter and a lengthy "Chinese Memorandum and Notes," dated Jan. 15, 1883, and signed by Capt. Arthur MacArthur, Jr., are *ibid.*, RG 165, War Dept. Staff, Historical Section. See Kenneth Ray Young, *The General's General: The Life and Times of Arthur MacArthur* (Boulder, 1994), pp. 127–29, 141–42.

On May 28, 1872, USG had written to ministers and consuls introducing MacArthur, Sr., "who proposes traveling in Europe. The Judge is one of our best Citizens and entitled to the respect and consideration of the representatives of our country abroad, and I commend him to your kind offices during his sojourn in your vicinity." Copy, DLC-USG, II, 1. See *PUSG*, 19, 495.

1. Born in 1845 in Mass., Arthur MacArthur, Jr., enlisted in the 24th Wis., mustered out as lt. col., and was nominated as 2nd lt. and promoted to capt. in 1866. On May 31, 1872, John H. Twombley, president, University of Wisconsin, wrote to USG requesting that MacArthur be assigned as military instructor. ALS, DNA, RG 94, ACP, M37 CB 1866. On June 17, John Potts, chief clerk, War Dept., wrote to Twombley that such assignments only went to 1st lts. of art. or retired officers. Copy, *ibid.*, RG 107, Letters Sent, Military Affairs. On July 2, Orville E. Babcock wrote to AG Edward D. Townsend. "The President directs me to say that he desires that you will extend the leave of absence of Capt. Arthur McArthur Jr., for thirty days." LS, *ibid.*, RG 94, ACP, M37 CB 1866. On July 25, U.S. Senator Matthew H. Carpenter of Wis., Milwaukee, wrote to USG. "You will remember the conversation we had at the White House about detailing Capt McArthur 13. Infty, as teacher of tactics &c at the University of Wisconsin, Madison Wis: and that you directed the Adjt General to extend the Captn's leave of absense so as to save him the nicessity of travelling to & from his regiment The leave was extended, but the order detailing him has not come. The Capt is anxious to have the matter determined and I hope you will direct it to be done." ALS, *ibid.* On July 28, USG endorsed this letter. "Refered to the Sec. of War. Capt. McArthur may be detailed as requested." AES, *ibid.* On Aug. 21, Secretary of War William W. Belknap wrote to Carpenter. "When the President had the conversation with you relative to the detail of Captain McArthur, 13th. Infantry, as professor of tactics, &c, in the Wisconsin University at Madison, alluded to by you in your letter of July 25th., 1872, he was unaware of the condition of Capt. McArthur's company, which is commanded by a 2nd Lieutenant of another company—its own 1st Lieutenant being absent sick, and no 2nd Lieutenant having been assigned to it. These facts having been brought to the attention of the President, he has directed me to say that under these circumstances Captain McArthurs services are imperatively needed with his company and to express his regrets that a Captain cannot be furnished the Institution as the interests of the service require that they should remain with their commands." Copy, *ibid.*, RG 107, Letters Sent, Military Affairs.

To Julia Dent Grant

————

Detroit June 14th *1882*

My Dear Mrs. G.

Fred & I arrived here about ten last night. Gn. & Mrs. Sheridan are here, the latter coming because she expected to meet you. This morning Mrs. Chandler[1] sent you a beautiful boquet, as large as a center table, and was coming herself to call in person. Sheridan Fred & I called on her however before she had a chance to come and told her you were not along. She sends much love. We also called on Mrs. Brush.[2] Mrs. Newberry[3] has also sent you an invitation to go with a number of ladies on a yacht excursion to-morrow. I have written her declining for myself by saying that I was sorry you were not here to accept. We will get home about breakfast saturday[4]—late breakfast.

U. S. G.

ALS, DLC-USG. Written on letterhead of the Russell House. Julia Dent Grant endorsed this letter. "I keep all of these as souveners of the past" AES (undated), *ibid.*

1. Probably Letitia G. Chandler, widow of Zachariah Chandler.
2. Probably Eliza H. Brush, widow of Edmund A. Brush.
3. Probably Helen P. Newberry, wife of former U.S. Representative John S. Newberry of Mich.
4. June 17, 1882.

Speech

————

[*Detroit, June 15, 1882*]

Mr. President: I cannot respond to your call to get upon the table. I am bad enough scared where I am. I have attended the Army meetings from Boston to Iowa, and I don't know but further West, and I have left every city where they have been held fully impressed with the hospitality of the City and State. I feel that it would be almost a blessing to be a native or a citizen of each of them as I have left them, but I have never expressed so strong a desire to make any change in regard to my citizenship until I have heard your Governor and your Mayor talk about your City and your State.[1] All that we as guests have experienced bears out all their statements about both the City and State, and I am proud to relate a fact which I never before thought of claiming, and that is, I was once a citizen of Michigan and of Detroit. At the time, I thought it was purely accidental, and I did not avail myself thoroughly of the benefits conferred upon me, but hereafter I shall claim that I was once a citizen of Detroit. I was stationed in this city from April, 1849, to April, 1851. During that time the present Constitution of the State was ratified, and by its terms it made every American citizen residing at that time within the State a citizen of Michigan. I was then in a small garrison, stationed not far from where we are. We were all made citizens, and an election following soon after, the most of them thought for the first time in their lives they would exercise one of the prerogatives of the citizen, which soldiers scarcely ever get an opportunity to exercise, and that was, to vote, and they marched down to the polls, and their ballots were received as citizens of the State and of the City. I myself abstained, because I rather thought I belonged to Ohio at that time.

I am now a little inclined to go back and claim my rights as a former citizen, yet I am glad that I abstained from voting on that occasion. The candidates for election for the office of Mayor were two very highly respectable citizens, one of them the late Senator of this State, Zachariah Chandler, and the other John R. Williams,[2] and if I had cast that vote I would have voted against Mr. Chandler.[3] I am very glad now that I did not do it. If we were going to stay here a day or two longer, I would suggest that, either by ratifying another constitution, or in some other way, you make General Sheridan a citizen, because he started out with the first command he had above that of the escort at the army headquarters, with Michigan troops. He never brought disgrace upon those troops, nor did the troops bring disgrace upon him. I therefore suggest General Sheridan for citizenship.

The Society of the Army of the Potomac. Report of the Thirteenth Annual Re-Union, . . . (New York, 1882), pp. 70–71. USG addressed the closing banquet.

On June 14, 1882, USG became an honorary member of the Society of the Army of the Potomac. *Ibid.*, p. 10. Later, he spoke about the army. "The Orator of the evening has said that it was reduced to a machine, with a thinking attachment; and that is the advantage that our volunteer armies all have over the standing armies of the world. They have the physical courage and the physical endurance of the machine armies that fight for pay, without any feeling at all in the cause they serve, and they have more. All our volunteer armies fought because they thought earnestly of what they were fighting for. The private was as much interested in the success of our arms as the general officer. The volunteers were not fighting for their generals or their rulers, but for a cause in which the generals and the privates were equally interested. As the Poet this evening has said, *that* illustrates the greater strength of our Republic, the great advantage in strength which it has over monarchical governments where all the people who fight are mere machines who get no benefit from their victories." *Ibid.*, pp. 39–40. Edward S. Bragg had delivered the oration. ". . . The material of the early volunteers has no equal in any standing army in the world; they readily assimilated to the professional soldier in discipline, and though rarely becoming the military model of a soldier—a machine—yet they were capable of assimilation to an extent that they might properly be called a machine with a 'thinking attachment'; the attachment when too obtrusive was noisome, but as a rule added largely to the *esprit de corps* of the command. . . ." *Ibid.*, pp. 31–32. Poet John Boyle O'Reilly read "America." *Ibid.*, pp. 20–24. USG remarked: "There is more meat in that poem than in any one I have ever heard." *Detroit Free Press*, June 16, 1882.

On June 15, USG received callers including James D. Elderkin, 4th Inf. veteran. "Mr. Elderkin was accompanied in his visit by his wife, and as soon as the General saw them he instantly recognized and advanced to receive them with evident gratification, recalling to Mrs. Elderkin the occasion when he sent her a coat to wear, an allusion which Mr. Elderkin, when subsequently questioned on the subject, explained as follows: 'I don't know that it's entirely fair to tell you the story, but since you insist, it will do no one any harm. When the Fourth Infantry went to California, Gen. Grant was Lieutenant and Regimental Quartermaster, and I was Drum-Major. The cholera broke out among the troops on the Isthmus, and Lieut. Grant came to me and said: "Sergeant, you must get your wife over to Panama if you can—if you can't get a jackass for her to ride, you had better let her walk; but she must wear men's clothes." He gave me a $20 gold piece to hire a jackass, and I rigged my wife out, managing to provide her with pants and everything else, but a coat. I told him of this and he said: "Why, I've got a coat that's just the thing," and gave it to me for her. She put it on and wore it across the Isthmus and into Panama, and that's how my wife borrowed the General's coat.'" *Detroit Free Press*, June 16, 1882.

1. Governor David H. Jerome of Mich. and Mayor William G. Thompson of Detroit addressed the banquet.

2. Born in 1782 in Detroit, a soldier and merchant, John R. Williams served six terms as mayor between 1824 and 1847. Zachariah Chandler defeated Williams in 1851.

3. In Jan., 1851, USG fell on an icy sidewalk and sued Chandler. See *PUSG*, 1, 195.

Endorsement

Referred to the President. Maj. Moore was an efficient and I believe thoroughly honest Treasury official I believe also that there are persons in the Treasury—who ought not to be there—who are willing to resort to any measure to keep him out of public appointment. I do not credit the report that Bliss[1] has pretended to represent me in this matter for I have had no conversation with him about Maj. Moore, nor have I ever had a conversation with any one which indicated that I took no interest in the Major.

U. S. GRANT

N. Y. JUNE 16TH 1882.

AES, DLC-Chester A. Arthur. Written on a letter of June 10, 1882, from William B. Moore, Washington, D. C., to [USG]. "It is just one month since you gave me a kind letter to President Arthur, and within a few days of that period since I handed the letter to Gen. Arthur in person. I enclose copy of letter to the President which explains the history of my case since that date. Every device has been resorted to to prevent action on your letter. The latest method comes to me second handed from the libeller George Bliss; assuming to be in the confidence of Sec'y Folger, he gives it out that you have no interest in my success and that the course of the administration meets your approbation. I only mention this because the Secretary's total disregard of your letters justify the presumption that he is influenced by such stuff. The clouds thicken around me and this crushing neglect by those for whom I threw myself into the breach when John Sherman sent his dirt flinging Committee to NewYork to put up a job on Collector Arthur in 1877, is driving me desperate when I see its consequences approaching My Wife and little ones. I appeal to you to ask the President whether I am to be ostracized and end my suspence. The Presidents kindly manner towards me on all occasions leads me to believe that if he understood your earnest wishes in my behalf, he would take immediate steps to right me of the injustice under which I suffer." ALS, *ibid.* Appointed deputy 4th auditor in 1875, Moore resigned after accepting an irregular payment from a naval paymaster. See *New York Times*, May 19, 1881, Jan. 7, 1894; *PUSG*, 27, 161–62, 164–67; Memorandum, Feb. 7, 1885.

1. Former U.S. attorney under USG, lead prosecutor for the Star Route mail fraud cases, George Bliss, Jr., was "known to be one of the closest political and personal friends" of President Chester A. Arthur. *New York Times*, Oct. 28, 1881. See *PUSG*, 23, 327–28.

To Edward F. Beale

Long Branch, N. J.
June 24th 1882

MY DEAR GENL BEALE:

Mrs. Grant & I will be glad to have a visit from you, Mrs. Beale & Emily, coming say about Monday, July ninth. I have asked General Cameron to come a week earlyer. If he cannot come then, and a

week earlyer would suit you better, I will let you know when I get
his answer, and invite you for the 2d of July.

    With love from Mrs. Grant & myself for you and family,

Very Truly yours

U. S. GRANT

ALS, DLC-Decatur House Papers. On June 29, 1882, USG, Elberon, N. J., telegraphed
to Edward F. Beale, Washington, D. C. "Can you not come by here & stop a day or two
on your way to California" Telegram received, *ibid.*

To Chester A. Arthur

———

New York City,
June 26th 1882.

THE PRESIDENT:

    Some two weeks since I promised Mrs. Coleman—the daugh-
ter of John J. Crittenden—that I would write you in behalf of her
brother, Gen. Crittenden,[1] late Marshal of Ky. and at the same time
say a word for her son, who has been for a long time second Sec.
at Berlin. General Crittenden as you probably know, has been a
Union man, and republican, from the start. He is very poor and
has a young family. If any position in his state can be given him
whereby he may make a living—at the same time rendering an
equivalent,—it will be a favor bestowed on a most worthy man.
Young Coleman[2] has been a long time second secretary. He is a
good French & German scholar, and when I was Berlin the Minister—Bayard Taylor—told me, almost indispensible. He would
like to go to Vienna as Secretary if he cannot be promoted where
he is. The old gentleman—Delaplain[3]—now in Austria is well off,
and has seased long since to be an American Citizen in the proper
sense. That is; he would not live in America probably for any office
that could be given him here. The first Secretary at Berlin[4] would
not live in the United States if he was out of office I do not think.
England he regards as his home.

    I write this in regard to the secretaries named more as infor-
mation—if you are not already in possession of it—than as a rec-

ommendation for a successor to either. But I would rather this letter should not filed as a part of the record for future refferences
while I do not mark it confidential. We Americans recognize the
right of self expatriation; but we do not recognize it as a claim for
recognition.

Very Truly yours

U. S. GRANT

ALS, DLC-Chester A. Arthur. For Ann Mary Coleman, see *PUSG*, 26, 156–58.

1. In [*April, 1869*], James Speed, Joshua F. Speed, and Silas F. Miller wrote to USG
recommending Robert H. Crittenden as marshal, Ky. ". . . We do it because we feel entire
Confidence in his integrity & ability, & further, because he has been from the beginning
of the war till now a true union man & a radical. Radically right in all his views & votes.
Mr Crittenden is a son of the late John. J. Crittenden" LS (docketed April 13), DNA, RG
60, Records Relating to Appointments. Appointed by President Rutherford B. Hayes,
Crittenden was replaced in March, 1882. See *New York Times*, March 1, 1884.

2. Chapman Coleman continued as 2nd secretary of legation, Berlin. See *PUSG*,
28, 439.

3. Born in New York City in 1815, heir to a shipping fortune, John F. Delaplaine
graduated from Columbia College and settled in Vienna, where he became secretary of
legation in 1869. See *New York Times*, April 4, 1884, Feb. 15, 1885.

4. A Harvard graduate (1855), son of Mass. statesman and orator Edward Everett, H. Sidney Everett was appointed secretary of legation, Berlin, in 1877. See *ibid.*,
April 18, 1885, Oct. 7, 1898.

To Adam Badeau

———

N. Y. June 26th /82

DEAR BADEAU.

I am sorry I have been out every time you called recently. I
want to see you before you go.—The very day after I saw you last
letters began to come in acknowledging the receipt of the book.
Nearly all have now been acknowledged—I will be in town again
on Thursday.[1] If you can come in then ~~and~~ go down and spend the
night with me at the Branch. If you cannot come then go to the
Branch on Saturday and stay over Sunday. If you can go on Thursday stay the balance of the week. We have no company invited for
this week, consequently plenty of room.

Very Truly Yours

U. S. GRANT.

P. S. The mail laying before me when you were in had the acknowledgement from Lytton, the first received. Next I believe was from the King of Siam.

U. S. G.

Copy, Munson-Williams-Proctor Institute, Utica, N. Y. USG sent complimentary copies of Adam Badeau's *Military History of Ulysses S. Grant* to dignitaries he had met in his travels abroad. See letter to Robert C. Napier, Jan. 16, 1882.

On April 10, 1882, Prince Bhanurangsi of Siam wrote to USG. "I have duly received the three volumes of the Military History of U. S. Grant, which you did me the honor of presenting to me and of superscribing with your own hand, and beg to express to you my warmest thanks for this interesting present. Since you left this country I have often been thinking and been reminded of you, though I have not been in correspondance with any one of the Gentlemen of your party except Dr. Keating, with whom I have frequently exchanged letters but who also has of late been silent. I am therefore the more agreeably surprised to receive your friendly lines for which I am exceedingly thankful to you, showing that the friendship we contracted some years ago has not been forgotten. I am very happy to have your assurance that you are well in every respect and to be able to state the same regarding myself and hope that you will always remember me with the same friendly sentiments I have always felt towards you ever since making your acquaintance, when thinking of me. Hoping that your well being and our friendly intercourse will continue for many years to come—. . ." LS, USG 3. On April 27, Chancellor Otto von Bismarck of Germany, Friedrichsruh, wrote to USG. "With great pleasure I have received here at Friedrichsruh during a few days retirement to the country your kind letter of the 16. of January accompanied by a complete set of General Badeau's History of your military exploits, the first volume of which is already adorning my library. I have great pleasure in accepting this kind of keepsake fully reciprocating, as I do, your pleasant recollection of our meeting." LS, *ibid.* On May 23, King Alfonso XII of Spain wrote to USG on the same subject. LS (in Spanish), Nellie C. Rothwell, La Jolla, Calif. On the same day, James O. Putnam, U.S. minister, Brussels, wrote to USG. "I have the honor to state that to-day I had the pleasure of presenting to His. Majesty, the King of Belgium, the 3 volumes of History of our War by General Badeau and of your letter—at an audience given me at his Summer Palace at Laeken. The King expressed great pleasure in this your remembrance, and desired me to express his thanks and to say that he should acknowledge the receipt of the volumes by letter very soon. He wished me to convey to you his sentiments of great respect and regard, stating that hoped you would revisit Belgium at some future day." ALS, USG 3. On May 25, King Oscar II of Sweden wrote to USG. "I just had the pleasure to receive the copy of Badeau's interesting work 'Military History of Ulysses S. Grant', you to me and I beg you now to accept my best thanks therefore." LS, *ibid.* On May 31, Caroline C. Marsh, Rome, wrote to [USG] transmitting the thanks of Queen Margherita of Italy for copies of Badeau's books. Doris Harris Autographs, Jan., 1983. On June 12, King George I of Greece wrote to USG. "I have received your letter dated January the 16th, and feel exceedingly obliged to you, for having sent me a copy of Adam Badeau's history of the rebellion, treating about your military life. This work I shall read with great pleasure, as every thing that concerns your noble country, the american nation, and yourself, is of the highest interest for me." LS, USG 3. On July 29, James R. Lowell, U.S. minister, London, wrote to USG. "I enclose a letter from

Colonel Noeli which will serve to show that I executed the Commission with which you honoured me. I am glad of the occasion to say how much General Badeau's book has interested, & how glad I was of the chance of retracing Connectedly a career so glorious for yourself & so serviceable to our Country." ALS, *ibid.* On Oct. 2, Viceroy Li Hung-chang of Chihli, Tientsin, wrote to John Russell Young, U.S. minister, Peking. "I am in receipt of General Grant's valuable present of his illustrious Military Life in three volumes forwarded to me through you from your consul, for which I thank General Grant very much. In perusing his wonderful career I shall take great pleasure to follow him in all his glorious campaign and gain wisdom and experience from his skilful generalship. Please tender to him my highest esteem and wish him every happiness and prosperity." Copy, DNA, RG 59, Diplomatic Despatches, China. Related papers are *ibid.*

On Jan. 5, 1883, Isaac J. Lansing, Stamford, Conn., wrote to USG. "I have just finished the History by Badeau of Your Military Campaigns. Permit me to Express to you my sense of personal obligation as an American Citizen for your Eminent services so unostentatiously performed for our country's welfare. That principle in your action which led you to do your duty undazzled by the gilded ambitions of political preferment, and equally to persist undeterred by the oppositions of an uninformed public deserves honest commendation. May I also be permitted to say that Mr. Badeaus declaration that he never heard you use a profane oath or tell an immodest story commands for you an admiration scarcely less than that called forth by your comprehensive military plans. Last Saturday I met Mrs. Dr. Cramer at the residence of my friend Oliver Hoyt Esq., to whom I remarked that I desired to express to you my unfeigned gratitude and respect, although my words might seem of small account among the many testimonials which you have received and to which you are justly entitled. She did not encourage me to follow my inclination as now I do. If I survive you, with a multitude of others I expect to eulogize your work when you have passed away. May I not then do what I judge equally appropriate and what your modesty will not count amiss, may I not say that your history inspires me with gratitude and admiration from an intellectual standpoint, no less than from a patriotic view—I wish you yet many years of life which I am sure will be made more satisfying to you by reason of the increasing regard entertained for you by your Countrymen among whom I am glad to be numbered. With sentiments of unfeigned goodwill, and high esteem, . . ." ALS, USG 3.

On March 29, Alonzo Flack, president, Claverack College and Hudson River Institute, Claverack, N. Y., wrote to USG. "When last in New York I asked Messers D Appleton & co. to publish a $1 50 School Edition of Badeau's Military History of General Grant. & told them I would use one hundred copies a year in this School and other schools would do the same I urged upon them, that the youth now in school knew nothing of Your Services to their Country before they were born, & that it was but justice to you that Every youth of the land be permitted to read such a work as a well prepared abridgement of your military History would make In answer to whether it would pay I offered money for privilege to publish it They replied, if there was money in it they needed it, & told me to See you & with your approbation they would publish it. Hence this letter. On the receipt of the three large volumes I read them through in nine days full of business & shed tears of Gratitude to God that Heaven had made you Such a man I read these volumes with this interest after I had followed you daily from first leaving Gelena until the Surrender at Appomattox. I was with the army (as a citizen) every few months from the beginning of the war until near the close. I came to the battlefield of the Wilderness a few days after the battle, & continued in the front until you crossed the James.—The day of the last charge at Cold Harbor a dying officer requested me to ask you to come & shake his hand & he would die happy—You were so busy I did not deliver the message, which I always regretted—One who knows & appreciates as I do your Services feels it a duty to have read such a book as I ask your publishers to issue" ALS, Munson-Williams-Proctor Institute, Utica, N. Y. On March 31, USG endorsed this letter to Badeau. "I have answered Mr. Flack approving his idea and told him that you had suggested the same thing yourself. I also told him that I would forward this letter to you." AE (initialed), *ibid.*

Between 1881 and 1883, USG wrote to Badeau. "In cleaning up my desk to go to the city I find Pleasantons criticisms on your book. You will find that after all it was Thomas and Rosecrans—principly Pleasanton—who captured Richmond" AN (initialed), *ibid.*

1. June 29, 1882.

To Charles J. Folger

New York City,
June 26th 1882.

Hon. Chas J. Folger;
Sec. of the Treas.
Dear sir:

I presume a new Surveyor for the port of St. Louis, Mo. will soon be designated. I have lived longer in St. Louis than in any other place, ~~fo~~ except Washington, for the last forty years and am better acquainted. Of the candidates for the Surveyorship Judge Jno. F. Long, in my opinion, is far the preferable. As I stated to you verbally when in Washington if he is appointed he will be the Surveyor himself, independent of assistants, and can give bonds without sacrificing his independence in the conduct of his office.—It will probably be urged against him that he voted for Hancock in the last election. He did, but as he wrote to me it was from sheer disgust with—well I will not say what—but if he could have separated the ticket he would have gladly voted for the second on the ticket. I have no doubt but the business men of St. Louis—without regard to party—will say that Judge Long made the best Collector St. Louis has had in forty years except possibly Breckenridge,[1] and inferior to none they have ever had. I hope the President will see his way clear to appoint him.

Very Truly yours

U. S. GRANT

ALS, University of Iowa, Iowa City, Iowa. On Aug. 3, 1882, President Chester A. Arthur nominated Charles M. Whitney as surveyor of customs, St. Louis. See letter to John F. Long, April 15, 1882.

1. Samuel M. Breckinridge, a St. Louis lawyer, served as surveyor of customs from 1867 to 1869. See *PUSG*, 20, 270.

To George W. Hayward

────────

New York, June 27 *1882*

GEO. W. HAYWARD ESQ.

CHAIRMAN &c

BUFFALO N. Y.

DEAR SIR:

I am today in receipt of your letter of the 26th inst, inviting me to attend the semi centennial celebration of the charter of the city of Buffalo. While thanking you for your kind invitation I regret that it will be impossible for me to attend. I have a partial engagement to attend a soldiers reunion in Vermont[1] which I must keep if I leave home at all at that time.

Truly yours.

U. S. GRANT

LS, Buffalo Historical Society, Buffalo, N. Y. George W. Hayward was a Buffalo grocer and selectman. Buffalo held its fiftieth anniversary on July 4, 1882.

1. On July 3, USG, Long Branch, had written to "Dear General," probably William W. Henry, former col., 10th Vt., and bvt. brig. gen. "I find that it will be impossible for me to meet the Vermont veterans at their approaching reunion, as I had looked to do. It has been been—and is—my expectation to pass through Vermont this Summer, and I would have been glad to happen in at the soldiers' reunion, I was not sure until within a day or two that I would not run up there especially for the occasion, but events have transpired which make it necessary for me to remain here for this week. Hoping the veterans a pleasant reunion and many returns of them, . . ." *Burlington Free Press & Times*, July 5, 1882. Vt. soldiers met at Burlington July 3–5.

On July 1, USG had written to Charles E. Lippincott, former col., 33rd Ill., Frank M. Davis, 2nd Ill. Light Art., and Finis E. Downing, circuit court clerk, Cass County, Ill. "I am much obliged for your invitation for me to be present on the occasion of the soldiers reunion, to be held in Virginia, Ill . . . but regret that I cannot accept. Even if I could attend I should be obliged to decline that part of your invitation which requests me to go prepared to speak on the occasion . . ." The Rendells, Catalog 136, 1978, no. 46; American Art Association, Nov. 30, 1927.

To Elizabeth M. Borie

———

Long Branch, N. J.
July 2d 1882.

My Dear Mrs. Borie:

Mrs. Grant is so anxious to see you that I write to ask if you can not come on Saturday next,[1] or the Monday after, and spend a week with us. We have plenty of room and it will be more quiet than later in the season.—We both hope that your trip abroad has been of benefit to you, though we sympathize deeply for the affliction which overtook you in the loss of such a promising young man as your nephew. We will hope to see you as above, and to make your time pass agreeably.

Very Truly yours
U. S. Grant

ALS, PHi. See letter to Elizabeth M. Borie, July 31, 1882.

1. July 8, 1882.

To James D. Fish

———

New York City, July 6, 1882.

My Dear Mr. Fish:—

On my arrival in the city this A. M. I find your letter of yesterday, with a letter from Thos. L. James, president of Lincoln National Bank, and a copy of your reply to the latter. Your understanding in regard to our liabilities in the firm of Grant & Ward are the same as mine. If you desire it I am entirely willing that the advertisement of the firm shall be so changed as to express this.

Not having been in the city for more than a week, I have a large accumulated mail to look over and some business appointments to meet, so that I may not be able to get down to see you to-day. But if I can I will go before three o'clock.

Very truly yours,

U. S. GRANT.

New York Herald, May 27, 1884. On July 5, 1882, James D. Fish wrote to USG. "(Private.) . . . You and I do not often meet to talk over our business matters or for any other purpose; but I trust you are well aware the failure to do so is not for any want of respect, esteem or friendship on my part. We are both pretty well occupied generally, which explains it. I think, however, it would not be amiss for you and me to counsel a little occasionally in regard to the business of Grant & Ward, as our conservative influence, if not beneficial, would do them no harm, as they are so much younger than ourselves. I have often been asked by friends and business men whether you and I were general or special partners   We were for a time advertised as special, but I think we are virtually and actually general partners, and I think, legally, we would find that to be our status. The enclosed letter to me from President James, of the Lincoln National Bank (to whom I sent a Grant & Ward note to be discounted), was received by me, and I send you a copy of my reply to his letter. You may be aware that I am on the notes of Grant & Ward as indorser—which I have discounted myself and have had to get negotiated to the extent of $200,000 in aggregate at the same time and at once, which is not a trifling amount for me. It is necessary that the credit of G. & W. should deservedly stand very high. These notes, as I understand it, are given for no other purpose than to rais[e] money for the payment of grain, &c., purchased to fill the government contracts. Under the circumstances, my dear General, you will see that it is of most vital importance to me particularly that the credit of the firm shall always be untarnished and unimpaired. I will be happy to meet you at almost any time you may name to talk these matters over. Please return me Mr. President James' letter at your convenience, with any suggestions you may have to make." *Ibid.* On July 1, Saturday, Thomas L. James, New York City, had written to Fish. "I will submit your favor to the Board of Directors on Wednesday next. Will you kindly inform me whether you are a general partner in the house of Grant & Ward?" *Ibid.* Fish then answered James. "In answer to your inquiry I have to say that both General Grant and myself are now general partners in the firm of Grant & Ward. We were originally special partners only, but by recent arrangement we have both become general partners." *Ibid.* See following letter.

To James D. Fish

New York, July 6th *1882*

My Dear Mr Fish,

In relation to the matter of discounts kindly made by you for account of Grant & Ward, I would say that I think the investments are safe and I am willing that Mr. Ward should derive what profit he can for the firm that the use of my name and influence may bring

yours very truly,

U. S. GRANT

LS (facsimile), *New York Sun*, May 30, 1884. "Gen. Grant made public yesterday letters to James D. Fish referring to the Government contracts of Ward & Grant and the profits thereon. . . . After the above letter of Mr. Fish, marked 'private,' had been answered and the correspondence had been closed, Mr. Ward prepared a draft of a letter and handed it to Mr. Spencer (who was in the employ of the firm) to copy. Mr. Spencer says he did copy it and delivered the copy to Mr. Ward, who went to Gen. Grant and obtained his signature to it. This letter and the signature were wholly disconnected with the preceding correspondence, so far as Gen. Grant knew, and nothing was told him from which he could suspect that the two things had any relation to each other, nor did the General scrutinize the letter, but signed it on the assurance that it was only an ordinary letter in the course of business. The incident made no impression, and the following copy of the letter, now obtained, is all the evidence of its contents the General has: . . ." *New York Times*, May 27, 1884. This incident was revisited in the trial of James D. Fish. "Cashier George E. Spencer, of Grant & Ward, was recalled. He stated that on July 6, 1882, he wrote the following letter from a memorandum on a small piece of paper handed to him by Mr. Ward, who told him to copy it the first thing on his arrival at the office that morning. The memorandum had no signature. . . . This was the letter which Mr. Fish received, signed by U. S. Grant, and which Gen. Grant had no recollection of writing. Mr. Spencer said it was the only time he had been called upon to copy a letter for Mr. Ward. That day Gen. Grant arrived at the office in the afternoon. He spoke to Mr. Ward, sat down at his desk a moment, and then went away. When the lithographed copy of the letter appeared in a morning paper with Gen. Grant's signature to it, Gen. Grant's attorney called and made some inquiries about the letter." *Ibid.*, April 10, 1885. See preceding letter; Memorandum, [*May, 1884*]; Henry Clews, *Fifty Years in Wall Street* (New York, 1908), pp. 219–21.

To Matías Romero

———

LONG BRANCH, N. J., July 12, 1882.

MY DEAR SIR: I am just in receipt of your letter of yesterday in regard to the arrival of President Barrios, of Guatemala. I had read in the morning papers of his reception in New-Orleans, and his intention of proceeding immediately to New-York. In my judgment, there is not the least ground for apprehension on account of his visit. He will unquestionably be received by the President and Secretary of State with great courtesy, as he ought to be as the representative of a neighboring republic; but annexation of territory will have but few advocates, and the treatment by the press of the country of such men as advocated interference in foreign countries, shows that any scheme of that kind would be extremely unpopular. As to our Government's interfering in the question of boundary between Mexico and Guatemala, I am sure there need not be any anxiety felt by Mexico. If Mexico and Guatemala should agree between themselves to refer any question between them to the United States as arbitrator, as Portugal and England did in regard to conflicting claims to territory on the east coast of Africa,[1] of course our Government would hear the statements of both parties, and give its judgment in the matter referred to it. But even then, I do not suppose that the United States would do any more than to use its "good offices" to have the contending parties accept her decision, if either should feel inclined to reject the decision. I am not, of course, authorized to say a word for the Administration on this subject. But I am certain that I know the sentiment of the country on the question of annexation. If the good offices of the United States could be used effectively to induce the Central American republics to consolidate into one I have no doubt but it would do so. But, then, the request would have to come from all of them. Certainty the United States would not attempt to coerce a consolidation at the instance of the President of one State and in his personal interest. The most that would likely be done would be to inquire through our representative to those countries as to the feeling of the people and officials on the subject of consolidation.

Very truly yours,
U. S. GRANT.

New York Times, July 20, 1882. Born in 1835 in western Guatemala, Justo Rufino Barrios joined an 1867 revolt, emerged as a military and political leader, and won election as president in 1873 and 1880, enacting liberal reform measures. On July 11, 1882, a correspondent reported from Washington, D. C. "In his Message to the Guatemalan Congress on April 24 Gen. Barrios said that he would not leave his country until there should be a definite settlement of the disputed question of boundary between Guatemala and Mexico. On May 22, however, Señor Montufar, the Guatemalan Minister in Washington, informed Secretary Frelinghuysen of Gen. Barri[o]s's intention to pay an official visit to the President of the United States. It is said that the objects of Gen. Barrios in coming to Washington are two in number—to obtain the support of this

Government and an exertion of its influence in favor of Guatemala in the disputed boundary question, and to bring about, with the aid of the United States, a consolidation of the five Central American States into one republic." *Ibid.*, July 12, 1882.

On Sept. 5 and 6, Matías Romero, Washington, D. C., wrote to USG, Long Branch. "I communicate in due time, to Señor Mariscal, Secretary of State of Mexico, both your letter to me of the 12th of July last about our then pending difficulties with Guatemala, and your subsequent permission to give it to the Press with the object that your views should be generally known and shape, in some degree, public opinion on this subject which object was, I believe satisfactorily accomplished. Señor Mariscal instructs me, in an official letter dated at the city of Mexico, on the 3d of August 1882, (No. 703) to inform you that President Gonzáles was very much pleased to see your consent for the publication of your letter, and desires me to formally thank you in his name for your friendship in this case. Although I had the pleasure of communicating this fact to you while I had the honor to stay with you at you house in Long Branch, it affords me great pleasure to make now this communication to you in writing." "I arrived to Washington yesterday morning and wrote you the enclosed letter, transmitting to you the thanks of the Mexican Government for your kind assistence to us in our difficulties with Guatemala. Sr. Balcarcel reminds me that in October next the time fixed in your cable grant for surveying the ground will expered, and that if the survey is not made, the deposit of $3,000 will be lost. I have thought that you might desire an extension of said grant and in that case it might be convenient to write Gen. Diaz on that subject. If you desire it, I will write him myself in your name. I presume the reason why he desired secrecy on the other subject, was to avoid that Guzman should hear about it and work to defeat his (Gen. Diaz') purpose." ALS, USG 3. On Sept. 21, James H. Work, New York City, telegraphed to Romero. "Telegram received, also letters to General. Opened by him this morning. General will be away tomorrow and I will be necessarily at Long Beach tomorrow & Saturday. will you come to LongBeach tomorrow night by four PM train and stay with me. You can get back to NewYork early in the morning, Saturday, if you wish Answer" Telegram received (facsimile), DLC-Matías Romero.

On Oct. 10, Work wrote to Romero. "I suppose it is unnecessary for me to say that I would like much to see you before you leave for Mexico about Mexican Southern matters. We are without an answer to Gen. Grants last telegram which leaves us still in a little uncertainty as to just what Gen Diaz is disposed to try to do for us. Maj. DeGress is on his way to Mexico and will, I believe, be on the same steamer that you go on, as I think it touches at Galveston, at which place he expects to take steamer. I have another reason for wishing to see you if you can arrange it with me before you meet Mr Barney and the Tehuantepec bond holders tomorrow. I have been personally and we have as an office here been a little embarassed by the course that Mr Barney has taken in this matter. As you will recollect I made some inquiries of you about the situation with a view to extending to some of the bond holders who were friends and clients of ours, our good offices, and those of Gen. Grant through you in Mexico. When I spoke to you on the subject I found that the matter had progressed more than I knew of and that you had what I understood to be some private communication from the Fomento department in Mexico which you thought would authorize you if you chose to do so, to meet and discuss the situation with the bondholders, or arrange for some reorganization of the company. You asked me to suggest the idea of some arrangement of this kind to these gentlemen and to say that I spoke as the result of a conversation with you. This I did, and afterwards saw you and told you that I understood that Mr Barney whose name you had mentioned to me as having been previously sent by you to these gentlemen had in the meantime called upon them, and I then said that it might be well to say to Mr Barney that so far as he appeared in the matter we did not wish to interfere with him, and would be very happy to co-operate with him in any negotiations which were to be had affecting this matter. I thought it only right to treat your wishes with delicacy and in my interviews with the bondholders did not feel authorized to go into any detail in stating what the Mexican Government would agree to, or to state that I was authorized to represent the Government, as I did not think that You would be pleased to have me take this position, although you did authorize me to say that I came personally from you. I was pleased with this position and thought it only natural in view of our railroad connections in your country and the fact that we have had the relations that we have had with you in connection with them,—that we should be the medium of communication and negotiation. However, on Mr Barneys meeting these gentlemen he has been very explicit in stating to them that he came as your representative and as the former representative of the Mexican government (so they tell me) and has so placed the matter that as a matter of courtesy to you, if for nothing else, they feel that it would be unnecessary to discuss the matter with us. I would not refer to the subject at all if I did not feel a little the embarassment which has been caused to me personally by having been as I think treated with some unintentional discourtesy by Mr B. in the matter. As it now stands we are placed in the position of having offered good offices which were wholly unnecessary, and having represented ourselves as authorized to speak for you when we were not." ALS (facsimile), *ibid.*

On Nov. 14, President Porfirio Díaz of Mexico wrote to USG introducing Robert R. Symon, a British financier active in Mexico. ALS (in Spanish), James S. Copley Library, La Jolla, Calif. See *New York Times*, Nov. 29, 1880, Jan. 30, 1899.

On Dec. 23, a correspondent reported from Panama. "The *Guatemal[t]eco* of Dec. 12 publishes a translation of a contract signed in New-York on Oct. 6 last, between Gen. Barrios and Gen. Ulysses S. Grant, President of the Mexican Southern Railroad Company, under which, in return for certain concessions, this company undertakes to build 250 miles of railroad in Guatemala within two years after the Mexican Southern line reaches the Guatemalan frontier." *Ibid.*, Jan. 4, 1883.

On Jan. 29 and Feb. 19 (twice), 1883, Work wrote to Romero. ". . . What I desire is that I shall have from you an expression of opinion in general terms that the Company's rights and privileges are of a favorable character, and that as matter of law in your opinion they are legally perfect and will remain so to the Company if we commence work at Anton Lizardo within the six months allowed us by the extension of our contracts. The General tells me that you intend to visit New York City before long—possibly some day this week, and if so you need not answer this letter except to let me know that you are going to be in New York, and I can talk with you about the subjects which I mention in it when you are here." "The General has just informed me that some few days ago while you were here, he had a visit from a gentleman who holds a bond upon what he calls the 'Bustamente property' in Mexico, which stretches along the line of the International Railroad, and which involves a very large tract of land, mines, settlements etc. He said nothing to me about it when the gentleman was in here because I think the General was not aware that we were in communication with English parties who would be very likely to take such a thing as this. Such however is the case, and if you know the gentleman in question and will ask him to be kind enough to come in and see me, I will talk with him a little about the project, and if he has sufficient length of time in his contract for the purchase to enable us to communicate with England, and meantime have an examination of a preliminary character made here, it is quite possible that we may be able to operate to our mutual advantage. . . ." "In relation to Anton Lizardo matters and our port contract there, I have just received from VeraCruz a statement of the schedule of charges for lighterage and the charges for what is called 'Introduction from the wharf.' I find that these charges in most cases, if not all, are considerably in excess of the sums which are allowed us by the 'port Contract', the contrast being so great as I think in most cases to make a comparison affect us unfavorably. I enclose you a slip giving the charges as sent to me. They are furnished by the house of Cos Castillo & Co. Would it not be desirable for us to have an amendment incorporated in our port contract allowing us to charge the same rates which are allowed for similar services at VeraCruz, or at least a provision which shall state that in addition to what is already allowed us we shall at all times be allowed at least as favorable charges for similar services as are allowed at the port of VeraCruz. There are one or two other points which I think could be covered to our advantage in case we were going to suggest an amendment, one being with reference to the transfer of the charter rights, and the other allowing us to separate the estimates for harbor improvement which are referred to in the contract so that a deficiency occurring in any portion of the work might be made to lap over on to another part. I can hardly explain what I mean by letter but would be glad if you would take an opportunity to speak with me on this point if you happen to be in NewYork City soon again" LS, DLC-Matías Romero.

On Feb. 26, Noble E. Dawson, Washington, D. C., wrote to Romero. "Personal . . . Do you remember a certain Mr. Peña, who was axious to get Gen. Grant's attention directed to some mines in the State of Guerero at the time we were in Mexico, two years ago? Do you know what he afterwards succeeded in doing with his mines? And if he did not succeed in disposing of them, could you tell me his present address,—or how I could be placed in communication with him? If you will be good enough to tell me all you can about him or the mines in which he is interested, I will consider it a great favor. . . ." ALS, *ibid.*

Also on Feb. 26, USG wrote to David D. Cone, Washington, D. C. "Your letter of Feby. 24, as also one of previous date were duly received, and were by me sent to Sr. Romero. I would therefore advise you to communicate directly with him upon the subject of their contents." LS, *ibid.* See *PUSG,* 23, 253.

1. On April 21, 1870, USG had awarded the island of Bolama to Portugal. See *PUSG,* 28, 329; *HMD,* 53-2-212, II, 1909–22.

To Gilbert A. Pierce

Long Branch, N. J.
July 17th 1882.

DEAR CAPT.

Your letter of the 4th of July reached me in due time; but not having time to answer it when received I put it in my pocket and forgot it for a time. There was talk at one time of purchasing the

Tribune as you say, by persons friendly to me. But I had no part in the matter. I do not know why the scheme fell through; probably the price was too high, or the owners would not sell.

I would not know who to go to in regard to the purchase of the Inter-Ocean, but I will give your letter to Col. Grant to see if he knows parties willing to invest in such an enterprize.

Very Truly yours
U. S. Grant

ALS, Goodspeed's Book Shop, Inc., Boston, Mass. A novelist and author of *The Dickens Dictionary* (1872), Gilbert A. Pierce edited the *Chicago Inter-Ocean* from 1871 until 1883, when he moved to the *Chicago Daily News*. See *PUSG*, 9, 239; *ibid.*, 22, 352–53; *New York Times*, Feb. 16, 1901.

To Charles G. Williams

Long Branch, N. J., July 24, 1882.

The Hon. C. G. Williams, Chairman Committee on Foreign Affairs:

Dear Sir: Seeing there is a disagreement in the conference committee of the Senate and House as to whether the refunding to Japan of the indemnity exacted from that Government—improperly, as I verily be[*l*]ieve, and I was strongly confirmed in that belief during my visit to that country—should include the interest received by our Government on the bonds purchased with the indemnity, or whether only the principal should be paid, I venture to write you a line on the subject. I am satisfied the money should never have been collected. Having been collected, it should now be refunded. Justice seems to me to dictate that interest as well as principal should be paid, just as the House by its action decided. But the principle involved is of much more importance to Japan than all the money in question, and I am satisfied Japan would be much better pleased with the refunding of the money exacted without any interest than with a gross amount larger than the original sum, but less than that with interest added. The Eastern countries have been so unaccustomed to "fair play" from the stronger powers of the world that this action of Congress—if consummated—will be such a new departure as will redound to our credit, if we receive no other benefit. I write, therefore, to express the hope that the conference committee will agree by one or the other of the two branches—one favoring the payment of interest in full, the other of paying only principal—yielding entirely and not compromise on a part of the interest. I hope you will not regard this as an attempt to interfere with the matters of legislation on my part; but as President I took an interest in this matter, and as a traveler since, I confirmed the views previously entertained on the subject. Expressing the sincere hope that this matter will be finally and creditably settled before Congress adjourns, I am very truly yours,

U. S. GRANT.

P. S.—If any rate of interest should be agreed upon in lieu[1] of what the Government has actually received from the bonds purchased with the indemnity, the principle involved would be preserved, even if the rate should be low. But the appropriation of a gross amount to be returned, without the amount being based on any calculation of what is due to Japan could not, in my opinion, be as well received as the admission that we hold, and have held for a number of years, funds actually the property of that country, and now we want to return it, and the question is, with or without interest, and if with interest, at what rate?

U. S. G.

New York Times, July 31, 1882. Born in 1829 in N. Y., Charles G. Williams settled in Janesville, Wis., in 1856, practiced law and was elected to the House of Representatives as a Republican in 1872.

Congress adjourned on Aug. 8, 1882, before House and Senate conferees could agree on a revised indemnity bill. On Feb. 15, 1883, a correspondent reported from Washington, D. C. "Mr. WILLIAMS, of Wisconsin, submitted the conference report on the Japanese Indemnity Fund bill. The effect of the bill as agreed to in conference is to return to Japan the original sum received from that Government ($785,000) without interest, to pay the officers and crews of the Wyoming and the Ta Kiang $140,000, and to cancel all the bonds comprising the Japanese indemnity fund. After a debate the report was agreed to." *New York Times,* Feb. 16, 1883. On Feb. 22, President Chester A. Arthur signed the bill. See letters to John Russell Young, [*March, 1881*], Nov. 28, 1882; James L. Huffman, "Edward H. House: questions of meaning and influence," *Japan Forum,* 13, 1 (2001), 15–25.

1. Another version has "view." *Washington Post,* July 31, 1882.

To Randolph Huntington

Long Branch, N. J., July 28, 1882.

Randolph Huntington, Rochester, N. Y.

Dear Sir,—About my Arabian horses, I cannot answer all your questions, but what I know I will give you.

I was in Constantinople in March, 1878, and visited the Sultan, and with him his stables.

All of his horses were of the most approved and purest blood (and there were about seventy horses in the stables I visited). I was told that the pedigrees of all of them ran back from five to seven hundred years (in breed).

Two of the horses that I then saw were sent to me as a present from the Sultan by the first steamer directly to the United States from that port. I do not know the name of the steamer, nor the date of its departure or arrival. They (the horses) were consigned to General E. F. Beale, of Washington City, who can probably inform you upon those points. Leopard was five years old when I first saw him, and Linden four, I think. I am certain as to the age of the first, and think I am right about the age of the second.

The fact of these horses being from the Sultan's own private stables, and being a present from him as an appreciation of our country among the nations of the earth, is the best proof of the purity of their blood.

Very truly yours,

U. S. Grant.

[Randolph Huntington], *History in Brief of "Leopard" and "Linden," General Grant's Arabian Stallions,* . . . (Philadelphia, 1885), p. 16. See *PUSG,* 28, 354, 356, 357; letter to Daniel Ammen, July 16, 1879. Born in 1828 in Mass., Randolph Huntington settled on a farm near Rochester, N. Y., where the 1880 census listed him as a retired druggist. On July 26 and 30, 1882, Huntington wrote to USG. "For more than a year I have been attempting to address you with inquiries of more interest to me, than yourself or others; nevertheless, am in hopes my subject may sufficiently call your attention as to reply to my questions. You may be aware that I am a little interested in the breeding of the 'American Road or Trotting Horse', and with years of patient study, arrived at the

conclusion we are more indebted to the Arabian horse for that trotting instinct & conformation, with adaptibility & action than very many would conceed. That Old Henry
Clay dicended thro' 'Andrew Jackson' & 'Young Bashaw' from the Arab, all breeders
know; and that all of the get by 'Andrew Jackson and his son 'Henry Clay' were pre-
disposed to trot, *I know*. Such being the case, I obtained permission through Genl
Beale, to study your arabs, which I did by the aid of the groom, in my way, after which
I bred to them, one daughter of 'Henry Clay' getting a black horse colt, marked with
three white pasterns and handsom star. I bred also a mare by 'Col Wadsworth' by
'Henry Clay,' getting a filly, black without marks, but will be *iron gray*. I bred also a
mare by 'Jack sheppard' by 'Henry Clay,' (the to first to 'Linden,' called the *Bedouine*)
getting a golden sorrel horse colt, marked with three white legs, and straight broad
white strip in the face, This colt was by 'Leopard,' and the dam was inbred to 'Jack
sheppard,' besides being in-bred to 'old Henry.' Annother mare by still annother son of
'Henry clay' out of an in-bred morgan mare, foaled a dark chestnut horse colt to 'Linden,' 4 colts in all, out of *6 mares stinted*. I am not thus far disappointed in the produce. I
think I can show as much size & substance in these colts, as is found in the majority of
colts of same age, and I also think I can show more trotting speed in the lot, than any
other man in N. Y. state. Two of these colts I might say were born trotting, for they
have never yet done anything else, & are a wonder to horsemen who have seen them.
All are at the stock Farm of the Messrs' Jewett of Buffalo, who is a relative of my wife,
as well as intimate friend of my own. I have made no publ[ic] mention of this experiment, knowing that developed facts are more interesting than boasted efforts, and time
will tell the story. I have a history of 'Old Henry clay' and his produce to be published
in due time, with some *60* odd sketches of sons & daughters of old Henry, also the only
perfect sketch of him-self ever made. I have pre-ceeded all these sketches with sketches
of *your two arabian* stallions, as fountain head blood or origin of old Henry Clay. My
sketches were made by one artist who outranked any native talent America has yet produced, and are all perfect to life. As I had largely educated, or assisted rather, the young
artist t[o] cultivate his genius into talent, and as my sketches were expensive to me, &
also valuable to my publication, I secured them by copy right as they were completed,
and intend their first appearance in public, shall be in connection with my publication.
Each sketch has a complete & correct history of the animal from day of foaling to its
death or the present time, except your two arabs, And of them I can get nothing satisfactory, only as I have seen & know myself. I knew when they were in NewHaven, upon
their arrival, & went there to see them &c, &c, but would like what I have not got. Pay
Inspector J. A. Smith U. S. Navy, at Washington D. C. tried to tell me about how, &
when you secured them; but I have nothing sufficintly authentic for publication in connection with my plates as yet. Will you please assist & oblige me, by writing me the
particulars of where they were obtained, from whom, & by whom, & the two families of
arabs they represent, what date they were shipped & from what port, on board what
vessel, commanded by whom, & to whom they were consigned, also exact ages when
shipped. The dark, or blue gray one that people like the *least*, is by all odds the best
horse, the *most* horse, & the best stock getter in *my* opinion, hence I bred most mares to
him. This horse called 'Linden' was represented to me to be from the Bedouine tribe of
arabs, and the other, called 'Leopard', was called to me, of the *Royal* tribe of Arabs,
which latter term I can neither understand or apply in my history. I have had my two
sketches of your horses copied, of the size they appear in my publication; and permit me
to present them to you. They are the first and only copies taken, & were taken expressly
for you. I have had two made I intend to send to Genl Beale, but as I have said, the

sketches are secured by copyright, and no copies can be taken under any circumstances. These pictures I send you, are platinum photographs, same size & exactly like the original sketches, and the sketches were exactly like the two horses themselves when taken in October 1880, by H. S. Kittredge, who is now dead. How the horses look now I do not know; but at the time the sketches were made, the likeness was perfect of each horse. All the sketches I have of the old Clay family are same size & and equally fine. It is my wish & intention there should be one family of horses in America without any lie, fraud, or deception in the breeding from the start. The mares I bred to the Arabians, were straight, clean, & free from fraud in their breeding, back to 'Henry Clay'; and from these three horse colts, and one filly, will come a family of horses which I trust will be a credit to all directly interested & to you first, as the importent owner of the Arabian Sires. I could do some pretty big talking about two of these colts if any good would come of it. Anxiously awaiting a reply from you, . . ." "Yours of the 28th inst' in hand, also the return check for picturs, signed by Mrs Grant, which latter my daughters have fastened into their Autographic Album, with delight. Your letter I shall prize highly as a souvenir, asside from its value in connection with the *Arabians,* and will undoubtedly always remain in my family as such. In regard to the horses, you may be sufficiently interested to know what I will write, as to cause you to read a lengthy letter. The 'American road & trotting horse' is a problem to which I have devoted a long life, not as a large breeder, but as an experimental student. Forty out of 54 years is not much, but that is the little time I have given to the study. . . . I had seen many Arabians, but wanted to see yours again, alone, for the purpose of study; so went to Washington, Genl Beale was in Calafornia, but J. Adams Smith, then Pay Inspector U. S. A. kindly took me to *Ash Hill.* I examined them (arabs) in physical conformation in the boxes. 'Leopard' was the type I had always seen, but 'Linden' was very different. I had them led out, and as usual the groom showed them in *play* which I soon made him stop, for any colt can be so taught. I thanked Inspector Smith for permitting me to manage them as I wished; so I made the groom lead them to & from me several times *upon a walk,* that I might study the action & natural play of the limbs & joints from feet up. From the view front & rear, I next took the side study, in both walking & trotting. Of the two horses, I prefered 'Linden'. First, he had more substance, and a superior frame for endurance. In action, all his joints from stiples down, promised *instinctive* trot, to harmonize with *motion.* Mr. Smith & the groom were surprised that my choice was 'Linden', as was also Genl Beale upon his return. The head of 'Linden' was *old,* & his disposition was not so good, & his form was not so graceful, & his color was not so good, nor could he *gambol* like *Leopard* in short they could not understand me in my choice. . . . As your son has 'Linden', I will have my sketch of him copied & sent to you, to tend to him with my compliments. 'Leopard' I will also have Copied and send to Genl Beale. They were *perfectly like* the *horses when taken* by young Kittridge, & I presume are to day if the horses are in same condition. They were fat at the time, & in prime shape. I intended Kittredge should paint them, but the poor boy died *too soon.* His associate, A. J. Schultz, who appeared to have equal genius, has been in Europe since Kittredge death, perfecting himself in manipulation of colors, but is expected by each German Steamer. Almost any artist can sketch a horse, but there was one *Bonheur* in Europe, & one *Kittredge* in America, although I am in hopes young ~~Sel~~ Shultz, (Kittredge associate,) will prove, as I have reason to believe he will, a second Kittredge in fidelity to life, in *Animal portraiture.*" ALS, USG 3. See George H. Conn, "Randolph Huntington; American Horse Breeder," *Western Horseman,* 14 (April, 1949), 10–11.

To Elizabeth M. Borie

———

Long Branch, N. J.
July 31st 1882.

My Dear Mrs. Borie:

Mrs. Grant wants me to acknowledge the receipt of your letter of the 25th inst. and say how sorry she is that we could not have you with us for a while this Summer. We will not probably leave here before late in September—except for a short trip in August—and if you feel like spending a little time by the Sea between this time and the 20th of Sept. we would be delighted to have you.

On the 2d of July I mailed three letters for Mrs. Grant, the one to you, one to Mrs. Rogers, the widow of an old and esteemed friend of mine,[1] inviting her and niece for the next week after you; and the third enclosing a check to a dressmaker. Mrs. Rogers only received her letter on the 22d of July—after the time she was invited to be here—postmarked July 21st. The letter with the check has not been received yet unless within the last week.

Mrs. Grant and I appreciate your great afflictions and sympathize with you and would be glad if we could in any way comfort you.—Hoping to see you before a great while.

Very Truly yours
U. S. Grant

ALS, PHi. See letter to Elizabeth M. Borie, July 2, 1882.

1. On Sept. 23, 1880, USG and Julia Dent Grant, Galena, telegraphed to Mary Rogers, New York City. "You have our heartfelt sympathy in your berevement The loss of your noble husband will be felt by all who knew him" Telegram received, DLC-USG. Charles H. Rogers died Sept. 22.

To Stephen B. Elkins

———

Long Branch, N. J.
Aug. 3d 1882.

My Dear Mr. Elkins;

Mr. Randall[1] communicated with the Commodore[2] yesterday. He says that if parties authorized to act will come to him he will say exactly what he will do. Mr. R. says however that it would be useless for parties to come to him to ascertain what he would do and then go off to consult with others to determine whether to accept or not. He says that if the Commodore makes one, or several propositions they must be accepted or rejected at once. If he says a million to-day, and it is not accepted it will likely be one and a quarter, or a rejection of all offers to-morrow.

Very Truly yours

U. S. GRANT

ALS, West Virginia University, Morgantown, West Va. Born in Ohio in 1841, Stephen B. Elkins earned his law degree in Mo., served in the Kan. militia, and settled in New Mexico Territory, where he held several offices including U.S. Delegate (1873–77). By 1880, Elkins was in New York City pursuing banking, railroad, and mining interests. See letter to Stephen B. Elkins, Aug. 10, 1882; John Alexander Williams, "New York's First Senator From West Virginia: How Stephen B. Elkins Found A New Political Home," *West Virginia History*, XXXI, II (Jan., 1970), 73–87.

1. An English immigrant, John M. Randell founded a successful hat and fur business in St. Louis. When his daughter Letitia married Cornelius K. Garrison in 1878, Randell moved to New York City and became active on Wall Street. "Mr. Randell was the last of that congenial card party who used to play nightly both in this city and at Elberon, which was made up of Gen. Grant, Commodore Garrison, Jerome Chaffee, and Mr. Randell." *New York Times*, June 1, 1888.

2. Born in 1809 in N. Y., Cornelius K. Garrison made a fortune in shipping in St. Louis, Panama, and San Francisco, where he served as mayor (1853–54). In 1859, Garrison settled in New York City and built a transportation and utilities empire. His son William died July 1, 1882, a victim of the June 29 train accident near Long Branch that injured USG. See *Calendar*, June 29, 1882; letter to Clarence A. Seward, Aug. 18, 1884.

To Stephen B. Elkins

———

Long Branch, N. J.

August 10, 1882.

MY DEAR MR. ELKINS:

I received your letter requesting the return of Mr. Keyser's[1] letters several days ago. This should have been attended to sooner, but I was in town yesterday and in Connecticut Monday[2] and Tuesday.

I have had [n]o further conversation with Mr. Randall about the B. matter, but if there is anything you or Mr. Keyser wish me to say or do, I will do it with pleasure.

I am expecting to go to Saratoga early week after next to be done two weeks or more.

Kind regards to Mrs. Elkins and Senator Davis[3] and family.

Very truly yours,
U. S. GRANT.

Typescript, West Virginia University, Morgantown, West Va. On Aug. 4, 1882, USG wrote to Stephen B. Elkins. "Mr. Randall come in again last evening, after another talk with the Commodore, to say that if the party wishing to treat for his Balt. property would come forward frankly that he would deal with them more favorably than if there was dickering attempted. He advised that whoever come should consult with me before going to the Commodore, and if necessary I could confer with him—Mr. Randall—before the parties would see the Commodore." ALS, *ibid.* Cornelius K. Garrison's extensive holdings included the Baltimore Equitable Gas Co. See letter to Stephen B. Elkins, Aug. 3, 1882; *New York Times*, June 21, 22, 1884.

1. Reputedly "the wealthiest man in Maryland," William Keyser was a Baltimore and Ohio Railroad executive, copper magnate, financier, and philanthropist. See *ibid.*, June 4, 1904.
2. Aug. 7.
3. Born in 1823 in Md., Henry G. Davis worked for the Baltimore and Ohio Railroad, became a banker, financed railroad, coal, and lumber operations, and entered West Va. Democratic politics, rising to U.S. Senator (1871–83). In 1875, his daughter Hallie married Elkins.

To Jesse Root Grant, Jr.

Saratoga Springs, N. Y. Aug. 28th *1882*

DEAR JESSE:

I send you receipt for trunk dispatched to-day to Long Branch. Your Ma says to have the trunk carried to her room.—We leave this pm—for Bucks. We will go down to the City Thursday morning, and to Long Branch by the 2 30 pm train unless I telegraph you to the contrary. We have had a very pleasant time here, but a week is enough of it for once.

Love to Lizzie and the babe from your Ma & me.

Yours
U. S. GRANT

ALS, Chapman Grant, Escondido, Calif. Written on letterhead of the Grand Union Hotel. USG enclosed an undated receipt. "Please return bill receipted to Mrs. U. S. Grant, Long Branch." ANS, *ibid.*

On Aug. 26, 1882, Saturday, USG wrote to Thomas R. Proctor on the same letter-head. "I regret that I will not be able to avail myself of your kind invitation of yesterday to visit Richfield Springs on this occasion. I leave here for Long Branch on Monday, to stop a couple of days on the road, which is as long as Mrs. Grant & I feel that we can stay away at this time. With many thanks for your kind invitation, . . ." ALS, Munson-Williams-Proctor Institute, Utica, N. Y. Proctor owned a hotel.

To Adam Badeau

N. Y. Sept. 21st 188[2]

DEAR BADEAU:

We moved to the city yesterday. I find on my desk your letters enclosing one from Col. Chesney[1]—herewith returned—and his lecture. I will read the latter when I go home this evening.

Green[2] was at my house, at the Branch, monday evening[3] and read the second part of his book. He will be up early next week to finish it. He has found a probable error of 4000 in his statement of numbers at Vicksburgh. The tri-monthly returns for the end of Apl. and the monthly return for same date disagree by that number. He finds that Scott[4] takes the monthly return as the correct one when the two disagree. This reduces the number. His second part was quite as interesting as the first. I will be much mistaken if his book is not regarded as far the best of the series. Green felt much com-plimented when I told him what you thought of his work.

yours very Truly
U. S. GRANT

P. S. We will be pleased to see you at the house when you come to town.

U. S. G.

ALS, Munson-Williams-Proctor Institute, Utica, N. Y.

1. "General Grant had met Colonel Chesney, the eminent British soldier and mili-tary critic, in India, and the letter and lecture which he forwarded contained some highly favorable comments on my history as well as on Grant's career." *Badeau*, p. 544. George T. Chesney was president of the Royal Indian Engineering College dur-ing USG's visit in 1879; his brother Charles, a col. and military historian, had died in 1876. See Charles Cornwallis Chesney, *Essays in Military Biography* (New York, 1874), pp. 1–80; "General Ulysses Simpson Grant," *The Edinburgh Review*, CXXIX, CCLXIII (Jan. 1869), 117–37.

2. 1st Lt. Francis V. Greene published *The Mississippi* in late 1882 as the eighth volume in Scribner's Campaigns of the Civil War series. Greene had attended Burlington College, N. J., with USG's two older sons and graduated first in his class from USMA in 1870. See *PUSG*, 16, 441; note to Frederick Dent Grant, June 15, 1885; *New York Times*, Dec. 4, 1882.

3. Sept. 18.

4. Maj. Robert N. Scott oversaw publication of the *O.R.*

To Chester A. Arthur

———

New York City,
Sept. 23d 1882

THE PRESIDENT:

I take pleasure in presenting Gen. John W. Fuller, Collector of the Port of Toledo, Ohio.

General Fuller served directly under me in the West, during my command there, and was appointed by me as Collector eight years ago. I believe he has given entire satisfaction to the Dept. in Washington and to the merchants having business with his office. At all events General Fuller is a man and Ex Soldier for whom I have a high regard and to whom I give this introduction with pleasure.

Very Truly yours
U. S. GRANT

ALS, DNA, RG 56, Collector of Customs Applications. John W. Fuller was not reappointed after his commission expired in Dec., 1882. See *PUSG*, 7, 142; *ibid.*, 25, 448.

To James M. Dalzell

———

New York City
Sept. 23d 1882

J. M. DALZELL, SEC. &c.
DEAR SIR:

I have your letter of the 21st inst. inviting me to be present at the soldiers re-union, to be held in Caldwell, Ohio, October 2d & 3d. It is with regret that I say that it will be impossible for me to attend. Many invitations have been sent me to attend re-unions of Veterans in the West this fall,[1] some of which I accepted conditionally, expecting to be able to go West during the season. But so far I have been unable to get away, and now fear that I shall not get off at all.

Very Truly yours
U. S. GRANT

ALS, ICHi. Born in 1838 near Pittsburgh, a private in the 116th Ohio, James M. Dalzell served two terms as a Republican in the Ohio legislature and practiced law in Caldwell. An early organizer of veterans' reunions, Dalzell was a prolific and widely published correspondent. See *Private Dalzell, His Autobiography, Poems and Comic War Papers . . .* (Cincinnati, 1888); *New York Times,* June 1, 1879, Oct. 25, 1881, Feb. 1, 1924.

On March 11, 1869, Dalzell, Caldwell, wrote to Secretary of State Elihu B. Washburne. "In September I resigned clerkship in Treasury, to take the stump for Grant. I was a private three years, and am a lawyer by profession, having graduated in Duff's College and also in Columbian College. Hon. Jno. A. Bingham knows all about my record as a soldier, clerk, and Republican. Upon this I apply for a fourth class clerkship, if private soldiers under Grant are to receive *different* treatment from what Johnson gave us. Under Johnson privates had back seats, traitors and civilians *all* the best desks, though *not* our superiors in qualifications, or in any essential element of manhood." ALS, DNA, RG 59, Letters of Application and Recommendation.

On Jan. 11, 1872, Dalzell wrote to USG. "Within a fortnight past in all the papers, You notice our—the Soldiers'—petition to Congress, asking equalization of bounty—land-warrants—back pensions to the cripples of '61—and equal pensions to all Soldiers of 1812—so as to make these laws all fair and Equal to all soldiers & widows, without the injustice now done 20.000 soldiers, & soldiers' heirs who have *no* benefit from these laws, though as deserving as those who are benefitted. Do you favor it—are you willing to see us all share alike? Your answer is requested for publication to the Boys in Blue now signing in every State by hundreds—Your obt svt for the private soldiers . . . If any understrapper open this letter—please hand it to our President himself." ALS, *ibid.,* RG 48, Miscellaneous Div., Letters Received. See *PUSG,* 23, 366; *SRC,* 48-1-368.

1. On Aug. 31, 1882, USG wrote to Frederick C. Winkler, Milwaukee. "Having been absent from the city for some days, I have only just received your kind invitation to attend the Reunion of the *Army of the Cumberland,* to be held in Milwaukee on the 20th and 21st prox. I am thinking of going West about that time; and, if I am able to get away in time, I certainly shall take very great pleasure in attending the Reunion of the *Society of the Army of the Cumberland;* but it is by no means certain that, with other engagements, I will be able to be there." *Society of the Army of the Cumberland Fourteenth Reunion, Milwaukee, Wisconsin, 1882* (Cincinnati, 1883), p. 161.

To John F. Long

New York City,
Oct. 3d 1882

MY DEAR JUDGE:

I have held on to my land in St. Louis Co. so long, and with such poor results, that I now want to offer it at a price that will secure a purchaser. If you think of any one likely to wish to buy you may offer it for $100.000 00, half cash, balance in one and two years, this to include the Carondelet property of—I believe—201 Arpents. If this cannot be obtained, and you can get an offer please inform me what it is.

With kind regards to all your family.

Very Truly yours

U. S. GRANT

ALS, InU. Grenville M. Dodge recorded an Oct. 27, 1882, conversation with USG. "I met General Grant at 58th St. Elevated Station, rode down to Rector Street and walked thence to the Union Bank Building with him. He first asked me how long Mr. Gould stayed in St. Louis. I soon saw he was desirous of knowing in order to learn whether Gould had looked at two pieces of land there, one of 168 acres, and one of 640 in Corondelet on main branch of the Missouri Pacific Railway. whih Gen Grant wished to sell him . . ." Typescript, IaHA.

To Col. Benjamin H. Grierson

New York, Oct 10 *1882*

GEN. B. H. GRIERSON,
JACKSONVILLE, ILL.
DEAR GENERAL:

I have your letter of the 7th inst, with enclosure, asking my aid in procuring for you the appointment of Brigadier General in the regular army on the retirement of Gen. McDowell. It will be impossible for me to make the recommendation you desire, because long ago, immediately on my return from abroad, and also since the incumbency of the Presidency by General Arthur, I recommended when a vacancy should occur that Gen. McKenzie should be advanced to the Brigadier Generalcy. To make any other recommendation now would be as a matter of course impossible, having made the former recommendation voluntarily, and believing it to be for the best interests of the public service.

Gen. McKenzie is an officer who, although he only graduated in 1862, one year after the war had commenced, without any political influence whatever, and without any application on his own part, won his way to a Major Generalcy during the remaining three years of the war, and at the close was commanding an army corps, and had scarcely a superior in the army for that position, although then so young.

Of course I am personally aware of your services in the war, and appreciate them highly, and it was in consequence of that appreciation that I suggested you for a colonelcy in the regular army at the reorganization; and I would be very glad to see you have any advancement not inconsistent with what I believe to be the just interests of others.

Very Truly Yours.
U. S. GRANT

LS, ICN. See letter to Chester A. Arthur, March 4, 1882; letter to Col. Benjamin H. Grierson, Dec. 17, 1884.

To Edwin D. Morgan

New York, Oct. 10th *1882*.

DEAR GOVERNOR:

I called to ask a personal favor, though not to press it in the least. I have to pay $50.000 to-morrow and can not do it without some ~~little~~ sacrefice. I want $30.000 on call to help me out, and which can certainly be paid by the end of the month, and will be paid if called at any time before the end of the month.

Grant & Ward will endorse my note. Mr. Jas. Fish, President of the Marine Nat. Bank, is a partner in the firm of Grant & Ward.

If you can let me have this accommodation will you be kind enough to send the note to Grant & Ward, for my & their signature, this afternoon. Their address is 2 Wall st.—United Bank building.

Very Truly yours
U. S. GRANT

ALS, Edwin D. Morgan Papers, New York State Library, Albany, N. Y. Written on Edwin D. Morgan's stationery.

USG wrote to Jesse Root Grant, Jr. "If you have received the money for Copper Stock I wish you would send me check for about $5000.00 until we can have a settlement." AN (initialed, undated), Chapman Grant, Escondido, Calif.

To Newton P. Frye

New York, Oct 17 *1882*

N. P. FRYE ESQ
253 ESSEX ST
LAWRENCE, MASS
DEAR SIR:

I have your letter of the 12th of October, in which you give me the substance of occurrences that were said to have taken place during the battle of the Wilderness. The statement as related is nearly without foundation. The full history of all that did occur, will be found accurately told in Badeau's history of my campaigns.

Truly Yours.
U. S. GRANT

LS, IHi. Newton P. Frye worked as a machinist before becoming a lawyer in 1877.

To Chester A. Arthur

New York City.
Oct. 19th, 1882

THE PRESIDENT:

Assuming that a change is likely to take place in the Governorship ~~of~~in New Mexico I venture to recommend General W. R. Rowley, of Galena, Ill. for the place. I would not ask this place for General Rowley if it is opposed by the republican Senator from the state, and the representative of the district in which General Rowley lives. I strongly commend General Rowley for the place knowing him intimately as a neighbor, and for about three years a member of my Military family during the War. General Rowley is a man of good ability, good education, brave, honest and incorruptible. As Governor of a territory making rapid strides towards Statehood he would be of immense value to the Government and Administration in frustrating the designs of smart and unscrupulous men in securing personal advantage and profit at the expense of the Government, and of the industrious and honest people who do most to build up the real interests of the Territory and state.

As stated in the begining I do not wish to urge the appointment of General Rowley if it is seriously opposed by his own representative and the republican senator from the state. General Rowley probably never thought of being an applicant for this, or any other, office until I suggested it. I made it to him believing that his appointment would be the best I could think of, and having a desire to recognize the services of a man whos past service has been so valuable.

Very Truly yours

U. S. GRANT

ALS, DNA, RG 48, Appointment Papers, New Mexico Territory. No appointment followed. Possibly at this time, USG wrote to William R. Rowley. "I send you copy of a letter I have just sent the President" ANS, Gilder Lehrman Collection, NNP.

Article

[*Oct. 24, 1882*]

AN UNDESERVED STIGMA.

ON the 27th of November, 1862, a court-martial was convened in the city of Washington, for the trial of Major-General Fitz John Porter, of the volunteer force. The court consisted of nine members and a judge-advocate,—the Judge-Advocate-General of the Army.

The charges against General Porter were:

First. Disobedience of orders under the 9th Article of War.

Second. Misbehavior before the enemy under the 52d Article of War.

Under the first charge there were three specifications of which the court found Porter guilty. These were, substantially:

First. Disobedience to the order of August 27th, requiring him to march from Warrenton Junction at one o'clock on the morning of the twenty-eighth and be at Bristoe Station by daylight.

Second. Disobedience on August 29th, while in front of the enemy, to the joint order to McDowell and Porter, directing them to march toward Gainesville and establish communication with the other corps.

Third. Disobedience on August 29th, while in front of the enemy, to what is known as the "4.30 P. M. Order," requiring Porter to attack the enemy's flank and rear.

Under the second charge the specifications upon which Porter was tried and convicted were, in substance:

First. Shameful disobedience to the 4.30 P. M. Order on August 29th, while in sight of the field and in full hearing of its artillery; and retreat from advancing forces of the enemy, without attempting to engage them or to aid the troops who were fighting greatly superior numbers, and who would have secured a decisive victory and captured the enemy's army, but for Porter's neglect to attack and his shameful disobedience.

Second. Failure of Porter all that day to bring his forces on the field when within sound of the guns and in presence of the enemy, and knowing that a severe action of great consequence was being fought, and that the aid of his corps was greatly needed; and his shameful falling back and retreat from the advance of unknown forces of the enemy without attempting to give them battle.

Third. Shameful failure of Porter on the same day, while a severe action was being fought, to go to the aid of General Pope's troops, when he believed that they were being defeated and were retiring from the field; and his shameful retreat away and falling back under these circumstances, leaving the army to the disasters of a presumed defeat; and failure, by any attempt to attack the enemy, to aid in averting a disaster which would have endangered the safety of the capital.

These are the accusations that were made against General Porter for his part and failure in the battles generally known as those of the second Bull Run campaign. The court found him guilty of the charges and specifications.[1] If he was so guilty, the punishment awarded was not commensurate with the offense committed. I believe lawyers have taken exception to the formation of the court and to some of its technical rulings; but neither at the time nor since has General Porter attempted to evade the consequences of his acts by any special pleading, or by taking advantage of any technical error in the composition of the court, or the method of its being ordered, but has relied entirely upon his innocence of all the charges and specifications, and would not be satisfied with an acquittal on any other ground than that of his entire innocence.

It will be seen from the foregoing that General Porter's alleged misconduct was embraced in three separate cases of disobedience of orders: one on the 27th of August, and two on the 29th of August; and in having retreated unnecessarily from the enemy, by that act endangering other portions of the army with which he was coöperating.

It will be seen that, though these offenses were alleged to have been committed in August of 1862, he was continued in the command of an army corps until some time in November following, taking an active part in the battles of the day following the date of the last charge, and in command of the defenses of Washington on the west bank of the Potomac, and also at the battle of Antietam, some weeks later. It would look at first very singular that an officer, so wantonly derelict in the performance of his duty as General Porter was alleged to have been on the 27th and 29th of August, should have been continued in so important a place as the command of an army corps, when so much was at stake as there was on the 30th of August, and in the defenses of Washington, and in the later battles in Maryland, when the invasion of the North was threatened. These facts would indicate to an unprejudiced mind that the charges against Porter were an after-thought, to shift the responsibilities of failure from other shoulders and to place them upon him.

In regard to his disobedience of the order of the 27th of August, he is alleged to have without justification deferred his march from Warrenton Junction to Bristoe Station from one o'clock until three of the morning of the 28th. It was about ten o'clock on the night of the 27th when Porter received the following order:

"HEAD-QUARTERS ARMY OF VIRGINIA,
BRISTOE STATION, August 27, 1862, 6.30 P. M.

GENERAL: The Major-General commanding directs that you start at one o'clock, and come forward with your whole corps, or such part of it as is with you, so as to be here by daylight to-morrow morning. Hooker has had a very severe action with the enemy, with a loss of about three hundred killed and wounded. The enemy has been driven back, but is retiring along the railroad. We must drive him from Manassas, and clear the country between that place and Gainesville, where McDowell is. If Morell has not joined you, send word to him to push forward immediately; also send word to Banks to hurry forward with all speed to take your place at Warrenton Junction. It is necessary, on all accounts, that you should be here by daylight. I send an officer with this dispatch, who will conduct you to this place. Be sure to send word to Banks, who is on the road from Fayetteville, probably in the direction of Bealton. Say to Banks, also, that he had best run back the railroad trains to this side of Cedar Run. If he is not with you, write him to that effect.

By command of Major-General Pope,

GEORGE D. RUGGLES,
Colonel and Chief-of-Staff.

Major-General F. J. Porter, Warrenton Junction.

P. S. If Banks is not at Warrenton Junction, leave a regiment of infantry and two pieces of artillery as a guard till he comes up, with instructions to follow you immediately. If Banks is not at the Junction, instruct Colonel Clary to run the trains back to this side of Cedar Run, and post a regiment and section of artillery with it.

By command of Major-General Pope.

GEORGE D. RUGGLES,
Colonel and Chief-of-Staff." [2]

His troops had been marching all day, were very much fatigued, some of them only having just arrived in camp and had their supper, when the order to march at one o'clock was received. The night, as shown in the testimony before the court which tried Porter, and as confirmed by the evidence given in what was known as the Schofield Board, [3] was extremely dark; the road very narrow, with numerous cuts and streams passing through it; bounded by woods on both sides in many places, with no place where the open country could be taken for the march of troops; and blocked up with about two thousand army wagons, many of them mired in the narrow road, so that the officer who conveyed this order to General Porter was over three hours, on horseback, in making the distance of ten miles. Porter was expected, with fatigued troops, worn with long marches, on scanty rations, to make a march on a very dark night, through a blockaded road, more rapidly than a single aide-de-camp, unincumbered, had been able to get through on horseback.

When he received the order, he showed it to his leading generals, and, apparently with one accord, they decided that the movement at that hour was impossible; further, that no time could possibly be gained by so early a start, and that if they should start at that hour and get through to Bristoe Station at the time designated, the troops would not be fit for either fighting or marching on their arrival at that point. Porter replied, however, "Here is the order, and it must be obeyed"; but, after further consultation, he decided, as did his generals, that a postponement of two hours in starting the march would enable them to get through as quick as if the men were kept on foot and under arms while the road was being cleared, and that the men would be in a much better condition for service on their arrival at their destination. He was entirely justified in exercising his own judgment in this matter, because the order shows that he was not to take part in any battle when he arrived there, but was wanted to pursue a fleeing enemy. He did not leave the commanding general in ignorance of his proposed delay, nor of the reasons for it, but at once sent a request that the general commanding should send back cavalry (he had none himself) and clear the road near him of incumbrances, so that the march might be unobstructed.

It is shown that a literal obedience to the order of the 27th of August was a physical impossibility. It is further shown that General Porter was desirous of obeying it literally, so far as was practicable, but was prevailed upon by his leading generals—against whom a suspicion of disloyalty to their commander, or to the cause, has never been entertained—to do what his own judgment approved as the best thing to do—to make a later start with a view of arriving at his destination as early as it was possible for him to arrive there, and to give to his jaded and worn troops two hours more of needed rest. If the night had been clear and the road an open one, there would not have been as much justification for the exercise of his discretion in the matter; but there is no doubt but that he would have arrived at Bristoe Station just as early, and with his troops in much better condition, if he had started at early dawn instead of at the hour he did, and the intervening time had been used in clearing the road for his troops when they did march. Where there were open spaces along the line of the road, they were either marshy, filled with stumps of trees, and impossible to march over, or were crowded with army wagons, so that the track of his army was limited to the incumbered narrow road between the two points designated in the order, which could be cleared only by the wagons being moved ahead, as requested of Pope.

Much of the testimony before the court and before the army board might be quoted to confirm what is here stated; but as this is all accessible to the reader, I will not lengthen this statement by quoting it.

I question very much whether there was an engagement during the war, or a series of engagements continuing over as much time as was consumed in the battles about Bull Run in August, 1862, when not only one, but a number of generals, did not exercise their discretion, as Porter did on this occasion, and with far less justification. The commanding general who gave the order desired to have the troops at a certain point by daylight, and he gave his orders so as to accomplish that result. Under the circumstances, his order required of the troops an impossibility. That was as evident to Porter, and those with him, before the attempt was made as it was after.

It is a little singular that any one high in rank, connected with the Army of Virginia, should be in ignorance of the arrival of at least a portion of Lee's army, by the very route designated by Pope, many hours before the 4.30 order was published. Porter was not in ignorance of that arrival. Between twelve and one o'clock, on arriving at his advanced position, Porter was shown by McDowell a dispatch from General Buford, sent at 9.30 on the morning of the 29th, stating that from seventeen to eighteen regiments of the enemy had passed through Gainesville three-quarters of an hour before, or at a quarter before nine o'clock, on their way to re-enforce Jackson,[4] so that the head of the column must have been not only in supporting distance of Jackson, but at the place of deployment by ten o'clock in the morning; and now it is known by others, as it was known by

Porter at the time, that Longstreet, with some twenty-five thousand men, was in position confronting Porter by twelve o'clock on the 29th of August, four hours and a half before the 4.30 order was written.

While at the head of their united forces, between twelve and one o'clock, and while Porter was preparing to attack the enemy in his immediate front, McDowell, then in command, showed Porter the "joint order"[5] and also Buford's dispatch. It was evident from this dispatch, corroborated by the enemy's movements in their immediate front, that the main forces of the enemy, which the "joint order" said were far distant, had not only arrived, but had formed a junction with Jackson and deployed in their front. Porter knew of this from another fact. He had prisoners from that force—Longstreet's troops. The object of moving toward Gainesville had been thus defeated, and any further advance, if practicable, would only the more widely separate them from Pope's forces then checked at Groveton, at least two miles distant, and with which they were ordered to "establish communication." McDowell, as he had the right, at once withdrew his troops, leaving Porter with ten thousand men to confront Longstreet's twenty-five thousand, while he went by a circuitous route to a point between Porter and Pope, to establish the communication enjoined.

Thus left alone, facing superior numbers advantageously posted, and ignorant of the needs of Pope, if indeed he had any, Porter had necessarily to bide McDowell's arrival on his right. In the meantime his duty was manifestly to engage Longstreet's attention and prevent him from moving against Pope, especially while McDowell was out of support of both Pope and Porter. Porter all that day did not hear of McDowell, or of what was taking place in front of Pope, though he kept the former well-informed of affairs with him,[6] and presumed that his dispatches were sent to the latter. He, however, engaged Longstreet's attention by demonstrations nearly harmless to himself, and so successfully as to cause Longstreet to take Wilcox's division from in front of Pope, in order to strengthen the line confronting Porter, who, at the time, was aware of this movement of forces coming from the right to his front, and notified McDowell of it. Thus Porter, without sacrifice of men, and without endangering any interests, did more for Pope's relief than if he had gone directly to that general's assistance. To have done so would probably have sacrificed his corps without any benefit, and jeoparded the safety of Pope's army.

So far as I have investigated the case—and I have studied it, I think, pretty thoroughly—I see no fact to base the charge of retreat upon. I do not see that any argument to prove this is necessary, because any reader of history may be defied now to find where and when General Porter retreated during the time specified.

In my judgment, this disposes of the charges, and consequently of all specifications under them, except the alleged disobedience of the 4.30 P. M. order.

In regard to the charge of disobedience of the 4.30 order, which is the principal one and the one that has most deeply impressed the mind of the general public, there are evidences which look to me important and conclusive, showing that the court-martial which tried General Porter found him guilty under a mistaken idea of the actual facts, now accessible to any one in search of the truth, and which Porter knew to be the facts at the time. As maintained by the prosecution, to the apparent satisfaction of the court, the situation of the belligerent forces were in numbers and position about as here given:

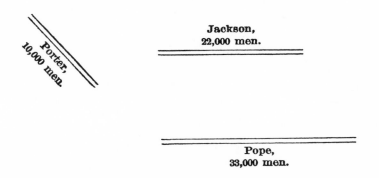

The 4.30 P. M. order of the 29th of August required Porter to attack the enemy's right flank and to get into his rear, if possible. This enemy, in the mind of the commanding general, and, no doubt, of the court, was Jackson's force of twenty-two thousand men. Porter was supposed to occupy, with ten thousand troops, the posi-

tion assigned to him in the diagram given. The court also seems to have been satisfied that the order to make this attack was received by Porter from five to half-past five o'clock in the afternoon, leaving him abundance of time to obey the order.

That the commanding general believed the positions as given in the foregoing diagram to be the positions of the different commands, is shown from the fact that in his joint order of that morning he stated that "the indications are that the whole force of the enemy is moving in this direction at a pace that will bring them here by to-morrow night or next day,"—that is, the evening of the 30th or the morning of the 31st of August,—and from the fact that in the 4.30 order he stated that "the enemy is massed in the woods in front of us," thus ignoring the presence of Longstreet. This is confirmed in his map No. 5, furnished to the Government. If these had been the facts of the case, there would have been no justification whatever for Porter's failing to make the attack as ordered; but, instead of the facts being as supposed by the commanding general and the court which tried General Porter, they were as shown by the following diagram. This Porter knew on indisputable evidence.

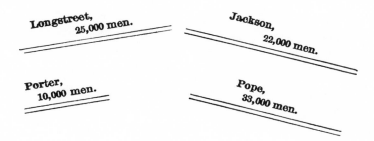

As shown by this diagram, Porter was not in a position to attack the right flank of Jackson, because he was at least three miles away, and not across his flank, as shown in the first diagram. With Longstreet's presence, to have obeyed that order he would have been obliged, with ten thousand men, to have defeated twenty-five thousand men in a chosen position, before he could have moved upon the flank of the enemy, as the order directed. But, even if the position of Lee's army had been thirty-six to forty-eight hours distant, as asserted in the joint order to McDowell and Porter, it would have been impossible for Porter to have obeyed the 4.30 order, because it did not contemplate a night attack, and was not received by Porter until about dark. To have obeyed it would have required some little preparation, movement of troops, and distribution of orders, so that it would have been some time after dark before he could have moved from the position he was then occupying, and at least as late as nine o'clock at night before he could have reached Jackson's flank to engage it. His efforts to execute the order, notwithstanding its apparent inappropriateness, demonstrate this assertion.

I consider that these facts, with many more that were brought to the knowledge of the Schofield Board, fully exonerate General Porter of the charge of disobedience of what is known as the 4.30 order, and also of the imputation of lukewarmness in his support of the commanding general.

A great deal that might be said of the movements, the marching and countermarching of troops between the date of the order of the 27th of August and the receipt of the order of the 29th, which would throw light upon this question; but I abstain from giving it, because I believe that what is stated here covers all the points wherein General Porter has been charged with being delinquent.

General Porter has now for twenty years been laboring under the disabilities and penalties inflicted upon him by the court-martial of 1862, all that time contending for a restoration to his position in the army and in society, and always, as stated in the beginning of this article, on the ground of his entire innocence. The investigation of the Schofield Board has, in my judgment, established his innocence of all the offenses for which he was tried and convicted. The sufferings of twenty years, under such findings, for himself and family and friends, is something it is now impossible to set right. Twenty years of the best part of his life have been consumed in trying to have his name and his reputation restored before his countrymen. In his application now before Congress,[7] he is asking only that he may be restored to the rolls of the army, with the rank that he would have if the court-martial had never been held. This, in my judgment, is a very small part of what it is possible to do in this case, and of what ought to be done. General Porter should, in the way of partial restitution, be declared by Congress to have been convicted on mistaken testimony, and, therefore, to have never been out of the army. This would make him a major-general of volunteers until the date might be fixed for his muster out as of that rank, after which he should be continued as a colonel of infantry, and brevet brigadier-general of the United States Army from the date of the act, when he could be placed upon the retired list with that rank.

In writing what I have here written, I mean no criticism upon the court which tried General Porter, nor upon the officers under whom or with whom he served. It is easy to understand, in the condition of the public mind as it was in 1862, when the nation was in great peril, and when the Union troops had met with some severe reverses, how the public were ready to condemn,—to death if need be,—any officer against whom even a suspicion might be raised. For many years, and till within a year,[8] I believed that the position and number of the troops on both sides were as stated in the first diagram given here, and that the order to attack was received at an hour in the day sufficiently early to have made the attack feasible; and, under that impression, it seemed to me that the enemy, unless through very bad generalship on the Union side, could not have been able to escape while a superior force confronted him and ten thousand men flanked him. But a study of the case not only has convinced me, but has clearly and conclusively established, that the position and numbers of the armies were as given in the second diagram.

If a solemn and sincere expression of my thorough understanding of and belief in the entire innocence of General Porter will tend to draw the public mind to the same conviction, I shall feel abundantly rewarded for my efforts. It will always be a pleasure to me, as well as a duty, to be the instrument, even in the smallest degree, of setting right any man who has been grossly wronged, especially if he has risked life and reputation in defense of his country. I feel, as stated on a previous occasion, a double interest in this particular case, because, directly after the war, as General of the Army, when I might have been instrumental in having justice done to General Porter, and later as President of the United States, when I certainly could have done so, I labored under the firm conviction that he was guilty;[9] that the facts of the receipt of the 4.30 order were as found by the court, and that the position of the troops and numbers were as given in the first of these diagrams. Having become better informed, I at once voluntarily gave, as I have continued to give, my earnest efforts to impress the minds of my countrymen with the justice of this case, and to secure from our Government, as far as it could grant it, the restitution due to General Fitz John Porter.

U. S. GRANT.

North American Review, CXXXV, cccxiii (Dec., 1882), 536–46. On Oct. 23, 1882, USG, New York City, wrote to Fitz John Porter. "A note from Gen. Mc.Clellan received since you were here this A. M. states that the editors of the North American can publish what I may have to say about your case if received by the 25th of this month—day after tomorrow. I did not take the papers with me yesterday, and today I have not had one minute to look at them. It is therefore very doubtful about my being able to submit the matter at so early a date." Copies (2), DLC-Fitz John Porter. See next letter.

On Nov. 16, Anthony J. Drexel, Philadelphia, wrote to USG. "That is a noble article of yours in the North American Review I know very few men who would have the courage & magnanimity to treat the subject as you do and to write that concluding paragraph. I cannot say that I am surprised at your action in the matter as you have done exactly what I would have expected you to do under the circumstances" ALS, DLC-Fitz John Porter. On the same day, U.S. Senator Thomas F. Bayard of Del., Wilmington, wrote to USG, New York City. "I have just read your article in the North American Review in relation to the case of General Fitz-John Porter—and yield to an instinctive impulse when I thus express to you my sense of personal respect and high appreciation for your efforts to repair, that which you now believe to have been a fearful injustice to a brave and ~~courageous~~ patriotic soldier— ~~While you were the President of the U. S a sense of public duty led me to oppose and condemn many measures of your administration, and much of your public action~~—and my judgment *then* of Porter's case ~~was~~ has always been that which you now so ably, frankly, and impressively have expressed. As your fellow citizen I am glad and grateful that you have so placed yourself on record—as one not hesitating to remedy injustice when disclosed to your mind even though it involved an admission of your own error in consenting for a long time to its continuance—Your action now is so simply magnanimous, manly and just that it must increase the admiration and esteem ~~of~~ felt for you by all right-minded men—and be most valuable as a public example ~~to your countrymen~~—Wishing you prolonged health and prosperity . . ." ADfS, DLC-Thomas F. Bayard. See Charles Callan Tansill, *The Congressional Career of Thomas Francis Bayard 1869–1885* (Washington, 1946), pp. 257–58, 302–3.

On Nov. 17, Charles F. McKenna, Pittsburgh, wrote to USG. "As one who carried a musket for three years in the Army of the Potomac in the Fifth Army Corps down until the surrender allow me to tender you my heartfelt thanks for the frank, honorable, soldierly words written by you in the current number of the 'North American' in favor of Gen'l. FitzJohn Porter. As one of his Corps, it did not require ~~for me~~ the Schofield Board or the proofs from the rebel archives to vindicate the integrity, loyalty and courage of Genl Porter. Mexico, Malvern Hill, Gaines Mill and Antietam were sufficient names to resent the insult put upon Genl. Porter—by Genl Pope. According to the latter General's report of operations of the army in Virginia every General cooperating with him from the day he assumed command blundered or disobeyed orders. Many of Porter's regiments were recruited in this part of Pennsylvania and in our G. A. R. Posts his case has often been discussed and your able article I know will be warmly welcomed. Since ~~I~~ my return from the Army and reading law I have closely studied the case of Gen'l. Porter and rejoice that your study of the case has resulted in the gain of so able and fearless an advocate for national justice to a gallant and skilful soldier who has suffered so much unmerited and cruel wrong for the incompetency of others. Accept dear General, my most grateful thanks for your manly plea for justice— which will commend itself to men of all parties worthy of the name of American—and more than this, will because of the earnest demand for reparation of a great wrong call forth the approval of a just God." ALS, DLC-Fitz John Porter.

On Nov. 18, George Hoyt, *Cleveland Plain Dealer*, wrote to USG. "Permit me to thank you for your noble generosity in the Porter case. Having looked into it a good deal, & done what I humbly could to set it properly before the country I feel that I can appreciate what you have done." ALS, *ibid.*

On Nov. 19, Brig. Gen. Alfred H. Terry, Fort Snelling, Minn., wrote to USG. "Will you permit me to express to you the very great gratification with which I have read your article in the North American Review? Dealing, as it does, with only the great essential points of Porter's case, and brushing aside as unworthy of serious notice all the petty sophistries with which his opponents have sought to confuse the public mind, it seems to me that it must carry conviction to every fair, unprejudiced man. The questions involved in Porter's case are, of course, partly legal and partly military. Long ago the best legal authority of the country—such men as B. R. Curtis, Charles O'Conor and Daniel Lord—declared that the rules of law were violated by the conviction of Porter, even as the case stood before the court-martial; and now that the highest military authority of the nation has pronounced in his favor upon the military questions, what is there left for the Government and the people to do except to hasten to make such reparation as may yet be possible for the wrong which has been done? As perhaps you may know, I once, like yourself, believed Porter to be guilty. I believed that he had committed a crime so great that mere human law could provide no adequate punishment for it. But when it became my duty to examine into the case carefully I found that I had grossly erred. I found that instead of being a criminal he was a martyr. So believing, it is a source of very great satisfaction to me that I have borne some small part in his vindication. Looking back over the years that have elapsed since I entered the military service, I find nothing that gives me so much pleasure as the fact that I have had some part in that vindication, and I can think of nothing in the future which would be so grateful to me as to be able to do something more in behalf of one who has suffered so grievously and so unjustly. While I feel thus, you may imagine the gratification with which I find that the opinion which I now entertain, that what I believe to be the cause of truth, of right, and of justice, is so strongly supported by yourself; and you will pardon me, I am sure, for expressing to you my feelings." Copy (illegibly faint), *ibid.*; SRC, 48-1-74, 33–34.

On Nov. 20, Horace B. Sargent, Salem, Mass., wrote to USG. "I take the liberty of expressing my admiration of your article on Fitz John Porter in the North American Review. The public has not the patience or capacity to collate the facts that make a chain of evidence. Even jurors let the summing-up Judge do their thinking, if they absolutely trust him. If not presumptuous in me to express any opinion on the manner of condensing facts, and stating their necessary consequence in the briefest form of inevitable conclusion, I think you would have been a Lord Chancellor if you had not been a General. Your statement seems to me masterly, in form, and manner. That this, and foreign Nations will accept it, without further proof, as they would accept it from no other living man,—as a vindication of General Porter,—must reward even you. From the first, I believed his statement of facts; and I have no small pleasure in knowing, that, when you also believed the same facts, you have justified my long belief in his innocence—" ALS, DLC-Fitz John Porter.

On Nov. 23, Maj. Gen. John M. Schofield, San Francisco, wrote to USG. "I have read with great interest and satisfaction your article in the North American Review for December on the case of Fitz John Porter. It is a remarkably clear concise and exact statement of the essential facts of the case. Next to Porter himself, Terry, Getty and I have a right to feel gratified by your powerful vindication of our judgement, and to thank you for it." Copy, *ibid.* See Schofield, *Forty-Six Years in the Army* (New York, 1897), pp. 462–63.

On Nov. 27, Theodore Lyman *et al.*, Boston, wrote to USG. "The undersigned, once Soldiers under your command, desire to express their hearty and grateful thanks for your recent paper in vindication of Gen. Fitz John Porter. They feel that no act, whether of valor or of policy, which has marked your great career should bring you more honor than the moral courage and the spirit of fairness and justice exhibited in this defense of a gallant Union Soldier, condemned on insufficient or mistaken evidence" LS (12 signatures), DLC-Fitz John Porter. On the same day, Francis A. Walker, Boston, wrote to USG. "I have the honor, on behalf of some of your former soldiers, to inclose a note expressive of their sentiments respecting your recent article in the North American Review. No circulation has been given to this note with a view to securing signatures. It is written and sent only as a spontaneous utterance of hearty thanks for your justice and courage in defending an unfortunate but honorable and gallant soldier." *SRC*, 48-1-74, 34.

On Dec. 30, James Longstreet, Atlanta, wrote to USG. "It occurs to me that an account of parallel circumstances passing in the Army of Northern Virginia, before and during the Second Manassas, to those leading to the Fitz John Porter trial, may be a proper ~~segment~~ sequel to your recently published paper referring to his case. It is but just, however, to admit that the argument of those who hold to the finding of the Court Martial, is, from their strictly military stand point, conclusive. But they seem to ignore the well recognized custom of war, that Superior Officers are not confined to the rule that holds an army as a grand machine, limited, under all circumstances, to the letter of the orders of its Chief, but are expected and required to exercise due discretion, when not in his immediate presence. No doubt, cases have occurred in your experience where officers, were as deserving reproof for failing to exercise such discretion as for failing to obey orders. Early on the 29th of August, 1862, at the head of my column, I arrived in striking distance of the battle, in progress, between part of the Army of the Potomac and General Jackson's wing of the Army of Northern Virginia. Upon seeing the approach of our column the Federal troops were withdrawn to a defensive position, a little retired. Before noon, as testified by myself and others before the Schofield Board, my command was deployed and formed on Jackson's right, at right angles to the Warrenton Pike and extending to and beyond the Mannassas Gap railroad. As soon as deployed, General Lee indicated his purpose to have me attack. Intending to execute his plan I asked time to reconnoitre the new position, and the ground intervening. After the reconnoisance, I reported the position strong and that the sacrifice was likely to be such as to cause apprehension of failure. He did not seem satisfied, and was considering the propriety of making his orders more definite when information was received from General Stuart of the approach of Federal troops upon my right. This drew attention to that part of the field, for the time, but when it appeared that this force was hardly strong enough for attack, the question of attack by the First Corps was resumed. As the day was far spent I suggested, a forced reconnoisance at nightfall, and preparations for the action of the day following. This was accepted. The reconnoisance however satisfied General Lee and myself that the battle should not be made at this point. So I withdrew about midnight to the ground we had occupied before our advance. The next day the Federals renewed the battle against Jackson. As we were not engaged on 30th, nor seriously threatened, I rode out in advance of my line in search of opportunity to take my share of the battle; and found a number of my officers collected at a point from which they had fair view of the masses welling up against Jackson. From this point it was evident that a few batteries, having enfilade fire, could disperse the attack, and some of our batteries were ordered forward for the position, and prepare. Meanwhile a message came from General Jackson asking for re-inforcements, and almost immediately after came an order from General Lee to send some of my brigades to Jackson. It did not seem probable that the troops could reach Jackson in time, if sent; at the same time there was no doubt of our dispersing the attack by the fire of our Artillery. Under the circumstances I felt impelled to disregard the orders, and to operate on my own judgment. The fire of our batteries produced results anticipated. When the attacking forces were dispersed, my command was sprung to the charge and swept the field. Had I thus engaged the day before it is more than probable that Porter would have been in good season to take me on the wing, and would in all probability have crushed me. Had I stopped to re-inforce on the second day, it is hardly probable that Jackson could have held till my troops could have reached him. As you state it was not possible for Porter to attack under the 4.30 order the failure to do which was alleged to be his high crime. If we may suppose that he received the order at 4.50 and had attacked he would have given us the opportunity that we were so earnestly seeking all of that day, and in the disjointed condition of their army on that day, the result might have been more serious than that of the next day—30th. Now if we suppose that my attack on the afternoon of the 30th had failed, we shall see that the evidence against me would have been stronger than that against Porter. Yet, with an earnest desire to meet the orders of my Chief, I felt that it would be more culpable to execute than to disobey them. As we were successful there was no room to question of my motives. And this brings us to the only safe rule to guide the judgment in such cases. If in the exercise of discretion one becomes the direct cause of failure, he should only be adjudged as failing in generalship. If the intention is to bring discomfiture upon the arms it is criminal. Soon after this campaign I was promoted, and assigned as Senior Lieutenant General of the Confederate Army." Typed copies (2), DLC-Fitz John Porter. On [*Jan. 10, 1883*], one copy of this letter was endorsed. "The following letter asked of the writer by the National Republican of Washington City has been sent to that paper and is now published for the first time—" E, *ibid.* See *Washington National Republican*, Jan. 10, 1883.

On Nov. 23, U.S. Senator John A. Logan of Ill. had written "*To the Editor of The Chicago Tribune.*" "You call my attention to the article in the December number of the

North American Review, written by Gen. U. S. Grant, in justification of the conduct of Fitz John Porter in disobeying the orders of his commanding General on the 27th, 28th, and 29th of August, 1862. I dislike very much to enter into any discussion with Gen. Grant on matters pertaining to military movements, as I must do so knowing I am contesting ground with a man of great military renown. But, inasmuch as Gen. Grant has so recently changed his opinion on this subject, after having the case before him when General of the Army, and during eight years while President of the United States, based upon Porter's own statement of the case, and after careful examination of the case concluded that he was guilty, and having more than once impressed his then opinion upon my mind, which very strongly confirmed me in my own conclusions of Porter's guilt, therefore I take it that the General's generosity will be sufficient to pardon me if I shall now differ with him and trust my own judgment in the case, instead of accepting his present conclusions—especially when I feel confident that I can clearly demonstrate that his present opinions are based upon a misapprehension of the facts as they did exist and were understood by those understanding them at the time. . . . Suppose his [o]fficers had taken it upon themselves to determine the manner of obeying imperative commands, how long does any one suppose they would have kept their commands? And suppose Gen. Grant's justification of the disobedience of orders, as he has stated it now in defense of Porter, had been published by him (Grant) to his armies and been so understood by his Generals, does any one suppose by such discipline he would ever have made the success he did and become the hero he is? No, sir! His officers did not stop to write letters of criticism against him. They obeyed his orders and fought the enemy with a good will. If they failed to obey his orders they failed to retain their commands longer under him. The General's present justification of the disobedience of a peremptory order if followed out by Generals would make any army a mob, and the commanding General a laughing stock. It would authorize every officer, down to the lower officers in rank, to determine how and when they would act under orders. . . . I wish to call Gen. Grant's attention to one little thing which occurred during the War, under his command. He remembers the march that McPherson's troops made in the night from Jackson to Baker's Creek. Does he not remember that while Pemberton, with nearly his whole army, was attacking Hovey's division, my division was moved in on the right of Hovey, and Crocker supporting Hovey, these three divisions receiving nearly the whole force of Pemberton's 30,000 men? Does he not remember of one small brigade sent by me (with his assent) down through a strip of wood[s], a distance of a mile or a mile and a half away from the balance of the force, getting in on the left flank of Pemberton's army? Does he not remember that that one little brigade of not more than 2,000 men attacked the left flank of Pemberton's army, and that the latter became so panic-stricken that the whole army fled, and we captured all the artillery and drove them that night across Black River? If a brigade of 2,000 men could do this by striking the flank of the enemy, what does Gen. Grant think Porter with his corps could have done by striking Longstreet in flank on that afternoon? There may be this difference, however: Gen. Grant will remember that his Generals were in earnest, and supported him in all things that he required. . . . I now wish to call attention to another proposition of Gen. Grant's which is equally as astounding as anything in reference to Porter's conduct. . . . This proposition would give him over $70,000 out of the Treasury of the United States for no act performed, for no duty done, for no service rendered, except the failure in performance of his duty on the 29th day of August, 1862. Gen. Grant ought to know whether Porter was dismissed or not from the army on what he considers 'mistaken evidence': that he was dismissed and put out of the army, his place was filled, and he has been a citizen ever since, is today a citizen, and not a soldier. I know of no rule of law, no rule of justice, that would give this to Gen. Porter, or to any other man dismissed from the army. This rule would establish a precedent that would pay money back to every man dismissed from the army that might ever afterwards be placed back again, whether dismissed at the beginning of the War for disloyalty or not, if they could get up testimony such as is wanted. Some have been put back into the army by act of Congress since, and, under this rule of Gen. Grant's, they could come and claim pay for the whole time they have been out of the army, saying that they were not disloyal and were improperly dismissed. Every officer that may be convicted for misconduct in office, civil or military, and removed from office, if afterwards on examination of the evidence obtains a decision that he was improperly dismissed, on this proposition would he be entitled to pay while he was out of his office. A proposition of this kind and a principle of this sort should not not be entertained for a moment, and I am very much surprised to find a suggestion of this kind coming from the pen of Gen. Grant. I believe I have answered fully the propositions laid down by Gen. Grant in justification of Fitz John Porter, and merely wish to add that, after twenty years have passed and the country has been raked and scraped for some kind of flimsy testimony for an excuse to restore this man to the army, no such testimony has been found. The effort to vindicate Porter at the expense of the reputations of such men as Gen. Garfield, Gen. Hunter, and their associates, all honorable gentlemen, who found him guilty, and also to cloud the reputation of Abraham Lincoln, who approved the findings, cannot succeed. This is asking too much, even though it be asked by such men as Gen. Grant." *Chicago Tribune*, Nov. 26, 1882. A related editorial is *ibid.*, Nov. 27, 1882.

1. See *O.R.*, I, xii, part 2 (Supplement).
2. See *ibid.*, p. 825.
3. See *SED*, 46-1-37.
4. See *O.R.*, I, xii, part 3, 730.
5. See *ibid.*, part 2 (Supplement), 825.
6. See *ibid.*, part 3, 959–61.
7. See letter to James D. Cameron, May 29, 1882.
8. See letter to Fitz John Porter, Dec. 9, 1881.
9. See *PUSG*, 17, 327–40; *ibid.*, 25, 91–93; *ibid.*, 26, 71–74.

To Fitz John Porter

New York City,
[*Oct.*] 25th 1882

DEAR GENERAL;

With this I send you the matter prepared by me yesterday touching upon the findings of the Court Martial of 1862 upon charges against you. You are at liberty to do with it as you think best. I will suggest however that it does not appear to me worthy of a place in a magazine of the standing of the North American Review. As you know it was dictated from notes prepared hastily, and they were departed from largely. The subject however has become so familiar to me recently that I think I have committed no error in the statement of facts. I am sorry that I did not have more time to prepare the article; but I have had my time so taken up with callers at my office since I consented to write this that I carsely got an opportunity to look at the papers referring to your case until I took them home with me on Monday afternoon[1] and spent the evening over them. This must be my excuse for so limited an amount of detail, and other imperfections.

Very Truly yours
U. S. GRANT

GEN. F J. PORTER

ALS (misdated Nov.), InU. See previous text.

    1. Oct. 23, 1882.

To Edward F. Beale

———

New York City,
Nov. 3d 1882

MY DEAR GENERAL BEALE:

I gave Mrs. Grant last evening Emilys letter saying that she and Truxton[1] would be up on the 15th if convenient for us to have them at that time. It will be entirely convenient for us to have Emily, and Truxton too except for the lodging. Buck come in yesterday and with his family will remain with us until he sails for Europe about the last of the month. Jesse & wife isare with us, and Bessie Sharp also. Tell Emily & Truxton to come however and the latter take a room some place and make our house his home except for sleeping

Very Truly yours
U. S. GRANT

ALS, DLC-Decatur House Papers. See letter to Edward F. Beale, Nov. 25, 1882.

    1. Truxton Beale, born in 1856. See *New York Times,* June 3, 1936.

To Julia K. Fish

——————

New York City,
Nov. 6th 1882.

MY DEAR MRS. FISH:

Mrs. Grant, who did not hear of your sad accident until long after it occurred, asks me to write and say how sorry she was to hear of it, and how much she hopes you are recovering, and will recover without a trace of bad effect from it. I go to Boston[1] to-morrow evening to be absent a couple of days, but soon after my return I will run up for an hour or two to see the Governor and to learn more particularly how you are.

With best wishes for your speedy recovery,

Very Truly yours
U. S. GRANT

ALS, ICarbS. Julia K. Fish broke two ribs in an Oct. 16, 1882, carriage accident. See *New York Times*, Oct. 20, 1882.

1. On Nov. 8, USG toured the New England Manufacturers' and Mechanics' Institute fair. ". . . I look upon what it is doing as of great importance in filling up the breach which was caused between the two sections of the country by the conflict which has passed. I saw today a very good showing from our Southern States alongside of exhibits from the North, showing, perhaps, more ingenuity and skill, but less of the natural resources of the country. This bringing of their resources into the markets of your manufacturers should go a long way, and will undoubtedly go a long way, towards creating that feeling of friendship between the people of the two sections which will make all alike equally good citizens. . . ." *Boston Evening Transcript*, Nov. 9, 1882.

To Lt. Col. Henry C. Hodges

——————

New York City,
Nov. 21st 1882

MY DEAR HODGES:

I wish you would bear in mind Ed. C. Marshall for a Clerkship when you can make a vacancy. He is a brother Gen. Marshall, retired, and a very correct and competant man. Mr. Marshall is a man of literary tastes and ability, and I think could be implicitly trusted.

Truly yours

U. S. GRANT

ALS, Union League Club, New York, N. Y. Lt. Col. Henry C. Hodges, USMA 1851, took command of the q. m. dept., New York City, as of April 10, 1882.

On Oct. 6, 1881, Elisha G. Marshall, USMA 1850, Lehigh Gap, Pa., had written to USG. "I must earnestly request you will take an interest in my only Brother Edward C. Marshall & request that he receive some permanent position that you deem fitted for him! As a Clerk in the Quarter Masters Department at Washington." R. M. Smythe & Co., Inc., Sale No. 99, Oct. 23, 1991, no. 151; Superior Galleries, June 1993, no. 1437. On Oct. 12, USG endorsed this letter. "Referred to Gen. Ingalls. If a position as clerk,—or in the Dept. in this City in other capacity—can be given to Mr. Marshall I think a he will be found a competant and worthy man." AES (facsimile), *ibid.* No appointment followed. See *PUSG*, 22, 242.

To Chester A. Arthur

———

New York City,
Nov. 22d 1882

THE PRESIDENT;

While the country is in the midst of unusual prosperity I am satisfied it is on the brink of a great and widespread catastrophy unless the Administration comes to the aid of the people. I can write to you freely on this subject I think because there are but few who will be so little effected by it as myself. The disaster, if it comes will be caused—indirectly—by the prosperity. The farmers have large crops and the laborer employment at present. This makes them free purchasers and consequently money comes into the Treasury more rapidly than it can be paid out as now conducted. Soon there will be less money in circulation than is necessary for conducting the business of the country while it will be laying idle in the Treasury. Calling bonds will not relieve this pressure because so many of the called bonds are held by institutions that cannot surrender them without replacing by other bonds not called. They can not purchase others without the money for those called. Hence they are compelled to keep their called bonds and forego the receipt of interest on their capital. Another thing that is producing this stringency is the fact that all banks—National—that have gone into liquidation have been obliged to deposite the amount of their outstanding circulation in the Treasury to redeem it as presented. It is only a matter of time, under the present system, when all the money in the country will be so held from circulation. It is a known fact that large amounts of the paper currency of the country is destroyed and lost every year. For every dollar so lost, sooner or later, a corresponding amount is locked up. Now it seems to me the remedy for this is in purchasing, at the lowest bid, say five or ten million of bonds weekly with the money held for the redemption of currency until the amount locked up is reduced to five millions. When this amount become reduced so as to make it necessary these bonds could be sold again in sufficient amount to bring the balance in the hand of the Treasurer up to the standard. In this way the government would be getting interest on this idle capital and the country would have the benefit of the circulation.

Very Truly yours
U. S. GRANT

P. S. I have written this without the knowledge or advice of any one and would be please if it could have no publicity.

U. S. G.

ALS, DLC-Chester A. Arthur. On Nov. 25, 1882, President Chester A. Arthur wrote to USG. "I read your letter of the 22d inst with much interest & am much impressed with your suggestions. I have talked with the Secretary in regard to them & will have further conference with him in the matter" ALS, USG 3. On the same day, Secretary of the Treasury Charles J. Folger telegraphed to Thomas C. Acton, asst. treasurer, New York City, pledging to redeem $10,000,000 of uncalled bonds on or before Feb. 28, 1883. "The information contained in the dispatch was sent over the tapes early in the afternoon, and its effect upon the market was immediately strengthening." _New York Times_, Nov. 26, 1882. See _ibid._, Dec. 7, 1882, March 17, 1883.

To Hamilton Fish

New York City
Nov. 24th 1882

My Dear Governor Fish,

Since my return from Boston it has so happened that every day I have had some one little thing to attend to to occupy an hour in the midde of the day so that I could not pay my desired visit to you and

Mrs. Fish and return the same evening. It is now getting so late in the season that I will defer my call until you come to the City.—I hope Mrs. Fish is so far recovered as to be able to move without pain.

Very Truly yours

U. S. GRANT

ALS, King V. Hostick, Springfield, Ill.

To Edward F. Beale

————

New York City

Nov. 25th 1882

MY DEAR GENERAL BEALE:

I telegraphed for Emily & Truxton to come up to-day or Monday[1] because Mrs Grant was anxious to have Truxton as well as Emily visit us. Buck had expected to leave earlyer for Michigan for the purpose of depositing his young coupon with his wifes aunt preparitory to sailing for Europe. His wifes sickness delayed his going west as well as his day of sailing. On their return from the west they will be at our house again until they do sail—probably about the 4th of Nov. [*Dec.*] though it may be a few days later.[2] Fred and his family will also be with us. Bessie Sharp being with us leaves but one spare room after Buck leaves. We want Emily to take that and have Truxton make our house head quarters. If Buck sails on the 4th I will telegraph you in time so that Emily can come the day they have fixed upon. If they are detained a few days beyond I will notify you. They have their state rooms secured for the 4th of Dec. but Mrs. U. S. Jr. has been quite indisposed for the last few weeks, causing one postponement of their departure.

Very Truly yours

U. S. GRANT

ALS, DLC-Decatur House Papers.

1. Nov. 27, 1882. On Nov. 24, Friday, USG had telegraphed to Edward F. Beale, Washington, D. C. "Let Emily and Truxton come tomorrow or Monday. We are now all ready for them." Telegram received, *ibid.*

2. See letter to Ellen Grant Sartoris, Dec. 12, 1882.

To Ellen Grant Sartoris

New York City.
Nov. 28th 1882

Dear Nellie:

Your Ma and the girls write to you so often that it is not necessary for me to do so to keep you advised of how we are and what
we are doing. I suppose you may expect to see Buck & Fanny over
about the last of November [*December*]. Jesse and Lizzyie are talking either of going to Europe or Mexico. It will probably be the
latter unless some business Jesse has in contemplation takes him
the other way. We all miss our little pets Algy and Vivie. Tell them
they must come to see their grand pa & Grand ma in America soon,
unless we go there, and they must bring their little sister Rosa with
them.—I think there is but little doubt but we will go over about
the last of May. Senator and Mrs. Cameron and Will Smith expect
to go with us. We want you to go too. We expect to drive over the
Austrian & Swiss Alps most of the time for three months. Kiss all
the children for me.

Yours affectionately
U. S. Grant

ALS, ICHi.

To John Russell Young

New York City
Nov. 28th 1882.

My Dear Commodore:

Your very welcome letter come to hand about ten days ago. I
should have written to you before, and have no excuse for not having done so except chronic laziness. But there has not been anything of special interest to write about that you do not get from the
papers. The result of the elections you have heard from and were

no doubt surprized.[1] The defeat was expected, but the magnitude of the defeat was a surprize. It was deserved, and it is to be hope the lesson will be appreciated. The fact is—aside from the half breed and mock reform defection—the country has grown tired of war taxation in time of peace. The democrats have been about as much to blame for the continuance of this taxation as the republicans; but the latter having controll of the government are of course held responsible.—My family are all well and all enjoyed reading your letter. I hope my old friend, Viceroy Li Hung Chang is well. I have no idea of the cause of the delay in manufacturing the gun which I ordered for him.[2] If it is ever made I will forward it by the first opportunity.—We were all sorry to hear of Mrs. Youngs indisposition and inability to accompany you to Pekin. I hope the winter in Shanghai will restore her. Please present to her Mrs. Grant and my kindest regards.

It is gratifying to me that the Corea question passed off without a conflict between China and Japan.[3] a war between those two Nations would be as disastrous to both—no matter which come out victorious—as a civil war in any other country. I hope Prince Kung & Li Hung Chang will see this.

With the kind regards of all my family,

Very Truly yours
U. S. GRANT

ALS, DLC-John Russell Young. On Sept. 23, 1882, and Jan. 27, 1883, John Russell Young, U.S. minister, Peking, wrote to USG. "*Private.* . . . I have been intending to write you ever since I left Japan, but have been on the move nearly all the time. When I came to Peking I was taken with a kind of remittent fever, caught on the Peiho, and I have not thrown it off. The only work I can do, is general official work and this is the first private letter I have written for an age.—I wrote you about Iwakura, and all his kindness. I hope you received his message and also the mementoes for Mrs. Grant. Yoshida's appointment as Vice-Foreign Minister was especially pleasant. Yoshida was not well, but he seemed pleased with his place. It presages his entrance into the cabinet. In my talks with Iwakura I urged his government to send an envoy to Peking. Japan has not had an envoy here for three years, simply a Chargé, while all the time China has had one in Tokio. I pointed out the disadvantage under which this placed Japan. Yoshida writes me that my advice was taken & Admiral Enemoto, whom you ~~will~~ will remember, comes as full minister. The Japanese felt aggrieved about the Corean business.—Whether their grievance was real or a sentiment I could not quite say. Our treaty, however, was a Chinese measure. Li planned it, practically wrote it, and ordered the Coreans to sign it. He meant to spite Japan. Shufeldt did not care much what he signed,—or he signed something before I came out here.—Nor did he care about the emotions of the Japanese.—I found that Holcombe shared this feeling, as would be natural to one living under Chinese influence.—My own idea was to be friends to both, and so when the outbreak came in Corea, and Inouye telegraphed me, I saw my chance.—I telegraphed for permission to send the *Monocacy* to Corea She was lying at Chafoo eighteen hours away doing nothing.—The President consented, and I instructed the commander *to convey to the Japanese our sincere sympathies* in the outrage upon their legation, and *to offer our aid in restoring order and protecting life.* I explained my motives in an elaborate despatch to the department of state. The result was as I expected. The Japanese were pleased with our friendly words, and the presence of our vessel, as Holcombe was told at the Yamen had a powerful influence in the peaceful settlement. The situation was most critical. Japan was in a flame,—and justly so, as the outrage was atrocious. China became alarmed and the Emperor ordered Li out of retirement at once & to come north. It looked as if war was inevitable, so my advice and influence was for peace and a settlement, upon *any honorable terms.*—Before Li reached Tientsin an agreement had been made. I have an impression that if Li had been in power, a settlement would have been more difficult.—I first saw the Viceroy at Chefoo about three weeks ago. He was very cordial,—could not have been more so. Asked a thousand questions about you,—all about you,—what you were doing,—why you did not insist upon being President—how you looked.—He asked about Frederick & Mrs. Grant,—and seemed pleased to hear of your grandson & namesake.—I saw him again at Tientsin, twice, and on each occasion found him as you did. He was angry with Shufeldt, but said he was too good a friend of yours and of America to cherish resentment towards America because of Shufeldt—He brought up the LooChoo Question, and all you did, and wanted to know if I would not try and settle it. His bitterness against Japan was marked, as he has, as you know the un-Oriental way of speaking plainly.—He said he was ready to fight Japan, and rather wanted to, unless Japan behaved herself.—Japan had humiliated China in Formosa,—had taken LooChoo, and now was meddling with Corea. I told the Viceroy that I should be proud and happy to be of any service in securing peace.—I could not think of any calamity more horrible than a war between China & Japan,—a war that would leave them at the mercy of Russia or England. There was a good deal of talk in that vein. I think Li meant it, and that is why I was glad that we brought Corea to a settlement before he came from mourning.—He would I am afraid have precipitated things. And the situation was like what one sees in the Alps sometimes,—a shout would have brought down the avalanche. Li talked about the opium question. He said the Angell-Trescott treaty had been of immense moral service to China by prohibiting American trade in opium.—Wanted to know if I could help him in England. He had heard fabulous stories about my ability as a writer & wondered if I could write anything that would awaken English thought. I said that my pen was at his command if I could serve China in that best of causes,—that I thought opium as great a curse as slavery. I said, further, that the main arguments relied upon in the English parliament for this trade came from the customs reports of Sir Robt Hart,—who was a Chinese official,—and it threw doubt upon China's sincerity in wishing to stop the traffic. Li said he was sincere and so was his government.—He thought of sending a special embassy to present the case,—~~to g~~ going through the U. S. to England.—I asked him why he did not go himself as Mr. Iwakura did,—and it would have a tenfold effect. He laughed & said, that the only reason which would induce him to go to the U. S. would be to 'see General Grant.' I said, I knew that Gen. Grant would be only too glad to receive a visit from him & that he would be well-received in America.—These are all the useful points in our talk. I found Badeau's books here awaiting his coming out of mourning—and sent them to him. My reception by Prince Kung was most cordial. The Prince asked about you, and wanted me to ask you for your picture. I told him I would write you. If you would send Marshall's large steel-plate, I ~~could~~ could have it framed in Shanghae, and send it to him. I had no talk with the Prince beyond formal courtesies in taking the legation. Mrs. Y. is at Chefoo not very well. The doctors fear that her lungs are in danger & I fear she cannot come to Pekin this winter. I am living in the legation & am slowly getting the house in order.— I have bought no curios yet beyond a vase of old blue.—The stories about Denny & myself are mischievous and nonsensical. We are on the very best terms, and so far from my being 'ostracized,' no minister was ever more cordially received.—Denny goes home for a leave.—Mosby is sore about Mahone. Hill is here worrying about his claim. I hope I can arrange it, as China owes him the money. I hope Mrs. Grant is well, & that she can think of something I can do for her in China. Give the kindest remembrances to her & to all of your family, & believe me always with affection & respect, . . ." "Personal. . . . I was very glad indeed to have your letter of November, which was a long time coming on account of the winter blockade.—Mails have to come all the way from Shanghae, 800 miles, on ponies, and are sixteen days coming.—I have enjoyed the winter very much. The weather is cold, but a steady, constant cold, with endless sunshine, and an even temperature.—I do not think I ever spent a winter more pleasantly so far as climate is concerned. There is society enough to go around.—Most of the legations are vacant.—Wade has gone home, presumably to talk about opium.—The agitation on this subject is alarming the government of India, and well it may.—Opium pays $50.000.000 a year revenue to India, and the budget even then is hard to balance.—I think opium is worse than slavery, and have written one or two despatches home on the subject.—Van Brandt is still delicate and does not go out.—There are some incorrigible whist players, three or four who play chess badly, and a number who know how to waltz. I have had a very quiet and very busy winter.—There is in the Legation a good deal of work to do anyhow, and I have made a good deal.—Since I have been in charge in August, I have written over six hundred letters, despatches, and so on, public and private,—which implies a steady volume of ~~mail~~ work whatever the quality may be.—I correspond freely with Li and Yoshida, and think I have succeeded in establishing once more good relations between Japan and ourselves.—We did treat Japan rather shabbily in that Corean business, ignored and slighted her, which you know annoys a nation, more than downright enmity. The Japanese confer with me upon all their affairs and confidentially. I am, sometimes afraid their confidence will embarrass me,—but as I have only one aim in view, the peace of both China and Japan, I need not have any special anxiety.—I wish the two nations had a better feeling to each other. Enomotto the envoy has not been as well-received by the Chinese as he should have been, but he does not seem to care.—He is a fair and a brave man, and I like him very much.—The Shanghae difficulty about which I wrote you fully has rather subsided. The necessity of speaking rather plainly about the conduct of the Nanking Viceroy Tso, was disagreeable. The argument of the Chinese that foreign machinery will ruin the industries of millions, and bring starvation is pathetic, and while we may not agree with them, and know from our own experience the contrary, still we must respect their anxieties.— After all, they are no farther wrong than Mr. Kelley who would protect sunshine by a high duty, or Gen. Butler who would pay our debts in paper.—I suppose I shall separate from my colleagues on this point, and there will be an end of the co-operative policy.—I don't much believe in that. It means practically that we do what other nations

would like us to do. At the same time, before one ventures upon an independent policy
here, you should have some encouragement from China. Just now, the government is in
a helpless condition. Kung is ill,—chronic kidney trouble. Li is apprehensive of cabals,
and is timid. The palace is said to be a bedlam of eunuchs and conspirators. The government seems to have no fibre, no sinew, but to be entirely flabby and weak.—I am
glad you are so philosophical over the elections. Republicanism has been politics, not a
policy for years past. I am not surprised at the overthrow.—I have very little hopes of a
union. The half-breeds will only consent provided they can run the party. Then we
shall have a Pecksniff party.—I have been a Republican since I could think, but would
rather vote for Jeff. Davis than for one of these men. They are not honest, not patriotic.
I want to see an *American* party now. Not American in a proscriptive sense, as against
~~for~~ aliens and Catholics, but a party that believes in [*build*]ing up the country, extending its influence,—a party of self-respect and patriotism—The half-breeds live on li-
bels and slander.—Affairs will be interesting at home.—I am sorry for Arthur. What
little thanks he receives for his conciliation and courtesy I read with deep interest
your article on Porter. It seems to be as clear as a problem in geometry.—I glanced
over Logan's article in the *Chicago Tribune*, and when I came to the part, that it would
not do to overrule the sainted Lincoln, Garfield & Hunter, did not see any use in reading further.—How can as firm and true a man as Logan slip into such demagogu-
ery?—Lincoln may have erred,—and had he lived would have said so—The best of
men, even Peter the apostle, are only fallible, and it is no reflection upon these men, to
say that in the light of new evidence, they made a mistake. What was done in 1863 was
in the darkness, now we have light. Mrs. Y. sends her love to Mrs Grant and the ladies.
The stories about her health have been exaggerated. She only needs care and time, will
bring her health.—Remember me to all at home, to your wife most especially, . . ."
ALS, USG 3. See note 3, below; *Foreign Relations, 1883*, pp. 123–29; Article, [*Oct. 24,
1882*]. Before Young arrived in China, a correspondent had reported from Hong Kong.
"A curious intrigue exists against the agreeable reception of Mr. Young, United States
Minister. The friends of Mr. Denny, United States Consul at Shanghai, declare that
Gen. Grant promised him the Peking mission, and that Li Hung Chang urged the appointment. Intelligent foreigners disbelieve that Gen. Grant made any definite promises, and doubt the expediency of accepting Chinese statements regarding the recommendation of a candidate for such a post, but several unpleasant newspaper articles
have been published upholding Mr. Denny and threatening Mr. Young with social and
diplomatic ostracism, &c. Mr. Denny denies having authorized the attack." *New York
Times*, July 24, 1882. See letter to Chester A. Arthur, Dec. 5, 1881.

On Sept. 23, 1882, Saturday, Takahira Kogoro, chargé d'affaires, Washington,
D. C., wrote to USG. "I beg to offer you my thanks most sincerely for the kind reception you gave me the other day, and as I had immediately upon my return to Washington, reported to my Government of the result of my interview with you, I can now
assure you that they feel once again greatly indebted to you for the good offices you
would render in the matter in such effective manner as you mentioned to me. The importance of the ratification of the treaty by the United States Government was made
plain to you, if my impression is right, at our last interview and I now desire for your
information to apprise you of the important facts, to which my attention has subsequently been called regarding the Corean matter. The Honorable Secretary of State
at last found the letter of the King of Corea and had it read to me when I saw him on
Thursday last. Although I do not exactly remember the phraseology used in that letter, I am almost positive that declarations are therein made to the following effect; that

Corea has been tributary to China from the Ancient time, and also that the treaty was made with the equality (by virtue of the equal sovereign rights?) between the United States and Corea. So, the letter contains at least two points which seem to me conflicting ~~to~~ and incompatible with each other, and as I mentioned to you the other day, the treaty has no provisions of such kind, and therefore it is plain enough that when the treaty was exchanged, the United States did not recognize Corea's dependency to any other country. The question is therefore whether the United States will treat Corea as a tributary nation according to the sense of the King's letter which was written to the President after having concluded the treaty in such manner as is usually observed by and between independent nations. This question is not only a matter of Corea's sovereignty, but of great concern with the public interest and general welfare of the eastern countries, and if the Far East is equally to be benefited with justice and wisdom, which have always distinguished the United States in their relations with foreign countries, I have reason to believe that the United States Government must already know how they will dispose of the question at last. I am however sorry to say that I have not been able as yet to find out from Mr Frelinghuysen the opinions entertained by the Department of State regarding the matter, but as he kindly desired to see me on the subject before the next session of the Senate, it will be hereafter my earnest endeavor to fully exchange the views with him in due time, so that if I could come to some agreement with him in the opinion, our ends may be finally attained for the general benefit of the eastern countries. In the meantime, I shall be greatly obliged to you, if you kindly impart to me your opinion on the subject for my own information. With my best compliments to Mrs Grant, . . ." ALS, USG 3. See *New York Times,* July 14, 1900.

On Nov. 6, Edward H. House, Tokyo, wrote to USG. ". . . You can remember that soon after your visit here, the Foreign Office was placed in the hands of an official named Inouye Kaoru. I doubt if any particulars as to his reputation ever reached you. He had been dismissed from the Ministry ten years ago, for causing a national panic by openly proclaiming that the nation was bankrupt, and after his expulsion, was found guilty of financial irregularities so grave that fine and imprisonment had to be imposed upon him. It would seem as if that ought to be sufficient to keep him forever from reentering official life,—but they sometimes do strange things in Japan. He had numerous powerful friends, at the head of whom was Ito Hirobumi, whom you saw much of, when you were here. The strong clan spirit enabled Inouye to keep quite a party about him, and his ability (which every one says is remarkable) gave him almost as much influence as if he had been actually in the Cabinet. When Okubo was killed, his partisans saw their opportunity. They sent for him to England, where he then was, and on his return brought him back into the Government, as Minister of Public Works. While Okubo lived, such a thing would hardly have been possible. Okuma, (then Finance Minister) was not strong enough to prevent it, and so he pretended to approve. Inouye immediately set himself to the work of controlling the administration. Nobody but Okuma had cleverness enough to match him, and in less than two years, Okuma was forced to retire in a most ignominious way. From that time, Inouye has been supreme. He is the government, all by himself. Every department yields to him. The first sign of resistance is followed by instant deposition. He is more of a dictator than Okubo would ever have dreamed of being, without, apparently, possessing a particle of Okubo's patriotism or integrity. The danger of the situation lies in the circumstance that Inouye is, as he always has been, a wild and reckless speculator. Not a speculator in politics, scheming for power, especially, but a *money* speculator—a man filled with ambition to accumulate great wealth. It is universally charged against him that his report declaring the Empire bankrupt, (or virtually so) when he was Finance Minister, ten years ago, was part of a grand *coup* by which he laid the foundation of his large fortune. While he was out of office, he was a merchant;—a 'sleeping partner,' apparently, but in fact the active head of the Mitsui Bussan Kaisha—a trading company of which Mr. R. H. Irwin is foreign adviser and one of the directors. Through his friends in the Ministry, (Ito, Yamagata, and others, all Chosiu men) he obtained large Government support. Now, he *is* the Government, and he still remains at the head of his company,— secretly, as far as he can—[That is to say, everybody knows it, but few would be able to prove it.] It is only too obvious what an unscrupulous man may do, with the tremendous opportunities he has. Here is one example. A vast steamboat enterprise (vast for Japan) has been started, in rivalry of the Mitsu Bishi Company. This new company belongs to the trading firm of which Inouye is the soul. The Department of Commerce, at Inouye's behest, declares it essential to the welfare of the country. The Treasury, at his command, supplies millions to endow it. The Post Office clamors for its immediate establishment, because the Post Office has been ground down into obedience at the absolute cost of all its fine prestige. I do not enlarge upon this, nor bring forward other instances of the same kind, for I should hardly know where to stop. The scandal is of course widespread, but nobody can give it effective utterance, the press being muzzled, and public meetings forbidden. The means which Inouye has taken to secure connivance, or cooperation, are simple, but thoroughly injurious. He has virtually removed all restraint from the several heads of Departments, in their own methods of expenditure. This is a return to the bad system of ten years ago. *Eight* years ago, by a great effort, certain officers succeeded in instituting the rule that every Department should send in a careful estimate of its needs, annually, and that no over draft on the Treasury should be made—*i. e.* in excess of the stated estimate. This was one of the finest reforms ever effected here. Under Inouye, that principle is abandoned, and Departments are held accountable only once in three years, to begin with. In point of fact, however, it seems to be understood that each Minister may draw whatever he chooses, after consultation with the all-potent Inouye. They are all his willing tools. Men who were too high minded to assist in such schemes were set aside, no matter what their claims. Mr. Yoshida, whom I believe to be an honest official, came home fully warranted in expecting to be made Minister of Finance. He was not pliant enough, and after being held in idleness for six months, was put in the second place to Inouye—Vice Minister of Foreign Affairs—a position no higher than he held in 1874, when he was Vice Minister of the Treasury. And I could tell the same about many, in higher or lower degree. These things are painful, especially as there seems to be no hope of any change while Inouye remains without a rival. The system of Japan—positive arbitrary rule by a small body of officials,—renders it a tolerably easy matter for one peculiarly adroit man, at any time, to get the control into his own hands—where it will be likely to stay, unless some stronger or cleverer man appears, to dispute his supremacy. Thus Okubo was the main spring of the Government, up to his death; and it seems certain that he used his strength honorably, at least, and with pure intentions. After him, Okuma took the lead; but he never commanded the same confidence, and he could not keep the mastery. He may not have been the most high-minded of men, but he certainly did his best to keep the finances from utter chaos, and to maintain proper dignity and decorum in public business. Now, there is no serious effort to restore the currency to a correct standard, or to keep it from flying about at the will of any petty speculator. Whether successful or not, Okuma did strain every nerve to maintain the national credit,—which is now regarded as an unnecessary and too troublesome task. There is only one thing, besides making money, that Inouye appears to take an interest in, and that is to keep up a good show in external relations. In that respect, Japan is always fortunate. It is her best and brightest point—witness the successful issue of the Corean business, which is greatly to Japan's credit;—(although perhaps, the lavishing of affectionate demonstrations upon the Corean visitors, is a little overdone.) Inouye seems to anticipate fine results, too, from his scheme for Treaty Revision, but here I doubt the efficacy of his management. Before Yoshida took office, four months ago, he told me unhesitatingly that he thought the whole thing a failure; that the little good accomplished on the Japanese side was more than counteracted by the ingenious combinations of the European envoys. Now, of course, Yoshida is silent. But excepting in the matter of Treaty Revision, and one other (the recovery of the Simonoseki money) Inouye bestirs himself little, in the concerns of his own special department. As to the Simonoseki fund, I feel much mortified, for Japan itself, at the turn things are taking. You know how proper and discreet the attitude of the Government used to be. That is all changed. There is no concealment of an intense desire to get the money back. Steps have been taken which, I should think, must have a very bad effect in America—for they will assuredly be known, sooner or later, through the imprudence of certain new agents appointed to 'engineer' the restitution. I do not believe that what is now going on could have been carried through if Yoshida had remained in Washington;—but Yoshida was summoned home more peremptorily than ever any other Japanese envoy. Four successive telegrams, ordering his return, were sent him in one month, he told me, and when he arrived here, nobody wanted him. Now Terashima is in Washington, (a weak, soft creature, ready and anxious to be instructed in every thing), with young Mr. Stevens as his adviser. I have not a word to say against Mr. Stevens, except, perhaps, that I am sorry he is willing to undertake what is expected of him, but it is the common talk of Tokio, both among Japanese and foreigners, that he was detached from our Legation, and added to the Japanese Legation in Washington, with the one express purpose of getting the Simonoseki money, or as much of it as he could. I don't believe *he* ever claimed the power to 'work it through,' but such things have been said on his behalf that the Japanese appear to have not the faintest doubt that he will gather in the cash and transmit it (or a portion of it) without any delay. It gives me no pleasure to have to add that their belief was strengthened and confirmed by assurances from a quarter whence no such assurances should proceed; but though I do not care to circulate disagreeable truths, I see no reason why I should conceal them entirely—particularly as you have the best right to know what the situation really is. I have nothing to allege against our Minister's uprightness, but his feebleness and blindness to certain requisites of his position are obvious; and indeed there are too many voices raised against his official honesty. Much of this I assume to be malice, but some of his recent acts unluckily give malice a hold upon him. Among these are his forcing a son in law (Fraser) into Japanese employ from which he retired after proofs of incompetency, and subsequently getting him the post of Legation interpreter, when the poor fellow does not even know *English* creditably, cannot utter a syllable of Japanese, and is a general butt for his ignorance and loose habits—although, I am told, he was once a clergyman. Also, his obtaining, by direct and urgent application, a place for another son-in-law (Wasson) in the Japanese War Department. Wasson is a young man whom everybody likes, so far as I hear, and no one begrudges him his good luck; but the Japanese openly declare they do not want him, and yielded only to pressure in appointing him. Again, his arranging this transfer of his young friend and protegé, Stevens, from American to Japanese service. These things, I fancy, would not be so irritably criticized, by the Americans here, but for the fact, as many emphatically declare, that Mr. Bingham can never be brought to serve anybody outside of his own family. The complainants are doubtless interested complainants, but it is a pity they should have *any* ground to stand upon. Returning to the Simonoseki matter, I can only hope that Stevens's good sense will restrain him from committing himself, or the Japanese, in any way; but there is a prospect of a worse complication. Mr. Irwin, the business associate of Inouye, is preparing to go to America, to assist in the labor of getting through the Simonoseki Bill. It may yet be that adverse warnings will prevent his going on this errand, but just now it seems a settled thing. When I tell you that this gentleman is a brother of the Irwin who did the 'lobbying' for the Pacific Mail Company, some years ago, and that he makes no secret of his conviction that bribery, and nothing else, can do the work, you can see the false—or at least the discreditable—position in which Japan may be placed. The only thing to meet the exigency, in this matter as in others, would be the application of earnest, resolute, unimpeachable foreign counsel, from some quarter entitled to respect and able to command it. I don't *know*, of course, that this would suffice, but I can conceive of nothing more likely to. But the Japanese do not get it. Their ears are filled with interested persuasions from English, French and particularly (just now) German sources, and that is all. No impartial voice reaches them. Mr. Bingham grows more and more inactive, and it may be that he is disqualified from the position of an impartial and disinterested adviser. I have never ceased to lament the circumstances that prevented Mr. Young from coming here. Nothing can be certain about it, but I should have had great hopes from his energetic action. In China, by the bye, his station is already secure. He has gained excellent opinions, on all sides, in spite of a mean attempt to put him at a disadvantage, before his arrival. But he is very unpleasantly situated there. Mrs. Young has suffered from an unexpected throat or lung complaint, and has not joined him in Peking. It is doubted if she can ever reside there. And in his official life, he finds absolutely nobody who is not directly opposed to every view he entertains. In every sense, he is quite alone, and he suffers a good deal, in these first months of isolation. I wish events could yet turn so as to bring him here. For my own part, if I may say a word of myself, in this connection, I am convinced matters are far better than if your kind wishes and intentions had proved practicable. In no position, away from the capital, could any person, desirous of harmonizing American and Japanese interests, perform useful service while the Central Government continues as at present, and the connecting diplomatic link is as good as broken. In point of fact, I see no reason why I should ever, at any time, take any office that, in the nature of things, could be offered me by the United States. I should find it morally impossible to hold a place in which it would be certain that I could do no good, nor contribute to any lasting beneficial results. I have detained you far too long, but with the belief that you would wish to know the state of affairs here, which could hardly be explained briefly. I wish only that I had a more cheerful story to tell. No one has had higher hopes than I, for Japan, and it goes severely against me to see how the country is misgoverned and to note the growing gloom and discontent of the people. About American affairs I have not said much, and there is only one practical subject in which I think you would be interested— namely, the proposal for establishing a system of United States judiciary, similar to the British, both in Japan and China. This may turn out a matter of considerable importance, and I have taken the liberty of giving a note of introduction to a gentleman, Mr. G. W. Hill, who has the subject thoroughly under command. I have always steadily refused to give such an introduction to anybody—for I am very particular about making myself responsible for intrusions upon your time—and I have done so in this instance only because I think you may wish to hear the outline of this scheme, which Mr. Hill can give better than I, or any other, as he was its originator. The idea is to fill up the time (ten years, I think) of the interim to be allowed before Japan takes over control of everything, under the terms of the new Treaty. I am acquainted with few details, and I have no opinion in the case;—although I am free to admit that nothing could be worse than our present method of holding Courts. General Van Buren has gone home partly to see what will come of the project, and if it turns out well, he will undoubtedly claim to be the author, and seek to become a judge, instead of a consul general. I suppose Mr. Hill will try for a seat, also, though he has not said so to me. Any way, he can put you in possession of the facts without wasting time, and that is my justification for sending him to you. I have no sort of idea that he will ask any favor of you, and I trust you will kindly understand that, if he should do so, I have no knowledge of it. But I can safely say the information he gives will be sound, if you care to receive it. Pray do me the favor to give my compliments to Mrs. Grant, and to remember me to any of your family who may have me in recollection—as I am sure Colonel Grant will. I hope they are all, as well as yourself, in the best health—as they were when I last had opportunity of hearing directly about them and you,—that was when Mr. Young came. Again asking you to excuse the great length of this letter, . . ." ALS (brackets in original), USG 3.

On Dec. 11, Inoue Kaoru, foreign minister, Tokyo, wrote to USG. "The great interest you have always manifested in matters affecting my country and the East generally, and the kind remembrances and wishes which I have been charged by your host of friends here to convey to you justifies me, I hope, in writing this letter. Their Excellencies Sanjo, Iwakura and all the other members of the Government who were so fortunate as to have the pleasure of meeting you, remember with lively satisfaction your visit to Japan and they have one and all especially requested me to express to you their sentiments of high esteem and regard coupled with their good wishes for your future health and happiness and that of Mrs. Grant and in their sentiments and wishes I cordially join. We have by no means forgotten the good offices in the interest of peace and a friendly understanding between Japan and her neighbors, which you were kind enough to extend to us, and I may be permitted to assure you that so far as circumstances would admit, our course has been shaped by your wise advice. Since that time however, events have occurred which could not be foreseen and could not therefore be provided for. Through Messrs. Terashima, Takahira and Stevens, you have heard of the unfortunate Corean difficulty and its happy solution so far as Japan and Corea are concerned. In settling the matter we have endeavored to be guided by the principles of right, justice and moderation—while we have not, by any means, been unmindful of the importance of maintaining peace between Oriental Powers. Our efforts, I am convinced, would have been crowned with complete success so far as all powers are concerned, had China pursued that policy of non-interference in the affairs of Corea, which her past course fully justified us in believing she would follow. China has repeatedly declared to the United States and France that Corea was alone responsible for her acts; she actively assisted the United States, Great Britain and Germany, in concluding treaties of friendship and commerce with Corea and although she was well aware of the existence of a treaty between Japan and Corea in which the complete independence of the latter power was fully recognized, she made no protest. Notwithstanding these several acts which would have been conclusive against any other state in the same position, she at once, upon becoming possessed of the information that we intended to despatch a mission to Corea to demand satisfaction for the outrage, sent a body of troops to Corea which still remain at the Capital, and assumed that active suzerainty over the kingdom, which she had always before consistently denied. You will, I am convinced, believe me when I assure you that we have no designs against the integrity of the Corean Kingdom, and that our interests lie in the direction of peace and a good understanding with all surrounding countries. To secure this latter end we are persuaded that all jealousies and entangling alliances are to be as much deprecated as mutual accommodation is to be encouraged. The end which we are striving to bring about, and that which we know would have your hearty approval, namely, the perpetuation of peace and friendly relations, demands that the complete independence of Corea be recognized. The more general this recognition is, the stronger and more effective it will be. If the United States, Great Britain and Germany ratify the treaties concluded with Corea, I can not doubt that China will regard such action as an intimation that she must for the future govern herself according to the declarations she has in the past so freely made. Corea has now concluded treaties with three of the Western Powers, and is I have no doubt prepared to make treaties with such other states as may desire to enter into relations with her, and I firmly believe she will endeavour faithfully to discharge the obligations which those treaties impose upon her. The treaty between the United States and Corea, I understand now only awaits the action of the Senate. I trust I have made it clear to you that the interests of all parties would be subserved by its ratification. If I have been successful in my endeavours, I hope you will not fail to urge its speedy approval. Our aim is to avoid all misunderstandings with China and to cultivate friendly relations with her. The task is difficult, but to show you how firmly impressed is your advice upon our minds, I may mention that at a Cabinet meeting held just after the Corean outrage, His Majesty the Emperor said that 'remembering the wise advice of General Grant endeavour to maintain the peace of Asia.' I do not mention these things for the purpose of convincing you of the high esteem in which you are held by the Sovereign and people of Japan, because of that you are already assured, but I recall them in order to show you that in all our dealings with China and Corea our policy has been controlled by principles which I am sure would command the approval of the enlightened world. Mr. Sugi, H. I. M's Vice-Minister of the Household has been appointed as Envoy Extraordinary and Minister Plenipotentiary to Hawaii to be present at the Coronation ceremonials of His Hawaiian Majesty which are to take place on the 12th February next. Upon his return from the Islands, Mr. Sugi will, by command of H. M. the Emperor, visit the eastern states of the United States and he will avail himself of earliest opportunity to meet you and personally deliver to you His Majesty's cordial sentiments and high esteem. I shall take advantage of Mr. Sugi's visit to request him to explain to you the situation of all pending questions in which Japan is interested. I bespeak for Mr Sugi your kind attention. I have received from Mr Terashima a telegram to the effect that the President has recommended in his annual message the return of the Shimonoseki Indemnity, and had stated that the ratification of the Corean treaty awaited the action of the Senate. I know the interest you have taken in these matters and I can not doubt that we are right in attributing to your powerful influence the favorable recommendations of the Executive. I sincerely hope that the questions will be finally disposed of this Session, and that you will continue to interest yourself in the subjects. With the kindest wishes and high esteem to yourself and Mrs. Grant in which Mr. Yoshida heartily joins, . . ." LS, *ibid.* See letter to Charles G. Williams, July 24, 1882. Sugi Magoshichirō and his embassy arrived in New York City on March 9, 1883. On Aug. 2, Sugi, Tokyo, wrote to USG. "I have the honor to inform you of my safe arrival in my country after a pleasant voyage and to offor you my most

sincere acknowlegements for all the courtesies I received at your hands while I was in
New York. I beg you to accept my most sincere thanks for all your kindness and best
wishes for your health and welfare   pray give my compliments to Mrs Grant and all
the familis" LS, USG 3.

On Dec. 12, 1882, Tuesday, Young had written to USG. "I have been looking in
all the corners of the very few newspapers that come to Peking to see whether you are
in the United States or not.—I presume you are in Mexico,—and shall send this to the
care of the Colonel in that supposition. Ever since I wrote you I have been quite busy,—
studying up the archives, and trying to know my trade.—I find it very interesting.—I
have the legation in fairly good order,—although it has cost me some money. Holcombe
says it never looked so well.—On Saturday we gave our first diplomatic dinner, and
had all the legations present.—Mrs. Young falls into her new honors as if she had been
born a diplomatist, and as she speaks French, German and Italian, her accomplish-
ments make the legation attractive. The society here is small but select,—and all the
people you meet have some quality about them. I get along fairly well with Holcombe.
He feels that he should have been minister, and that having been secretary for eleven
years he had earned promotion. I sympathize with the feeling,—but think his promotion should be in another country than where he began as a missionary. His place here
is really a good one, better than Belgium or Holland. He has $5000 a year, and his
house. I have an impression he adds to his income by purchasing curios for his friends.
I do not know this, as it is none of my business, but he told me once that he had bought
some things for Mr. Barlow and sold them at 400 per cent to that gentleman,—that
Mr B. was glad to pay the advance.—This is far better than a second-class mission.—I
do not like, however, the arrangement which unites the secretary and the interpreter in
one office.—I would prefer it, as it is in Japan,—a secretary who *is* secretary, and an
interpreter likewise.—As it now is, we have two ministers and no secretary. I have expressed this view to the department, not in any unfriendly or even critical way so far as
Holcombe is concerned, because I wish him well, and want to see him advanced—But
the arrangement was made by Williams when interpreters were few, and ministers
came and went, and a knowledge of Chinese was essential in a secretary.—Interpreters
can readily be found.—Long service in China has thrown Holcombe's mind into a rut,
especially of antipathy to Japan. I have had to combat this in many ways:—I think Holcombe is not conscious of this feeling,—that it has grown upon him, and he would be
surprised to think he had it.—Long contact with Chinese ways and Chinese statesmen
has infected him, just as a magnet would infect iron, and with his positive nature, an
impression is apt to become a conviction.—A very important question has arisen in
China in reference to the right of foreigners to manufacture at the treaty ports.—It
came up in Shghae where Wetmore, whom you will remember, proposed a cotton-yarn
company.—The Chinese contended that there was no provision in the treaties that gave
foreigners permission to manufacture.—The treaty with the French is very clear on
this subject, and under the favored-nations clause we enjoy its benefits. The Chinese,
however, are embarrassed by their redundant population, and any new machine, or new
mechanical influence which threatens to deprive the laborer of the means of earning
his pinch of salt or his handfull of rice is a serious problem.—The course of the Chinese
in the matter was furtive and insincere;—weaknesses you see in a weak and oppressed
nation.—Instead of pointing out to our government that the treaty was oppressive, and
asking us to remodel it, as we asked China on the emigration question, an order was
issued to arrest Mr. Wetmore's compradore on the charge of having been a partisan of
the rebels in the TaiPing rebellion,—which collapsed the same year that Lee did—!—

Mr. Wetmore complained that the charge was false, and that the real motive for the warrant was to punish the compradore for having purchased shares in the company, and thus by an act of terror prevent other Chinamen from doing the same thing.—I hated to do it, but no way seemed open, and so I directed the consulate to disregard the warrant and protect the compradore until I was satisfied that the forms of Chinese law were not being degraded to injure an American interest. As soon as my decision was known, and as showing the curious, innocent ways of this people, a proposition was made to Mr. Wetmore to the effect that if he would withdraw his company, the viceroy would withdraw his warrant!—I said that this was a degrading, ignominious proposition, really black-mail. That if this compradore was a criminal, he should answer for his crime, but to punish him because he had been thirty years in Mr. Wetmore's service, and chose to buy some shares in his company could never be permitted. So I forbade the warrant absolutely and if the viceroy insists upon carrying it out shall send the compradore on board a gunboat.—I am so sorry over it all because you know my feelings towards the Chinese and they know them too. But my impression is that the Viceroy will be disavowed.—The Germans have sent for men of war and propose a policy of violence. I do not propose to be drawn into another Simonoseki affair, and while I shall be glad to have the moral aid of the other powers, shall only go so far as to make strong appeals to the Yamen. I have just finished a despatch to the dep't. It makes with enclosures about 200 pages. I suppose no one will read it,—but should Congress call for it,—the whole story will be there told.—I had a three hours talk with Li the other day in the room where you met him. He was as cordial as ever, and talked about you a good deal & about F. D. G. He has been relieved of his viceroyalty but given a higher place in the direction of foreign affairs. He was anxious to have the Corean treaty ratified and went on to assail Japan. I preached peace to him like a Quaker,—but I do not feel comfortable about the relations between the two countries. He has taken Corea into his own hands, and has done some things which will make it very difficult for us to regard Corea as independent.—My own position in the matter is peculiar and I think will be useful.—I have the confidence of Li, & the Japanese minister Mr Enemotto, a handsome black-whiskered fellow whom you will remember evidently comes with instructions to have the most intimate relations with me.—I see him a great deal, and have smoothed many rough ways.—I have the suspicion that England & Russia are urging a war-policy. This I combat at every point, and next spring, if matters do not mend shall go over to Japan and see Iwakura—The responsibility is a serious one,—but I am very proud of it, and do not mind the trouble. I shall feel that I have not lived entirely in vain if I can do some good here. We have little news from home, and it is all bad.—I see a paragraph to the effect that you are 'out of politics.' I am very glad of it.—I hope you will resign that 'boys in Blue' command in a letter saying to the American people, what you have so often said to me. You are too great, and your name is too illustrious to be thrown into the arena in every campaign.—I wish I could see an American party,—not American in the sense of proscripted and proscription, but believing in the Union, our nation's credit, & in conserving the fame of the men our children will honor. I am tired of patching up a truce every four years with hypocrites & reformers and cattle of that kind.—That was the Henry Wilson way, and we were always in trouble.—I would rather be in a minority all my life than act with such people.—The river is about to freeze up. Home life is very pleasant.—I read a good deal.— The work is not hard,—enough to do however—Matters here fell into confusion on account of the feud between Denny & Holcombe, and I am gradually unwinding the tangled threads. I have had to take some—responsibilities I would rather have avoided,

but as Thiers say an omelette cannot be made until you break the eggs.—I am sure Arthur will give me his confidence, and I do not think I will disappoint him. I wish I could bring about a new system here as to my consular & minor diplomatic appointments. But little can be hoped from a Democratic congress.—Mrs. Young sends her love to Mrs. Grant & yourself likewise to Mrs. Colonel Grant. She is homesick now & then but likes her new life. I tell your friends here that you may come again as far as Japan. I wish you could think of something I could do for Mrs. Grant & yourself.—I need not say how much I should enjoy the opportunity. Remember me to all at home, and give my regards to Mr Trescott should this find him with you. Above all give Mrs. Grant the tribute of my affection & friendship,—a tribute I am always proud to yield . . ."
ALS, *ibid.* For William S. Wetmore, see *Foreign Relations, 1883*, pp. 129–41, 152–68.

1. In the 1882 election, Democrats won a near eighty vote majority in the House of Representatives.
2. See letter to Li Hung-chang, April 1, 1881; letter to Edwards Pierrepont, Dec. 23, 1883.
3. Young had assumed his post amid a dispute between China and Japan over Korea. In May, assisted by Chinese advisors, Commodore Robert W. Shufeldt had negotiated the first treaty between the U.S. and Korea. Japan protested that the treaty tacitly recognized Chinese claims to hegemony over the peninsula. In July, an uprising in Korea targeted Japanese diplomats and escalated tensions. See *New York Times*, June 11, July 7, 1882; Martina Deuchler, *Confucian Gentlemen and Barbarian Envoys: The Opening of Korea, 1875–1885* (Seattle, 1977), pp. 129–47; Robert R. Swartout, Jr., *Mandarins, Gunboats, and Power Politics: Owen Nickerson Denny and the International Rivalries in Korea* (Honolulu, 1980), pp. 31–35, 39–40.

To Edward F. Beale

New York City,
Dec. 6th 1882.

DEAR GENERAL BEALE:

I owe you an apology for not answering your letter of a few days ago sooner. I could not answer it just at the time and it escaped my memory that there was one request in it that you might wish an immediate answer to until last night I happened to think of it. You speak of sending Leopard to California and want my permission to do so. Leopard is yours to do with as you please. I place no restriction whatever except that some day a few years from this you and Buck may have filleys ~~that you wo~~ from the horses you now have that you would like to breed back nearer to the Arabian. In that event you might want to "swap" horses. But you need not even keep Leopard for so remote a contingency.

Mrs. Grant & I will not be going to Washington so early as you speak of in your letter. We can not say now just when we can go, but I will let you know in time. When we do go we have accepted an invitation—this was some months ago—to spend a few days with Senator & Mrs. Cameron. We will go to your house from there if it is not inconvenient for you when the time comes.

Very Truly yours
U. S. Grant

ALS, DLC-Decatur House Papers. See letter to Randolph Huntington, July 28, 1882.

To Chester A. Arthur

New York City,
Dec. 9th 1882.

The President:

In view of the early retirement of Gen. Z. B. Tower I take the liberty of writing you suggesting a recommendation to Congress that he be retired with the rank of Brigadier General. I put this on the ground of his valuable services in the Mexican War, in the late rebellion, and all the time since 1841 as one of the ablest officers of the Engineer Corps of the Army. Gen. Tower has been breveted for gallantry in the two wars—with Mexico and the Civil War—I believe through every grade from 2d Lieut. to Major General. There was also a hardship inflicted upon General Tower in the promotion to the chiefship of his corps. There was no possible objection to the present head of the corps, and there is no man in it who Gen. Tower would prefer to him. But they were classmates at West Point Gen. Tower was head of his class, and always above General Wright[1] in the Corps of Engineers until his overslaugh, the latters promotion to Chief and his professional ability or qualifications were never questioned. It is proper that I should state here that General Wright have always and General Tower have always—since their Cadetship—been the closest of friends, and no one except the former was probably more pleased with the promotion than General

Tower. But I thought at the time, and so expressed myself, that I thought that the passing over of General Tower was a hardship entirely undeserved. This could be set right now by retiring him as a Brigadier General. In view of the retirement of General Tower in January early, it is very desirable that early action should be taken, if you consent to do this, and I strongly recommend and urge it.

Very Truly yours
U. S. GRANT

P. S. I neglected to state that General Tower was severely wounded both in the Mexican War and in the War of the rebellion. He was a Brigadier General of Volunteers when he was so wounded as to keep him out of the field for near two years, which kept him out of the rank that he might have had, and from all his past services probably would have had but for this wound in 1862.

U. S. G.

ALS, DNA, RG 94, ACP, 1537 1882. On Dec. 10, 1882, U.S. Senator James D. Cameron of Pa. wrote to USG. "I am in receipt of your letter of yesterday and note what you say in reference to the retirement of Genls Tower Hunt & Getty. It is possible that if the President should ask for the power to retire Tower as a Brigadier General that Congress might grant it, but I dont think it could be done without such a request. When the proposition was before the military committee to retire Ord as a Major General, I voted for it as did Logan, but when Logan asked that you should be placed on the retired list, the proposition did not meet with the approval of our Democratic friends, who had been active in the Ord case. We afterwards passed a bill through the Senate placing Meiggs upon the retired list as a Maj Genl and that is still pending in the house, and I am told that there is great doubt about its becoming a law. A few days since after the Comtee had agreed to report favorably in favor of Pope, the question of retiring Hunt & Getty as Brigadiers was informally discussed, and from what was said by the different members of the Comtee upon that subject I am very sure that it would be very difficult to accomplish any thing in their behalf" ALS, USG 3. Zealous B. Tower was retired as col. as of Jan. 10, 1883. See *PUSG*, 13, 329; letter to John A. Logan, April 25, 1884.

1. Horatio G. Wright graduated second, USMA 1841, behind Tower.

To Adam Badeau

———

New York City,
Dec. 11th 1882.

MY DEAR GENERAL BADEAU:

I have your letter of the 1st instant, enclosing one from Hughes and also your previous letter. I did not write to you before because I expected to see your Vice Consul, Williams,[1] but he has not called on me yet. Of course I will help you if I can to obtain the appointment you ask.[2] In regard to the matter Hughes speaks of,[3] I wrote the letter he requested long ago, just after you spoke to me about possibly the second time, and in time I should think for them to have received it, and informed their father before the date of his letter to you. If however they have not received my letter—it was a general letter to rail-road officials connecting with international roads between this country and Mexico—I will be glad to write them another.

I have no special news to write you from here. Congress has met and the overwhelming defeat of the republicans seems to have put both parties on their guard. It looks now as if the interests of the country were to be more considered—by many I fear as the best means of serving a party—than party interest. But there is abundant time for either party to do foolish things, and both parties have men capable of them.

I hope you will find your new station an agreeable one. I believe you will, for a time, and wish for you a more pleasant one in the near future. But I can hardly say I expect much from this Administration. It is too slow.

Buck sails for Europe day after to-morrow. Jesse & wife think of going to Mexico this Winter. If they do they may drop in upon you.

Hurry up your book on English Life.[4] It will be interesting I think to many readers.

With kind regards from all my family,

Very Truly yours
U. S. GRANT

ALS, Munson-Proctor-Williams Institute, Utica, N. Y.

1. Ramon O. Williams, listed in the 1880 census as a sugar planter, was vice consul gen., Havana.
2. "The appointment mentioned by General Grant was the Vice-Presidency of the international telegraph line between the United States and Cuba. The position was held by an Englishman, and the control of all telegraphic messages between the Consul-General of the United States and his own Government was thus in the hands of a foreigner. It was proposed that this should be transferred to the Consul-General, *ex officio.* Mr. Jay Gould was the principal owner of the stock of the company, and General Grant's business relations with Gould at that time warranted him in making the request. He did apply to Gould, who referred him to Dr. Norvin Green, the President

of the Western Union, as well as of the Cuban Telegraph Company. General Grant made the application to Dr. Green, who paid no attention to his request, and the place with its powers and appurtenances remained in the hands of an Englishman." *Badeau,* pp. 545–46.

    3. "Mr. Thomas Hughes, the well-known English author and political economist, had a son in Texas, and I had asked General Grant for letters to some of the important people in that region for the young man, who was an especial favorite and friend of mine." *Ibid.,* p. 545. See *PUSG,* 28, 222–23; Thomas Hughes, ed., *G. T. T.: Gone to Texas: Letters from Our Boys* (New York, 1884).

    4. Adam Badeau published *Aristocracy in England* in 1886.

To Ellen Grant Sartoris

————

N Y. Dec. 12th 1882

DEAR NELLIE:

    I send you by Algy, as my Christmas present a copy of Badeau's book. I thought of sending it to Mr Sartoris, Sr. but I do not know that he cares to read it, and if he does he can do so as well if it is yours as if sent direct to him. You will see Algy, Buck and Fanny as soon as you get this, and will get all the news from them. I[n] May I think you will see your Ma and I in England. Give our love to the children an[d] do'nt let Algy & Vivian forget their Grand pa & grand ma in America.

AL (signature clipped), ICHi. Ulysses S. Grant, Jr., Fannie C. Grant, and Algernon Sartoris sailed for Liverpool aboard the *Servia* on Dec. 13, 1882.

To Elizabeth King

————

2 Broadway
New York City
Dec. 20th 1882.

MY DEAR MRS. KING:

    I received your last letter in due time. I have deferred answering so that it—the answer—might reach you about Christmas with my offering. Please accept the enclosed check with my best wishes.

I hope to visit Georgetown again though I will not probably be able to do so the coming Spring. It is my expectation now to go to Europe in May to spend about four months.—With my kind regards to my Georgetown friends,

Very Truly yours
U. S. GRANT

ALS (facsimile), Candace Scott, Victorville, Calif.

To Ferdinand Ward

NEW YORK, December 21, 1882.

DEAR WARD—Please explain to the president of the Brooklyn New England Society that I hope my absence this evening will be no disappointment. It is, however, now so late—quarter to nine— the distance so great and the night so bad that I think it better not to go.

I hope the society will have a most pleasant gathering, and from my experience with it—the society—on former occasions[1] like the present I do not doubt but all the members will enjoy their reunion.

Very truly yours,
U. S. GRANT.

Brooklyn Eagle, Dec. 22, 1882.

1. On Dec. 21, 1881, USG addressed the Brooklyn New England Society. *Ibid.*, Dec. 22, 1881. See Speech, [*Dec. 21, 1880*].

Speech

[*New York City, Dec. 22, 1882*]

MR. PRESIDENT AND GENTLEMEN OF THE NEW-ENGLAND SOCI- ETY OF NEW-YORK CITY: I will say that General Grant would not have been present this evening if he had known he was going to be called upon to respond to this or any other toast. He was invited to be here this evening and accepted the invitation a good while ago. About a week ago he received notice that he would be called upon to respond to this toast and replied that it was agony enough for him to be called upon suddenly, and to have it over directly. He notified them in advance that if he had to speak to that or anything else it would be a week of agony, which he was not willing to endure, and he would not do it for the descendants of all the Pilgrims. He supposed he was simply to come here and listen to other people's discomfiture and not his own, and I think now in retaliation that I shall not say a word about anything so insignificant as the United States. It is a small Republic on the Western Hemisphere, and has men who think they have carried it on their own shoulders a good while and have been making something of it. But there are other parts of the Western Hemisphere who look upon us as being very weak sisters—that we have not taken an active part in defending what they think we ought to, being what we profess to be, the first Power on the Western continent; and they sometimes question whether we have taken the part in defending ourselves even in the Eastern Hemisphere, and taken that stand that our numbers and the intelligence of the Pilgrim descendants would entitle us to take there. So I will say that while there are a great many good things that could be said of the United States—and I could have said some of them if I had been called upon without being notified—I will designate now some of these orators that have been referred to, to speak of some of her virtues in the elaborate speeches they have already prepared to deliver to us this evening. I would not like to be quite so personal as the orator of the evening has been in designating any two persons, for instance, but I will be a little personal, and I will take one of those orators of the evening and I will designate him to add to the speech which he has given to the reporters and I will give a name that you are all familiar with, and will add also a name that a few of you have heard of.

The familiar name that the people of this country all know is "Mark Twain." There are some people near the Charter Oak, just around the roots of that celebrated tree, who know him by the name of Clemens, and I will ask him to say what there is to be said in favor of this little, weak country here with only 100,000 miles of railroad and a few other public improvements. We have some navigable rivers; in fact there are canals also that have been built by individual skill, labor, enterprise and capital, and then it is surrounded and interspersed with lakes and has some agriculture. In addition to the descendants of the Pilgrim fathers, it has some other people too, but they don't want to have much voice in the Government of the United States but then they would like to be considered while the Pilgrim descendants are making laws for them. They don't want to be suppressed. Mr. Twain says he will say what I was going to say.

New York Tribune, Dec. 23, 1882. USG responded to the toast, "The United States of America," during a banquet at Delmonico's. Mark Twain did not mention USG's subject in his response to the toast, "Woman. God Bless Her!" *Ibid.*

To Fitz John Porter

New York City,
Dec. 27th 1882.

DEAR GENERAL:

I have just opened your letter of the 25th inst. Bragg[1] is right in saying that your bill[2] and mine should not go to-gether. If any friend—or enemy—should be guilty of the bad taste of so associating the two bills I should certainly write or telegraph some friend to withdraw mine entirely. I care nothing about mine whatever. It will depend much upon the discussion that takes place in Congress whether I accept even if it does pass. In yours I feel a much deeper interest and am ready to say now that if yours can be advanced by laying mine "on the table," or withdrawing it, I am ready to ask it.

Very Truly yours
U. S. GRANT

GN. F. J. PORTER

ALS, DLC-Fitz John Porter. On Dec. 5, 1881, U.S. Senator John A. Logan of Ill. introduced a bill to place USG on the army retired list. *CR*, 47-1, 4. On Feb. 20, 1882,

U.S. Senator George G. Vest of Mo., a Democrat, spoke against the measure because USG did not "need the proposed legislation. He is in robust health, in the prime of life, and beyond pecuniary want. The first American soldier to receive the rank of General, he was the first American citizen to seek for a third term, the highest office within the gift of the Republic. During his second term as President the salary of that office was doubled for his benefit; and he is to-day surrounded by wealthy connections, living luxuriously in the city of New York, and possessed, besides other fortune, of the income from $250,000 donated to him by the public. To give General Grant the full measure of glory as a great soldier is one thing; to tax the people of this country $13,500 annually in order to enrich a man already in affluence is a different proposition. . . ." *Ibid.*, p. 1289. On the same day, U.S. Senator John A. Logan of Ill. criticized Vest for opposing this bill while supporting similar legislation for Fitz John Porter. *Ibid.*, pp. 1290–92. On Feb. 23, the Senate passed the bill. *Ibid.*, pp. 1376–83. On March 21, U.S. Representative Thomas M. Browne of Ind. presented petitions from "ex-soldiers and citizens of the sixth Congressional district of Indiana, remonstrating against placing General U. S. Grant on the retired list." *Ibid.*, p. 2140. On July 31, the House of Representatives sent the Senate bill to committee, where it died. *Ibid.*, p. 6698. See *New York Times*, Feb. 21, 1882; letter to John A. Logan, Feb. 9, 1881; letter to Fitz John Porter, Feb. 21, 1883; letter to Edward F. Beale, June 26, 1884.

1. Raised in upstate N. Y., Edward S. Bragg moved to Fond du Lac, Wis. (1850) to practice law. After extensive Civil War service with the 6th Wis., he mustered out as a brig. gen. and began a political career that led to his election as Democratic U.S. Representative (1877). On May 8, 1882, Bragg introduced a bill to relieve Porter. *CR*, 47-1, 3705.

2. On Dec. 28, the Senate began debate on a bill to restore Porter to the army. Additional debate, with references to USG's support for Porter, preceded passage on Jan. 11, 1883. The bill then died in the House of Representatives. See *ibid.*, 47-2, 671–86, 692–701, 715–36, 752–86, 1091–97, 1195; letter to James D. Cameron, Feb. 4, 1882. On Jan. 2, Tuesday, a correspondent had reported from Washington, D. C. "Gen. and Mrs. Grant arrived on the limited express from New-York this afternoon, and were taken to the residence of Gen. E. F. Beale, on Lafayette-square. . . . It is said that the object of Gen. Grant's visit here is to maintain the position taken by him in his recent article on the Fitz John Porter case against the vigorous assaults upon it made by Senator Logan in his argument on Friday and to-day." *New York Times*, Jan. 3, 1883.

On Feb. 13, Governor Lucius F. Hubbard of Minn. *et al.* wrote to USG, Washington, D. C. "The undersigned, citizens of Minnesota, without distinction of party, take this method of expressing to you our high appreciation of your efforts in securing for Genl Fitz John Porter that simple measure of justice which a misapprehension of the facts bearing on his case has been so long and largely instrumental in withholding from him. Whatever may have been public sentiment touching the merits of Gen. Porter's case as presented to the country from time to time by the several tribunals that have been charged with its determination, there is, in the opinion of the undersigned, no denying the fact that at the present time the great body of the American people demand his restoration to the position in the army of which he has been, in the light of more recent disclosures, for twenty years unjustly deprived. Not unmindful of the fact that the representatives in both houses of Congress from New Jersey—the home of Gen. Porter—have ignored party considerations and united invain in an appeal to

Congress to do a simple act of justice to this wronged soldier and citizen of the Republic, the undersigned ex-soldiers and citizens generally of Minnesota, having full faith
in the patriotism and integrity of Gen'l Porter, while thanking you for your efforts in
his behalf, express the hope that the example and co-operation in this case of one so
illustrious as yourself may lead to the prompt and full vindication of Gen. Porter at
the hands of the present Congress" DS (121 signatures), DLC-Fitz John Porter. On
Feb. 16, Fabius J. Mead, St. Paul, wrote to USG. "I enclose you an address from the
United States, & State officials, bankers, clergy and business men of this State, thanking you for your disinterested efforts in securing Gen. Fitz John Porter's restoration to
his old position in the army. The character of the men whose signatures are attached
to this address furnishes the most ample assurance of the hearty endorsement your
course has met with in this State, regardless of party. The signature of Senator-elect
Sabin is especially gratifying, reversing as it does, the vote of his predecessor on this
case in the Senate. I know of nothing that has given me more pleasure than this opportunity to second your efforts in this case. I desire to say also that to the efforts of our
mutual friend Gen. R. W. Johnson is largely due the success of the movement which
has resulted in this handsome vindication of your course. Since I saw you my health
has improved, but Mrs. Mead suffers from the rheumatism in this climate. Accept my
best wishes . . ." ALS, *ibid.* Richard W. Johnson, USMA 1849, endorsed this letter. "In
my opinion if this matter is placed in the hands of some discreet person I believe the
Fitz John Porter bill can be brought up this session by a two-thirds vote. With many
wishes for your continued good health . . ." AES (undated), *ibid.* On Feb. 24, USG
wrote to Porter, New York City. "In reply to your note of this morning, I too fail to call
to mind Mr Mead, and cannot say therefore whether he has rank or not. Probably if I
was to see him, I would recall him." LS, ICarbS.

To Edward F. Beale

New York City,
Dec. 28th 1882

MY DEAR GEN. BEALE:

Unexpectedly to me I shall be going to Washington on Tuesday next[1] to remain I cannot tell how long. Mrs. Grant & I had
accepted an invitation from both Cameron & yourself to visit you
during the winter. As I am going on business however—connected
with framing a Commercial treaty with Mexico—and will want
to consult with Senators, particularly with members of the Committee on Foreign Relations and Commerce, both Mrs. Grant and
I think we had better take rooms at a hotel until that business is
settled. I think of taking ~~my~~ Mrs. Grant's carriage & team as we
may be delayed much longer than we now think. I wish I could

take mine also which have shewn a 2 25 gate with my driving. But this latter I will forego.

With best regards to all your family.

yours Truly

U. S. GRANT

Would you advise me to take rooms at the Arlington or where? please telegraph me. Our stay in Washington may be for a month or more, or the business part of it may be completed in a few days. Of course if we find there is no disposition on the part of the Senate to ratify such a treaty as can be made that will end the matter at once.

U. S. G.

ALS, DLC-Decatur House Papers.

On Aug. 7, 1882, President Chester A. Arthur commissioned USG to negotiate a commercial treaty with Mexico. DS, Smithsonian Institution. On Aug. 9 and Dec. 12, Secretary of State Frederick T. Frelinghuysen wrote to USG. "A provision in the Sundry Civil Bill authorized the President to appoint Commissioners to negotiate a commercial treaty with Mexico, and he hastened to avail himself of your valuable aid by nominating you to serve as one of them. He felt the less hesitation in doing so as it was thought that such duties might not be uncongenial to you and because of your familiarity with Mexican affairs. I take pleasure in informing you that at the first executive session of the Senate held after the nomination you were unanimously confirmed without reference. It was believed that Mr. Trescot's large experience in the negotiation of treaties and in the management of diplomatic matters would be valuable to the government and of assistance to you. He was therefore associated with you on the Commission. Mexico has not consented to the negotiation of such treaty. In the course of a fortnight, I hope to be able to give you more full information. It is unnecessary for me to assure you that the President and I will be greatly gratified should you decide to accept the position." "Referring to previous correspondence upon the subject, I have now the pleasure to enclose to you herewith, your commission as a Commissioner on the part of the United States to negotiate a Commercial Treaty with Mexico. Asking that you will properly execute and return to this Department the blank oath of office herewith enclosed, . . ." LS, USG 3. See Interview, [*Jan. 22, 1883*].

On Dec. 25, Matías Romero, Washington, D. C., telegraphed to USG. "I leave this evening ~~for New York~~ and ~~would~~ desire ~~like~~ to see you tomorrow ~~morning~~ at your house, or office. Send word to 5th Avenue hotel when and where can I ~~see you~~ call." Telegram sent, DLC-Matías Romero.

1. Jan. 2, 1883. On Dec. 30, [*1882*], USG, New York City, had telegraphed to Edward F. Beale, Washington, D. C. "MRS. GRANT SAYS SHE WILL BE READY TO GO ON TUESDAY." Telegram received, DLC-Decatur House Papers. On Jan. 2, [*1883*], USG, Philadelphia, telegraphed to Beale. "Mrs Grant asks me to say she would like to have a room on floor with Emily" Telegram received, *ibid.*

Calendar

1880, OCT. 2.   To H. C. Tuttle, from Chicago. "I have your letter of the 29th ult. with enclosure and thank you for it. It is only in character & keeping with all the acts of its author towards all who try to befriend him."—ALS (facsimile), Early American History Auctions, Inc., June 10, 2000, no. 82.

1880, OCT. 2.   USG application for membership in the Chicago Union Veteran Club, an organization committed to "the principles of the Republican Party."—DS, IC.

1880, Nov. 3.   Speech, New York Loyal Legion reception.—*New York Herald*, Nov. 4, 1880.

1880, Nov. 15.   USG authorization. "Chas. S. Brown, Real Estate Agt. 77 Liberty Street, New York City is authorized to receive the money for my Long Branch property, west of Ocean Avenue, & to receipt for the same. . . . Please deposit in the Marine Bank, to my credit, after deducting commissions and other dues."—ADS, Mrs. Walter Love, Flint, Mich.
     On April 11, 1873, Levi P. Luckey had written to Frank G. Brown and Davison Brown, New York City. "The President directs me to acknowledge the receipt of your letter of yesterday and say that he will be obliged to you if you will see Mr. John Hoey and ascertain if Mr. Thompson, President of the Penna. R. R. wishes to rent, as he had said something in relation to it. If you find that Mr. Thompson does not want the cottage, you may rent as you suggest and let the sale be made later."—Copy, DLC-USG, II, 2. On April 22, 1875, Orville E. Babcock wrote to Frank G. Brown and Charles S. Brown. "Enclosed please find lease of the President's Long Branch Cottage to Mr. Seligman, and to say that the repairs required will all be attended to before the time specified for occupation. Please excuse delay in answering your letter. I have been absent."—Copy, *ibid.* On Jan. 19, 1876, Culver C. Sniffen wrote to the same agents. "In reply to your favor of the 17th instant the President directs me to say that he does desire to rent his west Long Branch Cottage the coming summer"—Copy, *ibid.*, II, 3. On Oct. 25, 1876, Ulysses S. Grant, Jr., wrote to the agents. "Yours of the 23d instant received—The Presidents directions are to insure for three years and for $10.000—or $12.000—in whatever companies you see fit—"—Copy, *ibid.* On June 14, 1877, the agents wrote twice to Grant, Jr. "We enclose you our check for $375 and receipted bill for $125 making $500 received this day from H. A. C. Taylor for second payment of rent Long Branch Cottage." "Received from Mr U. S. Grant One hundred & twenty five dollars in full for commission for renting L. Branch Cottage to H A. C Taylor—for $2500—"—L, USG 3. Later correspondence regarding the cottage is *ibid.*

1880, Nov. 16.   To Hamilton Fish, from New York City. "I leave by Eleven o'clock train"—Telegram received, DLC-Hamilton Fish. On Nov. 17, Fish wrote to J. C. Bancroft Davis, Washington, D. C. ". . . Genl Grant paid me a visit here yesterday—he had telegraphed the day before that he wished to see me—he is well—thoroughly hopeful as to the future of the Country, & delighted with the result of the Election. . . ."—ALS (press), *ibid.*

1880, Nov. 21. To Silas Farmer, from New York City. "Your letter of the 17th making enquiry of the time I was stationed in Detroit was duly received. I was there for a few days in Nov. 1848 and then ordered to Sacketts Harbor, N. Y. In Apl. /49 I was returned to Detroit, and remained there until Apl. /51."—ALS (facsimile), Silas Farmer, *The History of Detroit and Michigan or the Metropolis Illustrated* (Detroit, 1884), p. 105.

1880, Nov. 23. To George W. Schaefer. "It would afford me much pleasure to be with the 17th Ward Garfield & Arthur Club this evening to celebrate the recent political victory in this land, but I have a previous engagement for the evening to dine at the Union League Club. Thanking you for the invitation, . . ."—ALS, Union League Club, New York, N. Y. See Schaefer to James A. Garfield, Nov. 20, 1880, DLC-James A. Garfield.

1880, Dec. 19. To David M. Simmons, postmaster, Jacksonville, Ill., from New York City. "I have a letter of the 14 14th instant, requesting my presence in Jacksonville, Illinois, at a mass meeting to be held for the purpose of raising funds for the erection of a monument over Illinois' distinguished citizen and war governor, the Honorable Richard Yates, I regret that it will not be possible for me to be present at that time, but I wish the enterprise every success, and will contribute, according to my means, to secure success."—Typescript, IHi.

1880, Dec. 20. USG calling card. "*U. S. Grant.* & Mrs. Grant will be in this evening from 8 to 10 O'clock, and in the morning from 9 30 to 11 and will be pleased to see Mr. & Mrs. at their convenience during these hours"—AN, Gallery of History, Las Vegas, Nev.

1880, Dec. 24. To Frederick Cocheu, former capt., 61st N. Y., from New York City. "I accept with pleasure the invitation of the Harry Lee Post No 21, G. A. R. of Brooklyn to attend the entertainment to be given Jan.y 24th 1881."—ALS, USG 3. See *New York Times*, Jan. 3, 1897.

On Jan. 24, 1881, USG greeted veterans at the Bedford Avenue Reformed Church in Brooklyn, then briefly attended a reception in his honor at the nearby home of insurance magnate Joseph F. Knapp. Earlier, USG attended the annual dinner of the New York Horticultural Society at Delmonico's but failed to return in time to make a scheduled address. See *Reception tendered to General U. S. Grant, by Harry Lee Post, No. 21, G. A. R., Department of New York, Monday Evening, January 24, 1881, . . .* (New York, 1881), p. 23; *Brooklyn Eagle*, Jan. 25, 1881; *New York Tribune*, Jan. 25, 1881.

1881, Jan. 10. USG endorsement. "Respectfully forwarded to the Sec. of State. Dr. Jones I believe served through the rebellion, but I do not recollect him well enough to add further recommendation."—AES, DNA, RG 59, Applications and Recommendations, Hayes-Arthur. Written on a letter of Jan. 3, 1881, from Wesley Jones, Marshfield, Ind., to Secretary of State William M. Evarts. "I would hereby respectfully apply for the position Of Consul—in

Mexico, Central, America or South America. I desire to Secure position nearer the South Pacific or Atlantic. by reason Of physical defects, resulting from injuries incured during my term Of Service. in the late rebellion Humbly hoping that I may receive your favorable consideration. for which I Shall arduously labor to reflect credit and merit confidence"—ALS, *ibid.*

1881, JAN. 18.   Janet Macfarlan, Philadelphia, to USG, President Rutherford B. Hayes, and others alleging mistreatment over debts contracted in S. C.—ALS, OFH.

1881, JAN. 21.   Richard P. Evans, Washington, D. C., to USG, New York City. "Senate Bill, *No. 496,* is considered as ruinous to the interests of the *disabled soldiers* of the country—and their dependent ones,—as it would be impossible for *nine* out of *ten* Pension claimants to prove up their claims under its provisions. In behalf of the *thousands* of worthy claimants, who will be forced to abandon their claims should this Bill become law, I take the liberty of enclosing the same for your attention. The most objectionable '*Sections*' have remarks attached which are thought to be appropriate and a printed criticism is attached to the last page of the Bill. The Political status of our firm is shown by the accompanying papers. Our *personal* interests might be *served* by the passage of this Bill, as it would relieve us from completing the claims we have in hand, in which most of our claimants have already paid our fees, in whole or in part, but it is an *outrage* upon the rights of the claimants and should be defeated. The '*Arrears*' bill was for their *benefit*: this measure will *prevent* their becoming *beneficiaries* thereunder. Your objection to this Bill would assuredly defeat it."—ALS, USG 3. Enclosures are *ibid.*

1881, FEB. 9.   USG endorsement. "Respectfully referred to the War Dept. This will be ~~accompanied~~ supplimented later with an application for a pension for the widow & orphan children of a gallant officer who served faithfully during the war, and ever since."—AES, DNA, RG 94, ACP, 1020 1881. Written on the official announcement of the death on Jan. 30, 1881, of Capt. Joseph Lawson, 3rd Cav.—*Ibid.* See Mark E. Miller, *Hollow Victory: The White River Expedition of 1879 and the Battle of Milk Creek* (Boulder, Colo., 1997), pp. 149–51.

1881, FEB. 14.   USG testimonial. ". . . a very authentic account of my journey and what transpired. Mr. Young was personally of my party most of the time in Europe, and all the time in Asia and Africa. This is the only authentic account yet written."—"Americana," *Quarterly Journal of the Library of Congress,* 34, 3 (July, 1977), 230. Written in a salesman's dummy copy of *Young.*

1881, MARCH 12.   USG endorsement. "Although Mr. Delano was absent from China during my visit to that country I heard the highest testimonials to his administration of the Consulate under his charge. This was the evidence of Americans & Europeans."—AES, DNA, RG 59, Applications and Recommendations, Hayes-Arthur. Written on a letter of Jan. 20, 1881, from

John P. Newman, New York City, to Milton M. De Lano.—ALS, *ibid.* On
Dec. 31, De Lano, New York City, wrote to Secretary of State Frederick T.
Frelinghuysen. "I have the honor most respectfully to represent to you as follows. In the spring of 1869 I was appointed United States Consul at Foochow
China, which office I held until the end of July 1880, when I was relieved on
account of a slight disagreement which I had with Mr Minister Seward . . .
I was appointed by President Grant upon my personal application and on
the Strength of his personal knowledge of me, and I have been credibly informed that at an interview which he had with the late President Garfield
in March last, he recommended my restoration to the Consular Service in
China, . . ."—ALS, *ibid.* Related papers are *ibid.* No appointment followed.
See *PUSG,* 19, 181–83.

1881, MARCH 23.   USG endorsement. "Respectfully referred to the Sec. of
War."—AES, DNA, RG 94, ACP, 1820 1881. Written on a letter of March
21 from Zadok T. Daniel, Washington, D. C., to USG, New York City. "I
am a son-in-Law of the Hon. E. M. Keils of Alabama. You probably know
something of our family history. His son, (my wifes brother) assassinated by
rebel democrats, loss of property, and all other evils concomitant to general
proscription in the South. I want a commission in the Military service of our
Country, and I ask for your endorsement."—ALS, *ibid.* As of July 1, Daniel
clerked in the Treasury Dept. See *PUSG,* 25, 197–98.

1881, MARCH 26.   USG endorsement. "The writer of this letter I met in Canton, China, as U. S. Consul, and was entertained by him as his guest during
my stay in that City. I was favorably impressed with him and his family, and
understand his record in the State Dept. is good. I would be very glad if such
position as he requests under the Treasury Dept. could be given him."—AES,
DNA, RG 56, Applications. Written on a letter of March 19 from Charles P.
Lincoln, Washington, D. C., to USG, New York City, seeking a recommendation. ". . . But for your time being so taken up with more important matters, I should have mentioned this subject to you when in Washington last
week . . ."—ALS, *ibid.* Related papers are *ibid.* No appointment followed.
    On May 15, 1875, Governor Adelbert Ames of Miss., Bay St. Louis, had
written to USG. "I take great pleasure in recommending Mr C. P. Lincoln
of Grenada of this state as a suitable competent and in every sense worthy
person for appointment as consul to Canton China in place of Dr Tindall who
has resigned. Mr Lincoln was a union officer—he has been a true unflinch-
ing republican against whom nothing has or can be said even though he lives
where political animosities shadow all else. Our State has, I believe few if any
representatives abroad and I can but believe that she can expect this consul-
ateship which she has held for some five years"—AL, *ibid.,* RG 59, Letters of
Application and Recommendation. Related papers are *ibid.* On Dec. 9, USG
nominated Lincoln as consul, Canton.

1881, MARCH 26.   Charles H. Blair, Union League Club, New York City,
to USG. "Your kind memoranda referring to the Tourgee Dinner reached
me last evening—If you can not be with us in person I would be glad to

receive a formal note of regrets—to be read by the President—Mr Fish—I presume"—ALS, USG 3. At a March 29 dinner honoring Albion W. Tourgee, "Letters of regret were read from Gen. Grant, Gen. Horace Porter, and the Hon. Hamilton Fish."—*New York Times,* March 30, 1881.

[*1881, March*]. USG endorsement. "General Badeau's book, now in the hands of the printer, will give the exact truth of the matter referred to in this letter. There was no demand made for Gen. Lee's sword and no tender of it offered."—AES, Appomattox Court House National Historic Park, Appomattox, Va. Written on a letter of March 11, 1881, from Thomas D. Jeffress, Buffalo Lithia Springs, Va., to USG, New York City. "In a friendly discussion between several gentlemen, of northern and southern proclivities, as to the 'truth of history,' a question arose *whether Gen. Lee at the surrender actually tendered and you took his sword.* It was mutually agreed that you be written to for a decision. There is no idle curiosity or desire for notoriety in regard to this request, and a reply from you would be highly appreciated"—ALS, *ibid.* See *Southern Historical Society Papers,* IX, 3 (March, 1881), 139–40.

1881, July 27.   To Edward W. Bok.—Ben Bloomfield, *Autographs of Distinction,* List DI-5, no. 83. For his autograph collection, Bok, an office boy at Western Union Telegraph Co., had written to USG and other notables asking "one man why he did this or why some other man did that. Most interesting were, of course, the replies. Thus General Grant sketched on an improvised map the exact spot where General Lee surrendered to him."—*The Americanization of Edward Bok: The Autobiography of a Dutch Boy Fifty Years After* (New York, 1921), p. 19. See *ibid.,* pp. 21–25; *New York Tribune,* Nov. 9, 1881.

On Jan. 4, [*1882*], USG wrote to Bok acknowledging a Western Union frank for 1882. "I have thanked the company for this courtesy."—Charles Hamilton Auction No. 103, Feb. 24, 1977, no. 97.

On June 11, 1883, William J. Bok, Brooklyn, wrote to Hamilton Fish seeking his autograph. ". . . Prests' Grant, Hayes, Garfield and Arthur have conferred this honor upon me."—ALS, DLC-Hamilton Fish.

1881, July 27.   To Ira H. Palmer, from New York City. "In answer to yours of July 21st in regard to the Palmer Reunion, I will say that I shall be very glad to attend at Stonington for one of the days mentioned if it is possible for me to do so at that time."—*Stonington Mirror* (Conn.), July 30, 1881. Earlier, USG had written to [Ira Palmer]. "It would afford me pleasure to be present on that occasion, but I have been running about so much for the last four years, with nothing else to do, that now, when I have employment for my time, I feel loth to accept invitations that take me away from it."—*New York Times,* July 25, 1881. Ira Palmer replied. "As to ancestry, the blood of Walter Palmer of 1629 runs in no Palmer's veins of this generation any more than in yours." *Ibid.* On Aug. 10, Palmer read a telegram from USG to those assembled at the reunion. "Domestic reasons prevent my attending the Palmer family reunion." *Ibid.,* Aug. 11, 1881. USG descended from Walter Palmer on his father's side.

1881, JULY 29.   To William A. Barrett, Philadelphia, stating that at the failure of Cooke's Bank, Washington D. C., in 1873, "it was found that I had
overdrawn my account and I paid up immediately for the benefit of the credi-
tors the amount overdrawn. I had no more knowledge or expectation of their
failure than anybody else, and it so happened that if I had had money at the
time it would have been in their bank."—Quoted in E. Garfield Perkins to
Ulysses S. Grant 3rd, April 7, 1941, USG 3.

1881, AUG. 31.   Brig. Gen. Oliver O. Howard to USG. "This will introduce
to you Mr F. O. Von Fritsch a gentleman of much experience in Railroad
Engineering and business, a brave and worthy soldier during our Civil War
and a man of good character and deserving of any assistance that you may
be able to render him."—LS (press), MeB. In May, 1874, Otto Von Fritsch,
former capt., 68th N. Y., Chicago, had written to Secretary of State Hamilton Fish seeking a consulship in Nicaragua.—ALS, DNA, RG 59, Letters
of Application and Recommendation. Related papers are *ibid.* No appointment followed. See Joseph Tyler Butts, ed., *A Gallant Captain of the Civil War:
Being the Record of the Extraordinary Adventures of Frederick Otto Baron Von
Fritsch* . . . (New York, 1902).

1881, SEPT. 22.   Brig. Gen. Oliver O. Howard, superintendent, USMA, to
USG, Long Branch. "The Hon. Epes Sargent, who has been long & favorably
known to me, desires a letter of introduction to you. Mr Sargent was a true
friend to our Government at the Port of Nassau N. P. during the war of rebellion and he was enabled among enemies & lukewarm friends, to do us many
a loyal service, free of charge. He was well known to our Naval Dept. which
he assisted to the capture of several blockade runners and to the saving of
money & life. He served as the Government Agent then at Nassau, but has
since for some reason moved to our country. He wishes to see you about some
business connected with himself & thinks you can render him some good
turn. My brother visited him once at his home & judging by what I know of
him & what I hear I believe him to be a man of honor & integrity."—ALS,
DNA, RG 59, Applications and Recommendations, Hayes-Arthur; (press),
MeB. See *New York Times,* April 5, 1902.

1881, SEPT. 30.   George M. Pullman receipt. "Received of General U. S.
Grant Thirtyseven hundred and fifty dollars being the first installment of
fifty per cent on his subscription to the increase of capital of the Pullman
Land Ass'n as per my circular of September 10 1881. $3750.00/100"—DS,
USG 3. See *New York Times,* Sept. 10, 12, 1881; Stanley Buder, *Pullman: An
Experiment in Industrial Order and Community Planning 1880–1930* (New
York, 1967), pp. 49–50.

1881, OCT. 8.   Margaret J. Lovell, Louisville, to USG. "After the lapse of
many years of suffering; trial & bereavement; I again present myself to you
as a petitioner—begging you earnestly to use your influence for *me*; in behalf
of my Son Lieut R. A. Lovell, 14th U S Infty he is a great sufferer from acute

rheumatism, & neuralgia—and has disease of the heart!—Oh Genl for his Fathers sake do something for us, for I know he will die if he joins his Regt *This Winter*!—Dear General I am an old woman now & seen much trouble—will you try; either to get his 'Leave extended for an *indefinite* period, until his health is *reestablished*; or try to get him on some *detail East*, where he can do duty and *not* be subject to exposure &—Will you try to help us & answer Hoping you will give this petition your favorable consideration and earnestly try to help us with your influence—. . ." —ALS, DNA, RG 94, ACP, 5676 1876. USG endorsed this letter. "Respectfully forwarded to Gen Sherman—" —ES (undated), *ibid.* On Oct. 24, Gen. William T. Sherman denied leave to 2nd Lt. Robert A. Lovell. See *PUSG*, 24, 333–34.

1881, OCT. 10.   USG endorsement. "Respectfully forwarded to the President. The applicant, Chas Trowbridge, for the Vera cruz Consulate is the son of the present Consul. He has lived in Vera Cruz for a number of years and is therefore thoroughly acclimated, and having been in the office with his father, is well acquainted with ~~histhe~~ the duties of ~~the offi~~ it."—AES, DNA, RG 59, Applications and Recommendations, Hayes-Arthur. Written on a petition of Aug. 4 from ninety "merchants and business men of Vera Cruz," recommending the promotion of Charles Trowbridge, vice consul.—DS, *ibid.* No appointment followed.

On March 6, 1869, U.S. Representative Jesse H. Moore of Ill. had written to USG. "I respectfully present to you the application of *Dr. S. T. Trobridge* of Decatur Ill, to be appointed Consul to *Rio de. Janeiro.* Dr. Trobridge, I think, is not unknown to you. He was surgeon of the Eighth Ill. Vols. Infty. and was the especial friend and companion of Gov. Oglesby was with him when wounded, and remained in the service for nearly four years, . . ."—ALS, *ibid.*, Letters of Application and Recommendation. Related papers are *ibid.* On April 13, USG nominated Silas T. Trowbridge as consul, Vera Cruz. See *PUSG*, 6, 145.

1881, OCT. 12.   Secretary of War Robert T. Lincoln to USG. "I have the honor to acknowledge the receipt of your letter of October 10th, enclosing communications from the Rev. Preston Nash, of Richmond, Virginia, making application for appointment as Post Chaplain in the Army. In accordance with the terms of your letter, I will place his papers on file for examination by the President upon the happening of a vacancy."—LS (press), Robert T. Lincoln Letterbooks, IHi. On July 12, 1876, USG had nominated Preston G. Nash, Jr., as post chaplain; Nash resigned as of May 14, 1878.

1881, OCT. 17.   To Ethel C. Hine, president, Jewelers Association, New York City. "Your kind invitation of the 10th of October for me to meet the Association of which you are President at dinner at Delmonicos on the 20th inst was no doubt duly received, but I have just found it in my pocket unopened, and apologize for the apparent neglect. It would afford me pleasure to meet your Association on this occasion, but I will have to decline and Express my regrets because of other engagements which I cannot say was previous but was before I was aware yours had been received"—Hudson Rogue Co., May 1994, no. 38.

1881, OCT. 31.   To Abram Merritt, Nyack, N. Y. "Yours of the 28th inst. was duly received, and in answer I desire to say that I have no objection to the department naming a post of the G. A. R. after my father, 'Jesse Grant?'"— *New York Times*, Nov. 7, 1881. On Oct. 28, Merritt, dept. commander, Grand Army of the Republic, had written to USG. "The rules and regulations of the G. A. R. read that 'No post shall be named after any living person.' Would you object to having a Grand Army post in this department named after your illustrious father, 'Jesse Grant?'"—*Ibid.* No such post was organized. See *ibid.*, April 27, 1888.

1881, Nov. 16.   USG endorsement. "A. J. Perry is the son of an Officer of the Army who has served faithfully & efficiently since his graduation at West Point, before the War. I cheerfully endorse his application."—AES, DNA, RG 94, ACP, 6199 1880. Written on a letter of Nov. 14, 1881, from Lt. Col. Alexander J. Perry, deputy q. m. gen., New York City, to President Chester A. Arthur. "I have the honor to make application for the appointment of my son *John Adams Perry* to the position of second Lieutenant in the Army. He is of proper age and I believe well qualified to perform most satisfactorily the duties of an officer of the Army."—ALS, *ibid.* Col. Rufus Ingalls, asst. q. m. gen., also favorably endorsed this letter.—AES (undated), *ibid.* John A. Perry was appointed 2nd lt., 10th Inf., as of Oct. 10, 1883.

1881, Nov. 28.   To Edward F. Beale. "Will Gen. Beale please deliver the enclosed papers to the Sec. of the Treas, *at his hotel*, into his own hands."—ANS, DLC-Decatur House Papers.

1881, Nov.   USG endorsement. "Referred to the Atty. General. General Vandever served with distinction during the entire rebellion, and would, I think make a most excellent Governor for Arizona."—AES, DNA, RG 48, Appointment Papers, Arizona Territory. Written on a letter of Nov. 11 from William Vandever, Maricopa, Arizona Territory, to USG. "I am spending some time with my sons who are established in business in Arizona—There being a vacancy in the Governorship of this Territory I have an ambition to fill it. Senator Allison writes me that he has spoken to the President about appointing me—If it is not inconsistent with your ideas of propriety, or with what you desire for any other friend, pleas give me an endorsement;"—ALS, *ibid.* No appointment followed. See *PUSG*, 13, 89; *ibid.*, 23, 278.

1881, DEC. 2.   USG endorsement. "I take pleasure in endorsing Mr. S. Millers recommendation for appointment from Ky. Mr. Nunez, I understand has been a faithful worker and writer ~~for~~ in the republican cause and I do not doubt is well qualified for such position as he asks."—AES, DNA, RG 59, Applications and Recommendations, Hayes-Arthur. Written on a letter of Nov. 28 from Silas F. Miller, Louisville, to President Chester A. Arthur recommending Joseph A. Nunes for a consulship.—ALS, *ibid.* On Feb. 18, 1869,

U.S. Representative Leonard Myers of Pa. had written to USG. "Joseph A. Nunes of Phila desires to be Consul to Rio Janeiro. I have known him for a number of years as a most deserving gentleman. He is a fine writer and the author of several works of great interest, has taken a prominent part towards securing the triumph of our cause—served honorably four years as Paymaster in our Army—and is conversant with the Spanish language. The latter fact will make him of service to us & to Americans generally who visit the South American governments. I sincerely hope he may be appointed"—ALS, *ibid.* Related papers are *ibid.* No appointment followed. Nunes published *"Let Us Have Peace." A Poem* (Philadelphia, 1869). See *PUSG,* 19, 408.

1881, DEC. 5. USG endorsement. "Referred to the Atty. General. As an ex-union soldier, and lawyer recommended by his immediate representative, and one of the Senators in his state, I commend Mr. Glasgow for a Judgeship in one of the territories."—AES, eBay, June 4, 2005. On Feb. 10 and 24, Samuel L. Glasgow, Huntingdon, Pa., had written to President-elect James A. Garfield seeking appointment as associate justice, Utah Territory or Dakota Territory.—ALS, DLC-James A. Garfield. No appointment followed.

1882, JAN. 1. Alexander R. Shepherd, Consolidated Batopilas Silver Mining Co., Batopilas, Mexico, to USG. "I desire to recommend to your notice and favorable consideration, Mr A. Willard U. S. Consul at Guaymas, Sonora Mexico and to ask your assistance in having him retain his present position which he desires From business relations on the part of this company I can testify to his capacity, integrity and fitness for the office with the influx of our citizens into this part of Mexico, efforts are being made on the part of several persons to oust Mr W. and to secure his position and I feel satisfied that any change in the office would not benefit the public service I trust you will do me the favor to ask his retention, knowing your deep interest in the building up of trade between our country and Mexico"—ALS, DNA, RG 59, Applications and Recommendations, Hayes-Arthur. Related papers are *ibid.*; *ibid.,* Letters of Application and Recommendation. Alexander Willard continued as consul, Guaymas.

1882, JAN. 4. To Julia K. Fish. "Mrs. Grant asks me to say that it will give her & me pleasure to dine with you on the 17th inst. at ½ past seven O'Clock."—ALS, King V. Hostick, Springfield, Ill.

1882, JAN. 11. Frederick J. Phillips to USG. "The President directs me to acknowledge the receipt, by your reference and favorable endorsement, of a letter from Mr Ward H. Lamon, whose P. O. address is Boulder, Colorado, which will receive due consideration."—ALS, CSmH. For Ward H. Lamon's unsuccessful effort to become Denver postmaster, see Benjamin P. Thomas, *Portrait for Posterity: Lincoln and His Biographers* (New Brunswick, N. J., 1947), pp. 85–88.

1882, FEB. 9. To William E. Strong. "Will not be able to be present on March 6."—Richard Robins, comp., *Toasts and Responses at Banquets Given*

Lieut.-Gen. P. H. Sheridan . . . (Chicago, 1883), p. 84. Read when Lt. Gen. Philip H. Sheridan celebrated his birthday in Chicago.

1882, FEB. 16, Thursday.   To James B. Fry. "Any day next week after Tuesday that may suit you best I will be disengaged and will be happy to meet your company at dinner."—ALS, PPRF.

1882, FEB. 23.   USG endorsement. "This application is from the son of an officer in the regular Army, and the grandson also of an officer who spent all his manhood in the Army. I would be very glad to see him receive the appointment he asks."—AES, DNA, RG 94, ACP, 3029 1893. Written on papers including a letter of Feb. 20 from Robert A. Forsyth, Washington, D. C., to President Chester A. Arthur. "I have the honor to solicit from your Excellency, the appointment of Lieutenant in the Marine Corps.—I am a citizen of the District of Columbia,—aged twenty years,—and a son of Capt. L. Cass Forsyth, A. Q. M.—U. S. A."—ALS, *ibid.* On April 13, 1883, Forsyth, Buffalo, wrote to Arthur seeking an army appointment.—AES, *ibid.* No appointment followed.

1882, MARCH 3.   To Hubert O. Thompson, New York City public works commissioner, introducing Ricardo Orozco, ". . . who has been engaged, and is now largely interested in the public works about the City of Mexico. Mr. Orozco desires to examine the Water Works . . . with a view of acquiring information which he may make available in the work to be accomplished about the Capital of his own country . . ."—Charles Hamilton Auction No. 67, May 3, 1973, no. 115.

1882, MARCH 11.   To Adam Badeau. "The story about my failure was all a pure fiction, invented with many others lies on the Stock board to depress stocks. I have nothing to do with their speculations and I think it great presumption to use my name in any way to effect their purposes."—ALS, George N. Meissner Collection, Washington University, St. Louis, Mo. On March 9, USG had written to "Dear General." "The Stock jobing report referred to— or rather which gave the idea of my losses—had no foundation whatever. I have nothing to do in this world which can cause me any loss except that in a great depression what I have might depreciate in value—but then I would still have the same, but of less value than before the depression."—ALS, Gallery of History, Las Vegas, Nev. On March 8, a correspondent had reported from Wall Street. "The bears made a determined raid on the market to-day, and by circulating all sorts of alarming and improbable stories, such as the bankruptcy of Gen. Grant, . . . succeeded in thoroughly frightening the general run of speculators."—*New York Times,* March 9, 1882.

1882, MARCH 20.   Secretary of the Navy William H. Hunt to USG. "In compliance with your request of the 13th inst. I take pleasure in enclosing a permit for Mr. F. D. Casey to appear before the Board for examination as to his qualifications for appointment as an assistant paymaster in the Navy"—

Copy, DNA, RG 45, Miscellaneous Letters Sent. Frederick Dent Casey, USG's nephew, served as weigher, U.S. mint, New Orleans, as of July 1, 1885. See *PUSG*, 3, 271.

1882, March 25.   Henry R. Jackson, Savannah, to USG, "Executive Mansion Washington City." "The friends of Hon. H. K. McCay, of Atlanta, are anxious to secure for him the judgeship of the Northern District of Georgia—the Bill establishing the new District having recently become a law. They think that a letter from me to yourself will aid them in their efforts. The bare possibility that I may be able to render service in the matter is sufficient to overcome the reluctance I naturally feel to trouble you about the application. As one of the oldest members of the Bar in Georgia I realize a simple discharge of duty in saying that I know of no man in the State so thoroughly qualified for the place as Judge McCay. As a Republican (he has always been a steadfast Republican) he was raised to the Supreme Bench of the State. He there exhibited judicial ability of the very highest order. His withdrawal from the Bench was a public calamity. I have no hesitation whatever in saying that the appointment by the President of no one in Georgia would give more or as general satisfaction to the people and the profession of our State."—ALS, DNA, RG 60, Records Relating to Appointments. USG endorsed this letter. "Referred to the Atty. General. I do not know Mr. McCay but I know the writer of this letter to be a lawyer of high professional and social standing in Georgia. He is not a republican himself, but if all were like him it would be a matter of supreme indifference which political party was in power."—AES (undated), *ibid.* On Aug. 3, President Chester A. Arthur made this nomination. See Alexander A. Lawrence, "Henry Kent McCay—Forgotten Jurist," *Journal of Southern Legal History*, III (1994), 297–326.

[*1882, March*].   USG endorsement. "General Trevenio was Sec. of War when I was last in Mexico. He is the son-in-law of General Ord, and a citizen of Monterey."—AES (undated), DNA, RG 59, Letters of Application and Recommendation, Hayes-Arthur. Written on a telegram of March 17, 1882, from Geronimo Trevino, "commanding General in chief of the H. division M. A.," Monterey, Mexico, to USG, care of James H. Work, New York City. "Please to give your influency on favor of the appointment of mr Frank C. Thompson for the Consulate of the United States in this City"—Telegram received, *ibid.* Related papers are *ibid.* No appointment followed for Frank P. Thompson, whose sister Mary had married Edward O. C. Ord. See *New York Times*, July 26, 1880.

1882, April 2.   To U.S. Senator John P. Jones of Nev. "Will you and Mrs. Jones come and take family dinner with Mrs Grant & I. I left a card at the hotel for Conkling asking him to come also. Please say to the bearer if we may expect you."—ALS, R & R Enterprises, Feb., 2007.

1882, April 3.   To Secretary of the Treasury Charles J. Folger. "The circumstances under which I understand Col. D. McD. Lindsay was discharged

from the Treasury—before you went into the office—are such that I venture
to ask if if you will see the Colonel, and if consistent and practicable restore
him to employment."—ALS, DNA, RG 56, Applications. In an undated memorandum, Daniel McDonald Lindsey, former C.S.A. capt., alleged that he had
been removed from his Treasury Dept. clerkship in June, 1880, because he
supported USG at the Republican National Convention in Chicago.—ADS,
ibid. Related papers are *ibid.* In June, 1882, Lindsey was reappointed to the
Treasury Dept.

1882, APRIL 6.   To Daniel B. Whittier, Boston. "Will comply with your request of March 11th with pleasure. I apologize for not seeing your letter before, though it must have been delivered in due time."—Doris Harris Mail
Auction Sale No. 2, March 17, 1982, no. 36. Whittier, a Mass. homeopathic
physician, was a temperance advocate.

1882, APRIL 12.   To Edward Browne, Grand Army of the Republic. "I regret
that I cannot now accept the kind invitation contained in your letter of the
8th inst. to take part in the Parade & Review on Decoration Day. I think
I shall be absent from the city at that time."—ALS, Richard Schrodermier,
Cedar Rapids, Iowa. USG reviewed the New York City parade but declined
to speak because of a severe cold. See *New York Times,* May 31, 1882, Oct. 20,
1883.

1882, APRIL 15.   USG endorsement. "Referred to the Sec. of State. Mr. Morans
services are known to the State Department both as Sec. of Legation, to
London, during the rebellion, and as representative to Lisbond."—AES,
DNA, RG 59, Applications and Recommendations, Hayes-Arthur. Written
on a letter of March 30 from Benjamin Moran, U.S. chargé d'affaires, Lisbon,
to USG. "I learn that on the 5th inst, by an amendment offered in the House
during the discussion on the Diplomatic Appropriation bill the clause making provision for a Consul at Lisbon was struck out; and that Mr Burrows
who had charge of the bill, said, 'We have by this bill made the Minister
Resident at that port consul General.' In the general debate which followed
on the amendment Mr Neal of Ohio spoke of the Consular duties superadded
to those already performed by me; and of me, as a 'confirmed invalid,' and
that I would not be able to discharge the duties of Consul if they should be
imposed upon me &c &c. Mr Robeson followed advocating the adoption of
Mr Burrows's amendment; and it was ultimately agreed to, and on the 6th
instant the whole bill was passed and sent to the Senate. Should the Senate
sustain the amendment which does away with the consul here, and imposes
new functions, and confers another title upon the Chargé, a new Commission
will be required, as well as a nomination to the Senate and confirmation by
that body. The object of my letter is that I may appeal to your friendship for
me, to advocate with the President my retention in my post. I have no timid-
ity in regard to my strength supporting me under the superadded duties as
contemplated by the new bill. I am not better in health than when you saw me
in Lisbon, but I hope that the record of my work since that time; to be found
in the State Department, will prove conclusively that I am not unable to per-

form the duties of my office—it is almost a matter of life or death for me to retain it, for I have no means sufficient for a comfortable livelihood without it. I hope, that in one sense you will find a warrant for your advocacy, in the fact that I have been for 27 years a devoted servant to my country in Europe and I trust that President Arthur will permit me to continue to devote to it the ability and strength which I yet possess. I beg of you to remember me to Mrs Grant, . . . P. S. I received several weeks since a letter addressed to His Majesty enclosed to me by Mr Young to be transmitted to The King with the three volumes by Genl Badeau. As soon as they reach me, I will forward them to their destination."—LS, *ibid.* Related papers are *ibid.* On April 20, President Chester A. Arthur nominated John M. Francis to succeed Moran, who had resigned.

1882, APRIL 18. USG endorsement. "Respectfully referred to the Sec. of State. The Sec. will probably recollect the writer of this letter as the widow of Mr. Judd who represented his country at Berlin during Mr. Lincolns Administration, and afterward his district—Chicago—in Congress for four or six years."—AES, DNA, RG 59, Letters of Application and Recommendation, Hayes-Arthur. Written on a letter of April 15 from Adeline R. Judd, Moline, Ill., to USG. "I think you will recollect having met my son-in-law Mr S. S. Gould Jr. of Seneca Falls. New York, when he was a guest of Mrs Honore, at the 'Grant, Honore' wedding. He is one of the largest manufacturers of Hydraulic machinery of all kinds, in America, & as such is very much interested in the International Exposition which will open in Amsterdam in 1883. He would like exceedingly to receive the app, from President Arthur of Commissioner to the Exposition. . . ."—ALS, *ibid.* Related papers are *ibid.* On April 18, USG wrote to Judd. "I have forwarded your letter of the 15th inst. with indorsement, to the Sec. of State calling his attention to your husbands services which I know—with your husband himself—he will remember."—ALS, King V. Hostick, Springfield, Ill. Norman B. Judd died on Nov. 10, 1878. No appointment followed for Seabury S. Gould, Jr.

1882, APRIL 27. To Fitch & Fox. "You are authorized to draw on me at three days sight for the amt. due Mr Greene, and which Mr. Olmstead owes. I hope you will push O to a settlement of this amount, and also of what I previously paid."—ALS (facsimile), Raleigh De Geer Amyx Catalog 1085, Nov. 1, 1985, p. 41.

1882, MAY 4. USG endorsement. "Respectfully referred to the Sec. of War. Mrs. Hooe is the widow of an officer who lost an arm at the battle of Resaca de la Palma,—the second battle of the war with Mexico—and who died in the service."—AES, DNA, RG 56, Applications. Written on a letter of May 3 from Emilie R. Hooe, Washington, D. C., to USG seeking an appointment for her son, Alexander S. Hooe, Jr.—ALS, *ibid.* Related papers are *ibid.*

1882, MAY 4. Lt. Gen. Philip H. Sheridan to USG. "I take pleasure in introducing to you Major Sawyer formerly a paymaster in the Army during the War under my command. He was well off in business but met with some reverses & now has to go to work to earn his living. He thinks your influence will get him a place in the customhouse in NewYork if you could help him it would be a kindly act to a worthy man."—ADfS and copy (press), DLC-Philip H. Sheridan. As of July 1, 1883, Nathaniel C. Sawyer clerked at the pension office in Washington, D. C.

1882, MAY 15.   USG endorsement. "Capt. Gardner lost a leg in the service of his country and deserves therefore the support of the Govt. where he can render service in his crippled condition. My sympathy goes out in behalf of such veterans and I therefore hope he may not be disappointed."—AES, DLC-USG, IB. Written on a letter of the same day from Francis B. Thurber, New York City, to President Chester A. Arthur. "I beg to call your attention to a case which I think will appeal strongly to your sympathies as a soldier and a citizen. Major H. Gardner was in the Union Army (100th Illinois Regiment) and lost a leg at Missionary Ridge Chattanooga. He held a commission in the 44th Regiment Regular Army from the time of its organization in 1867 to its consolidation in 1869, since which time he has been on the retired list and has been making a gallant struggle to eke out a slender income by selling goods for various commercial houses. Being crippled through the loss of his leg he cannot of course fill every position. His lungs are not very strong and he recently took a trip to Bermuda for his health and while there conceived the idea of getting an appointment at Hamilton, Bermuda, as United States Counsul. The present incumbent has filled that position 20 years. I do not know that there is anything against him as a representative of the United States at that place, but I do know that there is no more deserving man than Major Gardner and I believe that in point of character, habits and ability to fill the position creditably Major Gardner is eminently fitted for the position. I would ask if possible something more than your usual official consideration of this case."—TLS, *ibid.* No appointment followed.

1882, JUNE 7.   To Edward L. Jellinek, Buffalo. "Yours of April 5th advising me of my election as an honorary member of the Philomaths Club, was duly received. Please accept my thanks for your kind consideration."—LS, DLC-USG, IB. See *New York Times*, May 21, 1943.

1882, JUNE 8.   To unknown recipient. "I have your very kind note of the 5th inst. for the flattering expressions of which please accept my thanks."—ALS (facsimile), Nate D. Sanders Autographs, May 10, 2005, Lot 19.

1882, JUNE 29.   Gen. William T. Sherman to USG, Long Branch. "I congratulate you on your escape from the RailRoad accident which is reported to have been serious to our friends Raymond & Garrison"—Telegram received (at 8:00 P.M.), USG 3. At 8:15 A.M., USG had boarded a New York and Long Branch Railroad train that derailed while crossing a trestle bridge about four miles from Long Branch, killing three and injuring about seventy, including William R. Garrison, railroad and shipping magnate, who died July 1. After the derailment, "Gen. Grant was one of the first to attract attention.

He was getting his body out of one of the windows of the smoking car. He had lost his hat, but still had his morning's cigar between his teeth. He had received no other injury than a slight cut on the leg, and to somebody who asked him if he was hurt, he replied, 'No, I'm all right.' Then he began to direct the movements of the workmen, . . ."—*New York Times*, June 30, 1882. Another passenger reported. "I was sitting in the smoking car, . . . The train was fairly under way, and we were nearing the bridge, when we felt a slight quivering of our car, which soon became a disagreeable jolting. I knew the car was off the track and had not made up my mind what to do about it when Gen. Grant got up, and stooping down in the aisle, grasped the iron work of the seat on each side. I said to myself, 'Old man, your head is level, if you are a General,' and I got up and followed his example. Hardly had I changed my position when the car gave a lurch to the right, and then went down what seemed to be an interminable distance. It finally settled into the water, lying on its left side. The right side was above water, and Gen. Grant, poking out the window, drew himself up and climbed out of the car. . . ."—*Ibid.*

On July 3, USG testified at a coroner's inquest. "I really haven't anything of value to tell the jury, . . . I was in the train that was wrecked at Little Silver, and I sat in the smoking car—the forward one of those that left the track. When the cars leaped from the track I advised the passengers to keep their seats, but, as a general thing, they didn't follow my advice. I was on the west side of the car, which was the uppermost side after the fall, and I fell down in the water. I made no special examination of the bridge. I saw no unsound ties. I noticed that the ties were close together, and that a person walking on them would step on every other one."—*Ibid.*, July 4, 1882. USG collected fifty cents as a witness fee. Jurors found the railroad guilty of gross and culpable negligence.—*Ibid.*

On June 29, Matías Romero, Washington, D. C., had telegraphed to USG. "I congratulate you and your country for your escaping of todays accident"— Telegram received (at 8:15 P.M.), USG 3. On June 30, John F. Long, St. Louis, telegraphed to Julia Dent Grant, New York City. "Please accept my familys rejoicings at your husbands escape"—Telegram received (at 2:15 A.M.), *ibid.* On July 6, [*Ignacio*] Mariscal, Mexico City, telegraphed to USG, Long Branch. "Just informed of the accident I congratulate you on happy escape"— Telegram received, *ibid.* On July 7, John C. Hamilton, Long Branch, wrote to USG. "I could not have been the latest in tendering to you and to Mrs Grant and to every member of your family upon your delivery from this great exigency which touched the heart of the nation and which I now do. But I am lying here doubtfully ill and can do no more than to repeat the expression of my sincerest respect and warmest regard."—LS, Nellie C. Rothwell, La Jolla, Calif. Hamilton died July 25.

In Oct., 1885, an engraved knife belonging to USG, found at the scene of the accident, was sold to benefit the Grant Monument fund. See *New York Tribune*, Oct. 21, 1885.

1882, JULY 8. To Alfred May, Washington, D. C., from Long Branch. "I am very sorry to have retained your papers so long. I forgot the m[atter] until your second letter come. I have sent your papers to the Sec. of the Treas. with my endorsement." "I mail your papers today care Senator Jones"—ALS and telegram received (at 11:12 A.M.), USGA.

1882, JULY 20. USG endorsement. "Respectfully referred to the Sec. of State."—AES, DNA, RG 59, Applications and Recommendations, Hayes-Arthur. Written on a letter of July 18 from Charles B. Norton, Washington, D. C., to USG. "The Committee on Foreign Affairs of the House have reccomended the establishment of Diplomatic and Commercial relations with the Empire of Persia. When you were President I had the honor of then bringing the matter to the attention of our Govermt having had personal relations which enabled me to state that the Schah was desirous of carrying out such a programme and it was at the suggestion of Genl Dix that I then presented the subject. It has been suggested that I should apply for the position of Special Agent to go to Persia and report upon the condition of affairs. To secure such an appointment (controlled by the State Dept) a letter from yourself to Mr Frlinghuysen would be invaluable and it is for that reason I take the liberty of writing you. I have given the subject much study and am conversant with foreign languages. Your kind attention will confer a special favour . . ."—ALS, *ibid.* Also on July 18, Brig. Gen. Rufus Ingalls wrote to USG recommending Norton.—ALS, *ibid.* Related papers are *ibid.* No appointment followed. See *New York Times*, Jan. 30, 1891.

1882, AUG. 3. To Secretary of the Treasury Charles J. Folger. "We the undersigned take great pleasure in recommending Capt. A. J. Russell, to the Position of Chief Photographer in the Supervising Architects Office of the Treasury Department Washington D. C. Capt A. J. Russell has had long experience and is a thoroughly competant and superior artist, and also an honorable and trustworthy man."—LS (6 signatures), DNA, RG 56, Applications. On Nov. 22, Frank H. Norton, Washington, D. C., wrote to President Chester A. Arthur. ". . . Capt. Russell was one of the three photographers in government employ during the war; and was afterwards employed as an expert by the Union Pacific RR Company. . . ."—ALS, *ibid.* Related papers are *ibid.* No appointment followed. See David Haward Bain, *Empire Express: Building the First Transcontinental Railroad* (New York, 1999), pp. 518, 659–62. In 1869–70, Norton had sought a consulship in Nova Scotia. See DNA, RG 59, Letters of Application and Recommendation.

1882, AUG. 3. To A. S. Wright, from Long Branch, expressing regret that he cannot attend the McHenry County (Ill.) fair, and apologizing for not answering Wright's July 3 letter sooner. ". . . But it has been carried in my coat pocket—which often happens with letters that I cannot attend to at once—until this time. . . ."—*The Collector*, No. 10–12 (1964), E-361.

1882, AUG. 11. To William Chatfield, from Long Branch. ". . . let me thank you now for your kind invitation and to express the regret that I can not accept for this summer."—Sotheby's, April 24, 1985.

1882, AUG. 15.   Bishop Henry B. Whipple, Faribault, Minn., to USG. "You
have always been most kind to me & do dislike troubling you—May I ask
a great favor? Both myself & my dear wife are growing old and in broken
health. I often feel that it may not be long before I go home. My son Maj
Charles H. Whipple is a Paymaster in the U. S. Army stationed in San
Francisco—whenever it is practicable to do so, I should be very glad if
he could be stationed at Fort Snelling—I do not know Sec Lincoln altho'
I knew his honored father well. If you can with propriety prefer this request for your old friend I shall be grateful"—ALS, DNA, RG 94, ACP,
1578 1881.

1882, AUG. 16.   To Joab N. Patterson, Concord, N. H. "Your letter of the
14th . . . inviting me to be present at the 6th annual reunion of the Soldiers
and Sailors of New Hampshire on September 13th and 15th, was duly received, and in reply I must express my regrets that my engagements are such
that I will not be able to attend. . . ."—Paul C. Richards, Catalog 250, April,
1990, no. 86. Patterson, former col., 2nd N. H., was a Grand Army of the
Republic official.

1882, SEPT. 29.   USG endorsement. "Respectfully referred to the Sec. of
state."—AES, DNA, RG 59, Applications and Recommendations, Hayes-
Arthur. Written on a letter of Sept. 20 from 1st Lt. William W. Robinson, Jr.,
"Camp near Billings M. T.," to USG. "Some years ago, upon my earnest solicitation and the recommendation of the Wisconsin delegation, or certain
members of it, you kindly appointed my father—Col W. W. Robinson as
Consul at the port of Tamatave Madagascar—which position he has filled
ever since I have recently heard from him that his health has failed, owing
to hardships to which he was subjected as Colonel of the 7th Wis during the
War and to the climate of his post and he has expressed fears that he would
be compelled to resign. Since his time of service there he has made himself
master of several languages including French, Malagasse, and German I believe. May I ask that if the records of the State Department warrant such
action you will kindly recommend his transfer to some other post nearer his
home where for the remaining years of his service he may not be subjected
to the depressing influences of a tropical climate. You will perhaps pardon
the liberty I have taken in addressing you when you consider that it simply
prompted by a sons love and respect for his father and that long service on
the frontier as an officer has not given me political friends upon whom I can
call for favors—"—ALS, *ibid.* William W. Robinson continued as consul, Tamatave. See *PUSG*, 25, 438.

1882, OCT. 30.   To Mr. [*Isaac H.*] Bailey. "Will you be kind enough to send a
verbal message by bearer, 'Yes' or 'No' if you can come and dine with me to-
morrow, at seven pm. Beside my family present there will be but six people,
all friends of yours except [Conkling] and Horace Porter"—ALS (facsimile),
Superior Galleries Manuscript Auction, May 29, 1993, no. 288. See *PUSG*,
23, 329–30.

1882, Nov. 23.   USG endorsement. "Respectfully referred to the Sec. of State. The writer of this letter is one of the ablest republicans in W. Va and was strongly suggested for a seat on the supreme Court bench by his party and friends. He was a Confederate soldier but became a strong supporter of the party of progress—as he considers—when the war was over"—AES, DNA, RG 59, Letters of Application and Recommendation, Hayes-Arthur. Written on a letter of Oct. 23 from Thomas B. Swann, Charleston, West Va., to USG. "The Papers State that our Consul General for Rumania has resigned. You appreciate the propriety of this Place being filled by an Israelite. Dr Daniel Mayer, a union soldier, an accomplished gentleman & every way a thorough Man—for many years a citizen of this Place—will apply for the Position. It appears to me he has every needed qualification for the Place. He is cultivated, correct & energetic (45 years of age). I have no acquaintance with the President: & would not like to ask any favor for that reason. I thought if you could endorse this note approvingly, & send it to the President, it might meet with some favor. Dr Mayer is endorsed by Dr Wise of Cincinnati for the Place & by the Rep. Ex. Com. of WV for this Place."—ALS, *ibid.* Related papers are *ibid.* No appointment followed.

1882, Dec. 15.   Lt. Gen. Philip H. Sheridan, Chicago, to USG. "It has been so frequently asserted in the newspapers that Meade, Thomas and Hancock were my seniors at the time I was made Lieut. Gen. that some good people are commencing to believe it. I have therefore made out the accompanying statement from the records of the War Department, and find it only incomplete in the telegram or letter you sent to me from City Point, asking me or suggesting to me to secure Mead's confirmation by consenting to his taking date from the occupation of the Weldon road. If you have lost the correspondence, as I have in the Chicago fire, will you write me a note on the subject. We are all well out here and send our warm regards and unfaltering attachment to you and Mrs. Grant."—Copy, DLC-Philip H. Sheridan. See *Chicago Times*, Dec. 22, 1882; *PUSG*, 28, 426, 435–37.

1882, Dec. 20.   Secretary of War Robert T. Lincoln to USG. "Your letter of the 17th reached me yesterday. I regret very much that I was not advised either officially or privately of the expected arrival of the Japanese Prince as it would have given me pleasure to provide for his receiving a salute. The Secretary of State informs me that some little time ago the Japanese Minister in an informal way mentioned to him that when he arrived in Washington he would wish to have him presented to the President. He seems however not to have made any formal communication or to have indicated the probable time of his arrival or of his movements in this country. I understand that Secretary Frelinghuysen will at once have a conference with the Japanese Minister on this subject. I am very glad you have written, and I trust that such attention will be paid the Prince here as may be agreeable to him and creditable to ourselves."—LS (press), Robert T. Lincoln Letterbooks, IHi. On Dec. 15, Prince Arisugawa Taruhito, uncle to Emperor Meiji, had arrived in New York City on the *Scythia*, from Liverpool. On Dec. 16, Arisugawa lunched with USG. On Dec. 19, USG gave a dinner for Arisugawa at the Union League Club, attended by John Jacob Astor, Edwards Pierrepont, Leland Stanford, and others. Invitations are in OHi (Pierrepont) and the Edwin D. Morgan Papers, New York State Library, Albany, N. Y. See *New York Times,* Dec. 16, 17, 19, 20, 1882. For protocol complications during Arisugawa's visit to Washington, D. C., see *ibid.,* Jan. 5, 1883.

[*1882*].   USG endorsement. "Very correct history."—George F. Williams, *Bullet and Shell. War as the Soldier Saw it:* . . . (New York, 1882), advertisement opposite p. 454. See *New York Times,* Jan. 1, 1921.

Index

All letters written by USG of which the text was available for use in this volume are indexed under the names of the recipients. The dates of these letters are included in the index as an indication of the existence of text. Abbreviations used in the index are explained on pp. xvii–xxii. Individual regts. are indexed under the names of the states in which they originated.